See map of the Roman Empire in the age of the Antonines, pages 692-93.

The Portable

GIBBON:

The

DECLINE AND FALL

of the

ROMAN EMPIRE

Edited, and with an Introduction, by
DERO A. SAUNDERS

Preface by
CHARLES ALEXANDER ROBINSON, JR.

PENGUIN BOOKS

Penguin Books Ltd, Harmondsworth,
Middlesex, England
Penguin Books, 625 Madison Avenue,
New York, New York 10022, U.S.A.
Penguin Books Australia Ltd, Ringwood,
Victoria, Australia
Penguin Books Canada Limited, 2801 John Street,
Markham, Ontario, Canada L3R 1B4
Penguin Books (N.Z.) Ltd, 182–190 Wairau Road,
Auckland 10, New Zealand

First published in the United States of America
by The Viking Press 1944
Paperbound edition published 1956
Reprinted 1958, 1959, 1960, 1961, 1963, 1965, 1967,
1970 (twice), 1971, 1974, 1976
Published in Penguin Books 1977

ISBN 0 14 015.008 0

Printed in the United States of America by
Kingsport Press, Inc., Kingsport, Tennessee
Set in Linotype Caledonia

Contents

Preface

Winston Churchill's majestic phrases, as we all know, have been inspired, at least in part, by close familiarity with Gibbon's *Decline and Fall of the Roman Empire.* I doubt, however, whether it is equally well known that another British prime minister, Clement R. Attlee, re-read the *Decline and Fall* during the critical summer of 1949. "No significance, his admirers say, should be attached to his selection at that time of the particular work," *The New York Times* reported.

Be that as it may, there is a certain thrill, as well as comfort, in the knowledge that these two great leaders of Western democracy have steeped themselves in antiquity's most terrible and most instructive lesson. The history of Rome, after all, is the story of a remarkable city-state which seemed to pile success upon monumental success and then, having conquered the world, enmeshed itself and civilization in catastrophe. The question of exactly why this disaster occurred has occupied historians ever since, and none more eloquently than Gibbon.

Gibbon's immediacy and importance for us—aside from his virtue and worth as a literary artist—result primarily from a vision and perspective that were refined by long toil with more than a thousand years of eventful history. As a historian and philosopher of the eighteenth century, he had a deeper concern with human thought, creativeness, and moral corrosion than with economics or archæology, specialties of a later day; but his researches into the available materials were very thorough

ix

even when his judgments failed of impartiality. Gibbon was passionately interested in politics, war, and religion. "I have described," he says, "the triumph of barbarism and religion"; and in a somber moment he remarks that history is "little more than the register of the crimes, follies, and misfortunes of mankind."

Doubtless it has been the all-embracing length of Gibbon's triumphant march through the centuries that has caused many persons to hesitate before joining him on this fruitful and fascinating voyage of exploration. Dero A. Saunders, by his urbane Introduction and his editing of an embarrassing abundance of riches, has now performed a signal public service. With the journalist's skill he has compressed Gibbon into reasonable compass and yet has managed to preserve the vivid expositions of the glories of ancient civilization, its decay and final, overwhelming tragedy. More to the point, perhaps, is the fact that he has maintained the flow of the original by devoting most of his volume to a single great period— that which ends early in the fifth century. The centuries leading up to the collapse of the Roman empire in the West are the ones that mainly interest us and indeed constitute half of Gibbon's work.

Nevertheless, Mr. Saunders gives us later events as well, and very particularly the epochal capture of Constantinople by the Turks. In short, he has made it easy for us all to enjoy, together with the Churchills and Attlees of our world, a penetrating and sustained account of the greatest phenomenon in history.

CHARLES ALEXANDER ROBINSON, JR.
Professor of Classics
Brown University

April 6, 1952

Editor's Introduction

1.

THE historian of the Roman empire was born in April 1737, at Putney in the county of Surrey, of a well-to-do family whose wealth had been amassed by Gibbon's grandfather, a tough-minded army contractor. (Gibbon notes that "even his opinions were subordinate to his interest; and I find him in Flanders clothing King William's troops, while he would have contracted with more pleasure, though not perhaps at a cheaper rate, for the service of King James.") The family would have been richer but for his grandfather's involvement in the collapse of the South Sea Bubble in 1720, when an angry Parliament confiscated all but £10,000 of a fortune totalling £106,500. However, the resourceful old man had put considerable landed property beyond legal reach, and he also managed by his death in 1736 to recoup much of what had been taken from him. Thereafter the family fortunes began a steady decline under the mismanagement of the historian's amiable but erratic father.

Edward Gibbon gave formal thanks that he was born not a slave, savage, or peasant, but "in a free and civilized country, in an age of science and philosophy, in a family of honourable rank, and decently endowed with the gifts of fortune." But nature's bounty was strictly measured. The first of seven children, he was the only one to survive past infancy. Physically frail and forever ill, he was dragged in desperation from doctor to doc-

1

tor; their unsuccessful treatments yielded only scars that he carried to his grave, and a resistance to personal medical care that helped to put him there. His first formal education, at a boarding school at Kingston-upon-Thames, was interrupted before he was ten by his mother's death, from the exhaustion and complications of frequent child-bearing. In later years, fat with fame and adult satisfactions, he could still lash out at "the trite and lavish praise of the happiness of our boyish years, which is echoed with so much affectation in the world. That happiness I have never known, that time I have never regretted. . . ."

His mere survival was probably due to a kindly aunt, Miss Catherine Porten, upon whose death Gibbon wrote a letter combining a tender memorial with a scarifying picture of his own youth: "To her care I am indebted in earliest infancy for the preservation of my life and health. I was a puny child, neglected by my Mother, starved by my nurse, and of whose being very little care or expectation was entertained; without her maternal vigilance I should either have been in my grave, or imperfectly lived a crooked ricketty monster, a burthen to myself and others. To her instructions I owe the first rudiments of knowledge, the first exercise of reason, and a taste for books which is still the pleasure and glory of my life; and though she taught me neither language nor science, she was certainly the most useful preceptor I have ever had."

One rare reward from the *History of the Decline and Fall of the Roman Empire*, if close-read with an eye to the author's life, is discovering those eloquent lines where the historian, speaking of someone else, unconsciously describes himself. Thus of Mohammed he remarks, "Conversation enriches the understanding, but solitude is the school of genius." The frail little boy knew much of solitude, which he slowly learned to twist to his own self-reliant purposes. At Kingston-upon-Thames he was first captured by two books, Pope's translation of Homer ("a portrait endowed with every merit excepting that of likeness to the original") and the Arabian Nights. For some nine months after his mother's death he lived in his maternal grandfather's house, where he "rioted without control" in the unlocked library.

Still cursed with recurrent illness, dragged or sent here and there by a father still grief-stricken over his wife's death, attended by this tutor or doctor and that, in the next five years he somehow managed to read much of Horace, Virgil, Terence, and Ovid; to master everything on Oriental history then available in English; to plough through the formidable Latin of such tomes as Pococke's *Abulpharagius;* and to reflect so deeply over ancient geography and chronology that he could lie awake nights trying to reconcile the chronology of the Hebrew Old Testament with the Greek. He arrived at Magdalen College, Oxford, in April of 1752, with "a stock of erudition which might have puzzled a doctor, and a degree of ignorance of which a schoolboy would have been ashamed."

Gibbon's brief stay at Magdalen coincided with his blessed delivery from childhood ailments; but beyond that happenstance, he considered his fourteen months at Oxford "the most idle and unprofitable of my whole life." The institution was at its lowest ebb, and neither faculty nor student body contained anyone anxious or able to assist the precocious young student. Reading widely on religion, and probably influenced most by the French Catholic scholar Bossuet, Gibbon converted himself to Roman Catholicism and was privately baptized in London in early June of 1753.

His outraged father responded by withdrawing him precipitately from Oxford and demanding to know who had converted him; anyone who had would have faced possible execution. (Such was the temper of the times that a few years later a London mob, incensed by proposals to relax the discriminatory Penal Laws against Roman Catholics, burned sections of the city and had to be put down by armed force.) Scarce ten days elapsed before Gibbon's father had arranged to entrust the correction of his errant son to one M. Pavillard, a Calvinist minister of Lausanne, Switzerland. Gibbon arrived in Lausanne at the end of June 1753, "a thin little figure with a large head [so Pavillard described him], disputing and urging with the greatest ability all the best arguments that had ever been used in favor of popery."

In his autobiography written years later, Gibbon blesses his "childish revolt against the religion of my own country"; for otherwise those five wonderful years at Lausanne would have been spent "steeped in port and prejudice among the monks of Oxford." The blessing was certainly well disguised at the time. He was in a strange country, without friends, the object of family censure, boarded at a niggardly figure, badly fed and housed by Pavillard's pinch-penny wife, and short of clothes and spending money. And he was further isolated by his almost total ignorance of French.

Fortunately M. Pavillard was no ordinary gaoler. Perceiving instantly that his strange charge was not to be browbeaten into anything, he talked when Gibbon wanted to talk, respected his silence, and gently encouraged him to discover his own way back to Protestant orthodoxy. That was accomplished by Christmas Day, 1754, when Gibbon received the sacrament at the Calvinist church in Lausanne. But there is no such thing as complete return. Despite the sharp charges of irreligion that have been hurled ever since the first volume of the *Decline and Fall* appeared (the waspish Boswell called him "an infidel puppet"), Gibbon achieved at Lausanne the religious philosophy from which he never again wavered—a moderate scepticism that was quite willing to accept the existence of a Deity, but with no stipulations about the precise mechanics of the operation of the Divine Will.

More important, as a man of some learning and taste, Pavillard taught method to the young scholar without cramping his interest or range. For example, in 1756 Gibbon resolved to review *all* the Latin classics—historians, poets, orators, and philosophers—from Plautus and Sallust down to "the decline of the language and empire of Rome"; and in fourteen months he did just about that. With Pavillard's help he set out to learn Greek, and read half the *Iliad* and most of Herodotus and Xenophon before putting the job aside for later completion. Nor was his reading skimpy. He kept voluminous notes, though agreeing with Dr. Johnson that what is "twice read is commonly better remembered than what is transcribed." Before each new book he would assess carefully "all that I knew or believed or had thought on the subject," then after completion tote up his intellectual balance sheet to estimate his net profit.

Gibbon learned more than the classics in those five Lausanne years. He became so fluent in French that his first published work was in that language, as were his last words on his deathbed. (To improve both his French and his Latin he would translate Cicero into French, put it aside for a time, translate the French back into Latin, and then compare the result with the original.) He began his friendship with "the most extraordinary man of the age," Voltaire; and he acquired such a taste for the French theatre that it "perhaps abated my idolatry for the gigantic genius of Shakespeare, which is inculcated from our infancy as the first duty of an Englishman." At Lausanne he also met the two staunchest friends of his life: Georges Deyverdun, a young Swiss with whom he set up a Lausanne bachelor establishment in later years; and J. B. Holroyd (later Lord Sheffield), who became his literary executor.

He also fell completely in love, for the first and only time. Suzanne Curchod was the intelligent, personable daughter of a Calvinist minister in the nearby French village of Crassy. Within months the two twenty-year-olds were exchanging visits and fervent letters; and when he left Lausanne in April 1758 to return to England, his first objective was to secure his father's consent to the marriage.

It was not his only purpose. His father had remarried, and Gibbon had visions of a new brood cutting him off from an already shrinking patrimony. (Characteristically, his father had not even written about his second marriage.) But when his stepmother proved a warm and amiable soul—with no immediate prospects of producing—Gibbon got down to the question of Mlle. Curchod. His father was adamant, and his father held the purse strings. Gibbon reports the outcome with shamefaced brevity: "I sighed as a lover, I obeyed as a son." He put Suzanne Curchod (he thought) out of his life forever and became the wary bachelor, a favourite with all the ladies but intimate with few, if any.

In the next few months (the psychoanalyst might detect sublimation) he completed a remarkable little volume in French, his *Essai sur l'étude de la littérature*. The tool must ever be sharper and more precise than its work, and Gibbon's *Essai* is the only place where he exhibits, though in early form, the tools of his trade.

To demonstrate that full appreciation of the classics requires a thorough knowledge of their times, this amazing twenty-one-year-old propounded that Virgil wrote his *Georgics* at the request of Augustus Cæsar, to impress the unruly veterans of the civil war with the beauties of agriculture. "Taken in this light, Virgil is no longer to be considered as a mere writer describing the business of a rural life, but as another Orpheus, who strikes his lyre only to disarm savages of their ferocity, and unite them in the peaceful bonds of society. His *Georgics* actually produced this admirable effect. His veterans became insensibly reconciled to a quiet life and passed without disturbance the thirty years that slipt away before Augustus had established, not without much difficulty, a military fund to pay them in money."

As for understanding history in general, "Among a multitude of historical facts there are some, and those by much the majority, which prove nothing more than that they are facts. There are others that may be useful in drawing a partial conclusion, whereby the philosopher may be enabled to judge of the motives of an action, or some particular features in a character; these relate only to single links of the chain. Those whose influence extends throughout the whole system, and which are so intimately connected as to give motion to the springs of action, are very rare; and what is still more rarely to be met with is a genius who knows how to distinguish them, amidst the vast chaos of events wherein they are jumbled, and deduce them pure and unmixt from the rest."

If detecting and evaluating those facts is the true job of the critical historian, his highest art is understanding the irrational in human history. "We see that minds, the

most exempt from prejudice, cannot altogether shake it
off. Their ideas have an air of paradox; and we perceive
by their broken chains that they have worn them. . . .
We should hence learn not only to acknowledge but
to feel the force of prejudice; we should learn never to
be surprised at apparent absurdity, and often to suspect
the truth of what might appear to want no confirmation.
I must own that I like to see the reasonings of mankind
take a tincture from their prejudices; to take a view of
[those who] are afraid to deduce, even from principles
they acknowledge to be just, conclusions they know to
be logically exact. I like to detect those who detest in a
barbarian what they admire in a Greek, and who would
call the same history impious if written by a heathen
and sacred if penned by a Jew."

By the time the *Essai* appeared in 1761 (it was well
received on the Continent, but an English translation
passed almost unnoticed), Gibbon had for over a year
held an utterly unlikely post—that of captain in the
Hampshire militia. For England was at war and had
been in danger of invasion, though the danger was fast
disappearing. Superficially the years from May 1760
to December 1762 were the least productive of Gibbon's
mature life. But he learned much about men in rough
surroundings, and nothing could altogether halt his
studies. Moreover, he remarks wryly that "the discipline
and evolutions of a modern battalion gave me a clearer
notion of the phalanx and the legion; and the captain
of the Hampshire grenadiers (the reader may smile) has
not been useless to the historian of the Roman empire."

As a reward for this good behaviour his father agreed
to Gibbon's cherished plan of an extensive European
tour. Within barely a month of the battalion's demobi-
lization he was on the Continent; and, after a short stay

in Paris, he proceeded to Lausanne—where he ran
smack into Suzanne Curchod. She apparently still entertained expectations or hopes that, despite the formal
break between them, a marriage might yet be possible.
Suzanne's friends were incensed at Gibbon's coolness
and asked Rousseau to speak to the young man; but
Rousseau declined to interfere, on the grounds that Gibbon was too cold-blooded for his taste or Suzanne's happiness. Rousseau was uncomfortably close to being right.
Shortly afterward Suzanne Curchod became Mme.
Necker, wife of the great French minister of finance
who called the session of the Estates General that led
to the French Revolution; and her daughter was Mad-
ame de Staël. It was Gibbon's courage that was wanting, not his taste.[1]

But Gibbon already had his other love, whom he
approached with slow and diffident steps, as if to prolong the pleasures of anticipation. He dallied in Lausanne for nearly a year before proceeding to Italy and,
in the fall of 1764, at last to Rome itself. His autobiography eloquently recounts "the strong emotions which
agitated my mind as I first approached and entered the
eternal city," where "several days of intoxication were
lost or enjoyed before I could descend to a cool and
minute investigation." But still more persuasive is his
private letter to his father at the time: "I have already
found such a fund of entertainement for a mind some-

1. Of course, there were times when Gibbon wanted it
both ways. After visiting the Neckers in Paris a few years
later, he wrote his friend Lord Sheffield: "She is very fond
of me, and the husband particularly civil. Could they insult
me more cruelly? Ask me every evening to supper; go to bed,
and leave me alone with his wife—what an impertinent security! It is making an old lover of mighty little consequence."

what prepared for it by an acquaintance with the Romans that I am really almost in a dream. Whatever ideas books may have given us of the greatness of that people, their accounts of the most flourishing state of Rome fall infinitely short of the picture of its ruins. I am convinced that there never before existed such a nation, and I hope for the happiness of mankind there never will again."

With characteristic precision Gibbon marks the exact moment when the idea of his history was born: "It was at Rome, on the 15th of October 1764, as I sat musing amid the ruins of the Capitol, while the barefooted friars were singing vespers in the temple of Jupiter, that the idea of writing the decline and fall of the city first started to my mind." He observes, however, that the idea was originally limited to the city alone, and only later extended to include the empire—not the last time the *Decline and Fall* was broadened before its completion.

This is altogether too precise. Edward Gibbon did not write his history because he happened to visit Rome in 1764, or because (as he remarks elsewhere) thirteen years earlier he had stumbled across a copy of Eachard's *History of the Later Roman Empire*. In retrospect, almost everything he ever did seems immutably pointed in one direction. His earliest surviving letter, written at the age of thirteen, records that "after Church and upon our Return home we viewed the Remains of an ancient Camp which pleased me vastly." His voracious reading, even during the militia period, seemed to contribute to a single end. (In the militia his copy of Horace "was always in my pocket, and often in my hand"; and it was there that he completed his earlier design of learning Greek.) As D. M. Low very properly observes in his excellent biography of Gibbon, one accident is as good as another, and "by one channel or another the swelling stream must find its way to the tracts it is destined to flood and fertilize."

The five years after Gibbon's return from Italy in the summer of 1765 were divided between London and Putney and spent in a number of apparently aimless pursuits. He began a history of the Swiss republic, then dropped it; he helped his friend Deyverdun put together two volumes of a review of British literature, to be published in French on the Continent; he published anonymously a contentious little essay entitled *Critical Observations on the Sixth Book of the Aeneid*. But mainly he chafed at continued dependence on his father (Gibbon was passing thirty). Even his father's death late in 1770 did not immediately release him: over two years were spent in putting the tangled estate into some kind of order before he could establish himself, with relative permanence, in a house of his own at No. 7 Bentinck Street, London.

The wine of personal independence produced the first volume of the *Decline and Fall* in rather short order; but the outside world at the time saw only the new phenomenon of Gibbon, the man-about-town. He was a self-made man-about-town, for he had neither wealth nor family rank to deserve automatic status. Yet he made his way among what was certainly one of the most brilliant literary sets in English history.

His social-literary status is adequately documented by his election, over a year before the first volume of the *Decline and Fall* was published, to the famous Literary Club founded by Samuel Johnson in 1765. In addition to Johnson, during the years of Gibbon's active membership, it included Gibbon's enemy Boswell; Sir Joshua Reynolds, the painter; Oliver Goldsmith; Edmund Burke; David Garrick, the actor; the great Opposition statesman Charles Fox; playwright-politico

Richard Sheridan; Gibbon's warm friend Adam Smith. And Gibbon's social and literary acquaintance of course extended far beyond the club.

A seat in Parliament was a desirable attribute for any man-about-town; Gibbon secured one in 1774 through the help of a wealthy cousin and remained a member, without once making a speech, through the eight most productive years of his life. He generally supported the government, though occasionally sliding into opposition over the critical American question. (Early in 1775 he was "convinced that we have both the right and the power on our side"; but by late 1777 he was saying, "What a wretched piece of work do we seem to be making of it in America!") However, his restiveness was eventually discouraged by his appointment to the Board of Trade and Plantations, a sinecure that he held for some three years at £750 a year.[2]

2. The following anonymous verse, possibly by Charles Fox, was circulated on the occasion of Gibbon's appointment:

> King George in a fright
> Lest Gibbon should write
> The story of England's disgrace,
> Thought no way so sure,
> His pen to secure,
> As to give the historian a place.
>
> But the caution is vain—
> 'Tis the curse of his reign
> That his projects should never succeed;
> Though he wrote not a line,
> Yet a course of decline
> In the author's example we read.
>
> His book well describes
> How corruption and bribes
> O'erthrew the great empire of Rome;
> And his ratings declare
> A degeneracy there
> That his conduct exhibits at home.

Throughout his adult life Gibbon was a painfully easy target for ridicule. Most personal descriptions of him date from later years, when fame permitted him to indulge his foibles freely. Yet so marked were his later idiosyncrasies that they must have been glaringly apparent even in the first years of his London independence. He was already putting on the weight that ultimately became gross corpulence; and on a man of small bones who was probably less than five feet tall, one pound did the work of several. His dress was at the very least elegant: one observer, recounting his boyhood meeting with Gibbon, recalled him dressed "in a suit of flower'd velvet, with a bag and sword"—a costume noted as "a little overcharged, perhaps, if his *person* be considered."

The same observer continues that Gibbon condescended "once or twice, in the course of the evening, to talk with me; the great historian was light and playful, suiting his matter to the capacity of the boy; but . . . still his mannerism prevail'd, still he tapp'd his snuff-box, still he smirk'd and smiled; and rounded his periods with the same air of good breeding as if he were conversing with men. His mouth, mellifluous as Plato's, was a round hole, nearly in the center of his visage."

Or consider this description of a "conversation" with Gibbon: "There was no interchange of ideas, for no one had a chance of replying, so fugitive, so variable, was his mode of discoursing, which consisted of points, anecdotes, and epigrammatic thrusts, all more or less to the purpose, and all pleasantly said with a French air and manner which gave them great piquancy, but which were withal so desultory and unconnected that, though each separately was extremely amusing, the attention of his auditors sometimes flagged before his own resources were exhausted. . . "

Gibbon appears to have been most chary of discussing his history in these years, when he was writing the first volume. His letters make very infrequent mention of it, and he did not tell his stepmother precisely what he was up to until the first volume was practically ready for the compositor. His London acquaintances may well have known that he was engaged in some historical project; but they too were literary men, busy on ambitious schemes of their own. Before the event, they had no reason to assume that the little fat man with the red hair, the high voice, the fancy clothes, and the absurd mannerisms was writing the greatest history that has ever been published in any of the languages of mankind.

2.

There is a possibly apocryphal story to the effect that when Gibbon presented the second volume of the *Decline and Fall* to the Duke of Gloucester, the duke exclaimed good-naturedly, "Another damned thick, square book! Always scribble, scribble, scribble! Eh, Mr. Gibbon?" The duke's reaction (which is also the reason for this Portable) inadvertently touches one of Gibbon's great strengths—the enormous scope of his history. It covers not merely Rome from the days of the early and "virtuous" emperors to the extinction of the empire in the west. It also includes the eastern empire, which survived for another thousand years; all the peoples and nations, both civilized and barbarian, which bordered on the empire; the rise of Mohammedanism; the Holy Roman empire; the crusades—in short, the history of the West (and also of the East, where it significantly affected the West) from A.D. 100 to A.D. 1500. For Gibbon correctly judged that these were all parts of a single great interlocking process. Though he has accused himself of displaying sometimes "a minute and superfluous diligence," he can certainly be pardoned for allotting three thousand pages to fourteen hundred years of western history.

The English are at their best in the writing of the spoken word, and Gibbon's style taps the same springs that have given English literature its greatest pre-eminence in drama and poetry. This may seem strange, applied to a man who sat in Parliament for eight years a "mute." But although he admits to writing his first chapter three times, and the second twice, his usual method of composition was to "cast a long paragraph in a single mould, to try it by my ear, to deposit it in my memory, but to suspend the action of the pen 'til I had given the last polish to my work." Hence the splendid sonority of the Gibbonian sentence, which echoes in the ear even when read silently.

Gibbon himself professed to detect certain variations in style among the six volumes in which the work was originally published. The first he judged "somewhat crude and elaborate," the second and third "ripened into ease [and] correctness"; but in the last three, for the most part composed in Lausanne, he feared that he "may have been seduced by the facility of my pen, and the constant habit of speaking one language and writing another may have infused some mixture of Gallic idioms."

It is possible, barely possible, that a meticulous reader might agree. But with minor variations in frequency, the sparkling sentences, paragraphs, and pages are to be found throughout, to the very end. Nor is this a matter of mere style. It is also a matter of wit, of delicately chosen words, of sardonic asides, of an occasional raciness that has caused Philip Guedalla to remark that Gibbon lived out most of his sex life in his footnotes. And above all it is a matter of thorough familiarity with and complete immersion in his subject: when Gibbon places something "beyond the Alps," he always means beyond the Alps from Rome or Constantinople, not from London or Lausanne.

Yet scope and style alone would not have given him audience among succeeding generations but for his massive underlying integrity. He was addicted to passionate description—his characters are haughty, bold, crafty, credulous, cowardly, etc.,—and he had his strong beliefs and prejudices. He delighted, for example, to reveal the shortcomings of some dubious figure of the early church. But underneath lay the calm historian, dealing out a full measure of censure to his favourite emperor, Julian, and praising St. Athanasius of Alexandria to the point of panegyric. In an age when it was fashionable to maintain that the historian's function was to point an instructive moral, Gibbon was out to prove nothing. Moreover, unlike some historians whose studied impartiality seems but a screen, his predilections are always in plain view. There are no hidden-ball tricks in Gibbon.

Rarely has a writer exercised so strong an attraction for his enemies, who have spent patient years of scholarship prying at the solid structure of the *Decline and Fall*. One long-used edition was edited and annotated by Dean Milman of St. Paul's Cathedral, who characterized the work as "a bold and disingenuous attack on Christianity." A second, perhaps the most widely read within the United States, was prepared by one Oliphant Smeaton, a Victorian worthy who snapped at Gibbon's heels for three thousand pages in a manner reminiscent of a small, active terrier on a parade ground. Another proper Victorian, by the engaging name of Birkbeck Hill, who edited a volume of Gibbon's memoirs, was shocked at the "indecency of his writing" and his "cold and erudite obscenity." And the original Thomas Bowdler, who gave his name to the language in the word "bowdlerized," prepared a special edition of the *Decline and Fall* with all the religious material expurgated.

Perhaps the most competent judgment of Gibbon's present stature was made by the great Cambridge scholar J. B. Bury, who prepared the best edition of the *Decline and Fall,* and who also wrote a classic *History of Greece.* Professor Bury warns that for a detailed description of early Christian theology and institutions, "neither the historian nor the man of letters will any longer subscribe, without a thousand reserves, to the theological chapters of the *Decline and Fall*"; but the most exhaustive subsequent inquiry "has neither reversed nor blunted the point" of Gibbon's slowly unfolding theme, that the destruction of the Roman empire was the joint triumph of barbarism and Christianity. The tremendous researches of the great German historian Mommsen and his school have perhaps slightly dated Gibbon's picture of the early empire; "but on the other hand his admirable description of the change from the Principate to absolute Monarchy, and the system of Diocletian and Constantine, is still most valuable." And Bury is almost tempted to rejoice that Gibbon leaned heavily on a now-discredited source for his description of Mohammed and the early Mohammedan expansion, since the resulting chapters in the *Decline and Fall* "would alone be enough to win perpetual literary fame."

More serious is Gibbon's contemptuous characterization of the later eastern empire as a "uniform tale of weakness and misery"—which Bury condemns as "one of the most untrue, and most effective, judgments ever uttered by a thoughtful historian." And Gibbon was "most conspicuously inadequate" in his description of the Slavonic peoples and kingdoms within and just without the eastern empire. On the whole, however, Gibbon himself could rest his case with Professor Bury's concluding verdict:

"That Gibbon is behind date in many details, and in some departments of importance, simply signifies that we and our fathers have not lived in an absolutely incompetent world. But in the main things he is still our master, above and beyond 'date.' It is needless to dwell on the obvious qualities which secure to him immunity from the common lot of historian writers—such as the bold and accurate measure of his progress through the ages; his accurate vision, and his tact in managing perspective; his discreet reserves of judgment and timely scepticism; the immortal affectation of his unique manner. By virtue of these superiorities he can defy the danger with which the activity of successors must always threaten the worthies of the past."

3.

Gibbon was immediately famous from the publication of the first volume of the *Decline and Fall* in February 1776. However, it was not until the entire work was finally completed (the second and third volumes appeared in 1781, the last three in 1788) that he received perhaps his two most impressive compliments. At that time Adam Smith (whose *Wealth of Nations* had also been published in 1776) wrote that "by the universal assent of every man of taste and learning, whom I either know or correspond with," the *Decline and Fall* "sets you at the very head of the whole literary tribe at present existing in Europe." And at the most famous public spectacle of the age, when people paid fifty guineas for a visitor's seat, Richard Sheridan denounced the mal-

feasances of Warren Hastings in India by charging that
"nothing equal in criminality was to be traced in ancient
or modern history, in the correct periods of Tacitus or
the luminous page of Gibbon." To be sure, Sheridan
later maintained—perhaps to prick the little man's vanity—that he had said "voluminous," not "luminous." But
in such a setting mere mention was enough.

The *Decline and Fall* also aroused a great theological
rancour against Gibbon, especially his famous chapters
fifteen and sixteen (see p. 260), which were the concluding chapters of the first volume. (Late in 1776 Gibbon wrote his stepmother that he was very well, "and I
think unhurt amidst as hot a cannonading as can be
pointed at Washington.") His single public reaction, in
reply to a pamphlet by one H. E. Davis, was to publish
*A Vindication of Some Passages in the Fifteenth and Six-
teenth Chapters;* thereafter he maintained a discreet and
on the whole effective silence. But in his autobiography
he remarks that had he foreseen their effect upon "the
pious, the timid, and the prudent," he might have been
tempted to soften the chapters in question.

The remainder of Gibbon's life can be told briefly.
The fall of Lord North's government in the spring of
1782 brought an end to the Board of Trade, and with it
Gibbon's £750 stipend that made living in London
possible. The next year he retired to Lausanne, where
he shared a handsome house with his friend Deyverdun;
lived sumptuously; grew fatter and fatter, troubled with
increasingly frequent and severe attacks of gout; argued
with Deyverdun about which of them should marry
(each nominated the other); remained the favourite of
Lausanne society; and became mellower and more philosophical by the minute. "I was never a very warm
patriot," he wrote to his friend Lord Sheffield in 1785,

"and I grow every day more a Citizen of the World. The scramble for power and profit at Westminster or St. James's, and the names of Pitt and Fox, become less interesting to me than those of Cæsar and Pompey."

For there was still study and work, until the great task was done. "It was on the day, or rather night, of the 27th of June 1787, between the hours of eleven and twelve, that I wrote the last lines of the last page, in a summerhouse in my garden. After laying down my pen, I took several turns in a *berceau*, or covered walk of acacias, which command a prospect of the country, the lake, and the mountains. The air was temperate, the sky was serene, the silver orb of the moon was reflected from the waters, and all nature was silent. I will not dissemble my first emotions of joy on recovery of my freedom, and, perhaps, the establishment of fame. But my pride was soon humbled, and a sober melancholy was spread over my mind, by the idea that I had taken an everlasting leave of an old and agreeable companion, and that, whatever might be the future of my *History*, the life of the historian must be short and precarious."

The completion of the *Decline and Fall* emptied his life. For a time he seems to have been held together by his mounting alarm at the French Revolution. He warned Lord Sheffield that "if you do not resist the spirit of innovation in the first attempt, if you admit the smallest and most specious change in our parliamentary system, you are lost." And his pleasure over the publication of Burke's *Reflections on the Revolution in France* caused him to write elatedly, "I admire his eloquence, I approve his politics, I adore his chivalry, and I can forgive even his superstition." However, the old historian's reverence for fact was still there. Passing in 1793 near Mainz, where the Prussian and Austrian forces were besieging the French, he observed that "the French fight with a courage worthy of a better cause," and noted that their artillery was admirable.

But being the dyspeptic onlooker, even of a great revolution, is no substitute for the daily task. Therefore he wrote Lord Sheffield confidentially in 1793 that he was considering a series of biographical sketches of eminent Englishmen since Henry VIII, and that he would like Sheffield to ask a certain Pall Mall bookseller whether such a work done in, say, the style of Gibbon might not be popular. If the bookseller rose to the bait, Gibbon continued, then Sheffield was to reply as follows: "'I am afraid, Mr. Nichols, that we shall hardly persuade my friend to engage in so great a work. Gibbon is old, and rich, and lazy. However, you may make the trial, and if you have a mind to write to Lausanne (as I do not know when he will be in England), I will send the application.'"

The sad truth about this project, Gibbon went on to explain, was "that my habits of industry are much impaired, and that I have reduced my studies to be the loose amusement of my morning hours, the repetition of which will insensibly lead me to the last term of existence. And for this very reason I shall not be sorry to bind myself by a liberal engagement, from which I may not with honour recede." It is always a question which is the more tragic, to fail in one's great ambition, or to succeed.

Gibbon died in January 1794, at the age of fifty-six, in London, on a visit occasioned by the death of Lord Sheffield's wife. The cause of his death was a vastly enlarged hydrocele, or collection of fluid in the area of the scrotum, perhaps complicated by a hernia. The condition seems to have existed in lesser degree during all his adult life, for at the age of twenty-four he visited a surgeon about it. The surgeon urged him to return for treatment, but he never did.

4.

In preparing this Portable version of the *Decline and Fall* I have sought to form a connected narrative while using as many as possible of Gibbon's bricks and as little as possible of my own mortar. Quantitatively, the pages following consist of about 96 per cent Gibbon and 4 per cent Saunders. But the reader has a right to know the exact techniques by which the condensation was effected. There were four:

1. All except the last chapter of this Portable has been drawn from the first half of the *Decline and Fall* —roughly, from the age of the Antonines to the end of the empire in the West. (The last chapter is composed of brief selections from the second half, chosen for literary merit and general interest.) This coincides with the general definition of the Roman empire, and Gibbon himself seriously considered halting his history at that point. Only by this limitation of scope was it possible even to dream of keeping within the bounds of a single Portable volume.

2. Within this narrower scope, it still proved feasible to omit a number of chapters in their entirety without, I hope, doing serious damage to the thread of Gibbon's narrative. A few of these omitted chapters (such as chapters viii and ix in the original, giving background on Persia and Germany, respectively) are not an integral part of the basic narrative and could be dropped with only a footnote marking their omission. Others, containing some material essential to the understanding of later chapters, have been abridged by me in italicized sec-

tions a few pages in length. In these abridgments I have of course attempted to follow faithfully the form and spirit of the original, and have sought to retain some of its flavour by a liberal sprinkling of quotations.

3. Within chapters that are otherwise included in their entirety, brief passages consisting of a paragraph to a page or so have occasionally seemed dispensable. (The possibility had been noted by Gibbon himself, who suggested that his fifteenth and sixteenth chapters "might still be compressed, without any loss of facts or sentiments.") Where the internal continuity of the chapter does not suffer, these brief omissions are marked merely by a footnote, which also mentions the nature of the omitted material. In all other cases the omitted section is condensed within an italicized section of text.

4. Nearly one fourth of the original *Decline and Fall* consists of footnotes, which D. M. Low aptly calls Gibbon's "table talk." Nearly all of them had to go; but only a lover of Gibbon will understand the pain involved in their deletion, and how hard it was to choose the few that could remain. (The footnotes are Gibbon's unless otherwise noted.) I cannot say that I used any rigorous rule in deciding which ones to keep. A few seemed necessary to understand the text sections to which they referred; others illustrated Gibbon's continual complaints at the prejudice, ignorance, stupidity, of the ancient writers whom he had to use as sources; and I certainly tried to retain all those whose raciness would have displeased Thomas Bowdler or Birkbeck Hill.

In addition, I have also taken the liberty of repunctuating and reparagraphing Gibbon throughout. By today's standards, a reader would have every right to complain that Gibbon used too much punctuation and too few paragraphs.

A final word. The *History of the Decline and Fall of the Roman Empire* has something special in it for everyone, and it had a special something for me. In the conclusion of his second chapter, where he discusses Roman literature and learning in the age of the Antonines, Gibbon remarks that "a crowd of critics, of compilers, of commentators, darkened the face of learning." I have often winced at those words while preparing this Portable, and my only claim to Gibbon's forgiveness lies in what I am trying to do. This book is designed to give the reader a taste for Gibbon, in the hope that he will go out and make a glutton of himself.

DERO A. SAUNDERS

March 1952

THE DECLINE AND FALL
OF THE ROMAN EMPIRE

Chapter I

(A.D. 98-180)

The extent and military force of the empire in the age of the Antonines

IN THE second century of the Christian era the empire of Rome comprehended the fairest part of the earth and the most civilized portion of mankind. The frontiers of that extensive monarchy were guarded by ancient renown and disciplined valour. The gentle but powerful influence of laws and manners had gradually cemented the union of the provinces. Their peaceful inhabitants enjoyed and abused the advantages of wealth and luxury. The image of a free constitution was preserved with decent reverence: the Roman senate appeared to possess the sovereign authority and devolved on the emperors all the executive powers of government. During a happy period of more than fourscore years, the public administration was conducted by the virtue and abilities of Nerva, Trajan, Hadrian, and the two Antonines. It is the design of this and of the two succeeding chapters to describe the prosperous condition of their empire, and afterwards, from the death of Marcus Antoninus, to deduce the most important circumstances of its decline and fall, a revolution which will ever be remembered and is still felt by the nations of the earth.

The principal conquests of the Romans were achieved under the republic; and the emperors, for the most part, were satisfied with preserving those dominions which had been acquired by the policy of the senate, the active emulation of the consuls, and the martial enthusiasm of the people. The seven first centuries were filled with a rapid succession of triumphs; but it was reserved for Augustus to relinquish the ambitious design of subduing the whole earth and to introduce a spirit of moderation into the public councils. Inclined to peace by his temper and situation, it was easy for him to discover that Rome, in her present exalted situation, had much less to hope than to fear from the chance of arms; and that, in the prosecution of remote wars, the undertaking became every day more difficult, the event more doubtful, and the possession more precarious and less beneficial. The experience of Augustus added weight to these salutary reflections and effectually convinced him that, by the prudent vigour of his counsels, it would be easy to secure every concession which the safety or the dignity of Rome might require from the most formidable barbarians. Instead of exposing his person and his legions to the arrows of the Parthians, he obtained, by an honourable treaty, the restitution of the standards and prisoners which had been taken in the defeat of Crassus.

His generals, in the early part of his reign, attempted the reduction of Æthiopia and Arabia Felix [Yemen]. They marched near a thousand miles to the south of the tropic; but the heat of the climate soon repelled the invaders and protected the unwarlike natives of those sequestered regions. The northern countries of Europe scarcely deserved the expense and labour of conquest. The forests and morasses of Germany were filled with a hardy race of barbarians, who despised life when it was separated from freedom; and though on the first attack they seemed to yield to the weight of the Roman power, they soon, by a signal act of despair, regained their independence and reminded Augustus of the vi-

cissitude of fortune.[1] On the death of that emperor
his testament was publicly read in the senate. He bequeathed, as a valuable legacy to his successors, the
advice of confining the empire within those limits which
Nature seemed to have placed as its permanent bul-
warks and boundaries: on the west the Atlantic Ocean;
the Rhine and Danube on the north; the Euphrates on
the east; and towards the south, the sandy deserts of
Arabia and Africa.

Happily for the repose of mankind, the moderate system recommended by the wisdom of Augustus was
adopted by the fears and vices of his immediate successors. Engaged in the pursuit of pleasure or in the
exercise of tyranny, the first Cæsars seldom showed
themselves to the armies or to the provinces; nor were
they disposed to suffer that those triumphs which *their*
indolence neglected should be usurped by the conduct
and valour of their lieutenants. The military fame of a
subject was considered as an insolent invasion of the
Imperial prerogative; and it became the duty as well
as interest of every Roman general to guard the frontiers
entrusted to his care, without aspiring to conquests
which might have proved no less fatal to himself than
to the vanquished barbarians.

The only accession which the Roman empire received during the first century of the Christian era was
the province of Britain. In this single instance the successors of Cæsar and Augustus were persuaded to follow the example of the former rather than the precept
of the latter. The proximity of its situation to the coast

1. By the slaughter of Varus and his three legions. Augustus
did not receive the melancholy news with all the temper and
firmness that might have been expected from his character.
[Footnotes are Gibbon's unless otherwise noted.]

of Gaul seemed to invite their arms; the pleasing though doubtful intelligence of a pearl fishery attracted their avarice;[2] and as Britain was viewed in the light of a distinct and insulated world, the conquest scarcely formed any exception to the general system of continental measures. After a war of about forty years, undertaken by the most stupid, maintained by the most dissolute, and terminated by the most timid of all the emperors, the far greater part of the island submitted to the Roman yoke.[3] The various tribes of Britons possessed valour without conduct, and the love of freedom without the spirit of union. They took up arms with savage fierceness; they laid them down or turned them against each other with wild inconstancy; and while they fought singly, they were successively subdued. Neither the fortitude of Caractacus, nor the despair of Boadicea, nor the fanaticism of the Druids, could avert the slavery of their country or resist the steady progress of the Imperial generals, who maintained the national glory when the throne was disgraced by the weakest or the most vicious of mankind. At the very time when Domitian, confined to his palace, felt the terrors which he inspired, his legions, under the command of the virtuous Agricola, defeated the collected force of the Caledonians at the foot of the Grampian hills; and his fleets, venturing to explore an unknown and dangerous navigation, displayed the Roman arms round every part of the island. The conquest of Britain was considered as already achieved; and it was the design of Agricola to complete and ensure his success by the easy reduction of Ireland, for which in his opinion one legion and a

2. Cæsar himself conceals that ignoble motive, but it is mentioned by Suetonius. The British pearls proved, however, of little value, on account of their dark and livid colour.
3. Claudius, Nero, and Domitian.

few auxiliaries were sufficient. The western isle might be improved into a valuable possession, and the Britons would wear their chains with the less reluctance if the prospect and example of freedom were on every side removed from before their eyes.

But the superior merit of Agricola soon occasioned his removal from the government of Britain, and forever disappointed this rational though extensive scheme of conquest. Before his departure the prudent general had provided for security as well as for dominion. He had observed that the island is almost divided into two unequal parts by the opposite gulfs or, as they are now called, the Firths of Scotland. Across the narrow interval of about forty miles he had drawn a line of military stations, which was afterwards fortified in the reign of Antoninus Pius by a turf rampart erected on foundations of stone. This wall of Antoninus, at a small distance beyond the modern cities of Edinburgh and Glasgow, was fixed as the limit of the Roman province. The native Caledonians preserved in the northern extremity of the island their wild independence, for which they were not less indebted to their poverty than to their valour. Their incursions were frequently repelled and chastised, but their country was never subdued. The masters of the fairest and most wealthy climates of the globe turned with contempt from gloomy hills assailed by the winter tempest, from lakes concealed in a blue mist, and from cold and lonely heaths over which the deer of the forest were chased by a troop of naked barbarians.

Such was the state of the Roman frontiers, and such the maxims of Imperial policy, from the death of Augustus to the accession of Trajan. That virtuous and active prince had received the education of a soldier and possessed the talents of a general. The peaceful system of his predecessors was interrupted by scenes of war and conquest; and the legions, after a long interval, beheld a military emperor at their head. The first exploits of Trajan were against the Dacians, the most warlike of men, who dwelt beyond the Danube, and who, during the reign of Domitian, had insulted with impunity the majesty of Rome. To the strength and fierceness of barbarians they added a contempt for life, which was derived from a warm persuasion of the immortality and transmigration of the soul. Decebalus, the Dacian king, approved himself a rival not unworthy of Trajan; nor did he despair of his own and the public fortune till, by the confession of his enemies, he had exhausted every resource both of valour and policy. This memorable war, with a very short suspension of hostilities, lasted five years; and as the emperor could exert without control the whole force of the state, it was terminated by an absolute submission of the barbarians. The new province of Dacia, which formed a second exception to the precept of Augustus, was about thirteen hundred miles in circumference. Its natural boundaries were the Dniester, the Theiss or Tibiscus,[4] the Lower Danube, and the Euxine Sea [Black Sea]. The vestiges of a military road may still be traced from the banks of the Danube to the neighbourhood of Bender, a place famous in modern history, and the actual frontier of the Turkish and Russian empires.

Trajan was ambitious of fame; and as long as mankind shall continue to bestow more liberal applause on their destroyers than on their benefactors, the thirst of military glory will ever be the vice of the most exalted characters. The praises of Alexander, transmitted by a succession of poets and historians, had

4. *Editor's note:* Now known as the Tisza, a river that rises in the Carpathian Mountains and empties into the Danube.

kindled a dangerous emulation in the mind of Trajan. Like him, the Roman emperor undertook an expedition against the nations of the East, but he lamented with a sigh that his advanced age scarcely left him any hopes of equalling the renown of the son of Philip. Yet the success of Trajan, however transient, was rapid and specious. The degenerate Parthians, broken by intestine discord, fled before his arms. He descended the river Tigris in triumph, from the mountains of Armenia to the Persian gulf. He enjoyed the honour of being the first, as he was the last, of the Roman generals who ever navigated that remote sea. His fleets ravaged the coasts of Arabia; and Trajan vainly flattered himself that he was approaching towards the confines of India. Every day the astonished senate received the intelligence of new names and new nations that acknowledged his sway. They were informed that the kings of Bosphorus, Colchos, Iberia, Albania, Osrhoene, and even the Parthian monarch himself, had accepted their diadems from the hands of the emperor; that the independent tribes of the Median and Carduchian hills had implored his protection; and that the rich countries of Armenia, Mesopotamia, and Assyria were reduced into the state of provinces. But the death of Trajan soon clouded the splendid prospect; and it was justly to be dreaded that so many distant nations would throw off the unaccustomed yoke when they were no longer restrained by the powerful hand which had imposed it.

It was an ancient tradition that when the Capitol was founded by one of the Roman kings, the god Terminus (who presided over boundaries and was represented according to the fashion of that age by a large stone) alone among all the inferior deities refused to yield his place to Jupiter himself. A favourable inference was drawn from his obstinacy, which was inter-

preted by the augurs as a sure presage that the boundaries of the Roman power would never recede. During
many ages the prediction, as it is usual, contributed to
its own accomplishment. But though Terminus had
resisted the majesty of Jupiter, he submitted to the authority of the emperor Hadrian. The resignation of all
the eastern conquests of Trajan was the first measure
of his reign. He restored to the Parthians the election
of an independent sovereign, withdrew the Roman garrisons from the provinces of Armenia, Mesopotamia,
and Assyria, and in compliance with the precept of
Augustus once more established the Euphrates as the
frontier of the empire. Censure, which arraigns the
public actions and the private motives of princes, has
ascribed to envy a conduct which might be attributed
to the prudence and moderation of Hadrian. The various character of that emperor, capable by turns of the
meanest and the most generous sentiments, may afford
some colour to the suspicion. It was, however, scarcely
in his power to place the superiority of his predecessor
in a more conspicuous light than by thus confessing
himself unequal to the task of defending the conquests
of Trajan.

The martial and ambitious spirit of Trajan formed
a very singular contrast with the moderation of his successor. The restless activity of Hadrian was not less
remarkable when compared with the gentle repose
of Antoninus Pius. The life of the former was almost
a perpetual journey; and as he possessed the various
talents of the soldier, the statesman, and the scholar,
he gratified his curiosity in the discharge of his duty.
Careless of the difference of seasons and of climates,
he marched on foot and bareheaded over the snows of
Caledonia and the sultry plains of the Upper Egypt;
nor was there a province of the empire which, in the

course of his reign, was not honoured with the presence of the monarch. But the tranquil life of Antoninus Pius was spent in the bosom of Italy; and during the twenty-three years that he directed the public administration the longest journeys of that amiable prince extended no farther than from his palace in Rome to the retirement of his Lanuvian villa.

Notwithstanding this difference in their personal conduct, the general system of Augustus was equally adopted and uniformly pursued by Hadrian and by the two Antonines. They persisted in the design of maintaining the dignity of the empire without attempting to enlarge its limits. By every honourable expedient they invited the friendship of the barbarians and endeavoured to convince mankind that the Roman power, raised above the temptation of conquest, was actuated only by the love of order and justice. During a long period of forty-three years their virtuous labours were crowned with success; and if we except a few slight hostilities that served to exercise the legions of the frontier, the reigns of Hadrian and Antoninus Pius offer the fair prospect of universal peace. The Roman name was revered among the most remote nations of the earth. The fiercest barbarians frequently submitted their differences to the arbitration of the emperor; and we are informed by a contemporary historian that he had seen ambassadors who were refused the honour, which they came to solicit, of being admitted into the rank of subjects.

The terror of the Roman arms added weight and dignity to the moderation of the emperors. They preserved peace by a constant preparation for war; and while justice regulated their conduct, they announced to the nations on their confines that they were as little disposed to endure as to offer an injury. The military strength which it had been sufficient for Hadrian and the elder Antoninus to display was exerted against the Parthians and the Germans by the emperor Marcus. The hostilities of the barbarians provoked the resentment of that philosophic monarch, and in the prosecution of a just defence Marcus and his generals obtained many signal victories both on the Euphrates and on the Danube. The military establishment of the Roman empire, which thus assured either its tranquillity or success, will now become the proper and important object of our attention.

In the purer ages of the commonwealth the use of arms was reserved for those ranks of citizens who had a country to love, a property to defend, and some share in enacting those laws which it was their interest as well as duty to maintain. But in proportion as the public freedom was lost in extent of conquest, war was gradually improved into an art and degraded into a trade. The legions themselves, even at the time when they were recruited in the most distant provinces, were supposed to consist of Roman citizens. That distinction was generally considered either as a legal qualification or as a proper recompense for the soldier; but a more serious regard was paid to the essential merit of age, strength, and military stature. In all levies a just preference was given to the climates of the North over those of the South; the race of men born to the exercise of arms was sought for in the country rather than in cities; and it was very reasonably presumed that the hardy occupations of smiths, carpenters, and huntsmen would supply more vigour and resolution than the sedentary trades which are employed in the service of luxury. After every qualification of property had been laid aside, the armies of the Roman emperors were still commanded for the most part by officers of a liberal birth and education; but the common soldiers, like the mercenary troops of modern Europe, were drawn from the meanest and very frequently from the most profligate of mankind.

That public virtue which among the ancients was denominated patriotism is derived from a strong sense of our own interest in the preservation and prosperity of the free government of which we are members. Such a sentiment, which had rendered the legions of the republic almost invincible, could make but a very feeble impression on the mercenary servants of a despotic prince; and it became necessary to supply that defect by other motives of a different but not less forcible nature—honour and religion. The peasant or mechanic imbibed the useful prejudice that he was advanced to the more dignified profession of arms, in which his rank and reputation would depend on his own valour; and that, although the prowess of a private soldier must often escape the notice of fame, his own behaviour might sometimes confer glory or disgrace on the company, the legion, or even the army to whose honours he was associated. On his first entrance into the service an oath was administered to him with every circumstance of solemnity. He promised never to desert his standard, to submit his own will to the commands of his leaders, and to sacrifice his life for the safety of the emperor and the empire. The attachment of the Roman troops to their standards was inspired by the united influence of religion and of honour. The golden eagle which glittered in the front of the legion was the object of their fondest devotion; nor was it esteemed less impious than it was ignominious to abandon that sacred ensign in the hour of danger. These motives, which derived their strength from the imagination, were enforced by fears and hopes of a more substantial kind.

Regular pay, occasional donatives, and a stated recompense after the appointed time of service alleviated the hardships of the military life,[5] whilst on the other hand it was impossible for cowardice or disobedience to escape the severest punishment. The centurions were authorized to chastise with blows, the generals had a right to punish with death; and it was an inflexible maxim of Roman discipline that a good soldier should dread his officers far more than the enemy. From such laudable arts did the valour of the Imperial troops receive a degree of firmness and docility unattainable by the impetuous and irregular passions of barbarians.

And yet so sensible were the Romans of the imperfection of valour without skill and practice that in their language the name of an army was borrowed from the word which signified exercise. Military exercises were the important and unremitted object of their discipline. The recruits and young soldiers were constantly trained both in the morning and in the evening, nor was age or knowledge allowed to excuse the veterans from the daily repetition of what they had completely learned. Large sheds were erected in the winter-quarters of the troops that their useful labours might not receive any interruption from the most tempestuous weather; and it was carefully observed that the arms destined to this imitation of war should be of double the weight which was required in real action. It is not the purpose of this work to enter into any minute description of the Roman exercises. We shall only remark that they com-

5. The emperor Domitian raised the annual stipend of the legionaries to twelve pieces of gold, which in his time was equivalent to about ten of our guineas. After twenty years' service, the veteran received three thousand denarii (about one hundred pounds sterling), or a proportionable allowance of land. The pay and advantages of the guards were in general about double those of the legions.

prehended whatever could add strength to the body, activity to the limbs, or grace to the motions. The soldiers were diligently instructed to march, to run, to leap, to swim, to carry heavy burdens; to handle every species of arms that was used either for offence or for defence, either in distant engagement or in a closer onset; to form a variety of evolutions; and to move to the sound of flutes in the Pyrrhic or martial dance. In the midst of peace the Roman troops familiarized themselves with the practice of war; and it is prettily remarked by an ancient historian [Josephus] who had fought against them that the effusion of blood was the only circumstance which distinguished a field of battle from a field of exercise. It was the policy of the ablest generals, and even of the emperors themselves, to encourage these military studies by their presence and example; and we are informed that Hadrian as well as Trajan frequently condescended to instruct the unexperienced soldiers, to reward the diligent, and sometimes to dispute with them the prize of superior strength or dexterity. Under the reigns of those princes the science of tactics was cultivated with success; and as long as the empire retained any vigour their military instructions were respected as the most perfect model of Roman discipline.[6]

We have attempted to explain the spirit which moderated and the strength which supported the power of Hadrian and the Antonines. We shall now endeavour with clearness and precision to describe the provinces once united under their sway but at present divided into so many independent and hostile states.

Spain, the western extremity of the empire, of Europe,

6. *Editor's note:* Omitted here is Gibbon's precise description of the composition, armament, tactics, etc., of the Roman forces.

and of the ancient world, has in every age invariably preserved the same natural limits: the Pyrenæan mountains, the Mediterranean, and the Atlantic Ocean. That great peninsula, at present so unequally divided between two sovereigns, was distributed by Augustus into three provinces, Lusitania, Bætica, and Tarraconensis. The kingdom of Portugal now fills the place of the warlike country of the Lusitanians; and the loss sustained by the former on the side of the east is compensated by an accession of territory towards the north. The confines of Grenada and Andalusia correspond with those of ancient Bætica. The remainder of Spain, Gallicia and the Asturias, Biscay and Navarre, León and the two Castilles, Murcia, Valencia, Catalonia, and Aragon, all contributed to form the third and most considerable of the Roman governments, which from the name of its capital was styled the province of Tarragona. Of the native barbarians, the Celtiberians were the most powerful, as the Cantabrians and Asturians proved the most obstinate. Confident in the strength of their mountains, they were the last who submitted to the arms of Rome and the first who threw off the yoke of the Arabs.

Ancient Gaul, as it contained the whole country between the Pyrenees, the Alps, the Rhine, and the Ocean, was of greater extent than modern France. To the dominions of that powerful monarchy, with its recent acquisitions of Alsace and Lorraine, we must add the duchy of Savoy, the cantons of Switzerland, the four electorates of the Rhine, and the territories of Liége, Luxembourg, Hainault, Flanders, and Brabant. When Augustus gave laws to the conquests of his father, he introduced a division of Gaul equally adapted to the progress of the legions, to the course of the rivers, and to the principal national distinctions, which had comprehended above an hundred independent states. The seacoast of the Mediterranean, Languedoc, Provence, and Dauphiné, received their provincial appellation from the colony of Narbonne. The government of Aquitaine was extended from the Pyrenees to the Loire. The country between the Loire and the Seine was styled the Celtic Gaul, and soon borrowed a new denomination from the celebrated colony of Lugdunum, or Lyons. The Belgic lay beyond the Seine, and in more ancient 'times had been bounded only by the Rhine; but a little before the age of Cæsar the Germans, abusing their superiority of valour, had occupied a considerable portion of the Belgic territory. The Roman conquerors very eagerly embraced so flattering a circumstance, and the Gallic frontier of the Rhine, from Basel to Leyden, received the pompous names of the Upper and the Lower Germany. Such, under the reign of the Antonines, were the six provinces of Gaul: the Narbonnese, Aquitaine, the Celtic or Lyonnese, the Belgic, and the two Germanies.

We have already had occasion to mention the conquest of Britain and to fix the boundary of the Roman province in this island. It comprehended all England, Wales, and the Lowlands of Scotland as far as Dumbarton and Edinburgh. Before Britain lost her freedom the country was irregularly divided between thirty tribes of barbarians, of whom the most considerable were the Belgæ in the West, the Brigantes in the North, the Silures in South Wales, and the Iceni in Norfolk and Suffolk. As far as we can either trace or credit the resemblance of manners and language, Spain, Gaul, and Britain were peopled by the same hardy race of savages. Before they yielded to the Roman arms, they often disputed the field, and often renewed the contest. After their submission they constituted the western

division of the European provinces, which extended
from the columns of Hercules to the wall of Antoninus,
and from the mouth of the Tagus to the sources of the
Rhine and Danube.

Before the Roman conquest the country which is
now called Lombardy was not considered as a part of
Italy. It had been occupied by a powerful colony of
Gauls, who, settling themselves along the banks of the
Po from Piedmont to Romagna, carried their arms and
diffused their name from the Alps to the Apennine.
The Ligurians dwelt on the rocky coast which now
forms the republic of Genoa. Venice was yet unborn;
but the territories of that state, which lie to the east
of the Adige, were inhabited by the Venetians. The
middle part of the peninsula that now composes the
duchy of Tuscany and the ecclesiastical state was
the ancient seat of the Etruscans and Umbrians, to the
former of whom Italy was indebted for the first rudiments of civilized life. The Tiber rolled at the foot of
the seven hills of Rome, and the country of the Sabines,
the Latins, and the Volsci, from that river to the frontiers of Naples, was the theatre of her infant victories.
On that celebrated ground the first consuls deserved
triumphs, their successors adorned villas, and *their* posterity have erected convents. Capua and Campania possessed the immediate territory of Naples; the rest of
the kingdom was inhabited by many warlike nations,
the Marsi, the Samnites, the Apulians, and the Lucanians; and the seacoasts had been covered by the
flourishing colonies of the Greeks. We may remark that
when Augustus divided Italy into eleven regions the
little province of Istria was annexed to that seat of
Roman sovereignty.

The European provinces of Rome were protected by
the course of the Rhine and the Danube. The latter

of those mighty streams, which rises at the distance
of only thirty miles from the former, flows above thirteen hundred miles, for the most part to the southeast,
collects the tribute of sixty navigable rivers, and is at
length, through six mouths, received into the Euxine,
which appears scarcely equal to such an accession of
waters. The provinces of the Danube soon acquired
the general appellation of Illyricum, or the Illyrian
frontier, and were esteemed the most warlike of the
empire; but they deserve to be more particularly considered under the names of Rhætia, Noricum, Pannonia,
Dalmatia, Dacia, Mæsia, Thrace, Macedonia, and
Greece.

The province of Rhætia, which soon extinguished the
name of the Vindelicians, extended from the summit of
the Alps to the banks of the Danube; from its source, as
far as its conflux with the Inn. The greatest part of the
flat country is subject to the elector of Bavaria; the city
of Augsburg is protected by the constitution of the German empire; the Grisons are safe in their mountains,
and the country of Tyrol is ranked among the numerous
provinces of the house of Austria.

The wide extent of territory which is included between the Inn, the Danube, and the Save—Austria,
Styria, Carinthia, Carniola, the Lower Hungary, and
Sclavonia—was known to the ancients under the names
of Noricum and Pannonia. In their original state of
independence, their fierce inhabitants were intimately
connected. Under the Roman government they were
frequently united, and they still remain the patrimony
of a single family. They now contain the residence of
a German prince, who styles himself Emperor of the
Romans, and form the centre as well as strength of the
Austrian power. It may not be improper to observe that
if we except Bohemia, Moravia, the northern skirts of

Austria, and a part of Hungary between the Theiss and the Danube, all the other dominions of the house of Austria were comprised within the limits of the Roman empire.

Dalmatia, to which the name of Illyricum more properly belonged, was a long but narrow tract between the Save and the Adriatic. The best part of the seacoast, which still retains its ancient appellation, is a province of the Venetian state and the seat of the little republic of Ragusa. The inland parts have assumed the Sclavonian names of Croatia and Bosnia; the former obeys an Austrian governor, the latter a Turkish pasha; but the whole country is still infested by tribes of barbarians whose savage independence irregularly marks the doubtful limit of the Christian and Mahometan power.

After the Danube had received the waters of the Theiss and the Save, it acquired, at least among the Greeks, the name of Ister. It formerly divided Mæsia and Dacia, the latter of which, as we have already seen, was a conquest of Trajan, and the only province beyond the river. If we inquire into the present state of those countries, we shall find that, on the left hand of the Danube, Temeswar and Transylvania have been annexed, after many revolutions, to the crown of Hungary; whilst the principalities of Moldavia and Wallachia acknowledge the supremacy of the Ottoman Porte. On the right hand of the Danube, Mæsia, which during the middle ages was broken into the barbarian kingdoms of Servia and Bulgaria, is again united in Turkish slavery.

The appellation of Roumelia, which is still bestowed by the Turks on the extensive countries of Thrace, Macedonia, and Greece, preserves the memory of their ancient state under the Roman empire. In the time of the Antonines the martial regions of Thrace, from the mountains of Hæmus and Rhodope to the Bosphorus and the Hellespont, had assumed the form of a province. Notwithstanding the change of masters and of religion, the new city of Rome, founded by Constantine on the banks of the Bosphorus, has ever since remained the capital of a great monarchy. The kingdom of Macedonia, which under the reign of Alexander gave laws to Asia, derived more solid advantages from the policy of the two Philips, and with its dependencies of Epirus and Thessaly extended from the Ægean to the Ionian Sea. When we reflect on the fame of Thebes and Argos, of Sparta and Athens, we can scarcely persuade ourselves that so many immortal republics of ancient Greece were lost in a single province of the Roman empire, which from the superior influence of the Achæan league was usually denominated the province of Achaia.

Such was the state of Europe under the Roman emperors. The provinces of Asia, without excepting the transient conquests of Trajan, are all comprehended within the limits of the Turkish power. But instead of following the arbitrary divisions of despotism and ignorance, it will be safer for us, as well as more agreeable, to observe the indelible characters of nature. The name of Asia Minor is attributed with some propriety to the peninsula which, confined betwixt the Euxine and the Mediterranean, advances from the Euphrates towards Europe. The most extensive and flourishing district, westward of Mount Taurus and the river Halys,[7] was dignified by the Romans with the exclusive title of Asia. The jurisdiction of that province extended over the ancient monarchies of Troy, Lydia, and Phrygia, the maritime countries of the Pamphylians, Lycians, and Carians, and the Grecian colonies of Ionia, which equalled in arts, though not in arms, the glory of their

7. *Editor's note:* Now known as the Kizilirmak, a river that rises in central Turkey and flows into the Black Sea.

parent. The kingdoms of Bithynia and Pontus possessed the northern side of the peninsula from Constantinople to Trebizond. On the opposite side, the province of Cilicia was terminated by the mountains of Syria; the inland country, separated from the Roman Asia by the river Halys, and from Armenia by the Euphrates, had once formed the independent kingdom of Cappadocia. In this place we may observe that the northern shores of the Euxine, beyond Trebizond in Asia and beyond the Danube in Europe, acknowledged the sovereignty of the emperors and received at their hands either tributary princes or Roman garrisons. Budzak, Crim Tartary, Circassia, and Mingrelia are the modern appellations of those savage countries.

Under the successors of Alexander, Syria was the seat of the Seleucidæ, who reigned over Upper Asia till the successful revolt of the Parthians confined their dominions between the Euphrates and the Mediterranean. When Syria became subject to the Romans it formed the eastern frontier of their empire; nor did that province, in its utmost latitude, know any other bounds than the mountains of Cappadocia to the north, and towards the south the confines of Egypt and the Red Sea. Phœnicia and Palestine were sometimes annexed to, and sometimes separated from, the jurisdiction of Syria. The former of these was a narrow and rocky coast; the latter was a territory scarcely superior to Wales either in fertility or extent. Yet Phœnicia and Palestine will forever live in the memory of mankind, since America as well as Europe has received letters from the one and religion from the other. A sandy desert alike destitute of wood and water skirts along the doubtful confine of Syria from the Euphrates to the Red Sea. The wandering life of the Arabs was inseparably connected with their independence; and wherever, on some spots less barren than the rest, they ventured to form any settled habitation, they soon became subjects to the Roman empire.

The geographers of antiquity have frequently hesitated to what portion of the globe they should ascribe Egypt. By its situation that celebrated kingdom is included within the immense peninsula of Africa; but it is accessible only on the side of Asia, whose revolutions in almost every period of history Egypt has humbly obeyed. A Roman præfect was seated on the`splendid throne of the Ptolemies, and the iron sceptre of the Mamalukes is now in the hands of a Turkish pasha. The Nile flows down the country, above five hundred miles from the Tropic of Cancer to the Mediterranean, and marks on either side the extent of fertility by the measure of its inundations. Cyrene, situate towards the west and along the seacoast, was first a Greek colony, afterwards a province of Egypt, and is now lost in the desert of Barca.

From Cyrene to the ocean the coast of Africa extends above fifteen hundred miles; yet so closely is it pressed between the Mediterranean and the Sahara, or sandy desert, that its breadth seldom exceeds fourscore or an hundred miles. The eastern division was considered by the Romans as the more peculiar and proper province of Africa. Till the arrival of the Phœnician colonies that fertile country was inhabited by the Libyans, the most savage of mankind. Under the immediate jurisdiction of Carthage it became the centre of commerce and empire; but the republic of Carthage is now degenerated into the feeble and disorderly states of Tripoli and Tunis. The military government of Algiers oppresses the wide extent of Numidia, as it was once united under Massinissa and Jugurtha; but in the time of Augustus the limits of Numidia were contracted, and at least two-thirds of the country acquiesced in the name of Mauritania, with the epithet of Cæsariensis. The genuine Mauritania, or country of the Moors, which from the ancient city of Tingi (or Tangier) was distinguished by the appellation of Tingitana, is represented by the modern kingdom of Fez. Sallè, on the ocean, long infamous for its piratical depredations, was noticed by the Romans as the extreme object of their power and almost of their geography. A city of their foundation may still be discovered near Mequinez, the residence of the barbarian whom we condescend to style the Emperor of Morocco; but it does not appear that his more southern dominions, Morocco itself, and Segelmessa, were ever comprehended within the Roman province. The western parts of Africa are intersected by the branches of Mount Atlas, a name so idly celebrated by the fancy of poets, but which is now diffused over the immense ocean that rolls between the ancient and the new continent.[8]

Having now finished the circuit of the Roman empire, we may observe that Africa is divided from Spain by a narrow strait of about twelve miles, through which the Atlantic flows into the Mediterranean. The columns of Hercules, so famous among the ancients, were two mountains which seemed to have been torn asunder by some convulsion of the elements, and at the foot of the European mountain the fortress of Gibraltar is now seated. The whole extent of the Mediterranean Sea, its coasts, and its islands, were comprised within the Roman dominion. Of the larger islands, the two Baleares, which derive their name of Majorca and Minorca from their respective size, are subject at present, the former to Spain, the latter to Great Britain. It is easier to deplore

8. M. de Voltaire, unsupported by either fact or probability, has generously bestowed the Canary Islands on the Roman empire.

the fate than to describe the actual condition of Corsica.
Two Italian sovereigns assume a regal title from Sardinia
and Sicily. Crete, or Candia, with Cyprus, and most of
the smaller islands of Greece and Asia, have been subdued by the Turkish arms; whilst the little rock of
Malta defies their power and has emerged, under the
government of its military Order, into fame and opulence.

This long enumeration of provinces, whose broken
fragments have formed so many powerful kingdoms,
might almost induce us to forgive the vanity or ignorance of the ancients. Dazzled with the extensive sway,
the irresistible strength, and the real or affected moderation of the emperors, they permitted themselves to despise, and sometimes to forget, the outlying countries
which had been left in the enjoyment of a barbarous
independence; and they gradually usurped the license
of confounding the Roman monarchy with the globe of
the earth. But the temper as well as knowledge of a
modern historian requires a more sober and accurate
language. He may impress a juster image of the greatness of Rome by observing that the empire was above
two thousand miles in breadth, from the wall of Antoninus and the northern limits of Dacia to Mount Atlas
and the Tropic of Cancer; that it extended in length
more than three thousand miles from the Western Ocean
to the Euphrates; that it was situated in the finest part
of the Temperate Zone, between the twenty-fourth and
fifty-sixth degrees of northern latitude; and that it was
supposed to contain above sixteen hundred thousand
square miles, for the most part of fertile and well-
cultivated land.

Chapter II

*Of the union and internal prosperity of the Roman
empire in the age of the Antonines*

IT IS not alone by the rapidity or extent of conquest
that we should estimate the greatness of Rome. The
sovereign of the Russian deserts commands a larger
portion of the globe. In the seventh summer after his
passage of the Hellespont, Alexander erected the Macedonian trophies on the banks of the Hyphasis. Within
less than a century the irresistible Zingis and the Mogul
princes of his race spread their cruel devastations and
transient empire from the sea of China to the confines
of Egypt and Germany. But the firm edifice of Roman
power was raised and preserved by the wisdom of ages.
The obedient provinces of Trajan and the Antonines
were united by laws and adorned by arts. They might
occasionally suffer from the partial abuse of delegated
authority; but the general principle of government was
wise, simple, and beneficent. They enjoyed the religion
of their ancestors, whilst in civil honours and advantages
they were exalted, by just degrees, to an equality with
their conquerors.

The policy of the emperors and the senate, as far as
it concerned religion, was happily seconded by the reflections of the enlightened, and by the habits of the
superstitious, part of their subjects. The various modes
of worship which prevailed in the Roman world were
all considered by the people as equally true, by the
philosopher as equally false, and by the magistrate as

equally useful. And thus toleration produced not only mutual indulgence but even religious concord.

The superstition of the people was not embittered by any mixture of theological rancour, nor was it confined by the chains of any speculative system. The devout polytheist, though fondly attached to his national rites, admitted with implicit faith the different religions of the earth. Fear, gratitude, and curiosity, a dream or an omen, a singular disorder or a distant journey, perpetually disposed him to multiply the articles of his belief and to enlarge the list of his protectors. The thin texture of the pagan mythology was interwoven with various but not discordant materials. As soon as it was allowed that sages and heroes who had lived or who had died for the benefit of their country were exalted to a state of power and immortality, it was universally confessed that they deserved, if not the adoration, at least the reverence, of all mankind. The deities of a thousand groves and a thousand streams possessed in peace their local and respective influence; nor could the Roman who deprecated the wrath of the Tiber deride the Egyptian who presented his offering to the beneficent genius of the Nile. The visible powers of Nature, the planets, and the elements were the same throughout the universe. The invisible governors of the moral world were inevitably cast in a similar mould of fiction and allegory. Every virtue, and even vice, acquired its divine representative, every art and profession its patron, whose attributes, in the most distant ages and countries, were uniformly derived from the character of their peculiar votaries. A republic of gods of such opposite tempers and interest required, in every system, the moderating hand of a supreme magistrate, who by the progress of knowledge and flattery was gradually invested with the sublime perfections of an Eternal Parent and an Omnipotent Monarch. Such was the mild spirit of antiquity that the nations were less attentive to the difference than to the resemblance of their religious worship. The Greek, the Roman, and the barbarian, as they met before their respective altars, easily persuaded themselves that under various names and with various ceremonies they adored the same deities. The elegant mythology of Homer gave a beautiful and almost a regular form to the polytheism of the ancient world.[1]

The philosophers of Greece deduced their morals from the nature of man rather than from that of God. They meditated, however, on the Divine Nature as a very curious and important speculation; and in the profound inquiry they displayed the strength and weakness of the human understanding. Of the four most celebrated schools, the Stoics and the Platonists endeavoured to reconcile the jarring interests of reason and piety. They have left us the most sublime proofs of the existence and perfections of the first cause; but, as it was impossible for them to conceive the creation of matter, the workman in the Stoic philosophy was not sufficiently distinguished from the work; whilst, on the contrary, the spiritual God of Plato and his disciples resembled an idea rather than a substance. The opinions of the Academics and Epicureans were of a less religious cast; but whilst the modest science of the former induced them to doubt, the positive ignorance of the latter urged them to deny, the providence of a Supreme Ruler. The spirit of inquiry, prompted by emulation and supported by freedom, had divided the public teachers of philosophy into a variety of contending sects; but the ingenuous youth, who from every part resorted to

1. Within a century or two the Gauls themselves applied to their gods the names of Mercury, Mars, Apollo, etc.

Athens and the other seats of learning in the Roman empire, were alike instructed in every school to reject and to despise the religion of the multitude. How, indeed, was it possible that a philosopher should accept as divine truths the idle tales of the poets and the incoherent traditions of antiquity, or that he should adore as gods those imperfect beings whom he must have despised as men! Against such unworthy adversaries Cicero condescended to employ the arms of reason and eloquence, but the satire of Lucian was a much more adequate as well as more efficacious weapon. We may be well assured that a writer conversant with the world would never have ventured to expose the gods of his country to public ridicule had they not already been the objects of secret contempt among the polished and enlightened orders of society.

Notwithstanding the fashionable irreligion which prevailed in the age of the Antonines, both the interests of the priests and the credulity of the people were sufficiently respected. In their writings and conversation the philosophers of antiquity asserted the independent dignity of reason; but they resigned their actions to the commands of law and of custom. Viewing with a smile of pity and indulgence the various errors of the vulgar, they diligently practised the ceremonies of their fathers, devoutly frequented the temples of the gods; and sometimes condescending to act a part on the theatre of superstition, they concealed the sentiments of an atheist under the sacerdotal robes. Reasoners of such a temper were scarcely inclined to wrangle about their respective modes of faith or of worship. It was indifferent to them what shape the folly of the multitude might choose to assume; and they approached with the same inward contempt and the same external reverence the altars of the Libyan, the Olympian, or the Capitoline Jupiter.

It is not easy to conceive from what motives a spirit of persecution could introduce itself into the Roman councils. The magistrates could not be actuated by a blind though honest bigotry, since the magistrates were themselves philosophers; and the schools of Athens had given laws to the senate. They could not be impelled by ambition or avarice, as the temporal and ecclesiastical powers were united in the same hands. The pontiffs were chosen among the most illustrious of the senators, and the office of supreme pontiff was constantly exercised by the emperors themselves. They knew and valued the advantages of religion as it is connected with civil government. They encouraged the public festivals which humanize the manners of the people. They managed the arts of divination as a convenient instrument of policy; and they respected as the firmest bond of society the useful persuasion that, either in this or in a future life, the crime of perjury is most assuredly punished by the avenging gods. But whilst they acknowledged the general advantages of religion, they were convinced that the various modes of worship contributed alike to the same salutary purposes, and that in every country the form of superstition which had received the sanction of time and experience was the best adapted to the climate and to its inhabitants. Avarice and taste very frequently despoiled the vanquished nations of the elegant statues of their gods and the rich ornaments of their temples; but in the exercise of the religion which they derived from their ancestors they uniformly experienced the indulgence and even protection of the Roman conquerors. The province of Gaul seems, and indeed only seems, an exception to this universal toleration. Under the specious pretext of abolishing human sacrifices, the emperors Tiberius and Claudius suppressed the dangerous power of the Druids; but the

priests themselves, their gods and their altars, subsisted
in peaceful obscurity till the final destruction of paganism.

Rome, the capital of a great monarchy, was incessantly filled with subjects and strangers from every part
of the world, who all introduced and enjoyed the favourite superstitions of their native country. Every city
in the empire was justified in maintaining the purity of
its ancient ceremonies; and the Roman senate, using the
common privilege, sometimes interposed to check this
inundation of foreign rites. The Egyptian superstition,
of all the most contemptible and abject, was frequently
prohibited, the temples of Serapis and Isis demolished,
and their worshippers banished from Rome and Italy.
But the zeal of fanaticism prevailed over the cold and
feeble efforts of policy. The exiles returned, the proselytes multiplied, the temples were restored with
increasing splendour, and Isis and Serapis at length
assumed their place among the Roman deities. Nor was
this indulgence a departure from the old maxims of
government. In the purest ages of the commonwealth
Cybele and Æsculapius had been invited by solemn embassies; and it was customary to tempt the protectors
of besieged cities by the promise of more distinguished
honours than they possessed in their native country.
Rome gradually became the common temple of her subjects, and the freedom of the city was bestowed on all
the gods of mankind.

The narrow policy of preserving, without any foreign
mixture, the pure blood of the ancient citizens had
checked the fortune and hastened the ruin of Athens
and Sparta. The aspiring genius of Rome sacrificed vanity to ambition and deemed it more prudent as well as
honourable to adopt virtue and merit for her own wheresoever they were found, among slaves or strangers,

enemies or barbarians. During the most flourishing era
of the Athenian commonwealth the number of citizens
gradually decreased from about thirty to twenty-one
thousand. If, on the contrary, we study the growth of
the Roman republic, we may discover that, notwithstanding the incessant demands of wars and colonies,
the citizens who, in the first census of Servius Tullius,
amounted to no more than eighty-three thousand were
multiplied, before the commencement of the social war,
to the number of four hundred and sixty-three thousand
men able to bear arms in the service of their country.
When the allies of Rome claimed an equal share of
honours and privileges, the senate indeed preferred the
chance of arms to an ignominious concession. The
Samnites and the Lucanians paid the severe penalty of
their rashness; but the rest of the Italian states, as they
successively returned to their duty, were admitted into
the bosom of the republic and soon contributed to the
ruin of public freedom. Under a democratical government the citizens exercise the powers of sovereignty;
and those powers will be first abused and afterwards
lost if they are committed to an unwieldy multitude.
But when the popular assemblies had been suppressed
by the administration of the emperors, the conquerors
were distinguished from the vanquished nations only as
the first and most honourable order of subjects; and their
increase, however rapid, was no longer exposed to the
same dangers. Yet the wisest princes, who adopted the
maxims of Augustus, guarded with the strictest care
the dignity of the Roman name and diffused the freedom of the city with a prudent liberality.

Till the privileges of Romans had been progressively
extended to all the inhabitants of the empire, an important distinction was preserved between Italy and the
provinces. The former was esteemed the centre of public

unity and the firm basis of the constitution. Italy claimed the birth, or at least the residence, of the emperors and the senate. The estates of the Italians were exempt from taxes, their persons from the arbitrary jurisdiction of governors. Their municipal corporations, formed after the perfect model of the capital, were entrusted, under the immediate eye of the supreme power, with the execution of the laws. From the foot of the Alps to the extremity of Calabria all the natives of Italy were born citizens of Rome. Their partial distinctions were obliterated, and they insensibly coalesced into one great nation, united by language, manners, and civil institutions, and equal to the weight of a powerful empire. The republic gloried in her generous policy and was frequently rewarded by the merit and services of her adopted sons. Had she always confined the distinction of Romans to the ancient families within the walls of the city, that immortal name would have been deprived of some of its noblest ornaments. Virgil was a native of Mantua; Horace was inclined to doubt whether he should call himself an Apulian or a Lucanian; it was in Padua that an historian [Livy] was found worthy to record the majestic series of Roman victories. The patriot family of the Catos emerged from Tusculum; and the little town of Arpinum claimed the double honour of producing Marius and Cicero, the former of whom deserved, after Romulus and Camillus, to be styled the Third Founder of Rome; and the latter, after saving his country from the designs of Catiline, enabled her to contend with Athens for the palm of eloquence.

The provinces of the empire (as they have been described in the preceding chapter) were destitute of any public force or constitutional freedom. In Etruria, in Greece, and in Gaul, it was the first care of the senate to dissolve those dangerous confederacies which taught mankind that as the Roman arts prevailed by division they might be resisted by union. Those princes whom the ostentation of gratitude or generosity permitted for a while to hold a precarious sceptre were dismissed from their thrones as soon as they had performed their appointed task of fashioning to the yoke the vanquished nations. The free states and cities which had embraced the cause of Rome were rewarded with a nominal alliance and insensibly sunk into real servitude. The public authority was everywhere exercised by the ministers of the senate and of the emperors, and that authority was absolute and without control. But the same salutary maxims of government which had secured the peace and obedience of Italy were extended to the most distant conquests. A nation of Romans was gradually formed in the provinces by the double expedient of introducing colonies and of admitting the most faithful and deserving of the provincials to the freedom of Rome.

"Wheresoever the Roman conquers, he inhabits," is a very just observation of Seneca, confirmed by history and experience. The natives of Italy, allured by pleasure or by interest, hastened to enjoy the advantages of victory; and we may remark that about forty years after the reduction of Asia eighty thousand Romans were massacred in one day by the cruel orders of Mithridates. These voluntary exiles were engaged for the most part in the occupations of commerce, agriculture, and the farm of the revenue. But after the legions were rendered permanent by the emperors, the provinces were peopled by a race of soldiers; and the veterans, whether they received the reward of their service in land or in money, usually settled with their families in the country where they had honourably spent their youth. Throughout the empire, but more particularly in the western parts, the most fertile districts and the most convenient situations were reserved for the establishment of colonies, some of which were of a civil and others of a military nature.

In their manners and internal policy the colonies formed a perfect representation of their great parent; and as they were soon endeared to the natives by the ties of friendship and alliance, they effectually diffused a reverence for the Roman name and a desire, which was seldom disappointed, of sharing in due time its honours and advantages. The municipal cities insensibly equalled the rank and splendour of the colonies; and in the reign of Hadrian it was disputed which was the preferable condition, of those societies which had issued from, or those which had been received into, the bosom of Rome. The right of Latium, as it was called, conferred on the cities to which it had been granted a more partial favour. The magistrates only, at the expiration of their office, assumed the quality of Roman citizens; but as those offices were annual, in a few years they circulated round the principal families. Those of the provincials who were permitted to bear arms in the legions, those who exercised any civil employment—all, in a word, who performed any public service or displayed any personal talents were rewarded with a present whose value was continually diminished by the increasing liberality of the emperors. Yet even in the age of the Antonines, when the freedom of the city had been bestowed on the greater number of their subjects, it was still accompanied with very solid advantages. The bulk of the people acquired, with that title, the benefit of the Roman laws, particularly in the interesting articles of marriage, testaments, and inheritances; and the road of fortune was open to those whose pretensions were seconded by favour or merit. The grandsons of the Gauls who had besieged Julius Cæsar in Alesia commanded legions, governed provinces, and were admitted into the senate of Rome. Their ambition, instead of disturbing the tranquillity of the state, was intimately connected with its safety and greatness.

So sensible were the Romans of the influence of language over national manners that it was their most serious care to extend, with the progress of their arms, the use of the Latin tongue. The ancient dialects of Italy, the Sabine, the Etruscan, and the Venetian, sunk into oblivion; but in the provinces the east was less docile than the west to the voice of its victorious preceptors. This obvious difference marked the two portions of the empire with a distinction of colours which, though it was in some degree concealed during the meridian splendour of prosperity, became gradually more visible as the shades of night descended upon the Roman world. The western countries were civilized by the same hands which subdued them. As soon as the barbarians were reconciled to obedience, their minds were opened to any new impressions of knowledge and politeness. The language of Virgil and Cicero, though with some inevitable mixture of corruption, was so universally adopted in Africa, Spain, Gaul, Britain, and Pannonia that the faint traces of the Punic or Celtic idioms were preserved only in the mountains or among the peasants. Education and study insensibly inspired the natives of those countries with the sentiments of Romans; and Italy gave fashions as well as laws to her Latin provincials. They solicited with more ardour, and obtained with more facility, the freedom and honours of the state, supported the national dignity in letters[2] and in arms, and at length, in the person of Trajan, produced an emperor whom the Scipios would not have disowned for their countryman.

2. Spain alone produced Columella, the Senecas, Lucan, Martial, and Quintilian.

The situation of the Greeks was very different from that of the barbarians. The former had been long since civilized and corrupted. They had too much taste to relinquish their language, and too much vanity to adopt any foreign institutions. Still preserving the prejudices after they had lost the virtues of their ancestors, they affected to despise the unpolished manners of the Roman conquerors whilst they were compelled to respect their superior wisdom and power.[3] Nor was the influence of the Grecian language and sentiments confined to the narrow limits of that once celebrated country. Their empire, by the progress of colonies and conquest, had been diffused from the Hadriatic to the Euphrates and the Nile. Asia was covered with Greek cities, and the long reign of the Macedonian kings had introduced a silent revolution into Syria and Egypt. In their pompous courts those princes united the elegance of Athens with the luxury of the East; and the example of the court was imitated at an humble distance by the higher ranks of their subjects. Such was the general division of the Roman empire into the Latin and Greek languages. To these we may add a third distinction for the body of the natives in Syria and especially in Egypt. The use of their ancient dialects, by secluding them from the commerce of mankind, checked the improvements of those barbarians. The slothful effeminacy of the former exposed them to the contempt, the sullen ferociousness of the latter excited the aversion, of the conquerors. Those nations had submitted to the Roman power, but they seldom desired or deserved the freedom of the city; and it was remarked that more than two hundred and thirty years elapsed after the ruin of the Ptolemies

3. There is not, I believe, from Dionysius to Libanius, a single Greek critic who mentions Virgil or Horace. They seem ignorant that the Romans had any good writers.

before an Egyptian was admitted into the senate of
Rome.

It is a just though trite observation that victorious
Rome was herself subdued by the arts of Greece. Those
immortal writers who still command the admiration of
modern Europe soon became the favourite object of
study and imitation in Italy and the western provinces.
But the elegant amusements of the Romans were not
suffered to interfere with their sound maxims of policy.
Whilst they acknowledged the charms of the Greek,
they asserted the dignity of the Latin tongue, and the
exclusive use of the latter was inflexibly maintained in
the administration of civil as well as military government.[4] The two languages exercised at the same time
their separate jurisdiction throughout the empire, the
former as the natural idiom of science, the latter as the
legal dialect of public transactions. Those who united
letters with business were equally conversant with both;
and it was almost impossible in any province to find a
Roman subject of a liberal education who was at once
a stranger to the Greek and to the Latin language.

It was by such institutions that the nations of the
empire insensibly melted away into the Roman name
and people. But there still remained, in the centre of
every province and of every family, an unhappy condition of men who endured the weight, without sharing
the benefits, of society. In the free states of antiquity
the domestic slaves were exposed to the wanton rigour
of despotism. The perfect settlement of the Roman empire was preceded by ages of violence and rapine. The
slaves consisted for the most part of barbarian captives,
taken in thousands by the chance of war, purchased at

4. The emperor Claudius disfranchised an eminent Grecian for not understanding Latin.

a vile price,[5] accustomed to a life of independence, and impatient to break and to revenge their fetters. Against such internal enemies, whose desperate insurrections had more than once reduced the republic to the brink of destruction, the most severe regulations and the most cruel treatment seemed almost justified by the great law of self-preservation. But when the principal nations of Europe, Asia, and Africa were united under the laws of one sovereign, the source of foreign supplies flowed with much less abundance, and the Romans were reduced to the milder but more tedious method of propagation. In their numerous families, and particularly in their country estates, they encouraged the marriage of their slaves. The sentiments of nature, the habits of education, and the possession of a dependent species of property contributed to alleviate the hardships of servitude. The existence of a slave became an object of greater value, and though his happiness still depended on the temper and circumstances of the master, the humanity of the latter, instead of being restrained by fear, was encouraged by the sense of his own interest. The progress of manners was accelerated by the virtue or policy of the emperors; and by the edicts of Hadrian and the Antonines the protection of the laws was extended to the most abject part of mankind. The jurisdiction of life and death over the slaves, a power long exercised and often abused, was taken out of private hands and reserved to the magistrates alone. The subterraneous prisons were abolished, and, upon a just complaint of intolerable treatment, the injured slave obtained either his deliverance or a less cruel master.

Hope, the best comfort of our imperfect condition,

5. In the camp of Lucullus an ox sold for a drachma, and a slave for four drachmæ, or about three shillings.

was not denied to the Roman slave; and if he had any opportunity of rendering himself either useful or agreeable, he might very naturally expect that the diligence and fidelity of a few years would be rewarded with the inestimable gift of freedom. The benevolence of the master was so frequently prompted by the meaner suggestions of vanity and avarice that the laws found it more necessary to restrain than to encourage a profuse and undistinguishing liberality, which might degenerate into a very dangerous abuse. It was a maxim of ancient jurisprudence that, [as] a slave had not any country of his own, he acquired with his liberty an admission into the political society of which his patron was a member. The consequences of this maxim would have prostituted the privileges of the Roman city to a mean and promiscuous multitude. Some seasonable exceptions were therefore provided; and the honourable distinction was confined to such slaves only as for just causes, and with the approbation of the magistrate, should receive a solemn and legal manumission. Even these chosen freedmen obtained no more than the private rights of citizens, and were rigorously excluded from civil or military honours. Whatever might be the merit or fortune of their sons, *they* likewise were esteemed unworthy of a seat in the senate; nor were the traces of a servile origin allowed to be completely obliterated till the third or fourth generation. Without destroying the distinction of ranks, a distant prospect of freedom and honours was presented even to those whom pride and prejudice almost disdained to number among the human species.

It was once proposed to discriminate the slaves by a peculiar habit; but it was justly apprehended that there might be some danger in acquainting them with their own numbers. Without interpreting in their utmost strictness the liberal appellations of legions and myriads, we may venture to pronounce that the proportion of slaves, who were valued as property, was more considerable than that of servants, who can be computed only as an expense. The youths of a promising genius were instructed in the arts and sciences, and their price was ascertained by the degree of their skill and talents. Almost every profession, either liberal [6] or mechanical, might be found in the household of an opulent senator. The ministers of pomp and sensuality were multiplied beyond the conception of modern luxury. It was more for the interest of the merchant or manufacturer to purchase than to hire his workmen; and in the country slaves were employed as the cheapest and most laborious instruments of agriculture. To confirm the general observation and to display the multitude of slaves, we might allege a variety of particular instances. It was discovered, on a very melancholy occasion, that four hundred slaves were maintained in a single palace of Rome.[7] The same number of four hundred belonged to an estate which an African widow, of a very private condition, resigned to her son, whilst she reserved for herself a much larger share of her property. A freedman under the reign of Augustus, though his fortune had suffered great losses in the civil wars, left behind him three thousand six hundred yoke of oxen, two hundred and fifty thousand head of smaller cattle, and, what was almost included in the description of cattle, four thousand one hundred and sixteen slaves.

The number of subjects who acknowledged the laws of Rome, of citizens, of provincials, and of slaves, cannot now be fixed with such a degree of accuracy as the importance of the object would deserve. We are in-

6. Many of the Roman physicians were slaves.
7. They were all executed for not preventing their master's murder.

formed that when the emperor Claudius exercised the office of censor, he took an account of six million nine hundred and forty-five thousand Roman citizens, who, with the proportion of women and children, must have amounted to about twenty millions of souls. The multitude of subjects of an inferior rank was uncertain and fluctuating. But after weighing with attention every circumstance which could influence the balance, it seems probable that there existed in the time of Claudius about twice as many provincials as there were citizens, of either sex and of every age, and that the slaves were at least equal in number to the free inhabitants of the Roman world. The total amount of this imperfect calculation would rise to about one hundred and twenty millions of persons, a degree of population which possibly exceeds that of modern Europe and forms the most numerous society that has ever been united under the same system of government.

Domestic peace and union were the natural consequences of the moderate and comprehensive policy embraced by the Romans. If we turn our eyes towards the monarchies of Asia, we shall behold despotism in the centre and weakness in the extremities, the collection of the revenue or the administration of justice enforced by the presence of an army, hostile barbarians established in the heart of the country, hereditary satraps usurping the dominion of the provinces, and subjects inclined to rebellion though incapable of freedom. But the obedience of the Roman world was uniform, voluntary, and permanent. The vanquished nations, blended into one great people, resigned the hope, nay even the wish, of resuming their independence, and scarcely considered their own existence as distinct from the existence of Rome. The established authority of the emperors pervaded without an effort the wide extent of their dominions and was exercised with the same facility on the banks of the Thames or of the Nile as on those of the Tiber. The legions were destined to serve against the public enemy, and the civil magistrate seldom required the aid of a military force. In this state of general security the leisure as well as opulence both of the prince and people were devoted to improve and to adorn the Roman empire.

Among the innumerable monuments of architecture constructed by the Romans, how many have escaped the notice of history, how few have resisted the ravages of time and barbarism! And yet even the majestic ruins that are still scattered over Italy and the provinces would be sufficient to prove that those countries were once the seat of a polite and powerful empire. Their greatness alone, or their beauty, might deserve our attention; but they are rendered more interesting by two important circumstances, which connect the agreeable history of the arts with the more useful history of human manners. Many of those works were erected at private expense, and almost all were intended for public benefit.

It is natural to suppose that the greatest number, as well as the most considerable, of the Roman edifices were raised by the emperors, who possessed so unbounded a command both of men and money. Augustus was accustomed to boast that he had found his capital of brick and that he had left it of marble. The strict economy of Vespasian was the source of his magnificence. The works of Trajan bear the stamp of his genius. The public monuments with which Hadrian adorned every province of the empire were executed not only by his orders, but under his immediate inspection. He was himself an artist; and he loved the arts, as they conduced to the glory of the monarch. They were encouraged by the Antonines, as they contributed to the happiness of the people. But if the emperors were the first, they were not the only architects of their dominions. Their example was universally imitated by their principal subjects, who were not afraid of declaring to the world that they had spirit to conceive and wealth to accomplish the noblest undertakings. Scarcely had the proud structure of the Coliseum been dedicated at Rome before the edifices of a smaller scale, indeed, but of the same design and materials, were erected for the use and at the expense of the cities of Capua and Verona. The inscription of the stupendous bridge of Alcantara attests that it was thrown over the Tagus by the contribution of a few Lusitanian communities. When Pliny was entrusted with the government of Bithynia and Pontus, provinces by no means the richest or most considerable of the empire, he found the cities within his jurisdiction striving with each other in every useful and ornamental work that might deserve the curiosity of strangers or the gratitude of their citizens. It was the duty of the proconsul to supply their deficiencies, to direct their taste, and sometimes to moderate their emulation. The opulent senators of Rome and the provinces esteemed it an honour, and almost an obligation, to adorn the splendour of their age and country; and the influence of fashion very frequently supplied the want of taste or generosity. Among a crowd of these private benefactors we may select Herodes Atticus, an Athenian citizen who lived in the age of the Antonines. Whatever might be the motive of his conduct, his magnificence would have been worthy of the greatest kings.

The family of Herod, at least after it had been favoured by fortune, was lineally descended from Cimon and Miltiades, Theseus and Cecrops, Æacus and Jupiter. But the posterity of so many gods and heroes was fallen into the most abject state. His grandfather had suffered by the hands of justice; and Julius Atticus, his father, must have ended his life in poverty and contempt had he not discovered an immense treasure buried under an old house, the last remains of his patrimony. According to the rigour of law, the emperor might have asserted his claim, and the prudent Atticus prevented, by a frank confession, the officiousness of informers. But the equitable Nerva, who then filled the throne, refused to accept any part of it and commanded him to use without scruple the present of fortune. The cautious Athenian still insisted that the treasure was too considerable for a subject and that he knew not how to *use it*. *Abuse it, then*, replied the monarch with a good-natured peevishness, *for it is your own*. Many will be of opinion that Atticus literally obeyed the emperor's last instructions, since he expended the greatest part of his fortune, which was much increased by an advantageous marriage, in the service of the public. He had obtained for his son Herod the præfecture of the free cities of Asia; and the young magistrate, observing that the town of Troas was indifferently supplied with water, obtained from the munificence of Hadrian three hundred myriads of drachms (about a hundred thousand pounds) for the construction of a new aqueduct. But in the execution of the work the charge amounted to more than double the estimate, and the officers of the revenue began to murmur, till the generous Atticus silenced their complaints by requesting that he might be permitted to take upon himself the whole additional expense.

The ablest preceptors of Greece and Asia had been invited by liberal rewards to direct the education of young Herod. Their pupil soon became a celebrated orator according to the useless rhetoric of that age, which, confining itself to the schools, disdained to visit either the Forum or the senate. He was honoured with the consulship at Rome; but the greatest part of his life was spent in a philosophic retirement at Athens and his adjacent villas, perpetually surrounded by sophists, who acknowledged without reluctance the superiority of a rich and generous rival. The monuments of his genius have perished; [but] some considerable ruins still preserve the fame of his taste and munificence, [and] modern travellers have measured the remains of the stadium which he constructed at Athens. It was six hundred feet in length, built entirely of white marble, capable of admitting the whole body of the people, and finished in four years whilst Herod was president of the Athenian games. To the memory of his wife Regilla he dedicated a theatre scarcely to be paralleled in the empire; no wood except cedar, very curiously carved, was employed in any part of the building. The Odeum, designed by Pericles for musical performances and the rehearsal of new tragedies, had been a trophy of the victory of the arts over barbaric greatness, as the timbers employed in the construction consisted chiefly of the masts of the Persian vessels. Notwithstanding the repairs bestowed on that ancient edifice by a king of Cappadocia, it was again fallen to decay. Herod restored its ancient beauty and magnificence. Nor was the liberality of that illustrious citizen confined to the walls of Athens. The most splendid ornaments bestowed on the temple of Neptune in the Isthmus, a theatre at Corinth, a stadium at Delphi, a bath at Thermopylæ, and an aqueduct at Canusium in Italy were insufficient to exhaust his treasures. The people of Epirus, Thessaly, Eubœa, Bœotia, and Peloponnesus experienced his favours, and many inscriptions of the cities of Greece and Asia gratefully style Herodes Atticus their patron and benefactor.

In the commonwealths of Athens and Rome the

modest simplicity of private houses announced the equal condition of freedom, whilst the sovereignty of the people was represented in the majestic edifices destined to the public use; nor was this republican spirit totally extinguished by the introduction of wealth and monarchy. It was in works of national honour and benefit that the most virtuous of the emperors affected to display their magnificence. The golden palace of Nero excited a just indignation, but the vast extent of ground which had been usurped by his selfish luxury was more nobly filled under the succeeding reigns by the Coliseum, the baths of Titus, the Claudian portico, and the temples dedicated to the goddess of Peace and to the genius of Rome. These monuments of architecture, the property of the Roman people, were adorned with the most beautiful productions of Grecian painting and sculpture; and in the temple of Peace a very curious library was open to the curiosity of the learned. At a small distance from thence was situated the Forum of Trajan. It was surrounded with a lofty portico, in the form of a quadrangle, into which four triumphal arches opened a noble and spacious entrance; in the centre arose a column of marble, whose height of one hundred and ten feet denoted the elevation of the hill that had been cut away. This column, which still subsists in its ancient beauty, exhibited an exact representation of the Dacian victories of its founder. The veteran soldier contemplated the story of his own campaigns, and by an easy illusion of national vanity, the peaceful citizen associated himself to the honours of the triumph.

All the other quarters of the capital and all the provinces of the empire were embellished by the same liberal spirit of public magnificence, and were filled with amphitheatres, theatres, temples, porticos, triumphal arches, baths, and aqueducts, all variously conducive to the health, the devotion, and the pleasures of the meanest citizen. The last mentioned of those edifices deserve our peculiar attention. The boldness of the enterprise, the solidity of the execution, and the uses to which they were subservient rank the aqueducts among the noblest monuments of Roman genius and power. The aqueducts of the capital claim a just pre-eminence; but the curious traveller who, without the light of history, should examine those of Spoleto, of Metz, or of Segovia would very naturally conclude that those provincial towns had formerly been the residence of some potent monarch. The solitudes of Asia and Africa were once covered with flourishing cities, whose populousness and even whose existence was derived from such artificial supplies of a perennial stream of fresh water.

We have computed the inhabitants and contemplated the public works of the Roman empire. The observation of the number and greatness of its cities will serve to confirm the former and to multiply the latter. It may not be unpleasing to collect a few scattered instances relative to that subject, without forgetting, however, that from the vanity of nations and the poverty of language the vague appellation of city has been indifferently bestowed on Rome and upon Laurentum. *Ancient* Italy is said to have contained eleven hundred and ninety-seven cities; and for whatsoever era of antiquity the expression might be intended, there is not any reason to believe the country less populous in the age of the Antonines than in that of Romulus. The petty states of Latium were contained within the metropolis of the empire, by whose superior influence they had been attracted. Those parts of Italy which have so long languished under the lazy tyranny of priests and viceroys had been afflicted only by the more tolerable calamities of war; and the first symptoms of decay which *they* experienced were amply

Chapter III

Of the constitution of the Roman empire in the age of the Antonines

THE obvious definition of a monarchy seems to be that of a state in which a single person, by whatsoever name he may be distinguished, is entrusted with the execution of the laws, the management of the revenue, and the command of the army. But unless public liberty is protected by intrepid and vigilant guardians, the authority of so formidable a magistrate will soon degenerate into despotism. The influence of the clergy, in an age of superstition, might be usefully employed to assert the rights of mankind; but so intimate is the connection between the throne and the altar that the banner of the church has very seldom been seen on the side of the people. A martial nobility and stubborn commons, possessed of arms, tenacious of property, and collected into constitutional assemblies, form the only balance capable of preserving a free constitution against enterprises of an aspiring prince.

Every barrier of the Roman constitution had been levelled by the vast ambition of the dictator, every fence had been extirpated by the cruel hand of the Triumvir. After the victory of Actium the fate of the Roman world depended on the will of Octavianus, surnamed Cæsar by his uncle's adoption, and afterwards Augustus by the flattery of the senate. The conqueror was at the head of forty-four veteran legions, conscious of their own strength and of the weakness of the constitution, habituated during twenty years' civil war to every act of blood and violence, and passionately devoted to the house of Cæsar, from whence alone they had received, and expected, the most lavish rewards. The provinces, long oppressed by the ministers of the republic, sighed for the government of a single person who would be the master, not the accomplice, of those petty tyrants. The people of Rome, viewing with a secret pleasure the humiliation of the aristocracy, demanded only bread and public shows, and were supplied with both by the liberal hand of Augustus. The rich and polite Italians, who had almost universally embraced the philosophy of Epicurus, enjoyed the present blessings of ease and tranquillity, and suffered not the pleasing dream to be interrupted by the memory of their old tumultuous freedom. With its power, the senate had lost its dignity; many of the most noble families were extinct. The republicans of spirit and ability had perished in the field of battle or in the proscription. The door of the assembly had been designedly left open for a mixed multitude of more than a thousand persons, who reflected disgrace upon their rank instead of deriving honour from it.

The reformation of the senate was one of the first steps in which Augustus laid aside the tyrant and professed himself the father of his country. He was elected censor; and, in concert with his faithful Agrippa, he examined the list of the senators, expelled a few members whose vices or whose obstinacy required a public example, persuaded near two hundred to prevent the shame of an expulsion by a voluntary retreat, raised the qualification of a senator to about ten thousand pounds, created a sufficient number of patrician families, and accepted for himself the honourable title of Prince of the Senate, which had always been bestowed by the censors on the citizen the most eminent for his honours and services. But whilst he thus restored the dignity, he destroyed the independence of the senate. The principles of a free constitution are irrevocably lost when the legislative power is nominated by the executive.

Before an assembly thus modelled and prepared, Augustus pronounced a studied oration which displayed his patriotism and disguised his ambition. "He lamented, yet excused, his past conduct. Filial piety had required at his hands the revenge of his father's murder; the humanity of his own nature had sometimes given way to the stern laws of necessity and to a forced connection with two unworthy colleagues: as long as Antony lived, the republic forbade him to abandon her to a degenerate Roman and a barbarian queen. He was now at liberty to satisfy his duty and his inclination. He solemnly restored the senate and people to all their ancient rights, and wished only to mingle with the crowd of his fellow-citizens and to share the blessings which he had obtained for his country."

It would require the pen of Tacitus (if Tacitus had assisted at this assembly) to describe the various emotions of the senate—those that were suppressed and those that were affected. It was dangerous to trust the sincerity of Augustus; to seem to distrust it was still more dangerous. The respective advantages of monarchy and a republic have often divided speculative inquirers; the present greatness of the Roman state, the corruption of manners, and the licence of the soldiers supplied new arguments to the advocates of monarchy; and these general views of government were again warped by the hopes and fears of each individual. Amidst this confusion of sentiments the answer of the senate was unanimous and decisive. They refused to accept the resignation of Augustus; they conjured him not to desert the republic, which he had saved. After a decent resistance the crafty tyrant submitted to the orders of the senate and consented to receive the government of the provinces and the general command of the Roman armies under the well-known names of *proconsul* and *imperator*. But he would receive them only for ten years. Even before the expiration of that period he hoped that the wounds of civil discord would be completely healed and that the republic, restored to its pristine health and vigour, would no longer require the dangerous interposition of so extraordinary a magistrate. The memory of this comedy, repeated several times during the life of Augustus, was preserved to the last ages of the empire by the peculiar pomp with which the perpetual monarchs of Rome always solemnized the tenth years of their reign.

Without any violation of the principles of the constitution, the general of the Roman armies might receive and exercise an authority almost despotic over the soldiers, the enemies, and the subjects of the republic. With regard to the soldiers, the jealousy of freedom had, even from the earliest ages of Rome, given way to the hopes of conquest and a just sense of military discipline. The dictator, or consul, had a right to command the service of the Roman youth, and to punish an obstinate or cowardly disobedience by the most severe and ignominious penalties, by striking the offender out of the list of citizens, by confiscating his property, and by selling his person into slavery. The most sacred rights of freedom, confirmed by the Porcian and Sempronian laws, were suspended by the military engagement. In his camp the general exercised an absolute power of life and death; his jurisdiction was not confined by any forms of trial or rules of proceeding, and the execution of the sentence was immediate and without appeal. The choice of the enemies of Rome was regularly decided by the legislative authority. The most important resolutions of peace and war were seriously debated in the senate and solemnly ratified by the people. But when the arms of the legions were carried to a great distance from Italy, the generals assumed the liberty of directing them against whatever people and in whatever manner they judged most advantageous for the public service. It was from the success, not from the justice, of their enterprises that they expected the honours of a triumph. In the use of victory, especially after they were no longer controlled by the commissioners of the senate, they exercised the most unbounded despotism. When Pompey commanded in the East he rewarded his soldiers and allies, dethroned princes, divided kingdoms, founded colonies, and distributed the treasures of Mithridates. On his return to Rome he obtained, by a single act of the senate and people, the universal ratification of all his proceedings. Such was the power over the soldiers and over the enemies of Rome which was either granted to, or assumed by, the generals of the republic. They were at the same time the governors, or rather monarchs, of the conquered provinces, united the civil with the military character, administered justice as well as the finances, and exercised both the executive and legislative power of the state.

From what has been already observed in the first chapter of this work, some notion may be formed of the armies and provinces thus entrusted to the ruling hand of Augustus. But as it was impossible that he could personally command the legions of so many distant frontiers, he was indulged by the senate, as Pompey had already been, in the permission of devolving the execution of his great office on a sufficient number of lieutenants. In rank and authority these officers seemed not inferior to the ancient proconsuls; but their station was dependent and precarious. They received and held their commissions at the will of a superior, to whose *auspicious* influence the merit of their action was legally attributed. They were the representatives of the emperor. The emperor alone was the general of the republic, and his jurisdiction, civil as well as military, extended over all the conquests of Rome. It was some satisfaction, however, to the senate that he always delegated his power to the members of their body. The Imperial lieutenants were of consular or prætorian dignity, the legions were commanded by senators, and the præfecture of Egypt was the only important trust committed to a Roman knight.

Within six days after Augustus had been compelled to accept so very liberal a grant, he resolved to gratify the pride of the senate by an easy sacrifice. He represented to them that they had enlarged his powers even beyond that degree which might be required by the melancholy condition of the times. They had not permitted him to refuse the laborious command of the armies and the frontiers; but he must insist on being allowed to restore the more peaceful and secure provinces to the mild administration of the civil magistrate. In the division of the provinces Augustus provided for his own power and for the dignity of the republic. The proconsuls of the senate, particularly those of Asia, Greece, and Africa, enjoyed a more honourable character than the lieutenants of the emperor, who commanded in Gaul or Syria. The former were attended by lictors, the latter by soldiers. A law was passed that wherever the emperor was present, his extraordinary commission should supersede the ordinary jurisdiction of the governor; a custom was introduced that the new conquest belonged to the Imperial portion; and it was soon discovered that the authority of the Prince, the favourite epithet of Augustus, was the same in every part of the empire.

In return for this imaginary concession Augustus obtained an important privilege which rendered him master of Rome and Italy. By a dangerous exception to the ancient maxims he was authorized to preserve his military command, supported by a numerous body of guards, even in time of peace and in the heart of the capital. His command, indeed, was confined to those citizens who were engaged in the service by the military oath; but such was the propensity of the Romans to servitude that the oath was voluntarily taken by the magistrates, the senators, and the equestrian order, till the homage of flattery was insensibly converted into an annual and solemn protestation of fidelity.

Although Augustus considered a military force as the firmest foundation, he wisely rejected it as a very odious instrument of government. It was more agreeable to his temper, as well as to his policy, to reign under the venerable names of ancient magistracy and artfully to collect, in his own person, all the scattered rays of civil jurisdiction. With this view he permitted the senate to confer upon him, for his life, the powers of the consular and tribunitian offices, which were in the same manner continued to all his successors. The consuls had succeeded to the kings of Rome and represented the dignity of the state. They superintended the ceremonies of religion, levied and commanded the legions, gave audience to foreign ambassadors, and presided in the assemblies both of the senate and people. The general control of the finances was entrusted to their care; and though they seldom had leisure to administer justice in person, they were considered as the supreme guardians of law, equity, and the public peace. Such was their ordinary jurisdiction; but whenever the senate empowered the first magistrate to consult the safety of the common-wealth, he was raised by that degree above the laws and exercised, in the defence of liberty, a temporary despotism.

The character of the tribunes was in every respect different from that of the consuls. The appearance of the former was modest and humble, but their persons were sacred and inviolable. Their force was suited rather for opposition than for action. They were instituted to defend the oppressed, to pardon offences, to arraign the enemies of the people, and, when they judged it necessary, to stop by a single word the whole machine of government. As long as the republic subsisted, the dangerous influence which either the consul or the tribune might derive from their respective jurisdiction was diminished by several important restrictions. Their authority expired with the year in which they were elected; the former office was divided between two, the latter among ten, persons; and as both in their private and public interest they were averse to each other, their mutual conflicts contributed for the most part to strengthen rather than to destroy the balance of the constitution. But when the consular and tribunitian powers were united, when they were vested for life in a single person, when the general of the army was at the same time the minister of the senate and the representative of the Roman people, it was impossible to resist the exercise, nor was it easy to define the limits, of his Imperial prerogative.

To these accumulated honours the policy of Augustus soon added the splendid as well as important dignities of supreme pontiff and of censor. By the former he acquired the management of the religion, and by the latter a legal inspection over the manners and fortunes, of the Roman people. If so many distinct and independent

powers did not exactly unite with each other, the com-
plaisance of the senate was prepared to supply every
deficiency by the most ample and extraordinary concessions. The emperors, as the first ministers of the republic, were exempted from the obligation and penalty of
many inconvenient laws: they were authorized to con-
voke the senate, to make several motions in the same
day, to recommend candidates for the honours of the
state, to enlarge the bounds of the city, to employ the
revenue at their discretion, to declare peace and war, to
ratify treaties; and by a most comprehensive clause they
were empowered to execute whatsoever they should
judge advantageous to the empire and agreeable to the
majesty of things private or public, human or divine.

When all the various powers of executive government
were committed to the *Imperial magistrate,* the ordinary
magistrates of the commonwealth languished in obscurity, without vigour and almost without business. The
names and forms of the ancient administration were preserved by Augustus with the most anxious care. The
usual number of consuls, prætors, and tribunes were
annually invested with their respective ensigns of office
and continued to discharge some of their least important
functions. Those honours still attracted the vain ambition of the Romans; and the emperors themselves,
though invested for life with the powers of the consulship, frequently aspired to the title of that annual
dignity, which they condescended to share with the
most illustrious of their fellow-citizens. In the election
of these magistrates the people, during the reign of
Augustus, were permitted to expose all the inconveniences of a wild democracy. That artful prince, instead
of discovering the least symptom of impatience, humbly
solicited their suffrages for himself or his friends and
scrupulously practised all the duties of an ordinary

candidate. But we may venture to ascribe to his councils the first measure of the succeeding reign, by which the elections were transferred to the senate. The assemblies of the people were forever abolished, and the emperors were delivered from a dangerous multitude who, without restoring liberty, might have disturbed and perhaps endangered the established government.

By declaring themselves the protectors of the people, Marius and Cæsar had subverted the constitution of their country. But as soon as the senate had been humbled and disarmed, such an assembly, consisting of five or six hundred persons, was found a much more tractable and useful instrument of dominion. It was on the dignity of the senate that Augustus and his successors founded their new empire; and they affected, on every occasion, to adopt the language and principles of patricians. In the administration of their own powers they frequently consulted the great national council and *seemed* to refer to its decision the most important concerns of peace and war. Rome, Italy, and the internal provinces were subject to the immediate jurisdiction of the senate. With regard to civil objects it was the supreme court of appeal; with regard to criminal matters, a tribunal constituted for the trial of all offences that were committed by men in any public station or that affected the peace and majesty of the Roman people. The exercise of the judicial power became the most frequent and serious occupation of the senate; and the important causes that were pleaded before them afforded a last refuge to the spirit of ancient eloquence. As a council of state, and as a court of justice, the senate possessed very considerable prerogatives; but in its legislative capacity, in which it was supposed virtually to represent the people, the rights of sovereignty were acknowledged to reside in that assembly. Every power was derived from their authority, every law was ratified by their sanction. Their regular meetings were held on three stated days in every month, the Calends, the Nones, and the Ides. The debates were conducted with decent freedom; and the emperors themselves, who gloried in the name of senators, sat, voted, and divided with their equals.

To resume, in a few words, the system of the Imperial government as it was instituted by Augustus and maintained by those princes who understood their own interest and that of the people, it may be defined an absolute monarchy disguised by the forms of a commonwealth. The masters of the Roman world surrounded their throne with darkness, concealed their irresistible strength, and humbly professed themselves the accountable ministers of the senate, whose supreme decrees they dictated and obeyed.

The face of the court corresponded with the forms of the administration. The emperors, if we except those tyrants whose capricious folly violated every law of nature and decency, disdained that pomp and ceremony which might offend their countrymen but could add nothing to their real power. In all the offices of life they affected to confound themselves with their subjects and maintained with them an equal intercourse of visits and entertainments. Their habit, their palace, their table, were suited only to the rank of an opulent senator. Their family, however numerous or splendid, was composed entirely of their domestic slaves and freedmen.[1] Augustus or Trajan would have blushed at employing the

1. A weak prince will always be governed by his domestics. The power of slaves aggravated the shame of the Romans; and the senate paid court to a Pallas or a Narcissus. There is a chance that a modern favourite may be a gentleman.

meanest of the Romans in those menial offices which, in the household and bed-chamber of a limited monarch, are so eagerly solicited by the proudest nobles of Britain.

The deification of the emperors is the only instance in which they departed from their accustomed prudence and modesty. The Asiatic Greeks were the first inventors, the successors of Alexander the first objects, of this servile and impious mode of adulation. It was easily transferred from the kings to the governors of Asia; and the Roman magistrates very frequently were adored as provincial deities, with the pomp of altars and temples, of festivals and sacrifices. It was natural that the emperors should not refuse what the proconsuls had accepted; and the divine honours which both the one and the other received from the provinces attested rather the despotism than the servitude of Rome. But the conquerors soon imitated the vanquished nations in the arts of flattery; and the imperious spirit of the first Cæsar too easily consented to assume, during his lifetime, a place among the tutelar deities of Rome.

The milder temper of his successor declined so dangerous an ambition, which was never afterwards revived except by the madness of Caligula and Domitian. Augustus permitted, indeed, some of the provincial cities to erect temples to his honour, on condition that they should associate the worship of Rome with that of the sovereign; he tolerated private superstition of which he might be the object; but he contented himself with being revered by the senate and people in his human character and wisely left to his successor the care of his public deification. A regular custom was introduced that on the decease of every emperor who had neither lived nor died like a tyrant, the senate by a solemn decree should place him in the number of the gods; and the ceremonies of his apotheosis were blended with those of his funeral. This legal and, as it should seem, injudicious profanation, so abhorrent to our stricter principles, was received with a faint murmur by the easy nature of polytheism; but it was received as an institution not of religion but of policy. We should disgrace the virtues of the Antonines by comparing them with the vices of Hercules or Jupiter. Even the character of Cæsar or Augustus was far superior to those of the popular deities. But it was the misfortune of the former to live in an enlightened age, and their actions were too faithfully recorded to admit of such a mixture of fable and mystery as the devotion of the vulgar requires. As soon as their divinity was established by law it sunk into oblivion, without contributing either to their own fame or to the dignity of succeeding princes.

In the consideration of the Imperial government we have frequently mentioned the artful founder, under his well-known title of Augustus, which was not however conferred upon him till the edifice was almost completed. The obscure name of Octavianus he derived from a mean family in the little town of Aricia. It was stained with the blood of the proscription; and he was desirous, had it been possible, to erase all memory of his former life. The illustrious surname of Cæsar he had assumed as the adopted son of the dictator; but he had too much good sense either to hope to be confounded, or to wish to be compared, with that extraordinary man. It was proposed in the senate to dignify their minister with a new appellation; and after a very serious discussion that of Augustus was chosen, among several others, as being the most expressive of the character of peace and sanctity which he uniformly affected. Augustus was therefore a personal, Cæsar a family distinction. The former should naturally have expired with the prince on whom it was bestowed; and however the latter was diffused by adoption and female alliance, Nero was the last prince who could allege any hereditary claim to the honours of the Julian line. But at the time of his death the practice of a century had inseparably connected those appellations with the Imperial dignity, and they have been preserved by a long succession of emperors, Romans, Greeks, Franks, and Germans, from the fall of the republic to the present time. A distinction was, however, soon introduced. The sacred title of Augustus was always reserved for the monarch, whilst the name of Cæsar was more freely communicated to his relations; and, from the reign of Hadrian at least, was appropriated to the second person in the state, who was considered as the presumptive heir of the empire.

The tender respect of Augustus for a free constitution which he had destroyed can only be explained by an attentive consideration of the character of that subtle tyrant. A cool head, an unfeeling heart, and a cowardly disposition prompted him, at the age of nineteen, to assume the mask of hypocrisy, which he never afterwards laid aside. With the same hand, and probably with the same temper, he signed the proscription of Cicero and the pardon of Cinna. His virtues, and even his vices, were artificial; and according to the various dictates of his interest, he was at first the enemy, and at last the father, of the Roman world. When he framed the artful system of the Imperial authority, his moderation was inspired by his fears. He wished to deceive the people by an image of civil liberty, and the armies by an image of civil government.

The death of Cæsar was ever before his eyes. He had lavished wealth and honours on his adherents, but the most favoured friends of his uncle were in the number of the conspirators. The fidelity of the legions might defend his authority against open rebellion, but their vigilance could not secure his person from the dagger of a determined republican; and the Romans, who revered the memory of Brutus,[2] would applaud the imitation of his virtue. Cæsar had provoked his fate as much by the ostentation of his power as by his power itself. The consul or the tribune might have reigned in peace: the title of king had armed the Romans against his life. Augustus was sensible that mankind is governed by names; nor was he deceived in his expectation that the senate and people would submit to slavery, provided they were respectfully assured that they still enjoyed their ancient freedom. A feeble senate and enervated people cheerfully acquiesced in the pleasing illusion as long as it was supported by the virtue, or even by the prudence, of the successors of Augustus. It was a motive of self-preservation, not a principle of liberty, that animated the conspirators against Caligula, Nero, and Domitian. They attacked the person of the tyrant without aiming their blow at the authority of the emperor.

There appears, indeed, one memorable occasion in which the senate, after seventy years of patience, made an ineffectual attempt to reassume its long-forgotten rights. When the throne was vacant by the murder of Caligula, the consuls convoked that assembly in the Capitol, condemned the memory of the Cæsars, gave the watchword *liberty* to the few cohorts who faintly adhered to their standard, and during eight and forty hours acted as the independent chiefs of a free commonwealth. But while they deliberated, the Prætorian Guards had resolved. The stupid Claudius, brother of Germanicus, was already in their camp, invested with

2. Two centuries after the establishment of monarchy, the emperor Marcus Antoninus recommends the character of Brutus as a perfect model of Roman virtue.

the Imperial purple and prepared to support his election by arms. The dream of liberty was at an end, and the senate awoke to all the horrors of inevitable servitude. Deserted by the people and threatened by a military force, that feeble assembly was compelled to ratify the choice of the Prætorians and to embrace the benefit of an amnesty, which Claudius had the prudence to offer and the generosity to observe.

The insolence of the armies inspired Augustus with fears of a still more alarming nature. The despair of the citizens could only attempt what the power of the soldiers was, at any time, able to execute. How precarious was his own authority over men whom he had taught to violate every social duty! He had heard their seditious clamours; he dreaded their calmer moments of reflection. One revolution had been purchased by immense rewards; but a second revolution might double those rewards. The troops professed the fondest attachment to the house of Cæsar; but the attachments of the multitude are capricious and inconstant. Augustus summoned to his aid whatever remained in those fierce minds of Roman prejudices; enforced the rigour of discipline by the sanction of law; and, interposing the majesty of the senate between the emperor and the army, boldly claimed their allegiance as the first magistrate of the republic.[3]

During a long period of two hundred and twenty years, from the establishment of this artful system to the death of Commodus, the dangers inherent to a military government were in a great measure suspended. The soldiers were seldom roused to that fatal sense of their own strength and of the weakness of the civil authority

3. Augustus restored the ancient severity of discipline. After the civil wars, he dropped the endearing name of *fellow-soldiers,* and called them only *soldiers.*

which was, before and afterwards, productive of such
dreadful calamities. Caligula and Domitian were assassinated in their palace by their own domestics; the convulsions which agitated Rome on the death of the former
were confined to the walls of the city. But Nero involved
the whole empire in his ruin. In the space of eighteen
months four princes perished by the sword, and the
Roman world was shaken by the fury of the contending
armies. Excepting only this short though violent eruption of military licence, the two centuries from Augustus
to Commodus passed away unstained with civil blood
and undisturbed by revolutions. The emperor was
elected by *the authority of the senate* and *the consent
of the soldiers*. The legions respected their oath of
fidelity; and it requires a minute inspection of the Roman annals to discover three inconsiderable rebellions,
which were all suppressed in a few months and without
even the hazard of a battle.

In elective monarchies the vacancy of the throne is
a moment big with danger and mischief. The Roman
emperors, desirous to spare the legions that interval of
suspense and the temptation of an irregular choice, invested their designed successor with so large a share of
present power as should enable him, after their decease,
to assume the remainder without suffering the empire
to perceive the change of masters. Thus Augustus, after
all his fairer prospects had been snatched from him by
untimely deaths, rested his last hopes on Tiberius, obtained for his adopted son the censorial and tribunitian
powers, and dictated a law by which the future prince
was invested with an authority equal to his own over
the provinces and the armies. Thus Vespasian subdued
the generous mind of his eldest son. Titus was adored
by the eastern legions, which under his command had
recently achieved the conquest of Judæa. His power was

dreaded, and, as his virtues were clouded by the intemperance of youth, his designs were suspected. Instead of listening to such unworthy suspicions, the prudent monarch associated Titus to the full powers of the Imperial dignity; and the grateful son ever approved himself the humble and faithful minister of so indulgent a father.

The good sense of Vespasian engaged him indeed to embrace every measure that might confirm his recent and precarious elevation. The military oath and the fidelity of the troops had been consecrated by the habits of an hundred years to the name and family of the Cæsars; and although that family had been continued only by the fictitious rite of adoption, the Romans still revered, in the person of Nero, the grandson of Germanicus and the lineal successor of Augustus. It was not without reluctance and remorse that the Prætorian Guards had been persuaded to abandon the cause of the tyrant. The rapid downfall of Galba, Otho, and Vitellius taught the armies to consider the emperors as the creatures of *their* will and the instruments of *their* licence. The birth of Vespasian was mean; his grandfather had been a private soldier, his father a petty officer of the revenue; his own merit had raised him, in an advanced age, to the empire; but his merit was rather useful than shining, and his virtues were disgraced by a strict and even sordid parsimony. Such a prince consulted his true interest by the association of a son whose more splendid and amiable character might turn the public attention from the obscure origin to the future glories of the Flavian house. Under the mild administration of Titus the Roman world enjoyed a transient felicity, and his beloved memory served to protect, above fifteen years, the vices of his brother Domitian.

Nerva had scarcely accepted the purple from the as-

sassins of Domitian before he discovered that his feeble
age was unable to stem the torrent of public disorders,
which had multiplied under the long tyranny of his
predecessor. His mild disposition was respected by the
good; but the degenerate Romans required a more vigorous character, whose justice should strike terror into
the guilty. Though he had several relations, he fixed his
choice on a stranger. He adopted Trajan, then about
forty years of age, and who commanded a powerful
army in the Lower Germany, and immediately, by a
decree of the senate, declared him his colleague and
successor in the empire. It is sincerely to be lamented
that whilst we are fatigued with the disgustful relation
of Nero's crimes and follies, we are reduced to collect
the actions of Trajan from the glimmerings of an abridgment or the doubtful light of a panegyric. There remains, however, one panegyric far removed beyond the
suspicion of flattery. Above two hundred and fifty years
after the death of Trajan the senate, in pouring out the
customary acclamations on the accession of a new emperor, wished that he might surpass the felicity of
Augustus and the virtue of Trajan.

We may readily believe that the father of his country
hesitated whether he ought to entrust the various and
doubtful character of his kinsman Hadrian with sovereign power. In his last moments the arts of the empress
Plotina either fixed the irresolution of Trajan or boldly
supposed a fictitious adoption, the truth of which could
not be safely disputed, and Hadrian was peaceably
acknowledged as his lawful successor. Under his reign,
as has been already mentioned, the empire flourished in
peace and prosperity. He encouraged the arts, reformed
the laws, asserted military discipline, and visited all his
provinces in person. His vast and active genius was
equally suited to the most enlarged views and the mi-

nute details of civil policy. But the ruling passions of his soul were curiosity and vanity. As they prevailed, and as they were attracted by different objects, Hadrian was by turns an excellent prince, a ridiculous sophist, and a jealous tyrant. The general tenor of his conduct deserved praise for its equity and moderation. Yet in the first days of his reign he put to death four consular senators, his personal enemies and men who had been judged worthy of empire; and the tediousness of a painful illness rendered him, at last, peevish and cruel. The senate doubted whether they should pronounce him a god or a tyrant; and the honours decreed to his memory were granted to the prayers of the pious Antoninus.

The caprice of Hadrian influenced his choice of a successor. After revolving in his mind several men of distinguished merit, whom he esteemed and hated, he adopted Ælius Verus, a gay and voluptuous nobleman, recommended by uncommon beauty to the lover of Antinous.[4] But while Hadrian was delighting himself with his own applause and the acclamations of the soldiers, whose consent had been secured by an immense donative, the new Cæsar was ravished from his embraces by an untimely death. He left only one son. Hadrian commended the boy to the gratitude of the Antonines. He was adopted by Pius and, on the accession of Marcus, was invested with an equal share of sovereign power. Among the many vices of this younger Verus he possessed one virtue: a dutiful reverence for his wiser colleague, to whom he willingly abandoned the ruder cares of empire. The philosophic emperor dissembled his fol-

---

4. The deification of Antinous, his medals, statues, temples, city, oracles, and constellation, are well known and still dishonour the memory of Hadrian. Yet we may remark that of the first fifteen emperors Claudius ...s the only one whose taste in love was entirely correct.

lies, lamented his early death, and cast a decent veil over his memory.

As soon as Hadrian's passion was either gratified or disappointed, he resolved to deserve the thanks of posterity by placing the most exalted merit on the Roman throne. His discerning eye easily discovered a senator about fifty years of age, blameless in all the offices of life, and a youth of about seventeen, whose riper years opened the fair prospect of every virtue. The elder of these was declared the son and successor of Hadrian, on condition, however, that he himself should immediately adopt the younger. The two Antonines (for it is of them that we are now speaking) governed the Roman world forty-two years with the same invariable spirit of wisdom and virtue. Although Pius had two sons, he preferred the welfare of Rome to the interest of his family, gave his daughter Faustina in marriage to young Marcus, obtained from the senate the tribunitian and proconsular powers, and with a noble disdain, or rather ignorance of jealousy, associated him to all the labours of government. Marcus, on the other hand, revered the character of his benefactor, loved him as a parent, obeyed him as his sovereign, and, after he was no more, regulated his own administration by the example and maxims of his predecessor. Their united reigns are possibly the only period of history in which the happiness of a great people was the sole object of government.

Titus Antoninus Pius has been justly denominated a second Numa. The same love of religion, justice, and peace was the distinguishing characteristic of both princes. But the situation of the latter opened a much larger field for the exercise of those virtues. Numa could only prevent a few neighbouring villages from plundering each other's harvests. Antoninus diffused order and tranquillity over the greatest part of the earth. His reign is marked by the rare advantage of furnishing very few materials for history, which is, indeed, little more than the register of the crimes, follies, and misfortunes of mankind. In private life he was an amiable as well as a good man. The native simplicity of his virtue was a stranger to vanity or affectation. He enjoyed with moderation the conveniencies of his fortune and the innocent pleasures of society;[5] and the benevolence of his soul displayed itself in a cheerful serenity of temper.

The virtue of Marcus Aurelius Antoninus was of a severer and more laborious kind. It was the well-earned harvest of many a learned conference, of many a patient lecture, and many a midnight lucubration. At the age of twelve years he embraced the rigid system of the Stoics, which taught him to submit his body to his mind, his passions to his reason; to consider virtue as the only good, vice as the only evil, all things external as things indifferent. His meditations, composed in the tumult of a camp, are still extant, and he even condescended to give lessons of philosophy in a more public manner than was perhaps consistent with the modesty of a sage or the dignity of an emperor. But his life was the noblest commentary on the precepts of Zeno. He was severe to himself, indulgent to the imperfections of others, just and beneficent to all mankind. He regretted that Avidius Cassius, who excited a rebellion in Syria, had disappointed him, by a voluntary death, of the pleasure of converting an enemy into a friend; and he justified the sincerity of that sentiment by moderating the zeal of the senate against the adherents of the traitor. War he detested as the disgrace and calamity of human nature; but when the necessity of a just defence called upon him to take up arms, he readily exposed his person to

5. He was fond of the theatre and not insensible to the charms of the fair sex.

eight winter campaigns on the frozen banks of the Danube, the severity of which was at last fatal to the weakness of his constitution. His memory was revered by a grateful posterity, and above a century after his death many persons preserved the image of Marcus Antoninus among those of their household gods.

If a man were called to fix the period in the history of the world during which the condition of the human race was most happy and prosperous, he would, without hesitation, name that which elapsed from the death of Domitian to the accession of Commodus. The vast extent of the Roman empire was governed by absolute power, under the guidance of virtue and wisdom. The armies were restrained by the firm but gentle hand of four successive emperors whose characters and authority commanded involuntary respect. The forms of the civil administration were carefully preserved by Nerva, Trajan, Hadrian, and the Antonines, who delighted in the image of liberty and were pleased with considering themselves as the accountable ministers of the laws. Such princes deserved the honour of restoring the republic, had the Romans of their days been capable of enjoying a rational freedom.

The labours of these monarchs were overpaid by the immense reward that inseparably waited on their success; by the honest pride of virtue and by the exquisite delight of beholding the general happiness of which they were the authors. A just but melancholy reflection embittered, however, the noblest of human enjoyments. They must often have recollected the instability of a happiness which depended on the character of a single man. The fatal moment was perhaps approaching when some licentious youth or some jealous tyrant would abuse, to the destruction, that absolute power which they had exerted for the benefit of their people. The

ideal restraints of the senate and the laws might serve
to display the virtues, but could never correct the vices,
of the emperor. The military force was a blind and irresistible instrument of oppression; and the corruption of
Roman manners would always supply flatterers eager to
applaud and ministers prepared to serve the fear or the
avarice, the lust or the cruelty, of their masters.

These gloomy apprehensions had been already justified by the experience of the Romans. The annals of
the emperors exhibit a strong and various picture of
human nature, which we should vainly seek among the
mixed and doubtful characters of modern history. In
the conduct of those monarchs we may trace the utmost
lines of vice and virtue, the most exalted perfection and
the meanest degeneracy of our own species. The golden
age of Trajan and the Antonines had been preceded
by an age of iron. It is almost superfluous to enumerate
the unworthy successors of Augustus. Their unparalleled
vices, and the splendid theatre on which they were
acted, have saved them from oblivion. The dark unrelenting Tiberius, the furious Caligula, the feeble
Claudius, the profligate and cruel Nero, the beastly
Vitellius,[6] and the timid, inhuman Domitian are condemned to everlasting infamy. During fourscore years
(excepting only the short and doubtful respite of Vespasian's reign) Rome groaned beneath an unremitting
tyranny, which exterminated the ancient families of the
republic and was fatal to almost every virtue and every
talent that arose in that unhappy period.

Under the reign of these monsters the slavery of the

6. Vitellius consumed, in mere eating, at least six millions
of our money in about seven months. It is not easy to express
his vices with dignity or even decency. Tacitus fairly calls
him a hog; but it is by substituting to a coarse word a very
fine image.

Romans was accompanied with two peculiar circumstances, the one occasioned by their former liberty, the
other by their extensive conquests, which rendered their
condition more completely wretched than that of the
victims of tyranny in any other age or country. From
these causes were derived: I. the exquisite sensibility
of the sufferers: and II. the impossibility of escaping
from the hand of the oppressor.

I. When Persia was governed by the descendants
of Sefi, a race of princes whose wanton cruelty often
stained their divan, their table, and their bed with the
blood of their favourites, there is a saying recorded of
a young nobleman that he never departed from the
sultan's presence without satisfying himself whether
his head was still on his shoulders. The experience of
every day might almost justify the scepticism of Rustan.
Yet the fatal sword, suspended above him by a single
thread, seems not to have disturbed the slumbers or
interrupted the tranquillity of the Persian. The monarch's frown, he well knew, could level him with the
dust; but the stroke of lightning or apoplexy might be
equally fatal; and it was the part of a wise man to
forget the inevitable calamities of human life in the
enjoyment of the fleeting hour. He was dignified with
the appellation of the king's slave; had, perhaps, been
purchased from obscure parents in a country which
he had never known; and was trained up from his
infancy in the severe discipline of the seraglio. His
name, his wealth, his honours were the gift of a master
who might, without injustice, resume what he had bestowed. Rustan's knowledge, if he possessed any, could
only serve to confirm his habits by prejudices. His language afforded not words for any form of government
except absolute monarchy. The history of the East informed him that such had ever been the condition of

mankind. The Koran, and the interpreters of that divine book, inculcated to him that the sultan was the descendant of the prophet and the vice-regent of heaven, that patience was the first virtue of a Mussulman, and unlimited obedience the great duty of a subject.

The minds of the Romans were very differently prepared for slavery. Oppressed beneath the weight of their own corruption and of military violence, they for a long while preserved the sentiments, or at least the ideas, of their free-born ancestors. The education of Helvidius and Thrasea, of Tacitus and Pliny, was the same as that of Cato and Cicero. From Grecian philosophy they had imbibed the justest and most liberal notions of the dignity of human nature and the origin of civil society. The history of their own country had taught them to revere a free, a virtuous, and a victorious commonwealth; to abhor the successful crimes of Cæsar and Augustus; and inwardly to despise those tyrants whom they adored with the most abject flattery. As magistrates and senators, they were admitted into the great council which had once dictated laws to the earth, whose name still gave a sanction to the acts of the monarch, and whose authority was so often prostituted to the vilest purposes of tyranny. Tiberius and those emperors who adopted his maxims attempted to disguise their murders by the formalities of justice, and perhaps enjoyed a secret pleasure in rendering the senate their accomplice as well as their victim. By this assembly the last of the Romans were condemned for imaginary crimes and real virtues. Their infamous accusers assumed the language of independent patriots, who arraigned a dangerous citizen before the tribunal of his country; and the public service was rewarded by riches and honours. The servile judges professed to assert the majesty of the commonwealth, violated in the person of its first magistrate, whose clemency they most applauded when they trembled the most at his inexorable and impending cruelty.[7] The tyrant beheld their baseness with just contempt and encountered their secret sentiments of detestation with sincere and avowed hatred for the whole body of the senate.

II. The division of Europe into a number of independent states, connected, however, with each other by the general resemblance of religion, language, and manners, is productive of the most beneficial consequences to the liberty of mankind. A modern tyrant, who should find no resistance either in his own breast or in his people, would soon experience a gentle restraint from the example of his equals, the dread of present censure, the advice of his allies, and the apprehension of his enemies. The object of his displeasure, escaping from the narrow limits of his dominions, would easily obtain, in a happier climate, a secure refuge, a new fortune adequate to his merit, the freedom of complaint, and perhaps the means of revenge. But the empire of the Romans filled the world, and when that empire fell into the hands of a single person, the world became a safe and dreary prison for his enemies. The slave of Imperial despotism, whether he was condemned to drag his gilded chain in Rome and the senate, or to wear out a life of exile on the barren rock of Seriphus or the frozen banks of the Danube, expected his fate in silent despair. To resist was fatal, and it was impossible to fly. On every side he was encompassed with a vast extent of sea and land, which he could never hope to traverse without

7. After the virtuous and unfortunate widow of Germanicus had been put to death, Tiberius received the thanks of the senate for his clemency. She had not been publicly strangled; nor was the body drawn with a hook to the Gemoniæ, where those of common malefactors were exposed.

being discovered, seized, and restored to his irritated master. Beyond the frontiers his anxious view could discover nothing except the ocean, inhospitable deserts, hostile tribes of barbarians of fierce manners and unknown language, or dependent kings who would gladly purchase the emperor's protection by the sacrifice of an obnoxious fugitive. "Wherever you are," said Cicero to the exiled Marcellus, "remember that you are equally within the power of the conqueror."

Chapter IV

(A.D. 180-248)

*The cruelty, follies, and murder of Commodus –
His successor Pertinax is slain by the Prætorian
Guards – Public sale of the empire to Didius
Julianus – Triumph and harsh reign of Septimius
Severus – Tyranny of Caracalla and the follies of
Elagabalus – General unrest and rapid succession
of emperors – Usurpation and secular games of
Philip[1]*

THE mildness of Marcus, which the rigid discipline
of the Stoics was unable to eradicate, formed at the
same time the most amiable and the only defective part
of his character. His excellent understanding was often
deceived by the unsuspecting goodness of his heart.
Artful men, who study the passions of princes and conceal their own, approached his person in the disguise
of philosophic sanctity and acquired riches and honours
by affecting to despise them. His excessive indulgence
to his brother, his wife, and his son exceeded the bounds
of private virtue and became a public injury by the example and consequences of their vices.

Faustina, the daughter of Pius and the wife of Marcus, has been as much celebrated for her gallantries as
for her beauty. The grave simplicity of the philosopher

1. *Editor's note:* Chapters IV through VII of the original.
Not included in the condensation are Chapters VIII and IX,
which give the historical background of Persia and Germany,
respectively—nations destined to bulk large in the empire's
subsequent history.

was ill calculated to engage her wanton levity or to
fix that unbounded passion for variety which often discovered personal merit in the meanest of mankind.
The Cupid of the ancients was, in general, a very sensual deity; and the amours of an empress, as they
exact on her side the plainest advances, are seldom
susceptible of much sentimental delicacy. Marcus was
the only man in the empire who seemed ignorant or
insensible of the irregularities of Faustina, which, according to the prejudices of every age, reflected some
disgrace on the injured husband. He promoted several
of her lovers to posts of honour and profit, and during
a connection of thirty years invariably gave her proofs
of the most tender confidence and of a respect which
ended not with her life. In his Meditations he thanks
the gods who had bestowed on him a wife so faithful,
so gentle, and of such a wonderful simplicity of manners. The obsequious senate, at his earnest request,
declared her a goddess. She was represented in her
temples with the attributes of Juno, Venus, and Ceres;
and it was decreed that on the day of their nuptials the youth of either sex should pay their vows before the altar of their chaste patroness.

The monstrous vices of the son have cast a shade on
the purity of the father's virtues. It has been objected
to Marcus that he sacrificed the happiness of millions
to a fond partiality for a worthless boy, and that he
chose a successor in his own family rather than in the
republic. Nothing, however, was neglected by the anxious father, and by the men of virtue and learning whom
he summoned to his assistance, to expand the narrow
mind of young Commodus, to correct his growing vices,
and to render him worthy of the throne for which he
was designed. But the power of instruction is seldom
of much efficacy except in those happy dispositions

where it is almost superfluous. The distasteful lesson of a grave philosopher was in a moment obliterated by the whisper of a profligate favourite; and Marcus himself blasted the fruits of this laboured education by admitting his son, at the age of fourteen or fifteen, to a full participation of the Imperial power. He lived but four years afterwards; but he lived long enough to repent a rash measure which raised the impetuous youth above the restraint of reason and authority.

Most of the crimes which disturb the internal peace of society are produced by the restraints which the necessary but unequal laws of property have imposed on the appetites of mankind, by confining to a few the possession of those objects that are coveted by many. Of all our passions and appetites, the love of power is of the most imperious and unsociable nature, since the pride of one man requires the submission of the multitude. In the tumult of civil discord the laws of society lose their force, and their place is seldom supplied by those of humanity. The ardour of contention, the pride of victory, the despair of success, the memory of past injuries, and the fear of future dangers, all contribute to inflame the mind and to silence the voice of pity. From such motives almost every page of history has been stained with civil blood; but these motives will not account for the unprovoked cruelties of Commodus, who had nothing to wish and everything to enjoy. The beloved son of Marcus succeeded (A.D. 180) to his father, amidst the acclamations of the senate and armies; and when he ascended the throne the happy youth saw round him neither competitor to remove nor enemies to punish. In this calm, elevated station it was surely natural that he should prefer the love of mankind to their detestation, the mild glories of his five predecessors to the ignominious fate of Nero and Domitian.

Yet Commodus was not, as he has been represented, a tiger born with an insatiate thirst of human blood and capable from his infancy of the most inhuman actions. Nature had formed him of a weak rather than a wicked disposition. His simplicity and timidity rendered him the slave of his attendants, who gradually corrupted his mind. His cruelty, which at first obeyed the dictates of others, degenerated into habit and at length became the ruling passion of his soul.

Upon the death of his father, Commodus found himself embarrassed with the command of a great army and the conduct of a difficult war against the Quadi and Marcomanni. The servile and profligate youths whom Marcus had banished soon regained their station and influence about the new emperor. They exaggerated the hardships and dangers of a campaign in the wild countries beyond the Danube; and they assured the indolent prince that the terror of his name and the arms of his lieutenants would be sufficient to complete the conquest of the dismayed barbarians or to impose such conditions as were more advantageous than any conquest. By a dexterous application to his sensual appetites, they compared the tranquillity, the splendour, the refined pleasures of Rome with the tumult of a Pannonian camp, which afforded neither leisure nor materials for luxury. Commodus listened to the pleasing advice; but whilst he hesitated between his own inclination and the awe which he still retained for his father's counsellors, the summer insensibly elapsed, and his triumphal entry into the capital was deferred till the autumn. His graceful person, popular address, and imagined virtues attracted the public favour; the honourable peace which he had recently granted to the barbarians diffused an universal joy; his impatience to revisit Rome was fondly ascribed to the love of his country; and his dissolute course of amusements was faintly condemned in a prince of nineteen years of age.

During the three first years of his reign the forms, and even the spirit, of the old administration were maintained by those faithful counsellors to whom Marcus had recommended his son, and for whose wisdom and integrity Commodus still entertained a reluctant esteem. The young prince and his profligate favourites revelled in all the licence of sovereign power; but his hands were yet unstained with blood, and he had even displayed a generosity of sentiment which might perhaps have ripened into solid virtue. A fatal incident decided his fluctuating character.

One evening (A.D. 183), as the emperor was returning to the palace through a dark and narrow portico in the amphitheatre, an assassin who waited his passage rushed upon him with a drawn sword, loudly exclaiming, *"The senate sends you this."* The menace prevented the deed; the assassin was seized by the guards and immediately revealed the authors of the conspiracy. It had been formed not in the state but within the walls of the palace. Lucilla, the emperor's sister and widow of Lucius Verus, impatient of the second rank and jealous of the reigning empress, had armed the murderer against her brother's life. She had not ventured to communicate the black design to her second husband, Claudius Pompeianus, a senator of distinguished merit and unshaken loyalty; but among the crowd of her lovers (for she imitated the manners of Faustina) she found men of desperate fortunes and wild ambition who were prepared to serve her more violent as well as her tender passions. The conspirators experienced the rigour of justice, and the abandoned princess was punished, first with exile and afterwards with death.

But the words of the assassin sunk deep into the mind

of Commodus and left an indelible impression of fear
and hatred against the whole body of the senate. Those
whom he had dreaded as importunate ministers he now
suspected as secret enemies. The Delators, a race of men
discouraged and almost extinguished under the former
reigns, again became formidable as soon as they discovered that the emperor was desirous of finding disaffection and treason in the senate. That assembly,
whom Marcus had ever considered as the great council
of the nation, was composed of the most distinguished
of the Romans, and distinction of every kind soon became criminal. The possession of wealth stimulated the
diligence of the informers; rigid virtue implied a tacit
censure of the irregularities of Commodus; important
services implied a dangerous superiority of merit; and
the friendship of the father always insured the aversion
of the son. Suspicion was equivalent to proof, trial to
condemnation. The execution of a considerable senator
was attended with the death of all who might lament
or revenge his fate; and when Commodus had once
tasted human blood, he became incapable of pity or
remorse.

Of these innocent victims of tyranny, none died more
lamented than the two brothers of the Quintilian family,
Maximus and Condianus, whose fraternal love has saved
their names from oblivion and endeared their memory
to posterity. Their studies and their occupations, their
pursuits and their pleasures, were still the same. In
the enjoyment of a great estate they never admitted
the idea of a separate interest; some fragments are now
extant of a treatise which they composed in common;
and in every action of life it was observed that their
two bodies were animated by one soul. The Antonines,
who valued their virtues and delighted in their union,
raised them in the same year to the consulship; and

Marcus afterwards entrusted to their joint care the civil administration of Greece and a great military command, in which they obtained a signal victory over the Germans. The kind cruelty of Commodus united them in death.

The tyrant's rage, after having shed the noblest blood of the senate, at length recoiled on the principal instrument of his cruelty. Whilst Commodus was immersed in blood and luxury he devolved the detail of the public business on Perennis, a servile and ambitious minister who had obtained his post by the murder of his predecessor, but who possessed a considerable share of vigour and ability. By acts of extortion and the forfeited estates of the nobles sacrificed to his avarice, he had accumulated an immense treasure. The Prætorian Guards were under his immediate command; and his son, who already discovered a military genius, was at the head of the Illyrian legions. Perennis aspired to the empire; or what, in the eyes of Commodus, amounted to the same crime: he was capable of aspiring to it, had he not been prevented, surprised, and (A.D. 186) put to death. The fall of a minister is a very trifling incident in the general history of the empire; but it was hastened by an extraordinary circumstance which proved how much the nerves of discipline were already relaxed. The legions of Britain, discontented with the administration of Perennis, formed a deputation of fifteen hundred select men, with instructions to march to Rome and lay their complaints before the emperor. These military petitioners, by their own determined behaviour, by inflaming the divisions of the guards, by exaggerating the strength of the British army, and by alarming the fears of Commodus, exacted and obtained tne minister's death as the only redress of their grievances. This presumption of a distant army and their discovery of the weakness of government were a sure presage of the most dreadful convulsions.

The negligence of the public administration was betrayed soon afterwards by a new disorder which arose from the smallest beginnings. A spirit of desertion began to prevail among the troops, and the deserters, instead of seeking their flight in safety or concealment, infested the highways. Maternus, a private soldier of a daring boldness above his station, collected these bands of robbers into a little army, set open the prisons, invited the slaves to assert their freedom, and plundered with impunity the rich and defenceless cities of Gaul and Spain. The governors of the provinces, who had long been the spectators and perhaps the partners of his depredations, were at length roused from their supine indolence by the threatening commands of the emperor. Maternus found that he was encompassed and foresaw that he must be overpowered. A great effort of despair was his last resource. He ordered his followers to disperse, to pass the Alps in small parties and various disguises, and to assemble at Rome during the licentious tumult of the festival of Cybele. To murder Commodus and to ascend the vacant throne was the ambition of no vulgar robber. His measures were so ably concerted that his concealed troops already filled the streets of Rome. The envy of an accomplice discovered and ruined this singular enterprise in the moment when it was ripe for execution.

Suspicious princes often promote the last of mankind, from a vain persuasion that those who have no dependence except on their favour will have no attachment except to the person of their benefactor. Cleander, the successor of Perennis, was a Phrygian by birth, of a nation over whose stubborn but servile temper blows only could prevail. He had been sent from his native

country to Rome in the capacity of a slave. As a slave
he entered the Imperial palace, rendered himself useful to his master's passions, and rapidly ascended to
the most exalted station which a subject could enjoy.
His influence over the mind of Commodus was much
greater than that of his predecessor, for Cleander was
devoid of any ability or virtue which could inspire the
emperor with envy or distrust. Avarice was the reigning passion of his soul and the great principle of his
administration. The rank of consul, of patrician, of senator was exposed to public sale; and it would have been
considered as disaffection if anyone had refused to purchase these empty and disgraceful honours with the
greatest part of his fortune.[2] In the lucrative provincial
employments the minister shared with the governor the
spoils of the people. The execution of the laws was
venal and arbitrary. A wealthy criminal might obtain
not only the reversal of the sentence by which he was
justly condemned, but might likewise inflict whatever
punishment he pleased on the accuser, the witnesses,
and the judge.

By these means Cleander, in the space of three years,
had accumulated more wealth than had ever yet been
possessed by any freedman. Commodus was perfectly
satisfied with the magnificent presents which the artful
courtier laid at his feet in the most seasonable moments.
To divert the public envy, Cleander, under the emper-
or's name, erected baths, porticos, and places of exercise
for the use of the people. He flattered himself that the
Romans, dazzled and amused by this apparent liberality, would be less affected by the bloody scenes which
were daily exhibited; that they would forget the death
of Byrrhus, a senator to whose superior merit the late

2. One of these dear-bought promotions occasioned a current *bon mot* that Julius Solon was *banished* into the senate.

emperor had granted one of his daughters; and that they would forgive the execution of Arrius Antoninus, the last representative of the name and virtues of the Antonines. The former, with more integrity than prudence, had attempted to disclose to his brother-in-law the true character of Cleander. An equitable sentence pronounced by the latter, when proconsul of Asia, against a worthless creature of the favourite proved fatal to him. After the fall of Perennis, the terrors of Commodus had for a short time assumed the appearance of a return to virtue. He repealed the most odious of his acts, loaded his memory with the public execration, and ascribed to the pernicious counsels of that wicked minister all the errors of his inexperienced youth. But his repentance lasted only thirty days, and under Cleander's tyranny the administration of Perennis was often regretted.

Pestilence and famine contributed to fill up the measure of the calamities of Rome. The first could be imputed only to the just indignation of the gods; but (A.D. 189) a monopoly of corn, supported by the riches and power of the minister, was considered as the immediate cause of the second. The popular discontent, after it had long circulated in whispers, broke out in the assembled circus. The people quitted their favourite amusements for the more delicious pleasure of revenge, rushed in crowds towards a palace in the suburbs, one of the emperor's retirements, and demanded with angry clamours the head of the public enemy. Cleander, who commanded the Prætorian Guards, ordered a body of cavalry to sally forth and disperse the seditious multitude. The multitude fled with precipitation towards the city; several were slain, and many more were trampled to death; but when the cavalry entered the streets their pursuit was checked by a shower of

stones and darts from the roofs and windows of the
houses. The foot guards, who had been long jealous of
the prerogatives and insolence of the Prætorian cavalry,
embraced the party of the people. The tumult became
a regular engagement and threatened a general massacre. The Prætorians at length gave way, oppressed
with numbers; and the tide of popular fury returned
with redoubled violence against the gates of the palace,
where Commodus lay dissolved in luxury and alone
unconscious of the civil war. It was death to approach
his person with the unwelcome news. He would have
perished in this supine security had not two women, his
elder sister Fadilla and Marcia, the most favoured of
his concubines, ventured to break into his presence.
Bathed in tears and with dishevelled hair, they threw
themselves at his feet and, with all the pressing eloquence of fear, discovered to the affrighted emperor
the crimes of the minister, the rage of the people, and
the impending ruin which in a few minutes would burst
over his palace and person. Commodus started from
his dream of pleasure and commanded that the head of
Cleander should be thrown out to the people. The
desired spectacle instantly appeased the tumult; and
the son of Marcus might even yet have regained the
affection and confidence of his outraged subjects.

But every sentiment of virtue and humanity was extinct in the mind of Commodus. Whilst he thus abandoned the reins of empire to these unworthy favourites,
he valued nothing in sovereign power except the unbounded licence of indulging his sensual appetites. His
hours were spent in a seraglio of three hundred beautiful women and as many boys, of every rank and of every
province; and wherever the arts of seduction proved
ineffectual, the brutal lover had recourse to violence.
The ancient historians have expatiated on these aban-

doned scenes of prostitution, which scorned every restraint of nature or modesty; but it would not be easy
to translate their too faithful descriptions into the decency of modern language. The intervals of lust were
filled up with the basest amusements. The influence of
a polite age and the labour of an attentive education
had never been able to infuse into his rude and brutish
mind the least tincture of learning; and he was the first
of the Roman emperors totally devoid of taste for the
pleasures of the understanding. Nero himself excelled,
or affected to excel, in the elegant arts of music and
poetry; nor should we despise his pursuits had he not
converted the pleasing relaxation of a leisure hour into
the serious business and ambition of his life. But Commodus from his earliest infancy discovered an aversion
to whatever was rational or liberal, and a fond attachment to the amusements of the populace—the sports
of the circus and amphitheatre, the combats of gladiators, and the hunting of wild beasts. The masters in
every branch of learning whom Marcus provided for
his son were heard with inattention and disgust; whilst
the Moors and Parthians, who taught him to dart the
javelin and to shoot with the bow, found a disciple who
delighted in his application and soon equalled the most
skilful of his instructors in the steadiness of the eye
and the dexterity of the hand.

The servile crowd, whose fortune depended on their
master's vices, applauded these ignoble pursuits. The
perfidious voice of flattery reminded him that by exploits of the same nature, by the defeat of the Nemæan
lion and the slaughter of the wild boar of Erymanthus,
the Grecian Hercules had acquired a place among the
gods and an immortal memory among men. They only
forgot to observe that in the first ages of society, when
the fiercer animals often dispute with man the possession

of an unsettled country, a successful war against those savages is one of the most innocent and beneficial labours of heroism. In the civilized state of the Roman empire, the wild beasts had long since retired from the face of man and the neighbourhood of populous cities. To surprise them in their solitary haunts and to transport them to Rome that they might be slain in pomp by the hand of an emperor was an enterprise equally ridiculous for the prince and oppressive for the people. Ignorant of these distinctions, Commodus eagerly embraced the glorious resemblance and styled himself (as we still read on his medals) the Roman Hercules. The club and the lion's hide were placed by the side of the throne amongst the ensigns of sovereignty; and statues were erected in which Commodus was represented in the character and with the attributes of the god, whose valour and dexterity he endeavoured to emulate in the daily course of his ferocious amusements.

Elated with these praises, which gradually extinguished the innate sense of shame, Commodus resolved to exhibit before the eyes of the Roman people those exercises which till then he had decently confined within the walls of his palace and to the presence of a few favourites. On the appointed day the various motives of flattery, fear, and curiosity attracted to the amphitheatre an innumerable multitude of spectators; and some degree of applause was deservedly bestowed on the uncommon skill of the Imperial performer. Whether he aimed at the head or heart of the animal, the wound was alike certain and mortal. With arrows whose point was shaped into the form of a crescent, Commodus often intercepted the rapid career and cut asunder the long bony neck of the ostrich. A panther was let loose, and the archer waited till he had leaped upon a trembling malefactor. In the same instant the shaft flew, the beast

dropped dead, and the man remained unhurt. The dens
of the amphitheatre disgorged at once a hundred lions;
a hundred darts from the unerring hand of Commodus
laid them dead as they ran raging around the arena.
Neither the huge bulk of the elephant nor the scaly
hide of the rhinoceros could defend them from his
stroke. Ethiopia and India yielded their most extraordinary productions, and several animals were slain in
the amphitheatre which had been seen only in the representations of art, or perhaps of fancy. In all these
exhibitions the securest precautions were used to protect the person of the Roman Hercules from the desperate spring of any savage who might possibly disregard the dignity of the emperor and the sanctity of the
god.

But the meanest of the populace were affected with
shame and indignation when they beheld their sovereign enter the lists as a gladiator and glory in a profession which the laws and manners of the Romans
had branded with the justest note of infamy. He chose
the habit and arms of the *secutor*, whose combat with
the *retiarius* formed one of the most lively scenes in the
bloody sports of the amphitheatre. The *secutor* was
armed with an helmet, sword, and buckler; his naked
antagonist had only a large net and a trident; with the
one he endeavoured to entangle, with the other to dispatch, his enemy. If he missed the first throw, he was
obliged to fly from the pursuit of the *secutor* till he
had prepared his net for a second cast. The emperor
fought in this character seven hundred and thirty-five
times. These glorious achievements were carefully recorded in the public acts of the empire; and that he
might omit no circumstance of infamy, he received from
the common fund of gladiators a stipend so exorbitant
that it became a new and most ignominious tax upon

the Roman people. It may be easily supposed that in
these engagements the master of the world was always
successful. In the amphitheatre his victories were not
often sanguinary; but when he exercised his skill in the
school of gladiators or his own palace, his wretched
antagonists were frequently honoured with a mortal
wound from the hand of Commodus and obliged to seal
their flattery with their blood.[3] He now disdained the
appellation of Hercules. The name of Paulus, a celebrated Secutor, was the only one which delighted his
ear. It was inscribed on his colossal statues and repeated
in the redoubled acclamations of the mournful and applauding senate. Claudius Pompeianus, the virtuous
husband of Lucilla, was the only senator who asserted
the honour of his rank. As a father, he permitted his
sons to consult their safety by attending the amphitheatre. As a Roman he declared that his own life was
in the emperor's hands, but that he would never behold
the son of Marcus prostituting his person and dignity.
Notwithstanding his manly resolution, Pompeianus
escaped the resentment of the tyrant, and with his
honour had the good fortune to preserve his life.

Commodus had now attained the summit of vice and
infamy. Amidst the acclamations of a flattering court
he was unable to disguise from himself that he had
deserved the contempt and hatred of every man of
sense and virtue in his empire. His ferocious spirit was
irritated by the consciousness of that hatred, by the
envy of every kind of merit, by the just apprehension
of danger, and by the habit of slaughter which he contracted in his daily amusements. History has preserved
a long list of consular senators sacrificed to his wanton

3. Victor tells us that Commodus only allowed his antagonists a leaden weapon, dreading most probably the consequences of their despair.

suspicion, which sought out with peculiar anxiety those unfortunate persons connected, however remotely, with the family of the Antonines, without sparing even the ministers of his crimes or pleasures. His cruelty proved at last fatal to himself. He had shed with impunity the noblest blood of Rome; he perished as soon as he was dreaded by his own domestics. Marcia his favourite concubine, Eclectus his chamberlain, and Lætus his Prætorian præfect, alarmed by the fate of their companions and predecessors, resolved to prevent the destruction which every hour hung over their heads, either from the mad caprice of the tyrant or the sudden indignation of the people. Marcia seized the occasion of presenting a draught of wine to her lover, after he had fatigued himself with hunting some wild beasts. Commodus retired to sleep; but whilst he was labouring with the effects of poison and drunkenness, a robust youth, by profession a wrestler, entered his chamber and strangled him without resistance. The body was secretly conveyed out of the palace before the least suspicion was entertained in the city, or even in the court, of the emperor's death. Such was the fate of the son of Marcus, and so easy was it to destroy a hated tyrant, who, by the artificial powers of government, had oppressed during thirteen years so many millions of subjects, each of whom was equal to his master in personal strength and personal abilities.

In the original, the remainder of this chapter and the three following are a melancholy record of growing military unrest, especially among the Prætorian Guards, the only effective military force stationed near Rome. Upon Commodus's assassination, the Imperial power was thrust upon Pertinax, a long-time official under Marcus Aurelius; but his "hasty zeal to reform the cor-

rupted state" brought his assassination (A.D. 193) *by the Prætorian Guards after a rule of only eighty-six days.* It is difficult to fix the lowest point in Roman political history; but one of them certainly occurred when, after the murder of Pertinax, the Prætorian Guards sold the empire at public auction to a wealthy and foolish senator named Didius Julianus. The resulting revolt of three generals, in Britain, on the Danube, and in the East, limited the reign of Julianus to a mere sixty-six days.

The ultimately victorious general, Septimius Severus, gave the empire nearly eighteen years of peace, but at a fearful cost. A *"haughty and inflexible"* man who *"considered the Roman empire as his personal property,"* he disdained to use the senate as an instrument of policy and *"issued his commands where his request would have proved as effectual."* And while he banished the Prætorian Guards from Rome for their murder of Pertinax and contemptible transaction with Julianus, he soon found it expedient to re-establish the Guards at four times the earlier number. For thus discarding even the forms of self-government, and for leaving the capital at the mercy of the soldiers, Gibbon regards Septimius Severus *"the principal author of the decline of the Roman empire."*

He was succeeded (A.D. 211) jointly by his two sons, Caracalla and Geta, whose implacable enmity led the former to murder the latter scarcely a year after their father's death; and Caracalla's guilt apparently drove him to wild cruelties and excesses that made him *"the common enemy of mankind."* His death (A.D. 217) came from a plot by a high official named Opilius Macrinus, who assumed with the purple the difficult task of reforming the very military power whose pliant cupidity had confirmed his own position. He perished a little more than a year later in a military revolt that brought

to power that incredible creature known to history as
Elagabalus.

Elagabalus, who took his name from a Syrian sun god,
"abandoned himself to the grossest pleasures with un-
governed fury." But a "confused multitude of women,
of wines, and of dishes" were inadequate to his tastes.
He also "affected to copy the dress and manners of the
female sex . . . and dishonoured the principal dignities
of the empire by distributing them among his numerous
lovers, one of whom was publicly invested with the
title and authority of the emperor's, or, as he more
properly styled himself, of the empress's, husband."
The death of Elagabalus (A.D. 222) came when he foolishly presumed to punish the Prætorian Guards for their
partiality to a young cousin, Alexander Severus, who
succeeded him.

During a moderately properous reign of thirteen years
(A.D. 222-235), Alexander Severus used his considerable
talents in an incessant struggle against military mutinies
from one end of the empire to the other, in one of
which his closest friend and counsellor, the celebrated
lawyer Ulpian, was pursued into the Imperial palace
and murdered at the emperor's feet for some fancied
slight to the Prætorian Guards. Alexander's death came
at the hands of one Maximin, a savage Thracian peasant whose eight-foot stature and amazing strength had
first brought him to the notice of Septimius Severus and
started him on his rise in the military order.

Maximin's only loyalty, says Gibbon, was to the army;
his only fear was the fear of contempt, which led him
to act with equally implacable cruelty toward those
who had spurned and those who had helped him in
humbler years. Maximin's attempt (A.D. 237) to seize
the independent revenues of every city in the empire,
for use by the military, caused a rash of small revolts;

and one of these in Africa claimed the purple for Gordianus, an eighty-year-old Roman of illustrious and ver-
satile family, who was then proconsul of Africa, and
his son.[4] In the absence of Maximin, who was campaign-
ing on the Danubian frontier, the senate boldly confirmed the Imperial claims of the Gordians. Nor did the
early death of the two Gordians, at the hands of one of
Maximin's African lieutenants, quell this exercise of
senatorial independence. Two senators, a magistrate
named Balbinus and a soldier named Maximus, were
proclaimed joint emperors, and with them was associated a third Gordianus, the thirteen-year-old grandson
of the African proconsul.

Their joint strategy was sufficient to dispatch Maximin
(A.D. 238), who, returning to Rome, saw the loyalty of
his troops evaporate in the fruitless siege of the fortified city of Aquileia; but it was no protection against
the sullen Prætorian Guards. Within three months the
Guards, taking advantage of the popular preoccupation
with the Capitoline games, invaded the imperial palace,
killed both Maximus and Balbinus, and carried the
young Gordianus back to their camp as a kind of hos-
tage. During a reign of six years the young Gordianus
showed much promise, especially in his attachment to
a gifted lieutenant named Misitheus. But the death of
Misitheus (A.D. 243) soon led, in the following year, to
the death of the nineteen-year-old Gordianus at the
hands of the Prætorian præfect, an Arab named Philip.
Philip's chief claim to the attention of history was

4. *Editor's note:* Of the son Gibbon remarks: "Twenty-two
acknowledged concubines and a library of sixty-two thousand
volumes attested to the variety of his inclinations; and from
the productions which he left behind him, it appears that
the former as well as the latter were for use rather than
ostentation."

his elaborate celebration (A.D. 248) *of the great secular games of Rome, the fifth such celebration since the founding of the city some ten centuries earlier. But his total powerlessness to dispell the empire's gathering political instability is abundantly shown in the gloomy events so soon to follow.*

Chapter V
(A.D. 248-285)

The Emperors Decius, Gallus, Æmilianus, Valerian, and Gallienus — General irruption of the barbarians — The thirty tyrants — Reigns and victories of Claudius and Aurelian — Peaceful respite after the death of Aurelian — Reigns of Tacitus, Probus, Carus, and Carus's sons[1]

FROM the great secular games celebrated by Philip to the death of the emperor Gallienus there elapsed (A.D. 248-268) twenty years of shame and misfortune. During that calamitous period every instant of time was marked, every province of the Roman world was afflicted by barbarous invaders and military tyrants, and the ruined empire seemed to approach the last and fatal moment of its dissolution. The confusion of the times and the scarcity of authentic memorials oppose equal difficulties to the historian who attempts to preserve a clear and unbroken thread of narration. Surrounded with imperfect fragments, always concise, often obscure, and sometimes contradictory, he is reduced to collect, to compare, and to conjecture; and though he ought never to place his conjectures in the rank of facts, yet the knowledge of human nature, and of the sure operation of its fierce and unrestrained passions, might on some occasions supply the want of historical materials.

There is not, for instance, any difficulty in conceiv-

1. *Editor's note:* Chapters X through XII of the original.

ing that the successive murders of so many emperors had loosened all the ties of allegiance between the prince and people; that all the generals of Philip were disposed to imitate the example of their master; and that the caprice of armies, long since habituated to frequent and violent revolutions, might any day raise to the throne the most obscure of their fellow-soldiers. History can only add that the rebellion against the emperor Philip broke out in the summer of the year 249 among the legions of Mæsia, and that a subaltern officer named Marinus was the object of their seditious choice. Philip was alarmed. He dreaded lest the treason of the Mæsian army should prove the first spark of a general conflagration. Distracted with the consciousness of his guilt and of his danger, he communicated the intelligence to the senate. A gloomy silence prevailed, the effect of fear and perhaps of disaffection; till at length Decius, one of the assembly, assuming a spirit worthy of his noble extraction, ventured to discover more intrepidity than the emperor seemed to possess. He treated the whole business with contempt as a hasty and inconsiderate tumult, and Philip's rival as a phantom of royalty who in a very few days would be destroyed by the same inconstancy that had created him.

The speedy completion of the prophecy inspired Philip with a just esteem for so able a counsellor; and Decius appeared to him the only person capable of restoring peace and discipline to an army whose tumultuous spirit did not immediately subside after the murder of Marinus. Decius, who long resisted his own nomination, seems to have insinuated the danger of presenting a leader of merit to the angry and apprehensive minds of the soldiers; and his prediction was again confirmed by the event. The legion of Mæsia forced their judge to become (A.D. 249) their accomplice. They left him only the alternative of death or the purple. His subsequent conduct, after that decisive measure, was unavoidable. He conducted or followed his army to the confines of Italy, whither Philip, collecting all his force to repel the formidable competitor whom he had raised up, advanced to meet him. The Imperial troops were superior in number, but the rebels formed an army of veterans commanded by an able and experienced leader. Philip was either killed in the battle or put to death a few days afterwards at Verona. His son and associate in the empire was massacred at Rome by the Prætorian Guards; and the victorious Decius, with more favourable circumstances than the ambition of that age can usually plead, was universally acknowledged by the senate and provinces. It is reported that, immediately after his reluctant acceptance of the title of Augustus, he had assured Philip by a private message of his innocence and loyalty, solemnly protesting that on his arrival in Italy he would resign the Imperial ornaments and return to the condition of an obedient subject. His professions might be sincere. But in the situation where fortune had placed him it was scarcely possible that he could either forgive or be forgiven.

The emperor Decius had employed a few months in the works of peace and the administration of justice when (A.D. 250) he was summoned to the banks of the Danube by the invasion of the Goths. This is the first considerable occasion in which history mentions that great people, who afterwards broke the Roman power, sacked the Capitol, and reigned in Gaul, Spain, and Italy. So memorable was the part which they acted in the subversion of the western empire that the name of Goths is frequently but improperly used as a general appellation of rude and warlike barbarism.

In the beginning of the sixth century, and after the

conquest of Italy, the Goths, in possession of present greatness, very naturally indulged themselves in the prospect of past and of future glory. They wished to preserve the memory of their ancestors and to transmit to posterity their own achievements. The principal minister of the court of Ravenna, the learned Cassiodorus, gratified the inclination of the conquerors in a Gothic history which consisted of twelve books, now reduced to the imperfect abridgment of Jornandes. These writers passed with the most artful conciseness, over the misfortunes of the nation, celebrated its successful valour, and adorned the triumph with many Asiatic trophies that more properly belonged to the people of Scythia. On the faith of ancient songs, the uncertain but the only memorials of barbarians, they deduced the first origin of the Goths from the vast island or peninsula of Scandinavia. That extreme country of the north was not unknown to the conquerors of Italy; the ties of ancient consanguinity had been strengthened by recent offices of friendship; and a Scandinavian king had cheerfully abdicated his savage greatness that he might pass the remainder of his days in the peaceful and polished court of Ravenna. Many vestiges, which cannot be ascribed to the arts of popular vanity, attest the ancient residence of the Goths in the countries beyond the Baltic. From the time of the geographer Ptolemy the southern part of Sweden seems to have continued in the possession of the less enterprising remnant of the nation, and a large territory is even at present divided into east and west Gothland. During the middle ages (from the ninth to the twelfth century), whilst Christianity was advancing with a slow progress into the north, the Goths and the Swedes composed two distinct and sometimes hostile members of the same monarchy. The latter of these two names has prevailed

without extinguishing the former. The Swedes, who
might well be satisfied with their own fame in arms,
have in every age claimed the kindred glory of the
Goths. In a moment of discontent against the court of
Rome, Charles the Twelfth insinuated that his victorious
troops were not degenerated from their brave ancestors
who had already subdued the mistress of the world.[2]

If so many successive generations of Goths were capable of preserving a faint tradition of their Scandinavian origin, we must not expect from such unlettered
barbarians any distinct account of the time and circumstances of their emigration. To cross the Baltic was
an easy and natural attempt. The inhabitants of Sweden
were masters of a sufficient number of large vessels with
oars, and the distance is little more than one hundred
miles from Carlscrona to the nearest ports of Pomerania
and Prussia. Here, at length, we land on firm and his-
toric ground. At least as early as the Christian era, and
as late as the age of the Antonines, the Goths were
established towards the mouth of the Vistula, and in
that fertile province where the commercial cities of
Thorn, Elbing, Königsberg, and Dantzig were long afterwards founded. Westward of the Goths, the numerous tribes of the Vandals were spread along the banks
of the Oder and the seacoast of Pomerania and Meck-
lenburg. A striking resemblance of manners, complexion,
religion, and language seemed to indicate that the
Vandals and the Goths were originally one great people.
The latter appear to have been subdivided into Ostrogoths, Visigoths, and Gepidæ. The distinction among
the Vandals was more strongly marked by the independent names of Heruli, Burgundians, Lombards, and a
variety of other petty states, many of which, in a future

2. *Editor's note:* Here is omitted a brief passage drawing
upon mythological references to trace the origin of the Goths.

age, expanded themselves into powerful monarchies.

In the age of the Antonines the Goths were still seated in Prussia. About the reign of Alexander Severus, the Roman province of Dacia had already experienced their proximity by frequent and destructive inroads. In this interval, therefore, of about seventy years, we must place the second migration of the Goths from the Baltic to the Euxine; but the cause that produced it lies concealed among the various motives which actuate the conduct of unsettled barbarians. Either a pestilence or a famine, a victory or a defeat, an oracle of the gods or the eloquence of a daring leader, was sufficient to impel the Gothic arms on the milder climates of the south. Besides the influence of a martial religion, the numbers and spirit of the Goths were equal to the most dangerous adventures. The use of round bucklers and short swords rendered them formidable in a close engagement; the manly obedience which they yielded to hereditary kings gave uncommon union and stability to their councils; and the renowned Amala, the hero of that age and the tenth ancestor of Theodoric, king of Italy, enforced by the ascendant of personal merit the prerogative of his birth, which he derived from the *Anses,* or demigods, of the Gothic nation.

The fame of a great enterprise excited the bravest warriors from all the Vandalic states of Germany, many of whom are seen a few years afterwards combating under the common standard of the Goths. The first motions of the emigrants carried them to the banks of the Prypec [Pripet], a river universally conceived by the ancients to be the southern branch of the Borysthenes [Dnieper]. The windings of that great stream through the plains of Poland and Russia gave a direction to their line of march and a constant supply of fresh water and pasturage to their numerous herds of cattle. They fol-

lowed the unknown course of the river, confident in
their valour and careless of whatever power might oppose their progress. The Bastarnæ and the Venedi were
the first who presented themselves; and the flower of
their youth, either from choice or compulsion, increased
the Gothic army. The Bastarnæ dwelt on the northern
side of the Carpathian mountains; the immense tract
of land that separated the Bastarnæ from the savages
of Finland was possessed, or rather wasted, by the
Venedi; we have some reason to believe that the first
of these nations, which distinguished itself in the Macedonian war and was afterwards divided into the formidable tribes of the Peucini, the Borani, the Carpi, etc.,
derived its origin from the Germans. With better
authority, a Sarmatian extraction may be assigned to
the Venedi, who rendered themselves so famous in the
middle ages. But the confusion of blood and manners
on the doubtful frontier often perplexed the most
accurate observers. As the Goths advanced near the
Euxine Sea, they encountered a purer race of Sarmatians, the Jazyges, the Alani, and the Roxolani; and they
were probably the first Germans who saw the mouth
of the Borysthenes and of the Tanais [Don]. If we inquire into the characteristic marks of the people of
Germany and of Sarmatia, we shall discover that those
two great portions of humankind were principally distinguished by fixed huts or movable tents, by a close
dress of flowing garments, by the marriage of one or of
several wives, by a military force consisting for the most
part either of infantry or cavalry, and above all by the
use of the Teutonic or of the Sclavonian language,
the last of which has been diffused by conquest from
the confines of Italy to the neighbourhood of Japan.

The Goths were now in possession of the Ukraine,
a country of considerable extent and uncommon fer-

tility, intersected with navigable rivers which from either side discharge themselves into the Borysthenes, and interspersed with large and lofty forests of oaks. The plenty of game and fish, the innumerable beehives deposited in the hollows of old trees and in the cavities of rocks (and forming, even in that rude age, a valuable branch of commerce), the size of the cattle, the temperature of the air, the aptness of the soil for every species of grain, and the luxuriancy of the vegetation, all displayed the liberality of Nature and tempted the industry of man. But the Goths withstood all these temptations and still adhered to a life of idleness, of poverty, and of rapine.

The Scythian hordes, which towards the east bordered on the new settlements of the Goths, presented nothing to their arms except the doubtful chance of an unprofitable victory. But the prospect of the Roman territories was far more alluring; and the fields of Dacia were covered with rich harvests, sown by the hands of an industrious, and exposed to be gathered by those of a warlike, people. It is probable that the conquests of Trajan, maintained by his successors less for any real advantage than for ideal dignity, had contributed to weaken the empire on that side. The new and unsettled province of Dacia was neither strong enough to resist, nor rich enough to satiate, the rapaciousness of the barbarians. As long as the remote banks of the Dniester were considered as the boundary of the Roman power, the fortifications of the Lower Danube were more carelessly guarded; and the inhabitants of Mæsia lived in supine security, fondly conceiving themselves at an inaccessible distance ᴜin any barbarian invaders. The irruptions of the Goths, under [i.e., during] the reign of Philip, fatally convinced them of their mistake. The king, or leader, of that fierce nation traversed with contempt the province of Dacia and passed both the Dniester and the Danube without encountering any opposition capable of retarding his progress. The relaxed discipline of the Roman troops betrayed the most important posts where they were stationed, and the fear of deserved punishment induced great numbers of them to enlist under the Gothic standard. The various multitude of barbarians appeared, at length, under the walls of Marcianopolis, a city built by Trajan in honour of his sister, and at that time the capital of the second Mæsia. The inhabitants consented to ransom their lives and property by the payment of a large sum of money, and the invaders retreated back into their deserts, animated rather than satisfied with the first success of their arms against an opulent but feeble country. Intelligence was soon transmitted to the emperor Decius that Cniva, king of the Goths, had passed the Danube a second time with more considerable forces; that his numerous detachments scattered devastation over the province of Mæsia, whilst the main body of the army, consisting of seventy thousand Germans and Sarmatians, a force equal to the most daring achievements, required the presence of the Roman monarch and the exertion of his military power.

Decius found (A.D. 250) the Goths engaged before Nicopolis, on the Jatrus, one of the many monuments of Trajan's victories. On his approach they raised the siege, but with a design only of marching away to a conquest of greater importance, the siege of Philippopolis, a city of Thrace, founded by the father of Alexander, near the foot of Mount Hæmus. Decius followed them through a difficult country and by forced marches; but when he imagined himself at a considerable distance from the rear of the Goths, Cniva turned with rapid fury on his pursuers. The camp of the Romans was surprised and pillaged, and for the first time their emperor fled in disorder before a troop of half-armed barbarians. After a long resistance Philippopolis, destitute of succour, was taken by storm. A hundred thousand persons are reported to have been massacred in the sack of that great city. Many prisoners of consequence became a valuable accession to the spoil; and Priscus, a brother of the late emperor Philip, blushed not to assume the purple under the protection of the barbarous enemies of Rome. The time, however, consumed in that tedious siege enabled Decius to revive the courage, restore the discipline, and recruit the numbers of his troops. He intercepted several parties of Carpi and other Germans who were hastening to share the victory of their countrymen, entrusted the passes of the mountains to officers of approved valour and fidelity, repaired and strengthened the fortifications of the Danube, and exerted his utmost vigilance to oppose either the progress or the retreat of the Goths. Encouraged by the return of fortune, he anxiously waited for an opportunity to retrieve by a great and decisive blow his own glory and that of the Roman arms.

At the same time when Decius was struggling with the violence of the tempest, his mind, calm and deliberate amidst the tumult of war, investigated the more general causes that since the age of the Antonines had so impetuously urged the decline of the Roman greatness. He soon discovered that it was impossible to replace that greatness on a permanent basis without restoring public virtue, ancient principles and manners, and the oppressed majesty of the laws. To execute this noble but arduous design he first resolved to revive the obsolete office of censor, an office which, as long as it had subsisted in its pristine integrity, had so much contributed to the perpetuity of the state till it was usurped and gradually neglected by the Cæsars. Conscious that the favour of the sovereign may confer power but that the esteem of the people can alone bestow authority, he submitted the choice of the censor to the unbiased voice of the senate. By their unanimous votes, or rather acclamations, Valerian, who was afterwards emperor, and who then served with distinction in the army of Decius, was declared (A.D. 251, 27 Oct.) the most worthy of that exalted honour. As soon as the decree of the senate was transmitted to the emperor, he assembled a great council in his camp, and before the investiture of the censor-elect he apprised him of the difficulty and importance of his great office.

"Happy Valerian," said the prince to his distinguished subject, "happy in the general approbation of the senate and of the Roman republic! Accept the censorship of mankind, and judge of our manners. You will select those who deserve to continue members of the senate; you will restore the equestrian order to its ancient splendour; you will improve the revenue, yet moderate the public burdens. You will distinguish into regular classes the various and infinite multitude of citizens, and accurately review the military strength, the wealth, the virtue, and the resources of Rome. Your decisions shall obtain the force of laws. The army, the palace, the ministers of justice, and the great officers of the empire are all subject to your tribunal. None is exempted, excepting only the ordinary consuls, the præfect of the city, the king of the sacrifices, and (as long as she preserves her chastity inviolate) the eldest of the vestal virgins. Even these few, who may not dread the severity, will anxiously solicit the esteem of the Roman censor."

A magistrate invested with such extensive powers would have appeared not so much the minister as the colleague of his sovereign. Valerian justly dreaded an elevation so full of envy and of suspicion. He modestly urged the alarming greatness of the trust, his own insufficiency, and the incurable corruption of the times. He artfully insinuated that the office of censor was inseparable from the Imperial dignity, and that the feeble hands of a subject were unequal to the support of such an immense weight of cares and of power. The approaching event of war soon put an end to the prosecution of a project so specious but so impracticable; and whilst it preserved Valerian from the danger, [it] saved the emperor Decius from the disappointment which would most probably have attended it. A censor may maintain, he can never restore, the morals of a state. It is impossible for such a magistrate to exert his authority with benefit, or even with effect, unless he is supported by a quick sense of honour and virtue in the minds of the people, by a decent reverence for the public opinion, and by a train of useful prejudices combating on the side of national manners. In a period when these principles are annihilated, the censorial jurisdiction must either sink into empty pageantry or be converted into a partial instrument of vexatious oppression. It was easier to vanquish the Goths than to eradicate the public vices; yet even in the first of these enterprises Decius lost his army and his life.

The Goths were now, on every side, surrounded and pursued by the Roman arms. The flower of their troops had perished in the long siege of Philippopolis, and the exhausted country could no longer afford subsistence for the remaining multitude of licentious barbarians. Reduced to this extremity, the Goths would gladly have purchased, by the surrender of all their booty and prisoners, the permission of an undisturbed retreat. But the emperor, confident of victory and resolving, by the chastisement of these invaders, to strike a salutary terror into the nations of the North, refused to listen to any terms of accommodation.

The high-spirited barbarians preferred death to slavery. An obscure town of Mæsia, called Forum Terebronii, was the scene of the battle. The Gothic army was drawn up in three lines, and, either from choice or accident, the front of the third line was covered by a morass. In the beginning of the action the son of Decius, a youth of the fairest hopes and already associated to the honours of the purple, was slain by an arrow in the sight of his afflicted father, who, summoning all his fortitude, admonished the dismayed troops that the loss of a single soldier was of little importance to the republic. The conflict was terrible; it was the combat of despair against grief and rage. The first line of the Goths at length gave way in disorder; the second, advancing to sustain it, shared its fate; and the third only remained entire, prepared to dispute the passage of the morass, which was imprudently attempted by the presumption of the enemy. "Here the fortune of the day turned, and all things became adverse to the Romans: the place deep with ooze, sinking under those who stood, slippery to such as advanced; their armour heavy, the waters deep; nor could they wield, in that uneasy situation, their weighty javelins. The barbarians, on the contrary, were enured to encounters in the bogs, their persons tall, their spears long, such as could wound at a distance." In the morass the Roman army, after an ineffectual struggle, was irrecoverably lost; nor could the body of the emperor ever be found. Such was the fate of Decius, in the fiftieth year of his age; an accomplished prince, active in war and affable in peace, who together with his son has deserved to be compared, both in life and death, with the brightest examples of ancient virtue.

This fatal blow humbled, for a very little time, the insolence of the legions. They appear to have patiently expected, and submissively obeyed, the decree of the senate which regulated the succession to the throne. From a just regard for the memory of Decius, the Imperial title was conferred (A.D. 251, Dec.) on Hostilianus, his only surviving son; but an equal rank, with more effectual power, was granted to Gallus, whose experience and ability seemed equal to the great trust of guardian to the young prince and the distressed empire. The first care of the new emperor was to deliver the Illyrian provinces from the intolerable weight of the victorious Goths. He (A.D. 252) consented to leave in their hands the rich fruits of their invasion, an immense booty, and, what was still more disgraceful, a great number of prisoners of the highest merit and quality. He plentifully supplied their camp with every conveniency that could assuage their angry spirits or facilitate their so much wished-for departure; and he even promised to pay them annually a large sum of gold, on condition they should never afterwards infest the Roman territories by their incursions.

In the age of the Scipios the most opulent kings of the earth, who courted the protection of the victorious commonwealth, were gratified with such trifling presents as could only derive a value from the hand that bestowed them: an ivory chair, a coarse garment of purple, an inconsiderable piece of plate, or a quantity of copper coin. After the wealth of nations had centred in Rome, the emperors displayed their greatness, and even their policy, by the regular exercise of a steady and moderate liberality towards the allies of the state. They relieved the poverty of the barbarians, honoured their merit, and recompensed their fidelity. These voluntary marks of bounty were understood to flow not from the fears but merely from the generosity or the gratitude of the Romans; and whilst presents and subsidies were liberally distributed among friends and suppliants, they were sternly refused to such as claimed them as a debt. But this stipulation of an annual payment to a victorious enemy appeared without disguise in the light of an ignominious tribute; the minds of the Romans were not yet accustomed to accept such unequal laws from a tribe of barbarians; and the prince, who by a necessary concession had probably saved his country, became the object of the general contempt and aversion. The death of Hostilianus, though it happened in the midst of a raging pestilence, was interpreted as the personal crime of Gallus; and even the defeat of the late emperor was ascribed by the voice of suspicion to the perfidious counsels of his hated successor. The tranquillity which the empire enjoyed during the first year of his admin-istration served rather to inflame than to appease the public discontent; and as soon as the apprehensions of war were removed, the infamy of the peace was more deeply and more sensibly felt.

But the Romans were irritated to a still higher degree when they discovered that they had not even secured their repose, though at the expense of their honour. The dangerous secret of the wealth and weakness of the em-pire had been revealed to the world. New swarms of barbarians, encouraged (A.D. 253) by the success and not conceiving themselves bound by the obligation of their brethren, spread devastation through the Illyrian provinces and terror as far as the gates of Rome. The defence of the monarchy, which seemed abandoned by the pusillanimous emperor, was assumed by Æmilianus, governor of Pannonia and Mæsia, who rallied the scat-tered forces and revived the fainting spirits of the troops. The barbarians were unexpectedly attacked, routed, chased, and pursued beyond the Danube. The victorious leader distributed as a donative the money collected for the tribute, and the acclamations of the

soldiers proclaimed him emperor on the field of battle.
Gallus, who, careless of the general welfare, indulged
himself in the pleasures of Italy, was almost in the
same instant informed of the success of the revolt and
of the rapid approach of his aspiring lieutenant. He
advanced to meet him as far as the plains of Spoleto.
When the armies came in sight of each other, the soldiers of Gallus compared the ignominious conduct of
their sovereign with the glory of his rival. They admired
the valour of Æmilianus; they were attracted by his
liberality, for he offered a considerable increase of pay
to all deserters. The murder of Gallus, and of his son
Volusianus, put an end to the civil war; and the senate
(A.D. 253, May) gave a legal sanction to the rights of
conquest. The letters of Æmilianus to that assembly
displayed a mixture of moderation and vanity. He
assured them that he should resign to their wisdom the
civil administration, and, contenting himself with the
quality of their general, would in a short time assert
the glory of Rome and deliver the empire from all the
barbarians both of the North and of the East. His pride
was flattered by the applause of the senate; and medals
are still extant representing him with the name and attributes of Hercules and Victor and of Mars the Avenger.

If the new monarch possessed the abilities, he wanted
the time necessary to fulfil these splendid promises.
Less than four months intervened between his victory
and his fall. He had vanquished Gallus: he sank under
the weight of a competitor more formidable than Gallus.
That unfortunate prince had sent Valerian, already distinguished by the honourable title of censor, to bring
the legions of Gaul and Germany to his aid. Valerian
executed that commission with zeal and fidelity; and as
he arrived too late to save his sovereign, he resolved to
revenge him. The troops of Æmilianus, who still lay

encamped in the plains of Spoleto, were awed by the sanctity of his character, but much more by the superior strength of his army; and as they were now become as incapable of personal attachment as they had always been of constitutional principle, they (A.D. 253, Aug.) readily imbrued their hands in the blood of a prince who had so lately been the object of their partial choice. The guilt was theirs, but the advantage of it was Valerian's, who obtained the possession of the throne by the means indeed of a civil war, but with a degree of innocence singular in that age of revolutions, since he owned neither gratitude nor allegiance to his predecessor whom he dethroned.

Valerian was about sixty years of age when he was invested with the purple, not by the caprice of the populace or the clamours of the army, but by the unanimous voice of the Roman world. In his gradual ascent through the honours of the state, he had deserved the favour of virtuous princes and had declared himself the enemy of tyrants. His noble birth, his mild but unblemished manners, his learning, prudence, and experience, were revered by the senate and people; and if mankind (according to the observation of an ancient writer) had been left at liberty to choose a master, their choice would most assuredly have fallen on Valerian. Perhaps the merit of this emperor was inadequate to his reputation; perhaps his abilities, or at least his spirit, were affected by the languor and coldness of old age. The consciousness of his decline engaged him to share the throne with a younger and more active associate; the emergency of the times demanded a general no less than a prince; and the experience of the Roman censor might have directed him where to bestow the Imperial purple, as the reward of military merit. But instead of making a judicious choice which would have confirmed his reign and endeared his memory, Valerian, consulting only the dictates of affection or vanity, immediately invested with the supreme honours his son Gallienus, a youth whose effeminate vices had been hitherto concealed by the obscurity of a private station. The joint government of the father and the son subsisted about seven, and the sole administration of Gallienus continued about eight years (A.D. 253-268). But the whole period was one uninterrupted series of confusion and calamity. As the Roman empire was at the same time, and on every side, attacked by the blind fury of foreign invaders and the wild ambition of domestic usurpers, we shall consult order and perspicuity by pursuing not so much the doubtful arrangement of dates as the more natural distribution of subjects. The most dangerous enemies of Rome, during the reigns of Valerian and Gallienus, were: I. the Franks; II. the Alemanni; III. the Goths; and IV. the Persians. Under these general appellations we may comprehend the adventures of less considerable tribes, whose obscure and uncouth names would only serve to oppress the memory and perplex the attention of the reader.

I. THE FRANKS. As the posterity of the Franks compose one of the greatest and most enlightened nations of Europe, the powers of learning and ingenuity have been exhausted in the discovery of their unlettered ancestors. To the tales of credulity have succeeded the systems of fancy. Every passage has been sifted, every spot has been surveyed, that might possibly reveal some faint traces of their origin. It has been supposed that Pannonia, that Gaul, that the northern parts of Germany, gave birth to that celebrated colony of warriors. At length the most rational critics, rejecting the fictitious emigrations of ideal conquerors, have acquiesced in a sentiment whose simplicity persuades us of its truth.

They suppose that, about the year 240, a new confederacy was formed, under the name of Franks, by the old inhabitants of the Lower Rhine and the Weser. The present circle of Westphalia, the Landgraviate of Hesse, and the duchies of Brunswick and Luneburg were the ancient seat of the Chauci, who in their inaccessible morasses defied the Roman arms; of the Cherusci, proud of the fame of Arminius; of the Catti, formidable by their firm and intrepid infantry; and of several other tribes of inferior power and renown. The love of liberty was the ruling passion of these Germans; the enjoyment of it their best treasure; the word that expressed that enjoyment the most pleasing to their ear. They deserved, they assumed, they maintained the honourable epithet of Franks or Freemen, which concealed, though it did not extinguish, the peculiar names of the several states of the confederacy. Tacit consent and mutual advantage dictated the first laws of the union; it was gradually cemented by habit and experience. The league of the Franks may admit of some comparison with the Helvetic body, in which every canton, retaining its independent sovereignty, consults with its brethren in the common cause without acknowledging the authority of any supreme head or representative assembly. But the principle of the two confederacies were extremely different. A peace of two hundred years has rewarded the wise and honest policy of the Swiss. An inconstant spirit, the thirst of rapine, and a disregard to the most solemn treaties disgraced the character of the Franks.

The Romans had long experienced the daring valour of the people of Lower Germany. The union of their strength threatened Gaul with a more formidable invasion and required the presence of Gallienus, the heir and colleague of imperial power. Whilst that prince and his infant son Salonius displayed in the court of Treves the majesty of the empire, its armies were ably conducted by their general Posthumus, who, though he afterwards betrayed the family of Valerian, was ever faithful for the great interest of the monarchy. The treacherous language of panegyrics and medals darkly announces a long series of victories. Trophies and titles attest (if such evidence can attest) the fame of Posthumus, who is repeatedly styled the Conqueror of the Germans and the saviour of Gaul.

But a single fact, the only one indeed of which we have any distinct knowledge, erases in a great measure these monuments of vanity and adulation. The Rhine, though dignified with the title of safeguard of the provinces, was an imperfect barrier against the daring spirit of enterprise with which the Franks were actuated. Their rapid devastations stretched from the river to the foot of the Pyrenees; nor were they stopped by those mountains. Spain, which had never dreaded, was unable to resist, the inroads of the Germans. During twelve years, the greatest part of the reign of Gallienus, that opulent country was the theatre of unequal and destructive hostilities. Tarragona, the flourishing capital of a peaceful province, was sacked and almost destroyed; and so late as the days of Orosius, who wrote in the fifth century, wretched cottages scattered amidst the ruins of magnificent cities still recorded the rage of the barbarians. When the exhausted country no longer supplied a variety of plunder, the Franks seized on some vessels in the ports of Spain and transported themselves into Mauritania. The distant province was astonished with the fury of these barbarians, who seemed to fall from a new world, as their name, manners, and complexion were equally unknown on the coast of Africa.

II. THE ALÉMANNI. In that part of Upper Saxony beyond the Elbe which is at present called the Marquisate of Lusace, there existed in ancient times a sacred wood, the awful seat of the superstition of the Suevi. None was permitted to enter the holy precincts without confessing, by his servile bonds and suppliant posture, the immediate presence of the sovereign deity. Patriotism contributed as well as devotion to consecrate the Sonnenwald, or wood of the Semnones. It was universally believed that the nation had received its first existence on that sacred spot. At stated periods the numerous tribes who gloried in the Suevic blood resorted thither by their ambassadors; and the memory of their common extraction was perpetuated by barbaric rites and human sacrifices. The wide-extended name of Suevi filled the interior countries of Germany from the banks of the Oder to those of the Danube. They were distinguished from the other Germans by their peculiar mode of dressing their long hair, which they gathered into a rude knot on the crown of the head; and they delighted in an ornament that showed their ranks more lofty and terrible in the eyes of the enemy. Jealous as the Germans were of military renown, they all confessed the superior valour of the Suevi; and the tribes of the Usipetes and Tencteri, who with a vast army encountered the dictator Cæsar, declared that they esteemed it not a disgrace to have fled before a people to whose arms the immortal gods themselves were unequal.

In the reign of the emperor Caracalla an innumerable swarm of Suevi appeared on the banks of the Main and in the neighbourhood of the Roman provinces, in quest either of food, of plunder, or of glory. The hasty army of volunteers gradually coalesced into a great and permanent nation and, as it was composed from so many different tribes, assumed the name of Alemanni, or *All-men,* to denote at once their various lineage and their common bravery. The latter was soon felt by the Ro-

mans in many a hostile inroad. The Alemanni fought
chiefly on horseback; but their cavalry was rendered
still more formidable by a mixture of light infantry,
selected from the bravest and most active of the youth,
whom frequent exercise had enured to accompany the
horsemen in the longest march, the most rapid charge,
or the most precipitate retreat.

This warlike people of Germans had been astonished
by the immense preparations of Alexander Severus; they
were dismayed by the arms of his successor, a barbarian
equal in valour and fierceness to themselves. But still
hovering on the frontiers of the empire, they increased
the general disorder that ensued after the death of
Decius. They inflicted severe wounds on the rich provinces of Gaul; they were the first who removed the veil
that covered the feeble majesty of Italy. A numerous
body of the Alemanni penetrated across the Danube
and through the Rhætian Alps into the plains of Lombardy, advanced as far as Ravenna, and displayed the
victorious banners of barbarians almost in sight of Rome.
The insult and the danger rekindled in the senate some
sparks of their ancient virtue. Both the emperors were
engaged in far distant wars, Valerian in the East and
Gallienus on the Rhine. All the hopes and resources of
the Romans were in themselves. In this emergency the
senators resumed the defence of the republic, drew out
the Prætorian Guards who had been left to garrison the
capital, and filled up their numbers by enlisting into
the public service the stoutest and most willing of the
plebeians. The Alemanni, astonished with the sudden
appearance of an army more numerous than their own,
retired into Germany laden with spoil; and their retreat
was esteemed as a victory by the unwarlike Romans.

When Gallienus received the intelligence that his capital was delivered from the barbarians, he was much less

delighted than alarmed with the courage of the senate, since it might one day prompt them to rescue the public from domestic tyranny as well as from foreign invasion. His timid ingratitude was published to his subjects in an edict which prohibited the senators from exercising any military employment, and even from approaching the camps of the legions. But his fears were groundless. The rich and luxurious nobles, sinking into their natural character, accepted as a favour this disgraceful exemption from military service; and as long as they were indulged in the enjoyment of their baths, their theatres, and their villas, they cheerfully resigned the more dangerous cares of empire to the rough hands of peasants and soldiers.

Another invasion of the Alemanni, of a more formidable aspect but more glorious event, is mentioned by a writer of the lower empire. Three hundred thousand of that warlike people are said to have been vanquished in a battle near Milan by Gallienus in person, at the head of only ten thousand Romans. We may, however, with great probability ascribe this incredible victory either to the credulity of the historian or to some exaggerated exploits of one of the emperor's lieutenants. It was by arms of a very different nature that Gallienus endeavoured to protect Italy from the fury of the Germans. He espoused Pipa, the daughter of a king of the Marcomanni, a Suevic tribe, which was often confounded with the Alemanni in their wars and conquests. To the father, as the price of his alliance, he granted an ample settlement in Pannonia. The native charms of unpolished beauty seem to have fixed the daughter in the affections of the inconstant emperor, and the bands of policy were more firmly connected by those of love. But the haughty prejudice of Rome still refused the name of marriage to the profane mixture of a citizen and a barbarian, and has stigmatized the German princess with the opprobrious title of concubine of Gallienus.

III. THE GOTHS. We have already traced the emigration of the Goths from Scandinavia, or at least from Prussia, to the mouth of the Borysthenes, and have followed their victorious arms from the Borysthenes to the Danube. Under the reigns of Valerian and Gallienus the frontier of the last-mentioned river was perpetually infested by the inroads of Germans and Sarmatians, but it was defended by the Romans with more than usual firmness and success. The provinces that were the seat of war recruited the armies of Rome with an inexhaustible supply of hardy soldiers; and more than one of these Illyrian peasants attained the station and displayed the abilities of a general. Though flying parties of the barbarians, who incessantly hovered on the banks of the Danube, penetrated sometimes to the confines of Italy and Macedonia, their progress was commonly checked, or their return intercepted, by the Imperial lieutenants. But the great stream of the Gothic hostilities was diverted into a very different channel. The Goths, in their new settlement of the Ukraine, soon became masters of the northern coast of the Euxine; to the south of that inland sea were situated the soft and wealthy provinces of Asia Minor, which possessed all that could attract, and nothing that could resist, a barbarian conqueror.

The banks of the Borysthenes are only sixty miles distant from the narrow entrance of the peninsula of Crim Tartary, known to the ancients under the name of Chersonesus Taurica. On that inhospitable shore Euripides, embellishing with exquisite art the tales of antiquity, has placed the scene of one of his most affecting tragedies. The bloody sacrifices of Diana, the arrival of Orestes and Pylades, and the triumph of virtue and religion over savage fierceness, serve to represent an historical truth that the Tauri, the original inhabitants of the peninsula, were in some degree reclaimed from their brutal manners by a gradual intercourse with the Grecian colonies which settled along the maritime coast.

The little kingdom of Bosphorus, whose capital was situated on the Straits through which the Mæotis communicates itself to the Euxine, was composed of degenerate Greeks and half-civilized barbarians. It subsisted as an independent state from the time of the Peloponnesian war, was at last swallowed up by the ambition of Mithridates, and with the rest of his dominions sank under the weight of the Roman arms. From the reign of Augustus the kings of Bosphorus were the humble but not useless allies of the empire. By presents, by arms, and by a slight fortification drawn across the Isthmus, they effectually guarded against the roving plunderers of Sarmatia the access of a country which, from its peculiar situation and convenient harbours, commanded the Euxine Sea and Asia Minor. As long as the sceptre was possessed by a lineal succession of kings, they acquitted themselves of their important charge with vigilance and success. Domestic factions and the fears or private interest of obscure usurpers who seized on the vacant throne admitted the Goths into the heart of Bosphorus. With the acquisition of a superfluous waste of fertile soil, the conquerors obtained the command of a naval force sufficient to transport their armies to the coast of Asia.

The ships used in the navigation of the Euxine were of a very singular construction. They were slight flat-bottomed barks framed of timber only, without the least mixture of iron, and occasionally covered with a shelving roof on the appearance of a tempest. In these floating houses the Goths carelessly trusted themselves to the mercy of an unknown sea, under the conduct of sailors pressed into the service, and whose skill and fidelity were equally suspicious. But the hopes of plunder had banished every idea of danger, and a natural fearlessness of temper supplied in their minds the more rational confidence which is the just result of knowledge and experience. Warriors of such a daring spirit must have often murmured against the cowardice of their guides, who required the strongest assurances of a settled calm before they would venture to embark, and would scarcely ever be tempted to lose sight of the land. Such, at least, is the practise of the modern Turks; and they are probably not inferior in the art of navigation to the ancient inhabitants of Bosphorus.

The fleet of the Goths, leaving the coast of Circassia on the left hand, first appeared before Pityus, the utmost limits of the Roman provinces, a city provided with a convenient port and fortified with a strong wall. Here they met with a resistance more obstinate than they had reason to expect from the feeble garrison of a distant fortress. They were repulsed, and their disappointment seemed to diminish the terror of the Gothic name. As long as Successianus, an officer of superior rank and merit, defended that frontier, all their efforts were ineffectual; but as soon as he was removed by Valerian to a more honourable but less important station, they resumed the attack of Pityus, and by the destruction of that city obliterated the memory of their former disgrace.

Circling round the eastern extremity of the Euxine Sea, the navigation from Pityus to Trebizond is about three hundred miles. The course of the Goths carried them in sight of the country of Colchis, so famous by the expedition of the Argonauts; and they even attempted, though without success, to pillage a rich

temple at the mouth of the river Phasis [now Rion].
Trebizond, celebrated in the retreat of the Ten Thousand as an ancient colony of Greeks, derived its wealth
and splendour from the munificence of the emperor
Hadrian, who had constructed an artificial port on a
coast left destitute by nature of secure harbours. The
city was large and populous; a double enclosure of
walls seemed to defy the fury of the Goths, and the
usual garrison had been strengthened by a reinforcement of ten thousand men. But there are not any advantages capable of supplying the absence of discipline
and vigilance. The numerous garrison of Trebizond,
dissolved in riot and luxury, disdained to guard their
impregnable fortifications. The Goths soon discovered
the supine negligence of the besieged, erected a lofty
pile of fascines, ascended the walls in the silence of
the night, and entered the defenceless city sword in
hand. A general massacre of the people ensued, whilst
the affrighted soldiers escaped through the opposite
gates of the town. The most holy temples and the most
splendid edifices were involved in a common destruction. The booty that fell into the hands of the Goths
was immense; the wealth of the adjacent countries had
been deposited in Trebizond as in a secure place of
refuge. The number of captives was incredible, as the
victorious barbarians ranged without opposition through
the extensive province of Pontus. The rich spoils of
Trebizond filled a great fleet of ships that had been
found in the port. The robust youth of the seacoast were
chained to the oar; and the Goths, satisfied with the
success of their first naval expedition, returned in triumph to their new establishments in the kingdom of
Bosphorus.

The second expedition of the Goths was undertaken
with greater powers of men and ships; but they steered

a different course and, disdaining the exhausted provinces of Pontus, followed the western coast of the
Euxine, passed before the wide mouths of the Borysthenes, the Dniester, and the Danube, and, increasing
their fleet by the capture of a great number of fishing
barks, they approached the narrow outlet through which
the Euxine Sea pours its waters into the Mediterranean
and divides the continents of Europe and Asia. The
garrison of Chalcedon was encamped near the temple
of Jupiter Urius, on a promontory that commanded the
entrance of the Strait; and so inconsiderable were the
dreaded invasions of the barbarians that this body of
troops surpassed in number the Gothic army. But it was
in numbers alone that they surpassed it. They deserted
with precipitation their advantageous post and abandoned the town of Chalcedon, most plentifully stored
with arms and money, to the discretion of the conquerors. Whilst they hesitated whether they should prefer
the sea or land, Europe or Asia, for the scene of their
hostilities, a perfidious fugitive pointed out Nicomedia,
once the capital of the kings of Bithynia, as a rich and
easy conquest. He guided the march, which was only
sixty miles from the camp of Chalcedon, directed the
resistless attack, and partook of the booty; for the Goths
had learned sufficient policy to reward the traitor whom
they detested. Nice, Prusa, Apamæa, Cius, cities that
had sometimes rivalled or imitated the splendour of
Nicomedia, were involved in the same calamity, which
in a few weeks raged without control through the whole
province of Bithynia. Three hundred years of peace,
enjoyed by the soft inhabitants of Asia, had abolished
the exercise of arms and removed the apprehension of
danger. The ancient walls were suffered to moulder
away, and all the revenue of the most opulent cities was

reserved for the construction of baths, temples, and theatres.

When the city of Cyzicus withstood the utmost effort of Mithridates it was distinguished by wise laws, a naval power of two hundred galleys, and three arsenals: of arms, of military engines, and of corn. It was still the seat of wealth and luxury; but of its ancient strength nothing remained except the situation, in a little island of the Propontis, connected with the continent of Asia only by two bridges. From the recent sack of Prusa, the Goths advanced within eighteen miles of the city, which they had devoted to destruction; but the ruin of Cyzicus was delayed by a fortunate accident. The season was rainy, and the lake Apolloniates, the reservoir of all the springs of Mount Olympus, rose to an uncommon height. The little river of Rhyndacus, which issues from the lake, swelled into a broad and rapid stream and stopped the progress of the Goths. Their retreat to the maritime city of Heraclea, where the fleet had probably been stationed, was attended by a long train of waggons, laden with the spoils of Bithynia, and was marked by the flames of Nice and Nicomedia, which they wantonly burned. Some obscure hints are mentioned of a doubtful combat that secured their retreat. But even a complete victory would have been of little moment, as the approach of the autumnal equinox summoned them to hasten their return. To navigate the Euxine before the month of May or after that of September is esteemed by the modern Turks the most unquestionable instance of rashness and folly.

When we are informed that the third fleet equipped by the Goths in the ports of Bosphorus consisted of five hundred sail of ships, our ready imagination instantly computes and multiplies the formidable arma-

ment; but as we are assured by the judicious Strabo
that the piratical vessels used by the barbarians of
Pontus and the Lesser Scythia were not capable of containing more than twenty-five or thirty men, we may
safely affirm that fifteen thousand warriors at the most
embarked in this great expedition. Impatient of the
limits of the Euxine, they steered their destructive
course from the Cimmerian to the Thracian Bosphorus.
When they had almost gained the middle of the Straits,
they were suddenly driven back to the entrance of them,
till a favourable wind springing up the next day carried
them in a few hours into the placid sea, or rather lake,
of the Propontis. Their landing on the little island of
Cyzicus was attended with the ruin of that ancient and
noble city. From thence issuing again through the narrow passage of the Hellespont, they pursued their winding navigation amidst the numerous islands scattered
over the Archipelago, or the Ægean Sea. The assistance
of captives and deserters must have been very necessary to pilot their vessels and to direct their various
incursions, as well on the coast of Greece as on that of
Asia. At length the Gothic fleet anchored in the port of
Piræus, five miles distant from Athens, which had
attempted to make some preparations for a vigorous
defence. Cleodamus, one of the engineers employed by
the emperor's orders to fortify the maritime cities against
the Goths, had already begun to repair the ancient walls
fallen to decay since the time of Sylla. The efforts of his
skill were ineffectual, and the barbarians became masters of the native seat of the muses and the arts. But
while the conquerors abandoned themselves to the licence of plunder and intemperance, their fleet, which
lay with a slender guard in the harbour of Piræus, was
unexpectedly attacked by the brave Dexippus, who,
flying with the engineer Cleodamus from the sack of

Athens, collected a hasty band of volunteers, peasants as well as soldiers, and in some measure avenged the calamities of his country.

But this exploit, whatever lustre it might shed on the declining age of Athens, served rather to irritate than to subdue the undaunted spirit of the northern invaders. A general conflagration blazed out at the same time in every district of Greece. Thebes and Argos, Corinth and Sparta, which had formerly waged such memorable wars against each other, were now unable to bring an army into the field, or even to defend their ruined fortifications. The rage of war, both by land and by sea, spread from the eastern point of Sunium to the western coast of Epirus. The Goths had already advanced within sight of Italy when the approach of such imminent danger awakened the indolent Gallienus from his dream of pleasure. The emperor appeared in arms; and his presence seems to have checked the ardour and to have divided the strength of the enemy. Naulobatus, a chief of the Heruli, accepted an honourable capitulation, entered with a large body of his countrymen into the service of Rome, and was invested with the ornaments of the consular dignity, which had never before been profaned by the hands of a barbarian. Great numbers of the Goths, disgusted with the perils and hardships of a tedious voyage, broke into Mæsia with a design of forcing their way over the Danube to their settlements in the Ukraine. The wild attempt would have proved inevitable destruction if the discord of the Roman generals had not opened to the barbarians the means of an escape. The small remainder of this destroying host returned on board their vessels and, measuring back their way through the Hellespont and the Bosphorus, ravaged in their passage the shores of Troy, whose fame, immortalized by Homer, will probably survive the memory

of the Gothic conquests. As soon as they found themselves in safety within the basin of the Euxine, they
landed at Anchialus in Thrace, near the foot of Mount
Hæmus, and after all their toils indulged themselves in
the use of those pleasant and salutary hot baths. What
remained of the voyage was a short and easy navigation.
Such was the various fate of this third and greatest of
their naval enterprises.

It may seem difficult to conceive how the original
body of fifteen thousand warriors could sustain the
losses and divisions of so bold an adventure. But as
their numbers were gradually wasted by the sword, by
shipwrecks, and by the influence of a warm climate,
they were perpetually renewed by troops of banditti
and deserters, who flocked to the standard of plunder,
and by a crowd of fugitive slaves, often of German or
Sarmatian extraction, who eagerly seized the glorious
opportunity of freedom and revenge. In these expeditions the Gothic nation claimed a superior share of
honour and danger, but the tribes that fought under
the Gothic banners are sometimes distinguished and
sometimes confounded in the imperfect histories of that
age; and as the barbarian fleets seemed to issue from
the mouth of the Tanais, the vague but familiar appellation of Scythians was frequently bestowed on the
mixed multitude.

In the general calamities of mankind the death of an
individual, however exalted, the ruin of an edifice, however famous, are passed over with careless inattention.
Yet we cannot forget that the temple of Diana at
Ephesus, after having risen with increasing splendour
from seven repeated misfortunes, was finally burned by
the Goths in their third naval invasion. The arts of
Greece and the wealth of Asia had conspired to erect
that sacred and magnificent structure. It was supported

by an hundred and twenty-seven marble columns of the
Ionic order. They were the gifts of devout monarchs,
and each was sixty feet high. The altar was adorned
with the masterly sculptures of Praxiteles, who had,
perhaps, selected from the favourite legends of the place
the birth of the divine children of Latona, the concealment of Apollo after the slaughter of the Cyclops, and
the clemency of Bacchus to the vanquished Amazons.
Yet the length of the temple of Ephesus was only four
hundred and twenty-five feet, about two-thirds of the
measure of the church of St. Peter's at Rome. In the
other dimensions it was still more inferior to that sublime production of modern architecture. The spreading
arms of a Christian cross require a much greater breadth
than the oblong temples of the pagans; and the boldest
artists of antiquity would have been startled at the
proposal of raising in the air a dome of the size and proportions of the Pantheon. The temple of Diana was,
however, admired as one of the wonders of the world.
Successive empires, the Persian, the Macedonian, and
the Roman, had revered its sanctity and enriched its
splendour. But the rude savages of the Baltic were destitute of a taste for the elegant arts, and they despised
the ideal terrors of a foreign superstition.

Another circumstance is related of these invasions,
which might deserve our notice were it not justly to be
suspected as the fanciful conceit of a recent sophist.
We are told that in the sack of Athens the Goths had
collected all the libraries and were on the point of setting fire to this funeral pile of Grecian learning, had not
one of their chiefs, of more refined policy than his
brethren, dissuaded them from the design by the profound observation that as long as the Greeks were addicted to the study of books they would never apply
themselves to the exercise of arms. The sagacious

counsellor (should the truth of the fact be admitted) reasoned like an ignorant barbarian. In the most polite and powerful nations, genius of every kind has displayed itself about the same period; and the age of science has generally been the age of military virtue and success.

IV. THE PERSIANS. The new sovereigns of Persia, Artaxerxes and his son Sapor, had triumphed over the house of Arsaces. Of the many princes of that ancient race, Chosroes, king of Armenia, had alone preserved both his life and his independence. He defended himself by the natural strength of his country, by the perpetual resort of fugitives and malcontents, by the alliance of the Romans, and above all, by his own courage. Invincible in arms during a thirty years' war, he was at length assassinated by the emissaries of Sapor, king of Persia. The patriotic satraps of Armenia, who asserted the freedom and dignity of the crown, implored the protection of Rome in favour of Tiridates, the lawful heir. But the son of Chosroes was an infant, the allies were at a distance, and the Persian monarch advanced towards the frontier at the head of an irresistible force. Young Tiridates, the future hope of his country, was saved by the fidelity of a servant, and Armenia continued above twenty-seven years a reluctant province of the great monarchy of Persia. Elated with this easy conquest, and presuming on the distresses or the degeneracy of the Romans, Sapor obliged the strong garrisons of Carrhæ and Nisibis to surrender, and spread devastation and terror on either side of the Euphrates.

The loss of an important frontier, the ruin of a faithful and natural ally, and the rapid success of Sapor's ambition affected Rome with a deep sense of the insult as well as of the danger. Valerian flattered himself that the vigilance of his lieutenants would sufficiently provide for the safety of the Rhine and of the Danube; but he resolved, notwithstanding his advanced age, to march in person to the defence of the Euphrates. During his progress through Asia Minor the naval enterprises of the Goths were suspended, and the afflicted province enjoyed a transient and fallacious calm. He passed the Euphrates, encountered the Persian monarch near the walls of Edessa, was vanquished (A.D. 260) and taken prisoner by Sapor.

The particulars of this great event are darkly and imperfectly represented; yet by the glimmering light which is afforded us, we may discover a long series of imprudence, of error, and of deserved misfortunes on the side of the Roman emperor. He reposed an implicit confidence in Macrinus, his Prætorian præfect. That worthless minister rendered his master formidable only to the oppressed subjects, and contemptible to the enemies of Rome. By his weak or wicked counsels the Imperial army was betrayed into a situation where valour and military skill were equally unavailing. The vigorous attempt of the Romans to cut their way through the Persian host was repulsed with great slaughter; and Sapor, who encompassed the camp with superior numbers, patiently waited till the increasing rage of famine and pestilence had ensured his victory. The licentious murmurs of the legions soon accused Valerian as the cause of their calamities; their seditious clamours demanded an instant capitulation. An immense sum of gold was offered to purchase the permission of a disgraceful retreat. But the Persian, conscious of his superiority, refused the money with disdain and, detaining the deputies, advanced in order of battle to the foot of the Roman rampart and insisted on a personal conference with the emperor. Valerian was reduced to the necessity of entrusting his life and dignity to the faith of an enemy. The interview ended as it was natural to expect. The emperor was made a prisoner, and his astonished troops laid down their arms. In such a moment of triumph the pride and policy of Sapor prompted him to fill the vacant throne with a successor entirely dependent on his pleasure. Cyriades, an obscure fugitive of Antioch, stained with every vice, was chosen to dishonour the Roman purple; and the will of the Persian victor could not fail of being ratified by the acclamations, however reluctant, of the captive army.

The Imperial slave was eager to secure the favour of his master by an act of treason to his native country. He conducted Sapor over the Euphrates and by the way of Chalcis to the metropolis of the East. So rapid were the motions of the Persian cavalry that, if we may credit a very judicious historian, the city of Antioch was surprised when the idle multitude was fondly gazing on the amusements of the theatre. The splendid buildings of Antioch, private as well as public, were either pillaged or destroyed, and the numerous inhabitants were put to the sword or led away into captivity. The tide of devastation was stopped for a moment by the resolution of the high priest of Emesa. Arrayed in his sacerdotal robes, he appeared at the head of a great body of fanatic peasants, armed only with slings, and defended his god and his property from the sacrilegious hands of the followers of Zoroaster. But the ruin of Tarsus and many other cities furnishes a melancholy proof that, except in this single instance, the conquest of Syria and Cilicia scarcely interrupted the progress of the Persian arms. The advantages of the narrow passes of Mount Taurus were abandoned, in which an invader whose principal force consisted in his cavalry would have been engaged in a very unequal combat; and Sapor was permitted to form the siege of Cæsarea, the capital of Cappadocia, a city (though of the second rank) which was supposed to contain four hundred thousand inhabitants. Demosthenes commanded in the place, not so much by the commission of the emperor as in the voluntary defence of his country. For a long time he deferred its fate; and when at last Cæsarea was betrayed by the perfidy of a physician, he cut his way through the Persians, who had been ordered to exert their utmost diligence to take him alive. This heroic chief escaped the power of a foe who might either have honoured or punished his obstinate valour; but many thousands of his fellow-citizens were involved in a general massacre, and Sapor is accused of treating his prisoners with wanton and unrelenting cruelty. Much should undoubtedly be allowed for national animosity, much for humbled pride and impotent revenge; yet upon the whole it is certain that the same prince who in Armenia had displayed the mild aspect of a legislator showed himself to the Romans under the stern features of a conqueror. He despaired of making any permanent establishment in the empire and sought only to leave behind him a wasted desert, whilst he transported into Persia the people and the treasures of the provinces.

At the time when the East trembled at the name of Sapor, he received a present not unworthy of the greatest kings: a long train of camels laden with the most rare and valuable merchandises. The rich offering was accompanied with an epistle, respectful but not servile, from Odenathus, one of the noblest and most opulent senators of Palmyra. "Who is this Odenathus," said the haughty victor, and he commanded that the presents should be cast into the Euphrates, "that he thus insolently presumes to write to his lord? If he entertains a hope of mitigating his punishment, let him fall prostrate before the foot of our throne with his hands bound behind his back. Should he hesitate, swift destruction shall be poured on his head, on his whole race, and on his country." The desperate extremity to which the Palmyrenian was reduced called into action all the latent powers of his soul. He met Sapor, but he met him in arms. Infusing his own spirit into a little army collected from the villages of Syria and the tents of the desert, he hovered round the Persian host, harassed their retreat, carried off part of the treasure, and, what was dearer than any treasure, several of the women of the Great King, who was at last obliged to repass the Euphrates with some marks of haste and confusion. By this exploit Odenathus laid the foundations of his future fame and fortunes. The majesty of Rome, oppressed by a Persian, was protected by a Syrian or Arab of Palmyra.

The voice of history, which is often little more than the organ of hatred or flattery, reproaches Sapor with a proud abuse of the rights of conquest. We are told that Valerian, in chains but invested with the Imperial purple, was exposed to the multitude, a constant spectacle of fallen greatness; and that whenever the Persian monarch mounted on horseback he placed his foot on the neck of a Roman emperor. Notwithstanding all the remonstrances of his allies, who repeatedly advised him to remember the vicissitude of fortune, to dread the returning power of Rome, and to make his illustrious captive the pledge of peace not the object of insult, Sapor still remained inflexible. When Valerian sank under the weight of shame and grief, his skin, stuffed with straw and formed into the likeness of a human figure, was preserved for ages in the most celebrated temple of Persia, a more real monument of triumph than the fancied trophies of brass and marble so often erected by Roman vanity. The tale is moral and pathetic, but the truth of it may very fairly be called in question. The letters still extant from the princes of the East to Sapor are manifest forgeries; nor is it natural to suppose that a jealous monarch should, even in the person of a rival, thus publicly degrade the majesty of kings. Whatever treatment the unfortunate Valerian might experience in Persia, it is at least certain that the only emperor of Rome who had ever fallen into the hands of the enemy languished away his life in hopeless captivity.

The emperor Gallienus, who had long supported with impatience the censorial severity of his father and colleague, received the intelligence of his misfortunes with secret pleasure and avowed indifference. "I knew that my father was a mortal," said he, "and since he has acted as becomes a brave man, I am satisfied." Whilst Rome lamented the fate of her sovereign, the savage coldness of his son was extolled by the servile courtiers as the perfect firmness of a hero and a Stoic.

It is difficult to paint the light, the various, the inconstant character of Gallienus, which he displayed without constraint as soon as he became sole possessor of the empire. In every art that he attempted his lively genius enabled him to succeed; and as his genius was destitute of judgment, he attempted every art except the important ones of war and government. He was a master of several curious but useless sciences, a ready orator and elegant poet, a skilful gardener, an excellent cook, and most contemptible prince. When the great emergencies of the state required his presence and attention, he was engaged in conversation with the philosopher Plotinus, wasting his time in trifling or licentious pleasures, preparing his initiation to the Grecian mysteries, or soliciting a place in the Areopagus of Athens. His profuse magnificence insulted the general poverty; the solemn ridicule of his triumphs impressed a deeper sense of the public disgrace. The repeated intelligence of invasions, defeats, and rebellions he received with a careless smile; and singling out with affected contempt some particular production of the lost province, he carelessly asked whether Rome must be ruined unless it was supplied with linen from Egypt and Arras cloth from Gaul? There were, however, a few short moments in the life of Gallienus when, exasperated by some recent injury, he suddenly appeared the intrepid soldier and the cruel tyrant, till, satiated with blood or fatigued by resistance, he insensibly sank into the natural mildness and indolence of his character.

At a time when the reins of government were held with so loose a hand, it is not surprising that a crowd of usurpers should start up in every province of the empire against the son of Valerian. It was probably some ingenious fancy, of comparing the thirty tyrants of Rome with the thirty tyrants of Athens, that induced the writers of the Augustan History to select that celebrated number which has been gradually received into a popular appellation. But in every light the parallel is idle and defective. What resemblance can we discover between a council of thirty persons, the united oppressors of a single city, and an uncertain list of independent rivals who rose and fell in irregular succession through the extent of a vast empire? Nor can the number of thirty be completed unless we include in the account the women and children who were honoured with the Imperial title. The reign of Gallienus, distracted as it was, produced only nineteen pretenders to the throne: Cyriades, Macrianus, Balista, Odenathus, and Zenobia in the East; in Gaul and the western provinces, Posthumus, Lollianus, Victorinus and his mother Victoria, Marius, and Tetricus; in Illyricum and the confines of the Danube, Ingenuus, Regillianus, and Aureolus; in Pontus, Saturninus; in Isauria, Trebellianus; Piso in

Thessaly; Valens in Achaia; Æmilianus in Egypt; and Celsus in Africa. To illustrate the obscure monuments of the life and death of each individual would prove a laborious task, alike barren of instruction and of amusement. We may content ourselves with investigating some general characters that most strongly mark the condition of the times and the manners of the men, their pretensions, their motives, their fate, and the destructive consequences of their usurpation.

It is sufficiently known that the odious appellation of *Tyrant* was often employed by the ancients to express the illegal seizure of supreme power, without any reference to the abuse of it. Several of the pretenders who raised the standard of rebellion against the emperor Gallienus were shining models of virtue, and almost all possessed a considerable share of vigour and ability. Their merit had recommended them to the favour of Valerian and gradually promoted them to the most important commands of the empire. The generals who assumed the title of Augustus were either respected by their troops for their able conduct and severe discipline, or admired for valour and success in war, or beloved for frankness and generosity. The field of victory was often the scene of their election; and even the armourer Marius, the most contemptible of all the candidates for the purple, was distinguished, however, by intrepid courage, matchless strength, and blunt honesty. His mean and recent trade cast indeed an air of ridicule on his elevation; but his birth could not be more obscure than was that of the greater part of his rivals, who were born of peasants and enlisted in the army as private soldiers. In times of confusion every active genius finds the place assigned him by Nature; in a general state of war, military merit is the road to glory and to greatness. Of the nineteen tyrants, Tetricus only was a senator, Piso alone was a noble. The blood of Numa, through twenty-eight successive generations, ran in the veins of Calphurnius Piso, who by female alliances claimed a right of exhibiting in his house the images of Crassus and of the great Pompey. His ancestors had been repeatedly dignified with all the honours which the commonwealth could bestow; and of all the ancient families of Rome the Calphurnian alone had survived the tyranny of the Cæsars. The personal qualities of Piso added new lustre to his race. The usurper Valens, by whose order he was killed, confessed with deep remorse that even an enemy ought to have respected the sanctity of Piso; and although he died in arms against Gallienus, the senate, with the emperor's generous permission, decreed the triumphal ornaments to the memory of so virtuous a rebel.

The lieutenants of Valerian were grateful to the father, whom they esteemed. They disdained to serve the luxurious indolence of his unworthy son. The throne of the Roman world was unsupported by any principle of loyalty, and treason against such a prince might easily be considered as patriotism to the state. Yet if we examine with candour the conduct of these usurpers, it will appear that they were much oftener driven into rebellion by their fears than urged to it by their ambition. They dreaded the cruel suspicions of Gallienus; they equally dreaded the capricious violence of their troops. If the dangerous favour of the army had imprudently declared them deserving of the purple, they were marked for sure destruction; and even prudence would counsel them to secure a short enjoyment of empire, and rather to try the fortune of war than to expect the hand of an executioner. When the clamour of the soldiers invested the reluctant victims with the ensigns of sovereign authority they sometimes mourned in secret their approaching fate. "You have lost," said Saturninus on the day of his elevation, "you have lost a useful commander, and you have made a very wretched emperor."

The apprehensions of Saturninus were justified by the repeated experience of revolutions. Of the nineteen tyrants who started up under the reign of Gallienus, there was not one who enjoyed a life of peace or a natural death. As soon as they were invested with the bloody purple, they inspired their adherents with the same fears and ambition which had occasioned their own revolt. Encompassed with domestic conspiracy, military sedition, and civil war, they trembled on the edge of precipices in which, after a longer or shorter term of anxiety, they were inevitably lost. The precarious monarchs received, however, such honours as the flattery of their respective armies and provinces could bestow; but their claim, founded on rebellion, could never obtain the sanction of law or history. Italy, Rome, and the senate constantly adhered to the cause of Gallienus, and he alone was considered as the sovereign of the empire. That prince condescended indeed to acknowledge the victorious arms of Odenathus, who deserved the honourable distinction by the respectful conduct which he always maintained towards the son of Valerian. With the general applause of the Romans and the consent of Gallienus, the senate conferred the title of Augustus on the brave Palmyrenian and seemed to entrust him with the government of the East, which he already possessed in so independent a manner that, like a private succession, he bequeathed it to his illustrious widow Zenobia.

The rapid and perpetual transitions from the cottage

to the throne and from the throne to the grave might have amused an indifferent philosopher, were it possible for a philosopher to remain indifferent amidst the general calamities of humankind. The election of these precarious emperors, their power, and their death were equally destructive to their subjects and adherents. The price of their fatal elevation was instantly discharged to the troops by an immense donative, drawn from the bowels of the exhausted people. However virtuous was their character, however pure their intentions they found themselves reduced to the hard necessity of supporting their usurpation by frequent acts of rapine and cruelty. When they fell, they involved armies and provinces in their fall. There is still extant a most savage mandate from Gallienus to one of his ministers after the suppression of Ingenuus, who had assumed the purple in Illyricum. "It is not enough," says that soft but inhuman prince, "that you exterminate such as have appeared in arms; the chance of battle might have served me as effectually. The male sex of every age must be extirpated—provided that, in the execution of the children and old men, you can contrive means to save our reputation. Let everyone die who has dropped an expression, who has entertained a thought, against me, against *me*, the son of Valerian, the father and brother of so many princes. Remember that Ingenuus was made emperor: tear, kill, hew in pieces. I write to you with my own hand and would inspire you with my own feelings." Whilst the public forces of the state were dissipated in private quarrels, the defenceless provinces lay exposed to every invader. The bravest usurpers were compelled by the perplexity of their situation to conclude ignominious treaties with the common enemy, to purchase with oppressive tributes the neutrality or services of the barbarians, and to introduce hostile and independent nations into the heart of the Roman monarchy.[3]

Our habits of thinking so fondly connect the order of the universe with the fate of man that this gloomy period of history has been decorated with inundations, earthquakes, uncommon meteors, preternatural darkness, and a crowd of prodigies fictitious or exaggerated. But a long and general famine was a calamity of a more serious kind. It was the inevitable consequence of rapine and oppression, which extirpated the produce of the present and the hope of future harvests. Famine is almost always followed by epidemical diseases, the effect of scanty and unwholesome food. Other causes must, however, have contributed to the furious plague which from the year 250 to the year 265 raged without interruption in every province, every city, and almost every family of the Roman empire. During some time five thousand persons died daily in Rome, and many towns that had escaped the hands of the barbarians were entirely depopulated.

We have the knowledge of a very curious circumstance, of some use perhaps in the melancholy calculation of human calamities. An exact register was kept at Alexandria of all the citizens entitled to receive the distribution of corn. It was found that the ancient number of those comprised between the ages of forty and seventy had been equal to the whole sum of claimants, from fourteen to fourscore years of age, who remained alive after the reign of Gallienus. Applying this authentic fact to the most correct tables of mortality, it evidently proves that above half the people of Alexandria had perished; and could we venture to extend the anal-

3. *Editor's note:* A short section is omitted here describing three typical examples of civil disturbances, in Sicily, in Alexandria, and in the province of Isauria in Asia Minor.

ogy to the other provinces, we might suspect that war, pestilence, and famine had consumed, in a few years, the moiety of the human species.

The amazing strength and vitality of the empire was demonstrated by its remarkable recovery under a series of rulers beginning with Claudius,[4] whose reigns are recounted in the next two chapters of the original. After the fall of Gallienus—at the hands of his own soldiers, it need hardly be added—the first exploit of his successor was the delivery of the empire from a great Gothic horde that had flooded down through the Black Sea and over both the European and Asiatic coasts of the Mediterranean. The Goths, whose army was almost entirely destroyed by a combination of war, pestilence, and starvation, apparently had come with some idea of settlement, for each Roman soldier was allotted two or three female slaves from the numerous captives. But the pestilence that had ravaged the Goths presently (A.D. 270) claimed Claudius as well, who passed on the sceptre to a distinguished general named Aurelian.

Aurelian's first task was a final settlement with the Goths, who had returned with fresh numbers upon the death of Claudius. After an inconclusive test of arms the issue was settled by negotiation, as a result of which the Romans relinquished the trans-Danubian province of Dacia to Gothic settlement; and those Romans who remained in Dacia served the useful purpose of introducing the Goths to the arts of civilization. Aurelian had then to deal with a vast invasion of Italy by the Alemanni. They were eventually routed after a series of doubtful engagements; but the fear they spread in-

4. *Editor's note:* Not to be confused with the earlier inept Claudius, whose history has been fictionalized by Robert Graves.

duced the first serious effort in several centuries to fortify the city of Rome itself.

The first triumph of Claudius over the Goths was rendered more memorable by the slender resources at his disposal; for the effective power in Gaul, Spain, and Britain had for several years been wielded by a usurper named Tetricus, while that remarkable woman named Zenobia, the widow of Odenathus (see p. 175), ruled the Roman provinces of Egypt and Asia Minor. Aurelian set about recovering these dismembered elements of the empire. Tetricus connived at his own defeat, preferring the chance (in this case justified) of mercy at Aurelian's hands to remaining "the sovereign and slave of a licentious army"; but Zenobia resisted skilfully and resolutely throughout a series of battles and a long siege of her capital until she was at last defeated, captured, and brought to Rome as the center of attention ("she almost fainted under the intolerable weight of jewels") in perhaps the greatest and certainly one of the best-deserved triumphs ever celebrated by a Roman emperor. Both Zenobia and Tetricus were permitted a private life of wealth and ease and the luxury of a death in bed; but Aurelian himself died violently through the wiles of a knavish secretary. Accused of extortion, the secretary counterfeited a long list of names allegedly marked for execution, and a group of army officers on the list did Aurelian to death in A.D. 275.

His death led to "one of the best-attested but most improbable events in the history of mankind," in which the legions, "as if satiated in the exercise of power," steadily importuned the senate to select a new emperor, while the senate as steadily urged that the choice be made by the legions. After eight months "during which the Roman world remained without a sovereign, without an usurper, and without a sedition," the senate finally *(in September of the year* A.D. *275) chose an aged and illustrious senator named Tacitus, a descendant of the great historian. But the cares and exertions of empire hastened his death within scarce six months of his accession; and he was succeeded (in* A.D. *276, after a brief interregnum in which his brother snatched fitfully at the purple) by a general named Probus.*

In six short years Probus managed to beat back a succession of barbarian invasions, put down several military seditions, and even to bring the empire a measure of peace. But his zeal in employing the soldiers to perform useful public works—in this case draining a marsh near the emperor's birthplace—brought a sudden mutinous outburst that was fatal to him. His successor, Carus, pressed a great and successful war against the Persians until he was apparently killed by lightning; and the superstitious dread of the ancient world regarding lightning brought the immediate withdrawal of the Roman army from the Persian campaign.

*That army took several months in its slow retreat from the banks of the Tigris; and in the interval Carinus, the elder son of Carus, managed to gratify the Roman populace by the most spectacular games, and himself by the indulgence of a host of irregular and ultimately fatal appetites. The returning army invested a general named Diocletian with the purple. In the ensuing struggle the forces of Carinus seemed on the verge of triumph when "a tribune, whose wife he had seduced, seized the opportunity of revenge and by a single blow extinguished civil discord in the blood of the adulterer." Thus came to power (*A.D. *285) Diocletian, the most ambitious and successful reformer among the later emperors of Rome.*

Chapter VI

*The reign of Diocletian and his three associates,
Maximian, Galerius, and Constantius – General
re-establishment of order and tranquillity – The
Persian war, victory, and triumph – The new form
of administration – Abdication and retirement of
Diocletian and Maximian*[1]

A S THE reign of Diocletian was more illustrious than
that of any of his predecessors, so was his birth
more abject and obscure. The strong claims of merit and
of violence had frequently superseded the ideal prerogatives of nobility; but a distinct line of separation was
hitherto preserved between the free and the servile part
of mankind. The parents of Diocletian had been slaves
in the house of Anulinus, a Roman senator; nor was he
himself distinguished by any other name than that which
he derived from a small town in Dalmatia, from whence
his mother deduced her origin. It is, however, probable
that his father obtained the freedom of the family, and
that he soon acquired an office of scribe, which was
commonly exercised by persons of his condition. Favourable oracles, or rather the consciousness of superior
merit, prompted his aspiring son to pursue the profession of arms and the hopes of fortune; and it would be
extremely curious to observe the graduation of arts and
accidents which enabled him in the end to fulfil those
oracles and to display that merit to the world. Diocletian

1. *Editor's note:* Chapter XIII of the original.

was successively promoted to the government of Mæsia, the honours of the consulship, and the important command of the guards of the palace. He distinguished his abilities in the Persian war; and after the death of Numerian, the slave, by the confession and judgment of his rivals, was declared the most worthy of the Imperial throne.

The malice of religious zeal, whilst it arraigns the savage fierceness of his colleague Maximian, has affected to cast suspicion on the personal courage of the emperor Diocletian. It would not be easy to persuade us of the cowardice of a soldier of fortune who acquired and preserved the esteem of the legions, as well as the favour of so many warlike princes. Yet even calumny is sagacious enough to discover and to attack the most vulnerable part. The valour of Diocletian was never found inadequate to his duty or to the occasion; but he appears not to have possessed the daring and generous spirit of a hero who courts danger and fame, disdains artifice, and boldly challenges the allegiance of his equals. His abilities were useful rather than splendid: a vigorous mind improved by the experience and study of mankind; dexterity and application in business; a judicious mixture of liberality and economy, of mildness and rigour; profound dissimulation under the disguise of military frankness; steadiness to pursue his ends; flexibility to vary his means; and, above all, the great art of submitting his own passions, as well as those of others, to the interest of his ambition, and of colouring his ambition with the most specious pretences of justice and public utility. Like Augustus, Diocletian may be considered as the founder of a new empire. Like the adopted son of Cæsar, he was distinguished as a statesman rather than as a warrior; nor did either of those princes employ force whenever their purpose could be effected by policy.

The victory of Diocletian was remarkable for its singular mildness. A people accustomed to applaud the clemency of the conqueror if the usual punishments of death, exile, and confiscation were inflicted with any degree of temper and equity, beheld with the most pleasing astonishment a civil war, the flames of which were extinguished in the field of battle. Diocletian received into his confidence Aristobulus, the principal minister of the house of Carus, respected the lives, the fortunes, and the dignity of his adversaries, and even continued in their respective stations the greater number of the servants of Carinus. It is not improbable that motives of prudence might assist the humanity of the artful Dalmatian: of these servants, many had purchased his favour by secret treachery; in others he esteemed their grateful fidelity to an unfortunate master. The discerning judgment of Aurelian, of Probus, and of Carus had filled the several departments of the state and army with officers of approved merit, whose removal would have injured the public service without promoting the interest of the successor. Such a conduct, however, displayed to the Roman world the fairest prospect of the new reign, and the emperor affected to confirm this favourable prepossession by declaring that, among all the virtues of his predecessors, he was the most ambitious of imitating the humane philosophy of Marcus Antoninus.

The first considerable action of his reign seemed to evince his sincerity as well as his moderation. After the example of Marcus, he gave himself a colleague in the person of Maximian, on whom he bestowed at first the title of Cæsar and afterwards that of Augustus. But the motives of his conduct, as well as the object of his choice, were of a very different nature from those of his admired predecessor. By investing a luxurious youth with the honours of the purple, Marcus had discharged a debt of private gratitude at the expense, indeed, of the happiness of the state. By associating a friend and a fellow-soldier to the favours of government, Diocletian, in a time of public danger, provided for the defence both of the East and of the West.

Maximian was born a peasant, and, like Aurelian, in the territory of Sirmium. Ignorant of letters, careless of laws, the rusticity of his appearance and manners still betrayed in the most elevated fortune the meanness of his extraction. War was the only art which he professed. In a long course of service he had distinguished himself on every frontier of the empire; and though his military talents were formed to obey rather than to command, though perhaps he never attained the skill of a consummate general, he was capable, by his valour, constancy, and experience, of executing the most arduous undertakings. Nor were the vices of Maximian less useful to his benefactor. Insensible to pity and fearless of consequences, he was the ready instrument of every act of cruelty which the policy of that artful prince might at once suggest and disclaim. As soon as a bloody sacrifice had been offered to prudence or to revenge, Diocletian by his seasonable intercession saved the remaining few whom he had never designed to punish, gently censured the severity of his stern colleague, and enjoyed the comparison of a golden and an iron age, which was universally applied to their opposite maxims of government. Notwithstanding the difference of their characters, the two emperors maintained on the throne that friendship which they had contracted in a private station. The haughty, turbulent spirit of Maximian, so fatal afterwards to himself and to the public peace, was accustomed to respect the genius of Diocletian, and confessed the ascendant of reason over brutal violence. From a motive either of pride or superstition, the two emperors assumed the titles, the one of Jovius, the other of Herculius. Whilst the motion of the world (such was the language of their venal orators) was maintained by the all-seeing wisdom of Jupiter, the invincible arm of Hercules purged the earth from monsters and tyrants.

But even the omnipotence of Jovius and Herculius was insufficient to sustain the weight of the public administration. The prudence of Diocletian discovered that the empire, assailed on every side by the barbarians, required on every side the presence of a great army and of an emperor. With this view he resolved once more to divide his unwieldy power and, with the inferior title of Cæsar, to confer on two generals of approved merit an equal share of the sovereign authority. Galerius, surnamed Armentarius from his original profession of a herdsman, and Constantius, who from his pale complexion had acquired the denomination of Chlorus, were the two persons invested with the second honours of the Imperial purple. In describing the country, extraction, and manners of Herculius, we have already delineated those of Galerius, who was often, and not improperly, styled the younger Maximian, though in many instances both of virtue and ability he appears to have possessed a manifest superiority over the elder. The birth of Constantius was less obscure than that of his colleagues. Eutropius, his father, was one of the most considerable nobles of Dardania, and his mother was the niece of the emperor Claudius. Although the youth of Constantius had been spent in arms, he was endowed with a mild and amiable disposition, and the popular voice had long since acknowledged him worthy of the rank which he at last attained. To strengthen the bonds of political by those of domestic union, each of the emperors assumed the character of a father to one of the Cæsars, Diocletian to Galerius, and Maximian to Constantius; and each, obliging them to repudiate their former wives, bestowed his daughter in marriage on his adopted son.

These four princes distributed among themselves the wide extent of the Roman empire. The defence of Gaul, Spain, and Britain was intrusted to Constantius. Galerius was stationed on the banks of the Danube as the safeguard of the Illyrian provinces. Italy and Africa were considered as the department of Maximian; and for his peculiar portion Diocletian reserved Thrace, Egypt, and the rich countries of Asia. Every one was sovereign within his own jurisdiction; but their united authority extended over the whole monarchy, and each of them was prepared to assist his colleagues with his counsels or presence. The Cæsars, in their exalted rank, revered the majesty of the emperors, and the three younger princes invariably acknowledged, by their gratitude and obedience, the common parent of their fortunes. The suspicious jealousy of power found not any place among them; and the singular happiness of their union has been compared to a chorus of music, whose harmony was regulated and maintained by the skilful hand of the first artist.[2]

Notwithstanding the policy of Diocletian, it was impossible to maintain an equal and undisturbed tranquillity during a reign of twenty years and along a fron-

---

2. *Editor's note:* A section is omitted here recounting the earlier exploits of Maximian, particularly his crushing of the uprising of the peasants of Gaul known as the Bagaudæ, and his eventual success in recovering Britain from the hands of one Carausius, who had managed to subvert the Roman navy based at Boulogne as well as the legions stationed in Britain.

tier of many hundred miles. Sometimes the barbarians suspended their domestic animosities, and the relaxed vigilance of the garrisons sometimes gave a passage to their strength or dexterity. Whenever the provinces were invaded, Diocletian conducted himself with that calm dignity which he always affected or possessed, reserved his presence for such occasions as were worthy of his interposition, never exposed his person or reputation to any unnecessary danger, ensured his success by every means that prudence could suggest, and displayed with ostentation the consequences of his victory. In wars of a more difficult nature and more doubtful event he employed the rough valour of Maximian; and that faithful soldier was content to ascribe his own victories to the wise counsels and auspicious influence of his benefactor. But after the adoption of the two Cæsars the emperors, themselves retiring to a less laborious scene of action, devolved on their adopted sons the defence of the Danube and of the Rhine.

The vigilant Galerius was never reduced to the necessity of vanquishing an army of barbarians on the Roman territory. The brave and active Constantius delivered Gaul from a very furious inroad of the Alemanni, and his victories of Langres and Vindonissa appear to have been actions of considerable danger and merit. As he traversed the open country with a feeble guard, he was encompassed on a sudden by the superior multitude of the enemy. He retreated with difficulty towards Langres; but in the general consternation the citizens refused to open their gates, and the wounded prince was drawn up the wall by the means of a rope. But on the news of his distress the Roman troops hastened from all sides to his relief, and before the evening he had satisfied his honour and revenge by the slaughter of six thousand Alemanni. From the monuments of those times the obscure traces of several other victories over the barbarians of Sarmatia and Germany might possibly be collected; but the tedious search would not be rewarded either with amusement or with instruction.

The conduct which the emperor Probus had adopted in the disposal of the vanquished was imitated by Diocletian and his associates. The captive barbarians, exchanging death for slavery, were distributed among the provincials and assigned to those districts (in Gaul the territories of Amiens, Beauvais, Cambray, Treves, Langres, and Troyes are particularly specified) which had been depopulated by the calamities of war. They were usefully employed as shepherds and husbandmen but were denied the exercise of arms, except when it was found expedient to enroll them in the military service. Nor did the emperors refuse the property of lands with a less servile tenure to such of the barbarians as solicited the protection of Rome. They granted a settlement to several colonies of the Carpi, the Bastarnæ, and the Sarmatians, and by a dangerous indulgence permitted them in some measure to retain their national manners and independence. Among the provincials it was a subject of flattering exultation that the barbarian, so lately an object of terror, now cultivated their lands, drove their cattle to the neighbouring fair, and contributed by his labour to the public plenty. They congratulated their masters on the powerful accession of subjects and soldiers; but they forgot to observe that multitudes of secret enemies, insolent from favour or desperate from oppression, were introduced into the heart of the empire.[3]

3. *Editor's note:* A brief passage is omitted here, describing the repulse by Maximian of an invasion of North Africa by Moorish tribes to the South and Diocletian's vigorous suppression of an Egyptian revolt centered in Alexandria.

We have observed, under the reign of Valerian, that Armenia was subdued by the perfidy and the arms of the Persians, and that after the assassination of Chosroes his son Tiridates, the infant heir of the monarchy, was saved by the fidelity of his friends and educated under the protection of the emperors. Tiridates derived from his exile such advantages as he could never have obtained on the throne of Armenia—the early knowledge of adversity, of mankind, and of the Roman discipline.

He signalized his youth by deeds of valour and displayed a matchless dexterity, as well as strength, in every martial exercise and even in the less honourable contests of the Olympian games. Those qualities were more nobly exerted in the defence of his benefactor Licinius. That officer, in the sedition which occasioned the death of Probus, was exposed to the most imminent danger, and the enraged soldiers were forcing their way into his tent when they were checked by the single arm of the Armenian prince. The gratitude of Tiridates contributed soon afterwards to his restoration. Licinius was in every station the friend and companion of Galerius, and the merit of Galerius, long before he was raised to the dignity of Cæsar, had been known and esteemed by Diocletian. In the third year of that emperor's reign Tiridates was invested with the kingdom of Armenia. The justice of the measure was not less evident than its expediency. It was time to rescue from the usurpation of the Persian monarch an important territory which since the reign of Nero had been always granted under the protection of the empire to a younger branch of the house of Arsaces.

When Tiridates appeared on the frontiers of Armenia he was received with an unfeigned transport of joy and loyalty. During twenty-six years the country had experienced the real and imaginary hardships of a foreign

yoke. The Persian monarchs adorned their new conquest
with magnificent buildings; but those monuments had
been erected at the expense of the people and were
abhorred as badges of slavery. The apprehension of a
revolt had inspired the most rigorous precautions; oppression had been aggravated by insult; and the consciousness of the public hatred had been productive of
every measure that could render it still more implacable.
We have already remarked the intolerant spirit of the
Magian religion. The statues of the deified kings of
Armenia and the sacred images of the sun and moon
were broken in pieces by the zeal of the conqueror, and
the perpetual fire of Ormuzd was kindled and preserved
upon an altar erected on the summit of Mount Bagavan.

It was natural that a people exasperated by so many
injuries should arm with zeal in the cause of their independence, their religion, and their hereditary sovereign. The torrent bore down every obstacle, and the
Persian garrisons retreated before its fury. The nobles
of Armenia flew to the standard of Tiridates, all alleging
their past merit, offering their future service, and soliciting from the new king those honours and rewards from
which they had been excluded with disdain under the
foreign government. The command of the army was
bestowed on Artavasdes, whose father had saved the
infancy of Tiridates and whose family had been massacred for that generous action. The brother of Artavasdes obtained the government of a province. One of the
first military dignities was conferred on the satrap Otas,
a man of singular temperance and fortitude, who presented to the king his sister and a considerable treasure,
both of which, in a sequestered fortress, Otas had preserved from violation.

Among the Armenian nobles appeared an ally whose
fortunes are too remarkable to pass unnoticed. His name

was Mamgo, his origin was Scythian, and the horde
which acknowledged his authority had encamped a very
few years before on the skirts of the Chinese empire,
which at that time extended as far as the neighbourhood
of Sogdiana.[4] Having incurred the displeasure of his
master, Mamgo with his followers retired to the banks
of the Oxus and implored the protection of Sapor. The
emperor of China claimed the fugitive and alleged the
rights of sovereignty. The Persian monarch pleaded
the laws of hospitality and with some difficulty avoided
a war by the promise that he would banish Mamgo to
the uttermost parts of the West, a punishment, as he
described it, not less dreadful than death itself. Armenia
was chosen for the place of exile, and a large district
was assigned to the Scythian horde, on which they
might feed their flocks and herds and remove their en-
campment from one place to another according to the
different seasons of the year. They were employed to
repel the invasion of Tiridates; but their leader, after
weighing the obligations and injuries which he had received from the Persian monarch, resolved to abandon
his party. The Armenian prince, who was well acquainted with the merit as well as power of Mamgo,
treated him with distinguished respect, and by admitting him into his confidence acquired a brave and faithful servant who contributed very effectually to his
restoration.

For a while fortune appeared to favour the enterprising valour of Tiridates. He not only expelled the
enemies of his family and country from the whole extent
of Armenia, but in the prosecution of his revenge he
carried his arms, or at least his incursions, into the heart

4. *Editor's note:* A remote province of the Persian empire
first conquered by Cyrus the Great. Its capital was Samar-
kand.

of Assyria. The historian who has preserved the name of Tiridates from oblivion celebrates, with a degree of national enthusiasm, his personal prowess and in the true spirit of eastern romance describes the giants and the elephants that fell beneath his invincible arm. It is from other information that we discover the distracted state of the Persian monarchy, to which the king of Armenia was indebted for some part of his advantages. The throne was disputed by the ambition of contending brothers; and Hormuz, after exerting without success the strength of his own party, had recourse to the dangerous assistance of the barbarians who inhabited the banks of the Caspian Sea. The civil war was, however, soon terminated, either by a victory or by a reconciliation; and Narses, who was universally acknowledged as king of Persia, directed his whole force against the foreign enemy. The contest then became too unequal; nor was the valour of the hero able to withstand the power of the monarch. Tiridates, a second time expelled from the throne of Armenia, once more took refuge in the court of the emperors. Narses soon re-established his authority over the revolted province and, loudly complaining of the protection afforded by the Romans to rebels and fugitives, aspired to the conquest of the East.

Neither prudence nor honour could permit the emperors to forsake the cause of the Armenian king, and it was resolved to exert the force of the empire in the Persian war. Diocletian, with the calm dignity which he constantly assumed, fixed his own station in the city of Antioch, from whence he prepared and directed the military operations. The conduct of the legions was entrusted to the intrepid valour of Galerius, who for that important purpose was removed from the banks of the Danube to those of the Euphrates. The armies soon encountered each other in the plains of Mesopotamia, and two battles were fought with various and doubtful success; but the third engagement was of a more decisive nature, and the Roman army received a total overthrow, which is attributed to the rashness of Galerius, who with an inconsiderable body of troops attacked the innumerable host of the Persians.

But the consideration of the country that was the scene of action may suggest another reason for his defeat. The same ground on which Galerius was vanquished had been rendered memorable by the death of Crassus and the slaughter of ten legions. It was a plain of more than sixty miles, which extended from the hills of Carrhæ to the Euphrates, a smooth and barren surface of sandy desert without a hillock, without a tree, and without a spring of fresh water. The steady infantry of the Romans, fainting with heat and thirst, could neither hope for victory if they preserved their ranks, nor break their ranks without exposing themselves to the most imminent danger. In this situation they were gradually encompassed by the superior numbers, harassed by the rapid evolutions, and destroyed by the arrows of the barbarian cavalry. The king of Armenia had signalized his valour in the battle and acquired personal glory by the public misfortune. He was pursued as far as the Euphrates, his horse was wounded, and it appeared impossible for him to escape the victorious enemy. In this extremity Tiridates embraced the only refuge which he saw before him: he dismounted and plunged into the stream. His armour was heavy, the river very deep and at those parts at least half a mile in breadth; yet such was his strength and dexterity that he reached in safety the opposite bank. With regard to the Roman general, we are ignorant of the circumstances of his escape; but when he returned to Antioch, Diocletian received him not with the tenderness of a friend and colleague but with the indignation of an offended sovereign. The haughtiest of men, clothed in his purple but humbled by the sense of his fault and misfortune, was obliged to follow the emperor's chariot above a mile on foot and to exhibit before the whole court the spectacle of his disgrace.

As soon as Diocletian had indulged his private resentment and asserted the majesty of supreme power, he yielded to the submissive entreaties of the Cæsar and permitted him to retrieve his own honour as well as that of the Roman arms. In the room of the unwarlike troops of Asia, which had most probably served in the first expedition, a second army was drawn from the veterans and new levies of the Illyrian frontier, and a considerable body of Gothic auxiliaries were taken into the Imperial pay. At the head of a chosen army of twenty-five thousand men Galerius again passed the Euphrates; but instead of exposing his legions in the open plains of Mesopotamia he advanced through the mountains of Armenia, where he found the inhabitants devoted to his cause and the country as favourable to the operations of infantry as it was inconvenient for the motions of cavalry. Adversity had confirmed the Roman discipline, while the barbarians, elated by success, were become so negligent and remiss that in the moment when they least expected it they were surprised by the active conduct of Galerius, who, attended only by two horsemen, had with his own eyes secretly examined the state and position of their camp.

A surprise, especially in the night-time, was for the most part fatal to a Persian army. "Their horses were tied, and generally shackled, to prevent their running away; and if an alarm happened, a Persian had his housing to fix, his horse to bridle, and his corselet to put on before he could mount." On this occasion the impetuous attack of Galerius spread disorder and dismay over the camp of the barbarians. A slight resistance was followed by a dreadful carnage, and in the general confusion the wounded monarch (for Narses commanded his armies in person) fled towards the deserts of Media. His sumptuous tents and those of his satraps afforded an immense booty to the conqueror; and an incident is mentioned which proves the rustic but martial ignorance of the legions in the elegant superfluities of life. A bag of shining leather, filled with pearls, fell into the hands of a private soldier; he carefully preserved the bag, but he threw away its contents, judging that whatever was of no use could not possibly be of any value. The principal loss of Narses was of a much more affecting nature. Several of his wives, his sisters, and children, who had attended the army, were made captives in the defeat. But though the character of Galerius had in general very little affinity with that of Alexander, he imitated after his victory the amiable behaviour of the Macedonian towards the family of Darius. The wives and children of Narses were protected from violence and rapine, conveyed to a place of safety, and treated with every mark of respect and tenderness that was due from a generous enemy to their age, their sex, and their royal dignity.

While the East anxiously expected the decision of this great contest, the emperor Diocletian, having assembled in Syria a strong army of observation, displayed from a distance the resources of the Roman power and reserved himself for any future emergency of the war. On the intelligence of the victory he condescended to advance towards the frontier, with a view of moderating, by his presence and counsels, the pride of Galerius. The interview of the Roman princes at Nisibis was accompanied with every expression of respect on one side and of esteem on the other. It was in that city that they soon afterwards gave audience to the ambassador of the Great King. The power, or at least the spirit, of Narses had been broken by his last defeat; and he considered an immediate peace as the only means that could stop the progress of the Roman arms. He despatched Aphar- ban, a servant who possessed his favour and confidence, with a commission to negotiate a treaty, or rather to receive whatever conditions the conqueror should im- pose. Apharban opened the conference by expressing his master's gratitude for the generous treatment of his family and by soliciting the liberty of those illustrious captives. He celebrated the valour of Galerius without degrading the reputation of Narses, and thought it no dishonor to confess the superiority of the victorious Cæsar over a monarch who had surpassed in glory all the princes of his race. Notwithstanding the justice of the Persian cause, he was empowered to submit the present differences to the decision of the emperors them- selves, convinced as he was that in the midst of pros- perity they would not be unmindful of the vicissitudes of fortune. Apharban concluded his discourse in the style of eastern allegory by observing that the Roman and Persian monarchies were the two eyes of the world, which would remain imperfect and mutilated if either of them should be put out.

"It well becomes the Persians," replied Galerius, with a transport of fury which seemed to convulse his whole frame, "it well becomes the Persians to expatiate on the vicissitudes of fortune and calmly to read us lectures on the virtues of moderation. Let them remember their own *moderation* towards the unhappy Valerian. They van- quished him by fraud, they treated him with indignity. They detained him till the last moment of his life in shameful captivity, and after his death they exposed his body to perpetual ignominy." Softening, however, his tone, Galerius insinuated to the ambassador that it had never been the practice of the Romans to trample on a prostrate enemy and that on this occasion they should consult their own dignity rather than the Persian merit. He dismissed Apharban with a hope that Narses would soon be informed on what conditions he might obtain, from the clemency of the emperors, a lasting peace and the restoration of his wives and children. In this conference we may discover the fierce passions of Galerius, as well as his deference to the superior wisdom and authority of Diocletian. The ambition of the former grasped at the conquest of the East and had proposed to reduce Persia into the state of a province. The prudence of the latter, who adhered to the moderate policy of Augustus and the Antonines, embraced the favourable opportunity of terminating a successful war by an honourable and advantageous peace.

In pursuance of their promise the emperors soon afterwards appointed Sicorius Probus, one of their secretaries, to acquaint the Persian court with their final resolution. As the minister of peace he was received with every mark of politeness and friendship; but under the pretence of allowing him the necessary repose after so long a journey, the audience of Probus was deferred from day to day, and he attended the slow motions of the king till at length he was admitted to his presence, near the river Asprudus in Media. The secret motive of Narses in this delay had been to collect such a military force as might enable him, though sincerely desirous of peace, to negotiate with the greater weight and dignity. Three persons only assisted at this important conference: the minister Apharban, the præfect of the guards, and an officer who had commanded on the Armenian frontier. The first condition proposed by the ambassador is not at present of a very intelligible nature: that the city of Nisibis might be established for the place of mutual exchange, or, as we should formerly have termed it, for the staple of trade between the two empires. There is no difficulty in conceiving the intention of the Roman princes to improve their revenue by some restraints upon commerce; but as Nisibis was situated within their own dominions, and as they were masters both of the imports and exports, it should seem that such restraints were the objects of an internal law rather than of a foreign treaty. To render them more effectual, some stipulations were probably required on the side of the king of Persia, which appeared so very repugnant either to his interest or to his dignity that Narses could not be persuaded to subscribe them. As this was the only article to which he refused his consent, it was no longer insisted on; and the emperors either suffered the trade to flow in its natural channels or contented themselves with such restrictions as it depended on their own authority to establish.

As soon as this difficulty was removed a solemn peace was concluded and ratified between the two nations.[5] The East enjoyed a profound tranquillity during forty years, and the treaty between the rival monarchies was strictly observed till the death of Tiridates, when a new generation, animated with different views and different passions, succeeded to the government of the world, and the grandson of Narses undertook a long and memorable war against the princes of the house of Constantine.

The arduous work of rescuing the distressed empire from tyrants and barbarians had now been completely achieved by a succession of Illyrian peasants. As soon as Diocletian entered into the twentieth year of his

5. *Editor's note:* A description of the geographical boundaries and other conditions of the treaty is omitted here.

reign, he celebrated that memorable era, as well as the success of his arms, by the pomp of a Roman triumph. Maximian, the equal partner of his power, was his only companion in the glory of that day. The two Cæsars had fought and conquered, but the merit of their exploits was ascribed, according to the rigour of ancient maxims, to the auspicious influence of their fathers and emperors. The triumph of Diocletian and Maximian was less magnificent, perhaps, than those of Aurelian and Probus, but it was dignified by several circumstances of superior fame and good fortune. Africa and Britain, the Rhine, the Danube, and the Nile, furnished their respective trophies; but the most distinguished ornament was of a more singular nature, a Persian victory followed by an important conquest. The representations of rivers, mountains, and provinces were carried before the Imperial car. The images of the captive wives, the sisters, and the children of the Great King afforded a new and grateful spectacle to the vanity of the people. In the eyes of posterity this triumph is remarkable by a distinction of a less honourable kind. It was the last that Rome ever beheld. Soon after this period the emperors ceased to vanquish, and Rome ceased to be the capital of the empire.

The spot on which Rome was founded had been consecrated by ancient ceremonies and imaginary miracles. The presence of some god or the memory of some hero seemed to animate every part of the city, and the empire of the world had been promised to the Capitol. The native Romans felt and confessed the power of this agreeable illusion. It was derived from their ancestors, had grown up with their earliest habits of life, and was protected in some measure by the opinion of political utility. The form and the seat of government were intimately blended together; nor was it esteemed possible to transport the one without destroying the other. But the sovereignty of the capital was gradually annihilated in the extent of conquest, the provinces rose to the same level, and the vanquished nations acquired the name and privileges, without imbibing the partial affections, of Romans.

During a long period, however, the remains of the ancient constitution and the influence of custom preserved the dignity of Rome. The emperors, though perhaps of African or Illyrian extraction, respected their adopted country as the seat of their power and the centre of their extensive dominions. The emergencies of war very frequently required their presence on the frontiers, but Diocletian and Maximian were the first Roman princes who fixed, in time of peace, their ordinary residence in the provinces; and their conduct, however it might be suggested by private motives, was justified by very specious considerations of policy. The court of the emperor of the West was, for the most part, established at Milan, whose situation at the foot of the Alps appeared far more convenient than that of Rome for the important purpose of watching the motions of the barbarians of Germany. Milan soon assumed the splendour of an Imperial city. The houses are described as numerous and well built, the manners of the people as polished and liberal. A circus, a theatre, a mint, a palace, baths which bore the name of their founder Maximian, porticoes adorned with statues, and a double circumference of walls contributed to the beauty of the new capital; nor did it seem oppressed even by the proximity of Rome.

To rival the majesty of Rome was the ambition likewise of Diocletian, who employed his leisure and the wealth of the East in the embellishment of Nicomedia, a city placed on the verge of Europe and Asia almost at an equal distance between the Danube and the Euphrates. By the taste of the monarch, and at the expense of the people, Nicomedia acquired in the space of a few years a degree of magnificence which might appear to have required the labour of ages, and became inferior only to Rome, Alexandria, and Antioch in extent or populousness. The life of Diocletian and Maximian was a life of action, and a considerable portion of it was spent in camps or in their long and frequent marches; but whenever the public business allowed them any relaxation, they seemed to have retired with pleasure to their favourite residences of Nicomedia and Milan. Till Diocletian, in the twentieth year of his reign, cele-brated his Roman triumph, it is extremely doubtful whether he ever visited the ancient capital of the em-pire. Even on that memorable occasion his stay did not exceed two months. Disgusted with the licentious famil-iarity of the people, he quitted Rome with precipitation thirteen days before it was expected that he should have appeared in the senate, invested with the ensigns of the consular dignity.

The dislike expressed by Diocletian towards Rome and Roman freedom was not the effect of momentary caprice but the result of the most artful policy. The crafty prince had framed a new system of Imperial government, which was afterwards completed by the family of Constantine; and as the image of the old con-stitution was religiously preserved in the senate, he re-solved to deprive that order of its small remains of power and consideration. We may recollect, about eight years before the elevation of Diocletian, the transient greatness and the ambitious hopes of the Roman senate. As long as that enthusiasm prevailed, many of the nobles imprudently displayed their zeal in the cause of freedom; and after the successors of Probus had with-

drawn their countenance from the republican party, the
senators were unable to disguise their impotent resentment. As the sovereign of Italy, Maximian was entrusted
with the care of extinguishing this troublesome rather
than dangerous spirit, and the task was perfectly suited
to his cruel temper. The most illustrious members of the
senate, whom Diocletian always affected to esteem, were
involved by his colleague in the accusation of imaginary
plots; and the possession of an elegant villa or a well-
cultivated estate was interpreted as a convincing evidence of guilt. The camp of the Prætorians, which had
so long oppressed, began to protect, the majesty of
Rome; and as those haughty troops were conscious of
the decline of their power, they were naturally disposed
to unite their strength with the authority of the senate.
By the prudent measures of Diocletian the numbers of
the Prætorians were insensibly reduced, their privileges
abolished, and their place supplied by two faithful legions of Illyricum, who, under the new titles of Jovians
and Herculians, were appointed to perform the service
of the Imperial guards.

But the most fatal though secret wound which the
senate received from the hands of Diocletian and Maximian was inflicted by the inevitable operation of their
absence. As long as the emperors resided at Rome, that
assembly might be oppressed but it could scarcely be
neglected. The successors of Augustus exercised the
power of dictating whatever laws their wisdom or
caprice might suggest, but those laws were ratified by
the sanction of the senate. The model of ancient freedom was preserved in its deliberations and decrees; and
wise princes, who respected the prejudices of the Roman people, were in some measure obliged to assume
the language and behaviour suitable to the general and
first magistrate of the republic. In the armies and in the

provinces they displayed the dignity of monarchs; and when they fixed their residence at a distance from the capital they forever laid aside the dissimulation which Augustus had recommended to his successors. In the exercise of the legislative as well as the executive power, the sovereign advised with his ministers instead of consulting the great council of the nation. The name of the senate was mentioned with honour till the last period of the empire; the vanity of its members was still flattered with honorary distinctions; but the assembly, which had so long been the source and so long the instrument of power, was respectfully suffered to sink into oblivion. The senate of Rome, losing all connection with the Imperial court and the actual constitution, was left a venerable but useless monument of antiquity on the Capitoline hill.

When the Roman princes had lost sight of the senate and of their ancient capital they easily forgot the origin and nature of their legal power. The civil offices of consul, of proconsul, of censor, and of tribune, by the union of which it had been formed, betrayed to the people its republican extraction. Those modest titles were laid aside; and if they still distinguished their high station by the appellation of Emperor, or *Imperator*, that word was understood in a new and more dignified sense, and no longer denoted the general of the Roman armies but the sovereign of the Roman world. The name of Emperor, which was at first of a military nature, was associated with another of a more servile kind. The epithet of *Dominus*, or Lord, in its primitive signification, was expressive not of the authority of a prince over his subjects, or of a commander over his soldiers, but of the despotic power of a master over his domestic slaves. Viewing it in that odious light, it had been rejected with abhorrence by the first Cæsars. Their resistance insensibly became more feeble and the name less odious, till at length the style of *our Lord and Emperor* was not only bestowed by flattery but was regularly admitted into the laws and public monuments.

Such lofty epithets were sufficient to elate and satisfy the most excessive vanity; and if the successors of Diocletian still declined the title of King, it seems to have been the effect not so much of their moderation as of their delicacy. Wherever the Latin tongue was in use (and it was the language of government throughout the empire), the Imperial title, as it was peculiar to themselves, conveyed a more respectable idea than the name of king, which they must have shared with an hundred barbarian chieftains, or which at the best they could derive only from Romulus or from Tarquin. But the sentiments of the East were very different from those of the West. From the earliest period of history the sovereigns of Asia had been celebrated in the Greek language by the title of *Basileus,* or King; and since it was considered as the first distinction among men, it was soon employed by the servile provincials of the East in their humble addresses to the Roman throne. Even the attributes, or at least the titles, of the *Divinity* were usurped by Diocletian and Maximian, who transmitted them to a succession of Christian emperors. Such extravagant compliments, however, soon lose their impiety by losing their meaning; and when the ear is once accustomed to the sound, they are heard with indifference as vague though excessive professions of respect.

From the time of Augustus to that of Diocletian the Roman princes, conversing in a familiar manner among their fellow-citizens, were saluted only with the same respect that was usually paid to senators and magistrates. Their principal distinction was the Imperial or military robe of purple, whilst the senatorial garment was marked by a broad, and the equestrian by a narrow, band or stripe of the same honourable colour. The pride, or rather the policy, of Diocletian engaged that artful prince to introduce the stately magnificence of the court of Persia. He ventured to assume the diadem, an ornament detested by the Romans as the odious ensign of royalty, and the use of which had been considered as the most desperate act of the madness of Caligula. It was no more than a broad white fillet set with pearls, which encircled the emperor's head. The sumptuous robes of Diocletian and his successors were of silk and gold; and it is remarked with indignation that even their shoes were studded with the most precious gems. The access to their sacred person was every day rendered more difficult by the institution of new forms and ceremonies. The avenues of the palace were strictly guarded by the various *schools,* as they began to be called, of domestic officers. The interior apartments were entrusted to the jealous vigilance of the eunuchs, the increase of whose numbers and influence was the most infallible symptom of the progress of despotism. When a subject was at length admitted to the Imperial presence he was obliged, whatever might be his rank, to fall prostrate on the ground and to adore, according to the eastern fashion, the divinity of his lord and master.

Diocletian was a man of sense who, in the course of private as well as public life, had formed a just estimate both of himself and of mankind; nor is it easy to conceive that in substituting the manners of Persia to those of Rome he was seriously actuated by so mean a principle as that of vanity. He flattered himself that an ostentation of splendour and luxury would subdue the imagination of the multitude; that the monarch would be less exposed to the rude licence of the people and the soldiers as his person was secluded from the public view; and that habits of submission would insensibly be productive of sentiments of veneration. Like the modesty affected by Augustus, the state maintained by Diocletian was a theatrical representation; but it must be confessed that of the two comedies the former was of a much more liberal and manly character than the latter. It was the aim of the one to disguise, and the object of the other to display, the unbounded power which the emperors possessed over the Roman world.

Ostentation was the first principle of the new system instituted by Diocletian. The second was division. He divided the empire, the provinces, and every branch of the civil as well as military administration. He multiplied the wheels of the machine of government and rendered its operations less rapid but more secure. Whatever advantages and whatever defects might attend these innovations, they must be ascribed in a very great degree to the first inventor; but as the new frame of policy was gradually improved and completed by succeeding princes, it will be more satisfactory to delay the consideration of it till the season of its full maturity and perfection. Reserving, therefore, for the reign of Constantine a more exact picture of the new empire, we shall content ourselves with describing the principal and decisive outline as it was traced by the hand of Diocletian. He had associated three colleagues in the exercise of the supreme power; and as he was convinced that the abilities of a single man were inadequate to the public defence, he considered the joint administration of four princes not as a temporary expedient but as a fundamental law of the constitution. It was his intention that the two elder princes should be distinguished by the use of the diadem and the title of Augusti; that, as affection or esteem might direct their choice, they should regularly call to their assistance two subordinate colleagues;

and that the Cæsars, rising in their turn to the first rank, should supply an uninterrupted succession of emperors. The empire was divided into four parts. The East and Italy were the most honourable, the Danube and the Rhine the most laborious stations. The former claimed the presence of the Augusti, the latter were entrusted to the administration of the Cæsars. The strength of the legions was in the hands of the four partners of sovereignty, and the despair of successively vanquishing four formidable rivals might intimidate the ambition of an aspiring general. In their civil government the emperors were supposed to exercise the undivided power of the monarch, and their edicts, inscribed with their joint names, were received in all the provinces as promulgated by their mutual councils and authority. Notwithstanding these precautions the political union of the Roman world was gradually dissolved, and a principle of division was introduced which in the course of a few years occasioned the perpetual separation of the eastern and western empires.

The system of Diocletian was accompanied with another very material disadvantage, which cannot even at present be totally overlooked: a more expensive establishment, and consequently an increase of taxes and the oppression of the people. Instead of a modest family of slaves and freedmen, such as had contented the simple greatness of Augustus and Trajan, three or four magnificent courts were established in the various parts of the empire, and as many Roman *kings* contended with each other and with the Persian monarch for the vain superiority of pomp and luxury. The number of ministers, of magistrates, of officers, and of servants who filled the different departments of the state was multiplied beyond the example of former times; and (if we may borrow the warm expression of a contemporary), "when the proportion of those who received exceeded the proportion of those who contributed, the provinces were oppressed by the weight of tributes." From this period to the extinction of the empire it would be easy to deduce an uninterrupted series of clamours and complaints. According to his religion and situation, each writer chooses either Diocletian, or Constantine, or Valens, or Theodosius for the object of his invectives; but they unanimously agree in representing the burden of the public impositions, and particularly the land-tax and capitation, as the intolerable and increasing grievance of their own times. From such a concurrence an impartial historian, who is obliged to extract truth from satire as well as from panegyric, will be inclined to divide the blame among the princes whom they accuse and to ascribe their exactions much less to their personal vices than to the uniform system of their administration. The emperor Diocletian was indeed the author of that system; but during his reign the growing evil was confined within the bounds of modesty and discretion, and he deserves the reproach of establishing pernicious precedents rather than of exercising actual oppression. It may be added that his revenues were managed with prudent economy, and that, after all the current expenses were discharged, there still remained in the Imperial treasury an ample provision either for judicious liberality or for any emergency of the state.

It was in the twenty-first year of his reign that Diocletian executed his memorable resolution of abdicating the empire, an action more naturally to have been expected from the elder or the younger Antoninus than from a prince who had never practised the lessons of philosophy either in the attainment or in the use of supreme power. Diocletian acquired the glory of giving to the world the first example of a resignation, which has not been very frequently imitated by succeeding monarchs. The parallel of Charles the Fifth, however, will naturally offer itself to our mind, not only since the eloquence of a modern historian has rendered that name so familiar to an English reader, but from the very striking resemblance between the characters of the two emperors, whose political abilities were superior to their military genius and whose specious virtues were much less the effect of nature than of art. The abdication of Charles appears to have been hastened by the vicissitude of fortune, and the disappointment of his favourite schemes urged him to relinquish a power which he found inadequate to his ambition. But the reign of Diocletian had flowed with a tide of uninterrupted success; nor was it till after he had vanquished all his enemies and accomplished all his designs that he seems to have entertained any serious thoughts of resigning the empire. Neither Charles nor Diocletian was arrived at a very advanced period of life, since the one was only fifty-five and the other was no more than fifty-nine years of age; but the active life of those princes, their wars and journeys, the cares of royalty, and their application to business had already impaired their constitutions and brought on the infirmities of a premature old age.

Notwithstanding the severity of a very cold and rainy winter, Diocletian left Italy soon after the ceremony of his triumph and began his progress towards the East round the circuit of the Illyrian provinces. From the inclemency of the weather and the fatigue of the journey he soon contracted a slow illness; and though he made easy marches and was generally carried in a close litter, his disorder, before he arrived at Nicomedia about the end of the summer, was become very serious and alarming. During the whole winter he was confined to his palace; his danger inspired a general and unaffected concern; but the people could only judge of the various alterations of his health from the joy or consternation which they discovered in the countenances and behaviour of his attendants. The rumour of his death was for some time universally believed, and it was supposed to be concealed with a view to prevent the troubles that might have happened during the absence of the Cæsar Galerius. At length, however, on the first of March, Diocletian once more appeared in public, but so pale and emaciated that he could scarcely have been recognized by those to whom his person was the most familiar. It was time to put an end to the painful struggle, which he had sustained during more than a year, between the care of his health and that of his dignity. The former required indulgence and relaxation; the latter compelled him to direct, from the bed of sickness, the administration of a great empire. He resolved to pass the remainder of his days in honourable repose, to place his glory beyond the reach of fortune, and to relinquish the theatre of the world to his younger and more active associates.

The ceremony of his abdication was performed in a spacious plain about three miles from Nicomedia. The emperor ascended a lofty throne and, in a speech full of reason and dignity, declared his intention both to the people and to the soldiers who were assembled on this extraordinary occasion. As soon as he had divested himself of the purple he withdrew from the gazing multitude and, traversing the city in a covered chariot, proceeded without delay to the favourite retirement which he had chosen in his native country of Dalmatia. On the same day, which was the first of May, Maximian, as it had been previously concerted, made his resignation of the Imperial dignity at Milan. Even in the splendour of the Roman triumph Diocletian had meditated his design of abdicating the government. As he wished to secure the obedience of Maximian, he exacted from him either a general assurance that he would submit his actions to the authority of his benefactor or a particular promise that he would descend from the throne whenever he should receive the advice and the example. This engagement, though it was confirmed by the solemnity of an oath before the altar of the Capitoline Jupiter, would have proved a feeble restraint on the fierce temper of Maximian, whose passion was the love of power and who neither desired present tranquillity nor future reputation. But he yielded, however reluctantly, to the ascendant which his wiser colleague had acquired over him and retired immediately after his abdication to a villa in Lucania, where it was almost impossible that such an impatient spirit could find any lasting tranquillity.

Diocletian, who from a servile origin had raised himself to the throne, passed the nine last years of his life in a private condition. Reason had dictated, and content seems to have accompanied, his retreat, in which he enjoyed for a long time the respect of those princes to whom he had resigned the possession of the world. It is seldom that minds long exercised in business have formed any habits of conversing with themselves, and in the loss of power they principally regret the want of occupation. The amusements of letters and of devotion, which afford so many resources in solitude, were incapable of fixing the attention of Diocletian; but he had preserved, or at least he soon recovered, a taste for the most innocent as well as natural pleasures, and his leisure hours were sufficiently employed in building, planting, and gardening. His answer to Maximian is deservedly celebrated. He was solicited by that restless old man to reassume the reins of government and the Imperial purple. He rejected the temptation with a smile of pity, calmly observing that if he could show Maximian the cabbages which he had planted with his own hands at Salona, he should no longer be urged to relinquish the enjoyment of happiness for the pursuit of power.

In his conversations with his friends he frequently acknowledged that of all arts the most difficult was the art of reigning; and he expressed himself on that favourite topic with a degree of warmth which could be the result only of experience. "How often," was he accustomed to say, "is it the interest of four or five ministers to combine together to deceive their sovereign! Secluded from mankind by his exalted dignity, the truth is concealed from his knowledge; he can see only with their eyes, he hears nothing but their misrepresentations. He confers the most important offices upon vice and weakness, and disgraces the most virtuous and deserving among his subjects. By such infamous arts," added Diocletian, "the best and wisest princes are sold to the venal corruption of their courtiers."

A just estimate of greatness and the assurance of immortal fame improve our relish for the pleasures of retirement; but the Roman emperor had filled too important a character in the world to enjoy without alloy the comforts and security of a private condition. It was impossible that he could remain ignorant of the troubles which afflicted the empire after his abdication. It was impossible that he could be indifferent to their consequences. Fear, sorrow, and discontent sometimes pursued him into the solitude of Salona. His tenderness, or at least his pride, was deeply wounded by the misfortunes of his wife and daughter; and the last moments of Diocletian were embittered by some affronts, which

Licinius and Constantine might have spared the father of so many emperors and the first author of their own fortune. A report, though of a very doubtful nature, has reached our times that he prudently withdrew himself from their power by a voluntary death.[6]

It is almost unnecessary to remark that the civil distractions of the empire, the licence of the soldiers, the inroads of the barbarians, and the progress of despotism had proved very unfavourable to genius, and even to learning. The succession of Illyrian princes restored the empire without restoring the sciences. Their military education was not calculated to inspire them with the love of letters; and even the mind of Diocletian, however active and capacious in business, was totally uninformed by study or speculation. The professions of law and physic are of such common use and certain profit that they will always secure a sufficient number of practitioners endowed with a reasonable degree of abilities and knowledge; but it does not appear that the students in those two faculties appeal to any celebrated masters who have flourished within that period. The voice of poetry was silent. History was reduced to dry and confused abridgments, alike destitute of amusement and instruction. A languid and affected eloquence was still retained in the pay and service of the emperors, who encouraged not any arts except those which contributed to the gratification of their pride or the defence of their power.

The declining age of learning and of mankind is marked, however, by the rise and rapid progress of the new Platonists. The school of Alexandria silenced those of Athens; and the ancient sects enrolled themselves under the banners of the more fashionable teachers,

6. *Editor's note:* A detailed description of Diocletian's place of retirement is omitted here.

who recommended their system by the novelty of their method and the austerity of their manners. Several of these masters—Ammonius, Plotinus, Amelius, and Porphyry—were men of profound thought and intense application; but by mistaking the true object of philosophy their labours contributed much less to improve than to corrupt the human understanding. The knowledge that is suited to our situation and powers, the whole compass of moral, natural, and mathematical science, was neglected by the new Platonists; whilst they exhausted their strength in the verbal disputes of metaphysics, attempted to explore the secrets of the invisible world, and studied to reconcile Aristotle with Plato on subjects of which both these philosphers were as ignorant as the rest of mankind. Consuming their reason in these deep but unsubstantial meditations, their minds were exposed to illusions of fancy. They flattered themselves that they possessed the secret of disengaging the soul from its corporeal prison, claimed a familiar intercourse with demons and spirits, and by a very singular revolution converted the study of philosophy into that of magic. The ancient sages had derided the popular superstition; after disguising its extravagance by the thin pretence of allegory, the disciples of Plotinus and Porphyry became its most zealous defenders. As they agreed with the Christians in a few mysterious points of faith, they attacked the remainder of their theological system with all the fury of civil war. The new Platonists would scarcely deserve a place in the history of science, but in that of the church the mention of them will very frequently occur.

Chapter VII
(A.D. 305-324)

Troubles after the abdication of Diocletian – Death of Constantius – Elevation of Constantine and Maxentius – Six emperors at the same time – Death of Maximian and Galerius – Victories of Constantine over Maxentius and Licinius – Reunion of the empire under the authority of Constantine[1]

THE balance of power established by Diocletian subsisted no longer than while it was sustained by the firm and dexterous hand of the founder. It required such a fortunate mixture of different tempers and abilities as could scarcely be found, or even expected, a second time—two emperors without jealousy, two Cæsars without ambition, and the same general interest invariably pursued by four independent princes. The abdication of Diocletian and Maximian was succeeded by eighteen years of discord and confusion. The empire was afflicted by five civil wars; and the remainder of the time was not so much a state of tranquillity as a suspension of arms between several hostile monarchs who, viewing each other with an eye of fear and hatred, strove to increase their respective forces at the expense of their subjects.

As soon as Diocletian and Maximian had resigned the purple, their station, according to the rules of the new constitution, was filled by the two Cæsars, Constantius

1. *Editor's note:* Chapter XIV of the original.

and Galerius, who immediately assumed the title of
Augustus. The honours of seniority and precedence
were allowed to the former of those princes, and he
continued under a new appellation to administer his ancient department of Gaul, Spain, and Britain. The government of those ample provinces was sufficient to exercise his talents and to satisfy his ambition. Clemency,
temperance, and moderation distinguished the amiable
character of Constantius, and his fortunate subjects had
frequently occasion to compare the virtues of their
sovereign with the passions of Maximian and even with
the arts of Diocletian. Instead of imitating their eastern
pride and magnificence, Constantius preserved the modesty of a Roman prince. He declared with unaffected
sincerity that his most valued treasure was in the hearts
of his people, and that whenever the dignity of the
throne or the danger of the state required any extraordinary supply he could depend with confidence on
their gratitude and liberality. The provincials of Gaul,
Spain, and Britain, sensible of his worth and of their
own happiness, reflected with anxiety on the declining health of the emperor Constantius and the tender
age of his numerous family, the issue of his second
marriage with the daughter of Maximian.

The stern temper of Galerius was cast in a very different mould; and while he commanded the esteem of
his subjects he seldom condescended to solicit their
affections. His fame in arms and, above all, the success
of the Persian war had elated his haughty mind, which
was naturally impatient of a superior, or even of an
equal. If it were possible to rely on the partial testimony
of an injudicious writer, we might ascribe the abdication of Diocletian to the menaces of Galerius and relate
the particulars of a *private* conversation between the
two princes, in which the former discovered as much

pusillanimity as the latter displayed ingratitude and arrogance. But these obscure anecdotes are sufficiently refuted by an impartial view of the character and conduct of Diocletian. Whatever might otherwise have been his intentions, if he had apprehended any danger from the violence of Galerius, his good sense would have instructed him to prevent the ignominious contest; and as he had held the sceptre with glory, he would have resigned it without disgrace.

After the elevation of Contantius and Galerius to the rank of Augusti two new Cæsars were required to supply their place and to complete the system of the Imperial government. Diocletian was sincerely desirous of withdrawing himself from the world; he considered Galerius, who had married his daughter, as the firmest support of his family and of the empire; and he consented without reluctance that his successor should assume the merit as well as the envy of the important nomination. It was fixed without consulting the interest or inclination of the princes of the West. Each of them had a son who was arrived at the age of manhood and who might have been deemed the most natural candidates for the vacant honour. But the impotent resentment of Maximian was no longer to be dreaded; and the moderate Constantius, though he might despise the dangers, was humanely apprehensive of the calamities of civil war. The two persons whom Galerius promoted to the rank of Cæsar were much better suited to serve the views of his ambition; and their principal recommendation seems to have consisted in the want of merit or personal consequence. The first of these was Daza, or, as he was afterwards called, Maximin, whose mother was the sister of Galerius. The inexperienced youth still betrayed by his manners and language his rustic education when, to his own astonishment as well as that of the world, he was invested by Diocletian with the purple, exalted to the dignity of Cæsar, and entrusted with the sovereign command of Egypt and Syria. At the same time Severus, a faithful servant, addicted to pleasure but not incapable of business, was sent to Milan to receive from the reluctant hands of Maximian the Cæsarian ornaments and the possession of Italy and Africa. According to the forms of the constitution, Severus acknowledged the supremacy of the western emperor; but he was absolutely devoted to the commands of his benefactor Galerius, who, reserving to himself the intermediate countries from the confines of Italy to those of Syria, firmly established his power over three-fourths of the monarchy. In the full confidence that the approaching death of Constantius would leave him sole master of the Roman world, we are assured that he arranged in his mind a long succession of future princes, and that he meditated his own retreat from public life after he should have accomplished a glorious reign of about twenty years.

But within less than eighteen months two unexpected revolutions overturned the ambitious schemes of Galerius. The hopes of uniting the western provinces to his empire were disappointed by the elevation of Constantine, whilst Italy and Africa were lost by the successful revolt of Maxentius.

I. THE ELEVATION OF CONSTANTINE. The fame of Constantine has rendered posterity attentive to the most minute circumstances of his life and actions. The place of his birth as well as the condition of his mother Helena have been the subject not only of literary but of national disputes. Notwithstanding the recent tradition which assigns for her father a British king, we are obliged to confess that Helena was the daughter of an innkeeper; but at the same time we may defend the

legality of her marriage against those who have represented her as the concubine of Constantius. The great
Constantine was most probably born at Naissus, in
Dacia; and it is not surprising that, in a family and province distinguished only by the profession of arms, the
youth should discover very little inclination to improve
his mind by the acquisition of knowledge. He was about
eighteen years of age when his father was promoted
to the rank of Cæsar; but that fortunate event was attended with his mother's divorce, and the splendour of
an Imperial alliance reduced the son of Helena to a
state of disgrace and humiliation. Instead of following
Constantius in the West, he remained in the service
of Diocletian, signalizing his valour in the wars of
Egypt and Persia, and gradually rose to the honourable
station of a tribune of the first order.

The figure of Constantine was tall and majestic; he
was dexterous in all his exercises, intrepid in war, affable
in peace; in his whole conduct the active spirit of youth
was tempered by habitual prudence; and while his mind
was engrossed by ambition, he appeared cold and insensible to the allurements of pleasure. The favour of
the people and soldiers, who had named him as a
worthy candidate for the rank of Cæsar, served only to
exasperate the jealousy of Galerius; and though prudence might restrain him from exercising any open
violence, an absolute monarch is seldom at a loss how
to execute a sure and secret revenge. Every hour increased the danger of Constantine and the anxiety of
his father, who by repeated letters expressed the warmest desire of embracing his son. For some time the
policy of Galerius supplied him with delays and excuses,
but it was impossible long to refuse so natural a request
of his associate without maintaining his refusal by arms.
The permission of the journey was reluctantly granted,

and whatever precautions the emperor might have taken to intercept a return, the consequences of which he with so much reason apprehended, they were effectually disappointed by the incredible diligence of Constantine. Leaving the palace of Nicomedia in the night, he travelled post through Bithynia, Thrace, Dacia, Pannonia, Italy, and, amidst the joyful acclamations of the people, reached the port of Boulogne in the very moment when his father was preparing to embark for Britain.

The British expedition, and an easy victory over the barbarians of Caledonia, were the last exploits of the reign of Constantius. He ended his life in the Imperial palace of York, fifteen months after he had received the title of Augustus and almost fourteen years and a half after he had been promoted to the rank of Cæsar. His death was immediately succeeded by the elevation of Constantine. The ideas of inheritance and succession are so very familiar that the generality of mankind consider them as founded not only in reason but in nature itself. Our imagination readily transfers the same principles from private property to public dominion; and whenever a virtuous father leaves behind him a son whose merit seems to justify the esteem, or even the hopes, of the people, the joint influence of prejudice and of affection operates with irresistible weight. The flower of the western armies had followed Constantius into Britain, and the national troops were reinforced by a numerous body of Alemanni, who obeyed the orders of Crocus, one of their hereditary chieftains.[2] The opinion of their own importance and the assurance that

2. This is perhaps the first instance of a barbarian king who assisted the Roman arms with an independent body of his own subjects. The practice grew familiar and at last became fatal.

Britain, Gaul, and Spain would acquiesce in their nomination were diligently inculcated to the legions by the adherents of Constantine. The soldiers were asked whether they could hesitate a moment between the honour of placing at their head the worthy son of their beloved emperor and the ignominy of tamely expecting the arrival of some obscure stranger, on whom it might please the sovereign of Asia to bestow the armies and provinces of the West? It was insinuated to them that gratitude and liberality held a distinguished place among the virtues of Constantine; nor did that artful prince show himself to the troops till they were prepared to salute him with the names of Augustus and Emperor. The throne was the object of his desires; and had he been less actuated by ambition, it was his only means of safety. He was well acquainted with the character and sentiments of Galerius and sufficiently apprised that, if he wished to live, he must determine to reign. The decent and even obstinate resistance which he chose to affect was contrived to justify his usurpation; nor did he yield to the acclamations of the army till he had provided the proper materials for a letter, which he immediately despatched to the emperor of the East. Constantine informed him of the melancholy event of his father's death, modestly asserted his natural claim to the succession, and respectfully lamented that the affectionate violence of his troops had not permitted him to solicit the Imperial purple in the regular and constitutional manner.

The first emotions of Galerius were those of surprise, disappointment, and rage; and, as he could seldom restrain his passions, he loudly threatened that he would commit to the flames both the letter and the messenger. But his resentment insensibly subsided; and when he recollected the doubtful chance of war, when he had weighed the character and strength of his adversary, he consented to embrace the honourable accommodation which the prudence of Constantine had left open to him. Without either condemning or ratifying the choice of the British army, Galerius accepted the son of his deceased colleague as the sovereign of the provinces beyond the Alps; but he gave him only the title of Cæsar and the fourth rank among the Roman princes, whilst he conferred the vacant place of Augustus on his favourite Severus. The apparent harmony of the empire was still preserved; and Constantine, who already possessed the substance, expected without impatience an opportunity of obtaining the honours of supreme power.

The children of Constantius by his second marriage were six in number, three of either sex, and whose Imperial descent might have solicited a preference over the meaner extraction of the son of Helena. But Constantine was in the thirty-second year of his age, in the full vigour both of mind and body, at the time when the eldest of his brothers could not possibly be more than thirteen years old. His claim of superior merit had been allowed and ratified by the dying emperor. In his last moments Constantius bequeathed to his eldest son the care of the safety as well as greatness of the family, conjuring him to assume both the authority and the sentiments of a father with regard to the children of Theodora. Their liberal education, advantageous marriages, the secure dignity of their lives, and the first honours of the state with which they were invested attest the fraternal affection of Constantine; and as those princes possessed a mild and grateful disposition, they submitted without reluctance to the superiority of his genius and fortune.

II. THE REVOLT OF MAXENTIUS. The ambitious spirit of Galerius was scarcely reconciled to the disappoint-

ment of his views upon the Gallic provinces before the
unexpected loss of Italy wounded his pride as well as
power in a still more sensible part. The long absence
of the emperors had filled Rome with discontent and indignation; and the people gradually discovered that the
preference given to Nicomedia and Milan was not to
be ascribed to the particular inclination of Diocletian,
but to the permanent form of government which he had
instituted. It was in vain that, a few months after his
abdication, his successors dedicated under his name
those magnificent baths whose ruins still supply the
ground as well as the materials for so many churches
and convents. The tranquillity of those elegant recesses
of ease and luxury was disturbed by the impatient
murmurs of the Romans, and a report was insensibly
circulated that the sums expended in erecting those
buildings would soon be required at their hands. About
that time the avarice of Galerius, or perhaps the exigencies of the state, had induced him to make a very
strict and rigorous inquisition into the property of his
subjects for the purpose of a general taxation, both on
their lands and on their persons. A very minute survey
appears to have been taken of their real estates; and
wherever there was the slightest suspicion of concealment, torture was very freely employed to obtain a
sincere declaration of their personal wealth. The privileges which had exalted Italy above the rank of the
provinces were no longer regarded, and the officers of
the revenue already began to number the Roman people
and to settle the proportion of the new taxes.

Even when the spirit of freedom had been utterly
extinguished, the tamest subjects have sometimes ventured to resist an unprecedented invasion of their property; but on this occasion the injury was aggravated
by the insult, and the sense of private interest was

quickened by that of national honour. The conquest
of Macedonia, as we have already observed, had delivered the Roman people from the weight of personal
taxes. Though they had experienced every form of
despotism, they had now enjoyed that exemption near
five hundred years; nor could they patiently brook the
insolence of an Illyrian peasant who, from his distant
residence in Asia, presumed to number Rome among
the tributary cities of his empire. The rising fury of the
people was encouraged by the authority, or at least
the connivance, of the senate; and the feeble remains
of the Prætorian Guards, who had reason to apprehend
their own dissolution, embraced so honourable a pretence and declared their readiness to draw their swords
in the service of their oppressed country. It was the
wish, and it soon became the hope, of every citizen
that, after expelling from Italy their foreign tyrants, they
should elect a prince who by the place of his residence
and by his maxims of government might once more
deserve the title of Roman emperor. The name as well
as the situation of Maxentius determined in his favour
the popular enthusiasm.

Maxentius was the son of the emperor Maximian,
and he had married the daughter of Galerius. His birth
and alliance seemed to offer him the fairest promise of
succeeding to the empire; but his vices and incapacity
procured him the same exclusion from the dignity of
Cæsar which Constantine had deserved by a dangerous
superiority of merit. The policy of Galerius preferred
such associates as would never disgrace the choice, nor
dispute the commands, of their benefactor. An obscure
stranger was therefore raised to the throne of Italy, and
the son of the late emperor of the West was left to
enjoy the luxury of a private fortune in a villa a few
miles distant from the capital The gloomy passions of

his soul, shame, vexation, and rage, were inflamed by envy on the news of Constantine's success; but the hopes of Maxentius revived with the public discontent, and he was easily persuaded to unite his personal injury and pretensions with the cause of the Roman people. Two Prætorian tribunes and a commissary of provisions undertook the management of the conspiracy; and as every order of men was actuated by the same spirit, the immediate event was neither doubtful nor difficult. The præfect of the city and a few magistrates who maintained their fidelity to Severus were massacred by the guards; and Maxentius, invested with the Imperial ornaments, was acknowledged by the applauding senate and people as the protector of the Roman freedom and dignity. It is uncertain whether Maximian was previously acquainted with the conspiracy; but as soon as the standard of rebellion was erected at Rome, the old emperor broke from the retirement, where the authority of Diocletian had condemned him to pass a life of melancholy solitude, and concealed his returning ambition under the disguise of paternal tenderness. At the request of his son and of the senate he condescended to reassume the purple. His ancient dignity, his experience, and his fame in arms added strength as well as reputation to the party of Maxentius.

According to the advice, or rather the orders, of his colleague, the emperor Severus immediately hastened to Rome, in the full confidence that by his unexpected celerity he should easily suppress the tumult of an unwarlike populace commanded by a licentious youth. But he found on his arrival the gates of the city shut against him, the walls filled with men and arms, an experienced general at the head of the rebels, and his own troops without spirit or affection. A large body of Moors deserted to the enemy, allured by the promise of a large donative, and, if it be true that they had been levied by Maximian in his African war, preferring the natural feelings of gratitude to the artificial ties of allegiance. Anulinus, the Prætorian præfect, declared himself in favour of Maxentius and drew after him the most considerable part of the troops accustomed to obey his commands. Rome, according to the expression of an orator, recalled her armies; and the unfortunate Severus, destitute of force and of counsel, retired, or rather fled, with precipitation to Ravenna.

Here he might for some time have been safe. The fortifications of Ravenna were able to resist the attempts, and the morasses that surrounded the town were sufficient to prevent the approach, of the Italian army. The sea, which Severus commanded with a powerful fleet, secured him an inexhaustible supply of provisions, and gave a free entrance to the legions which on the return of spring would advance to his assistance from Illyricum and the East. Maximian, who conducted the siege in person, was soon convinced that he might waste his time and his army in the fruitless enterprise, and that he had nothing to hope either from force or famine. With an art more suitable to the character of Diocletian than to his own, he directed his attack not so much against the walls of Ravenna as against the mind of Severus. The treachery which he had experienced disposed that unhappy prince to distrust the most sincere of his friends and adherents. The emissaries of Maximian easily persuaded his credulity that a conspiracy was formed to betray the town and prevailed upon his fears not to expose himself to the discretion of an irritated conqueror but to accept the faith of an honourable capitulation. He was at first received with humanity and treated with respect. Maximian conducted the captive emperor to Rome and gave him the most solemn assurances that he had secured his life by the resignation of the purple. But Severus could obtain only an easy death and an Imperial funeral. When the sentence was signified to him, the manner of executing it was left to his own choice; he preferred the favourite mode of the ancients, that of opening his veins; and as soon as he expired his body was carried to the sepulchre which had been constructed for the family of Gallienus.

Though the characters of Constantine and Maxentius had very little affinity with each other, their situation and interest were the same, and prudence seemed to require that they should unite their forces against the common enemy. Notwithstanding the superiority of his age and dignity, the indefatigable Maximian passed the Alps and, courting a personal interview with the sovereign of Gaul, carried with him his daughter Fausta as the pledge of the new alliance. The marriage was celebrated at Arles with every circumstance of magnificence; and the ancient colleague of Diocletian, who again asserted his claim to the western empire, conferred on his son-in-law and ally the title of Augustus. By consenting to receive that honour from Maximian, Constantine seemed to embrace the cause of Rome and of the senate; but his professions were ambiguous and his assistance slow and ineffectual. He considered with attention the approaching contest between the masters of Italy and the emperor of the East, and was prepared to consult his own safety or ambition in the event of the war.

The importance of the occasion called for the presence and abilities of Galerius. At the head of a powerful army collected from Illyricum and the East he entered Italy, resolved to revenge the death of Severus and to chastise the rebellious Romans, or, as he expressed his intentions in the furious language of a barbarian, to extirpate the senate and to destroy the people by the sword. But the skill of Maximian had concerted a prudent system of defence. The invader found every place hostile, fortified, and inaccessible; and though he forced his way as far as Narni, within sixty miles of Rome, his dominion in Italy was confined to the narrow limits of his camp. Sensible of the increasing difficulties of his enterprise, the haughty Galerius made the first advances towards a reconciliation and despatched two of his most considerable officers to tempt the Roman princes by the offer of a conference and the declaration of his paternal regard for Maxentius, who might obtain much more from his liberality than he could hope from the doubtful chance of war. The offers of Galerius were rejected with firmness, his perfidious friendship refused with contempt; and it was not long before he discovered that unless he provided for his safety by a timely retreat, he had some reason to apprehend the fate of Severus. The wealth which the Romans defended against his rapacious tyranny they freely contributed for his destruction. The name of Maximian, the popular arts of his son, the secret distribution of large sums, and the promise of still more liberal rewards checked the ardour and corrupted the fidelity of the Illyrian legions; and when Galerius at length gave the signal of the retreat, it was with some difficulty that he could prevail on his veterans not to desert a banner which had so often conducted them to victory and honour.[3]

The legions of Galerius exhibited a very melancholy proof of their disposition by the ravages which they committed in their retreat. They murdered, they ravished, they plundered, they drove away the flocks and

3. *Editor's note:* Gibbon derides, in a short passage deleted here, the improbable report that Galerius and his troops withdrew in awe at the size and magnificence of Rome.

herds of the Italians; they burned the villages through which they passed, and they endeavoured to destroy the country which it had not been in their power to subdue. During the whole march Maxentius hung on their rear, but he very prudently declined a general engagement with those brave and desperate veterans. His father had undertaken a second journey into Gaul, with the hope of persuading Constantine, who had assembled an army on the frontier, to join the pursuit and to complete the victory. But the actions of Constantine were guided by reason, and not by resentment. He persisted in the wise resolution of maintaining a balance of power in the divided empire, and he no longer hated Galerius when that aspiring prince had ceased to be an object of terror.

The mind of Galerius was the most susceptible of the sterner passions, but it was not, however, incapable of a sincere and lasting friendship. Licinius, whose manners as well as character were not unlike his own, seems to have engaged both his affection and esteem. Their intimacy had commenced in the happier period, perhaps, of their youth and obscurity. It had been cemented by the freedom and dangers of a military life; they had advanced almost by equal steps through the successive honours of the service; and as soon as Galerius was invested with the Imperial dignity he seems to have conceived the design of raising his companion to the same rank with himself. During the short period of his prosperity he considered the rank of Cæsar as unworthy of the age and merit of Licinius and rather chose to reserve for him the place of Constantius and the empire of the West. While the emperor was employed in the Italian war he entrusted his friend with the defence of the Danube; and immediately after his return from that unfortunate expedition he invested

Licinius with the vacant purple of Severus, resigning to his immediate command the provinces of Illyricum.

The news of his promotion was no sooner carried into the East than Maximin, who governed, or rather oppressed, the countries of Egypt and Syria, betrayed his envy and discontent, disdained the inferior name of Cæsar, and, notwithstanding the prayers as well as arguments of Galerius, exacted almost by violence the equal title of Augustus. For the first, and indeed for the last, time the Roman world was administered by six emperors. In the West, Constantine and Maxentius affected to reverence their father Maximian. In the East, Licinius and Maximin honoured with more real consideration their benefactor Galerius. The opposition of interest and the memory of a recent war divided the empire into two great hostile powers; but their mutual fears produced an apparent tranquillity and even a feigned reconciliation, till the death of Maximian and more particularly of Galerius, the elder princes, gave a new direction to the views and passions of their surviving associates.

When Maximian had reluctantly abdicated the empire the venal orators of the times applauded his philosophic moderation. When his ambition excited, or at least encouraged, a civil war they returned thanks to his generous patriotism and gently censured that love of ease and retirement which had withdrawn him from the public service. But it was impossible that minds like those of Maximian and his son could long possess in harmony an undivided power. Maxentius considered himself as the legal sovereign of Italy, elected by the Roman senate and people; nor would he endure the control of his father, who arrogantly declared that by *his* name and abilities the rash youth had been established on the throne. The cause was solemnly pleaded

before the Prætorian Guards; and those troops, who
dreaded the severity of the old emperor, espoused the
party of Maxentius. The life and freedom of Maximian
were, however, respected, and he retired from Italy
into Illyricum, affecting to lament his past conduct and
secretly contriving new mischiefs. But Galerius, who was
well acquainted with his character, soon obliged him
to leave his dominions, and the last refuge of the disappointed Maximian was the court of his son-in-law
Constantine. He was received with respect by that artful prince and with the appearance of filial tenderness
by the empress Fausta. That he might remove every
suspicion he resigned the Imperial purple a second
time, professing himself at length convinced of the vanity of greatness and ambition.

Had he persevered in this resolution he might have
ended his life with less dignity, indeed, than in his first
retirement; yet, however, with comfort and reputation.
But the near prospect of a throne brought back to his
remembrance the state from whence he was fallen; and
he resolved, by a desperate effort, either to reign or
to perish. An incursion of the Franks had summoned
Constantine, with a part of his army, to the banks of
the Rhine; the remainder of the troops was stationed
in the southern provinces of Gaul, which lay exposed
to the enterprises of the Italian emperor; and a considerable treasure was deposited in the city of Arles. Maximian either craftily invented or hastily credited a vain
report of the death of Constantine. Without hesitation
he ascended the throne, seized the treasure, and, scat-
tering it with his accustomed profusion among the soldiers, endeavoured to awake in their minds the memory
of his ancient dignity and exploits. Before he could establish his authority, or finish the negotiation which he
appears to have entered into with his son Maxentius,

the celerity of Constantine defeated all his hopes. On the first news of his perfidy and ingratitude, that prince returned by rapid marches from the Rhine to the Saône, embarked on the last-mentioned river at Chalons, and, at Lyons trusting himself to the rapidity of the Rhone, arrived at the gates of Arles with a military force which it was impossible for Maximian to resist and which scarcely permitted him to take refuge in the neighbouring city of Marseilles. The narrow neck of land which joined that place to the continent was fortified against the besiegers, whilst the sea was open either for the escape of Maximian or for the succours of Maxentius, if the latter should choose to disguise his invasion of Gaul under the honourable pretence of defending a distressed or, as he might allege, an injured father.

Apprehensive of the fatal consequences of delay, Constantine gave orders for an immediate assault; but the scaling-ladders were found too short for the height of the walls, and Marseilles might have sustained as long a siege as it formerly did against the arms of Cæsar if the garrison, conscious either of their fault or of their danger, had not purchased their pardon by delivering up the city and the person of Maximian. A secret but irrevocable sentence of death was pronounced against the usurper; he obtained only the same favour which he had indulged to Severus, and it was published to the world that, oppressed by the remorse of his repeated crimes, he strangled himself with his own hands. After he had lost the assistance and disdained the moderate counsels of Diocletian, the second period of his active life was a series of public calamities and personal mortifications, which were terminated in about three years by an ignominious death. He deserved his fate; but we should find more reason to applaud the humanity of Constantine if he had spared an old man, the benefactor of his father and the father of his wife. During the whole of this melancholy transaction, it appears that Fausta sacrificed the sentiments of nature to her conjugal duties.

The last years of Galerius were less shameful and unfortunate; and though he had filled with more glory the subordinate station of Cæsar than the superior rank of Augustus, he preserved till the moment of his death the first place among the princes of the Roman world. He survived his retreat from Italy about four years; and wisely relinquishing his views of universal empire, he devoted the remainder of his life to the enjoyment of pleasure and to the execution of some works of public utility, among which we may distinguish the discharging into the Danube the superfluous waters of the lake Pelso and the cutting down the immense forests that encompassed it—an operation worthy of a monarch, since it gave an extensive country to the agriculture of his Pannonian subjects. His death was occasioned by a very painful and lingering disorder. His body, swelled by an intemperate course of life to an unwieldy corpulence, was covered with ulcers and devoured by innumerable swarms of those insects who have given their name to a most loathsome disease; but as Galerius had offended a very zealous and powerful party among his subjects, his sufferings, instead of exciting their compassion, have been celebrated as the visible effects of divine justice.[4]

He had no sooner expired in his palace of Nicomedia than the two emperors who were indebted for their purple to his favour began to collect their forces, with

4. If any (like the late Dr. Jortin) still delight in recording the wonderful deaths of the persecutors, I would recommend to their perusal an admirable passage of Grotius concerning the last illness of Philip II of Spain.

the intention either of disputing or of dividing the dominions which he had left without a master. They were persuaded, however, to desist from the former design and to agree in the latter. The provinces of Asia fell to the share of Maximin, and those of Europe augmented the portion of Licinius. The Hellespont and the Thracian Bosphorus formed their mutual boundary, and the banks of those narrow seas, which flowed in the midst of the Roman world, were covered with soldiers, with arms, and with fortifications. The deaths of Maximian and of Galerius reduced the number of emperors to four. The sense of their true interest soon connected Licinius and Constantine; a secret alliance was concluded between Maximin and Maxentius; and their unhappy subjects expected with terror the bloody consequences of their inevitable dissensions, which were no longer restrained by the fear or the respect which they had entertained for Galerius.[5]

The virtues of Constantine were rendered more illustrious by the vices of Maxentius. Whilst the Gallic provinces enjoyed as much happiness as the condition of the times was capable of receiving, Italy and Africa groaned under the dominion of a tyrant as contemptible as he was odious. The zeal of flattery and faction has indeed too frequently sacrificed the reputation of the vanquished to the glory of their successful rivals; but even those writers who have revealed with the most freedom and pleasure the faults of Constantine unanimously confess that Maxentius was cruel, rapacious, and profligate. He had the good fortune to suppress a slight rebellion in Africa. The goverer and a few adherents

5. *Editor's note:* A brief passage concerning Constantine's partial remission of the taxes of the Gallic city of Autun is omitted at this point.

had been guilty; the province suffered for their crime. The flourishing cities of Cirtha and Carthage, and the whole extent of that fertile country, were wasted by fire and sword. The abuse of victory was followed by the abuse of law and justice. A formidable army of sycophants and delators invaded Africa; the rich and the noble were easily convicted of a connection with the rebels; and those among them who experienced the emperor's clemency were only punished by the confiscation of their estates. So signal a victory was celebrated by a magnificent triumph, and Maxentius exposed to the eyes of the people the spoils and captives of a Roman province.

The state of the capital was no less deserving of compassion than that of Africa. The wealth of Rome supplied an inexhaustible fund for his vain and prodigal expenses, and the ministers of his revenue were skilled in the arts of rapine. It was under his reign that the method of exacting a *free gift* from the senators was first invented; and as the sum was insensibly increased, the pretences of levying it—a victory, a birth, a marriage, or an Imperial consulship—were proportionately multiplied. Maxentius had imbibed the same implacable aversion to the senate which had characterized most of the former tyrants of Rome; nor was it possible for his ungrateful temper to forgive the generous fidelity which had raised him to the throne and supported him against all his enemies. The lives of the senators were exposed to his jealous suspicions, the dishonour of their wives and daughters heightened the gratification of his sensual passions. It may be presumed that an Imperial lover was seldom reduced to sigh in vain; but whenever persuasion proved ineffectual, he had recourse to violence; and there remains one memorable example of a noble matron who preserved her chastity by a voluntary death.[6]

The soldiers were the only order of men whom he appeared to respect or studied to please. He filled Rome and Italy with armed troops, connived at their tumults, suffered them with impunity to plunder and even to massacre the defenceless people; and indulging them in the same licentiousness which their emperor enjoyed, Maxentius often bestowed on his military favourites the splendid villa or the beautiful wife of a senator. A prince of such a character, alike incapable of governing either in peace or in war, might purchase the support, but he could never obtain the esteem, of the army. Yet his pride was equal to his other vices. Whilst he passed his indolent life either within the walls of his palace or in the neighbouring gardens of Sallust, he was repeatedly heard to declare that *he alone* was emperor and that the other princes were no more than his lieutenants, on whom he had devolved the defence of the frontier provinces that he might enjoy without interruption the elegant luxury of the capital. Rome, which had so long regretted the absence, lamented during the six years of his reign the presence of her sovereign.

Though Constantine might view the conduct of Maxentius with abhorrence and the situation of the Romans with compassion, we have no reason to presume that he would have taken up arms to punish the one or to relieve the other. But the tyrant of Italy rashly ventured to provoke a formidable enemy whose ambition had been hitherto restrained by considerations of prudence

6. The virtuous matron who stabbed herself to escape the violence of Maxentius was a Christian, wife to the præfect of the city, and her name was Sophronia. It still remains a question among the casuists whether, on such occasions, suicide is justifiable.

rather than by principles of justice. After the death of Maximian his titles, according to the established custom, had been erased and his statues thrown down with ignominy. His son, who had persecuted and deserted him when alive, affected to display the most pious regard for his memory and gave orders that a similar treatment should be immediately inflicted on all the statues that had been erected in Italy and Africa to the honour of Constantine. That wise prince, who sincerely wished to decline a war, with the difficulty and importance of which he was sufficiently acquainted, at first dissembled the insult and sought for redress by the milder expedients of negotiation, till he was convinced that the hostile and ambitious designs of the Italian emperor made it necessary for him to arm in his own defence. Maxentius, who openly avowed his pretensions to the whole monarchy of the West, had already prepared a very considerable force to invade the Gallic provinces on the side of Rhætia; and though he could not expect any assistance from Licinius, he was flattered with the hope that the legions of Illyricum, allured by his presents and promises, would desert the standard of that prince and unanimously declare themselves his soldiers and subjects. Constantine no longer hesitated. He had deliberated with caution, he acted with vigour. He gave a private audience to the ambassadors who, in the name of the senate and people, conjured him to deliver Rome from a detested tyrant; and without regarding the timid remonstrances of his council he resolved to prevent the enemy and to carry the war into the heart of Italy.

The enterprise was as full of danger as of glory, and the unsuccessful event of two former invasions was sufficient to inspire the most serious apprehensions. The veteran troops who revered the name of Maximian had embraced in both those wars the party of his son and

were now restrained by a sense of honour, as well as of
interest, from entertaining an idea of a second desertion.
Maxentius, who considered the Prætorian Guards as the
firmest defence of his throne, had increased them to
their ancient establishment; and they composed, including the rest of the Italians who were enlisted into his
service, a formidable body of fourscore thousand men.
Forty thousand Moors and Carthaginians had been
raised since the reduction of Africa. Even Sicily furnished its proportion of troops; and the armies of Maxentius amounted to one hundred and seventy thousand
foot and eighteen thousand horse. The wealth of Italy
supplied the expenses of the war; and the adjacent
provinces were exhausted to form immense magazines
of corn and every other kind of provisions.

The whole force of Constantine consisted of ninety
thousand foot and eight thousand horse; and as the defence of the Rhine required an extraordinary attention
during the absence of the emperor, it was not in his
power to employ above half his troops in the Italian
expedition, unless he sacrificed the public safety to his
private quarrel. At the head of about forty thousand
soldiers he marched to encounter an enemy whose numbers were at least four times superior to his own. But
the armies of Rome, placed at a secure distance from
danger, were enervated by indulgence and luxury. Habituated to the baths and theatres of Rome, they took
the field with reluctance, and were chiefly composed
of veterans who had almost forgotten, or of new levies
who had never acquired, the use of arms and the practice of war. The hardy legions of Gaul had long defended the frontiers of the empire against the barbarians
of the North; and in the performance of that laborious
service their valour was exercised and their discipline
confirmed. There appeared the same difference between

the leaders as between the armies. Caprice or flattery had tempted Maxentius with the hopes of conquest; but these aspiring hopes soon gave way to the habits of pleasure and the consciousness of his inexperience. The intrepid mind of Constantine had been trained from his earliest youth to war, to action, and to military command.

When Hannibal marched from Gaul into Italy he was obliged first to discover, and then to open, a way over mountains and through savage nations that had never yielded a passage to a regular army. The Alps were then guarded by nature; they are now fortified by art. Citadels, constructed with no less skill than labour and expense, command every avenue into the plain, and on that side render Italy almost inaccessible to the enemies of the king of Sardinia. But in the course of the intermediate period the generals who have attempted the passage have seldom experienced any difficulty or resistance. In the age of Constantine the peasants of the mountains were civilized and obedient subjects, the country was plentifully stocked with provisions, and the stupendous highways which the Romans had carried over the Alps opened several communications between Gaul and Italy. Constantine preferred the road of the Cottian Alps, or, as it is now called, of Mount Cenis, and led his troops with such active diligence that he descended into the plain of Piedmont before the court of Maxentius had received any certain intelligence of his departure from the banks of the Rhine. The city of Susa, however, which is situated at the foot of Mount Cenis, was surrounded with walls and provided with a garrison sufficiently numerous to check the progress of an invader; but the impatience of Constantine's troops disdained the tedious forms of a siege. The same day that they appeared before Susa they applied fire to the gates and ladders to the walls; and, mounting to the assault amidst a shower of stones and arrows, they entered the place sword in hand and cut in pieces the greatest part of the garrison. The flames were extinguished by the care of Constantine, and the remains of Susa preserved from total destruction.

About forty miles from thence a more severe contest awaited him. A numerous army of Italians was assembled, under the lieutenants of Maxentius, in the plains of Turin. Its principal strength consisted in a species of heavy cavalry, which the Romans, since the decline of their discipline, had borrowed from the nations of the East. The horses as well as the men were clothed in complete armour, the joints of which were artfully adapted to the motions of their bodies. The aspect of this cavalry was formidable, their weight almost irresistible; and as, on this occasion, their generals had drawn them up in a compact column or wedge with a sharp point and with spreading flanks, they flattered themselves that they should easily break and trample down the army of Constantine. They might, perhaps, have succeeded in their design had not their experienced adversary embraced the same method of defence which in similar circumstances had been practised by Aurelian. The skilful evolutions of Constantine divided and baffled this massy column of cavalry. The troops of Maxentius fled in confusion towards Turin; and as the gates of the city were shut against them, very few escaped the sword of the victorious pursuers. By this important service Turin deserved to experience the clemency and even favour of the conqueror. He made his entry into the Imperial palace of Milan, and almost all the cities of Italy between the Alps and the Po not only acknowledged the power but embraced with zeal the party of Constantine.

From Milan to Rome the Æmilian and Flaminian highways offered an easy march of about four hundred miles; but though Constantine was impatient to encounter the tyrant, he prudently directed his operations against another army of Italians, who by their strength and position might either oppose his progress or, in case of a misfortune, might intercept his retreat. Ruricius Pompeianus, a general distinguished by his valour and ability, had under his command the city of Verona and all the troops that were stationed in the province of Venetia. As soon as he was informed that Constantine was advancing towards him, he detached a large body of cavalry, which was defeated in an engagement near Brescia and pursued by the Gallic legions as far as the gates of Verona.

The necessity, the importance, and the difficulties of the siege of Verona immediately presented themselves to the sagacious mind of Constantine. The city was accessible only by a narrow peninsula towards the west, as the other three sides were surrounded by the Adige, a rapid river which covered the province of Venetia, from whence the besieged derived an inexhaustible supply of men and provisions. It was not without great difficulty, and after several fruitless attempts, that Constantine found means to pass the river at some distance above the city, and in a place where the torrent was less violent. He then encompassed Verona with strong lines, pushed his attacks with prudent vigour, and repelled a desperate sally of Pompeianus. That intrepid general, when he had used every means of defence that the strength of the place or that of the garrison could afford, secretly escaped from Verona, anxious not for his own but for the public safety. With indefatigable diligence he soon collected an army sufficient either to meet Constantine in the field or to attack him if he obsti-

nately remained within his lines. The emperor, attentive
to the motions and informed of the approach of so
formidable an enemy, left a part of his legions to continue the operations of the siege whilst, at the head of
those troops on whose valour and fidelity he more particularly depended, he advanced in person to engage the
general of Maxentius.

The army of Gaul was drawn up in two lines, according to the usual practice of war; but their experienced
leader, perceiving that the numbers of the Italians far
exceeded his own, suddenly changed his disposition and,
reducing the second, extended the front of his first line
to a just proportion with that of the enemy. Such evolutions, which only veteran troops can execute without
confusion in a moment of danger, commonly prove decisive; but as this engagement began towards the close
of the day and was contested with great obstinacy during the whole night, there was less room for the conduct
of the generals than for the courage of the soldiers.

The return of light displayed the victory of Constantine and a field of carnage covered with many
thousands of the vanquished Italians. Their general,
Pompeianus, was found among the slain; Verona immediately surrendered at discretion, and the garrison was
made prisoners of war. When the officers of the victorious army congratulated their master on this important success, they ventured to add some respectful
complaints, of such a nature, however, as the most
jealous monarchs will listen to without displeasure. They
represented to Constantine that, not contented with per-
forming all the duties of a commander, he had exposed
his own person with an excess of valour which almost
degenerated into rashness; and they conjured him for
the future to pay more regard to the preservation of a

life in which the safety of Rome and of the empire was involved.

While Constantine signalized his conduct and valour in the field, the sovereign of Italy appeared insensible of the calamities and danger of a civil war which raged in the heart of his dominions. Pleasure was still the only business of Maxentius. Concealing, or at least attempting to conceal, from the public knowledge the misfortunes of his arms, he indulged himself in a vain confidence which deferred the remedies of the approaching evil without deferring the evil itself. The rapid progress of Constantine was scarcely sufficient to awaken him from this fatal security; he flattered himself that his well-known liberality and the majesty of the Roman name, which had already delivered him from two invasions, would dissipate with the same facility the rebellious army of Gaul. The officers of experience and ability who had served under the banners of Maximian were at length compelled to inform his effeminate son of the imminent danger to which he was reduced, and, with a freedom that at once surprised and convinced him, to urge the necessity of preventing his ruin by a vigorous exertion of his remaining power.

The resources of Maxentius, both of men and money, were still considerable. The Prætorian Guards felt how strongly their own interest and safety were connected with his cause; and a third army was soon collected, more numerous than those which had been lost in the battles of Turin and Verona. It was far from the intention of the emperor to lead his troops in person. A stranger to the exercises of war, he trembled at the apprehension of so dangerous a contest; and as fear is commonly superstitious, he listened with melancholy attention to the rumours of omens and presages which seemed to menace his life and empire. Shame at length supplied the place of courage and forced him to take the field. He was unable to sustain the contempt of the Roman people. The circus resounded with their indignant clamours, and they tumultuously besieged the gates of the palace, reproaching the pusillanimity of their indolent sovereign and celebrating the heroic spirit of Constantine. Before Maxentius left Rome he consulted the Sibylline books. The guardians of these ancient oracles were as well versed in the arts of this world as they were ignorant of the secrets of fate; and they returned him a very prudent answer, which might adapt itself to the event and secure their reputation whatever should be the chance of arms.

The celerity of Constantine's march has been compared to the rapid conquest of Italy by the first of the Cæsars; nor is the flattering parallel repugnant to the truth of history, since no more than fifty-eight days elapsed between the surrender of Verona and the final decision of the war. Constantine had always apprehended that the tyrant would consult the dictates of fear and perhaps of prudence, and that, instead of risking his last hopes on a general engagement, he would shut himself up within the walls of Rome. His ample magazines secured him against the danger of famine; and as the situation of Constantine admitted not of delay, he might have been reduced to the sad necessity of destroying with fire and sword the Imperial city, the noblest reward of his victory, and the deliverance of which had been the motive, or rather indeed the pretence, of the civil war. It was with equal surprise and pleasure that, on his arrival at a place called Saxa Rubra, about nine miles from Rome, he discovered the army of Maxentius prepared to give him battle. Their long front filled a very spacious plain, and their deep array reached

to the banks of the Tiber, which covered their rear and
forbade their retreat.

We are informed, and we may believe, that Constantine disposed his troops with consummate skill, and
that he chose for himself the post of honour and danger.
Distinguished by the splendour of his arms, he charged
in person the cavalry of his rival; and his irresistible
attack determined the fortune of the day. The cavalry
of Maxentius was principally composed either of unwieldy cuirassiers or of light Moors and Numidians.
They yielded to the vigour of the Gallic horse, which
possessed more activity than the one, more firmness than
the other. The defeat of the two wings left the infantry
without any protection on its flanks, and the undisciplined Italians fled without reluctance from the standard
of a tyrant whom they had always hated and whom they
no longer feared. The Prætorians, conscious that their
offences were beyond the reach of mercy, were animated
by revenge and despair. Notwithstanding their repeated
efforts, those brave veterans were unable to recover the
victory; they obtained, however, an honourable death;
and it was observed that their bodies covered the same
ground which had been occupied by their ranks. The
confusion then became general, and the dismayed
troops of Maxentius, pursued by an implacable enemy,
rushed by thousands into the deep and rapid stream of
the Tiber. The emperor himself attempted to escape
back into the city over the Milvian bridge, but the
crowds which pressed together through that narrow
passage forced him into the river, where he was immediately drowned by the weight of his armour. His body,
which had sunk very deep into the mud, was found with
some difficulty the next day. The sight of his head, when
it was exposed to the eyes of the people, convinced them
of their deliverance and admonished them to receive

with acclamations of loyalty and gratitude the fortunate
Constantine, who thus achieved by his valour and ability
the most splendid enterprise of his life.[7]

Before Constantine marched into Italy he had secured
the friendship, or at least the neutrality, of Licinius, the
Illyrian emperor. He had promised his sister Constantia
in marriage to that prince; but the celebration of the
nuptials was deferred till after the conclusion of the war,
and the interview of the two emperors at Milan, which
was appointed for that purpose, appeared to cement the
union of their families and interests. In the midst of the
public festivity they were suddenly obliged to take leave
of each other. An inroad of the Franks summoned Constantine to the Rhine, and the hostile approach of the
sovereign of Asia demanded the immediate presence of
Licinius. Maximin had been the secret ally of Maxentius,
and, without being discouraged by his fate, he resolved
to try the fortune of a civil war. He moved out of Syria
towards the frontiers of Bithynia in the depth of winter.
The season was severe and tempestuous; great numbers
of men as well as horses perished in the snow; and as
the roads were broken up by incessant rains, he was
obliged to leave behind him a considerable part of the
heavy baggage, which was unable to follow the rapidity
of his forced marches. By this extraordinary effort of
diligence he arrived with a harassed but formidable
army on the banks of the Thracian Bosphorus before
the lieutenants of Licinius were apprised of his hostile
intentions. Byzantium surrendered to the power of Max-

7. *Editor's note:* Constantine's three major steps after his
victory are described in a section here omitted: he acted with
comparative clemency towards the adherents of Maxentius;
he dispersed forever the Prætorian Guards, thereby leaving
Rome a helpless and impotent capital; and he made permanent the heavy taxes which Maxentius had exacted from the
senatorial class under the guise of a free gift.

imin after a siege of eleven days. He was detained some days under the walls of Heraclea; and he had no sooner taken possession of that city than he was alarmed by the intelligence that Licinius had pitched his camp at the distance of only eighteen miles. After a fruitless negotiation, in which the two princes attempted to seduce the fidelity of each other's adherents, they had recourse to arms.

The emperor of the East commanded a disciplined and veteran army of above seventy thousand men; and Licinius, who had collected about thirty thousand Illyrians, was at first oppressed by the superiority of numbers. His military skill and the firmness of his troops restored the day and obtained a decisive victory. The incredible speed which Maximin exerted in his flight is much more celebrated than his prowess in the battle. Twenty-four hours afterwards he was seen pale, trembling, and without his Imperial ornaments at Nicomedia, one hundred and sixty miles from the place of his defeat. The wealth of Asia was yet unexhausted; and though the flower of his veterans had fallen in the late action he had still power, if he could obtain time, to draw very numerous levies from Syria and Egypt. But he survived his misfortune only three or four months. His death, which happened at Tarsus, was variously ascribed to despair, to poison, and to the divine justice. As Maximin was alike destitute of abilities and of virtue, he was lamented neither by the people nor by the soldiers. The provinces of the East, delivered from the terrors of civil war, cheerfully acknowledged the authority of Licinius.[8]

8. *Editor's note:* Licinius's cruelty in disposing of Maximin's family, as well as anyone else who might potentially threaten him (including the wife and daughter of Diocletian), is related in a brief passage omitted here.

The Roman world was now divided between Constantine and Licinius, the former of whom was master of the West, and the latter of the East. It might perhaps have been expected that the conquerors, fatigued with civil war and connected by a private as well as public alliance, would have renounced, or at least would have suspended, any further designs of ambition. And yet a year had scarcely elapsed after the death of Maximin before the victorious emperors turned their arms against each other. The genius, the success, and the aspiring temper of Constantine may seem to mark him out as the aggressor; but the perfidious character of Licinius justifies the most unfavourable suspicions, and by the faint light which history reflects on this transaction we may discover a conspiracy fomented by his arts against the authority of his colleague. Constantine had lately given his sister Anastasia in marriage to Bassianus, a man of a considerable family and fortune, and had elevated his new kinsman to the rank of Cæsar. According to the system of government instituted by Diocletian, Italy, and perhaps Africa, was designed for his department in the empire. But the performance of the promised favour was either attended with so much delay or accompanied with so many unequal conditions that the fidelity of Bassianus was alienated rather than secured by the honourable distinction which he had obtained. His nomination had been ratified by the consent of Licinius; and that artful prince, by the means of his emissaries, soon contrived to enter into a secret and dangerous correspondence with the new Cæsar, to irritate his discontents, and to urge him to the rash enterprise of extorting by violence what he might in vain solicit from the justice of Constantine. But the vigilant emperor discovered the conspiracy before it was ripe for execution; and after solemnly renouncing the alliance of Bassianus, despoiled him of the purple and inflicted the deserved punishment on his treason and ingratitude. The haughty refusal of Licinius, when he was required to deliver up the criminals who had taken refuge in his dominions, confirmed the suspicions already entertained of his perfidy; and the indignities offered at Æmona, on the frontiers of Italy, to the statues of Constantine became the signal of discord between the two princes.

The first battle was fought near Cibalis, a city of Pánnonia, situated on the river Save, about fifty miles above Sirmium. From the inconsiderable forces which in this important contest two such powerful monarchs brought into the field, it may be inferred that the one was suddenly provoked and that the other was unexpectedly surprised. The emperor of the West had only twenty thousand, and the sovereign of the East no more than five-and-thirty thousand, men. The inferiority of number was, however, compensated by the advantage of the ground. Constantine had taken post in a defile about half a mile in breadth, between a steep hill and a deep morass, and in that situation he steadily expected and repulsed the first attack of the enemy. He pursued his success and advanced into the plain. But the veteran legions of Illyricum rallied under the standard of a leader who had been trained to arms in the school of Probus and Diocletian. The missile weapons on both sides were soon exhausted; the two armies, with equal valour, rushed to a closer engagement of swords and spears; and the doubtful contest had already lasted from the dawn of the day to a late hour of the evening when the right wing, which Constantine led in person, made a vigorous and decisive charge. The judicious retreat of Licinius saved the remainder of his troops from a total defeat; but when he computed his loss, which amounted to more than twenty thousand men, he thought it unsafe to pass the night in the presence of an active and victorious enemy. Abandoning his camp and magazines, he marched away with secrecy and diligence at the head of the greatest part of his cavalry and was soon removed beyond the danger of a pursuit. His diligence preserved his wife, his son, and his treasures, which he had deposited at Sirmium. Licinius passed through that city and, breaking down the bridge on the Save, hastened to collect a new army in Dacia and Thrace. In his flight he bestowed the precarious title of Cæsar on Valens, his general of the Illyrian frontier.

The plain of Mardia in Thrace was the theatre of a second battle no less obstinate and bloody than the former. The troops on both sides displayed the same valour and discipline; and the victory was once more decided by the superior abilities of Constantine, who directed a body of five thousand men to gain an advantageous height from whence, during the heat of the action, they attacked the rear of the enemy and made a very considerable slaughter. The troops of Licinius, however, presenting a double front, still maintained their ground till the approach of night put an end to the combat and secured their retreat towards the mountains of Macedonia. The loss of two battles and of his bravest veterans reduced the fierce spirit of Licinius to sue for peace. His ambassador, Mistrianus, was admitted to the audience of Constantine; he expatiated on the common topics of moderation and humanity, which are so familiar to the eloquence of the vanquished; represented in the most insinuating language that the event of the war was still doubtful, whilst its inevitable calamities were alike pernicious to both the contending parties; and declared that he was authorized to propose a lasting and honourable peace in the name of the *two* emperors his masters. Constantine received the mention of Valens with indignation and contempt. "It was not for such a purpose," he sternly replied, "that we have advanced from the shores of the western ocean in an uninterrupted course of combats and victories, that, after rejecting an ungrateful kinsman, we should accept for our colleague a contemptible slave. The abdication of Valens is the first article of the treaty."

It was necessary to accept this humiliating condition; and the unhappy Valens, after a reign of a few days, was deprived of the purple and of his life. As soon as this obstacle was removed, the tranquillity of the Roman world was easily restored. The successive defeats of Licinius had ruined his forces, but they had displayed his courage and abilities. His situation was almost desperate, but the efforts of despair are sometimes formidable, and the good sense of Constantine preferred a great and certain advantage to a third trial of the chance of arms. He consented to leave his rival, or, as he again styled Licinius, his friend and brother, in the possession of Thrace, Asia Minor, Syria, and Egypt; but the provinces of Pannonia, Dalmatia, Dacia, Macedonia, and Greece were yielded to the western empire, and the dominions of Constantine now extended from the confines of Caledonia to the extremity of Peloponnesus. It was stipulated by the same treaty that three royal youths, the sons of the emperors, should be called to the hopes of the succession. Crispus and the young Constantine were soon afterwards declared Cæsars in the West, while the younger Licinius was invested with the same dignity in the East. In this double proportion of honours the conqueror asserted the superiority of his arms and power.

The reconciliation of Constantine and Licinius, though it was embittered by resentment and jealousy, by the remembrance of recent injuries, and by the apprehension of future dangers, maintained above eight years the tranquillity of the Roman world.[9] The civil administration was, however, sometimes interrupted by the military defence of the empire. Crispus, a youth of the most amiable character, who had received with the title of Cæsar the command of the Rhine, distinguished his conduct as well as valour in several victories over the Franks and Alemanni and taught the barbarians of that frontier to dread the eldest son of Constantine and the grandson of Constantius. The emperor himself had assumed the more difficult and important province of the Danube. The Goths, who in the time of Claudius and Aurelian had felt the weight of the Roman arms, respected the power of the empire even in the midst of its intestine divisions. But the strength of that warlike nation was now restored by a peace of near fifty years; a new generation had arisen, who no longer remembered the misfortunes of ancient days; the Sarmatians of the lake Mæotis followed the Gothic standard either as subjects or as allies, and their united force was poured upon the countries of Illyricum. Campona, Margus, and Bononia appear to have been the scenes of several memorable sieges and battles; and though Constantine encountered a very obstinate resistance, he prevailed at length in the contest, and the Goths were compelled to purchase an ignominious retreat by restoring the booty

9. *Editor's note:* A short section deleted here mentions two unusual laws promulgated by Constantine during this period: a law offering public financial assistance to families who might otherwise follow the common practice, in those distraught times, of abandoning or killing their newborn children; and a law against rape and even seduction, which imposed such brutal and severe punishments as burning alive, being torn by wild beasts in the amphitheatre, having melted lead poured down the throat, etc.

and prisoners which they had taken. Nor was this advantage sufficient to satisfy the indignation of the emperor. He resolved to chastise as well as to repulse the insolent barbarians who had dared to invade the territories of Rome. At the head of his legions he passed the Danube, after repairing the bridge which had been constructed by Trajan, penetrated into the strongest recesses of Dacia, and, when he had inflicted a severe revenge, condescended to give peace to the suppliant Goths on condition that, as often as they were required, they should supply his armies with a body of forty thousand soldiers. Exploits like these were no doubt honourable to Constantine and beneficial to the state; but it may surely be questioned whether they can justify the exaggerated assertion of Eusebius that *all Scythia*, as far as the extremity of the North, divided as it was into so many names and nations of the most various and savage manners, had been added by his victorious arms to the Roman empire.

In this exalted state of glory it was impossible that Constantine should any longer endure a partner in the empire. Confiding in the superiority of his genius and military power, he determined, without any previous injury, to exert them for the destruction of Licinius, whose advanced age and unpopular vices seemed to offer a very easy conquest. But the old emperor, awakened by the approaching danger, deceived the expectations of his friends as well as of his enemies. Calling forth that spirit and those abilities by which he had deserved the friendship of Galerius and the Imperial purple, he prepared himself for the contest, collected the forces of the East, and soon filled the plains of Hadrianople with his troops and the Straits of the Hellespont with his fleet. The army consisted of one hundred and fifty thousand foot and fifteen thousand horse; and as the cavalry was drawn for the most part from Phrygia and Cappadocia, we may conceive a more favourable opinion of the beauty of the horses than of the courage and dexterity of their riders. The fleet was composed of three hundred and fifty galleys of three ranks of oars. An hundred and thirty of these were furnished by Egypt and the adjacent coast of Africa; an hundred and ten sailed from the ports of Phœnicia and the isle of Cyprus; and the maritime countries of Bithynia, Ionia, and Caria were likewise obliged to provide an hundred and ten galleys.

The troops of Constantine were ordered to rendezvous at Thessalonica; they amounted to above an hundred and twenty thousand horse and foot. Their emperor was satisfied with their martial appearance, and his army contained more soldiers, though fewer men, than that of his eastern competitor. The legions of Constantine were levied in the warlike provinces of Europe; action had confirmed their discipline, victory had elevated their hopes; and there were among them a great number of veterans who, after seventeen glorious campaigns under the same leader, prepared themselves to deserve an honourable dismission by a last effort of their valour. But the naval preparations of Constantine were in every respect much inferior to those of Licinius. The maritime cities of Greece sent their respective quotas of men and ships to the celebrated harbour of Piræus, and their united forces consisted of no more than two hundred small vessels—a very feeble armament, if it is compared with those formidable fleets which were equipped and maintained by the republic of Athens during the Peloponnesian war. Since Italy was no longer the seat of government, the naval establishments of Misenum and Ravenna had been gradually neglected; and as the shipping and mariners of the em-

pire were supported by commerce rather than by war,
it was natural that they should the most abound in the
industrious provinces of Egypt and Asia. It is only surprising that the eastern emperor, who possessed so great
a superiority at sea, should have neglected the opportunity of carrying an offensive war into the centre of
his rival's dominions.

Instead of embracing such an active resolution, which
might have changed the whole face of the war, the
prudent Licinius expected the approach of his rival in
a camp near Hadrianople, which he had fortified with
an anxious care that betrayed his apprehension of the
event. Constantine directed his march from Thessalonica
towards that part of Thrace, till he found himself
stopped by the broad and rapid stream of the Hebrus
and discovered the numerous army of Licinius, which
filled the steep ascent of the hill from the river to the
city of Hadrianople. Many days were spent in doubtful
and distant skirmishes; but at length the obstacles of
the passage and of the attack were removed by the
intrepid conduct of Constantine.

In this place we might relate a wonderful exploit of
Constantine, which, though it can scarcely be paralleled
either in poetry or romance, is celebrated not by a venal
orator devoted to his fortune but by an historian, the
partial enemy of his fame. We are asssured that the
valiant emperor threw himself into the river Hebrus
accompanied only by *twelve* horsemen, and that by the
effort or terror of his invincible arm he broke, slaughtered, and put to flight a host of an hundred and fifty
thousand men. The credulity of Zosimus prevailed so
strongly over his passion that, among the events of the
memorable battle of Hadrianople, he seems to have
selected and embellished not the most important but
the most marvellous. The valour and danger of Con-

stantine are attested by a slight wound which he received in the thigh; but it may be discovered, even from an imperfect narration and perhaps a corrupted text, that the victory was obtained no less by the conduct of the general than by the courage of the hero; that a body of five thousand archers marched round to occupy a thick wood in the rear of the enemy, whose attention was diverted by the construction of a bridge; and that Licinius, perplexed by so many artful evolutions, was reluctantly drawn from his advantageous post to combat on equal ground in the plain. The contest was no longer equal. His confused multitude of new levies was easily vanquished by the experienced veterans of the West. Thirty-four thousand men are reported to have been slain. The fortified camp of Licinius was taken by assault the evening of the battle; the greater part of the fugitives, who had retired to the mountains, surrendered themselves the next day to the discretion of the conqueror; and his rival, who could no longer keep the field, confined himself within the walls of Byzantium.

The siege of Byzantium, which was immediately undertaken by Constantine, was attended with great labour and uncertainty. In the late civil wars the fortifications of that place, so justly considered as the key of Europe and Asia, had been repaired and strengthened; and as long as Licinius remained master of the sea, the garrison was much less exposed to the danger of famine than the army of the besiegers. The naval commanders of Constantine were summoned to his camp and received his positive orders to force the passage of the Hellespont, as the fleet of Licinius, instead of seeking and destroying their feeble enemy, continued inactive in those narrow straits where its superiority of numbers was of little use or advantage. Crispus, the emperor's eldest son, was entrusted with the execution of this daring enterprise, which he performed with so much courage and success that he deserved the esteem, and most probably excited the jealousy, of his father. The engagement lasted two days; and in the evening of the first the contending fleets, after a considerable and mutual loss, retired into their respective harbours of Europe and Asia. The second day about noon a strong south wind sprang up, which carried the vessels of Crispus against the enemy; and as the casual advantage was improved by his skilful intrepidity, he soon obtained a complete victory. An hundred and thirty vessels were destroyed, five thousand men were slain, and Amandus, the admiral of the Asiatic fleet, escaped with the utmost difficulty to the shores of Chalcedon.

As soon as the Hellespont was open a plentiful convoy of provisions flowed into the camp of Constantine, who had already advanced the operations of the siege. He constructed artificial mounds of earth of an equal height with the ramparts of Byzantium. The lofty towers which were erected on that foundation galled the besieged with large stones and darts from the military engines, and the battering rams had shaken the walls in several places. If Licinius persisted much longer in the defence, he exposed himself to be involved in the ruin of the place. Before he was surrounded he prudently removed his person and treasures to Chalcedon in Asia; and as he was always desirous of associating companions to the hopes and dangers of his fortune, he now bestowed the title of Cæsar on Martinianus, who exercised one of the most important offices of the empire.

Such were still the resources and such the abilities of Licinius that, after so many successive defeats, he collected in Bithynia a new army of fifty or sixty thousand men while the activity of Constantine was employed in the siege of Byzantium. The vigilant emperor

did not, however, neglect the last struggles of his antagonist. A considerable part of his victorious army was
transported over the Bosphorus in small vessels, and the
decisive engagement was fought soon after their landing
on the heights of Chrysopolis, or, as it is now called, of
Scutari. The troops of Licinius, though they were lately
raised, ill armed, and worse disciplined, made head
against their conquerors with fruitless but desperate valour, till a total defeat, and the slaughter of five-and-
twenty thousand men, irretrievably determined the fate
of their leader. He retired to Nicomedia, rather with
the view of gaining some time for negotiation than with
the hope of any effectual defence. Constantia, his wife
and the sister of Constantine, interceded with her
brother in favour of her husband and obtained from his
policy rather than from his compassion a solemn promise, confirmed by an oath, that after the sacrifice of
Martinianus and the resignation of the purple Licinius
himself should be permitted to pass the remainder of his
life in peace and affluence.

The behaviour of Constantia and her relation to the
contending parties naturally recall the remembrance of
that virtuous matron who was the sister of Augustus and
the wife of Antony. But the temper of mankind was
altered, and it was no longer esteemed infamous for a
Roman to survive his honour and independence. Licinius solicited and accepted the pardon of his offences,
laid himself and his purple at the feet of his *lord* and
master, was raised from the ground with insulting pity,
was admitted the same day to the imperial banquet, and
soon afterwards was sent away to Thessalonica, which
had been chosen for the place of his confinement. His
confinement was soon terminated by death, and it is
doubtful whether a tumult of the soldiers or a decree
of the senate was suggested as the motive for his execu-

tion. According to the rules of tyranny, he was accused of forming a conspiracy and of holding a treasonable correspondence with the barbarians; but as he was never convicted, either by his own conduct or by any legal evidence, we may perhaps be allowed, from his weakness, to presume his innocence. The memory of Licinius was branded with infamy; his statues were thrown down; and by a hasty edict, of such mischievous tendency that it was almost immediately corrected, all his laws and all the judicial proceedings of his reign were at once abolished. By this victory of Constantine the Roman world was again united under the authority of one emperor, thirty-seven years after Diocletian had divided his power and provinces with his associate Maximian.

The successive steps of the elevation of Constantine, from his first assuming the purple at York to the resignation of Licinius at Nicomedia, have been related with some minuteness and precision, not only as the events are in themselves both interesting and important, but still more as they contributed to the decline of the empire by the expense of blood and treasure, and by the perpetual increase as well of the taxes as of the military establishment. The foundation of Constantinople and the establishment of the Christian religion were the immediate and memorable consequences of this revolution.

Chapter VIII

*The progress of the Christian religion, and the senti-
ments, manners, numbers, and condition of the
primitive Christians – Persecution of the primitive
Christians*[1]

A CANDID but rational inquiry into the progress and
establishment of Christianity may be considered as
a very essential part of the history of the Roman empire.
While that great body was invaded by open violence or
undermined by slow decay, a pure and humble religion
gently insinuated itself into the minds of men, grew up
in silence and obscurity, derived new vigour from opposition, and finally erected the triumphant banner of
the Cross on the ruins of the Capitol. Nor was the
influence of Christianity confined to the period or to the
limits of the Roman empire. After a revolution of thirteen or fourteen centuries, that religion is still professed
by the nations of Europe, the most distinguished portion
of humankind in arts and learning as well as in arms.
By the industry and zeal of the Europeans it has been
widely diffused to the most distant shores of Asia and
Africa, and by the means of their colonies has been
firmly established from Canada to Chili in a world unknown to the ancients.

But this inquiry, however useful or entertaining, is
attended with two peculiar difficulties. The scanty and
suspicious materials of ecclesiastical history seldom enable us to dispel the dark cloud that hangs over the
first age of the church. The great law of impartiality too

1. *Editor's note:* Chapters XV and XVI of the original.

often obliges us to reveal the imperfections of the un-inspired teachers and believers of the Gospel; and, to a careless observer, *their* faults may seem to cast a shade on the faith which they professed. But the scandal of the pious Christian and the fallacious triumph of the infidel should cease as soon as they recollect not only *by whom*, but likewise *to whom*, the Divine Revelation was given. The theologian may indulge the pleasing task of describing Religion as she descended from Heaven, arrayed in her native purity. A more melancholy duty is imposed on the historian. He must discover the inevitable mixture of error and corruption which she contracted in a long residence upon earth, among a weak and degenerate race of beings.

Our curiosity is naturally prompted to inquire by what means the Christian faith obtained so remarkable a victory over the established religions of the earth. To this inquiry an obvious but satisfactory answer may be returned, that it was owing to the convincing evidence of the doctrine itself and to the ruling providence of its great Author. But as truth and reason seldom find so favourable a reception in the world, and as the wisdom of Providence frequently condescends to use the passions of the human heart and the general circumstances of mankind as instruments to execute its purpose, we may still be permitted (though with becoming submission) to ask, not indeed what were the first, but what were the secondary causes of the rapid growth of the Christian church? It will, perhaps, appear that it was most effectually favoured and assisted by the five following causes: I. The inflexible and, if we may use the expression, the intolerant zeal of the Christians—derived, it is true, from the Jewish religion but purified from the narrow and unsocial spirit which, instead of inviting, had deterred the Gentiles from embracing the law of Moses. II. The doctrine of a future life, improved by every additional circumstance which could give weight and efficacy to that important truth. III. The miraculous powers ascribed to the primitive church. IV. The pure and austere morals of the Christians. V. The union and discipline of the Christian republic, which gradually formed an independent and increasing state in the heart of the Roman empire.

I. THE ZEAL OF THE CHRISTIANS. We have already described the religious harmony of the ancient world and the facility with which the most different and even hostile nations embraced, or at least respected, each other's superstitions. A single people refused to join in the common intercourse of mankind. The Jews, who under the Assyrian and Persian monarchies had languished for many ages the most despised portion of their slaves, emerged from obscurity under the successors of Alexander; and as they multiplied to a surprising degree in the East and afterwards in the West, they soon excited the curiosity and wonder of other nations. The sullen obstinacy with which they maintained their peculiar rites and unsocial manners seemed to mark them out a distinct species of men, who boldly professed or faintly disguised their implacable hatred to the rest of humankind. Neither the violence of Antiochus, nor the arts of Herod, nor the example of the circumjacent nations, could ever persuade the Jews to associate with the institutions of Moses the elegant mythology of the Greeks.

According to the maxims of universal toleration, the Romans protected a superstition which they despised. The polite Augustus condescended to give orders that sacrifices should be offered for his prosperity in the temple of Jerusalem, while the meanest of the posterity of Abraham who should have paid the same homage to the Jupiter of the Capitol would have been an object of abhorrence to himself and to his brethren. But the moderation of the conquerors was insufficient to appease the jealous prejudices of their subjects, who were alarmed and scandalized at the ensigns of paganism which necessarily introduced themselves into a Roman province. The mad attempt of Caligula to place his own statue in the temple of Jerusalem was defeated by the unanimous resolution of a people who dreaded death much less than such an idolatrous profanation. Their attachment to the law of Moses was equal to their detestation of foreign religions. The current of zeal and devotion, as it was contracted into a narrow channel, ran with the strength, and sometimes with the fury, of a torrent.

This inflexible perseverance, which appeared so odious or so ridiculous to the ancient world, assumes a more awful character since Providence has deigned to reveal to us the mysterious history of the chosen people. But the devout and even scrupulous attachment to the Mosaic religion, so conspicuous among the Jews who lived under the second temple, becomes still more surprising if it is compared with the stubborn incredulity of their forefathers. When the law was given in thunder from Mount Sinai, when the tides of the ocean and the course of the planets were suspended for the convenience of the Israelites, and when temporal rewards and punishments were the immediate consequences of their piety or disobedience, they perpetually relapsed into rebellion against the visible majesty of their Divine King, placed the idols of the nations in the sanctuary of Jehovah, and imitated every fantastic ceremony that was practised in the tents of the Arabs or in the cities of Phœnicia. As the protection of Heaven was deservedly withdrawn from the ungrateful race, their faith acquired a proportionable degree of vigour and purity. The contemporaries of Moses and Joshua had beheld with careless indifference the most amazing miracles. Under the pressure of every calamity, the belief of those miracles has preserved the Jews of a later period from the universal contagion of idolatry; and in contradiction to every known principle of the human mind, that singular people seems to have yielded a stronger and more ready assent to the traditions of their remote ancestors than to the evidence of their own senses.

The Jewish religion was admirably fitted for defence, but it was never designed for conquest; and it seems probable that the number of proselytes was never much superior to that of apostates. The divine promises were originally made, and the distinguishing rite of circumcision was enjoined, to a single family. When the posterity of Abraham had multiplied like the sands of the sea, the Deity, from whose mouth they received a system of laws and ceremonies, declared himself the proper and, as it were, the national God of Israel, and with the most jealous care separated his favourite people from the rest of mankind. The conquest of the land of Canaan was accompanied with so many wonderful and with so many bloody circumstances that the victorious Jews were left in a state of irreconcilable hostility with all their neighbours. They had been commanded to extirpate some of the most idolatrous tribes, and the execution of the divine will had seldom been retarded by the weakness of humanity. With the other nations they were forbidden to contract any marriages or alliances; and the prohibition of receiving them into the congregation, which in some cases was perpetual, almost always extended to the third, to the seventh, or even to the tenth generation. The obligation of preaching to the Gentiles the faith of Moses had never been inculcated as a precept of the law, nor were the Jews inclined to impose it on themselves as a voluntary duty.[2]

Under these circumstances Christianity offered itself to the world armed with the strength of the Mosaic law and delivered from the weight of its fetters. An exclusive zeal for the truth of religion and the unity of God was as carefully inculcated in the new as in the ancient system; and whatever was now revealed to mankind concerning the nature and designs of the Supreme Being was fitted to increase their reverence for that mysterious doctrine. The divine authority of Moses and the prophets was admitted, and even established, as the firmest basis of Christianity. From the beginning of the world an uninterrupted series of predictions had announced and prepared the long-expected coming of the Messiah, who in compliance with the gross apprehensions of the Jews had been more frequently represented under the character of a king and conqueror than under that of a prophet, a martyr, and the Son of God. By his expiatory sacrifice the imperfect sacrifices of the temple were at once consummated and abolished. The ceremonial law, which consisted only of types and figures, was succeeded by a pure and spiritual worship equally adapted to all climates as well as to every condition of mankind; and to the initiation of blood was substituted a more harmless initiation of water. The promise of divine favour, instead of being partially confined to the posterity of Abraham, was universally proposed to the freeman and the slave, to the Greek and to the barbarian, to the Jew and to the Gentile. Every privilege that could raise the proselyte from earth to heaven, that could exalt his devotion, secure his happiness, or even

2. *Editor's note:* The steadfast refusal of the Jews to engage in proselytizing is the subject of a paragraph deleted here.

gratify that secret pride which, under the semblance of devotion, insinuates itself into the human heart, was still reserved for the members of the Christian church; but at the same time all mankind was permitted, and even solicited, to accept the glorious distinction, which was not only proffered as a favour but imposed as an obligation. It became the most sacred duty of a new convert to diffuse among his friends and relations the inestimable blessing which he had received, and to warn them against a refusal that would be severely punished as a criminal disobedience to the will of a benevolent but all-powerful Deity.

The enfranchisement of the church from the bonds of the synagogue was a work, however, of some time and of some difficulty. The Jewish converts, who acknowledged Jesus in the character of the Messiah foretold by their ancient oracles, respected him as a prophetic teacher of virtue and religion, but they obstinately adhered to the ceremonies of their ancestors and were desirous of imposing them on the Gentiles, who continually augmented the number of believers. These Judaizing Christians seem to have argued with some degree of plausibility from the divine origin of the Mosaic law and from the immutable perfections of its great Author. They affirmed *that* if the Being who is the same through all eternity had designed to abolish those sacred rites which had served to distinguish his chosen people, the repeal of them would have been no less clear and solemn than their first promulgation; *that,* instead of those frequent declarations which either suppose or assert the perpetuity of the Mosaic religion, it would have been represented as a provisionary scheme intended to last only till the coming of the Messiah, who should instruct mankind in a more perfect mode of faith and of worship; *that* the Messiah himself, and his disciples who conversed with him on earth, instead of authorizing by their example the most minute observances of the Mosaic law, would have published to the world the abolition of those useless and obsolete ceremonies without suffering Christianity to remain during so many years obscurely confounded among the sects of the Jewish church. Arguments like these appear to have been used in the defence of the expiring cause of the Mosaic law; but the industry of our learned divines has abundantly explained the ambiguous language of the Old Testament and the ambiguous conduct of the apostolic teachers. It was proper gradually to unfold the system of the Gospel and to pronounce with the utmost caution and tenderness a sentence of condemnation so repugnant to the inclination and prejudices of the believing Jews.[3]

While the orthodox church preserved a just medium between excessive veneration and improper contempt for the law of Moses, the various heretics deviated into equal but opposite extremes of error and extravagance. From the acknowledged truth of the Jewish religion, the Ebionites had concluded that it could never be abolished. From its supposed imperfections, the Gnostics as hastily inferred that it never was instituted by the wisdom of the Deity. There are some objections against the authority of Moses and the prophets which too readily present themselves to the sceptical mind, though

3. *Editor's note:* A short section omitted here discusses the dilemma of a small group of early Christians, known as Nazarenes, who continued for a time to insist on the necessity and validity of the Mosaic laws, but who ultimately relinquished their position and returned to the main body of the Christian church. A small Nazarene remnant, known as Ebionites, refused to take the step and called down upon their heads the hostility of both Christians and Jews for the two or three centuries that they persisted.

they can only be derived from our ignorance of remote antiquity and from our incapacity to form an adequate judgment of the divine economy. These objections were eagerly embraced and as petulantly urged by the vain science of the Gnostics. As those heretics were for the most part averse to the pleasures of sense, they morosely arraigned the polygamy of the patriarchs, the gallantries of David, and the seraglio of Solomon. The conquest of the land of Canaan and the extirpation of the unsuspecting natives they were at a loss how to reconcile with the common notions of humanity and justice. But when they recollected the sanguinary list of murders, of executions, and of massacres which stain almost every page of the Jewish annals, they acknowledged that the barbarians of Palestine had exercised as much compassion towards their idolatrous enemies as they had ever shown to their friends or countrymen.

Passing from the sectaries of the law to the law itself, they asserted that it was impossible that a religion which consisted only of bloody sacrifices and trifling ceremonies, and whose rewards as well as punishments were all of a carnal and temporal nature, could inspire the love of virtue or restrain the impetuosity of passion. The Mosaic account of the creation and fall of man was treated with profane derision by the Gnostics, who would not listen with patience to the repose of the Deity after six days' labour, to the rib of Adam, the garden of Eden, the trees of life and of knowledge, the speaking serpent, the forbidden fruit, and the condemnation pronounced against humankind for the venial offence of their first progenitors. The God of Israel was impiously represented by the Gnostics as a being liable to passion and to error, capricious in his favour, implacable in his resentment, meanly jealous of his superstitious worship, and confining his partial providence to a single people and to this transitory life. In such a character they could discover none of the features of the wise and omnipotent Father of the universe. They allowed that the religion of the Jews was somewhat less criminal than the idolatry of the Gentiles; but it was their fundamental doctrine that the Christ whom they adored as the first and brightest emanation of the Deity appeared upon earth to rescue mankind from their various errors and to reveal a *new* system of truth and perfection. The most learned of the fathers, by a very singular condescension, have imprudently admitted the sophistry of the Gnostics. Acknowledging that the literal sense is repugnant to every principle of faith as well as reason, they deem themselves secure and invulnerable behind the ample veil of allegory, which they carefully spread over every tender part of the Mosaic dispensation.[4]

But whatever difference of opinion might subsist between the Orthodox, the Ebionites, and the Gnostics concerning the divinity or the obligation of the Mosaic law, they were all equally animated by the same exclusive zeal and by the same abhorrence for idolatry which had distinguished the Jews from the other nations of the ancient world. The philosopher, who considered the system of polytheism as a composition of human fraud and error, could disguise a smile of contempt under the mask of devotion without apprehending that either the mockery or the compliance would expose him to the resentment of any invisible or, as he conceived them, imaginary powers. But the established religions of pa-

---

4. *Editor's note:* Gibbon remarks, in a brief passage omitted here, that the freedom of the Christian church from schism during its first hundred years was probably due to the great latitude allowed the early believers, as evidenced by the flourishing of a wide variety of Gnostic groups within the church.

ganism were seen by the primitive Christians in a much more odious and formidable light. It was the universal sentiment both of the church and of heretics that the demons were the authors, the patrons, and the objects of idolatry.

Those rebellious spirits, who had been degraded from the rank of angels and cast down into the infernal pit, were still permitted to roam upon earth, to torment the bodies and to seduce the minds of sinful men. The demons soon discovered and abused the natural propensity of the human heart towards devotion and, artfully withdrawing the adoration of mankind from their Creator, they usurped the place and honours of the Supreme Deity. By the success of their malicious contrivances they at once gratified their own vanity and revenge and obtained the only comfort of which they were yet susceptible, the hope of involving the human species in the participation of their guilt and misery. It was confessed, or at least it was imagined, that they had distributed among themselves the most important characters of polytheism, one demon assuming the name and attributes of Jupiter, another of Æsculapius, a third of Venus, and a fourth perhaps of Apollo; and that, by the advantage of their long experience and aerial nature, they were enabled to execute with sufficient skill and dignity the parts which they had undertaken. They lurked in the temples, instituted festivals and sacrifices, invented fables, pronounced oracles, and were frequently allowed to perform miracles. The Christians, who by the interposition of evil spirits could so readily explain every preternatural appearance, were disposed and even desirous to admit the most extravagant fictions of the pagan mythology. But the belief of the Christian was accompanied with horror. The most trifling mark of respect to the national worship he considered as *e* direct homage yielded to the demon and as an act of rebellion against the majesty of God.

In consequence of this opinion, it was the first but arduous duty of a Christian to preserve himself pure and undefiled by the practice of idolatry. The religion of the nations was not merely a speculative doctrine professed in the schools or preached in the temples. The innumerable deities and rites of polytheism were closely interwoven with every circumstance of business or pleasure, of public or of private life; and it seemed impossible to escape the observance of them without at the same time renouncing the commerce of mankind and all the offices and amusements of society. The important transactions of peace and war were prepared or concluded by solemn sacrifices in which the magistrate, the senator, and the soldier were obliged to preside or to participate. The public spectacles were an essential part of the cheerful devotion of the pagans, and the gods were supposed to accept as the most grateful offering the games that the prince and people celebrated in honour of their peculiar festivals. The Christian, who with pious horror avoided the abomination of the circus or the theatre, found himself encompassed with infernal snares in every convivial entertainment, as often as his friends, invoking the hospitable deities, poured out libations to each other's happiness. When the bride, struggling with well-affected reluctance, was forced in hymeneal pomp over the threshold of her new habitation, or when the sad procession of the dead slowly moved towards the funeral pile, the Christian on these interesting occasions was compelled to desert the persons who were the dearest to him rather than contract the guilt inherent to those impious ceremonies.

Every art and every trade that was in the least concerned in the framing or adorning of idols was polluted by the stain of idolatry—a severe sentence, since it devoted to eternal misery the far greater part of the community which is employed in the exercise of liberal or mechanic professions. If we cast our eyes over the numerous remains of antiquity we shall perceive that, besides the immediate representations of the gods and the holy instruments of their worship, the elegant forms and agreeable fictions consecrated by the imagination of the Greeks were introduced as the richest ornaments of the houses, the dress, and the furniture of the pagans. Even the arts of music and painting, of eloquence and poetry, flowed from the same impure origin. In the style of the fathers, Apollo and the Muses were the organs of the infernal spirit; Homer and Virgil were the most eminent of his servants; and the beautiful mythology which pervades and animates the compositions of their genius is destined to celebrate the glory of the demons. Even the common language of Greece and Rome abounded with familiar but impious expressions, which the imprudent Christian might too carelessly utter or too patiently hear.[5]

Such was the anxious diligence which was required to guard the chastity of the Gospel from the infectious breath of idolatry. The superstitious observances of public or private rites were carelessly practised, from education and habit, by the followers of the established religion. But as often as they occurred, they afforded the Christians an opportunity of declaring and confirming their zealous opposition. By these frequent protestations their attachment to the faith was continually fortified; and in proportion to the increase of zeal, they combated with the more ardour and success in the holy war which

5. *Editor's note:* Gibbon continues, in a paragraph omitted here, by enumerating the popular Roman festivals which were inextricably tied to the pagan religions.

they had undertaken against the empire of the demons.

II. THE BELIEF IN IMMORTALITY. The writings of Cicero represent in the most lively colours the ignorance, the errors, and the uncertainty of the ancient philosophers with regard to the immortality of the soul. When they are desirous of arming their disciples against the fear of death, they inculcate, as an obvious though melancholy position, that the fatal stroke of our dissolution releases us from the calamities of life, and that those can no longer suffer who no longer exist. Yet there were a few sages of Greece and Rome who had conceived a more exalted and in some respects a juster idea of human nature, though it must be confessed that in the sublime inquiry their reason had been often guided by their imagination, and that their imagination had been prompted by their vanity. When they viewed with complacency the extent of their own mental powers, when they exercised the various faculties of memory, of fancy, and of judgment in the most profound speculations or the most important labours, and when they reflected on the desire of fame, which transported them into future ages far beyond the bounds of death and of the grave, they were unwilling to confound themselves with the beasts of the field or to suppose that a being for whose dignity they entertained the most sincere admiration could be limited to a spot of earth and to a few years of duration.

With this favourable prepossession they summoned to their aid the science, or rather the language, of metaphysics. They soon discovered that, as none of the properties of matter will apply to the operations of the mind, the human soul must consequently be a substance distinct from the body, pure, simple, and spiritual, incapable of dissolution, and susceptible of a much higher degree of virtue and happiness after the release from its corporeal prison. From these specious and noble principles the philosophers who trod in the footsteps of Plato deduced a very unjustifiable conclusion, since they asserted not only the future immortality but the past eternity of the human soul, which they were too apt to consider as a portion of the infinite and self-existing spirit which pervades and sustains the universe. A doctrine thus removed beyond the senses and the experience of mankind might serve to amuse the leisure of a philosophic mind, or, in the silence of solitude, it might sometimes impart a ray of comfort to desponding virtue; but the faint impression which had been received in the schools was soon obliterated by the commerce and business of active life. We are sufficiently acquainted with the eminent persons who flourished in the age of Cicero and of the first Cæsars, with their actions, their characters, and their motives, to be assured that their conduct in this life was never regulated by any serious conviction of the rewards or punishments of a future state. At the bar and in the senate of Rome the ablest orators were not apprehensive of giving offence to their hearers by exposing that doctrine as an idle and extravagant opinion, which was rejected with contempt by every man of a liberal education and understanding.[6]

We might naturally expect that a principle so essential to religion would have been revealed in the clearest terms to the chosen people of Palestine and that it might safely have been entrusted to the hereditary priesthood of Aaron. It is incumbent on us to adore the mysterious dispensations of Providence, when we discover that the doctrine of the immortality of the soul is omit-

6. *Editor's note:* The original continues at this point by commenting on the inadequacy of the pagan religions of Greece and Rome to encompass the idea of the soul's immortality.

ted in the law of Moses; it is darkly insinuated by the
prophets; and during the long period which elapsed between the Egyptian and the Babylonian servitudes the
hopes as well as fears of the Jews appear to have been
confined within the narrow compass of the present life.
After Cyrus had permitted the exiled nation to return
into the promised land, and after Ezra had restored the
ancient records of their religion, two celebrated sects,
the Sadducees and the Pharisees, insensibly arose at
Jerusalem. The former, selected from the more opulent
and distinguished ranks of society, were strictly attached
to the literal sense of the Mosaic law; and they piously
rejected the immortality of the soul as an opinion that
received no countenance from the divine book, which
they revered as the only rule of their faith.

To the authority of Scripture the Pharisees added that
of tradition; and they accepted, under the name of
traditions, several speculative tenets from the philosophy
or religion of the eastern nations. The doctrines of fate
or predestination, of angels and spirits, and of a future
state of rewards and punishments were in the number of
these new articles of belief; and as the Pharisees by the
austerity of their manners had drawn into their party
the body of the Jewish people, the immortality of the
soul became the prevailing sentiment of the synagogue
under the reign of the Asmonæan princes and pontiffs.
The temper of the Jews was incapable of contenting
itself with such a cold and languid assent as might
satisfy the mind of a polytheist; and as soon as they
admitted the idea of a future state, they embraced it
with the zeal which has always formed the characteristic of the nation. Their zeal, however, added nothing
to its evidence, or even probability; and it was still
necessary that the doctrine of life and immortality,
which had been dictated by nature, approved by reason,

and received by superstition, should obtain the sanction of divine truth from the authority and example of Christ.

When the promise of eternal happiness was proposed to mankind on condition of adopting the faith and of observing the precepts of the Gospel, it is no wonder that so advantageous an offer should have been accepted by great numbers of every religion, of every rank, and of every province in the Roman empire. The ancient Christians were animated by a contempt for their present existence and by a just confidence of immortality, of which the doubtful and imperfect faith of modern ages cannot give us any adequate notion. In the primitive church the influence of truth was very powerfully strengthened by an opinion which, however it may deserve respect for its usefulness and antiquity, has not been found agreeable to experience. It was universally believed that the end of the world and the kingdom of heaven were at hand. The near approach of this wonderful event had been predicted by the apostles; the tradition of it was preserved by their earliest disciples; and those who understood in their literal sense the discourses of Christ himself were obliged to expect the second and glorious coming of the Son of Man in the clouds before that generation was totally extinguished which had beheld his humble condition upon earth, and which might still be witness of the calamities of the Jews under Vespasian or Hadrian. The revolution of seventeen centuries has instructed us not to press too closely the mysterious language of prophecy and revelation; but as long as, for wise purposes, this error was permitted to subsist in the church, it was productive of the most salutary effects on the faith and practice of Christians, who lived in the awful expectation of that moment when the globe itself and all the various race of mankind should tremble at the appearance of their divine Judge.[7]

Whilst the happiness and glory of a temporal reign were promised to the disciples of Christ, the most dreadful calamities were denounced against an unbelieving world. The edification of the new Jerusalem was to advance by equal steps with the destruction of the mystic Babylon; and as long as the emperors who reigned before Constantine persisted in the profession of idolatry, the epithet of Babylon was applied to the city and to the empire of Rome. A regular series was prepared of all the moral and physical evils which can afflict a flourishing nation: intestine discord and the invasion of the fiercest barbarians from the unknown regions of the North, pestilence and famine, comets and eclipses, earthquakes and inundations. All these were only so many preparatory and alarming signs of the great catastrophe of Rome, when the country of the Scipios and Cæsars should be consumed by a flame from Heaven, and the city of the seven hills, with her palaces, her temples, and her triumphal arches, should be buried in a vast lake of fire and brimstone. It might, however, afford some consolation to Roman vanity that the period of their empire would be that of the world itself, which, as it had once perished by the element of water, was destined to experience a second and a speedy destruction from the element of fire.[8]

7. *Editor's note:* Gibbon notes, in a brief passage omitted here, the early Christian belief that the final judgment would be preceded by the reign of Christ on earth, amid conditions of perfect plenty for all saints and true believers; but "when the edifice of the church was almost completed the temporary support was laid aside," and the doctrine of Christ's reign on earth was rejected by the church.

8. *Editor's note:* The belief in a great conflagration—as is noted in the original—not only coincided with the tenets of

The condemnation of the wisest and most virtuous of the pagans, on account of their ignorance or disbelief of the divine truth, seems to offend the reason and the humanity of the present age. But the primitive church, whose faith was of a much firmer consistence, delivered over, without hesitation, to eternal torture the far greater part of the human species. A charitable hope might perhaps be indulged in favour of Socrates or some other sages of antiquity who had consulted the light of reason before that of the Gospel had arisen. But it was unanimously affirmed that those who, since the birth or the death of Christ, had obstinately persisted in the worship of the demons neither deserved nor could expect a pardon from the irritated justice of the Deity.

These rigid sentiments, which had been unknown to the ancient world, appear to have infused a spirit of bitterness into a system of love and harmony. The ties of blood and friendship were frequently torn asunder by the difference of religious faith; and the Christians, who in this world found themselves oppressed by the power of the pagans, were sometimes seduced by resentment and spiritual pride to delight in the prospect of their future triumph. "You are fond of spectacles," exclaims the stern Tertullian, "expect the greatest of all spectacles, the last and eternal judgment of the universe. How shall I admire, how laugh, how rejoice, how exult, when I behold so many proud monarchs and fancied gods groaning in the lowest abyss of darkness; so many magistrates, who persecuted the name of the Lord, liquefying in fiercer fires than they ever kindled against the Christians; so many sage philosophers blushing in red-hot flames with their deluded scholars; so many

---

then existing eastern religions, but also agreed with the evidence of the senses of Romans who were familiar with Etna, Vesuvius, etc.

celebrated poets trembling before the tribunal not of Minos but of Christ; so many tragedians, more tuneful in the expression of their own sufferings; so many dancers—" But the humanity of the reader will permit me to draw a veil over the rest of this infernal description, which the zealous African pursues in a long variety of affected and unfeeling witticisms.

Doubtless there were many among the primitive Christians of a temper more suitable to the meekness and charity of their profession. There were many who felt a sincere compassion for the danger of their friends and countrymen, and who exerted the most benevolent zeal to save them from the impending destruction. The careless polytheist, assailed by new and unexpected terrors against which neither his priests nor his philosophers could afford him any certain protection, was very frequently terrified and subdued by the menace of eternal tortures. His fears might assist the progress of his faith and reason; and if he could once persuade himself to suspect that the Christian religion might possibly be true, it became an easy task to convince him that it was the safest and most prudent party that he could possibly embrace.

III. THE MIRACULOUS POWERS OF THE EARLY CHURCH. The supernatural gifts, which even in this life were ascribed to the Christians above the rest of mankind, must have conduced to their own comfort, and very frequently to the conviction of infidels. Besides the occasional prodigies, which might sometimes be effected by the immediate interposition of the Deity when he suspended the laws of Nature for the service of religion, the Christian church, from the time of the apostles and their first disciples, has claimed an uninterrupted succession of miraculous powers, the gift of tongues, of vision, and of prophecy, the power of expelling demons, of healing the sick, and of raising the dead. The knowledge of foreign languages was frequently communicated to the contemporaries of Irenæus, though Irenæus himself was left to struggle with the difficulties of a barbarous dialect whilst he preached the Gospel to the natives of Gaul. The divine inspiration, whether it was conveyed in the form of a waking or a sleeping vision, is described as a favour very liberally bestowed on all ranks of the faithful, on women as on elders, on boys as well as upon bishops. When their devout minds were sufficiently prepared by a course of prayer, of fasting, and of vigils to receive the extraordinary impulse, they were transported out of their senses and delivered in ecstasy that was inspired, being mere organs of the Holy Spirit, just as a pipe or flute is of him who blows into it. We may add that the design of these visions was for the most part either to disclose the future history or to guide the present administration of the church. The expulsion of the demons from the bodies of those unhappy persons whom they had been permitted to torment was considered as a signal though ordinary triumph of religion, and is repeatedly alleged by the ancient apologists as the most convincing evidence of the truth of Christianity. The awful ceremony was usually performed in a public manner and in the presence of a great number of spectators; the patient was relieved by the power or skill of the exorcist; and the vanquished demon was heard to confess that he was one of the fabled gods of antiquity who had impiously usurped the adoration of mankind.

But the miraculous cure of diseases of the most inveterate or even preternatural kind can no longer occasion any surprise when we recollect that in the days of Irenæus, about the end of the second century, the resurrection of the dead was very far from being esteemed an uncommon event; that the miracle was frequently performed on necessary occasions by great fasting and the joint supplication of the church of the place; and that the persons thus restored to their prayers had lived afterwards among them many years. At such a period, when faith could boast of so many wonderful victories over death, it seems difficult to account for the scepticism of those philosophers who still rejected and derided the doctrine of the resurrection. A noble Grecian had rested on this important ground the whole controversy and promised Theophilus, bishop of Antioch, that if he could be gratified with the sight of a single person who had been actually raised from the dead, he would immediately embrace the Christian religion. It is somewhat remarkable that the prelate of the first eastern church, however anxious for the conversion of his friend, thought proper to decline this fair and reasonable challenge.

The miracles of the primitive church, after obtaining the sanction of ages, have been lately attacked in a very free and ingenious inquiry, which, though it has met with the most favourable reception from the public, appears to have excited a general scandal among the divines of our own as well as of the other Protestant churches of Europe. Our different sentiments on this subject will be much less influenced by any particular arguments than by our habits of study and reflection, and above all by the degree of the evidence which we have accustomed ourselves to require for the proof of a miraculous event. The duty of an historian does not call upon him to interpose his private judgment in this nice and important controversy; but he ought not to dissemble the difficulty of adopting such a theory as may reconcile the interest of religion with that of reason, of making a proper application of that theory, and of defining with precision the limits of that happy period, exempt from error and from deceit, to which we might be disposed to extend the gift of supernatural powers.

From the first of the fathers to the last of the popes, a succession of bishops, of saints, of martyrs, and of miracles is continued without interruption; and the progress of superstition was so gradual and almost imperceptible that we know not in what particular link we should break the chain of tradition. Every age bears testimony to the wonderful events by which it was distinguished, and its testimony appears no less weighty and respectable than that of the preceding generation, till we are insensibly led on to accuse our own inconsistency if, in the eighth or in the twelfth century, we deny to the venerable Bede or to the holy Bernard the same degree of confidence which in the second century we had so liberally granted to Justin or to Irenæus.[9] If the truth of any of those miracles is appreciated by their apparent use and propriety, every age had unbelievers to convince, heretics to confute, and idolatrous nations to convert; and sufficient motives might always be produced to justify the interposition of Heaven. And yet, since every friend to revelation is persuaded of the reality, and every reasonable man is convinced of the cessation, of miraculous powers, it is evident that there must have been *some period* in which they were either suddenly or gradually withdrawn from the Christian church. Whatever era is chosen for that purpose—the

9. It may seem somewhat remarkable that Bernard of Clairvaux, who records so many miracles of his friend St. Malachi, never takes any notice of his own, which in their turn, however, are carefully related by his companions and disciples. In the long series of ecclesiastical history, does there exist a single instance of a saint asserting that he himself possessed the gift of miracles?

death of the apostles, the conversion of the Roman empire, or the extinction of the Arian heresy[10]—the insensibility of the Christians who lived at that time will equally afford a just matter of surprise. They still supported their pretensions after they had lost their power. Credulity performed the office of faith, fanaticism was permitted to assume the language of inspiration, and the effects of accident or contrivance were ascribed to supernatural causes. The recent experience of genuine miracles should have instructed the Christian world in the ways of Providence and habituated their eye (if we may use a very inadequate expression) to the style of the divine artist. Should the most skilful painter of modern Italy presume to decorate his feeble imitations with the name of Raphael or of Correggio, the insolent fraud would be soon discovered and indignantly rejected.[11]

IV. THE PURE AND AUSTERE MORALS OF THE CHRISTIANS. But the primitive Christian demonstrated his faith by his virtues; and it was very justly supposed that the divine persuasion which enlightened or subdued the understanding must at the same time purify the heart and direct the actions of the believer. The first apologists of Christianity who justify the innocence of their brethren, and the writers of a later period who celebrate the sanctity of their ancestors, display in the most lively colours the reformation of manners which was introduced into the world by the preaching of the Gospel. As it is my intention to remark only such human causes as were permitted to second the influence of revelation,

10. The conversion of Constantine is the era which is most usually fixed by Protestants. The more rational divines are unwilling to admit the miracles of the fourth, whilst the more credulous are unwilling to reject those of the fifth century.

11. *Editor's note:* In a concluding paragraph, omitted here, Gibbon summarizes the credulity of the ancients that "proved of some accidental benefit to the cause of truth and religion."

I shall slightly mention two motives which might naturally render the lives of the primitive Christians much purer and more austere than those of their pagan contemporaries or their degenerate successors—repentance for their past sins and the laudable desire of supporting the reputation of the society in which they were engaged.

It is a very ancient reproach, suggested by the ignorance or the malice of infidelity, that the Christians allured into their party the most atrocious criminals, who, as soon as they were touched by a sense of remorse, were easily persuaded to wash away in the water of baptism the guilt of their past conduct, for which the temples of the gods refused to grant them any expiation. But this reproach, when it is cleared from misrepresentation, contributes as much to the honour as it did to the increase of the church. The friends of Christianity may acknowledge without a blush that many of the most eminent saints had been before their baptism the most abandoned sinners. Those persons who in the world had followed, though in an imperfect manner, the dictates of benevolence and propriety, derived such a calm satisfaction from the opinion of their own rectitude as rendered them much less susceptible of the sudden emotions of shame, of grief, and of terror, which have given birth to so many wonderful conversions. After the example of their Divine Master, the missionaries of the Gospel disdained not the society of men, and especially of women, oppressed by the consciousness, and very often by the effects, of their vices. As they emerged from sin and superstition to the glorious hope of immortality, they resolved to devote themselves to a life not only of virtue but of penitence. The desire of perfection became the ruling passion of their soul; and it is well known that, while reason embraces a cold mediocrity, our passions hurry us with rapid violence over the space which lies between the most opposite extremes.

When the new converts had been enrolled in the number of the faithful and were admitted to the sacraments of the church, they found themselves restrained from relapsing into their past disorders by another consideration of a less spiritual, but of a very innocent and respectable, nature. Any particular society that has departed from the great body of the nation or the religion to which it belonged immediately becomes the object of universal as well as invidious observation. In proportion to the smallness of its numbers, the character of the society may be affected by the virtue and vices of the persons who compose it; and every member is engaged to watch with the most vigilant attention over his own behaviour and over that of his brethren, since, as he must expect to incur a part of the common disgrace, he may hope to enjoy a share of the common reputation.

When the Christians of Bithynia were brought before the tribunal of the younger Pliny they assured the proconsul that, far from being engaged in any unlawful conspiracy, they were bound by a solemn obligation to abstain from the commission of those crimes which disturb the private or public peace of society, from theft, robbery, adultery, perjury, and fraud. Near a century afterwards Tertullian with an honest pride could boast that very few Christians had suffered by the hand of the executioner except on account of their religion. Their serious and sequestered life, averse to the gay luxury of the age, inured them to chastity, temperance, economy, and all the sober and domestic virtues. As the greater number were of some trade or profession, it was incumbent on them, by the strictest integrity and the fairest dealing, to remove the suspicions which the

profane are too apt to conceive against the appearances
of sanctity. The contempt of the world exercised them
in the habits of humility, meekness, and patience. The
more they were persecuted, the more closely they
adhered to each other. Their mutual charity and unsuspecting confidence have been remarked by infidels
and were too often abused by perfidious friends.

It is a very honourable circumstance for the morals
of the primitive Christians that even their faults, or
rather errors, were derived from an excess of virtue.
The bishops and doctors of the church, whose evidence
attests and whose authority might influence the professions, the principles, and even the practice of their
contemporaries, had studied the Scriptures with less
skill than devotion; and they often received in the most
literal sense those rigid precepts of Christ and the
apostles to which the prudence of succeeding commentators has applied a looser and more figurative mode
of interpretation. Ambitious to exalt the perfection of
the Gospel above the wisdom of philosophy, the zealous
fathers have carried the duties of self-mortification, of
purity, and of patience to a height which it is scarcely
possible to attain, and much less to preserve, in our
present state of weakness and corruption. A doctrine
so extraordinary and so sublime must inevitably command the veneration of the people; but it was ill calculated to obtain the suffrage of those worldly philosophers who, in the conduct of this transitory life, consult
only the feelings of nature and the interest of society.[12]

The acquisition of knowledge, the exercise of our
reason or fancy, and the cheerful flow of unguarded con-

12. *Editor's note:* Gibbon comments, in a paragraph
omitted here, that the early church rejected two of the most
natural human propensities, the love of pleasure and the love
of action.

versation may employ the leisure of a liberal mind. Such
amusements, however, were rejected with abhorrence
or admitted with the utmost caution by the severity of
the fathers, who despised all knowledge that was not
useful to salvation and who considered all levity of discourse as a criminal abuse of the gift of speech. In our
present state of existence the body is so inseparably connected with the soul that it seems to be our interest to
taste with innocence and moderation the enjoyments of
which that faithful companion is susceptible. Very different was the reasoning of our devout predecessors;
vainly aspiring to imitate the perfection of angels, they
disdained, or they affected to disdain, every earthly and
corporeal delight. Some of our senses indeed are necessary for our preservation, others for our subsistence, and
others again for our information; and thus far it was
impossible to reject the use of them. The first sensation
of pleasure was marked as the first moment of their
abuse. The unfeeling candidate for heaven was instructed not only to resist the grosser allurements of the
taste or smell, but even to shut his ears against the
profane harmony of sounds and to view with indifference the most finished productions of human art. Gay
apparel, magnificent houses, and elegant furniture were
supposed to unite the double guilt of pride and of sensuality; a simple and mortified appearance was more
suitable to the Christian who was certain of his sins and
doubtful of his salvation.

In their censures of luxury the fathers are extremely
minute and circumstantial; and among the various articles which excite their pious indignation we may enumerate false hair, garments of any colour except white,
instruments of music, vases of gold or silver, downy
pillows (as Jacob reposed his head on a stone), white
bread, foreign wines, public salutations, the use of warm

baths, and the practice of shaving the beard, which, according to the expression of Tertullian, is a lie against our own faces and an impious attempt to improve the works of the Creator. When Christianity was introduced among the rich and the polite, the observation of these singular laws was left, as it would be at present, to the few who were ambitious of superior sanctity. But it is always easy as well as agreeable for the inferior ranks of mankind to claim a merit from the contempt of that pomp and pleasure which fortune has placed beyond their reach. The virtue of the primitive Christians, like that of the first Romans, was very frequently guarded by poverty and ignorance.

The chaste severity of the fathers in whatever related to the commerce of the two sexes flowed from the same principle—their abhorrence of every enjoyment which might gratify the sensual and degrade the spiritual nature of man. It was their favourite opinion that if Adam had preserved his obedience to the Creator, he would have lived forever in a state of virgin purity, and that some harmless mode of vegetation might have peopled paradise with a race of innocent and immortal beings. The use of marriage was permitted only to his fallen posterity as a necessary expedient to continue the human species and as a restraint, however imperfect, on the natural licentiousness of desire. The hesitation of the orthodox casuists on this interesting subject betrays the perplexity of men unwilling to approve an institution which they were compelled to tolerate.[13] The enumeration of the very whimsical laws which they most circumstantially imposed on the marriage bed would force a smile from the young and a blush from the fair. It was their unanimous sentiment that a first marriage was ade-

13. Some of the Gnostic heretics were more consistent; they rejected the use of marriage.

quate to all the purposes of nature and of society. The sensual connection was refined into a resemblance of the mystic union of Christ with his church and was pronounced to be indissoluble either by divorce or by death. The practice of second nuptials was branded with the name of a legal adultery; and the persons who were guilty of so scandalous an offence against Christian purity were soon excluded from the honours, and even from the arms, of the church.

Since desire was imputed as a crime and marriage was tolerated as a defect, it was consistent with the same principles to consider a state of celibacy as the nearest approach to the divine perfection. It was with the utmost difficulty that ancient Rome could support the institution of six vestals;[14] but the primitive church was filled with a great number of persons of either sex who had devoted themselves to the profession of perpetual chastity. A few of these, among whom we may reckon the learned Origen, judged it the most prudent to disarm the tempter.[15] Some were insensible and some were invincible against the assaults of the flesh. Disdaining an ignominious flight, the virgins of the warm climate of Africa encountered the enemy in the closest engagement: they permitted priests and deacons to share their bed and gloried amidst the flames in their unsullied purity. But insulted Nature sometimes vindicated her rights, and this new species of martyrdom served only to introduce a new scandal into the church. Among the Christian ascetics, however (a name which they soon

14. Notwithstanding the honours and rewards which were bestowed on those virgins, it was difficult to procure a sufficient number; nor could the dread of the most horrible death always restrain their incontinence.

15. As it was his general practice to allegorize Scripture, it seems unfortunate that, in this instance only, he should have adopted the literal sense.

acquired from their painful exercise), many, as they were less presumptuous, were probably more successful. The loss of sensual pleasure was supplied and compensated by spiritual pride. Even the multitude of pagans were inclined to estimate the merit of the sacrifice by its apparent difficulty; and it was in the praise of these chaste spouses of Christ that the fathers have poured forth the troubled stream of their eloquence.[16] Such are the early traces of monastic principles and institutions, which in a subsequent age have counterbalanced all the temporal advantages of Christianity.

The Christians were not less adverse to the business than to the pleasures of this world. The defence of our persons and property they knew not how to reconcile with the patient doctrine which enjoined an unlimited forgiveness of past injuries and commanded them to invite the repetition of fresh insults. Their simplicity was offended by the use of oaths, by the pomp of magistracy, and by the active contention of public life; nor could their humane ignorance be convinced that it was lawful on any occasion to shed the blood of our fellow-creatures, either by the sword of justice or by that of war, even though their criminal or hostile attempts should threaten the peace and safety of the whole community. It was acknowledged that, under a less perfect law, the powers of the Jewish constitution had been exercised with the approbation of Heaven by inspired prophets and by anointed kings. The Christians felt and confessed that such institutions might be necessary for the present system of the world, and they cheerfully submitted to the authority of their pagan governors. But while they inculcated the maxims of passive obedience, they re-

16. Dupin gives a particular account of the dialogue of the ten virgins, as it was composed by Methodius, bishop of Tyre. The praises of virginity are excessive.

fused to take any active part in the civil administration or the military defence of the empire. Some indulgence might perhaps be allowed to those persons who, before their conversion, were already engaged in such violent and sanguinary occupations; but it was impossible that the Christians, without renouncing a more sacred duty, could assume the character of soldiers, of magistrates, or of princes.[17]

This indolent or even criminal disregard to the public welfare exposed them to the contempt and reproaches of the pagans, who very frequently asked, What must be the fate of the empire, attacked on every side by the barbarians, if all mankind should adopt the pusillanimous sentiments of the new sect? To this insulting question the Christian apologists returned obscure and ambiguous answers, as they were unwilling to reveal the secret cause of their security—the expectation that before the conversion of mankind was accomplished war, government, the Roman empire, and the world itself would be no more. It may be observed that in this instance likewise the situation of the first Christians coincided very happily with their religious scruples, and that their aversion to an active life contributed rather to excuse them from the service than to exclude them from the honours of the state and army.

v. THE UNITY AND DISCIPLINE OF THE CHRISTIANS. But the human character, however it may be exalted or depressed by a temporary enthusiasm, will return by degrees to its proper and natural level and will resume those passions that seem the most adapted to its present condition. The primitive Christians were dead to the

17. Tertullian suggested to them the expedient of deserting —a counsel which, if it had been generally known, was not very proper to conciliate the favour of the emperors towards the Christian sect.

business and pleasures of the world; but their love of action, which could never be entirely extinguished, soon revived and found a new occupation in the government of the church. A separate society, which attacked the established religion of the empire, was obliged to adopt some form of internal policy and to appoint a sufficient number of ministers entrusted not only with the spiritual functions but even with the temporal direction of the Christian commonwealth. The safety of the society, its honour, its aggrandizement, were productive even in the most pious minds of a spirit of patriotism, such as the first of the Romans had felt for the republic, and sometimes of a similar indifference in the use of whatever means might probably conduce to so desirable an end. The ambition of raising themselves or their friends to the honours and offices of the church was disguised by the laudable intention of devoting to the public benefit the power and consideration which, for that purpose only, it became their duty to solicit. In the exercise of their functions they were frequently called upon to detect the errors of heresy or the arts of faction, to oppose the designs of perfidious brethren, to stigmatize their characters with deserved infamy, and to expel them from the bosom of a society whose peace and happiness they had attempted to disturb.

The ecclesiastical governors of the Christians were taught to unite the wisdom of the serpent with the innocence of the dove; but as the former was refined, so the latter was insensibly corrupted, by the habits of government. In the church as well as in the world, the persons who were placed in any public station rendered themselves considerable by their eloquence and firmness, by their knowledge of mankind, and by their dexterity in business; and while they concealed from others, and perhaps from themselves, the secret motives of their conduct, they too frequently relapsed into all the turbulent passions of active life, which were tinctured with an additional degree of bitterness and obstinacy from the infusion of spiritual zeal.

The government of the church has often been the subject as well as the prize of religious contention. The hostile disputants of Rome, of Paris, of Oxford, and of Geneva have alike struggled to reduce the primitive and apostolic model to the respective standards of their own policy. The few who have pursued this inquiry with more candour and impartiality are of opinion that the apostles declined the office of legislation and rather chose to endure some partial scandals and divisions than to exclude the Christians of a future age from the liberty of varying their forms of ecclesiastical government according to the changes of times and circumstances. The scheme of policy which under their approbation was adopted for the use of the first century may be discovered from the practice of Jerusalem, of Ephesus, or of Corinth. The societies which were instituted in the cities of the Roman empire were united only by the ties of faith and charity. Independence and equality formed the basis of their internal constitution. The want of discipline and human learning was supplied by the occasional assistance of the *prophets*, who were called to that function without distinction of age, of sex, or of natural abilities, and who, as often as they felt the divine impulse, poured forth the effusions of the Spirit in the assembly of the faithful. But these extraordinary gifts were frequently abused or misapplied by the prophetic teachers. They displayed them at an improper season, presumptuously disturbed the service of the assembly, and by their pride or mistaken zeal they introduced, particularly into the apostolic church of Corinth, a long and melancholy train of disorders. As the institution of prophets became useless, and even pernicious, their powers were withdrawn and their office abolished.

The public functions of religion were solely entrusted to the established ministers of the church, the *bishops* and the *presbyters,* two appellations which in their first origin appear to have distinguished the same office and the same order of persons. The name of presbyter was expressive of their age, or rather of their gravity and wisdom. The title of bishop denoted their inspection over the faith and manners of the Christians who were committed to their pastoral care. In proportion to the respective numbers of the faithful, a larger or smaller number of these episcopal presbyters guided each infant congregation with equal authority and with united counsels.

But the most perfect equality of freedom requires the directing hand of a superior magistrate; and the order of public deliberations soon introduces the office of a president, invested at least with the authority of collecting the sentiments and of executing the resolutions of the assembly. A regard for the public tranquillity, which would so frequently have been interrupted by annual or by occasional elections, induced the primitive Christians to constitute an honourable and perpetual magistracy and to choose one of the wisest and most holy among their presbyters to execute during his life the duties of their ecclesiastical governor. It was under these circumstances that the lofty title of bishop began to raise itself above the humble appellation of presbyter; and while the latter remained the most natural distinction for the members of every Christian senate, the former was appropriated to the dignity of its new president. The advantages of this episcopal form of government, which appears to have been introduced before the end of the first century, were so obvious, and so important for the future greatness as well as the present peace of Christianity, that it was adopted without delay by all the societies which were already scattered over the empire. It acquired in a very early period the sanction of antiquity, and is still revered by the most powerful churches both of the East and of the West as a primitive and even as a divine establishment.

It is needless to observe that the pious and humble presbyters who were first dignified with the episcopal title could not possess, and would probably have rejected, the power and pomp which now encircles the tiara of the Roman pontiff or the mitre of a German prelate. But we may define in a few words the narrow limits of their original jurisdiction, which was chiefly of a spiritual though in some instances of a temporal nature. It consisted in the administration of the sacraments and discipline of the church, the superintendency of religious ceremonies (which imperceptibly increased in number and variety), the consecration of ecclesiastical ministers (to whom the bishop assigned their respective functions), the management of the public fund, and the determination of all such differences as the faithful were unwilling to expose before the tribunal of an idolatrous judge. These powers, during a short period, were exercised according to the advice of the presbyteral college and with the consent and approbation of the assembly of Christians. The primitive bishops were considered only as the first of their equals and the honourable servants of a free people. Whenever the episcopal chair became vacant by death, a new president was chosen among the presbyters by the suffrage of the whole congregation, every member of which supposed himself invested with a sacred and sacerdotal character.

Such was the mild and equal constitution by which the Christians were governed more than an hundred years after the death of the apostles. Every society formed within itself a separate and independent republic; and although the most distant of these little states maintained a mutual as well as friendly intercourse of letters and deputations, the Christian world was not yet connected by any supreme authority or legislative assembly. As the numbers of the faithful were gradually multiplied, they discovered the advantages that might result from a closer union of their interest and designs. Towards the end of the second century the churches of Greece and Asia adopted the useful institutions of provincial synods; and they may justly be supposed to have borrowed the model of a representative council from the celebrated examples of their own country, the Amphictyons, the Achæan league, or the assemblies of the Ionian cities. It was soon established as a custom and as a law that the bishops of the independent churches should meet in the capital of the province at the stated periods of spring and autumn. Their deliberations were assisted by the advice of a few distinguished presbyters and moderated by the presence of a listening multitude. Their decrees, which were styled *canons*, regulated every important controversy of faith and discipline; and it was natural to believe that a liberal effusion of the Holy Spirit would be poured on the united assembly of the delegates of the Christian people. The institution of synods was so well suited to private ambition and to public interest that in the space of a few years it was received throughout the whole empire. A regular correspondence was established between the provincial councils, which mutually communicated and approved their respective proceedings; and the catholic church soon assumed the form and acquired the strength of a great federative republic.

As the legislative authority of the particular churches was insensibly superseded by the use of councils, the bishops obtained by their alliance a much larger share of executive and arbitrary power; and as soon as they were connected by a sense of their common interest, they were enabled to attack with united vigour the original rights of their clergy and people. The prelates of the third century imperceptibly changed the language of exhortation into that of command, scattered the seeds of future usurpations, and supplied, by Scripture allegories and declamatory rhetoric, their deficiency of force and of reason. They exalted the unity and power of the church as it was represented in the *episcopal office*, of which every bishop enjoyed an equal and undivided portion. Princes and magistrates, it was often repeated, might boast an earthly claim to a transitory dominion: it was the episcopal authority alone which was derived from the Deity and extended itself over this and over another world. The bishops were the vicegerents of Christ, the successors of the apostles, and the mystic substitutes of the high priest of the Mosaic law. Their exclusive privilege of conferring the sacerdotal character invaded the freedom both of clerical and of popular elections; and if in the administration of the church they still consulted the judgment of the presbyters or the inclination of the people, they most carefully inculcated the merit of such a voluntary condescension. The bishops acknowledged the supreme authority which resided in the assembly of their brethren; but in the government of his peculiar diocese each of them exacted from his flock the same implicit obedience as if that favourite metaphor had been literally just, and as if

the shepherd had been of a more exalted nature than
that of his sheep.

This obedience, however, was not imposed without
some efforts on one side and some resistance on the
other. The democratical part of the constitution was in
many places very warmly supported by the zealous or
interested opposition of the inferior clergy. But their
patriotism received the ignominious epithets of faction
and schism, and the episcopal cause was indebted for
its rapid progress to the labours of many active prelates,
who, like Cyprian of Carthage, could reconcile the arts
of the most ambitious statesman with the Christian
virtues which seem adapted to the character of a saint
and martyr.

The same causes which at first had destroyed the
equality of the presbyters introduced among the bishops
a pre-eminence of rank, and from thence a superiority
of jurisdiction. As often as in the spring and autumn
they met in provincial synod, the difference of personal
merit and reputation was very sensibly felt among the
members of the assembly, and the multitude was governed by the wisdom and eloquence of the few. But
the order of public proceedings required a more regular and less invidious distinction; the office of perpetual
presidents in the councils of each province was conferred on the bishops of the principal city; and these
aspiring prelates, who soon acquired the lofty titles of
metropolitans and *primates,* secretly prepared themselves to usurp over their episcopal brethren the same
authority which the bishops had so lately assumed above
the college of presbyters. Nor was it long before an
emulation of pre-eminence and power prevailed among
the metropolitans themselves, each of them affecting to
display, in the most pompous terms, the temporal honours and advantages of the city over which he presided,

the numbers and opulence of the Christians who were subject to their pastoral care, the saints and martyrs who had arisen among them, and the purity with which they preserved the tradition of the faith as it had been transmitted through a series of orthodox bishops from the apostle or the apostolic disciple to whom the foundation of their church was ascribed.

From every cause either of a civil or of an ecclesiastical nature, it was easy to foresee that Rome must enjoy the respect, and would soon claim the obedience, of the provinces. The society of the faithful bore a just proportion to the capital of the empire; and the Roman church was the greatest, the most numerous, and, in regard to the West, the most ancient of all the Christian establishments, many of which had received their religion from the pious labours of her missionaries. Instead of *one* apostolic founder, the utmost boast of Antioch, of Ephesus, or of Corinth, the banks of the Tiber were supposed to have been honoured with the preaching and martyrdom of the *two* most eminent among the apostles; and the bishops of Rome very prudently claimed the inheritance of whatsoever prerogatives were attributed either to the person or to the office of St. Peter.

The bishops of Italy and of the provinces were disposed to allow them a primacy of order and association (such was their very accurate expression) in the Christian aristocracy. But the power of a monarch was rejected with abhorrence, and the aspiring genius of Rome experienced from the nations of Asia and Africa a more vigorous resistance to her spiritual than she had formerly done to her temporal dominion. The patriotic Cyprian, who ruled with the most absolute sway the church of Carthage and the provincial synods, opposed with resolution and success the ambition of the Roman pontiff, artfully connected his own cause with that of the eastern bishops, and, like Hannibal, sought out new allies in the heart of Asia. If this Punic war was carried on without any effusion of blood, it was owing much less to the moderation than to the weakness of the contending prelates. Invectives and excommunications were *their* only weapons; and these, during the progress of the whole controversy, they hurled against each other with equal fury and devotion. The hard necessity of censuring either a pope or a saint and martyr distresses the modern Catholics whenever they are obliged to relate the particulars of a dispute in which the champions of religion indulged such passions as seem much more adapted to the senate or to the camp.

The progress of the ecclesiastical authority gave birth to the memorable distinction of the laity and of the clergy, which had been unknown to the Greeks and Romans. The former of these appellations comprehended the body of the Christian people; the latter, according to the signification of the word, was appropriated to the chosen portion that had been set apart for the service of religion, a celebrated order of men which has furnished the most important, though not always the most edifying, subjects for modern history. Their mutual hostilities sometimes disturbed the peace of the infant church, but their zeal and activity were united in the common cause; and the love of power, which under the most artful disguises could insinuate itself into the breasts of bishops and martyrs, animated them to increase the number of their subjects and to enlarge the limits of the Christian empire. They were destitute of any temporal force, and they were for a long time discouraged and oppressed rather than assisted by the civil magistrate; but they had acquired, and they employed within their own society, the two most efficacious instruments of government, rewards and punishments, the former derived from the pious liberality, the latter from the devout apprehensions, of the faithful.

1. *Rewards.* The community of goods, which had so agreeably amused the imagination of Plato and which subsisted in some degree among the austere sect of the Essenians, was adopted for a short time in the primitive church. The fervour of the first proselytes prompted them to sell those worldly possessions which they despised, to lay the price of them at the feet of the apostles, and to content themselves with receiving an equal share out of the general distribution. The progress of the Christian religion relaxed and gradually abolished this generous institution, which in hands less pure than those of the apostles would too soon have been corrupted and abused by the returning selfishness of human nature; and the converts who embraced the new religion were permitted to retain the possession of their patrimony, to receive legacies and inheritances, and to increase their separate property by all the lawful means of trade and industry. Instead of an absolute sacrifice, a moderate proportion was accepted by the ministers of the Gospel; and in their weekly or monthly assemblies every believer, according to the exigency of the occasion and the measure of his wealth and piety, presented his voluntary offering for the use of the common fund. Nothing, however inconsiderable, was refused; but it was diligently inculcated that in the article of tithes the Mosaic law was still of divine obligation; and that since the Jews, under a less perfect discipline, had been commanded to pay a tenth part of all that they possessed, it would become the disciples of Christ to distinguish themselves by a superior degree of liberality and to acquire some merit by resigning a

superfluous treasure, which must so soon be annihilated with the world itself.

It is almost unnecessary to observe that the revenue of each particular church, which was of so uncertain and fluctuating a nature, must have varied with the poverty or the opulence of the faithful, as they were dispersed in obscure villages or collected in the great cities of the empire. In the time of the emperor Decius it was the opinion of the magistrates that the Christians of Rome were possessed of very considerable wealth, that vessels of gold and silver were used in their religious worship, and that many among their proselytes had sold their lands and houses to increase the public riches of the sect—at the expense, indeed, of their unfortunate children, who found themselves beggars because their parents had been saints.

We should listen with distrust to the suspicions of strangers and enemies; on this occasion, however, they receive a very specious and probable colour from the two following circumstances, the only ones that have reached our knowledge which define any precise sums or convey any distinct idea. Almost at the same period the bishop of Carthage, from a society less opulent than that of Rome, collected an hundred thousand sesterces (above eight hundred and fifty pounds sterling) on a sudden call of charity to redeem the brethren of Numidia, who had been carried away captives by the barbarians of the desert. About an hundred years before the reign of Decius the Roman church had received, in a single donation, the sum of two hundred thousand sesterces from a stranger of Pontus, who proposed to fix his residence in the capital.

These oblations for the most part were made in money; nor was the society of Christians either desirous or capable of acquiring to any considerable degree the

encumbrance of landed property. It had been provided
by several laws, which were enacted with the same
design as our statutes of mortmain, that no real estates
should be given or bequeathed to any corporate body
without either a special privilege or a particular dispensation from the emperor or from the senate, who were
seldom disposed to grant them in favour of a sect at
first the object of their contempt and at last of their
fears and jealousy. A transaction, however, is related
under the reign of Alexander Severus, which discovers
that the restraint was sometimes eluded or suspended,
and that the Christians were permitted to claim and to
possess lands within the limits of Rome itself. The progress of Christianity and the civil confusion of the empire contributed to relax the severity of the laws; and
before the close of the third century many considerable
estates were bestowed on the opulent churches of Rome,
Milan. Carthage, Antioch, Alexandria, and the other
great cities of Italy and the provinces.

The bishop was the natural steward of the church;
the public stock was entrusted to his care without account or control; the presbyters were confined to their
spiritual functions, and the more dependent order of
deacons was solely employed in the management and
distribution of the ecclesiastical revenue. If we may
give credit to the vehement declamations of Cyprian,
there were too many among his African brethren who
in the execution of their charge violated every precept
not only of evangelic perfection but even of moral
virtue. By some of these unfaithful stewards the riches
of the church were lavished in sensual pleasures; by
others they were perverted to the purposes of private
gain, of fraudulent purchases, and of rapacious usury.
But as long as the contributions of the Christian people
were free and unconstrained, the abuse of their confi-

dence could not be very frequent, and the general uses to which their liberality was applied reflected honour on the religious society.

A decent portion was reserved for the maintenance of the bishop and his clergy; a sufficient sum was allotted for the expenses of the public worship, of which the feasts of love—the *agapœ,* as they were called—constituted a very pleasing part. The whole remainder was the sacred patrimony of the poor. According to the discretion of the bishop, it was distributed to support widows and orphans, the lame, the sick, and the aged of the community, to comfort strangers and pilgrims, and to alleviate the misfortunes of prisoners and captives, more especially when their sufferings had been occasioned by their firm attachment to the cause of religion. A generous intercourse of charity united the most distant provinces, and the smaller congregations were cheerfully assisted by the alms of their more opulent brethren.

Such an institution, which paid less regard to the merit than to the distress of the object, very materially conduced to the progress of Christianity. The pagans, who were actuated by a sense of humanity, while they derided the doctrines, acknowledged the benevolence, of the new sect. The prospect of immediate relief and of future protection allured into its hospitable bosom many of those unhappy persons whom the neglect of the world would have abandoned to the miseries of want, of sickness, and of old age. There is some reason likewise to believe that great numbers of infants who, according to the inhuman practice of the times, had been exposed by their parents, were frequently rescued from death, baptized, educated, and maintained by the piety of the Christians and at the expense of the public treasure.

2. *Punishments by the early church.* It is the undoubted right of every society to exclude from its communion and benefits such among its members as reject
or violate those regulations which have been established
by general consent. In the exercise of this power the
censures of the Christian church were chiefly directed
against scandalous sinners, and particularly those who
were guilty of murder, of fraud, or of incontinence;
against the authors or the followers of any heretical
opinions which had been condemned by the judgment
of the episcopal order; and against those unhappy persons who, whether from choice or from compulsion, had
polluted themselves after their baptism by any act of
idolatrous worship.

The consequences of excommunication were of a temporal as well as a spiritual nature. The Christian against
whom it was pronounced was deprived of any part in
the oblations of the faithful. The ties both of religious
and of private friendship were dissolved; he found himself a profane object of abhorrence to the persons whom
he the most esteemed, or by whom he had been the
most tenderly beloved; and as far as an expulsion from
a respectable society could imprint on his character
a mark of disgrace, he was shunned or suspected by
the generality of mankind. The situation of these unfortunate exiles was in itself very painful and melancholy; but, as it usually happens, their apprehensions
far exceeded their sufferings. The benefits of the Christian communion were those of eternal life; nor could
they erase from their minds the awful opinion that to
those ecclesiastical governors by whom they were condemned the Deity had committed the keys of Hell
and of Paradise. The heretics, indeed, who might be
supported by the consciousness of their intentions and
by the flattering hope that they alone had discovered

the true path of salvation, endeavoured to regain in their separate assemblies those comforts, temporal as well as spiritual, which they no longer derived from the great society of Christians. But almost all those who had reluctantly yielded to the power of vice or idolatry were sensible of their fallen condition and anxiously desirous of being restored to the benefits of the Christian communion.

With regard to the treatment of these penitents two opposite opinions, the one of justice, the other of mercy, divided the primitive church. The more rigid and inflexible casuists refused them forever, and without exception, the meanest place in the holy community which they had disgraced or deserted; and, leaving them to the remorse of a guilty conscience, indulged them only with a faint ray of hope that the contrition of their life and death might possibly be accepted by the Supreme Being. A milder sentiment was embraced, in practice as well as in theory, by the purest and most respectable of the Christian churches. The gates of reconciliation and of heaven were seldom shut against the returning penitent; but a severe and solemn form of discipline was instituted, which, while it served to expiate his crime, might powerfully deter the spectators from the imitation of his example. Humbled by a public confession, emaciated by fasting, and clothed in sackcloth, the penitent lay prostrate at the door of the assembly, imploring with tears the pardon of his offences and soliciting the prayers of the faithful. If the fault was of a very heinous nature, whole years of penance were esteemed an inadequate satisfaction to the divine justice; and it was always by slow and painful gradations that the sinner, the heretic, or the apostate was readmitted into the bosom of the church. A sentence of perpetual excommunication was, however, reserved for some crimes of

an extraordinary magnitude, and particularly for the in-
excusable relapses of those penitents who had already
experienced and abused the clemency of their ecclesiastical superiors.

According to the circumstances or the number of
the guilty, the exercise of the Christian discipline was
varied by the discretion of the bishops. The councils
of Ancyra and Illiberis were held about the same time,
the one in Galatia, the other in Spain; but their respective canons, which are still extant, seem to breathe a
very different spirit. The Galatian, who after his baptism had repeatedly sacrificed to idols, might obtain
his pardon by a penance of seven years; and if he had
seduced others to imitate his example, only three years
more were added to the term of his exile. But the unhappy Spaniard who had committed the same offence
was deprived of the hope of reconciliation even in the
article of death; and his idolatry was placed at the
head of a list of seventeen other crimes, against which
a sentence no less terrible was pronounced. Among
these we may distinguish the inexpiable guilt of calum-
niating a bishop, a presbyter, or even a deacon.

The well-tempered mixture of liberality and rigour,
the judicious dispensation of rewards and punishments,
according to the maxims of policy as well as justice,
constituted the *human* strength of the church. The
bishops, whose paternal care extended itself to the government of both worlds, were sensible of the importance of these prerogatives; and, covering their ambition with the fair pretence of the love of order, they
were jealous of any rival in the exercise of a discipline
so necessary to prevent the desertion of those troops
which had enlisted themselves under the banner of the
Cross and whose numbers every day became more considerable. From the imperious declamations of Cyprian

308 DECLINE AND FALL OF THE ROMAN EMPIRE

we should naturally conclude that the doctrines of excommunication and penance formed the most essential part of religion, and that it was much less dangerous for the disciples of Christ to neglect the observance of the moral duties than to despise the censures and authority of their bishops. Sometimes we might imagine that we were listening to the voice of Moses, when he commanded the earth to open and to swallow up in consuming flames the rebellious race which refused obedience to the priesthood of Aaron; and we should sometimes suppose that we heard a Roman consul asserting the majesty of the republic and declaring his inflexible resolution to enforce the rigour of the laws.

"If such irregularities are suffered with impunity" (it is thus that the bishop of Carthage chides the lenity of his colleague), "if such irregularities are suffered, there is an end of *episcopal vigour;* an end of the sublime and divine power of governing the Church; an end of Christianity itself." Cyprian had renounced those temporal honours which it is probable he would never have obtained; but the acquisition of such absolute command over the consciences and understanding of a congregation, however obscure or despised by the world, is more truly grateful to the pride of the human heart than the possession of the most despotic power imposed by arms and conquest on a reluctant people.[18]

It has been observed with truth as well as propriety that the conquests of Rome prepared and facilitated those of Christianity. In the second chapter of this work we have attempted to explain in what manner the most

18. *Editor's note:* The path of Christianity, as Gibbon remarks in a passage omitted here, was smoothed by the broad disbelief in the pagan religions, particularly among the wealthy or learned classes.

civilized provinces of Europe, Asia, and Africa were united under the dominion of one sovereign and gradually connected by the most intimate ties of laws, of manners, and of language. The Jews of Palestine, who had fondly expected a temporal deliverer, gave so cold a reception to the miracles of the divine prophet that it was found unnecessary to publish, or at least to preserve, any Hebrew Gospel. The authentic histories of the actions of Christ were composed in the Greek language, at a considerable distance from Jerusalem, and after the Gentile converts were grown extremely numerous. As soon as those histories were translated into the Latin tongue they were perfectly intelligible to all the subjects of Rome, excepting only to the peasants of Syria and Egypt, for whose benefit particular versions were afterwards made. The public highways which had been constructed for the use of the legions opened an easy passage for the Christian missionaries from Damascus to Corinth, and from Italy to the extremity of Spain or Britain; nor did those spiritual conquerors encounter any of the obstacles which usually retard or prevent the introduction of a foreign religion into a distant country.

There is the strongest reason to believe that before the reigns of Diocletian and Constantine the faith of Christ had been preached in every province and in all the great cities of the empire; but the foundation of the several congregations, the numbers of the faithful who composed them, and their proportion to the unbelieving multitude are now buried in obscurity or disguised by fiction and declamation. Such imperfect circumstances, however, as have reached our knowledge concerning the increase of the Christian name in Asia and Greece, in Egypt, in Italy, and in the West, we shall now proceed to relate, without neglecting the real or imaginary acquisitions which lay beyond the frontiers of the Roman empire.

The rich provinces that extend from the Euphrates to the Ionian Sea were the principal theatre on which the apostle of the Gentiles displayed his zeal and piety. The seeds of the Gospel, which he had scattered in a fertile soil, were diligently cultivated by his disciples; and it should seem that, during the two first centuries, the most considerable body of Christians was contained within those limits. Among the societies which were instituted in Syria, none were more ancient or more illustrious than those of Damascus, of Berœa or Aleppo, and of Antioch. The prophetic introduction of the Apocalypse had described and immortalized the seven churches of Asia—Ephesus, Smyrna, Pergamus, Thyatira, Sardis, Laodicea, and Philadelphia; and their colonies were soon diffused over that populous country. In a very early period the islands of Cyprus and Crete, the provinces of Thrace and Macedonia, gave a favourable reception to the new religion; and Christian republics were soon founded in the cities of Corinth, of Sparta, and of Athens. The antiquity of the Greek and Asiatic churches allowed a sufficient space of time for their increase and multiplication; and even the swarms of Gnostics and other heretics serve to display the flourishing condition of the orthodox church, since the appellation of heretics has always been applied to the less numerous party.

To these domestic testimonies we may add the confession, the complaints, and the apprehensions of the Gentiles themselves. From the writings of Lucian, a philosopher who had studied mankind and who describes their manners in the most lively colours, we may learn that under the reign of Commodus his native country of Pontus was filled with Epicureans and *Christians*. Within fourscore years after the death of Christ, the humane Pliny laments the magnitude of the evil which he vainly attempted to eradicate. In his very curious epistle to the emperor Trajan he affirms that the temples were almost deserted, that the sacred victims scarcely found any purchasers, and that the superstition had not only infected the cities but had even spread itself into the villages and the open country of Pontus and Bithynia.

Without descending into a minute scrutiny of the expressions or of the motives of those writers who either celebrate or lament the progress of Christianity in the East, it may in general be observed that none of them has left us any grounds from whence a just estimate might be formed of the real numbers of the faithful in those provinces. One circumstance, however, has been fortunately preserved, which seems to cast a more distinct light on this obscure but interesting subject. Under the reign of Theodosius, after Christianity had enjoyed during more than sixty years the sunshine of Imperial favour, the ancient and illustrious church of Antioch consisted of one hundred thousand persons, three thousand of whom were supported out of the public oblations. The splendour and dignity of the queen of the East, the acknowledged populousness of Cæsarea, Seleucia, and Alexandria, and the destruction of two hundred and fifty thousand souls in the earthquake which afflicted Antioch under the elder Justin are so many convincing proofs that the whole number of its inhabitants was not less than half a million, and that the Christians, however multiplied by zeal and power, did not exceed a fifth part of that great city.

How different a proportion must we adopt when we compare the persecuted with the triumphant church, the

West with the East, remote villages with populous towns, and countries recently converted to the faith with the place where the believers first received the appellation of Christians! It must not, however, be dissembled that in another passage Chrysostom, to whom we are indebted for this useful information, computes the multitude of the faithful as even superior to that of the Jews and pagans. But the solution of this apparent difficulty is easy and obvious. The eloquent preacher draws a parallel between the civil and the ecclesiastical constitution of Antioch, between the list of Christians who had acquired heaven by baptism and the list of citizens who had a right to share the public liberality. Slaves, strangers, and infants were comprised in the former; they were excluded from the latter.

The extensive commerce of Alexandria and its proximity to Palestine gave an easy entrance to the new religion. It was at first embraced by great numbers of the Therapeutæ, or Essenians, of the lake Mareotis, a Jewish sect which had abated much of its reverence for the Mosaic ceremonies. The austere life of the Essenians, their fasts and excommunications, the community of goods, the love of celibacy, their zeal for martyrdom, and the warmth though not the purity of their faith, already offered a very lively image of the primitive discipline. It was in the school of Alexandria that the Christian theology appears to have assumed a regular and scientifical form; and when Hadrian visited Egypt he found a church, composed of Jews and of Greeks, sufficiently important to attract the notice of that inquisitive prince. But the progress of Christianity was for a long time confined within the limits of a single city, which was itself a foreign colony; and till the close of the second century the predecessors of Demetrius were the only prelates of the Egyptian church. Three bishops were consecrated by the hands of Demetrius, and the number was increased to twenty by his successor Heraclas. The body of the natives, a people distinguished by a sullen inflexibility of temper, entertained the new doctrine with coldness and reluctance; and even in the time of Origen it was rare to meet with an Egyptian who had surmounted his early prejudices in favour of the sacred animals of his country. As soon, indeed, as Christianity ascended the throne, the zeal of those barbarians obeyed the prevailing impulsion; the cities of Egypt were filled with bishops, and the deserts of Thebais swarmed with hermits.

A perpetual stream of strangers and provincials flowed into the capacious bosom of Rome. Whatever was strange or odious, whoever was guilty or suspected, might hope in the obscurity of that immense capital to elude the vigilance of the law. In such a various conflux of nations, every teacher, either of truth or of falsehood, every founder, whether of a virtuous or a criminal association, might easily multiply his disciples or accomplices. The Christians of Rome, at the time of the accidental persecution of Nero, are represented by Tacitus as already amounting to a very great multitude, and the language of that great historian is almost similar to the style employed by Livy when he relates the introduction and the suppression of the rites of Bacchus. After the Bacchanals had awakened the severity of the senate, it was likewise apprehended that a very great multitude, as it were *another people,* had been initiated into those abhorred mysteries.

A more careful inquiry soon demonstrated that the offenders did not exceed seven thousand, a number indeed sufficiently alarming when considered as the object of public justice. It is with the same candid allowance that we should interpret the vague expressions of Tacitus, and in a former instance of Pliny, when they exaggerate the crowds of deluded fanatics who had forsaken the established worship of the gods. The church of Rome was undoubtedly the first and most populous of the empire; and we are possessed of an authentic record which attests the state of religion in that city about the middle of the third century, and after a peace of thirty-eight years. The clergy at that time consisted of a bishop, forty-six presbyters, seven deacons, as many sub-deacons, forty-two acolytes, and fifty readers, exorcists, and porters. The number of widows, of the infirm, and of the poor who were maintained by the oblations of the faithful amounted to fifteen hundred. From reason as well as from the analogy of Antioch, we may venture to estimate the Christians of Rome at about fifty thousand. The populousness of that great capital cannot perhaps be exactly ascertained; but the most modest calculation will not surely reduce it lower than a million of inhabitants, of whom the Christians might constitute at the most a twentieth part.

The western provincials appeared to have derived the knowledge of Christianity from the same source which had diffused among them the language, the sentiments, and the manners of Rome. In this more important circumstance, Africa as well as Gaul was gradually fashioned to the imitation of the capital. Yet notwithstanding the many favourable occasions which might invite the Roman missionaries to visit their Latin provinces, it was late before they passed either the sea or the Alps; nor can we discover in those great countries any assured traces either of faith or of persecution that ascend higher than the reign of the Antonines.

The slow progress of the Gospel in the cold climate of Gaul was extremely different from the eagerness with which it seems to have been received on the burning sands of Africa. The African Christians soon formed one of the principal members of the primitive church. The practice introduced into that province of appointing bishops to the most inconsiderable towns, and very frequently to the most obscure villages, contributed to multiply the splendour and importance of their religious societies, which during the course of the third century were animated by the zeal of Tertullian, directed by the abilities of Cyprian, and adorned by the eloquence of Lactantius. But if on the contrary we turn our eyes towards Gaul, we must content ourselves with discovering, in the time of Marcus Antoninus, the feeble and united congregations of Lyons and Vienne; and even as late as the reign of Decius we are assured that in a few cities only—Arles, Narbonne, Toulouse, Limoges, Clermont, Tours, and Paris—some scattered churches were supported by the devotion of a small number of Christians.

Silence is indeed very consistent with devotion; but as it is seldom compatible with zeal we may perceive and lament the languid state of Christianity in those provinces which had exchanged the Celtic for the Latin tongue, since they did not during the three first centuries give birth to a single ecclesiastical writer. From Gaul, which claimed a just pre-eminence of learning and authority over all the countries on this side of the Alps, the light of the Gospel was more faintly reflected on the remote provinces of Spain and Britain; and if we may credit the vehement assertions of Tertullian, they had already received the first rays of the faith when he addressed his Apology to the magistrates of the emperor Severus. But the obscure and imperfect origin of the western churches of Europe has been so negligently recorded that, if we would relate the time and manner of their foundation, we must supply the silence of antiquity by those legends which avarice or superstition long afterwards dictated to the monks in the lazy gloom of their convents. Of these holy romances, that of the apostle St. James can alone, by its singular extravagance, deserve to be mentioned. From a peaceful fisherman of the lake of Gennesareth he was transformed into a valorous knight, who charged at the head of the Spanish chivalry in their battles against the Moors. The gravest historians have celebrated his exploits; the miraculous shrine of Compostella displayed his power; and the sword of a military order, assisted by the terrors of the Inquisition, was sufficient to remove every objection of profane criticism.

The progress of Christianity was not confined to the Roman empire; and, according to the primitive fathers, who interpret facts by prophecy, the new religion, within a century after the death of its Divine Author, had already visited every part of the globe. "There exists not," says Justin Martyr, "a people, whether Greek or barbarian, or any other race of men, by whatsoever appellation or manners they may be distinguished, however ignorant of arts or agriculture, whether they dwell under tents, or wander about in covered waggons, among whom prayers are not offered up in the name of a crucified Jesus to the Father and Creator of all things." But this splendid exaggeration, which even at present it would be extremely difficult to reconcile with the real state of mankind, can be considered only as the rash sally of a devout but careless writer, the measure of whose belief was regulated by that of his wishes.

But neither the belief nor the wishes of the fathers can alter the truth of history. It will still remain an undoubted fact that the barbarians of Scythia and Germany, who afterwards subverted the Roman monarchy, were involved in the darkness of paganism, and that even the conversion of Iberia, of Armenia, or of Æthiopia was not attempted with any degree of success till the sceptre was in the hands of an orthodox emperor. Before that time the various accidents of war and commerce might indeed diffuse an imperfect knowledge of the Gospel among the tribes of Caledonia and among the borderers of the Rhine, the Danube, and the Euphrates. Beyond the last-mentioned river, Edessa was distinguished by a firm and early adherence to the faith. From Edessa the principles of Christianity were easily introduced into the Greek and Syrian cities which obeyed the successors of Artaxerxes; but they do not appear to have made any deep impression on the minds of the Persians, whose religious system, by the labours of a well-disciplined order of priests, had been constructed with much more art and solidity than the uncertain mythology of Greece and Rome.

From this impartial though imperfect survey of the progress of Christianity, it may perhaps seem probable that the number of its proselytes has been excessively magnified by fear on the one side and by devotion on the other. According to the irreproachable testimony of Origen, the proportion of the faithful was very inconsiderable when compared with the multitude of an unbelieving world; but as we are left without any distinct information, it is impossible to determine, and it is difficult even to conjecture, the real numbers of the primitive Christians. The most favourable calculation, however, that can be deduced from the examples of Antioch and of Rome will not permit us to imagine that more than a twentieth part of the subjects of the empire had enlisted themselves under the banner of the Cross before the important conversion of Constantine. But their habits of faith, of zeal, and of union seemed to multiply their numbers; and the same causes which contributed to their future increase served to render their actual strength more apparent and more formidable.

Such is the constitution of civil society that whilst a few persons are distinguished by riches, by honours, and by knowledge, the body of the people is condemned to obscurity, ignorance, and poverty. The Christian religion, which addressed itself to the whole human race, must consequently collect a far greater number of proselytes from the lower than from the superior ranks of life. This innocent and natural circumstance has been improved into a very odious imputation, which seems to be less strenuously denied by the apologists than it is urged by the adversaries of the faith, that the new sect of Christians was almost entirely composed of the dregs of the populace, of peasants and mechanics, of boys and women, of beggars and slaves, the last of whom might sometimes introduce the missionaries into the rich and noble families to which they belonged. These obscure teachers (such was the charge of malice and infidelity) are as mute in public as they are loquacious and dogmatical in private. Whilst they cautiously avoid the dangerous encounter of philosophers, they mingle with the rude and illiterate crowd and insinuate themselves into those minds whom their age, their sex, or their education has the best disposed to receive the impression of superstitious terrors.

This unfavourable picture, though not devoid of a faint resemblance, betrays by its dark colouring and distorted features the pencil of an enemy. As the humble faith of Christ diffused itself through the world, it was embraced by several persons who derived some consequence from the advantages of nature or fortune. Aristides, who presented an eloquent apology to the emperor Hadrian, was an Athenian philosopher. Justin

Martyr had sought divine knowledge in the schools of
Zeno, of Aristotle, of Pythagoras, and of Plato before
he fortunately was accosted by the old man, or rather
the angel, who turned his attention to the study of the
Jewish prophets. Clemens of Alexandria had acquired
much various reading in the Greek, and Tertullian in
the Latin, language. Julius Africanus and Origen possessed a very considerable share of the learning of their
times; and although the style of Cyprian is very different from that of Lactantius, we might almost discover
that both those writers had been public teachers of
rhetoric.

Even the study of philosophy was at length introduced among the Christians, but it was not always productive of the most salutary effects; knowledge was as
often the parent of heresy as of devotion, and the description which was designed for the followers of Arte-
mon may with equal propriety be applied to the various
sects that resisted the successors of the apostles. "They
presume to alter the holy Scriptures, to abandon the
ancient rule of faith, and to form their opinions according to the subtle precepts of logic. The science of the
church is neglected for the study of geometry, and they
lose sight of heaven while they are employed in measuring the earth. Euclid is perpetually in their hands.
Aristotle and Theophrastus are the objects of their admiration, and they express an uncommon reverence for
the works of Galen. Their errors are derived from the
abuse of the arts and sciences of the infidels, and they
corrupt the simplicity of the Gospel by the refinements
of human reason." [19]

Nor can it be affirmed with truth that the advantages

19. It may be hoped that none except the heretics gave
occasion to the complaint of Celsus that the Christians were
perpetually correcting and altering their Gospels.

of birth and fortune were always separated from the profession of Christianity. Several Roman citizens were brought before the tribunal of Pliny, and he soon discovered that a great number of persons of *every order* of men in Bithynia had deserted the religion of their ancestors. His unsuspected testimony may in this instance obtain more credit than the bold challenge of Tertullian, when he addresses himself to the fears as well as to the humanity of the proconsul of Africa, by assuring him that if he persists in his cruel intentions he must decimate Carthage, and that he will find among the guilty many persons of his own rank, senators and matrons of noblest extraction, and the friends or relations of his most intimate friends. It appears, however, that about forty years afterwards the emperor Valerian was persuaded of the truth of this assertion, since in one of his rescripts he evidently supposes that senators, Roman knights, and ladies of quality were engaged in the Christian sect. The church still continued to increase its outward splendour as it lost its internal purity; and in the reign of Diocletian the palace, the courts of justice, and even the army concealed a multitude of Christians, who endeavoured to reconcile the interests of the present with those of a future life.

And yet these exceptions are either too few in number or too recent in time entirely to remove the imputation of ignorance and obscurity which has been so arrogantly cast on the first proselytes of Christianity. Instead of employing in our defence the fictions of later ages, it will be more prudent to convert the occasion of scandal into a subject of edification. Our serious thoughts will suggest to us that the apostles themselves were chosen by Providence among the fishermen of Galilee, and that the lower we depress the temporal condition of the first Christians, the more reason we shall find to admire their merit and success. It is incumbent on us diligently to remember that the kingdom of Heaven was promised to the poor in spirit, and that minds afflicted by calamity and the contempt of mankind cheerfully listen to the divine promise of future happiness; while on the contrary the fortunate are satisfied with possession of this world, and the wise abuse in doubt and dispute their vain superiority of reason and knowledge.

We stand in need of such reflections to comfort us for the loss of some illustrious characters, which in our eyes might have seemed the most worthy of the heavenly present. The names of Seneca, of the elder and the younger Pliny, of Tacitus, of Plutarch, of Galen, of the slave Epictetus, and of the emperor Marcus Antoninus adorn the age in which they flourished and exalt the dignity of human nature. They filled with glory their respective stations, either in active or contemplative life; their excellent understandings were improved by study; philosophy had purified their minds from the prejudices of the popular superstition; and their days were spent in the pursuit of truth and the practice of virtue. Yet all these sages (it is no less an object of surprise than of concern) overlooked or rejected the perfection of the Christian system. Their language or their silence equally discover their contempt for the growing sect which in their time had diffused itself over the Roman empire. Those among them who condescend to mention the Christians consider them only as obstinate and perverse enthusiasts, who exacted an implicit submission to their mysterious doctrines without being able to produce a single argument that could engage the attention of men of sense and learning.

It is at least doubtful whether any of these philosophers perused the apologies which the primitive Christians repeatedly published in behalf of themselves and of their religion; but it is much to be lamented that such a cause was not defended by abler advocates. They expose with superfluous wit and eloquence the extravagance of polytheism. They interest our compassion by displaying the innocence and sufferings of their injured brethren. But when they would demonstrate the divine origin of Christianity, they insist much more strongly on the predictions which announced, than on the miracles which accompanied, the appearance of the Messiah. Their favourite argument might serve to edify a Christian or to convert a Jew, since both the one and the other acknowledge the authority of those prophecies, and both are obliged, with devout reverence, to search for their sense and their accomplishment.

But this mode of persuasion loses much of its weight and influence when it is addressed to those who neither understand nor respect the Mosaic dispensation and the prophetic style. In the unskilful hands of Justin and of the succeeding apologists, the sublime meaning of the Hebrew oracles evaporates in distant types, affected conceits, and cold allegories; and even their authenticity was rendered suspicious to an unenlightened Gentile by the mixture of pious forgeries which, under the names of Orpheus, Hermes, and the Sibyls,[20] were obtruded on him as of equal value with the genuine inspirations of Heaven. The adoption of fraud and sophistry in the defence of revelation too often reminds us of the

20. The philosophers, who derided the more ancient predictions of the Sibyls, would easily have detected the Jewish and Christian forgeries, which have been so triumphantly quoted by the fathers from Justin Martyr to Lactantius. When the Sibylline verses had performed their appointed task they, like the system of the millennium, were quietly laid aside. The Christian Sibyl had unluckily fixed the ruin of Rome for the year 195.

injudicious conduct of those poets who load their *invulnerable* heroes with a useless weight of cumbersome and brittle armour.

But how shall we excuse the supine inattention of the pagan and philosophic world to those evidences which were presented by the hand of Omnipotence not to their reason but to their senses? During the age of Christ, of his apostles, and of their first disciples, the doctrine which they preached was confirmed by innumerable prodigies. The lame walked, the blind saw, the sick were healed, the dead were raised, demons were expelled, and the laws of Nature were frequently suspended for the benefit of the church. But the sages of Greece and Rome turned aside from the awful spectacle and, pursuing the ordinary occupations of life and study, appeared unconscious of any alterations in the moral or physical government of the world. Under the reign of Tiberius the whole earth, or at least a celebrated province of the Roman empire, was involved in a preternatural darkness of three hours. Even this miraculous event, which ought to have excited the wonder, the curiosity, and the devotion of mankind, passed without notice in an age of science and history. It happened during the lifetime of Seneca and the elder Pliny, who must have experienced the immediate effects or received the earliest intelligence of the prodigy. Each of these philosophers, in a laborious work, has recorded all the great phenomena of Nature, earthquakes, meteors, comets, and eclipses, which his indefatigable curiosity could collect. Both the one and the other have omitted to mention the greatest phenomenon to which the mortal eye has been witness since the creation of the globe. A distinct chapter of Pliny is designed for eclipses of an extraordinary nature and unusual duration; but he contents himself with describing the singular defect of light which followed the murder of Cæsar, when, during the greatest part of a year, the orb of the sun appeared pale and without splendour. This season of obscurity, which cannot surely be compared with the preternatural darkness of the Passion, had been already celebrated by most of the poets and historians of that memorable age.

In the next chapter of the original Gibbon examines the apparent sternness towards Christianity of those same emperors "who beheld without concern a thousand forms of religion subsisting under their gentle sway"; and he suggests that it was based upon the intolerance of the primitive church, which disdained "every form of worship except its own as impious and idolatrous." Each new Christian convert "rejected with contempt the superstitions of his family, his city, and his province" and connected himself "in an indissoluble band of union with a peculiar society which everywhere assumed a different character from the rest of mankind."

Despite the resulting pagan resentment, Gibbon nonetheless concludes that a close reading and careful interpretation of history will indicate: (1) that the primitive church was for a considerable time too small and obscure to receive official notice; (2) that the authorities used great caution in proceeding against their Christian subjects; (3) that the punishments meted out were rare and, for the times, moderate; and (4) that the early church enjoyed long intervals of peace and tranquillity.

The first persecution of the Christians occurred after a great fire in Rome during the reign of the emperor Nero, who, to divert suspicion from himself about the origin of the fire, "resolved to substitute in his own place some fictitious criminals." But the outburst, though violent, was of brief duration and confined to the walls of Rome; and Gibbon speculates that the real object of the persecution may not have been the Christians at all, but a schismatic Jewish sect known as Gaulonites.

During the reign of Trajan, when the younger Pliny as governor of Bithynia and Pontus wrote the emperor asking for instructions in dealing with the numerous and growing sect of Christians, both the query itself as well as the nature of the answer implied that no general laws or decrees were in force against the Christians. Trajan's reply showed "much more solicitude to protect the security of the innocent than to prevent the escape of the guilty." Though persons convicted as Christians were to be punished, Trajan prohibited any inquiries designed to detect the supposed criminals and required that any charge of Christian leanings be made openly and directly, with the most severe penalties for false accusation.

Those charged were not always indicted; those indicted were not always convicted; those convicted were not always punished; and such punishments as were imposed were likely to be not execution but imprisonment, exile, etc., which might be, and frequently were, remitted in a general decree of amnesty accompanying some happy public event. Later ecclesiastical writers frequently "entertained themselves with diversifying the deaths and sufferings of the primitive martyrs." Christian maidens, for example, were allegedly abandoned to the embraces of youths who were instructed "to maintain the honor of Venus against the impious virgin who refused to burn incense on her altars." Gibbon dismisses such stories contemptuously, remarking that their inventors "ascribed to the magistrates the same degree of implacable and unrelenting zeal which filled their own breasts against the heretics or the idolators of their own time."

During the frequent peaceful intervals enjoyed by

the early church, many persons high in Imperial favour were themselves Christians or were friendly towards the foundling religion. Marcia, the favourite concubine of Commodus who eventually contrived his murder (see p. 128), was such a patroness, though her occupation ruled out the possibility of baptism. Septimus Severus was well disposed towards the new sect, at least in the early part of his reign, allegedly because one of his Christian slaves had anointed the emperor with a healing oil during a dangerous illness from which the emperor recovered; Caracalla's nurse was a Christian; the emperor Philip was so partial to the Christians as to give rise to the rumour, probably unfounded, that he himself was a convert; and following the accession of Gallienus the church enjoyed some four decades of uninterrupted peace and growth.

A severe repression of the early church came during, and shortly after, the rule of the emperor Decius, who exiled or executed the principal Christian bishops and for sixteen months prevented the election of a new bishop of Rome. But the greatest persecution occurred in the latter days of the emperor Diocletian. After some eighteen years of mild and tolerant rule, during which the wife and daughter of the emperor were much attracted to the Christian doctrine and the four principal eunuchs of the palace actually embraced the new religion, that great ruler at length succumbed to the anti-Christian prejudices of two of his associates, Maximian and Galerius. A series of increasingly harsh edicts led to the burning of churches, the withdrawal of all legal protection from Christians, the prohibition of Christian assemblies, the confiscation of church property, and the arrest, torture, exile, and execution of many of the faithful. The persecution persisted (though with widely varying degrees of severity in the different parts of the empire) for ten long years, until Galerius, somewhat softened by a painful and lingering illness, published an edict permitting the Christians "freely to profess their private opinions and to assemble in their conventicles without fear or molestation, provided always that they preserve a due respect to the established laws and government."

Yet it must not be supposed, Gibbon concludes, that any vast number of Christians perished even in these repressive circumstances. The zeal of the early Christians for martyrdom was so great that they sometimes "supplied by their voluntary declaration the want of an accuser, rudely disturbed the public service of paganism," called upon the magistrate "to pronounce and to inflict the sentence of the law," and then "cheerfully leaped into the fires that were kindled to consume them" —until the bishops themselves had to condemn such practices. ("Unhappy men!" exclaimed a proconsul of Asia, "if you are thus weary of your lives, is it so difficult to find ropes and precipices?") But according to a highly partial ecclesiastical historian, only nine bishops perished over the course of the decade of persecution begun by Diocletian; and Gibbon estimates the total number of Christians executed in that same period at about two thousand.

Chapter IX

(A.D. 300-500)

Foundation of Constantinople — Political system of Constantine and his successors — Military discipline — The palace — The finances — Brief review of the fate of the sons and nephews of Constantine, and the results of the legal establishment of the Christian church[1]

THE unfortunate Licinius was the last rival who opposed the greatness, and the last captive who adorned the triumph, of Constantine. After a tranquil and prosperous reign the conqueror bequeathed to his family the inheritance of the Roman empire, a new capital, a new policy, and a new religion; and the innovations which he established have been embraced and consecrated by succeeding generations. The age of the great Constantine and his sons is filled with important events; but the historian must be oppressed by their number and variety unless he diligently separates from each other the scenes which are connected only by the order of time. He will describe the political institutions that gave strength and stability to the empire before he proceeds to relate the wars and revolutions which hastened its decline. He will adopt the division, unknown to the ancients, of civil and ecclesiastical affairs. The victory of the Christians and their intestine discord will supply copious and distinct materials both for edification and for scandal.

After the defeat and abdication of Licinius his vic-

1. *Editor's note:* Chapters XVII through XX of the original.

torious rival proceeded to lay the foundations of a city
destined to reign in future times the mistress of the East,
and to survive the empire and religion of Constantine.
The motives, whether of pride or of policy, which first induced Diocletian to withdraw himself from the ancient
seat of government had acquired additional weight by the
example of his successors and the habits of forty years.
Rome was insensibly confounded with the dependent
kingdoms which had once acknowledged her supremacy; and the country of the Cæsars was viewed with
cold indifference by a martial prince, born in the neighbourhood of the Danube, educated in the courts and
armies of Asia, and invested with the purple by the
legions of Britain. The Italians, who had received Constantine as their deliverer, submissively obeyed the
edicts which he sometimes condescended to address to
the senate and people of Rome; but they were seldom
honoured with the presence of their new sovereign.
During the vigour of his age Constantine, according to
the various exigencies of peace and war, moved with
slow dignity or with active diligence along the frontiers
of his extensive dominions, and was always prepared to
take the field either against a foreign or a domestic
enemy. But as he gradually reached the summit of prosperity and the decline of life, he began to meditate the
design of fixing in a more permanent station the strength
as well as majesty of the throne.

In the choice of an advantageous situation he preferred the confines of Europe and Asia, to curb with a
powerful arm the barbarians who dwelt between the
Danube and the Tanais and to watch with an eye of
jealousy the conduct of the Persian monarch, who indignantly supported the yoke of an ignominious treaty.
With these views Diocletian had selected and embellished the residence of Nicomedia; but the memory of

Diocletian was justly abhorred by the protector of the church, and Constantine was not insensible to the ambition of founding a city which might perpetuate the glory of his own name. During the late operations of the war against Licinius he had sufficient opportunity to contemplate, both as a soldier and as a statesman, the incomparable position of Byzantium, and to observe how strongly it was guarded by nature against an hostile attack, whilst it was accessible on every side to the benefits of commercial intercourse. Many ages before Constantine one of the most judicious historians of antiquity had described the advantages of a situation from whence a feeble colony of Greeks derived the command of the sea and the honours of a flourishing and independent republic.[2]

We are at present qualified to view the advantageous position of Constantinople, which appears to have been formed by nature for the centre and capital of a great monarchy. Situated in the forty-first degree of latitude, the Imperial city commanded from her seven hills the opposite shores of Europe and Asia; the climate was healthy and temperate, the soil fertile, the harbour secure and capacious, and the approach on the side of the continent was of small extent and easy defence. The Bosphorus and the Hellespont may be considered as the two gates of Constantinople, and the prince who possessed those important passages could always shut them against a naval enemy and open them to the fleets of commerce. The preservation of the eastern provinces may in some degree be ascribed to the policy of Constantine, as the barbarians of the Euxine, who in the preceding age had poured their armaments into

2. *Editor's note:* The next section of the original is a minute description of the site of Constantinople and the surrounding area.

the heart of the Mediterranean, soon desisted from the exercise of piracy and despaired of forcing this insurmountable barrier. When the gates of the Hellespont and Bosphorus were shut, the capital still enjoyed within their spacious enclosure every production which could supply the wants or gratify the luxury of its numerous inhabitants. The seacoasts of Thrace and Bithynia, which languish under the weight of Turkish oppression, still exhibit a rich prospect of vineyards, of gardens, and of plentiful harvests; and the Propontis has ever been renowned for an inexhaustible store of the most exquisite fish, that are taken in their stated seasons without skill and almost without labour. But when the passages of the straits were thrown open for trade, they alternately admitted the natural and artificial riches of the North and South, of the Euxine and of the Mediterranean. Whatever rude commodities were collected in the forests of Germany and Scythia, as far as the sources of the Tanais and the Borysthenes; whatsoever was manufactured by the skill of Europe or Asia; the corn of Egypt, and the gems and spices of the farthest India, were brought by the varying winds into the port of Constantinople, which for many ages attracted the commerce of the ancient world.

The prospect of beauty, of safety, and of wealth united in a single spot was sufficient to justify the choice of Constantine. But as some decent mixture of prodigy and fable has in every age been supposed to reflect a becoming majesty on the origin of great cities, the emperor was desirous of ascribing his resolution not so much to the uncertain counsels of human policy as to the infallible and eternal decrees of divine wisdom. In one of his laws he has been careful to instruct posterity that, in obedience to the commands of God, he laid the everlasting foundations of Constantinople; and though he has not condescended to relate in what manner the celestial inspiration was communicated to his mind, the defect of his modest silence has been liberally supplied by the ingenuity of succeeding writers, who describe the nocturnal vision which appeared to the fancy of Constantine as he slept within the walls of Byzantium. The tutelar genius of the city, a venerable matron sinking under the weight of years and infirmities, was suddenly transformed into a blooming maid, whom his own hands adorned with all the symbols of Imperial greatness. The monarch awoke, interpreted the auspicious omen, and obeyed without hesitation the will of Heaven.

The day which gave birth to a city or colony was celebrated by the Romans with such ceremonies as had been ordained by a generous superstition; and though Constantine might omit some rites which savoured too strongly of their pagan origin, yet he was anxious to leave a deep impression of hope and respect on the minds of the spectators. On foot, with a lance in his hand, the emperor himself led the solemn procession and directed the line which was traced as the boundary of the destined capital, till the growing circumference was observed with astonishment by the assistants, who at length ventured to observe that he had already exceeded the most ample measure of a great city. "I shall still advance," replied Constantine, "till He, the invisible guide who marches before me, thinks proper to stop." Without presuming to investigate the nature or motives of this extraordinary conductor, we shall content ourselves with the more humble task of describing the extent and limits of Constantinople.

In the actual state of the city, the palace and gardens of the seraglio occupy the eastern promontory, the first of the seven hills, and cover about one hundred and fifty acres of our own measure. The seat of Turkish jealousy

and despotism is erected on the foundations of a Grecian
republic; but it may be supposed that the Byzantines
were tempted by the conveniency of the harbour to extend their habitations on that side beyond the modern
limits of the seraglio. The new walls of Constantine
stretched from the port to the Propontis across the enlarged breadth of the triangle, at the distance of fifteen
stadia from the ancient fortification, and with the city
of Byzantium they enclosed five of the seven hills,
which, to the eyes of those who approach Constantinople, appear to rise above each other in beautiful
order. About a century after the death of the founder
the new buildings, extending on one side up the harbour and on the other along the Propontis, already
covered the narrow ridge of the sixth and the broad
summit of the seventh hill. The necessity of protecting
those suburbs from the incessant inroads of the barbarians engaged the younger Theodosius to surround
his capital with an adequate and permanent enclosure
of walls. From the eastern promontory to the golden
gate the extreme length of Constantinople was about
three Roman miles, the circumference measured between ten and eleven, and the surface might be computed as equal to about two thousand English acres.
It is impossible to justify the vain and credulous exaggerations of modern travellers, who have sometimes
stretched the limits of Constantinople over the adjacent
villages of the European and even of the Asiatic coast.
But the suburbs of Pera and Galata, though situate beyond the harbour, may deserve to be considered as a
part of the city; and this addition may perhaps author-
ize the measure of a Byzantine historian who assigns
sixteen Greek (about fourteen Roman) miles for the
circumference of his native city. Such an extent may
seem not unworthy of an Imperial residence. Yet Con-

stantinople must yield to Babylon and Thebes, to ancient Rome, to London, and even to Paris.

The master of the Roman world who aspired to erect an eternal monument of the glories of his reign could employ in the prosecution of that great work the wealth, the labour, and all that yet remained of the genius of obedient millions. Some estimate may be formed of the expense bestowed with Imperial liberality on the foundation of Constantinople by the allowance of about two millions five hundred thousand pounds for the construction of the walls, the porticoes, and the aqueducts. The forests that overshadowed the shores of the Euxine and the celebrated quarries of white marble in the little island of Proconnesus supplied an inexhaustible stock of materials, ready to be conveyed, by the convenience of a short water-carriage, to the harbour of Byzantium. A multitude of labourers and artificers urged the conclusion of the work with incessant toil; but the impatience of Constantine soon discovered that, in the decline of the arts, the skill as well as numbers of his architects bore a very unequal proportion to the greatness of his designs. The magistrates of the most distant provinces were therefore directed to institute schools, to appoint professors, and, by the hopes of rewards and privileges, to engage in the study and practice of architecture a sufficient number of ingenious youths who had received a liberal education.

The buildings of the new city were executed by such artificers as the reign of Constantine could afford; but they were decorated by the hands of the most celebrated masters of the age of Pericles and Alexander. To revive the genius of Phidias and Lysippus surpassed indeed the power of a Roman emperor, but the immortal productions which they had bequeathed to posterity were exposed without defence to the rapacious

vanity of a despot. By his commands the cities of Greece
and Asia were despoiled of their most valuable ornaments. The trophies of memorable wars, the objects of
religious veneration, the most finished statues of the
gods and heroes, of the sages and poets of ancient
times, contributed to the splendid triumph of Constantinople and gave occasion to the remark of the historian
Cedrenus, who observes with some enthusiasm that
nothing seemed wanting except the souls of the illustrious men whom these admirable monuments were
intended to represent. But it is not in the city of Constantine, nor in the declining period of an empire, when
the human mind was depressed by civil and religious
slavery, that we should seek for the souls of Homer and
of Demosthenes.

During the siege of Byzantium the conqueror had
pitched his tent on the commanding eminence of the
second hill. To perpetuate the memory of his success
he chose the same advantageous position for the principal Forum, which appears to have been of a circular
or rather elliptical form. The two opposite entrances
formed triumphal arches; the porticoes, which enclosed
it on every side, were filled with statues; and the centre
of the Forum was occupied by a lofty column, of which
a mutilated fragment is now degraded by the appellation of the *burned pillar*. This column was erected on a
pedestal of white marble twenty feet high and was
composed of ten pieces of porphyry, each of which
measured about ten feet in height and about thirty-three
in circumference. On the summit of the pillar, above
one hundred and twenty feet from the ground, stood
the colossal statue of Apollo. It was of bronze, had
been transported either from Athens or from a town of
Phrygia, and was supposed to be the work of Phidias.
The artist had represented the god of day, or, as it was

afterwards interpreted, the emperor Constantine himself, with a sceptre in his right hand, the globe of the
world in his left, and a crown of rays glittering on his
head. The Circus, or Hippodrome, was a stately building about four hundred paces in length and one hundred
in breadth. The space between the two *metæ*, or goals,
was filled with statues and obelisks; and we may still
remark a very singular fragment of antiquity, the bodies
of three serpents twisted into one pillar of brass. Their
triple heads had once supported the golden tripod which
after the defeat of Xerxes was consecrated in the temple
of Delphi by the victorious Greeks. The beauty of the
Hippodrome has been long since defaced by the rude
hands of the Turkish conquerors, but under the similar
appellation of Atmeidan it still serves as a place of exercise for their horses. From the throne, whence the
emperor viewed the Circensian games, a winding staircase descended to the palace, a magnificent edifice
which scarcely yielded to the residence of Rome itself
and which, together with the dependent courts, gardens,
and porticoes, covered a considerable extent of ground
upon the banks of the Propontis between the Hippodrome and the church of St. Sophia. We might likewise
celebrate the baths, which still retained the name of
Zeuxippus, after they had been enriched by the munificence of Constantine with lofty columns, various
marbles, and above threescore statues of bronze. But
we should deviate from the design of this history if we
attempted minutely to describe the different buildings
or quarters of the city. It may be sufficient to observe
that whatever could adorn the dignity of a great capital
or contribute to the benefit or pleasure of its numerous
inhabitants was contained within the walls of Constantinople. A particular description, composed about a
century after its foundation, enumerates a capitol, or

school of learning, a circus, two theatres, eight public and one hundred and fifty-three private baths, fifty-two porticoes, five granaries, eight aqueducts or reservoirs of water, four spacious halls for the meetings of the senate or courts of justice, fourteen churches, fourteen palaces, and four thousand three hundred and eighty-eight houses which, for their size or beauty, deserved to be distinguished from the multitude of plebeian habitations.

The populousness of his favoured city was the next and most serious object of the attention of its founder. In the dark ages which succeeded the translation of the empire, the remote and the immediate consequences of that memorable event were strangely confounded by the vanity of the Greeks and the credulity of the Latins. It was asserted and believed that all the noble families of Rome, the senate, and the equestrian order, with their innumerable attendants, had followed their emperor to the banks of the Propontis; that a spurious race of strangers and plebeians was left to possess the solitude of the ancient capital; and that the lands of Italy, long since converted into gardens, were at once deprived of cultivation and inhabitants. In the course of this history such exaggerations will be reduced to their just value; yet, since the growth of Constantinople cannot be ascribed to the general increase of mankind and of industry, it must be admitted that this artificial colony was raised at the expense of the ancient cities of the empire. Many opulent senators of Rome and of the eastern provinces were probably invited by Constantine to adopt for their country the fortunate spot which he had chosen for his own residence. The invitations of a master are scarcely to be distinguished from commands, and the liberality of the emperor obtained a ready and cheerful obedience. He bestowed on his favourites the palaces which he had built in the several quarters of the city, assigned them lands and pensions for the support of their dignity, and alienated the demesnes of Pontus and Asia to grant hereditary estates by the easy tenure of maintaining a house in the capital. But these encouragements and obligations soon became superfluous and were gradually abolished. Wherever the seat of government is fixed, a considerable part of the public revenue will be expended by the prince himself, by his ministers, by the officers of justice, and by the domestics of the palace. The most wealthy of the provincials will be attracted by the powerful motives of interest and duty, of amusement and curiosity. A third and more numerous class of inhabitants will insensibly be formed of servants, of artificers, and of merchants, who derive their subsistence from their own labour and from the wants or luxury of the superior ranks. In less than a century Constantinople disputed with Rome itself the pre-eminence of riches and numbers. New piles of buildings, crowded together with too little regard to health or convenience, scarcely allowed the intervals of narrow streets for the perpetual throng of men, of horses, and of carriages. The allotted space of ground was insufficient to contain the increasing people, and the additional foundations, which on either side were advanced into the sea, might alone have composed a very considerable city.[3]

As Constantine urged the progress of the work with the impatience of a lover, the walls, the porticoes, and the principal edifices were completed in a few years, or, according to another account, in a few months; but this extraordinary diligence should excite the less admiration

3. *Editor's note:* In a paragraph omitted here, Gibbon remarks on several regulations of Constantine, especially the annual tribute of Egyptian grain to feed Constantinople's populace.

since many of the buildings were finished in so hasty
and imperfect a manner that under the succeeding reign
they were preserved with difficulty from impending
ruin. But while they displayed the vigour and freshness
of youth, the founder prepared to celebrate the dedication of his city. The games and largesses which crowned
the pomp of this memorable festival may easily be supposed; but there is one circumstance of a more singular
and permanent nature, which ought not entirely to be
overlooked. As often as the birthday of the city returned,
the statue of Constantine, framed by his order of gilt
wood and bearing in its right hand a small image of the
genius of the place, was erected on a triumphal car.
The guards, carrying white tapers and clothed in their
richest apparel, accompanied the solemn procession as
it moved through the Hippodrome. When it was opposite to the throne of the reigning emperor he rose from
his seat and with grateful reverence adored the memory
of his predecessor. At the festival of the dedication an
edict, engraved on a column of marble, bestowed the
title of *Second* or *New Rome* on the city of Constantine.
But the name of Constantinople has prevailed over that
honourable epithet, and after the revolution of fourteen
centuries still perpetuates the fame of its author.

The foundation of a new capital is naturally connected with the establishment of a new form of civil
and military administration. The distinct view of the
complicated system of policy introduced by Diocletian,
improved by Constantine, and completed by his immediate successors may not only amuse the fancy by the
singular picture of a great empire, but will tend to illustrate the secret and internal causes of its rapid decay.
In the pursuit of any remarkable institution, we may be
frequently led into the more early or the more recent
times of the Roman history; but the proper limits of this

inquiry will be included within a period of about one hundred and thirty years, from the accession of Constantine to the publication of the Theodosian code, from which, as well as from the *Notitia* of the East and West, we derive the most copious and authentic information of the state of the empire. This variety of objects will suspend for some time the course of the narrative; but the interruption will be censured only by those readers who are insensible to the importance of laws and manners, while they peruse with eager curiosity the transient intrigues of a court or the accidental event of a battle.

The manly pride of the Romans, content with substantial power, had left to the vanity of the East the forms and ceremonies of ostentatious greatness. But when they lost even the semblance of those virtues which were derived from their ancient freedom, the simplicity of Roman manners was insensibly corrupted by the stately affectation of the courts of Asia. The distinctions of personal merit and influence, so conspicuous in a republic, so feeble and obscure under a monarchy, were abolished by the despotism of the emperors, who substituted in their room a severe subordination of rank and office, from the titled slaves who were seated on the steps of the throne to the meanest instruments of arbitrary power. This multitude of abject dependents was interested in the support of the actual government from the dread of a revolution which might at once confound their hopes and intercept the reward of their services.

In this divine hierarchy (for such it is frequently styled) every rank was marked with the most scrupulous exactness, and its dignity was displayed in a variety of trifling and solemn ceremonies, which it was a study to learn and a sacrilege to neglect. The purity of the Latin language was debased by adopting, in the intercourse of pride and flattery, a profusion of epithets which Tully would scarcely have understood and which Augustus would have rejected with indignation. The principal officers of the empire were saluted, even by the sovereign himself, with the deceitful titles of your *Sincerity,* your *Gravity,* your *Excellency,* your *Eminence,* your *sublime and wonderful Magnitude,* your *illustrious and magnificent Highness.* The codicils or patents of their office were curiously emblazoned with such emblems as were best adapted to explain its nature and high dignity: the image or portrait of the reigning emperors; a triumphal car; the book of mandates placed on a table, covered with a rich carpet, and illuminated by four tapers; the allegorical figures of the provinces which they governed; or the appellations and standards of the troops whom they commanded. Some of these official ensigns were really exhibited in their hall of audience; others preceded their pompous march whenever they appeared in public; and every circumstance of their demeanour, their dress, their ornaments, and their train was calculated to inspire a deep reverence for the representatives of supreme majesty. By a philosophic observer the system of the Roman government might have been mistaken for a splendid theatre, filled with players of every character and degree, who repeated the language and imitated the passions of their original model.

All the magistrates of sufficient importance to find a place in the general state of the empire were accurately divided into three classes: The *Illustrious;* the *Spectabiles,* or *Respectable;* and the *Clarissimi,* whom we may translate by the word *Honourable.* In the times of Roman simplicity the last-mentioned epithet was used only as a vague expression of deference, till it became at length the peculiar and appropriated title of all who were members of the senate and consequently of all who, from that venerable body, were selected to govern the provinces. The vanity of those who from their rank and office might claim a superior distinction above the rest of the senatorial order was long afterwards indulged with the new appellation of *Respectable;* but the title of *Illustrious* was always reserved to some eminent personages who were obeyed or reverenced by the two subordinate classes. It was communicated only: I. to the consuls and patricians; II. to the Prætorian præfects, with the præfects of Rome and Constantinople; III. to the masters general of the cavalry and the infantry; and, IV. to the seven ministers of the palace, who exercised their *sacred* functions about the person of the emperor. Among those illustrious magistrates who were esteemed co-ordinate with each other, the seniority of appointment gave place to the union of dignities. By the expedient of honorary codicils the emperors, who were fond of multiplying their favours, might sometimes gratify the vanity, though not the ambition, of impatient courtiers.

I. THE CONSULS AND PATRICIANS. As long as the Roman consuls were the first magistrates of a free state, they derived their right to power from the choice of the people. As long as the emperors condescended to disguise the servitude which they imposed, the consuls were still elected by the real or apparent suffrage of the senate. From the reign of Diocletian even these vestiges of liberty were abolished, and the successful candidates, who were invested with the annual honours of the consulships, affected to deplore the humiliating condition of their predecessors. The Scipios and the Catos had been reduced to solicit the votes of plebeians, to pass through the tedious and expensive forms of a popular election, and to expose their dignity to the shame of a public refusal; while their own happier fate had reserved them for an age and government in which the rewards of virtue were assigned by the unerring wisdom of a gracious sovereign. In the epistles which the emperor addressed to the two consuls elect, it was declared that they were created by his sole authority. Their names and portraits, engraved on gilt tablets of ivory, were dispersed over the empire as presents to the provinces, the cities, the magistrates, the senate, and the people.

Their solemn inauguration was performed at the place of the Imperial residence; and during a period of one hundred and twenty years Rome was constantly deprived of the presence of her ancient magistrates. On the morning of the first of January the consuls assumed the ensigns of their dignity. Their dress was a robe of purple, embroidered in silk and gold, and sometimes ornamented with costly gems. On this solemn occasion they were attended by the most eminent officers of the state and army in the habit of senators; and the useless fasces, armed with the once formidable axes, were borne before them by the lictors. The procession moved from the palace to the Forum or principal square of the city, where the consuls ascended their tribunal and seated themselves in the curule chairs, which were framed after the fashion of ancient times. They immediately exercised an act of jurisdiction, by the manumission of a slave who was brought before them for that purpose; and the ceremony was intended to represent the celebrated action of the elder Brutus, the author of liberty and of the consulship, when he admitted among his fellow-citizens the faithful Vindex, who had revealed the conspiracy of the Tarquins.

The public festival was continued during several days in all the principal cities: in Rome from custom; in

Constantinople from imitation; in Carthage, Antioch, and Alexandria from the love of pleasure and the superfluity of wealth. In the two capitals of the empire the annual games of the theatre, the circus, and the amphitheatre cost four thousand pounds of gold, about one hundred and sixty thousand pounds sterling; and if so heavy an expense surpassed the faculties or the inclination of the magistrates themselves, the sum was supplied from the Imperial treasury.

As soon as the consuls had discharged these customary duties they were at liberty to retire into the shade of private life and to enjoy during the remainder of the year the undisturbed contemplation of their own greatness. They no longer presided in the national councils; they no longer executed the resolutions of peace or war. Their abilities (unless they were employed in more effective offices) were of little moment; and their names served only as the legal date of the year in which they had filled the chair of Marius and of Cicero. Yet it was still felt and acknowledged, in the last period of Roman servitude, that this empty name might be compared, and even preferred, to the possession of substantial power. The title of consul was still the most splendid object of ambition, the noblest reward of virtue and loyalty. The emperors themselves, who disdained the faint shadow of the republic, were conscious that they acquired an additional splendour and majesty as often as they assumed the annual honours of the consular dignity.

The proudest and most perfect separation which can be found in any age or country between the nobles and the people is perhaps that of the patricians and the plebeians, as it was established in the first age of the Roman republic. Wealth and honours, the offices of the state, and the ceremonies of religion were almost ex-

clusively possessed by the former, who, preserving the
purity of their blood with the most insulting jealousy,[4]
held their clients in a condition of specious vassalage.
But these distinctions, so incompatible with the spirit
of a free people, were removed after a long struggle by
the persevering efforts of the tribunes. The most active
and successful of the plebeians accumulated wealth,
aspired to honours, deserved triumphs, contracted alliances, and after some generations assumed the pride of
ancient nobility.

The patrician families, on the other hand, whose
original number was never recruited till the end of the
commonwealth, either failed in the ordinary course of
nature, or were extinguished in so many foreign and
domestic wars, or, through a want of merit or fortune,
insensibly mingled with the mass of the people. Very
few remained who could derive their pure and genuine
origin from the infancy of the city, or even from that of
the republic, when Cæsar and Augustus, Claudius and
Vespasian, created from the body of the senate a competent number of new patrician families in the hope of
perpetuating an order which was still considered as
honourable and sacred. But these artificial supplies (in
which the reigning house was always included) were
rapidly swept away by the rage of tyrants, by frequent
revolutions, by the change of manners, and by the in-
termixture of nations. Little more was left when Constantine ascended the throne than a vague and imperfect
tradition that the patricians had once been the first of
the Romans.

To form a body of nobles whose influence may re-

4. Intermarriages between the patricians and plebeians
were prohibited by the laws of the XII Tables; and the uniform operations of human nature may attest that the custom
survived the law.

strain while it secures the authority of the monarch would have been very inconsistent with the character and policy of Constantine; but, had he seriously entertained such a design, it might have exceeded the measure of his power to ratify by an arbitrary edict an institution which must expect the sanction of time and of opinion. He revived, indeed, the title of *Patricians,* but he revived it as a personal, not as an hereditary distinction. They yielded only to the transient superiority of the annual consuls; but they enjoyed the preeminence over all the great officers of state, with the most familiar access to the person of the prince. This honourable rank was bestowed on them for life; and, as they were usually favourites and ministers who had grown old in the Imperial court, the true etymology of the word was perverted by ignorance and flattery, and the patricians of Constantine were reverenced as the adopted *Fathers* of the emperor and the republic.

II. THE PRÆTORIAN PRÆFECTS. The fortunes of the Prætorian præfects were essentially different from those of the consuls and patricians. The latter saw their ancient greatness evaporate in a vain title. The former, rising by degrees from the most humble condition, were invested with the civil and military administration of the Roman world. From the reign of Severus to that of Diocletian the guards and the palace, the laws and the finances, the armies and the provinces, were entrusted to their superintending care; and, like the vizirs of the East, they held with one hand the seal, and with the other the standard, of the empire. The ambition of the præfects, always formidable and sometimes fatal to the masters whom they served, was supported by the strength of the Prætorian bands; but after those haughty troops had been weakened by Diocletian and finally suppressed by Constantine, the præfects who survived their fall were reduced without difficulty to the station of useful and obedient ministers. When they were no longer responsible for the safety of the emperor's person, they resigned the jurisdiction which they had hitherto claimed and exercised over all the departments of the palace. They were deprived by Constantine of all military command as soon as they had ceased to lead into the field, under their immediate orders, the flower of the Roman troops; and at length, by a singular revolution, the captains of the guards were transformed into the civil magistrates of the provinces.

According to the plan of government instituted by Diocletian, the four princes had each their Prætorian præfect; and after the monarchy was once more united in the person of Constantine, he still continued to create the same number of four præfects and entrusted to their care the same provinces which they already administered. 1. The præfect of the East stretched his ample jurisdiction into the three parts of the globe which were subject to the Romans, from the cataracts of the Nile to the banks of the Phasis, and from the mountains of Thrace to the frontiers of Persia. 2. The important provinces of Pannonia, Dacia, Macedonia, and Greece once acknowledged the authority of the præfect of Illyricum. 3. The power of the præfect of Italy was not confined to the country from whence he derived his title; it extended over the additional territory of Rhætia as far as the banks of the Danube, over the dependent islands of the Mediterranean, and over that part of the continent of Africa which lies between the confines of Cyrene and those of Tingitania. 4. The præfect of the Gauls comprehended under that plural denomination the kindred provinces of Britain and Spain, and his authority was obeyed from the wall of Antoninus to the foot of Mount Atlas.

After the Prætorian præfects had been dismissed from all military command, the civil functions which they were ordained to exercise over so many subject nations were adequate to the ambition and abilities of the most consummate ministers. To their wisdom was committed the supreme administration of justice and of the finances, the two objects which, in a state of peace, comprehend almost all the respective duties of the sovereign and of the people; of the former, to protect the citizens who are obedient to the laws; of the latter, to contribute the share of their property which is required for the expenses of the state. The coin, the highways, the posts, the granaries, the manufactures, whatever could interest the public prosperity, was moderated by the authority of the Prætorian præfects. As the immediate representatives of the Imperial majesty they were empowered to explain, to enforce, and on some occasions to modify the general edicts by their discretionary proclamations. They watched over the conduct of the provincial governors, removed the negligent, and inflicted punishments on the guilty. From all the inferior jurisdictions an appeal in every matter of importance, either civil or criminal, might be brought before the tribunal of the præfect; but *his* sentence was final and absolute, and the emperors themselves refused to admit any complaints against the judgment or the integrity of a magistrate whom they honoured with such unbounded confidence. His appointments were suitable to his dignity; and if avarice was his ruling passion he enjoyed frequent opportunities of collecting a rich harvest of fees, of presents, and of perquisites. Though the emperors no longer dreaded the ambition of their præfects, they were attentive to counterbalance the power of this great office by the uncertainty and shortness of its duration.

From their superior importance and dignity Rome and Constantinople were alone excepted from the jurisdiction of the Prætorian præfects. The immense size of the city and the experience of the tardy, ineffectual operation of the laws had furnished the policy of Augustus with a specious pretence for introducing a new magistrate, who alone could restrain a servile and turbulent populace by the strong arm of arbitrary power. Valerius Messalla was appointed the first præfect of Rome, that his reputation might countenance so invidious a measure; but at the end of a few days that accomplished citizen resigned his office, declaring, with a spirit worthy of the friend of Brutus, that he found himself incapable of exercising a power incompatible with public freedom. As the sense of liberty became less exquisite, the advantages of order were more clearly understood; and the præfect, who seemed to have been designed as a terror only to slaves and vagrants, was permitted to extend his civil and criminal jurisdiction over the equestrian and noble families of Rome. The prætors, annually created as the judges of law and equity, could not long dispute the possession of the Forum with a vigorous and permanent magistrate who was usually admitted into the confidence of the prince. Their courts were deserted; their number, which had once fluctuated between twelve and eighteen, was gradually reduced to two or three; and their important functions were confined to the expensive obligation of exhibiting games for the amusement of the people.

After the office of Roman consuls had been changed into a vain pageant, which was rarely displayed in the capital, the præfects assumed their vacant place in the senate and were soon acknowledged as the ordinary presidents of that venerable assembly. They received appeals from the distance of one hundred miles; and it

was allowed as a principle of jurisprudence that all
municipal authority was derived from them alone. In
the discharge of his laborious employment the governor
of Rome was assisted by fifteen officers, some of whom
had been originally his equals, or even his superiors.
The principal departments were relative to the command of a numerous watch, established as a safeguard
against fires, robberies, and nocturnal disorders; the
custody and distribution of the public allowance of corn
and provisions; the care of the port, of the aqueducts,
of the common sewers, and of the navigation and bed
of the Tiber; the inspection of the markets, the theatres,
and of the private as well as public works. Their vigilance ensured the three principal objects of a regular
police—safety, plenty, and cleanliness; and, as a proof
of the attention of government to preserve the splendour
and ornaments of the capital, a particular inspector was
appointed for the statues, the guardian as it were of
that inanimate people which, according to the extravagant computation of an old writer, was scarcely inferior
in number to the living inhabitants of Rome. About
thirty years after the foundation of Constantinople a
similar magistrate was created in that rising metropolis,
for the same uses and with the same powers. A perfect
equality was established between the dignity of the
two municipal and that of the four Prætorian præfects.

Those who in the Imperial hierarchy were distinguished by the title of *Respectable* formed an intermediate class between the *Illustrious* præfects and the
Honourable magistrates of the provinces. In this class
the proconsuls of Asia, Achaia, and Africa claimed a
pre-eminence, which was yielded to the remembrance
of their ancient dignity; and the appeal from their
tribunal to that of the præfects was almost the only
mark of their dependence. But the civil government

of the empire was distributed into thirteen great *dioceses*, each of which equalled the just measure of a powerful kingdom. The first of these dioceses was subject to the jurisdiction of the *count* of the East; and we may convey some idea of the importance and variety of his functions by observing that six hundred apparitors, who would be styled at present either secretaries, or clerks, or ushers, or messengers, were employed in his immediate office. The place of *Augustal præfect* of Egypt was no longer filled by a Roman knight, but the name was retained; and the extraordinary powers which the situation of the country and the temper of the inhabitants had once made indispensable were still continued to the governor. The eleven remaining dioceses —of Asiana, Pontica, and Thrace; of Macedonia, Dacia, and Pannonia, or Western Illyricum; of Italy and Africa; of Gaul, Spain, and Britain—were governed by twelve *vicars* or *vice-præfects*, whose name sufficiently explains the nature and dependence of their office. It may be added that the lieutenant generals of the Roman armies, the military counts and dukes, who will be hereafter mentioned, were allowed the rank and title of *Respectable*.

As the spirit of jealousy and ostentation prevailed in the councils of the emperors, they proceeded with anxious diligence to divide the substance and to multiply the titles of power. The vast countries which the Roman conquerors had united under the same simple form of administration were imperceptibly crumbled into minute fragments, till at length the whole empire was distributed into one hundred and sixteen provinces, each of which supported an expensive and splendid establishment. Of these, three were governed by *proconsuls*, thirty-seven by *consulars*, five by *correctors*, and seventy-one by *presidents*. The appellations of these magistrates were different; they ranked in successive order; the ensigns of their dignity were curiously varied; and their situation, from accidental circumstances, might be more or less agreeable or advantageous. But they were all (excepting only the proconsuls) alike included in the class of *Honourable* persons; and they were alike entrusted, during the pleasure of the prince, and under the authority of the præfects or their deputies, with the administration of justice and the finances in their respective districts.

The ponderous volumes of the Codes and Pandects would furnish ample materials for a minute inquiry into the system of provincial government, as in the space of six centuries it was improved by the wisdom of the Roman statesmen and lawyers. It may be sufficient for the historian to select two singular and salutary provisions, intended to restrain the abuse of authority.

1. For the preservation of peace and order the governors of the provinces were armed with the sword of justice. They inflicted corporal punishments, and they exercised in capital offences the power of life and death. But they were not authorized to indulge the condemned criminal with the choice of his own execution or to pronounce a sentence of the mildest and most honourable kind of exile. These prerogatives were reserved to the præfects, who alone could impose the heavy fine of fifty pounds of gold: their vicegerents were confined to the trifling weight of a few ounces. This distinction, which seems to grant the larger, while it denies the smaller, degree of authority, was founded on a very rational motive. The smaller degree was infinitely more liable to abuse. The passions of a provincial magistrate might frequently provoke him into acts of oppression which affected only the freedom or the fortunes of the

subject, though from a principle of prudence or perhaps of humanity he might still be terrified by the guilt of innocent blood. It may likewise be considered that exile, considerable fines, or the choice of an easy death relate more particularly to the rich and the noble; and the persons the most exposed to the avarice or resentment of a provincial magistrate were thus removed from his obscure persecution to the more august and impartial tribunal of the Prætorian præfect.

2. As it was reasonably apprehended that the integrity of the judge might be biased if his interest was concerned or his affections were engaged, the strictest regulations were established to exclude any person, without the special dispensation of the emperor, from the government of the province where he was born, and to prohibit the governor or his son from contracting marriage with a native or an inhabitant; or from purchasing slaves, lands, or houses within the extent of his jurisdiction. Notwithstanding these rigorous precautions the emperor Constantine, after a reign of twenty-five years, still deplores the venal and oppressive administration of justice and expresses the warmest indignation that the audience of the judge, his despatch of business, his seasonable delays, and his final sentence were publicly sold either by himself or by the officers of his court. The continuance, and perhaps the impunity, of these crimes is attested by the repetition of impotent laws and ineffectual menaces.

All the civil magistrates were drawn from the profession of the law. The celebrated Institutes of Justinian are addressed to the youth of his dominions who had devoted themselves to the study of Roman jurisprudence; and the sovereign condescends to animate their diligence by the assurance that their skill and ability would in time be rewarded by an adequate share in the

government of the republic. The rudiments of this lucrative science were taught in all the considerable cities
of the East and West; but the most famous school was
that of Berytus, on the coast of Phœnicia, which flourished above three centuries from the time of Alexander
Severus, the author perhaps of an institution so advantageous to his native country. After a regular course of
education, which lasted five years, the students dispersed themselves through the provinces in search of
fortune and honours; nor could they want an inexhaustible supply of business in a great empire already corrupted by the multiplicity of laws, of arts, and of vices.
The court of the Prætorian præfect of the East could
alone furnish employment for one hundred and fifty
advocates, sixty-four of whom were distinguished by
peculiar privileges, and two were annually chosen with
a salary of sixty pounds of gold to defend the causes of
the treasury. The first experiment was made of their
judicial talents by appointing them to act occasionally
as assessors to the magistrates; from thence they were
often raised to preside in the tribunals before which
they had pleaded. They obtained the government of a
province; and by the aid of merit, of reputation, or
of favour they ascended by successive steps to the
Illustrious dignities of the state.

In the practice of the bar these men had considered
reason as the instrument of dispute; they interpreted
the laws according to the dictates of private interest;
and the same pernicious habits might still adhere to
their characters in the public administration of the state.
The honour of a liberal profession has indeed been
vindicated by ancient and modern advocates, who have
filled the most important stations with pure integrity
and consummate wisdom; but in the decline of Roman
jurisprudence the ordinary promotion of lawyers was

pregnant with mischief and disgrace. The noble art, which had once been preserved as the sacred inheritance of the patricians, was fallen into the hands of freedmen and plebeians, who with cunning rather than with skill exercised a sordid and pernicious trade. Some of them procured admittance into families for the purpose of fomenting differences, of encouraging suits, and of preparing a harvest of gain for themselves or their brethren. Others, recluse in their chambers, maintained the gravity of legal professors by furnishing a rich client with subtleties to confound the plainest truth and with arguments to colour the most unjustifiable pretensions. The splendid and popular class was composed of the advocates who filled the Forum with the sound of their turgid and loquacious rhetoric. Careless of fame and of justice, they are described for the most part as ignorant and rapacious guides who conducted their clients through a maze of expense, of delay, and of disappointment, from whence, after a tedious series of years, they were at length dismissed when their patience and fortune were almost exhausted.

III. THE MASTERS GENERAL OF CAVALRY AND INFANTRY. In the system of policy introduced by Augustus, the governors, those at least of the Imperial provinces, were invested with the full powers of the sovereign himself. Ministers of peace and war, the distribution of rewards and punishments, depended on them alone; and they successively appeared on their tribunal in the robes of civil magistracy and in complete armour at the head of the Roman legions. The influence of the revenue, the authority of law, and the command of a military force concurred to render their power supreme and absolute; and whenever they were tempted to violate their allegiance, the loyal province which they involved in their rebellion was scarcely sensible of any change in its political state. From the time of Commodus to the reign of Constantine near one hundred governors might be enumerated who with various success erected the standard of revolt; and though the innocent were too often sacrificed, the guilty might be sometimes prevented, by the suspicious cruelty of their master.

To secure his throne and the public tranquillity from these formidable servants, Constantine resolved to divide the military from the civil administration and to establish, as a permanent and professional distinction, a practice which had been adopted only as an occasional expedient. The supreme jurisdiction exercised by the Prætorian præfects over the armies of the empire was transferred to the two *masters general* whom he instituted, the one for the cavalry, the other for the infantry; and though each of these *Illustrious* officers was more peculiarly responsible for the discipline of those troops which were under his immediate inspection, they both indifferently commanded in the field the several bodies, whether of horse or foot, which were united in the same army. Their number was soon doubled by the division of the East and West; and as separate generals of the same rank and title were appointed on the four important frontiers of the Rhine, of the Upper and the Lower Danube, and of the Euphrates, the defence of the Roman empire was at length committed to eight masters general of the cavalry and infantry.

Under their orders thirty-five military commanders were stationed in the provinces: three in Britain, six in Gaul, one in Spain, one in Italy, five on the Upper and four on the Lower Danube, in Asia eight, three in Egypt, and four in Africa. The titles of *counts* and *dukes*, by which they were properly distinguished, have obtained in modern languages so very different a sense

that the use of them may occasion some surprise. But
it should be recollected that the second of those appellations is only a corruption of the Latin word which was
indiscriminately applied to any military chief. All these
provincial generals were therefore *dukes;* but no more
than ten among them were dignified with the rank of
counts or companions, a title of honour, or rather of
favour, which had been recently invented in the court
of Constantine. A gold belt was the ensign which distinguished the office of the counts and dukes; and besides their pay they received a liberal allowance sufficient to maintain one hundred and ninety servants
and one hundred and fifty-eight horses. They were
strictly prohibited from interfering in any matter which
related to the administration of justice or the revenue;
but the command which they exercised over the troops
of their department was independent of the authority
of the magistrates.

About the same time that Constantine gave a legal
sanction to the ecclesiastical order, he instituted in the
Roman empire the nice balance of the civil and the
military powers. The emulation, and sometimes the discord, which reigned between two professions of opposite
interests and incompatible manners was productive of
beneficial and of pernicious consequences. It was seldom
to be expected that the general and the civil governoi
of a province should either conspire for the disturbance
or should unite for the service of their country. While
the one delayed to offer the assistance which the other
disdained to solicit, the troops very frequently remained
without orders or without supplies, the public safety
was betrayed, and the defenceless subjects were left
exposed to the fury of the barbarians. The divided
administration which had been formed by Constantine

relaxed the vigour of the state while it secured the tranquillity of the monarch.

The memory of Constantine has been deservedly censured for another innovation which corrupted military discipline and prepared the ruin of the empire. The nineteen years which preceded his final victory over Licinius had been a period of licence and intestine war. The rivals who contended for the possession of the Roman world had withdrawn the greatest part of their forces from the guard of the general frontier, and the principal cities which formed the boundary of their respective dominions were filled with soldiers who considered their countrymen as their most implacable enemies. After the use of these internal garrisons had ceased with the civil war, the conqueror wanted either wisdom or firmness to revive the severe discipline of Diocletian and to suppress a fatal indulgence which habit had endeared and almost confirmed to the military order. From the reign of Constantine a popular and even legal distinction was admitted between the *Palatines* and the *Borderers*—the troops of the court, as they were improperly styled, and the troops of the frontier. The former, elevated by the superiority of their pay and privileges, were permitted, except in the extraordinary emergencies of war, to occupy their tranquil stations in the heart of the provinces. The most flourishing cities were oppressed by the intolerable weight of quarters.

The soldiers insensibly forgot the virtues of their profession and contracted only the vices of civil life. They were either degraded by the industry of mechanic trades or enervated by the luxury of baths and theaters. They soon became careless of their martial exercises, curious in their diet and apparel, and, while they inspired terror to the subjects of the empire, they trembled at the hostile approach of the barbarians.[5] The chain of fortifications which Diocletian and his colleagues had extended along the banks of the great rivers was no longer maintained with the same care or defended with the same vigilance. The numbers which still remained under the name of the troops of the frontier might be sufficient for the ordinary defence; but their spirit was degraded by the humiliating reflection that *they,* who were exposed to the hardships and dangers of a perpetual warfare, were rewarded only with about two-thirds of the pay and emoluments which were lavished on the troops of the court. Even the bands or legions that were raised the nearest to the level of those unworthy favourites were in some measure disgraced by the title of honour which they were allowed to assume. It was in vain that Constantine repeated the most dreadful menaces of fire and sword against the Borderers who should dare to desert their colours, to connive at the inroads of the barbarians, or to participate in the spoil. The mischiefs which flow from injudicious counsels are seldom removed by the application of partial severities; and though succeeding princes laboured to restore the strength and numbers of the frontier garrisons, the empire, till the last moment of its dissolution, continued to languish under the mortal wound which had been so rashly or so weakly inflicted by the hand of Constantine.

The same timid policy of dividing whatever is united, of reducing whatever is eminent, of dreading every active power, and of expecting that the most feeble will prove the most obedient seems to pervade the institutions of several princes, and particularly those of Constantine. The martial pride of the legions, whose

5. Ammianus observes that they loved downy beds and houses of marble and that their cups were heavier than their swords.

victorious camps had so often been the scene of rebellion, was nourished by the memory of their past exploits and the consciousness of their actual strength. As long as they maintained their ancient establishment of six thousand men they subsisted, under the reign of Diocletian, each of them singly a visible and important object in the military history of the Roman empire. A few years afterwards these gigantic bodies were shrunk to a very diminutive size; and when *seven* legions, with some auxiliaries, defended the city of Amida against the Persians, the total garrison, with the inhabitants of both sexes and the peasants of the deserted country, did not exceed the number of twenty thousand persons. From this fact and from similar examples, there is reason to believe that the constitution of the legionary troops, to which they partly owed their valour and discipline, was dissolved by Constantine, and that the bands of Roman infantry, which still assumed the same names and the same honours, consisted only of one thousand or fifteen hundred men. The conspiracy of so many separate detachments, each of which was awed by the sense of its own weakness, could easily be checked; and the successors of Constantine might indulge their love of ostentation by issuing their orders to one hundred and thirty-two legions inscribed on the muster-roll of their numerous armies.

The remainder of their troops was distributed into several hundred cohorts of infantry and squadrons of cavalry. Their arms, titles, and ensigns were calculated to inspire terror and to display the variety of nations who marched under the Imperial standard. And not a vestige was left of that severe simplicity which, in the ages of freedom and victory, had distinguished the line of battle of a Roman army from the confused host of an Asiatic monarch. A more particular enumeration, drawn from the *Notitia*, might exercise the diligence of an antiquary; but the historian will content himself with observing that the number of permanent stations or garrisons established on the frontiers of the empire amounted to five hundred and eighty-three, and that under the successors of Constantine the complete force of the military establishment was computed at six hundred and forty-five thousand soldiers. An effort so prodigious surpassed the wants of a more ancient and the faculties of a later period.

In the various states of society armies are recruited from very different motives. Barbarians are urged by their love of war; the citizens of a free republic may be prompted by a principle of duty; the subjects, or at least the nobles, of a monarchy are animated by a sentiment of honour; but the timid and luxurious inhabitants of a declining empire must be allured into the service by the hopes of profit or compelled by the dread of punishment. The resources of the Roman treasury were exhausted by the increase of pay, by the repetition of donatives, and by the invention of new emoluments and indulgences, which, in the opinion of the provincial youth, might compensate the hardships and dangers of a military life. Yet, although the stature was lowered, although slaves, at least by a tacit connivance, were indiscriminately received into the ranks, the insurmountable difficulty of procuring a regular and adequate supply of volunteers obliged the emperors to adopt more effectual and coercive methods. The lands bestowed on the veterans as the free reward of their valour were henceforward granted under a condition which contains the first rudiment of the feudal tenures—that their sons who succeeded to the inheritance should devote themselves to the profession of arms as soon as they attained the age of manhood; and their cowardly refusal was punished by the loss of honour, of fortune, or even of life.

But as the annual growth of the sons of the veterans bore a very small proportion to the demands of the service, levies of men were frequently required from the provinces, and every proprietor was obliged either to take up arms, or to procure a substitute, or to purchase his exemption by the payment of a heavy fine. The sum of forty-two pieces of gold, to which it was *reduced,* ascertains the exorbitant price of volunteers and the reluctance with which the government admitted of this alternative. Such was the horror for the profession of a soldier which had affected the minds of the degenerate Romans that many of the youth of Italy and the provinces chose to cut off the fingers of their right hand to escape from being pressed into the service; and this strange expedient was so commonly practised as to deserve the severe animadversion of the laws and a peculiar name in the Latin language.[6]

The introduction of barbarians into the Roman armies became every day more universal, more necessary, and more fatal. The most daring of the Scythians, of the Goths, and of the Germans, who delighted in war and who found it more profitable to defend than to ravage the provinces, were enrolled not only in the auxiliaries of their respective nations but in the legions themselves and among the most distinguished of the Palatine troops. As they freely mingled with the subjects of the empire, they gradually learned to despise their manners and to imitate their arts. They abjured the implicit reverence which the pride of Rome had exacted from their ignorance, while they acquired the knowledge and

6. They were called *Murci.* The person and property of a Roman knight who had mutilated his two sons were sold at public auction by order of Augustus.

possession of those advantages by which alone she supported her declining greatness. The barbarian soldiers who displayed any military talents were advanced, without exception, to the most important commands; and the names of the tribunes, of the counts and dukes, and of the generals themselves betray a foreign origin, which they no longer condescended to disguise. They were often entrusted with the conduct of a war against their countrymen; and though most of them preferred the ties of allegiance to those of blood, they did not always avoid the guilt, or at least the suspicion, of holding a treasonable correspondence with the enemy, of inviting his invasion, or of sparing his retreat. The camps and the palace of the son of Constantine were governed by the powerful faction of the Franks, who preserved the strictest connection with each other and with their country, and who resented every personal affront as a national indignity.

When the tyrant Caligula was suspected of an intention to invest a very extraordinary candidate with the consular robes, the sacrilegious profanation would have scarcely excited less astonishment if, instead of a horse, the noblest chieftain of Germany or Britain had been the object of his choice. The revolution of three centuries had produced so remarkable a change in the prejudices of the people that, with the public approbation, Constantine showed his successors the example of bestowing the honours of the consulship on the barbarians who by their merit and services had deserved to be ranked among the first of the Romans. But as these hardy veterans, who had been educated in the ignorance or contempt of the laws, were incapable of exercising any civil offices, the powers of the human mind were contracted by the irreconcilable separation of talents as well as of professions. The accomplished citizens of the Greek and Roman republics, whose characters could adapt themselves to the bar, the senate, the camp, or the schools, had learned to write, to speak, and to act with the same spirit and with equal abilities.

IV. THE MINISTERS OF THE PALACE. Besides the magistrates and generals, who at a distance from the court diffused their delegated authority over the provinces and armies, the emperor conferred the rank of *Illustrious* on seven of his more immediate servants, to whose fidelity he entrusted his safety, or his counsels, or his treasures.

1. The private apartments of the palace were governed by a favourite eunuch who, in the language of that age, was styled the *præpositus*, or præfect of the sacred bedchamber. His duty was to attend the emperor in his hours of state or in those of amusement, and to perform about his person all those menial services which can only derive their splendour from the influence of royalty. Under a prince who deserved to reign, the great chamberlain (for such we may call him) was an useful and humble domestic; but an artful domestic, who improves every occasion of unguarded confidence, will insensibly acquire over a feeble mind that ascendant which harsh wisdom and uncomplying virtue can seldom obtain. The degenerate grandsons of Theodosius, who were invisible to their subjects and contemptible to their enemies, exalted the præfects of their bedchamber above the heads of all the ministers of the palace; and even his deputy, the first of the splendid train of slaves who waited in the presence, was thought worthy to rank before the *Respectable* proconsuls of Greece or Asia. The jurisdiction of the chamberlain was acknowledged by the *counts*, or superintendents, who regulated the two important provinces of the magnificence of the wardrobe and of the luxury of the Imperial table.

2. The principal administration of public affairs was committed to the diligence and abilities of the *master of the offices*. He was the supreme magistrate of the palace, inspected the discipline of the civil and military *schools*, and received appeals from all parts of the empire in the causes which related to that numerous army of privileged persons who, as the servants of the court, had obtained for themselves and families a right to decline the authority of the ordinary judges. The correspondence between the prince and his subjects was managed by the four *scrinia*, or offices of this minister of state. The first was appropriated to memorials, the second to epistles, the third to petitions, and the fourth to papers and orders of a miscellaneous kind. Each of these was directed by an inferior *master* of *Respectable* dignity, and the whole business was despatched by an hundred and forty-eight secretaries chosen for the most part from the profession of the law, on account of the variety of abstracts of reports and references which frequently occurred in the exercise of their several functions. From a condescension which in former ages would have been esteemed unworthy of the Roman majesty, a particular secretary was allowed for the Greek language, and interpreters were appointed to receive the ambassadors of the barbarians; but the department of foreign affairs, which constitutes so essential a part of modern policy, seldom diverted the attention of the master of the offices. His mind was more seriously engaged by the general direction of the posts and arsenals of the empire. There were thirty-four cities, fifteen in the East and nineteen in the West, in which regular companies of workmen were perpetually employed in fabricating defensive armour, offensive weapons of all sorts, and military engines, which were deposited in the

arsenals and occasionally delivered for the service of the troops.

3. In the course of nine centuries the office of *quæstor* had experienced a very singular revolution. In the infancy of Rome two inferior magistrates were annually elected by the people to relieve the consuls from the invidious management of the public treasure; a similar assistant was granted to every proconsul and to every prætor who exercised a military or provincial command; with the extent of conquest, the two quæstors were gradually multiplied to the number of four, of eight, of twenty, and for a short time, perhaps, of forty; and the noblest citizens ambitiously solicited an office which gave them a seat in the senate and a just hope of obtaining the honours of the republic. Whilst Augustus affected to maintain the freedom of election, he consented to accept the annual privilege of recommending, or rather indeed of nominating, a certain proportion of candidates; and it was his custom to select one of these distinguished youths to read his orations or epistles in the assemblies of the senate. The practice of Augustus was imitated by succeeding princes; the occasional commission was established as a permanent office; and the favoured quæstor, assuming a new and more illustrious character, alone survived the suppression of his ancient and useless colleagues. As the orations which he composed in the name of the emperor acquired the force and at length the form of absolute edicts, he was considered as the representative of the legislative power, the oracle of the council, and the original source of the civil jurisprudence. He was sometimes invited to take his seat in the supreme judicature of the Imperial consistory with the Præorian præfects and the master of the offices, and he was frequently requested to resolve the doubts of inferior judges; but as he was not oppressed

with a variety of subordinate business, his leisure and talents were employed to cultivate that dignified style of eloquence which, in the corruption of taste and language, still preserves the majesty of the Roman laws. In some respects the office of the Imperial quæstor may be compared with that of a modern chancellor; but the use of a great seal, which seems to have been adopted by the illiterate barbarians, was never introduced to attest the public acts of the emperors.

4. The extraordinary title of *count of the sacred largesses* was bestowed on the treasurer general of the revenue, with the intention perhaps of inculcating that every payment flowed from the voluntary bounty of the monarch. To conceive the almost infinite detail of the annual and daily expense of the civil and military administration in every part of a great empire would exceed the powers of the most vigorous imagination. The actual account employed several hundred persons distributed into eleven different offices, which were artfully contrived to examine and control their respective operations. The multitude of these agents had a natural tendency to increase; and it was more than once thought expedient to dismiss to their native homes the useless supernumeraries who, deserting their honest labours, had pressed with too much eagerness into the lucrative profession of the finances. Twenty-nine provincial receivers, of whom eighteen were honoured with the title of *count*, corresponded with the treasurer, and he extended his jurisdiction over the mines from whence the precious metals were extracted, over the mints in which they were converted into the current coin, and over the public treasuries of the most important cities, where they were deposited for the service of the state. The foreign trade of the empire was regulated by this minister, who directed likewise all the linen and woollen

manufactures, in which the successive operations of spinning, weaving, and dyeing were executed, chiefly by women of a servile condition, for the use of the palace and army. Twenty-six of these institutions are enumerated in the West, where the arts had been more recently introduced, and a still larger proportion may be allowed for the industrious provinces of the East.

5. Besides the public revenue which an absolute monarch might levy and expend according to his pleasure, the emperors, in the capacity of opulent citizens, possessed a very extensive property which was administered by the *count*, or treasurer, *of the private estate*. Some part had perhaps been the ancient demesnes of kings and republics; some accessions might be derived from the families which were successively invested with the purple; but the most considerable portion flowed from the impure source of confiscations and forfeitures. The Imperial estates were scattered through the provinces from Mauritania to Britain; but the rich and fertile soil of Cappadocia tempted the monarch to acquire in that country his fairest possessions, and either Constantine or his successors embraced the occasion of justifying avarice by religious zeal. They suppressed the rich temple of Comana, where the high priest of the goddess of war supported the dignity of a sovereign prince; and they applied to their private use the consecrated lands, which were inhabited by six thousand subjects or slaves of the deity and her ministers. But these were not the valuable inhabitants: the plains that stretch from the foot of Mount Argæus to the banks of the Sarus bred a generous race of horses, renowned above all others in the ancient world for their majestic shape and incomparable swiftness. These sacred animals, destined for the service of the palace and the Imperial games, were protected by the laws from the profanation of a vulgar

master. The demesnes of Cappadocia were important enough to require the inspection of a *count;* officers of an inferior rank were stationed in the other parts of the empire; and the deputies of the private as well as those of the public treasurer were maintained in the exercise of their independent functions and encouraged to control the authority of the provincial magistrates.

6, 7. The chosen bands of cavalry and infantry which guarded the person of the emperor were under the immediate command of the two counts of the domestics. The whole number consisted of three thousand and five hundred men divided into seven *schools,* or troops, of five hundred each; and in the East this honourable service was almost entirely appropriated to the Armenians. Whenever on public ceremonies they were drawn up in the courts and porticos of the palace, their lofty stature, silent order, and splendid arms of silver and gold displayed a martial pomp not unworthy of the Roman majesty. From the seven schools two companies of horse and foot were selected, of the *protectors,* whose advantageous station was the hope and reward of the most deserving soldiers. They mounted guard in the interior apartments and were occasionally despatched into the provinces to execute with celerity and vigour the orders of their master. The counts of the domestics had succeeded to the office of the Prætorian præfects; like the præfects, they aspired from the service of the palace to the command of armies.

The perpetual intercourse between the court and the provinces was facilitated by the construction of roads and the institution of posts. But these beneficial establishments were accidentally connected with a pernicious and intolerable abuse. Two or three hundred *agents,* or messengers, were employed, under the jurisdiction of the master of the offices, to announce the names of the annual consuls and the edicts or victories of the emperors. They insensibly assumed the licence of reporting whatever they could observe of the conduct either of magistrates or of private citizens, and were soon considered as the eyes of the monarch and the scourge of the people. Under the warm influence of a feeble reign they multiplied to the incredible number of ten thousand, disdained the mild though frequent admonitions of the laws, and exercised in the profitable management of the posts a rapacious and insolent oppression. These official spies, who regularly corresponded with the palace, were encouraged by favour and reward anxiously to watch the progress of every treasonable design, from the faint and latent symptoms of disaffection to the actual preparation of an open revolt. Their careless or criminal violation of truth and justice was covered by the consecrated mask of zeal; and they might securely aim their poisoned arrows at the breast either of the guilty or the innocent who had provoked their resentment or refused to purchase their silence. A faithful subject of Syria, perhaps, or of Britain, was exposed to the danger, or at least to the dread, of being dragged in chains to the court of Milan or Constantinople to defend his life and fortune against the malicious charge of these privileged informers. The ordinary administration was conducted by those methods which extreme necessity can alone palliate; and the defects of evidence were diligently supplied by the use of torture.

The deceitful and dangerous experiment of the criminal *quæstion,* as it is emphatically styled, was admitted rather than approved in the jurisprudence of the Romans. They applied this sanguinary mode of examination only to servile bodies, whose sufferings were seldom weighed by those haughty republicans in the scale of justice or humanity; but they would never consent to

violate the sacred person of a citizen till they possessed
the clearest evidence of his guilt. The annals of tyranny,
from the reign of Tiberius to that of Domitian, circumstantially relate the executions of many innocent victims; but as long as the faintest remembrance was kept
alive of the national freedom and honour, the last hours
of a Roman were secure from the danger of ignominious
torture.

The conduct of the provincial magistrates was not,
however, regulated by the practice of the city or the
strict maxims of the civilians. They found the use of
torture established not only among the slaves of oriental
despotism but among the Macedonians, who obeyed a
limited monarch; among the Rhodians, who flourished
by the liberty of commerce; and even among the sage
Athenians, who had asserted and adorned the dignity of
humankind. The acquiescence of the provincials encouraged their governors to acquire, or perhaps to usurp,
a discretionary power of employing the rack to extort
from vagrants or plebeian criminals the confession of
their guilt, till they insensibly proceeded to confound
the distinctions of rank and to disregard the privileges
of Roman citizens.

The apprehensions of the subjects urged them to
solicit, and the interest of the sovereign engaged him
to grant, a variety of special exemptions, which tacitly
allowed and even authorized the general use of torture.
They protected all persons of illustrious or honourable
rank, bishops and their presbyters, professors of the
liberal arts, soldiers and their families, municipal officers, and their posterity to the third generation, and all
children under the age of puberty. But a fatal maxim
was introduced into the new jurisprudence of the empire that in the case of treason, which included every
offence that the subtlety of lawyers could derive from

an *hostile intention* towards the prince or republic, all privileges were suspended and all conditions were reduced to the same ignominious level. As the safety of the emperor was avowedly preferred to every consideration of justice or humanity, the dignity of age and the tenderness of youth were alike exposed to the most cruel tortures; and the terrors of a malicious information, which might select them as the accomplices or even as the witnesses, perhaps, of an imaginary crime, perpetually hung over the heads of the principal citizens of the Roman world.

These evils, however terrible they may appear, were confined to the smaller number of Roman subjects whose dangerous situation was in some degree compensated by the enjoyment of those advantages, either of nature or of fortune, which exposed them to the jealousy of the monarch. The obscure millions of a great empire have much less to dread from the cruelty than from the avarice of their masters; and *their* humble happiness is principally affected by the grievance of excessive taxes, which, gently pressing on the wealthy, descend with accelerated weight on the meaner and more indigent classes of society. An ingenious philosopher has calculated the universal measure of the public impositions by the degrees of freedom and servitude and ventures to assert that, according to an invariable law of nature, it must always increase with the former and diminish in a just proportion to the latter. But this reflection, which would tend to alleviate the miseries of despotism, is contradicted at least by the history of the Roman empire, which accuses the same princes of despoiling the senate of its authority and the provinces of their wealth. Without abolishing all the various customs and duties on merchandises, which are imperceptibly discharged by the apparent choice of the purchaser, the policy of Constantine and his successors preferred a simple and direct mode of taxation, more congenial to the spirit of an arbitrary government.

The name and use of the *indictions,* which serve to ascertain the chronology of the middle ages, was derived from the regular practice of the Roman tributes. The emperor subscribed with his own hand, and in purple ink, the solemn edict or indiction which was fixed up in the principal city of each diocese during two months previous to the first day of September; and by a very easy connection of ideas the word *indiction* was transferred to the measure of tribute which it prescribed and to the annual term which it allowed for the payment. This general estimate of the supplies was proportioned to the real and imaginary wants of the state; but as often as the expense exceeded the revenue, or the revenue fell short of the computation, an additional tax, under the name of *superindiction,* was imposed on the people; and the most valuable attribute of sovereignty was communicated to the Prætorian præfects, who on some occasions were permitted to provide for the unforeseen and extraordinary exigencies of the public service.

The execution of these laws (which it would be tedious to pursue in their minute and intricate detail) consisted of two distinct operations: the resolving of the general imposition into its constituent parts, which were assessed on the provinces, the cities, and the individuals of the Roman world; and the collecting of the separate contributions of the individuals, the cities, and the provinces, till the accumulated sums were poured into the Imperial treasuries. But as the account between the monarch and the subject was perpetually open, and as the renewal of the demand anticipated the perfect discharge of the preceding obligation, the weighty machine of the finances was moved by the same hands round the circle of its yearly revolution. Whatever was honourable or important in the administration of the revenue was committed to the wisdom of the præfects and their provincial representatives; the lucrative functions were claimed by a crowd of subordinate officers, some of whom depended on the treasurer, others on the governor of the province, and who in the inevitable conflicts of a perplexed jurisdiction had frequent opportunities of disputing with each other the spoils of the people. The laborious offices, which could be productive only of envy and reproach, of expense and danger, were imposed on the *decurions,* who formed the corporations of the cities and whom the severity of the Imperial laws had condemned to sustain the burdens of civil society.

The whole landed property of the empire (without excepting the patrimonial estates of the monarch) was the object of ordinary taxation, and every new purchaser contracted the obligations of the former proprietor. An accurate *census,* or survey, was the only equitable mode of ascertaining the proportion which every citizen should be obliged to contribute for the public service; and from the well-known period of the indictions, there is reason to believe that this difficult and expensive operation was repeated at the regular distance of fifteen years. The lands were measured by surveyors who were sent into the provinces; their nature, whether arable or pasture, or vineyards or woods, was distinctly reported; and an estimate was made of their common value from the average produce of five years. The numbers of slaves and of cattle constituted an essential part of the report; an oath was administered to the proprietors which bound them to disclose the true state of their affairs; and their attempts to prevaricate or elude the intention

of the legislator were severely watched and punished as
a capital crime, which included the double guilt of treason and sacrilege.

A large portion of the tribute was paid in money; and
of the current coin of the empire, gold alone could be
legally accepted. The remainder of the taxes, according
to the proportions determined by the annual indiction,
was furnished in a manner still more direct and still
more oppressive. According to the different nature of
lands, their real produce in the various articles of wine
or oil, corn or barley, wood or iron, was transported by
the labour or at the expense of the provincials to the
Imperial magazines, from whence they were occasionally distributed for the use of the court, of the army,
and of the two capitals, Rome and Constantinople. The
commissioners of the revenue were so frequently obliged
to make considerable purchases that they were strictly
prohibited from allowing any compensation or from receiving in money the value of those supplies which were
exacted in kind.

In the primitive simplicity of small communities this
method may be well adapted to collect the almost voluntary offerings of the people; but it is at once susceptible
of the utmost latitude and of the utmost strictness,
which in a corrupt and absolute monarchy must introduce a perpetual contest between the power of oppression and the arts of fraud. The agriculture of the Roman
provinces was insensibly ruined; and in the progress of
despotism, which tends to disappoint its own purpose,
the emperors were obliged to derive some merit from
the forgiveness of debts or the remission of tributes
which their subjects were utterly incapable of paying.
According to the new division of Italy, the fertile and
happy province of Campania, the scene of the early victories and of the delicious retirements of the citizens of

Rome, extended between the sea and the Apennine from the Tiber to the Silarus. Within sixty years after the death of Constantine, and on the evidence of an actual survey, an exemption was granted in favour of three hundred and thirty thousand English acres of desert and uncultivated land, which amounted to one-eighth of the whole surface of the province. As the footsteps of the barbarians had not yet been seen in Italy, the cause of this amazing desolation, which is recorded in the laws, can be ascribed only to the administration of the Roman emperors.

Either from design or from accident, the mode of assessment seemed to unite the substance of a land-tax with the forms of a capitation. The returns which were sent of every province or district expressed the number of tributary subjects and the amount of the public impositions. The latter of these sums was divided by the former; and the estimate that such a province contained so many *capita*, or heads of tribute, and that each *head* was rated at such a price, was universally received not only in the popular but even in the legal computation. The value of a tributary head must have varied according to many accidental, or at least fluctuating, circumstances; but some knowledge has been preserved of a very curious fact, the more important since it relates to one of the richest provinces of the Roman empire and which now flourishes as the most splendid of the European kingdoms. The rapacious ministers of Constantius had exhausted the wealth of Gaul by exacting twenty-five pieces of gold for the annual tribute of every head. The humane policy of his successor reduced the capitation to seven pieces. A moderate proportion between these opposite extremes of extraordinary oppression and of transient indulgence may therefore be fixed at sixteen pieces of gold, or about nine pounds sterling, the common standard, perhaps, of the impositions of Gaul.[7]

But this tax, or capitation, on the proprietors of land would have suffered a rich and numerous class of free citizens to escape. With the view of sharing that species of wealth which is derived from art or labour, and which exists in money or in merchandise, the emperors imposed a distinct and personal tribute on the trading part of their subjects. Some exemptions, very strictly confined both in time and place, were allowed to the proprietors who disposed of the produce of their own estates. Some indulgence was granted to the profession of the liberal arts; but every other branch of commercial industry was affected by the severity of the law. The honourable merchant of Alexandria who imported the gems and spices of India for the use of the western world, the usurer who derived from the interest of money a silent and ignominious profit, the ingenious manufacturer, the diligent mechanic, and even the most obscure retailer of a sequestered village were obliged to admit the officers of the revenue into the partnership of their gain; and the sovereign of the Roman empire, who tolerated the profession, consented to share the infamous salary of public prostitutes.

As this general tax upon industry was collected every fourth year, it was styled the *Lustral Contribution;* and the historian Zosimus laments that the approach of the fatal period was announced by the tears and terrors of the citizens, who were often compelled by the impending scourge to embrace the most abhorred and unnat-

7. *Editor's note:* In the original, Gibbon continues by noting that the weight of the capitation was moderated by the fact that a number of poorer peasants might be grouped together for tax purposes as a single "head."

ural methods of procuring the sum at which their poverty had been assessed. The testimony of Zosimus cannot indeed be justified from the charge of passion and prejudice; but from the nature of this tribute it seems reasonable to conclude that it was arbitrary in the distribution and extremely rigorous in the mode of collecting. The secret wealth of commerce and the precarious profits of art or labour are susceptible only of a discretionary valuation, which is seldom disadvantageous to the interest of the treasury; and as the person of the trader supplies the want of a visible and permanent security, the payment of the imposition, which in the case of a land-tax may be obtained by the seizure of property, can rarely be extorted by any other means than those of corporal punishments. The cruel treatment of the insolvent debtors of the state is attested, and was perhaps mitigated, by a very humane edict of Constantine, who, disclaiming the use of racks and of scourges, allots a spacious and airy prison for the place of their confinement.

These general taxes were imposed and levied by the absolute authority of the monarch; but the occasional offerings of the *coronary gold* still retained the name and semblance of popular consent. It was an ancient custom that the allies of the republic, who ascribed their safety or deliverance to the success of the Roman arms, and even the cities of Italy, who admired the virtues of their victorious general, adorned the pomp of his triumph by their voluntary gifts of crowns of gold, which after the ceremony were consecrated in the temple of Jupiter to remain a lasting monument of his glory to future ages. The progress of zeal and flattery soon multiplied the number and increased the size of these popular donations; and the triumph of Cæsar was enriched with two thousand eight hundred and twenty-two massy

crowns, whose weight amounted to twenty thousand
four hundred and fourteen pounds of gold. This treasure was immediately melted down by the prudent dictator, who was satisfied that it would be more serviceable to his soldiers than to the gods; his example was
imitated by his successors, and the custom was introduced of exchanging these splendid ornaments for the
more acceptable present of the current gold coin of
the empire.

The spontaneous offering was at length exacted as
the debt of duty; and instead of being confined to the
occasion of a triumph, it was supposed to be granted by
the several cities and provinces of the monarchy as often
as the emperor condescended to announce his accession,
his consulship, the birth of a son, the creation of a
Cæsar, a victory over the barbarians, or any other real
or imaginary event which graced the annals of his reign.
The peculiar free gift of the senate of Rome was fixed
by custom at sixteen hundred pounds of gold, or about
sixty-four thousand pounds sterling. The oppressed subjects celebrated their own felicity that their sovereign
should graciously consent to accept this feeble but voluntary testimony of their loyalty and gratitude.

A people elated by pride or soured by discontent is
seldom qualified to form a just estimate of their actual
situation. The subjects of Constantine were incapable
of discerning the decline of genius and manly virtue,
which so far degraded them below the dignity of their
ancestors; but they could feel and lament the rage of
tyranny, the relaxation of discipline, and the increase of
taxes. The impartial historian, who acknowledges the
justice of their complaints, will observe some favourable
circumstances which tended to alleviate the misery of
their condition. The threatening tempest of barbarians,
which so soon subverted the foundations of Roman

greatness, was still repelled or suspended on the frontiers. The arts of luxury and literature were cultivated, and the elegant pleasures of society were enjoyed, by the inhabitants of a considerable portion of the globe. The forms, the pomp, and the expense of the civil administration contributed to restrain the irregular licence of the soldiers; and although the laws were violated by power or perverted by subtlety, the sage principles of the Roman jurisprudence preserved a sense of order and equity unknown to the despotic governments of the East. The rights of mankind might derive some protection from religion and philosophy; and the name of freedom, which could no longer alarm, might sometimes admonish the successors of Augustus that they did not reign over a nation of slaves or barbarians.

In the next chapters Gibbon remarks that Constantine, in the long unchallenged afternoon of his reign, appears to have degenerated into a "cruel but dissolute monarch," whose "opposite yet reconcilable vices of rapaciousness and prodigality" helped to induce the "secret but universal decay" felt throughout the empire. The charge is certainly supported by his execution of Crispus, his eldest son by a first wife, who had played a decisive part in Constantine's final victory over Licinius (see p. 257); of Licinius's son, who was Constantine's own nephew; and perhaps of Constantine's second wife, Fausta. Yet less than two years before death terminated his long reign, the founder of Constantinople could find the skill and vigour to chastise first the Goths and then the savage Sarmatians for their depredations along the Roman frontier. He died at sixty-four, leaving behind him seven princes of the blood: Constantius, Constans, and Constantine, the sons of his second wife, Fausta; and four nephews, Dalmatius, Hannibalianus,

Gallus, and Julian, all sons of his brother. The empire was apportioned among the three sons and the two older nephews (Dalmatius and Hannibalianus), all with the title of Cæsar.

Yet Constantine was scarcely cold in death before this numerous group of successors began to prey on one another. Constantius, who had been entrusted with his father's funeral, produced a forged will that was sufficient excuse for a "promiscuous massacre" which involved two of his uncles, seven of his cousins, "of whom Dalmatius and Hannibalianus were the most illustrious," and many of their friends and supporters. The three brothers then redivided the empire, with the younger Constantine acquiring the new capital, Constans the provinces of the West, and Constantius those in the East. The last-named was at once called to defend his patrimony against the alarming incursions of the Persian king Sapor. Some nine major battles were fought in a war that alternately flared and flickered throughout most of the long life of Constantius; and while the Romans were in most instances defeated, two circumstances contrive to prevent the apparently impending loss of the rich eastern provinces. The fortified city of Nisibis, in Mesopotamia, again and again tempted Sapor to break his strength in vain sieges; and the last of these was finally raised when Sapor was obliged to defend his own kingdom against a barbarian flood.

But the self-destruction of the line of Constantine proceeded inexorably. Three years after the division of the empire among the three brothers, the eldest (Constantine) led a "tumultuary band, suited for rapine rather than for conquest," against his brother Constans, and in so doing only contrived his own defeat and death. A decade later Constans was himself brought down by the revolt, in Gaul, of an ambitious soldier named Magnentius, who then alternately negotiated and contended with Constantius for the division or possession of the whole empire. Magnentius's first offer to relinquish the eastern provinces to Constantius, reserving the West for himself, was refused; then, when at a doubtful juncture in the ensuing civil war Constantius made the same offer, Magnentius refused. The issue was effectively decided at the battle of Mursa in Hungary, where the number of slain was estimated at fifty-four thousand; and though the outcome reunited the empire under the single authority of Constantius, the loss of so many veteran troops in civil strife was felt for decades.

The two youngest nephews of the great Constantine, Gallus and Julian, had been saved by their tender ages (twelve and six respectively) from the massacre that consumed Dalmatius and Hannibalianus; and eventually the burdens of government led Constantius to end their semi-confinement and raise Gallus to the rank of Cæsar, with jurisdiction over the five great provinces or dioceses of the East. Gallus proved, however, to have a temper "soured by solitude and adversity," while his wife, Constantina, "is described not as a woman but as one of the infernal furies tormented with an insatiate lust for human blood." (She is alleged, for the price of a pearl necklace, to have secured the murder of an Alexandrian nobleman whose sole crime was "a refusal to gratify the desires of his mother-in-law.") The eastern provinces were permitted to suffer under the yoke of Gallus until the end of the civil war with Magnentius, but soon thereafter Constantius managed to entice Gallus to his own destruction.

Julian, the other nephew, who is by all odds Gibbon's favourite character among the later Roman emperors, was exiled to Athens after the demise of his brother Gallus, and there studied well among the Greek teachers *and philosophers. Through the partiality of the empress Eusebia he was ultimately recalled from his studious exile and raised to the rank of Cæsar, to be stationed in the barbarian-distracted province of Gaul. Despite a total lack of military training and experience (after the clumsy performance of some routine exercise he is reported to have exclaimed, "O Plato, Plato, what a task for a philosopher!"), he surmounted immense difficulties to defeat first the Alemanni and then the Franks; and while Julius Cæsar could boast that he had twice passed the Rhine, Julian achieved three such expeditions before he was fated to assume the purple.*

Meanwhile the effective establishment of Christianity as the official religion, beginning with Constantine, was rapidly changing the social fabric of the empire. The conversion of Constantine seems to have been a gradual process, since he was not baptized until his last illness. (Gibbon dismisses as a fairy tale the traditional story of the great cross seen by Constantine in the sky and remarks of such historical omens that "if the eyes of the spectators were sometimes deceived by fraud, the understanding of the readers has much more frequently been insulted by fiction.") But from the time Constantine was ruler of Gaul, there could be no doubt where his sympathies lay.

As a result of this Imperial partiality, Christian bishops and teachers had constant and easy access to the throne; the church recovered, and in the process acquired perfect title to, all the land and property which it had lost under the severity of Diocletian; all subjects were given the right to bequeath property to the church; public moneys began to support the rapidly expanding religion; the ancient principle of sanctuary, once limited to the holiest of the pagan temples, was transferred to the Christian churches; and the bishops became powerful enough to censure and to excommunicate high civil officials who displeased them. From the time of Constantine on, the civil and religious affairs of the empire become so inextricably intermingled that it is seldom possible to understand the one without at least some grasp of the other.

Chapter X

(A.D. 312-362)

Persecution of heresy – The schism of the Donatists – The Arian controversy – Athanasius – Distracted state of the church and empire under Constantine and his sons – Toleration of paganism[1]

THE grateful applause of the clergy has consecrated the memory of a prince who indulged their passions and promoted their interest. Constantine gave them security, wealth, honours, and revenge; and the support of the orthodox faith was considered as the most sacred and important duty of the civil magistrate. The edict of Milan, the great charter of toleration, had confirmed to each individual of the Roman world the privilege of choosing and professing his own religion. But this inestimable privilege was soon violated; with the knowledge of truth the emperor imbibed the maxims of persecution; and the sects which dissented from the catholic church were afflicted and oppressed by the triumph of Christianity. Constantine easily believed that the heretics, who presumed to dispute *his* opinions or to oppose *his* commands, were guilty of the most absurd and criminal obstinacy, and that a seasonable application of moderate severities might save those unhappy men from the danger of an everlasting condemnation.

Not a moment was lost in excluding the ministers and teachers of the separated congregations from any share of the rewards and immunities which the emperor had so liberally bestowed on the orthodox clergy. But as the sec-

1. *Editor's note:* Chapter XXI of the original.

taries might still exist under the cloud of royal disgrace, the conquest of the East was immediately followed by an edict which announced their total destruction. After a preamble filled with passion and reproach, Constantine absolutely prohibits the assemblies of the heretics and confiscates their public property to the use either of the revenue or of the catholic church. The sects against whom the Imperial severity was directed appear to have been the adherents of Paul of Samosata; the Montanists of Phrygia, who maintained an enthusiastic succession of prophecy; the Novatians, who sternly rejected the temporal efficacy of repentance; the Marcionites and Valentinians, under whose leading banners the various Gnostics of Asia and Egypt had insensibly rallied; and perhaps the Manichæans, who had recently imported from Persia a more artful composition of oriental and Christian theology.

The design of extirpating the name, or at least of restraining the progress, of these odious heretics was prosecuted with vigour and effect. Some of the penal regulations were copied from the edicts of Diocletian; and this method of conversion was applauded by the same bishops who had felt the hand of oppression and had pleaded for the rights of humanity. Two immaterial circumstances may serve, however, to prove that the mind of Constantine was not entirely corrupted by the spirit of zeal and bigotry. Before he condemned the Manichæans and their kindred sects, he resolved to make an accurate inquiry into the nature of their religious principles. As if he distrusted the impartiality of his ecclesiastical counsellors, this delicate commission was entrusted to a civil magistrate whose learning and moderation he justly esteemed and of whose venal character he was probably ignorant. The emperor was soon convinced that he had too hastily proscribed the orthodox faith and the exemplary morals of the Novatians, who had dissented from the church in some articles of discipline which were not perhaps essential to salvation. By a particular edict he exempted them from the general penalties of the law, allowed them to build a church at Constantinople, respected the miracles of their saints, invited their bishop, Acesius, to the council of Nice, and gently ridiculed the narrow tenets of his sect by a familiar jest, which from the mouth of a sovereign must have been received with applause and gratitude.[2]

In the original, Gibbon continues with a brief account of the Donatist heresy, which began when a bitter dispute between two bishops, Cæcilian and Donatus, over the government of the African church led to the triumph of the former through Imperial preference. The followers of Donatus set themselves up as the only true Christians, distinguished equally by their inflexible zeal, their hatred of the orthodox creed, and their own tendency towards schism. They persisted for over three hundred years, disappearing only when the Moslems overran that part of Africa.

The schism of the Donatists was confined to Africa; the more diffusive mischief of the Trinitarian controversy successively penetrated into every part of the Christian world. The former was an accidental quarrel, occasioned by the abuse of freedom; the latter was a high and mysterious argument, derived from the abuse of philosophy. From the age of Constantine to that of Clovis and Theodoric, the temporal interests both of the Romans and barbarians were deeply involved in the theological

2. "Acesius, take a ladder, and get up to heaven by yourself." Most of the Christian sects have, by turns, borrowed the ladder of Acesius.

disputes of Arianism. The historian may therefore be permitted respectfully to withdraw the veil of the sanctuary and to deduce the progress of reason and faith, of error and passion, from the school of Plato to the decline and fall of the empire.

The genius of Plato, informed by his own meditation or by the traditional knowledge of the priests of Egypt, had ventured to explore the mysterious nature of the Deity. When he had elevated his mind to the sublime contemplation of the first self-existent, necessary cause of the universe, the Athenian sage was incapable of conceiving *how* the simple unity of his essence could admit the infinite variety of distinct and successive ideas which compose the model of the intellectual world; *how* a Being purely incorporeal could execute that perfect model and mould with a plastic hand the rude and independent chaos. The vain hope of extricating himself from these difficulties, which must ever oppress the feeble powers of the human mind, might induce Plato to consider the divine nature under the threefold modification: of the first cause; the reason, or *Logos;* and the soul or spirit of the universe. His poetical imagination sometimes fixed and animated these metaphysical abstractions; the three *archical* or original principles were represented in the Platonic system as three Gods, united with each other by a mysterious and ineffable generation; and the Logos was particularly considered under the more accessible character of the Son of an Eternal Father and the Creator and Governor of the world. Such appear to have been the secret doctrines which were cautiously whispered in the gardens of the Academy and which, according to the more recent disciples of Plato, could not be perfectly understood till after an assiduous study of thirty years.

The arms of the Macedonians diffused over Asia and

Egypt the language and learning of Greece, and the theological system of Plato was taught, with less reserve and perhaps with some improvements, in the celebrated school of Alexandria. A numerous colony of Jews had been invited, by the favour of the Ptolemies, to settle in their new capital. While the bulk of the nation practised the legal ceremonies and pursued the lucrative occupations of commerce, a few Hebrews of a more liberal spirit devoted their lives to religious and philosophical contemplation. They cultivated with diligence and embraced with ardour the theological system of the Athenian sage. But their national pride would have been mortified by a fair confession of their former poverty; and they boldly marked, as the sacred inheritance of their ancestors, the gold and jewels which they had so lately stolen from their Egyptian masters. One hundred years before the birth of Christ a philosophical treatise, which manifestly betrays the style and sentiments of the school of Plato, was produced by the Alexandrian Jews and unanimously received as a genuine and valuable relic of the inspired Wisdom of Solomon. A similar union of the Mosaic faith and the Grecian philosophy distinguishes the works of Philo, which were composed for the most part under the reign of Augustus. The material soul of the universe might offend the piety of the Hebrews; but they applied the character of the Logos to the Jehovah of Moses and the patriarchs; and the Son of God was introduced upon earth, under a visible and even human appearance, to perform those familiar offices which seem incompatible with the nature and attributes of the Universal Cause.

The eloquence of Plato, the name of Solomon, the authority of the school of Alexandria, and the consent of the Jews and Greeks were insufficient to establish the truth of a mysterious doctrine which might please, but could not satisfy, a rational mind. A prophet or apostle inspired by the Deity can alone exercise a lawful dominion over the faith of mankind; and the theology of Plato might have been forever confounded with the philosophical visions of the Academy, the Porch, and the Lyceum if the name and divine attributes of the Logos had not been confirmed by the celestial pen of the last and most sublime of the Evangelists. The Christian revelation, which was consummated under the reign of Nerva, disclosed to the world the amazing secret that the Logos, who was with God from the beginning and was God, who had made all things and for whom all things had been made, was incarnate in the person of Jesus of Nazareth, who had been born of a virgin and suffered death on the cross. Besides the general design of fixing on a perpetual basis the divine honours of Christ, the most ancient and respectable of the ecclesiastical writers have ascribed to the evangelic theologian a particular intention to confute two opposite heresies which disturbed the peace of the primitive church.

The faith of the Ebionites, perhaps of the Nazarenes, was gross and imperfect. They revered Jesus as the greatest of the prophets, endowed with supernatural virtue and power. They ascribed to his person and to his future reign all the predictions of the Hebrew oracles which relate to the spiritual and everlasting kingdom of the promised Messiah. Some of them might confess that he was born of a virgin; but they obstinately rejected the preceding existence and divine perfections of the Logos, or Son of God, which are so clearly defined in the Gospel of St. John. About fifty years afterwards the Ebionites, whose errors are mentioned by Justin Martyr with less severity than they seem to deserve, formed a very inconsiderable portion of the Christian name.

The Gnostics, who were distinguished by the epithet

of *Docetes,* deviated into the contrary extreme and betrayed the human, while they asserted the divine, nature of Christ. Educated in the school of Plato, accustomed to the sublime idea of the Logos, they readily conceived that the brightest *Æon,* or *Emanation* of the Deity, might assume the outward shape and visible appearances of a mortal; but they vainly pretended that the imperfections of matter are incompatible with the purity of a celestial substance. While the blood of Christ yet smoked on Mount Calvary, the Docetes invented the impious and extravagant hypothesis that, instead of issuing from the womb of the Virgin, he had descended on the banks of the Jordan in the form of perfect manhood; that he had imposed on the senses of his enemies and of his disciples; and that the ministers of Pilate had wasted their impotent rage on an airy phantom who *seemed* to expire on the cross and, after three days, to rise from the dead.

The divine sanction which the Apostle had bestowed on the fundamental principle of the theology of Plato encouraged the learned proselytes of the second and third centuries to admire and study the writings of the Athenian sage, who had thus marvellously anticipated one of the most surprising discoveries of the Christian revelation. The respectable name of Plato was used by the orthodox, and abused by the heretics, as the common support of truth and error; the authority of his skilful commentators and the science of dialectics were employed to justify the remote consequences of his opinions and to supply the discreet silence of the inspired writers.

The same subtle and profound questions concerning the nature, the generation, the distinction, and the equality of the three divine persons of the mysterious *Triad,* or *Trinity,* were agitated in the philosophical and in the Christian schools of Alexandria. An eager spirit of curiosity urged them to explore the secrets of the abyss, and the pride of the professors and of their disciples was satisfied with the science of words. But the most sagacious of the Christian theologians, the great Athanasius himself, has candidly confessed that whenever he forced his understanding to meditate on the divinity of the Logos, his toilsome and unavailing efforts recoiled on themselves; that the more he thought, the less he comprehended; and the more he wrote, the less capable was he of expressing his thoughts. In every step of the inquiry we are compelled to feel and acknowledge the immeasurable disproportion between the size of the object and the capacity of the human mind. We may strive to abstract the notions of time, of space, and of matter, which so closely adhere to all the perceptions of our experimental knowledge. But as soon as we presume to reason of infinite substance, of spiritual generation, as often as we deduce any positive conclusions from a negative idea, we are involved in darkness, perplexity, and inevitable contradiction.[3]

After the edict of toleration had restored peace and leisure to the Christians, the Trinitarian controversy was revived in the ancient seat of Platonism, the learned, the opulent, the tumultuous city of Alexandria; and the flame of religious discord was rapidly communicated from the schools to the clergy, the people, the provinces, and the East. The abstruse question of the eternity of the Logos was agitated in ecclesiastic conferences and

3. *Editor's note:* In an omitted paragraph, Gibbon notes two differences between the philosophical and ecclesiastical discussions of the same questions: the early Christians approached with zeal and passionate interest what the Platonist philosopher considered with wise moderation; and while the philosopher asserted the right of intellectual freedom, the extensive and growing organization of the church demanded a high degree of spiritual conformity from its members.

popular sermons; and the heterodox opinions of Arius were soon made public by his own zeal and by that of his adversaries. His most implacable adversaries have acknowledged the learning and blameless life of the eminent presbyter, who in a former election had declined, and perhaps generously declined, his pretensions to the episcopal throne. His competitor Alexander assumed the office of his judge. The important cause was argued before him; and if at first he seemed to hesitate, he at length pronounced his final sentence as an absolute rule of faith. The undaunted presbyter, who presumed to resist the authority of his angry bishop, was separated from the communion of the church.

But the pride of Arius was supported by the applause of a numerous party. He reckoned among his immediate followers two bishops of Egypt, seven presbyters, twelve deacons, and (what may appear almost incredible) seven hundred virgins. A large majority of the bishops of Asia appeared to support or favour his cause; and their measures were conducted by Eusebius of Cæsarea, the most learned of the Christian prelates, and by Eusebius of Nicomedia, who had acquired the reputation of a statesman without forfeiting that of a saint. Synods in Palestine and Bithynia were opposed to the synods of Egypt. The attention of the prince and people was attracted by this theological dispute; and the decision, at the end of six years, was referred to the supreme authority of the general council of Nice.[4]

If the bishops of the council of Nice had been permitted to follow the unbiased dictates of their conscience, Arius and his associates could scarcely have flattered themselves with the hopes of obtaining a ma-

4. *Editor's note:* In the original, Gibbon here speculates further upon three possible concepts regarding the nature of the Trinity

jority of votes in favour of an hypothesis so directly adverse to the two most popular opinions of the catholic world. The Arians soon perceived the danger of their situation and prudently assumed those modest virtues which, in the fury of civil and religious dissensions, are seldom practised or even praised except by the weaker party. They recommended the exercise of Christian charity and moderation, urged the incomprehensible nature of the controversy, disclaimed the use of any terms or definitions which could not be found in the Scriptures, and offered by very liberal concessions to satisfy their adversaries without renouncing the integrity of their own principles.

The victorious faction received all their proposals with haughty suspicion and anxiously sought for some irreconcilable mark of distinction, the rejection of which might involve the Arians in the guilt and consequences of heresy. A letter was publicly read and ignominiously torn, in which their patron, Eusebius of Nicomedia, ingenuously confessed that the admission of the *Homoousion,* or Consubstantial, a word already familiar to the Platonists, was incompatible with the principles of their theological system. The fortunate opportunity was eagerly embraced by the bishops who governed the resolutions of the synod; and, according to the lively expressions of Ambrose, they used the sword, which heresy itself had drawn from the scabbard, to cut off the head of the hated monster. The consubstantiality of the Father and the Son was established by the council of Nice and has been unanimously received as a fundamental article of the Christian faith by the consent of the Greek, the Latin, the Oriental, and the Protestant churches.

But if the same word had not served to stigmatize the heretics and to unite the catholics, it would have been inadequate to the purpose of the majority by whom it was introduced into the orthodox creed. This majority was divided into two parties, distinguished by a contrary tendency to the sentiments of the Tritheists and of the Sabellians. But as those opposite extremes seemed to overthrow the foundations either of natural or revealed religion, they mutually agreed to qualify the rigour of their principles and to disavow the just but invidious consequences which might be urged by their antagonists. The interest of the common cause inclined them to join their numbers and to conceal their differences; their animosity was softened by the healing counsels of toleration, and their disputes were suspended by the use of the mysterious Homoousion, which either party was free to interpret according to its peculiar tenets.

The Sabellian sense, which about fifty years before had obliged the council of Antioch to prohibit this celebrated term, had endeared it to those theologians who entertained a secret but partial affection for a nominal Trinity. But the more fashionable saints of the Arian times, the intrepid Athanasius, the learned Gregory Nazianzen, and the other pillars of the church who supported with ability and success the Nicene doctrine, appeared to consider the expression of *substance* as if it had been synonymous with that of *nature;* and they ventured to illustrate their meaning by affirming that three men, as they belong to the same common species, are consubstantial, or Homoousian, to each other. This pure and distinct equality was tempered on the one hand by the internal connection and spiritual penetration which indissolubly unites the divine persons, and on the other by the pre-eminence of the Father, which was acknowledged as far as it is compatible with the independence of the Son.

Within these limits the almost invisible and tremulous ball of orthodoxy was allowed securely to vibrate. On either side, beyond this consecrated ground, the heretics and the demons lurked in ambush to surprise and devour the unhappy wanderer. But as the degrees of theological hatred depend on the spirit of the war rather than on the importance of the controversy, the heretics who degraded were treated with more severity than those who annihilated the person of the Son. The life of Athanasius was consumed in irreconcilable opposition to the impious *madness* of the Arians, but he defended above twenty years the Sabellianism of Marcellus of Ancyra; and when at last he was compelled to withdraw himself from his communion, he continued to mention with an ambiguous smile the venial errors of his respectable friend.

The authority of a general council, to which the Arians themselves had been compelled to submit, inscribed on the banners of the orthodox party the mysterious characters of the word Homoousion, which essentially contributed, notwithstanding some obscure disputes, some nocturnal combats, to maintain and perpetuate the uniformity of faith, or at least of language. The Consubstantialists, who by their success have deserved and obtained the title of *Catholics*, gloried in the simplicity and steadiness of their own creed and insulted the repeated variations of their adversaries, who were destitute of any certain rule of faith. The sincerity or the cunning of the Arian chiefs, the fear of the laws or of the people, their reverence for Christ, their hatred of Athanasius, all the causes, human and divine, that influence and disturb the counsels of a theological faction, introduced among the sectaries a spirit of discord and inconstancy, which in the course of a few years erected eighteen different models of religion and avenged the violated dignity of the church. The zealous Hilary, who from the peculiar hardships of his situation was inclined to extenuate rather than to aggravate the errors of the Oriental clergy, declares that in the wide extent of the ten provinces of Asia to which he had been banished there could be found very few prelates who had preserved the knowledge of the true God. The oppression which he had felt, the disorders of which he was the spectator and the victim, appeased during a short interval the angry passions of his soul; and in the following passage, of which I shall transcribe a few lines, the bishop of Poitiers unwarily deviates into the style of a Christian philosopher. "It is a thing," says Hilary, "equally deplorable and dangerous, that there are as many creeds as opinions among men, as many doctrines as inclinations, and as many sources of blasphemy as there are faults among us; because we make creeds arbitrarily and explain them as arbitrarily. The Homoousion is rejected, and received, and explained away by successive synods. The partial or total resemblance of the Father and of the Son is a subject of dispute for these unhappy times. Every year, nay, every moon, we make new creeds to describe invisible mysteries. We repent of what we have done, we defend those who repent, we anathematize those whom we defended. We condemn either the doctrine of others in ourselves, or our own in that of others; and, reciprocally tearing one another to pieces, we have been the cause of each other's ruin." [5]

The provinces of Egypt and Asia, which cultivated the language and manners of the Greeks, had deeply

5. A brief passage is deleted here in which Gibbon discusses the faint differences between the orthodox creed and various shades of Arianism, symbolized by the difference between the words *Homoousian* and *Homoiousian*.

imbibed the venom of the Arian controversy. The familiar study of the Platonic system, a vain and argumentative disposition, a copious and flexible idiom, supplied the clergy and people of the East with an inexhaustible flow of words and distinctions; and in the midst of their fierce contentions they easily forgot the doubt which is recommended by philosophy and the submission which is enjoined by religion. The inhabitants of the West were of a less inquisitive spirit; their passions were not so forcibly moved by invisible objects, their minds were less frequently exercised by the habits of dispute; and such was the happy ignorance of the Gallican church that Hilary himself, above thirty years after the first general council, was still a stranger to the Nicene creed.

The Latins had received the rays of divine knowledge through the dark and doubtful medium of a translation. The poverty and stubbornness of their native tongue was not always capable of affording just equivalents for the Greek terms, for the technical words of the Platonic philosophy, which had been consecrated by the Gospel or by the church to express the mysteries of the Christian faith; and a verbal defect might introduce into the Latin theology a long train of error or perplexity. But as the western provincials had the good fortune of deriving their religion from an orthodox source, they preserved with steadiness the doctrine which they had accepted with docility; and when the Arian pestilence approached their frontiers, they were supplied with the seasonable preservative of the Homoousion by the paternal care of the Roman pontiff.

Their sentiments and their temper were displayed in the memorable synod of Rimini, which surpassed in numbers the council of Nice, since it was composed of above four hundred bishops of Italy, Africa, Spain, Gaul,

Britain, and Illyricum. From the first debates it appeared that only four score prelates adhered to the party, though *they* affected to anathematize the name and memory, of Arius. But this inferiority was compensated by the advantages of skill, of experience, and of discipline; and the minority was conducted by Valens and Ursacius, two bishops of Illyricum who had spent their lives in the intrigues of courts and councils and who had been trained under the Eusebian banner in the religious wars of the East. By their arguments and negotiations they embarrassed, they confounded, they at last deceived the honest simplicity of the Latin bishops, who suffered the palladium of the faith to be extorted from their hands by fraud and importunity rather than by open violence. The council of Rimini was not allowed to separate till the members had imprudently subscribed a captious creed, in which some expressions susceptible of an heretical sense were inserted in the room of the Homoousion. It was on this occasion that, according to Jerom, the world was surprised to find itself Arian. But the bishops of the Latin provinces had no sooner reached their respective dioceses than they discovered their mistake and repented of their weakness. The ignominious capitulation was rejected with disdain and abhorrence, and the Homoousian standard, which had been shaken but not overthrown, was more firmly replanted in all the churches of the West.

Such was the rise and progress, and such were the natural revolutions, of those theological disputes which disturbed the peace of Christianity under the reigns of Constantine and of his sons. But as those princes presumed to extend their despotism over the faith as well as over the lives and fortunes of their subjects, the weight of their suffrage sometimes inclined the ecclesiastical balance; and the prerogatives of the King of

Heaven were settled or changed or modified in the cabinet of an earthly monarch.

The unhappy spirit of discord which pervaded the provinces of the East interrupted the triumph of Constantine, but the emperor continued for some time to view with cool and careless indifference the object of the dispute. As he was yet ignorant of the difficulty of appeasing the quarrels of theologians, he addressed to the contending parties, to Alexander and to Arius, a moderating epistle, which may be ascribed with far greater reason to the untutored sense of a soldier and statesman than to the dictates of any of his episcopal counsellors. He attributes the origin of the whole controversy to a trifling and subtle question concerning an incomprehensible point of the law, which was foolishly asked by the bishop and imprudently resolved by the presbyter. He laments that the Christian people, who had the same God, the same religion, and the same worship, should be divided by such inconsiderable distinctions; and he seriously recommends to the clergy of Alexandria the example of the Greek philosophers, who could maintain their arguments without losing their temper and assert their freedom without violating their friendship.

The indifference and contempt of the sovereign would have been, perhaps, the most effectual method of silencing the dispute if the popular current had been less rapid and impetuous, and if Constantine himself, in the midst of faction and fanaticism, could have preserved the calm possession of his own mind. But his ecclesiastical ministers soon contrived to seduce the impartiality of the magistrate and to awaken the zeal of the proselyte. He was provoked by the insults which had been offered to his statues; he was alarmed by the real as well as the imaginary magnitude of the spreading mischief; and he extinguished the hope of peace and toleration from the moment that he assembled three hundred bishops within the walls of the same palace. The presence of the monarch swelled the importance of the debate; his attention multiplied the arguments; and he exposed his person with a patient intrepidity which animated the valour of the combatants.

Notwithstanding the applause which has been bestowed on the eloquence and sagacity of Constantine, a Roman general, whose religion might be still a subject of doubt and whose mind had not been enlightened either by study or by inspiration, was indifferently qualified to discuss in the Greek language a metaphysical question or an article of faith. But the credit of his favourite Osius, who appears to have presided in the council of Nice, might dispose the emperor in favour of the orthodox party; and a well-timed insinuation—that the same Eusebius of Nicomedia who now protected the heretic had lately assisted the tyrant—might exasperate him against their adversaries. The Nicene creed was ratified by Constantine; and his firm declaration that those who resisted the divine judgment of the synod must prepare themselves for an immediate exile annihilated the murmurs of a feeble opposition, which from seventeen, was almost instantly reduced to two, protesting bishops. Eusebius of Cæsarea yielded a reluctant and ambiguous consent to the Homoousion, and the wavering conduct of the Nicomedian Eusebius served only to delay about three months his disgrace and exile. The impious Arius was banished into one of the remote provinces of Illyricum; his person and disciples were branded by law with the odious name of *Porphyrians*; his writings were condemned to the flames, and a capital punishment was denounced against those in whose possession they should be found. The emperor had now imbibed the spirit of controversy, and the angry sarcastic style of his edicts was designed to inspire his subjects with the hatred which he had conceived against the enemies of Christ.

But, as if the conduct of the emperor had been guided by passion instead of principle, three years from the council of Nice were scarcely elapsed before he discovered some symptoms of mercy, and even of indulgence, towards the proscribed sect, which was secretly protected by his favourite sister. The exiles were recalled, and Eusebius, who gradually resumed his influence over the mind of Constantine, was restored to the episcopal throne from which he had been ignominiously degraded. Arius himself was treated by the whole court with respect which would have been due to an innocent and oppressed man. His faith was approved by the synod of Jerusalem; and the emperor seemed impatient to repair his injustice by issuing an absolute command that he should be solemnly admitted to the communion in the cathedral of Constantinople. On the same day which had been fixed for the triumph of Arius he expired; and the strange and horrid circumstances of his death might excite a suspicion that the orthodox saints had contributed more efficaciously than by their prayers to deliver the church from the most formidable of her enemies. The three principal leaders of the catholics, Athanasius of Alexandria, Eustathius of Antioch, and Paul of Constantinople, were deposed on various accusations by the sentence of numerous councils and were afterwards banished into distant provinces by the first of the Christian emperors, who in the last moments of his life received the rites of baptism from the Arian bishop of Nicomedia.

The ecclesiastical government of Constantine cannot be justified from the reproach of levity and weakness. But the credulous monarch, unskilled in the stratagems of theological warfare, might be deceived by the modest and specious professions of the heretics, whose sentiments he never perfectly understood; and while he protected Arius and persecuted Athanasius, he still considered the council of Nice as the bulwark of the Christian faith and the peculiar glory of his own reign.

The sons of Constantine must have been admitted from their childhood into the rank of catechumens, but they imitated, in the delay of their baptism, the example of their father. Like him, they presumed to pronounce their judgment on mysteries into which they had never been regularly initiated; and the fate of the Trinitarian controversy depended in a great measure on the sentiments of Constantius, who inherited the provinces of the East and acquired the possession of the whole empire. The Arian presbyter or bishop, who had secreted for his use the testament of the deceased emperor, improved the fortunate occasion which had introduced him to the familiarity of a prince whose public counsels were always swayed by his domestic favourites. The eunuchs and slaves diffused the spiritual poison through the palace, and the dangerous infection was communicated by the female attendants to the guards, and by the empress to her unsuspicious husband.

The partiality which Constantius always expressed towards the Eusebian faction was insensibly fortified by the dexterous management of their leaders; and his victory over the tyrant Magnentius increased his inclination as well as ability to employ the arms of power in the cause of Arianism. While the two armies were engaged in the plains of Mursa, and the fate of the two rivals depended on the chance of war, the son of Constantine passed the anxious moments in a church of the martyrs, under the walls of the city. His spiritual comforter, Valens, the Arian bishop of the diocese, employed the

most artful precautions to obtain such early intelligence
as might secure either his favour or his escape. A secret
chain of swift and trusty messengers informed him of the
vicissitudes of the battle; and while the courtiers stood
trembling round their affrighted master, Valens assured
him that the Gallic legions gave way and insinuated
with some presence of mind that the glorious event had
been revealed to him by an angel. The grateful emperor
ascribed his success to the merits and intercession of
the bishop of Mursa, whose faith had deserved the public and miraculous approbation of Heaven. The Arians,
who considered as their own the victory of Constantius,
preferred his glory to that of his father. Cyril, bishop of
Jerusalem, immediately composed the description of a
celestial cross encircled with a splendid rainbow, which
during the festival of Pentecost, about the third hour of
the day, had appeared over the Mount of Olives, to the
edification of the devout pilgrims and the people of
the holy city. The size of the meteor was gradually magnified; and the Arian historian has ventured to affirm
that it was conspicious to the two armies in the plains of
Pannonia and that the tyrant, who is purposely represented as an idolater, fled before the auspicious sign of
orthodox Christianity.

The sentiments of a judicious stranger, who has im-
partially considered the progress of civil or ecclesiastical
discord, are always entitled to our notice, and a short
passage of Ammianus, who served in the armies and
studied the character of Constantius, is perhaps of more
value than many pages of theological invectives. "The
Christian religion, which in itself," says that moderate
historian, "is plain and simple, *he* confounded by the
dotage of superstition. Instead of reconciling the parties
by the weight of his authority, he cherished and propagated, by verbal disputes, the differences which his vain

curiosity had excited. The highways were covered with troops of bishops galloping from every side to the assemblies, which they call synods; and while they laboured to reduce the whole sect to their own particular opinions, the public establishment of the posts was almost ruined by their hasty and repeated journies." Our more intimate knowledge of the ecclesiastical transactions of the reign of Constantius would furnish an ample commentary on this remarkable passage, which justifies the rational apprehensions of Athanasius that the restless activity of the clergy, who wandered round the empire in search of the true faith, would excite the contempt and laughter of the unbelieving world.

As soon as the emperor was relieved from the terrors of the civil war, he devoted the leisure of his winter quarters at Arles, Milan, Sirmium, and Constantinople to the amusement or toils of controversy; the sword of the magistrate, and even of the tyrant, was unsheathed to enforce the reasons of the theologian; and as he opposed the orthodox faith of Nice, it is readily confessed that his incapacity and ignorance were equal to his presumption. The eunuchs, the women, and the bishops who governed the vain and feeble mind of the emperor had inspired him with an insuperable dislike to the Homoousion; but his timid conscience was alarmed by the impiety of Aëtius. The guilt of that atheist was aggravated by the suspicious favour of the unfortunate Gallus, and even the deaths of the Imperial ministers who had been massacred at Antioch were imputed to the suggestions of that dangerous sophist.

The mind of Constantius, which could neither be moderated by reason nor fixed by faith, was blindly impelled to either side of the dark and empty abyss by his horror of the opposite extreme; he alternately embraced and condemned the sentiments, he successively banished and recalled the leaders, of the Arian and Semi-Arian factions. During the season of public business or festivity he employed whole days, and even nights, in selecting the words and weighing the syllables which composed his fluctuating creeds. The subject of his meditations still pursued and occupied his slumbers; the incoherent dreams of the emperor were received as celestial visions; and he accepted with complacency the lofty title of bishop of bishops from those ecclesiastics who forgot the interest of their order for the gratification of their passions. The design of establishing an uniformity of doctrine, which had engaged him to convene so many synods in Gaul, Italy, Illyricum, and Asia, was repeatedly baffled by his own levity, by the divisions of the Arians, and by the resistance of the catholics; and he resolved, as the last and decisive effort, imperiously to dictate the decrees of a general council. The destructive earthquake of Nicomedia, the difficulty of finding a convenient place, and perhaps some secret motives of policy produced an alteration in the summons. The bishops of the East were directed to meet at Seleucia, in Isauria, while those of the West held their deliberations at Rimini, on the coast of the Hadriatic; and instead of two or three deputies from each province, the whole episcopal body was ordered to march.

The eastern council, after consuming four days in fierce and unavailing debate, separated without any definite conclusion. The council of the West was protracted till the seventh month. Taurus, the Prætorian præfect, was instructed not to dismiss the prelates till they should all be united in the same opinion; and his efforts were supported by a power of banishing fifteen of the most refractory and a promise of the consulship if he achieved so difficult an adventure. His prayers and threats, the authority of the sovereign, the sophistry of

Valens and Ursacius, the distress of cold and hunger, and the tedious melancholy of a hopeless exile at length extorted the reluctant consent of the bishops of Rimini. The deputies of the East and of the West attended the emperor in the palace of Constantinople, and he enjoyed the satisfaction of imposing on the world a profession of faith which established the *likeness,* without expressing the *consubstantiality,* of the Son of God. But the triumph of Arianism had been preceded by the removal of the orthodox clergy, whom it was impossible either to intimidate or to corrupt; and the reign of Constantius was disgraced by the unjust and ineffectual persecution of the great Athanasius.

We have seldom an opportunity of observing, either in active or speculative life, what effect may be produced, or what obstacles may be surmounted, by the force of a single mind when it is inflexibly applied to the pursuit of a single object. The immortal name of Athanasius will never be separated from the catholic doctrine of the Trinity, to whose defence he consecrated every moment and every faculty of his being. Educated in the family of Alexander, he had vigorously opposed the early progress of the Arian heresy; he exercised the important functions of secretary under the aged prelate; and the fathers of the Nicene council beheld with surprise and respect the rising virtues of the young deacon. In a time of public danger the dull claims of age and of rank are sometimes superseded; and within five months after his return from Nice the deacon Athanasius was seated on the archiepiscopal throne of Egypt. He filled that eminent station above forty-six years, and his long administration was spent in a perpetual combat against the powers of Arianism. Five times was Athanasius expelled from his throne; twenty years he passed as an exile or a fugitive; and almost every province of the

Roman empire was successively witness to his merit and
his sufferings in the cause of the Homoousion, which he
considered as the sole pleasure and business, as the duty,
and as the glory of his life.

Amidst the storms of persecution the archbishop of
Alexandria was patient of labour, jealous of fame, careless of safety; and although his mind was tainted by the
contagion of fanaticism, Athanasius displayed a superiority of character and abilities which would have qualified him, far better than the degenerate sons of Constantine, for the government of a great monarchy. His
learning was much less profound and extensive than that
of Eusebius of Cæsarea, and his rude eloquence could
not be compared with the polished oratory of Gregory
or Basil; but whenever the primate of Egypt was called
upon to justify his sentiments or his conduct, his unpre-
meditated style, either of speaking or writing, was clear,
forcible, and persuasive. He has always been revered in
the orthodox school as one of the most accurate masters
of the Christian theology; and he was supposed to possess two profane sciences less adapted to the episcopal
character—the knowledge of jurisprudence and that of
divination. Some fortunate conjectures of future events,
which impartial reasoners might ascribe to the experience and judgment of Athanasius, were attributed by his
friends to heavenly inspiration and imputed by his
enemies to infernal magic.

But as Athanasius was continually engaged with the
prejudices and passions of every order of men, from the
monk to the emperor, the knowledge of human nature
was his first and most important science. He preserved a
distinct and unbroken view of a scene which was incessantly shifting, and never failed to improve those decisive moments which are irrecoverably past before they
are perceived by a common eye. The archbishop of

Alexandria was capable of distinguishing how far he might boldly command and where he must dexterously insinuate; how long he might contend with power and when he must withdraw from persecution; and while he directed the thunders of the church against heresy and rebellion, he could assume, in the bosom of his own party, the flexible and indulgent temper of a prudent leader.

The election of Athanasius has not escaped the reproach of irregularity and precipitation; but the propriety of his behaviour conciliated the affections both of the clergy and of the people. The Alexandrians were impatient to rise in arms for the defence of an eloquent and liberal pastor. In his distress he always derived support, or at least consolation, from the faithful attachment of his parochial clergy; and the hundred bishops of Egypt adhered with unshaken zeal to the cause of Athanasius. In the modest equipage which pride and policy would affect, he frequently performed the episcopal visitation of his provinces, from the mouth of the Nile to the confines of Æthiopia, familiarly conversing with the meanest of the populace and humbly saluting the saints and hermits of the desert. Nor was it only in ecclesiastical assemblies, among men whose education and manners were similar to his own, that Athanasius displayed the ascendancy of his genius. He appeared with easy and respectful firmness in the courts of princes; and in the various turns of his prosperous and adverse fortune he never lost the confidence of his friends or the esteem of his enemies.

In his youth the primate of Egypt resisted the great Constantine, who had repeatedly signified his will that Arius should be restored to the catholic communion. The emperor respected, and might forgive, this inflexible resolution; and the faction who considered Athana-

sius as their most formidable enemy were constrained to
dissemble their hatred and silently to prepare an indi-
rect and distant assault. They scattered rumours and
suspicions, represented the archbishop as a proud and
oppressive tyrant, and boldly accused him of violating
the treaty which had been ratified in the Nicene council
with the schismatic followers of Meletius. Athanasius
had openly disapproved that ignominious peace, and
the emperor was disposed to believe that he had abused
his ecclesiastical and civil power to persecute those odious sectaries; that he had sacrilegiously broken a chalice
in one of their churches of Maræotis; that he had
whipped or imprisoned six of their bishops; and that
Arsenius, a seventh bishop of the same party, had been
murdered, or at least mutilated, by the cruel hand of
the primate. These charges, which affected his honour
and his life, were referred by Constantine to his brother
Dalmatius, the censor, who resided at Antioch; the synods of Cæsarea and Tyre were successively convened;
and the bishops of the East were instructed to judge the
cause of Athanasius before they proceeded to consecrate
the new church of the Resurrection at Jerusalem.

The primate might be conscious of his innocence, but
he was sensible that the same implacable spirit which
had dictated the accusation would direct the proceeding
and pronounce the sentence. He prudently declined the
tribunal of his enemies, despised the summons of the
synod of Cæsarea, and after a long and artful delay submitted to the peremptory commands of the emperor,
who threatened to punish his criminal disobedience if
he refused to appear in the council of Tyre. Before
Athanasius, at the head of fifty Egyptian prelates, sailed
from Alexandria, he had wisely secured the alliance of
the Meletians; and Arsenius himself, his imaginary victim and his secret friend, was privately concealed in his

train. The synod of Tyre was conducted by Eusebius of
Cæsarea with more passion and with less art than his
learning and experience might promise; his numerous
faction repeated the names of homicide and tyrant; and
their clamours were encouraged by the seeming patience
of Athanasius, who expected at the decisive moment to
produce Arsenius alive and unhurt in the midst of the
assembly. The nature of the other charges did not admit
of such clear and satisfactory replies; yet the archbishop
was able to prove that in the village where he was accused of breaking a consecrated chalice neither church
nor altar nor chalice could really exist. The Arians, who
had secretly determined the guilt and condemnation of
their enemy, attempted, however, to disguise their injustice by the imitation of judicial forms; the synod
appointed an episcopal commission of six delegates to
collect evidence on the spot; and this measure, which
was vigorously opposed by the Egyptian bishops,
opened new scenes of violence and perjury. After the
return of the deputies from Alexandria, the majority of
the council pronounced the final sentence of degradation
and exile against the primate of Egypt. The decree, expressed in the fiercest language of malice and revenge,
was communicated to the emperor and the catholic
church; and the bishops immediately resumed a mild
and devout aspect, such as became their holy pilgrimage
to the Sepulchre of Christ.

But the injustice of these ecclesiastical judges had not
been countenanced by the submission, or even by the
presence, of Athanasius. He resolved to make a bold and
dangerous experiment, whether the throne was inaccessible to the voice of truth; and before the final sentence
could be pronounced at Tyre, the intrepid primate threw
himself into a bark which was ready to hoist sail for the
Imperial city. The request of a formal audience might

have been opposed or eluded; but Athanasius concealed his arrival, watched the moment of Constantine's return from an adjacent villa, and boldly encountered his angry sovereign as he passed on horseback through the principal street of Constantinople. So strange an apparition excited his surprise and indignation, and the guards were ordered to remove the importunate suitor; but his resentment was subdued by involuntary respect, and the haughty spirit of the emperor was awed by the courage and eloquence of a bishop who implored his justice and awakened his conscience.

Constantine listened to the complaints of Athanasius with impartial and even gracious attention; the members of the synod of Tyre were summoned to justify their proceedings; and the arts of the Eusebian faction would have been confounded if they had not aggravated the guilt of the primate by the dexterous supposition of an unpardonable offence—a criminal design to intercept and detain the corn fleet of Alexandria, which supplied the subsistence of the new capital. The emperor was satisfied that the peace of Egypt would be secured by the absence of a popular leader; but he refused to fill the vacancy of the archiepiscopal throne, and the sentence which, after long hesitation, he pronounced was that of a jealous ostracism rather than of an ignominious exile. In the remote province of Gaul, but in the hospitable court of Treves, Athanasius passed about twenty-eight months. The death of the emperor changed the face of public affairs; and amidst the general indulgence of a young reign the primate was restored to his country by an honourable edict of the younger Constantine, who expressed a deep sense of the innocence and merit of his venerable guest.

The death of that prince exposed Athanasius to a second persecution, and the feeble Constantius, the sovereign of the East, soon became the secret accomplice of the Eusebians. Ninety bishops of that sect or faction assembled at Antioch under the specious pretence of dedicating the cathedral. They composed an ambiguous creed, which is faintly tinged with the colours of Semi-Arianism, and twenty-five canons, which still regulate the discipline of the orthodox Greeks. It was decided, with some appearance of equity, that a bishop deprived by a synod should not resume his episcopal functions till he had been absolved by the judgment of an equal synod; the law was immediately applied to the case of Athanasius; the council of Antioch pronounced, or rather confirmed, his degradation; a stranger named Gregory was seated on his throne; and Philagrius, the præfect of Egypt, was instructed to support the new primate with the civil and military powers of the province.

Oppressed by the conspiracy of the Asiatic prelates, Athanasius withdrew from Alexandria and passed three years as an exile and a suppliant on the holy threshold of the Vatican. By the assiduous study of the Latin language he soon qualified himself to negotiate with the western clergy; his decent flattery swayed and directed the haughty Julius; the Roman pontiff was persuaded to consider his appeal as the peculiar interest of the Apostolic see; and his innocence was unanimously declared in a council of fifty bishops of Italy. At the end of three years the primate was summoned to the court of Milan by the emperor Constans, who, in the indulgence of unlawful pleasures, still professed a lively regard for the orthodox faith. The cause of truth and justice was promoted by the influence of gold, and the ministers of Constans advised their sovereign to require the convocation of an ecclesiastical assembly which might act as the representatives of the catholic church. Ninety-four bishops of the West, seventy-six bishops of the East, encountered each other at Sardica, on the verge of the two empires but in the dominions of the protector of Athanasius. Their debates soon degenerated into hostile altercations; the Asiatics, apprehensive for their personal safety, retired to Philippopolis in Thrace; and the rival synods reciprocally hurled their spiritual thunders against their enemies, whom they piously condemned as the enemies of the true God. Their decrees were published and ratified in their respective provinces; and Athanasius, who in the West was revered as a saint, was exposed as a criminal to the abhorrence of the East. The council of Sardica reveals the first symptoms of discord and schism between the Greek and Latin churches, which were separated by the accidental difference of faith and the permanent distinction of language.

During his second exile in the West, Athanasius was frequently admitted to the Imperial presence—at Capua, Lodi, Milan, Verona, Padua, Aquileia, and Treves. The bishop of the diocese usually assisted at these interviews; the master of the offices stood before the veil or curtain of the sacred apartment; and the uniform moderation of the primate might be attested by these respectable witnesses, to whose evidence he solemnly appeals. Prudence would undoubtedly suggest the mild and respectful tone that became a subject and a bishop. In these familiar conferences with the sovereign of the West, Athanasius might lament the error of Constantius; but he boldly arraigned the guilt of his eunuchs and his Arian prelates, deplored the distress and danger of the catholic church, and excited Constans to emulate the zeal and glory of his father. The emperor declared his resolution of employing the troops and treasures of Europe in the orthodox cause, and signified, by a concise and peremptory epistle to his brother Constantius, that unless he consented to the immediate restoration of Athanasius he himself, with a fleet and army, would seat the archbishop on the throne of Alexandria. But this religious war, so horrible to nature, was prevented by the timely compliance of Constantius; and the emperor of the East condescended to solicit a reconciliation with a subject whom he had injured.

Athanasius waited with decent pride till he had received three successive epistles full of the strongest assurances of the protection, the favour, and the esteem of his sovereign, who invited him to resume his episcopal seat and who added the humiliating precaution of engaging his principal ministers to attest the sincerity of his intentions. They were manifested in a still more public manner by the strict orders which were despatched into Egypt to recall the adherents of Athanasius, to restore their privileges, to proclaim their innocence, and to erase from the public registers the illegal proceedings which had been obtained during the prevalence of the Eusebian faction. After every satisfaction and security had been given which justice or even delicacy could require, the primate proceeded by slow journeys through the provinces of Thrace, Asia, and Syria; and his progress was marked by the abject homage of the Oriental bishops, who excited his contempt without deceiving his penetration. At Antioch he saw the emperor Constantius; sustained with modest firmness the embraces and protestations of his master; and eluded the proposal of allowing the Arians a single church at Alexandria by claiming in the other cities of the empire a similar toleration for his own party—a reply which might have appeared just and moderate in the mouth of an independent prince. The entrance of the archbishop into his capital was a triumphal procession; absence and persecution had endeared him to the

Alexandrians; his authority, which he exercised with rigour, was more firmly established; and his fame was diffused from Æthiopia to Britain, over the whole extent of the Christian world.

But the subject who has reduced his prince to the necessity of dissembling can never expect a sincere and lasting forgiveness; and the tragic fate of Constans soon deprived Athanasius of a powerful and generous protector. The civil war between the assassin and the only surviving brother of Constans, which afflicted the empire above three years, secured an interval of repose to the catholic church; and the two contending parties were desirous to conciliate the friendship of a bishop who by the weight of his personal authority might determine the fluctuating resolutions of an important province. He gave audience to the ambassadors of the tyrant, with whom he was afterwards accused of holding a secret correspondence; and the emperor Constantius repeatedly assured his dearest father, the most reverend Athanasius, that notwithstanding the malicious rumours which were circulated by their common enemies, he had inherited the sentiments as well as the throne of his deceased brother.

Gratitude and humanity would have disposed the primate of Egypt to deplore the untimely fate of Constans and to abhor the guilt of Magnentius; but as he clearly understood that the apprehensions of Constantius were his only safeguard, the fervour of his prayers for the success of the righteous cause might perhaps be somewhat abated. The ruin of Athanasius was no longer contrived by the obscure malice of a few bigoted or angry bishops, who abused the authority of a credulous monarch. The monarch himself avowed the resolution, which he had so long suppressed, of avenging his private injuries; and the first winter after his victory, which he passed at Arles, was employed against an enemy more odious to him than the vanquished tyrant of Gaul.

If the emperor had capriciously decreed the death of the most eminent and virtuous citizen of the republic, the cruel order would have been executed without hesitation by the ministers of open violence or of specious injustice. The caution, the delay, the difficulty with which he proceeded in the condemnation and punishment of a popular bishop discovered to the world that the privileges of the church had already revived a sense of order and freedom in the Roman government. The sentence which was pronounced in the synod of Tyre and subscribed by a large majority of the Eastern bishops had never been expressly repealed; and as Athanasius had been once degraded from his episcopal dignity by the judgment of his brethren, every subsequent act might be considered as irregular, and even criminal. But the memory of the firm and effectual support which the primate of Egypt had derived from the attachment of the Western church engaged Constantius to suspend the execution of the sentence till he had obtained the concurrence of the Latin bishops.

Two years were consumed in ecclesiastical negotiations; and the important cause between the emperor and one of his subjects was solemnly debated, first in the synod of Arles and afterwards in the great council of Milan, which consisted of above three hundred bishops. Their integrity was gradually undermined by the arguments of the Arians, the dexterity of the eunuchs, and the pressing solicitations of a prince who gratified his revenge at the expense of his dignity and exposed his own passions whilst he influenced those of the clergy. Corruption, the most infallible symptom of constitutional liberty, was successfully practised; honours, gifts, and immunities were offered and accepted as the price of an episcopal vote;[6] and the condemnation of the Alexandrian primate was artfully represented as the only measure which could restore the peace and union of the catholic church.

The friends of Athanasius were not, however, wanting to their leader or to their cause. With a manly spirit which the sanctity of their character rendered less dangerous, they maintained in public debate and in private conference with the emperor the eternal obligation of religion and justice. They declared that neither the hope of his favour nor the fear of his displeasure should prevail on them to join in the condemnation of an absent, an innocent, a respectable brother. They affirmed, with apparent reason, that the illegal and obsolete decrees of the council of Tyre had long since been tacitly abolished by the Imperial edicts, the honourable re-establishment of the archbishop of Alexandria, and the silence or recantation of his most clamorous adversaries. They alleged that his innocence had been attested by the unanimous bishops of Egypt and had been acknowledged in the councils of Rome and Sardica by the impartial judgment of the Latin church. They deplored the hard condition of Athanasius, who, after enjoying so many years his seat, his reputation, and the seeming confidence of his sovereign, was again called upon to confute the most groundless and extravagant accusations. Their language was specious, their conduct was honourable; but in this long and obstinate contest, which fixed the eyes of the whole empire on a single bishop, the ecclesiastical fac-

6. The honours, presents, feasts, which seduced so many bishops, are mentioned with indignation by those who were too pure or too proud to accept them. "We combat," says Hilary of Poitiers, "against Constantius the Antichrist, who strokes the belly instead of scourging the back."

tions were prepared to sacrifice truth and justice to the more interesting object of defending or removing the intrepid champion of the Nicene faith. The Arians still thought it prudent to disguise in ambiguous language their real sentiments and designs; but the orthodox bishops, armed with the favour of the people and the decrees of a general council, insisted on every occasion, and particularly at Milan, that their adversaries should purge themselves from the suspicion of heresy before they presumed to arraign the conduct of the great Athanasius.

But the voice of reason (if reason was indeed on the side of Athanasius) was silenced by the clamours of a factious or venal majority; and the councils of Arles and Milan were not dissolved till the archbishop of Alexandria had been solemnly condemned and deposed by the judgment of the Western as well as of the Eastern church. The bishops who had opposed were required to subscribe the sentence and to unite in religious communion with the suspected leaders of the adverse party. A formulary of consent was transmitted by the messengers of state to the absent bishops, and all those who refused to submit their private opinion to the public and inspired wisdom of the councils of Arles and Milan were immediately banished by the emperor, who affected to execute the decrees of the catholic church.

Among those prelates who led the honourable band of confessors and exiles, Liberius of Rome, Osius of Cordova, Paulinus of Treves, Dionysius of Milan, Eusebius of Vercellæ, Lucifer of Cagliari, and Hilary of Poitiers may deserve to be particularly distinguished. The eminent station of Liberius, who governed the capital of the empire, the personal merit and long experience of the venerable Osius, who was revered as the favourite of the great Constantine and the father of the Nicene

faith, placed those prelates at the head of the Latin
church; and their example, either of submission or resistance, would probably be imitated by the episcopal
crowds. But the repeated attempts of the emperor to
seduce or to intimidate the bishops of Rome and Cordova were for some time ineffectual. The Spaniard declared himself ready to suffer under Constantius as he
had suffered threescore years before under his grandfather Maximian. The Roman, in the presence of his
sovereign, asserted the innocence of Athanasius and his
own freedom. When he was banished to Beræa in
Thrace he sent back a large sum which had been offered
for the accommodation of his journey, and insulted the
court of Milan by the haughty remark that the emperor
and his eunuchs might want that gold to pay their soldiers and their bishops. The resolution of Liberius and
Osius was at length subdued by the hardships of exile
and confinement. The Roman pontiff purchased his return by some criminal compliances and afterwards expiated his guilt by a seasonable repentance. Persuasion
and violence were employed to extort the reluctant
signature of the decrepit bishop of Cordova, whose
strength was broken and whose faculties were perhaps
impaired by the weight of an hundred years; and the
insolent triumph of the Arians provoked some of the
orthodox party to treat with inhuman severity the character, or rather the memory, of an unfortunate old man
to whose former services Christianity itself was so
deeply indebted.

The fall of Liberius and Osius reflected a brighter
lustre on the firmness of those bishops who still adhered
with unshaken fidelity to the cause of Athanasius and
religious truth. The ingenious malice of their enemies
had deprived them of the benefit of mutual comfort and
advice, separated those illustrious exiles into distant

provinces, and carefully selected the most inhospitable spots of a great empire. Yet they soon experienced that the deserts of Libya and the most barbarous tracts of Cappadocia were less inhospitable than the residence of those cities in which an Arian bishop could satiate, without restraint, the exquisite rancour of theological hatred. Their consolation was derived from the consciousness of rectitude and independence, from the applause, the visits, the letters, and the liberal alms of their adherents, and from the satisfaction which they soon enjoyed of observing the intestine divisions of the adversaries of the Nicene faith. Such was the nice and capricious taste of the emperor Constantius, and so easily was he offended by the slightest deviation from his imaginary standard of Christian truth that he persecuted with equal zeal those who defended the *consubstantiality*, those who asserted the *similar substance*, and those who denied the *likeness* of the Son of God. Three bishops, degraded and banished for those adverse opinions, might possibly meet in the same place of exile and, according to the difference of their temper, might either pity or insult the blind enthusiasm of their antagonists, whose present sufferings would never be compensated by future happiness.

The disgrace and exile of the orthodox bishops of the West were designed as so many preparatory steps to the ruin of Athanasius himself. Six-and-twenty months had elapsed, during which the Imperial court secretly laboured by the most insidious arts to remove him from Alexandria and to withdraw the allowance which supplied his popular liberality. But when the primate of Egypt, deserted and proscribed by the Latin church, was left destitute of any foreign support, Constantius despatched two of his secretaries with a verbal commission to announce and execute the order of his banishment. As the justice of the sentence was publicly avowed by the whole party, the only motive which could restrain Constantius from giving his messengers the sanction of a written mandate must be imputed to his doubt of the event, and to a sense of the danger to which he might expose the second city and the most fertile province of the empire if the people should persist in the resolution of defending by force of arms the innocence of their spiritual father.

Such extreme caution afforded Athanasius a specious pretence respectfully to dispute the truth of an order which he could not reconcile either with the equity or with the former declarations of his gracious master. The civil powers of Egypt found themselves inadequate to the task of persuading or compelling the primate to abdicate his episcopal throne; and they were obliged to conclude a treaty with the popular leaders of Alexandria by which it was stipulated that all proceedings and all hostilities should be suspended till the emperor's pleasure had been more distinctly ascertained. By this seeming moderation the catholics were deceived into a false and fatal security, while the legions of the Upper Egypt and of Libya advanced by secret orders and hasty marches to besiege, or rather to surprise, a capital habituated to sedition and inflamed by religious zeal. The position of Alexandria, between the sea and the lake Mareotis, facilitated the approach and landing of the troops, who were introduced into the heart of the city before any effectual measures could be taken either to shut the gates or to occupy the important posts of defence.

At the hour of midnight, twenty-three days after the signature of the treaty, Syrianus, duke of Egypt, at the head of five thousand soldiers armed and prepared for an assault, unexpectedly invested the church of St. Theonas, where the archbishop, with a part of his clergy and people, performed their nocturnal devotions. The doors of the sacred edifice yielded to the impetuosity of the attack, which was accompanied with every horrid circumstance of tumult and bloodshed; but as the bodies of the slain and the fragments of military weapons remained the next day an unexceptionable evidence in the possession of the catholics, the enterprise of Syrianus may be considered as a successful irruption rather than as an absolute conquest. The other churches of the city were profaned by similar outrages; and during at least four months Alexandria was exposed to the insults of a licentious army, stimulated by the ecclesiastics of an hostile faction. Many of the faithful were killed, who may deserve the name of martyrs if their deaths were neither provoked nor revenged; bishops and presbyters were treated with cruel ignominy; consecrated virgins were stripped naked, scourged, and violated; the houses of wealthy citizens were plundered; and under the mask of religious zeal lust, avarice, and private resentment were gratified with impunity, and even with applause.

The pagans of Alexandria, who still formed a numerous and discontented party, were easily persuaded to desert a bishop whom they feared and esteemed. The hopes of some peculiar favours and the apprehension of being involved in the general penalties of rebellion engaged them to promise their support to the destined successor of Athanasius, the famous George of Cappadocia. The usurper, after receiving the consecration of an Arian synod, was placed on the episcopal throne by the arms of Sebastian, who had been appointed count of Egypt for the execution of that important design. In the use as well as in the acquisition of power, the tyrant George disregarded the laws of religion, of justice, and of humanity; and the same scenes of violence and scandal which had been exhibited in the capital were repeated in more than ninety episcopal cities of Egypt. Encouraged by success, Constantius ventured to approve the conduct of his ministers. By a public and passionate epistle the emperor congratulates the deliverance of Alexandria from a popular tyrant who deluded his blind votaries by the magic of his eloquence; expatiates on the virtues and piety of the most reverend George, the elected bishop; and aspires, as the patron and benefactor of the city, to surpass the fame of Alexander himself. But he solemnly declares his unalterable resolution to pursue with fire and sword the seditious adherents of the wicked Athanasius, who by flying from justice has confessed his guilt and escaped the ignominious death which he had so often deserved.

Athanasius had indeed escaped from the most imminent dangers; and the adventures of that extraordinary man deserve and fix our attention. On the memorable night when the church of St. Theonas was invested by the troops of Syrianus, the archbishop, seated on his throne, expected with calm and intrepid dignity the approach of death. While the public devotion was interrupted by shouts of rage and cries of terror, he animated his trembling congregation to express their religious confidence by chanting one of the psalms of David which celebrates the triumph of the God of Israel over the haughty and impious tyrant of Egypt. The doors were at length burst open; a cloud of arrows was discharged among the people; the soldiers, with drawn swords, rushed forward into the sanctuary; and the dreadful gleam of their armour was reflected by the holy luminaries which burned round the altar. Athanasius still rejected the pious importunity of the monks and presbyters who were attached to his person, and nobly refused to desert his episcopal station till he had dismissed in safety the last of the congregation. The darkness and tumult of the night favoured the retreat of the arch-bishop; and though he was oppressed by the waves of an agitated multitude, though he was thrown to the ground and left without sense or motion, he still recovered his undaunted courage and eluded the eager search of the soldiers, who were instructed by their Arian guides that the head of Athanasius would be the most acceptable present to the emperor. From that moment the primate of Egypt disappeared from the eyes of his enemies and remained above six years concealed in impenetrable obscurity.

The despotic power of his implacable enemy filled the whole extent of the Roman world; and the exasperated monarch had endeavoured, by a very pressing epistle to the Christian princes of Æthiopia, to exclude Athanasius from the most remote and sequestered regions of the earth. Counts, præfects, tribunes, whole armies were successively employed to pursue a bishop and a fugitive; the vigilance of the civil and military powers were excited by the Imperial edicts; liberal rewards were promised to the man who should produce Athanasius either alive or dead; and the most severe penalties were denounced against those who should dare to protect the public enemy. But the deserts of Thebaïs were now peopled by a race of wild yet submissive fanatics, who preferred the commands of their abbot to the laws of their sovereign. The numerous disciples of Antony and Pachomius received the fugitive primate as their father, admired the patience and humility with which he conformed to their strictest institutions, collected every word which dropped from his lips as the genuine effusions of inspired wisdom, and persuaded themselves that their prayers, their fasts, and their vigils were less meritorious than the zeal which they expressed and the dangers which they braved in the defence of truth and innocence.

The monasteries of Egypt were seated in lonely and desolate places, on the summit of mountains or in the islands of the Nile; and the sacred horn or trumpet of Tabenne was the well-known signal which assembled several thousand robust and determined monks, who for the most part had been the peasants of the adjacent country. When their dark retreats were invaded by a military force which it was impossible to resist, they silently stretched out their necks to the executioner and supported their national character, that tortures could never wrest from an Egyptian the confession of a secret which he was resolved not to disclose. The archbishop of Alexandria, for whose safety they eagerly devoted their lives, was lost among a uniform and well-disciplined multitude; and on the nearer approach of danger he was swiftly removed by their officious hands from one place of concealment to another, till he reached the formidable deserts, which the gloomy and credulous temper of superstition had peopled with demons and savage monsters.

The retirement of Athanasius, which ended only with the life of Constantius, was spent for the most part in the society of the monks, who faithfully served him as guards, as secretaries, and as messengers; but the importance of maintaining a more intimate connection with the catholic party tempted him, whenever the diligence of the pursuit was abated, to emerge from the desert, to introduce himself into Alexandria, and to trust his person to the discretion of his friends and adherents. His various adventures might have furnished the subject of a very entertaining romance. He was once secreted in a dry cistern, which he had scarcely left before he was betrayed by the treachery of a female slave; and he was once concealed in a still more extraordinary asylum, the house of a virgin only twenty years of age who was celebrated in the whole city for her exquisite beauty. At the hour of midnight, as she related her story many years afterwards, she was surprised by the appearance of the archbishop in a loose undress, who, advancing with hasty steps, conjured her to afford him the protection which he had been directed by a celestial vision to seek under her hospitable roof. The pious maid accepted and preserved the sacred pledge which was entrusted to her prudence and courage. Without imparting the secret to anyone, she instantly conducted Athanasius into her most sacred chamber and watched over his safety with the tenderness of a friend and the assiduity of a servant. As long as the danger continued she regularly supplied him with books and provisions, washed his feet, managed his correspondence, and dexterously concealed from the eye of suspicion this familiar and solitary intercourse between a saint whose character required the most unblemished chastity and a female whose charms might excite the most dangerous emotions.

During the six years of persecution and exile Athanasius repeated his visits to his fair and faithful companion; and the formal declaration that he *saw* the councils of Rimini and Seleucia forces us to believe that he was secretly present at the time and place of their convocation. The advantage of personally negotiating with his friends and of observing and improving the divisions of his enemies might justify in a prudent statesman so bold and dangerous an enterprise; and Alexandria was connected by trade and navigation with every seaport of the Mediterranean. From the depth of his inaccessible retreat the intrepid primate waged an incessant and offensive war against the protector of the Arians; and his seasonable writings, which were diligently circulated and eagerly perused, contributed to unite and animate the orthodox party. In his public apologies, which he addressed to the emperor himself, he sometimes affected the praise of moderation; whilst at the same time in secret and vehement invectives he exposed Constantius as a weak and wicked prince, the executioner of his family, the tyrant of the republic, and the Antichrist of the church. In the height of his prosperity the victorious monarch, who had chastised the rashness of Gallus and suppressed the revolt of Sylvanus, who had taken the diadem from the head of Vetranio and vanquished in the field the legions of Magnentius, received from an invisible hand a wound which he could neither heal nor revenge; and the son of Constantine was the first of the Christian princes who experienced the strength of those principles which, in the cause of religion, could resist the most violent exertions of the civil power.

The persecution of Athanasius and of so many respectable bishops who suffered for the truth of their opinions, or at least for the integrity of their conscience, was a just subject of indignation and discontent to all Christians except those who were blindly devoted to the Arian faction. The people regretted the loss of their faithful pastors, whose banishment was usually followed by the intrusion of a stranger into the episcopal chair, and loudly complained that the right of election was violated and that they were condemned to obey a mercenary usurper whose person was unknown and whose principles were suspected. The catholics might prove to the world that they were not involved in the guilt and heresy of their ecclesiastical governor by publicly testifying their dissent or by totally separating themselves from his communion. The first of these methods was invented at Antioch and practised with such success that it was soon diffused over the Christian world. The doxology, or sacred hymn, which celebrates the *glory* of the Trinity is susceptible of very nice but material inflections; and the substance of an orthodox or an heretical creed may be expressed by the difference of a disjunctive or a copulative particle. Alternate responses and a more regular psalmody were introduced into the public service by Flavianus and Diodorus, two devout and active laymen who were attached to the Nicene faith. Under their conduct a swarm of monks issued from the adjacent desert, bands of well-disciplined singers were stationed in the cathedral of Antioch, the Glory to the Father, *and* the Son, *and* the Holy Ghost was triumphantly chanted by a full chorus of voices, and the catholics insulted, by the purity of their doctrine, the Arian prelate who had usurped the throne of the venerable Eustathius.

The same zeal which inspired their songs prompted the more scrupulous members of the orthodox party to form separate assemblies, which were governed by the presbyters till the death of their exiled bishop allowed the election and consecration of a new episcopal pastor. The revolutions of the court multiplied the number of pretenders, and the same city was often disputed, under the reign of Constantius, by two or three or even four bishops, who exercised their spiritual jurisdiction over their respective followers and alternately lost and regained the temporal possessions of the church. The abuse of Christianity introduced into the Roman government new causes of tyranny and sedition; the bands of civil society were torn asunder by the fury of religious factions; and the obscure citizen, who might calmly have surveyed the elevation and fall of successive emperors, imagined and experienced that his own life and fortune were connected with the interests of a popular ecclesiastic.

Gibbon elaborates at this point in the original by describing the religious temper of two of the empire's greatest cities during the reign of Constantine's sons. In Rome the exile of the orthodox bishop Liberius caused such a public tumult that the emperor Constantius, on a visit to the Circus, was repeatedly assailed with roars of "One God, One Christ, One Bishop!" And the infuriated populace of Constantinople first burned the palace of the master general of the Imperial cavalry and then dragged his lifeless body by the heels through the streets, because he attempted to enforce a sentence of banishment against a popular bishop.

But such outbursts were mild compared to the madness of the Donatist sect known as Circumcellions, who, armed mainly with huge clubs known as Israelites and shouting their war cry of "Praise be to God!" preyed on the defenceless provincials of Africa. One of their major articles of devotion seems to have been a horror of life. "They frequently stopped travellers on the public highways and obliged them to inflict the stroke of martyrdom, by the promise of a reward if they consented and by the threat of instant death if they refused"; while others, on an announced day, would hurl themselves from some high precipice. The disappearance of the Circumcellions was speeded by this singular yearning for, and practice of, self-destruction.

The simple narrative of the intestine divisions which distracted the peace and dishonoured the triumph of the church will confirm the remark of a pagan historian and justify the complaint of a venerable bishop. The experience of Ammianus had convinced him that the enmity of the Christians towards each other surpassed the fury of savage beasts against man; and Gregory Nazianzen most pathetically laments that the Kingdom of Heaven was converted by discord into the image of chaos, of a nocturnal tempest, and of hell itself. The fierce and partial writers of the times, ascribing *all* virtue to themselves and imputing *all* guilt to their adversaries, have painted the battle of the angels and demons. Our calmer reason will reject such pure and perfect monsters of vice or sanctity and will impute an equal, or at least an indiscriminate, measure of good and evil to the hostile sectaries, who assumed and bestowed the appellations of orthodox and heretics. They had been educated in the same religion and the same civil society. Their hopes and fears in the present or in a future life were balanced in the same proportion. On either side the error might be innocent, the faith sincere, the practice meritorious or corrupt. Their passions were excited by similar objects, and they might alternately abuse the favour of the court or of the people. The metaphysical opinions of the Athanasians and the Arians could not influence their moral character, and they were alike actuated by the intolerant spirit which has been extracted from the pure and simple maxims of the Gospel.

A modern writer, who with a just confidence has prefixed to his own history the honourable epithets of political and philosophical, accuses the timid prudence of Montesquieu for neglecting to enumerate, among the causes of the decline of the empire, a law of Constantine by which the exercise of the pagan worship was absolutely suppressed and a considerable part of his subjects was left destitute of priests, of temples, and of any public religion. The zeal of the philosophic historian for the rights of mankind has induced him to acquiesce in the ambiguous testimony of those ecclesiastics who have too lightly ascribed to their favourite hero the *merit* of a general persecution. Instead of alleging this imaginary law, which would have blazed in the front of the Imperial codes, we may safely appeal to the original epistle which Constantine addressed to the followers of the ancient religion at a time when he no longer disguised his conversion nor dreaded the rivals of his throne. He invites and exhorts, in the most pressing terms, the subjects of the Roman empire to imitate the example of their master; but he declares that those who still refuse to open their eyes to the celestial light may freely enjoy their temples and their fancied gods. A report that the ceremonies of paganism were suppressed is formally contradicted by the emperor himself, who wisely assigns, as the principle of his moderation, the invincible force of habit, of prejudice, and of superstition.

Without violating the sanctity of his promise, without alarming the fears of the pagans, the artful monarch advanced by slow and cautious steps to undermine the irregular and decayed fabric of polytheism. The partial acts of severity which he occasionally exercised, though they were secretly prompted by a Christian zeal, were coloured by the fairest pretences of justice and the public good; and while Constantine designed to ruin the foundations, he seemed to reform the abuses, of the ancient religion. After the example of the wisest of his predecessors, he condemned under the most rigorous penalties the occult and impious arts of divination, which excited the vain hopes, and sometimes the criminal attempts, of those who were discontented with their present condition. An ignominious silence was imposed on the oracles, which had been publicly convicted of fraud and falsehood; the effeminate priests of the Nile were abolished; and Constantine discharged the duties

of a Roman censor when he gave orders for the demolition of several temples of Phœnicia, in which every
mode of prostitution was devoutly practised in the face
of day and to the honour of Venus. The Imperial city
of Constantinople was in some measure raised at the expense, and was adorned with the spoils, of the opulent
temples of Greece and Asia; the sacred property was
confiscated; the statues of gods and heroes were transported with rude familiarity among a people who considered them as objects not of adoration but of curiosity;
the gold and silver were restored to circulation; and the
magistrates, the bishops, and the eunuchs improved the
fortunate occasion of gratifying at once their zeal, their
avarice, and their resentment. But these depredations
were confined to a small part of the Roman world; and
the provinces had been long since accustomed to endure
the same sacrilegious rapine from the tyranny of princes
and proconsuls who could not be suspected of any design to subvert the established religion.

The sons of Constantine trod in the footsteps of their
father with more zeal and with less discretion. The pretences of rapine and oppression were insensibly multiplied; every indulgence was shown to the illegal behaviour of the Christians; every doubt was explained to
the disadvantage of paganism; and the demolition of the
temples was celebrated as one of the auspicious events
of the reign of Constans and Constantius. The name of
Constantius is prefixed to a concise law, which might
have superseded the necessity of any future prohibi-
tions. "It is our pleasure that in all places and in all cities
the temples be immediately shut and carefully guarded
that none may have the power of offending. It is likewise our pleasure that all our subjects should abstain
from sacrifices. If anyone should be guilty of such an
act, let him feel the sword of vengeance, and after his

execution let his property be confiscated to the public use. We denounce the same penalties against the governors of the provinces, if they neglect to punish the criminals."

But there is the strongest reason to believe that this formidable edict was either composed without being published or was published without being executed. The evidence of facts, and the monuments which are still extant of brass and marble, continue to prove the public exercise of the pagan worship during the whole reign of the sons of Constantine. In the East as well as in the West, in cities as well as in the country, a great number of temples were respected, or at least were spared; and the devout multitude still enjoyed the luxury of sacrifices, of festivals, and of processions by the permission or by the connivance of the civil government. About four years after the supposed date of his bloody edict, Constantius visited the temples of Rome; and the decency of his behaviour is recommended by a pagan orator as an example worthy of the imitation of succeeding princes. "That emperor," says Symmachus, "suffered the privileges of the vestal virgins to remain inviolate; he bestowed the sacerdotal dignities on the nobles of Rome, granted the customary allowance to defray the expenses of the public rites and sacrifices; and, though he had embraced a different religion, he never attempted to deprive the empire of the sacred worship of antiquity." The senate still presumed to consecrate by solemn decrees the *divine* memory of their sovereigns; and Constantine himself was associated after death to those gods whom he had renounced and insulted during his life. The title, the ensigns, the prerogatives of *Sovereign Pontiff*, which had been instituted by Numa and assumed by Augustus, were accepted without hesitation by seven Christian emperors, who were invested with a more absolute authority over the religion which they had deserted than over that which they professed.

The divisions of Christianity suspended the ruin of paganism; and the holy war against the infidels was less vigorously prosecuted by princes and bishops who were more immediately alarmed by the guilt and danger of domestic rebellion. The extirpation of idolatry might have been justified by the established principles of intolerance; but the hostile sects, which alternately reigned in the Imperial court, were mutually apprehensive of alienating and perhaps exasperating the minds of a powerful though declining faction. Every motive of authority and fashion, of interest and reason, now militated on the side of Christianity; but two or three generations elapsed before their victorious influence was universally felt. The religion which had so long and so lately been established in the Roman empire was still revered by a numerous people, less attached indeed to speculative opinion than to ancient custom. The honours of the state and army were indifferently bestowed on all the subjects of Constantine and Constantius, and a considerable portion of knowledge and wealth and valour was still engaged in the service of polytheism. The superstition of the senator and of the peasant, of the poet and the philosopher, was derived from very different causes; but they met with equal devotion in the temples of the gods. Their zeal was insensibly provoked by the insulting triumph of a proscribed sect; and their hopes were revived by the well-grounded confidence that the presumptive heir of the empire, a young and valiant hero who had delivered Gaul from the arms of the barbarians, had secretly embraced the religion of his ancestors.

Chapter XI

(A.D. 360-363)

*Julian is declared emperor by the legions of Gaul —
His march and success — The death of Constantius
— Civil administration of Julian — His attempt to
restore the pagan worship — Death of Julian in the
Persian campaign — His successor, Jovian, saves
the Roman army by a disgraceful treaty*[1]

WHILE the Romans languished under the ignominious tyranny of eunuchs and bishops, the praises of
Julian were repeated with transport in every part of the
empire except in the palace of Constantius. The barbarians of Germany had felt, and still dreaded, the arms
of the young Cæsar; his soldiers were the companions
of his victory; the grateful provincials enjoyed the blessings of his reign; but the favourites who had opposed
his elevation were offended by his virtues, and they
justly considered the friend of the people as the enemy
of the court. As long as the fame of Julian was doubtful,
the buffoons of the palace, who were skilled in the language of satire, tried the efficacy of those arts which
they had so often practised with success. They easily
discovered that his simplicity was not exempt from affectation: the ridiculous epithets of an hairy savage, of
an ape invested with the purple, were applied to the
dress and person of the philosophic warrior; and his
modest despatches were stigmatized as the vain and
elaborate fictions of a loquacious Greek, a speculative

1. *Editor's note:* Chapters XXII through XXIV of the
original.

soldier who had studied the art of war amidst the groves of the Academy.

The voice of malicious folly was at length silenced by the shouts of victory; the conqueror of the Franks and Alemanni could no longer be painted as an object of contempt; and the monarch himself was meanly ambitious of stealing from his lieutenant the honourable reward of his labours. In the letters crowned with laurel, which according to ancient custom were addressed to the provinces, the name of Julian was omitted. "Constantius had made his dispositions in person; *he* had signalized his valour in the foremost ranks; *his* military conduct had secured the victory; and the captive king of the barbarians was presented to *him* on the field of battle," from which he was at that time distant above forty days' journey.

So extravagant a fable was incapable, however, of deceiving the public credulity, or even of satisfying the pride of the emperor himself. Secretly conscious that the applause and favour of the Romans accompanied the rising fortunes of Julian, his discontented mind was prepared to receive the subtle poison of those artful sycophants who coloured their mischievous designs with the fairest appearances of truth and candour. Instead of depreciating the merits of Julian, they acknowledged, and even exaggerated, his popular fame, superior talents, and important services. But they darkly insinuated that the virtues of the Cæsar might instantly be converted into the most dangerous crimes if the inconstant multitude should prefer their inclinations to their duty, or if the general of a victorious army should be tempted from his allegiance by the hopes of revenge and independent greatness. The personal fears of Constantius were interpreted by his council as a laudable anxiety for the public safety, whilst in private, and perhaps in his own breast, he disguised under the less odious appellation of fear the sentiments of hatred and envy which he had secretly conceived for the inimitable virtues of Julian.

The apparent tranquillity of Gaul and the imminent danger of the eastern provinces offered a specious pretence for the design which was artfully concerted by the Imperial ministers. They resolved to disarm the Cæsar, to recall those faithful troops who guarded his person and dignity, and to employ, in a distant war against the Persian monarch, the hardy veterans who had vanquished on the banks of the Rhine the fiercest nations of Germany. While Julian used the laborious hours of his winter quarters at Paris in the administration of power, which in his hands was the exercise of virtue, he was surprised by the hasty arrival of a tribune and a notary with positive orders from the emperor, which *they* were directed to execute and *he* was commanded not to oppose. Constantius signified his pleasure that four entire legions—the Celtæ and Petulants, the Heruli and the Batavians—should be separated from the standard of Julian, under which they had acquired their fame and discipline; that in each of the remaining bands three hundred of the bravest youths should be selected; and that this numerous detachment, the strength of the Gallic army, should instantly begin their march, and exert their utmost diligence to arrive before the opening of the campaign on the frontiers of Persia.

The Cæsar foresaw and lamented the consequences of this fatal mandate. Most of the auxiliaries, who engaged their voluntary service, had stipulated that they should never be obliged to pass the Alps. The public faith of Rome and the personal honour of Julian had been pledged for the observance of this condition. Such an act of treachery and oppression would destroy the

confidence and excite the resentment of the independent
warriors of Germany, who considered truth as the noblest of their virtues and freedom as the most valuable
of their possessions. The legionaries, who enjoyed the
title and privileges of Romans, were enlisted for the
general defence of the republic; but those mercenary
troops heard with cold indifference the antiquated
names of the republic and of Rome. Attached either
from birth or long habit to the climate and manners of
Gaul, they loved and admired Julian; they despised and
perhaps hated the emperor; they dreaded the laborious
march, the Persian arrows, and the burning deserts of
Asia. They claimed as their own the country which they
had saved and excused their want of spirit by pleading
the sacred and more immediate duty of protecting their
families and friends.

The apprehensions of the Gauls were derived from
the knowledge of the impending and inevitable danger.
As soon as the provinces were exhausted of their military
strength, the Germans would violate a treaty which had
been imposed on their fears; and notwithstanding the
abilities and valour of Julian, the general of a nominal
army, to whom the public calamities would be imputed,
must find himself, after a vain resistance, either a prisoner in the camp of the barbarians or a criminal in the
palace of Constantius. If Julian complied with the orders
which he had received he subscribed his own destruction, and that of a people who deserved his affection.
But a positive refusal was an act of rebellion and a declaration of war. The inexorable jealousy of the emperor,
the peremptory and perhaps insidious nature of his commands, left not any room for a fair apology or candid
interpretation; and the dependent station of the Cæsar
scarcely allowed him to pause or to deliberate.

Solitude increased the perplexity of Julian; he could

no longer apply to the faithful counsels of Sallust, who had been removed from his office by the judicious malice of the eunuchs; he could not even enforce his representations by the concurrence of the ministers, who would have been afraid or ashamed to approve the ruin of Gaul. The moment had been chosen when Lupicinus, the general of the cavalry, was despatched into Britain to repulse the inroads of the Scots and Picts; and Florentius was occupied at Vienne by the assessment of the tribute. The latter, a crafty and corrupt statesman, declining to assume a responsible part on this dangerous occasion, eluded the pressing and repeated invitations of Julian, who represented to him that in every important measure the presence of the præfect was indispensable in the council of the prince. In the meanwhile the Cæsar was oppressed by the rude and importunate solicitations of the Imperial messengers, who presumed to suggest that if he expected the return of his ministers he could charge himself with the guilt of the delay and reserve for them the merit of the execution. Unable to resist, unwilling to comply, Julian expressed in the most serious terms his wish, and even his intention, of resigning the purple, which he could not preserve with honour but which he could not abdicate with safety.

After a painful conflict Julian was compelled to acknowledge that obedience was the virtue of the most eminent subject, and that the sovereign alone was entitled to judge of the public welfare. He issued the necessary orders for carrying into execution the commands of Constantius; a part of the troops began their march for the Alps; and the detachments from the several garrisons moved towards their respective places of assembly. They advanced with difficulty through the trembling and affrighted crowds of provincials, who attempted to excite their pity by silent despair or loud lamentations;

while the wives of the soldiers, holding their infants in
their arms, accused the desertion of their husbands in
the mixed language of grief, of tenderness, and of indignation.

This scene of general distress afflicted the humanity
of the Cæsar; he granted a sufficient number of post-
waggons to transport the wives and families of the soldiers, endeavoured to alleviate the hardships which he
was constrained to inflict, and increased by the most
laudable arts his own popularity and the discontent of
the exiled troops. The grief of an armed multitude is
soon converted into rage; their licentious murmurs
which every hour were communicated from tent to tent
with more boldness and effect, prepared their minds for
the most daring acts of sedition; and by the connivance
of their tribunes a seasonable libel was secretly dispersed, which painted in lively colours the disgrace of
the Cæsar, the oppression of the Gallic army, and the
feeble vices of the tyrant of Asia. The servants of Constantius were astonished and alarmed by the progress of
this dangerous spirit. They pressed the Cæsar to hasten
the departure of the troops; but they imprudently rejected the honest and judicious advice of Julian, who
proposed that they should not march through Paris, and
suggested the danger and temptation of a last interview.

As soon as the approach of the troops was announced,
the Cæsar went out to meet them and ascended his tribunal, which had been erected in a plain before the
gates of the city. After distinguishing the officers and
soldiers who by their rank or merit deserved a peculiar
attention, Julian addressed himself in a studied oration to the surrounding multitude: he celebrated their
exploits with grateful applause, encouraged them to accept with alacrity the honour of serving under the eyes
of a powerful and liberal monarch, and admonished

them that the commands of Augustus required an instant and cheerful obedience. The soldiers, who were
apprehensive of offending their general by an indecent
clamour or of belying their sentiments by false and venal
acclamations, maintained an obstinate silence, and after
a short pause were dismissed to their quarters. The
principal officers were entertained by the Cæsar, who
professed in the warmest language of friendship his desire and his inability to reward, according to their
deserts, the brave companions of his victories. They retired from the feast full of grief and perplexity, and
lamented the hardship of their fate which tore them
from their beloved general and their native country.

The only expedient which could prevent their separation was boldly agitated and approved; the popular resentment was insensibly moulded into a regular conspiracy; their just reasons of complaint were heightened
by passion, and their passions were inflamed by wine,
as on the eve of their departure the troops were indulged
in licentious festivity. At the hour of midnight the impetuous multitude, with swords and bows and torches in
their hands, rushed into the suburbs, encompassed the
palace, and, careless of future dangers, pronounced
the fatal and irrevocable words, *Julian Augustus!* The
prince, whose anxious suspense was interrupted by their
disorderly acclamations, secured the doors against their
intrusion, and as long as it was in his power secluded his
person and dignity from the accidents of a nocturnal
tumult. At the dawn of day the soldiers, whose zeal was
irritated by opposition, forcibly entered the palace,
seized with respectful violence the object of their choice,
guarded Julian with drawn swords through the streets
of Paris, placed him on the tribunal, and with repeated
shouts saluted him as their emperor.

Prudence as well as loyalty inculcated the propriety

of resisting their treasonable designs and of preparing
for his oppressed virtue the excuse of violence. Addressing himself by turns to the multitude and to individuals,
he sometimes implored their mercy and sometimes expressed his indignation; conjured them not to sully the
fame of their immortal victories; ventured to promise
that if they would immediately return to their allegiance
he would undertake to obtain from the emperor not
only a free and gracious pardon, but even the revocation
of the orders which had excited their resentment. But
the soldiers, who were conscious of their guilt, chose
rather to depend on the gratitude of Julian than on the
clemency of the emperor. Their zeal was insensibly
turned into impatience, and their impatience into rage.
The inflexible Cæsar sustained till the third hour of the
day their prayers, their reproaches, and their menaces;
nor did he yield till he had been repeatedly assured that
if he wished to live he must consent to reign. He was
exalted on a shield in the presence and amidst the unanimous acclamations of the troops; a rich military collar,
which was offered by chance, supplied the want of a
diadem; the ceremony was concluded by the promise
of a moderate donative; and the new emperor, overwhelmed with real or affected grief, retired into the
most secret recesses of his apartment.

The grief of Julian could proceed only from his innocence; but his innocence must appear extremely doubtful in the eyes of those who have learned to suspect the
motives and the professions of princes. His lively and
active mind was susceptible of the various impressions
of hope and fear, of gratitude and revenge, of duty and
of ambition, of the love of fame and of the fear of
reproach. But it is impossible for us to calculate the
respective weight and operation of these sentiments, or
to ascertain the principles of action which might escape

the observation while they guided, or rather impelled, the steps of Julian himself. The discontent of the troops was produced by the malice of his enemies; their tumult was the natural effect of interest and of passion; and if Julian had tried to conceal a deep design under the appearances of chance, he must have employed the most consummate artifice without necessity, and probably without success. He solemnly declares, in the presence of Jupiter, of the Sun, of Mars, of Minerva, and of all the other deities, that till the close of the evening which preceded his elevation he was utterly ignorant of the designs of the soldiers; and it may seem ungenerous to distrust the honour of a hero and the truth of a philosopher. Yet the superstitious confidence that Constantius was the enemy and that he himself was the favourite of the gods might prompt him to desire, to solicit, and even to hasten the auspicious moment of his reign, which was predestined to restore the ancient religion of mankind. When Julian had received the intelligence of the conspiracy he resigned himself to a short slumber; and afterwards related to his friends that he had seen the Genius of the empire waiting with some impatience at his door, pressing for admittance, and reproaching his want of spirit and ambition. Astonished and perplexed, he addressed his prayers to the great Jupiter, who immediately signified by a clear and manifest omen that he should submit to the will of heaven and of the army. The conduct which disclaims the ordinary maxims of reason excites our suspicion and eludes our inquiry. Whenever the spirit of fanaticism, at once so credulous and so crafty, has insinuated itself into a noble mind, it insensibly corrodes the vital principles of virtue and veracity.

To moderate the zeal of his party, to protect the persons of his enemies, to defeat and to despise the secret enterprises which were formed against his life and dignity were the cares which employed the first days of the reign of the new emperor. Although he was firmly resolved to maintain the station which he had assumed, he was still desirous of saving his country from the calamities of civil war, of declining a contest with the superior forces of Constantius, and of preserving his own character from the reproach of perfidy and ingratitude. Adorned with the designs of military and Imperial pomp, Julian showed himself in the field of Mars to the soldiers, who glowed with ardent enthusiasm in the cause of their pupil, their leader, and their friend. He recapitulated their victories, lamented their sufferings, applauded their resolution, animated their hopes, and checked their impetuosity; nor did he dismiss the assembly till he had obtained a solemn promise from the troops that if the emperor of the East would subscribe an equitable treaty, they would renounce any views of conquest and satisfy themselves with the tranquil possession of the Gallic provinces.

On this foundation he composed, in his own name and in that of the army, a specious and moderate epistle, which was delivered to Pentadius, his master of the offices, and to his chamberlain Eutherius, two ambassadors whom he appointed to receive the answer and observe the dispositions of Constantius. This epistle is inscribed with the modest appellation of Cæsar, but Julian solicits in a peremptory though respectful manner the confirmation of the title of Augustus. He acknowledges the irregularity of his own election, while he justifies in some measure the resentment and violence of the troops which had extorted his reluctant consent. He allows the supremacy of his brother Constantius and engages to send him an annual present of Spanish horses, to recruit his army with a select number of barbarian youths, and to accept from his choice a Prætorian præfect of approved discretion and fidelity. But he reserves for himself the nomination of his other civil and military officers, with the troops, the revenue, and the sovereignty of the provinces beyond the Alps. He admonishes the emperor to consult the dictates of justice, to distrust the arts of those venal flatterers who subsist only by the discord of princes, and to embrace the offer of a fair and honourable treaty, equally advantageous to the republic and to the house of Constantine.

In this negotiation Julian claimed no more than he already possessed. The delegated authority which he had long exercised over the provinces of Gaul, Spain, and Britain was still obeyed under a name more independent and august. The soldiers and the people rejoiced in a revolution which was not stained even with the blood of the guilty. Florentius was a fugitive, Lupicinus a prisoner. The persons who were disaffected to the new government were disarmed and secured, and the vacant offices were distributed, according to the recommendation of merit, by a prince who despised the intrigues of the palace and the clamours of the soldiers.

The negotiations of peace were accompanied and supported by the most vigorous preparations for war. The army, which Julian held in readiness for immediate action, was recruited and augmented by the disorders of the times. The cruel persecution of the faction of Magnentius had filled Gaul with numerous bands of outlaws and robbers. They cheerfully accepted the offer of a general pardon from a prince whom they could trust, submitted to the restraints of military discipline, and retained only their implacable hatred to the person and government of Constantius. As soon as the season of the year permitted Julian to take the field, he appeared at the head of his legions, threw a bridge over the Rhine in the neighbourhood of Cleves, and prepared to chastise the perfidy of the Attuarii, a tribe of Franks who presumed that they might ravage with impunity the frontiers of a divided empire. The difficulty as well as glory of this enterprise consisted in a laborious march; and Julian had conquered, as soon as he could penetrate into, a country which former princes had considered as inaccessible.

After he had given peace to the barbarians the emperor carefully visited the fortifications along the Rhine from Cleves to Basel; surveyed with peculiar attention the territories which he had recovered from the hands of the Alemanni; passed through Besançon, which had severely suffered from their fury; and fixed his headquarters at Vienne for the ensuing winter. The barrier of Gaul was improved and strengthened with additional fortifications; and Julian entertained some hopes that the Germans, whom he had so often vanquished, might in his absence be restrained by the terror of his name. Vadomair was the only prince of the Alemanni whom he esteemed or feared; and while the subtle barbarian affected to observe the faith of treaties, the progress of his arms threatened the state with an unseasonable and dangerous war. The policy of Julian condescended to surprise the prince of the Alemanni by his own arts; and Vadomair, who in the character of a friend had incautiously accepted an invitation from the Roman governors, was seized in the midst of the entertainment and sent away prisoner into the heart of Spain. Before the barbarians were recovered from their amazement the emperor appeared in arms on the banks of the Rhine and, once more crossing the river, renewed the deep impressions of terror and respect which had been already made by four preceding expeditions.

The ambassadors of Julian had been instructed to execute with the utmost diligence their important commission. But in their passage through Italy and Illyricum they were detained by the tedious and affected delays of the provincial governors; they were conducted by slow journeys from Constantinople to Cæsarea in Cappadocia; and when at length they were admitted to the presence of Constantius, they found that he had already conceived, from the despatches of his own officers, the most unfavourable opinion of the conduct of Julian and of the Gallic army. The letters were heard with impatience; the trembling messengers were dismissed with indignation and contempt; and the looks, the gestures, the furious language of the monarch expressed the disorder of his soul. The domestic connection which might have reconciled the brother and the husband of Helena was recently dissolved by the death of that princess, whose pregnancy had been several times fruitless and was at last fatal to herself. The empress Eusebia had preserved to the last moment of her life the warm and even jealous affection which she had conceived for Julian; and her mild influence might have moderated the resentment of a prince who, since her death, was abandoned to his own passions and to the arts of his eunuchs. But the terror of a foreign invasion obliged him to suspend the punishment of a private enemy; he continued his march towards the confines of Persia and thought it sufficient to signify the conditions which might entitle Julian and his guilty followers to the clemency of their offended sovereign. He required that the presumptuous Cæsar should expressly renounce the appellation and rank of Augustus which he had accepted from the rebels; that he should descend to his former station of a limited and dependent minister; that he should vest the powers of the state and army in the hands of those officers who were appointed by the Imperial court; and that he should trust his safety to the assurances of pardon, which were announced by Epictetus, a Gallic bishop and one of the Arian favourites of Constantius.

Several months were ineffectually consumed in a treaty which was negotiated at the distance of three thousand miles between Paris and Antioch; and as soon as Julian perceived that his moderate and respectful behaviour served only to irritate the pride of an implacable adversary, he boldly resolved to commit his life and fortune to the chance of a civil war. He gave a public and military audience to the quæstor Leonas; the haughty epistle of Constantius was read to the attentive multitude; and Julian protested with the most flattering deference that he was ready to resign the title of Augustus if he could obtain the consent of those whom he acknowledged as the authors of his elevation. The faint proposal was impetuously silenced; and the acclamations of "Julian Augustus, continue to reign, by the authority of the army, of the people, of the republic which you have saved," thundered at once from every part of the field and terrified the pale ambassador of Constantius. A part of the letter was afterwards read in which the emperor arraigned the ingratitude of Julian, whom he had invested with the honours of the purple, whom he had educated with so much care and tenderness, whom he had preserved in his infancy when he was left a helpless orphan.

"An orphan!" interrupted Julian, who justified his cause by indulging his passions. "Does the assassin of my family reproach me that I was left an orphan? He urges me to revenge those injuries which I have long studied to forget." The assembly was dismissed; and Leonas, who with some difficulty had been protected from the popular fury, was sent back to his master with an epistle in which Julian expressed, in a strain of the most vehement eloquence, the sentiments of contempt, of hatred, and of resentment which had been suppressed and embittered by the dissimulation of twenty years. After this message, which might be considered as a signal of irreconcilable war, Julian, who some weeks before had celebrated the Christian festival of the Epiphany, made a public declaration that he committed the care of his safety to the *Immortal Gods,* and thus publicly renounced the religion as well as the friendship of Constantius.

The situation of Julian required a vigorous and immediate resolution. He had discovered from intercepted letters that his adversary, sacrificing the interest of the state to that of the monarch, had again excited the barbarians to invade the provinces of the West. The position of two magazines, one of them collected on the banks of the lake of Constance, the other formed at the foot of the Cottian Alps, seemed to indicate the march of two armies; and the size of those magazines, each of which consisted of six hundred thousand quarters of wheat, or rather flour, was a threatening evidence of the strength and numbers of the enemy who prepared to surround him. But the Imperial legions were still in their distant quarters of Asia; the Danube was feebly guarded; and if Julian could occupy by a sudden incursion the important provinces of Illyricum, he might expect that a people of soldiers would resort to his standard and that the rich mines of gold and silver would contribute to the expenses of the civil war.

He proposed this bold enterprise to the assembly of the soldiers, inspired them with a just confidence in their general and in themselves, and exhorted them to maintain their reputation of being terrible to the enemy, moderate to their fellow-citizens, and obedient to their officers. His spirited discourse was received with the loudest acclamations; and the same troops which had taken up arms against Constantius when he summoned them to leave Gaul, now declared with alacrity that they would follow Julian to the farthest extremities of Europe or Asia. The oath of fidelity was administered; and the soldiers, clashing their shields and pointing their drawn swords to their throats, devoted themselves with horrid imprecations to the service of a leader whom they celebrated as the deliverer of Gaul and the conqueror of the Germans.

This solemn engagement, which seemed to be dictated by affection rather than by duty, was singly opposed by Nebridius, who had been admitted to the office of Prætorian præfect. That faithful minister, alone and unassisted, asserted the rights of Constantius in the midst of an armed and angry multitude, to whose fury he had almost fallen an honourable but useless sacrifice. After losing one of his hands by the stroke of a sword, he embraced the knees of the prince whom he had offended. Julian covered the præfect with his Imperial mantle and, protecting him from the zeal of his followers, dismissed him to his own house, with less respect than was perhaps due to the virtue of an enemy. The high office of Nebridius was bestowed on Sallust; and the provinces of Gaul, which were now delivered from the intolerable oppression of taxes, enjoyed the mild and equitable administration of the friend of Julian, who was permitted to practise those virtues which he had instilled into the mind of his pupil.

The hopes of Julian depended much less on the number of his troops than on the celerity of his motions. In the execution of a daring enterprise he availed himself of every precaution, as far as prudence could suggest; and where prudence could no longer accompany his steps, he trusted the event to valour and to fortune. In the neighbourhood of Basel he assembled and divided his army. One body, which consisted of ten thousand men, was directed, under the command of Nevitta, general of the cavalry, to advance through the midland parts of Rhætia and Noricum. A similar division of troops, under the orders of Jovius and Jovinus, prepared to follow the oblique course of the highways through the Alps and the northern confines of Italy. The instructions to the generals were conceived with energy and precision: to hasten their march in close and compact columns, which according to the disposition of the ground might readily be changed into any order of battle; to secure themselves against the surprises of the night by strong posts and vigilant guards; to prevent resistance by their unexpected arrival; to elude examination by their sudden departure; to spread the opinion of their strength and the terror of his name; and to join their sovereign under the walls of Sirmium.

For himself Julian had reserved a more difficult and extraordinary part. He selected three thousand brave and active volunteers resolved, like their leader, to cast behind them every hope of a retreat. At the head of this faithful band he fearlessly plunged into the recesses of the Marcian, or Black, Forest, which conceals the sources of the Danube; and for many days the fate of Julian was unknown to the world. The secrecy of his march, his diligence and vigour, surmounted every obstacle; he forced his way over mountains and morasses, occupied the bridges or swam the rivers, pursued his direct course without reflecting whether he traversed the territory of the Romans or of the barbarians, and at length emerged, between Ratisbon and Vienna, at the place where he designed to embark his troops on the Danube. By a well-concerted stratagem he seized a fleet

of light brigantines as it lay at anchor, secured a supply
of coarse provisions sufficient to satisfy the indelicate
but voracious appetite of a Gallic army, and boldly
committed himself to the stream of the Danube. The
labours of his mariners, who plied their oars with incessant diligence, and the steady continuance of a favourable wind carried his fleet above seven hundred miles
in eleven days; and he had already disembarked his
troops at Bononia, only nineteen miles from Sirmium,
before his enemies could receive any certain intelligence
that he had left the banks of the Rhine.

In the course of this long and rapid navigation the
mind of Julian was fixed on the object of his enterprise;
and though he accepted the deputation of some cities,
which hastened to claim the merit of an early submission, he passed before the hostile stations which were
placed along the river without indulging the temptation
of signalizing a useless and ill-timed valour. The banks
of the Danube were crowded on either side with spectators, who gazed on the military pomp, anticipated the
importance of the event, and diffused through the adjacent country the fame of a young hero, who advanced
with more than mortal speed at the head of the innumerable forces of the West.

Lucilian, who with the rank of general of the cavalry commanded the military powers of Illyricum, was
alarmed and perplexed by the doubtful reports, which
he could neither reject nor believe. He had taken some
slow and irresolute measures for the purpose of collecting his troops when he was surprised by Dagalaiphus,
an active officer whom Julian, as soon as he landed at
Bononia, had pushed forward with some light infantry.
The captive general, uncertain of his life or death, was
hastily thrown upon a horse and conducted to the presence of Julian, who kindly raised him from the ground

and dispelled the terror and amazement which seemed to stupefy his faculties. But Lucilian had no sooner recovered his spirits than he betrayed his want of discretion by presuming to admonish his conqueror that he had rashly ventured, with a handful of men, to expose his person in the midst of his enemies. "Reserve for your master Constantius these timid remonstrances," replied Julian with a smile of contempt; "when I gave you my purple to kiss, I received you not as a counsellor but as a suppliant."

Conscious that success alone could justify his attempt, and that boldness only could command success, he instantly advanced at the head of three thousand soldiers to attack the strongest and most populous city of the Illyrian provinces. As he entered the long suburb of Sirmium he was received by the joyful acclamations of the army and people, who, crowned with flowers and holding lighted tapers in their hands, conducted their acknowledged sovereign to the Imperial residence. Two days were devoted to the public joy, which was celebrated by the games of the Circus; but early on the morning of the third day Julian marched to occupy the narrow pass of Succi in the defiles of Mount Hæmus, which, almost in the midway between Sirmium and Constantinople, separates the provinces of Thrace and Dacia by an abrupt descent towards the former and a gentle declivity on the side of the latter. The defence of this important post was intrusted to the brave Nevitta, who, as well as the generals of the Italian division, successfully executed the plan of the march and junction which their master had so ably conceived.

The homage which Julian obtained from the fears or the inclination of the people extended far beyond the immediate effect of his arms. The præfectures of Italy and Illyricum were administered by Taurus and Floren-

tius, who united that important office with the vain honours of the consulship; and as those magistrates had
retired with precipitation to the court of Asia, Julian,
who could not always restrain the levity of his temper,
stigmatized their flight by adding, in all the Acts of the
Year, the epithet of *fugitive* to the names of the two
consuls. The provinces which had been deserted by their
first magistrates acknowledged the authority of an emperor who, conciliating the qualities of a soldier with
those of a philosopher, was equally admired in the
camps of the Danube and in the cities of Greece. From
his palace, or more properly from his headquarters of
Sirmium and Naissus, he distributed to the principal
cities of the empire a laboured apology for his own conduct; published the secret despatches of Constantius;
and solicited the judgment of mankind between two
competitors, the one of whom had expelled, and the
other had invited, the barbarians.

Julian, whose mind was deeply wounded by the reproach of ingratitude, aspired to maintain by argument
as well as by arms the superior merits of his cause, and
to excel not only in the arts of war but in those of composition. His epistle to the senate and people of Athens
seems to have been dictated by an elegant enthusiasm,
which prompted him to submit his actions and his motives to the degenerate Athenians of his own times with
the same humble deference as if he had been pleading
in the days of Aristides before the tribunal of the Areopagus. His application to the senate of Rome, which
was still permitted to bestow the titles of Imperial
power, was agreeable to the forms of the expiring republic. An assembly was summoned by Tertullus, præfect of the city; the epistle of Julian was read; and as he
appeared to be master of Italy, his claims were admitted
without a dissenting voice. His oblique censure of the

innovations of Constantine and his passionate invective against the vices of Constantius were heard with less satisfaction; and the senate, as if Julian had been present, unanimously exclaimed, "Respect, we beseech you, the author of your own fortune"—an artful expression, which, according to the chance of war, might be differently explained as a manly reproof of the ingratitude of the usurper, or as a flattering confession that a single act of such benefit to the state ought to atone for all the failings of Constantius.

The intelligence of the march and rapid progress of Julian was speedily transmitted to his rival, who, by the retreat of Sapor, had obtained some respite from the Persian war. Disguising the anguish of his soul under the semblance of contempt, Constantius professed his intention of returning into Europe and of giving chase to Julian; for he never spoke of this military expedition in any other light than that of a hunting party. In the camp of Hierapolis, in Syria, he communicated this design to his army, slightly mentioned the guilt and rashness of the Cæsar, and ventured to assure them that if the mutineers of Gaul presumed to meet them in the field they would be unable to sustain the fire of their eyes and the irresistible weight of their shout of onset. The speech of the emperor was received with military applause; and Theodotus, the president of the council of Hierapolis, requested with tears of adulation that *his* city might be adorned with the head of the vanquished rebel. A chosen detachment was despatched away in post-waggons to secure, if it were yet possible, the pass of Succi; the recruits, the horses, the arms, and the magazines which had been prepared against Sapor were appropriated to the service of the civil war; and the domestic victories of Constantius inspired his partisans with the most sanguine assurances of success. The notary Gaudentius had occupied in his name the provinces of Africa; the subsistence of Rome was intercepted; and the distress of Julian was increased by an unexpected event, which might have been productive of fatal consequences.

Julian had received the submission of two legions and a cohort of archers who were stationed at Sirmium; but he suspected, with reason, the fidelity of those troops which had been distinguished by the emperor, and it was thought expedient, under the pretence of the exposed state of the Gallic frontier, to dismiss them from the most important scene of action. They advanced with reluctance as far as the confines of Italy; but as they dreaded the length of the way and the savage fierceness of the Germans, they resolved, by the instigation of one of their tribunes, to halt at Aquileia and to erect the banners of Constantius on the walls of that impregnable city. The vigilance of Julian perceived at once the extent of the mischief and the necessity of applying an immediate remedy. By his order, Jovinus led back a part of the army into Italy, and the siege of Aquileia was formed with diligence and prosecuted with vigour. But the legionaries, who seemed to have rejected the yoke of discipline, conducted the defence of the place with skill and perseverance, invited the rest of Italy to imitate the example of their courage and loyalty, and threatened the retreat of Julian if he should be forced to yield to the superior numbers of the armies of the East.

But the humanity of Julian was preserved from the cruel alternative, which he pathetically laments, of destroying or of being himself destroyed; and the seasonable death of Constantius delivered the Roman empire from the calamities of civil war. The approach of winter could not detain the monarch at Antioch, and his favourites durst not oppose his impatient desire of revenge. A slight fever, which was perhaps occasioned by the agitation of his spirits, was increased by the fatigues of the journey; and Constantius was obliged to halt at the little town of Mopsucrene, twelve miles beyond Tarsus, where he expired after a short illness in the forty-fifth year of his age and the twenty-fourth of his reign. His genuine character, which was composed of pride and weakness, of superstition and cruelty, has been fully displayed in the preceding narrative of civil and ecclesiastical events. The long abuse of power rendered him a considerable object in the eyes of his contemporaries; but as personal merit can alone deserve the notice of posterity, the last of the sons of Constantine may be dismissed from the world with the remark that he inherited the defects without the abilities of his father.

Before Constantius expired, he is said to have named Julian for his successor; nor does it seem improbable that his anxious concern for the fate of a young and tender wife, whom he left with child, may have prevailed in his last moments over the harsher passions of hatred and revenge. Eusebius and his guilty associates made a faint attempt to prolong the reign of the eunuchs by the election of another emperor; but their intrigues were rejected with disdain by an army which now abhorred the thought of civil discord, and two officers of rank were instantly despatched to assure Julian that every sword in the empire would be drawn for his service. The military designs of that prince, who had formed three different attacks against Thrace, were prevented by this fortunate event. Without shedding the blood of his fellow-citizens, he escaped the dangers of a doubtful conflict and acquired the advantages of a complete victory. Impatient to visit the place of his birth and the new capital of the empire, he advanced from Naissus through the mountains of Hæmus and the cities of

Thrace. When he reached Heraclea, at the distance of sixty miles, all Constantinople was poured forth to receive him; and he made his triumphal entry amidst the dutiful acclamations of the soldiers, the people, and the senate. An innumerable multitude pressed around him with eager respect, and were perhaps disappointed when they beheld the small stature and simple garb of a hero whose inexperienced youth had vanquished the barbarians of Germany, and who had now traversed in a successful career the whole continent of Europe, from the shores of the Atlantic to those of the Bosphorus.

A few days afterwards, when the remains of the deceased emperor were landed in the harbour, the subjects of Julian applauded the real or affected humanity of their sovereign. On foot, without his diadem, and clothed in a mourning habit, he accompanied the funeral as far as the church of the Holy Apostles, where the body was deposited; and if these marks of respect may be interpreted as a selfish tribute to the birth and dignity of his Imperial kinsman, the tears of Julian professed to the world that he had forgot the injuries and remembered only the obligations which he had received from Constantius. As soon as the legions of Aquileia were assured of the death of the emperor they opened the gates of the city, and by the sacrifice of their guilty leaders obtained an easy pardon from the prudence or lenity of Julian, who in the thirty-second year of his age acquired the undisputed possession of the Roman empire.

Philosophy had instructed Julian to compare the advantages of action and retirement; but the elevation of his birth and the accidents of his life never allowed him the freedom of choice. He might perhaps sincerely have preferred the groves of the Academy and the society of Athens; but he was constrained, at first by the will and afterwards by the injustice of Constantius, to expose his person and fame to the dangers of Imperial greatness, and to make himself accountable to the world and to posterity for the happiness of millions. Julian recollected with terror the observation of his master Plato that the government of our flocks and herds is always committed to beings of a superior species and that the conduct of nations requires and deserves the celestial powers of the Gods or of the Genii. From this principle he justly concluded that the man who presumes to reign should aspire to the perfection of the divine nature; that he should purify his soul from her mortal and terrestrial part; that he should extinguish his appetites, enlighten his understanding, regulate his passions, and subdue the wild beast which, according to the lively metaphor of Aristotle, seldom fails to ascend the throne of a despot.

The throne of Julian, which the death of Constantius fixed on an independent basis, was the seat of reason, of virtue, and perhaps of vanity. He despised the honours, renounced the pleasures, and discharged with incessant diligence the duties of his exalted station; and there were few among his subjects who would have consented to relieve him from the weight of the diadem had they been obliged to submit their time and their actions to the rigorous laws which their philosophic emperor imposed on himself. One of his most intimate friends, who had often shared the frugal simplicity of his table, has remarked that his light and sparing diet (which was usually of the vegetable kind) left his mind and body always free and active for the various and important business of an author, a pontiff, a magistrate, a general, and a prince. In one and the same day he gave audience to several ambassadors and wrote or dictated a great number of letters to his generals, his civil magistrates, his private friends, and the different cities of his dominions. He listened to the memorials which had been received, considered the subject of the petitions, and signified his intentions more rapidly than they could be taken in shorthand by the diligence of his secretaries. He possessed such flexibility of thought and such firmness of attention that he could employ his hand to write, his ear to listen, and his voice to dictate, and pursue at once three several trains of ideas without hesitation and without error.

While his ministers reposed, the prince flew with agility from one labour to another, and after a hasty dinner retired into his library till the public business which he had appointed for the evening summoned him to interrupt the prosecution of his studies. The supper of the emperor was still less substantial than the former meal; his sleep was never clouded by the fumes of indigestion; and except in the short interval of a marriage which was the effect of policy rather than love, the chaste Julian never shared his bed with a female companion. He was soon awakened by the entrance of fresh secretaries, who had slept the preceding day; and his servants were obliged to wait alternately, while their indefatigable master allowed himself scarcely any other refreshment than the change of occupations.

The predecessors of Julian, his uncle, his brother, and his cousin, indulged their puerile taste for the games of the Circus under the specious pretence of complying with the inclinations of the people; and they frequently remained the greatest part of the day as idle spectators and as a part of the splendid spectacle, till the ordinary round of twenty-four races was completely finished. On solemn festivals, Julian, who felt and professed an unfashionable dislike to these frivolous amusements, condescended to appear in the Circus; and after bestowing a careless glance on five or six of the races, he hastily withdrew with the impatience of a philosopher who considered every moment as lost that was not devoted to the advantage of the public or the improvement of his own mind. By this avarice of time he seemed to protract the short duration of his reign; and if the dates were less securely ascertained, we should refuse to believe that only sixteen months elapsed between the death of Constantius and the departure of his successor for the Persian war. The actions of Julian can only be preserved by the care of the historian; but the portion of his voluminous writings which is still extant remains as a monument of the application as well as of the genius of the emperor. The Misopogon, the Cæsars, several of his orations, and his elaborate work against the Christian religion were composed in the long nights of the two winters, the former of which he passed at Constantinople and the latter at Antioch.[2]

The generality of princes, if they were stripped of their purple and cast naked into the world, would immediately sink to the lowest rank of society, without a hope of emerging from their obscurity. But the personal merit of Julian was in some measure independent of his fortune. Whatever had been his choice of life, by the force of intrepid courage, lively wit, and intense application he would have obtained, or at least he would have deserved, the highest honours of his profession; and Julian might have raised himself to the rank of minister

---

2. *Editor's note:* The reform of the Imperial court, described in detail in the original, was also attempted by Julian, who carried his affectation of simplicity so far as to take pride in "the length of his nails and the inky blackness of his hands," as well as a "shaggy and *populous* beard." He dismissed an army of Imperial servants and slaves, sought to restore the independence and strength of the civil magistrates, and often assumed the character of orator and judge, addressing the senate or hearing cases from the bench.

or general of the state in which he was born a private
citizen. If the jealous caprice of power had disappointed
his expectations, if he had prudently declined the paths
of greatness, the employment of the same talents in
studious solitude would have placed beyond the reach
of kings his present happiness and his immortal fame.
When we inspect with minute or perhaps malevolent
attention the portrait of Julian, something seems wanting
to the grace and perfection of the whole figure. His
genius was less powerful and sublime than that of Cæsar, nor did he possess the consummate prudence of
Augustus. The virtues of Trajan appear more steady and
natural, and the philosophy of Marcus is more simple
and consistent. Yet Julian sustained adversity with firmness and prosperity with moderation. After an interval of
one hundred and twenty years from the death of Alexander Severus, the Romans beheld an emperor who
made no distinction between his duties and his pleasures, who laboured to relieve the distress and to revive
the spirit of his subjects, and who endeavoured always
to connect authority with merit and happiness with
virtue. Even faction, and religious faction, was constrained to acknowledge the superiority of his genius in
peace as well as in war, and to confess with a sigh that
the apostate Julian was a lover of his country and that
he deserved the empire of the world.

*How Julian acquired the surname of "the Apostate,"
and his conflict with the Christians, are considered in
the next section of the original. Julian's "devout and
sincere attachment for the gods of Athens and Rome"
appears to have come as a reaction to the strict Christian
upbringing provided by his guardian-gaoler Constantius,
who gave him "the education not of a hero but of a
saint." But years of devout observations could not bring*

his active curiosity to "yield the passive and unresist-
ing obedience which was required . . . by the haughty
ministers of the church"; the rebukes he received merely
"provoked his impatient genius to disclaim the authority
of his ecclesiastical guides"; and his familiarity with the
Arian controversy further convinced him that the con-
testants "neither understood nor believed the religion for
which they so fiercely contended." His final conversion
to paganism came at about the age of twenty, during his
studies in Athens, though he dissimulated his beliefs for
over ten years.

And his conversion was thorough-going. Julian sincerely believed that the gods and goddesses spoke to
him constantly, touched his hand or hair during sleep,
warned him of danger, and guided his whole life—
superstitions which (remarks Gibbon angrily) "would almost degrade the emperor to the level of an Egyptian
monk." After he acquired the Imperial power, he filled
the palace and its gardens with pagan shrines and temples, gave regular sacrifices to the appropriate deities,
and himself performed the most menial and even dis-
gusting of the ceremonial acts. So great was the sacri-
ficial slaughter of oxen that, according to a popular jest,
if Julian should return victorious from the Persian war
"the breed of horned cattle must infallibly be extinguished."

Julian's conflict with the early church was not so
much a lack of tolerance as a question of whom was he
tolerant against. Having sensibly concluded that "neither
fire nor steel can eradicate the erroneous opinions of the
mind," Julian in one of his first edicts promised religious
freedom to all the inhabitants of the Roman world, recalled all the Ch istians of various sects who had been
exiled by Constantius, and ordered the reopening of all
closed pagan shrines. But his enthusiasm for his new-

*found religion led him consistently to favour the pagan
believers, both those who had maintained their beliefs
as well as "Christians who prudently embraced the religion of their sovereign." He made special efforts to
convert the legions, by such devices as requiring each
soldier to cast incense upon an altar before he received
his share of a general donative. There is even some evidence, though of doubtful validity, that he attempted
unsuccessfully the rebuilding of a great Jewish temple
in Jerusalem "which might eclipse the splendour of the
church of the Resurrection on the adjacent hill of Calvary."*

*One of Julian's weapons against the church was the
sarcastic wit which he used in his edicts and other writings against "the Galilæans," as he was fond of calling
the Christians, but there were other and more formidable discriminations. The clerical honours and immunities
were withdrawn; it was forbidden to bequeath money
to the church; Christians were excluded from the study
of grammar and rhetoric; they were gradually removed
from high employment in the army and civil government; and they were obliged to make restitution for the
pagan temples which they had destroyed—which often
meant destroying churches built on the same spot. Such
measures inevitably involved occasional violence against
prominent Christian leaders, which, as Gibbon notes,
was more likely to be carried out by provincial ministers
who "consulted the wishes rather than the commands of
their sovereign."*

*One cleric who was rendered famous by his death at
pagan hands during Julian's reign was George of Cappadocia, who had amassed a great fortune as a purveyor
of bacon to the army before he discovered a sudden attachment to the Arian cause. When Constantius drove
the great Athanasius from his ecclesiastical throne in*

Alexandria, George of Cappadocia was installed as his Arian successor, "qualified by nature and education to exercise the arts of persecution." He "oppressed with impartial hand" all the Alexandrian factions, acquired monopolies of such trades as salt, paper, and funerals, and often pillaged the rich pagan temples of the city. When Julian succeeded to the Imperial throne, George of Cappadocia was first thrown in prison and later done to death by an outraged mob of pagans. But after his death he was adopted by orthodox and Arian Christians alike as a saint, a martyr, and a hero; his fame was spread throughout Europe during the period of the Crusades; and it was he who was eventually transformed, over the working of centuries, into the shining figure of St. George of England.

The death of George of Cappadocia resulted in the return of Athanasius, who was soon exiled by Julian as he had been by Constantius before him. Athanasius once again vanished into the monasteries of the desert, and Julian also learned that all the resources of the empire were insufficient to effect his capture, in the face of resolute opposition from the powerful and growing church.

Had Julian persisted in his effort to re-establish paganism as the dominant Roman religion, he would surely have involved the empire in the horrors of a religious civil war. That dreadful eventuality was avoided by Julian's early death on the battlefield during a difficult retreat from a Persian campaign, which he had directed with great vigour and initial success. The chiefs of the harassed army, beset on all sides by the Persians, chose Jovian as their new emperor, who immediately negotiated a peace treaty that was perhaps necessary but certainly ingnominious. Under it the Persians regained the five Roman provinces beyond the Tigris as well as the

*impregnable city of Nisibis. But despite the public out-
cry at the treaty Jovian could be sure of powerful Christian support, for he was a devout believer who immediately re-established Christianity as the official religion.
That and the Persian treaty were the only monuments to
the brief reign of Jovian, who died an apparently natural
death a few months after his accession.*

Chapter XII

(A.D. 363-384)

Election of Valentinian, who associates his brother Valens and makes the final division of the eastern and western empires – Revolt of Procopius – Civil and ecclesiastical administration – Germany – Britain – Africa – The East – The Danube – Death of Valentinian – His two sons, Gratian and Valentinian II, succeed to the western empire[1]

AFTER the death of Jovian the throne of the Roman world remained ten days without a master. The ministers and generals still continued to meet in council, to exercise their respective functions, to maintain the public order, and peaceably to conduct the army to the city of Nice in Bithynia, which was chosen for the place of the election. In a solemn assembly of the civil and military powers of the empire, the diadem was again unanimously offered to the præfect Sallust. He enjoyed the glory of a second refusal; and when the virtues of the father were alleged in favour of the son, the præfect, with the firmness of a disinterested patriot, declared to the electors that the feeble age of the one and the inexperienced youth of the other were equally incapable of the laborious duties of government. Several candidates were proposed, and, after weighing the objections of character or situation, they were successively rejected; but as soon as the name of Valentinian was pronounced, the merit of that officer united the suffrages of the whole

1. *Editor's note:* Chapter XXV of the original.

assembly and obtained the sincere approbation of Sallust himself.

Valentinian was the son of Count Gratian, a native of Cibalis in Pannonia, who from an obscure condition had raised himself by matchless strength and dexterity to the military commands of Africa and Britain, from which he retired with an ample fortune and suspicious integrity. The rank and services of Gratian contributed, however, to smooth the first steps of the promotion of his son and afforded him an early opportunity of displaying those solid and useful qualifications which raised his character above the ordinary level of his fellow-soldiers. The person of Valentinian was tall, graceful, and majestic. His manly countenance, deeply marked with the impression of sense and spirit, inspired his friends with awe and his enemies with fear; and, to second the efforts of his undaunted courage, the son of Gratian had inherited the advantages of a strong and healthy constitution. By the habits of chasity and temperance, which restrain the appetites and invigorate the faculties, Valentinian preserved his own and the public esteem. The avocations of a military life had diverted his youth from the elegant pursuits of literature; he was ignorant of the Greek language and the arts of rhetoric; but, as the mind of the orator was never disconcerted by timid perplexity, he was able, as often as the occasion prompted him, to deliver his decided sentiments with bold and ready elocution. The laws of martial discipline were the only laws that he had studied, and he was soon distinguished by the laborious diligence and inflexible severity with which he discharged and enforced the duties of the camp.

In the time of Julian he provoked the danger of disgrace by the contempt which he publicly expressed for the reigning religion; and it should seem, from his subsequent conduct, that the indiscreet and unseasonable freedom of Valentinian was the effect of military spirit rather than of Christian zeal. He was pardoned, however, and still employed by a prince who esteemed his merit, and in the various events of the Persian war he improved the reputation which he had already acquired on the banks of the Rhine. The celerity and success with which he executed an important commission recommended him to the favour of Jovian and to the honourable command of the second *school,* or company, of Targeteers of the domestic guards. In the march from Antioch, he had reached his quarters at Ancyra when he was unexpectedly summoned, without guilt and without intrigue, to assume, in the forty-third year of his age, the absolute government of the Roman empire.

The invitation of the ministers and generals at Nice was of little moment unless it was confirmed by the voice of the army. The aged Sallust, who had long observed the irregular fluctuations of popular assemblies, proposed under pain of death that none of those persons whose rank in the service might excite a party in their favour should appear in public on the day of the inauguration. Yet such was the prevalence of ancient superstition that a whole day was voluntarily added to this dangerous interval because it happened to be the intercalation of the Bissextile.[2] At length, when the hour was supposed to be propitious, Valentinian showed himself from a lofty tribunal; the judicious choice was applauded, and the new prince was solemnly invested with the diadem and the purple amidst the acclamations of the troops, who were disposed in martial order round the tribunal. But when he stretched forth his hand to

2. *Editor's note:* That is, the repetition of the sixth day before the Calends of March, which in the Roman calendar was deemed to occur twice in a leap year.

address the armed multitude, a busy whisper was accidentally started in the ranks and insensibly swelled into a loud and imperious clamour that he should name without delay a colleague in the empire.

The intrepid calmness of Valentinian obtained silence and commanded respect, and he thus addressed the assembly: "A few minutes since it was in *your* power, fellow-soldiers, to have left me in the obscurity of a private station. Judging from the testimony of my past life that I deserved to reign, you have placed me on the throne. It is now *my* duty to consult the safety and interest of the public. The weight of the universe is undoubtedly too great for the hands of a feeble mortal. I am conscious of the limits of my abilities and the uncertainty of my life, and, far from declining, I am anxious to solicit, the assistance of a worthy colleague. But, where discord may be fatal, the choice of a faithful friend requires mature and serious deliberation. That deliberation shall be *my* care. Let *your* conduct be dutiful and consistent. Retire to your quarters; refresh your minds and bodies; and expect the accustomed donative on the accession of a new emperor." The astonished troops, with a mixture of pride, of satisfaction, and of terror, confessed the voice of their master. Their angry clamours subsided into silent reverence, and Valentinian, encompassed with the eagles of the legions and the various banners of the cavalry and infantry, was conducted in warlike pomp to the palace of Nice.

As he was sensible, however, of the importance of preventing some rash declaration of the soldiers, he consulted the assembly of the chiefs, and their real sentiments were concisely expressed by the generous freedom of Dagalaiphus. "Most excellent prince," said that officer, "if you consider only your family, you have a brother; if you love the republic, look round for the most deserving of the Romans." The emperor, who suppressed his displeasure without altering his intention, slowly proceeded from Nice to Nicomedia and Constantinople. In one of the suburbs of that capital, thirty days after his own elevation, he bestowed the title of Augustus on his brother Valens: and as the boldest patriots were convinced that their opposition, without being serviceable to their country, would be fatal to themselves, the declaration of his absolute will was received with silent submission.

Valens was now in the thirty-sixth year of his age, but his abilities had never been exercised in any employment, military or civil, and his character had not inspired the world with any sanguine expectations. He possessed, however, one quality which recommended him to Valentinian and preserved the domestic peace of the empire: a devout and grateful attachment to his benefactor, whose superiority of genius as well as of authority Valens humbly and cheerfully acknowledged in every action of his life.

Before Valentinian divided the provinces, he reformed the administration of the empire. All ranks of subjects who had been injured or oppressed under the reign of Julian were invited to support their public accusations. The silence of mankind attested the spotless integrity of the præfect Sallust, and his own pressing solicitations that he might be permitted to retire from the business of the state were rejected by Valentinian with the most honourable expressions of friendship and esteem. But among the favourites of the late emperor there were many who had abused his credulity or superstition and who could no longer hope to be protected either by favour or justice. The greater part of the ministers of the palace and the governors of the provinces were removed from their respective stations; yet the eminent merit of some officers was distinguished from the obnoxious crowd; and notwithstanding the opposite clamours of zeal and resentment, the whole proceedings of this delicate inquiry appear to have been conducted with a reasonable share of wisdom and moderation. The festivity of a new reign received a short and suspicious interruption from the sudden illness of the two princes, but as soon as their health was restored they left Constantinople in the beginning of the spring.

In the castle or palace of Mediana, only three miles from Naissus, they executed the solemn and final division of the Roman empire. Valentinian bestowed on his brother the rich præfecture of the East, from the Lower Danube to the confines of Persia; whilst he reserved for his immediate government the warlike præfectures of Illyricum, Italy, and Gaul, from the extremity of Greece to the Caledonian rampart and from the rampart of Caledonia to the foot of Mount Atlas. The provincial administration remained on its former basis, but a double supply of generals and magistrates was required for two councils and two courts; the division was made with a just regard to their peculiar merit and situation, and seven master generals were soon created either of the cavalry or infantry. When this important business had been amicably transacted, Valentinian and Valens embraced for the last time. The emperor of the West established his temporary residence at Milan, and the emperor of the East returned to Constantinople to assume the dominion of fifty provinces of whose language he was totally ignorant.

At this point in the original, Gibbon describes the revolt of one of Julian's generals named Procopius, who was driven into exile by the suspicions of Valens. Procopius attempted, with some initial success, to over-

throw Valens. But that "timid monarch was saved from disgrace and ruin by the firmness of his ministers," and Procopius "suffered the ordinary fate of an unsuccessful usurper."

Such indeed are the common and natural fruits of despotism and rebellion. But the inquisition into the crime of magic, which under the reign of the two brothers was so rigorously prosecuted both at Rome and Antioch, was interpreted as the fatal symptom either of the displeasure of Heaven or of the depravity of mankind.[3] Let us not hesitate to indulge a liberal pride that, in the present age, the enlightened part of Europe has abolished a cruel and odious prejudice which reigned in every climate of the globe and adhered to every system of religious opinions. The nations and the sects of the Roman world admitted, with equal credulity and similar abhorrence, the reality of that infernal art which was able to control the eternal order of the planets and the voluntary operations of the human mind. They dreaded the mysterious power of spells and incantations, of potent herbs and execrable rites, which could extinguish or recall life, inflame the passions of the soul, blast the works of creation, and extort from the reluctant demons the secrets of futurity. They believed, with the wildest inconsistency, that this preternatural dominion of the air, of earth, and of hell was exercised, from the vilest motives of malice or gain, by some wrinkled hags

3. *Editor's note:* "The persecution against philosophers and their libraries was carried on with such fury that from this time (A.D. 374) the names of the Gentile philosophers became almost extinct," said Dean Milman, one of Gibbon's editors. "Besides vast heaps of manuscripts publicly destroyed throughout the East, men of learning burned their whole libraries lest some fatal volume expose them to the malice of the informers and the extreme penalty of the law."

and itinerant sorcerers who passed their obscure lives in penury and contempt.

The arts of magic were equally condemned by the public opinion and by the laws of Rome; but, as they tended to gratify the most imperious passions of the heart of man, they were continually proscribed and continually practised. An imaginary cause is capable of producing the most serious and mischievous effects. The dark predictions of the death of an emperor or the success of a conspiracy were calculated only to stimulate the hopes of ambition and to dissolve the ties of fidelity, and the intentional guilt of magic was aggravated by the actual crimes of treason and sacrilege. Such vain terrors disturbed the peace of society and the happiness of individuals, and the harmless flame which insensibly melted a waxen image might derive a powerful and pernicious energy from the affrighted fancy of the person whom it was maliciously designed to represent. From the infusion of those herbs which were supposed to possess a supernatural influence it was an easy step to the use of more substantial poison, and the folly of mankind sometimes became the instrument and the mask of the most atrocious crimes.

As soon as the zeal of informers was encouraged by the ministers of Valens and Valentinian, they could not refuse to listen to another charge too frequently mingled in the scenes of domestic guilt, a charge of a softer and less malignant nature, for which the pious though excessive rigour of Constantine had recently decreed the punishment of death. This deadly and incoherent mixture of treason and magic, of poison and adultery, afforded infinite gradations of guilt and innocence, of excuse and aggravation, which in these proceedings appear to have been confounded by the angry or corrupt passions of the judges. They easily discovered that the

degree of their industry and discernment was estimated
by the Imperial court according to the number of executions that were furnished from their respective tribunals.
It was not without extreme reluctance that they pronounced a sentence of acquittal, but they eagerly admitted such evidence as was stained with perjury or
procured by torture to prove the most improbable
charges against the most respectable characters. The
progress of the inquiry continually opened new subjects
of criminal prosecution; the audacious informer whose
falsehood was detected retired with impunity; but the
wretched victim who discovered his real or pretended
accomplices was seldom permitted to receive the price
of his infamy. From the extremity of Italy and Asia the
young and the aged were dragged in chains to the
tribunals of Rome and Antioch. Senators, matrons, and
philosophers expired in ignominious and cruel tortures.
The soldiers who were appointed to guard the prisons
declared, with a murmur of pity and indignation, that
their numbers were insufficient to oppose the flight or
resistance of the multitude of captives. The wealthiest
families were ruined by fines and confiscations; the most
innocent citizens trembled for their safety; and we may
form some notion of the magnitude of the evil from
the extravagant assertion of an ancient writer that in the
obnoxious provinces the prisoners, the exiles, and the
fugitives formed the greatest part of the inhabitants.

When Tacitus describes the deaths of the innocent
and illustrious Romans who were sacrificed to the cruelty of the first Cæsars, the art of the historian or the
merit of the sufferers excites in our breasts the most
lively sensations of terror, of admiration, and of pity.
The coarse and undistinguishing pencil of Ammianus
has delineated his bloody figures with tedious and dis-
gusting accuracy. But as our attention is no longer en-

gaged by the contrast of freedom and servitude, of recent greatness and of actual misery, we should turn with horror from the frequent executions which disgraced, both at Rome and Antioch, the reign of the two brothers. Valens was of a timid, and Valentinian of a choleric, disposition. An anxious regard to his personal safety was the ruling principle of the administration of Valens. In the condition of a subject he had kissed with trembling awe the hand of the oppressor; and when he ascended the throne he reasonably expected that the same fears which had subdued his own mind would secure the patient submission of his people. The favourites of Valens obtained, by the privilege of rapine and confiscation, the wealth which his economy would have refused. They urged with persuasive eloquence that, in all cases of treason, suspicion is equivalent to proof; that the power supposes the intention of mischief; that the intention is not less criminal than the act; and that a subject no longer deserves to live if his life may threaten the safety or disturb the repose of his sovereign.

The judgment of Valentinian was sometimes deceived and his confidence abused; but he would have silenced the informers with a contemptuous smile had they presumed to alarm his fortitude by the sound of danger. They praised his inflexible love of justice; and in the pursuit of justice the emperor was easily tempted to consider clemency as a weakness and passion as a virtue. As long as he wrestled with his equals in the bold competition of an active and ambitious life, Valentinian was seldom injured and never insulted with impunity; if his prudence was arraigned, his spirit was applauded; and the proudest and most powerful generals were apprehensive of provoking the resentment of a fearless soldier.

After he became master of the world he unfortunately forgot that, where no resistance can be made, no cour-

age can be exerted; and instead of consulting the
dictates of reason and magnanimity, he indulged the
furious emotions of his temper at a time when they were
disgraceful to himself and fatal to the defenceless objects of his displeasure. In the government of his household or of his empire slight or even imaginary offences
—a hasty word, a casual omission, an involuntary delay
—were chastised by a sentence of immediate death. The
expressions which issued the most readily from the
mouth of the emperor of the West were, "Strike off his
head," "Burn him alive," "Let him be beaten with clubs
till he expires"; and his most favoured ministers soon
understood that by a rash attempt to dispute or suspend
the execution of his sanguinary commands, they might
involve themselves in the guilt and punishment of disobedience.

The repeated gratification of this savage justice hard-
ened the mind of Valentinian against pity and remorse;
and the sallies of passion were confirmed by the habits
of cruelty. He could behold with calm satisfaction the
convulsive agonies of torture and death; he reserved his
friendship for those faithful servants whose temper was
the most congenial to his own. The merit of Maximin,
who had slaughtered the noblest families. of Rome, was
rewarded with the royal approbation and the præfecture
of Gaul. Two fierce and enormous bears, distinguished
by the appellations of *Innocence* and *Mica Aurea,* could
alone deserve to share the favour of Maximin. The cages
of those trusty guards were always placed near the bedchamber of Valentinian, who frequently amused his eyes
with the grateful spectacle of seeing them tear and
devour the bleeding limbs of the malefactors who were
abandoned to their rage. Their diet and exercises were
carefully inspected by the Roman emperor; and when
Innocence had earned her discharge, by a long course

of meritorious service, the faithful animal was again restored to the freedom of her native woods.

But in the calmer moments of reflection, when the mind of Valens was not agitated by fear or that of Valentinian by rage, the tyrant resumed the sentiments or at least the conduct of the father of his country. The dispassionate judgment of the western emperor could clearly perceive and accurately pursue his own and the public interest; and the sovereign of the East, who imitated with equal docility the various examples which he received from his elder brother, was sometimes guided by the wisdom and virtue of the præfect Sallust. Both princes invariably retained in the purple the chaste and temperate simplicity which had adorned their private life; and under their reign the pleasures of the court never cost the people a blush or a sigh. They gradually reformed many of the abuses of the times of Constantius, judiciously adopted and improved the designs of Julian and his successor, and displayed a style and spirit of legislation which might inspire posterity with the most favourable opinion of their character and government. It is not from the master of *Innocence* that we should expect the tender regard for the welfare of his subjects which prompted Valentinian to condemn the exposition of new-born infants, and to establish fourteen skilful physicians, with stipends and privileges, in the fourteen quarters of Rome.

The good sense of an illiterate soldier founded an useful and liberal institution for the education of youth and the support of declining science. It was his intention that the arts of rhetoric and grammar should be taught, in the Greek and Latin languages, in the metropolis of every province; and as the size and dignity of the school was usually proportioned to the importance of the city, the academies of Rome and Constantinople claimed a just and singular pre-eminence. The fragments of the literary edicts of Valentinian imperfectly represent the school of Constantinople, which was gradually improved by subsequent regulations. That school consisted of thirty-one professors in different branches of learning: one philosopher and two lawyers; five sophists and ten grammarians for the Greek, and three orators and ten grammarians for the Latin, tongue; besides seven scribes or, as they were then styled, antiquarians, whose laborious pens supplied the public library with fair and correct copies of the classic writers.

The rule of conduct which was prescribed to the students is the more curious as it affords the first outlines of the form and discipline of a modern university. It was required that they should bring proper certificates from the magistrates of their native province. Their names, professions, and places of abode were regularly entered in a public register. The studious youth were severely prohibited from wasting their time in feasts or in the theatre, and the term of their education was limited to the age of twenty. The præfect of the city was empowered to chastise the idle and refractory by stripes or expulsion; and he was directed to make an annual report to the master of the offices that the knowledge and abilities of the scholars might be usefully applied to the public service.

The institutions of Valentinian contributed to secure the benefits of peace and plenty; and the cities were guarded by the establishment of the *Defensors*, freely elected as the tribunes and advocates of the people, to support their rights and to expose their grievances before the tribunals of the civil magistrates, or even at the foot of the Imperial throne. The finances were diligently administered by two princes who had been so long accustomed to the rigid economy of a private fortune;

but in the receipt and application of the revenue a discerning eye might observe some difference between the government of the East and of the West. Valens was persuaded that royal liberality can be supplied only by public oppression, and his ambition never aspired to secure, by their actual distress, the future strength and prosperity of his people. Instead of increasing the weight of taxes, which in the space of forty years had been gradually doubled, he reduced in the first years of his reign one-fourth of the tribute of the East. Valentinian appears to have been less attentive and less anxious to relieve the burthens of his people. He might reform the abuses of the fiscal administration; but he exacted without scruple a very large share of the private property, as he was convinced that the revenues which supported the luxury of individuals would be much more advantageously employed for the defence and improvement of the state. The subjects of the East, who enjoyed the present benefit, applauded the indulgence of their prince. The solid but less splendid merit of Valentinian was felt and acknowledged by the subsequent generation.

But the most honourable circumstance of the character of Valentinian is the firm and temperate impartiality which he uniformly preserved in an age of religious contention. His strong sense, unenlightened but uncorrupted by study, declined with respectful indifference the subtle questions of theological debate. The government of the *Earth* claimed his vigilance and satisfied his ambition; and while he remembered that he was the disciple of the church, he never forgot that he was the sovereign of the clergy. Under the reign of an apostate, he had signalized his zeal for the honour of Christianity; he allowed to his subjects the privilege which he had assumed for himself, and they might accept with grati-

tude and confidence the general toleration which was
granted by a prince addicted to passion but incapable
of fear or of disguise. The pagans, the Jews, and all the
various sects which acknowledged the divine authority
of Christ were protected by the laws from arbitrary
power or popular insult; nor was any mode of worship
prohibited by Valentinian, except those secret and criminal practices which abused the name of religion for the
dark purposes of vice and disorder.

The art of magic, as it was more cruelly punished,
was more strictly proscribed; out the emperor admitted
a formal distinction to protect the ancient methods of
divination, which were approved by the senate and exercised by the Tuscan haruspices. He had condemned,
with the consent of the most rational pagans, the licence
of nocturnal sacrifices; but he immediately admitted the
petition of Prætextatus, proconsul of Achaia, who represented that the life of the Greeks would become dreary
and comfortless if they were deprived of the invaluable
blessing of the Eleusinian mysteries. Philosophy alone
can boast (and perhaps it is no more than the boast of
philosophy) that her gentle hand is able to eradicate
from the human mind the latent and deadly principle of
fanaticism. But this truce of twelve years, which was
enforced by the wise and vigorous government of Valentinian, by suspending the repetition of mutual injuries
contributed to soften the manners and abate the prejudices of the religious factions.[4]

The strict regulations which have been framed by the
wisdom of modern legislators to restrain the wealth and

4. *Editor's note:* Unfortunately, Gibbon continues, Valens
showed no such enlightenment, and his reign in the East
was marked by continuous internecine warfare between the
Arians, whom he supported, and the orthodox.

avarice of the clergy may be originally deduced from the example of the emperor Valentinian. His edict addressed to Damasus, bishop of Rome, was publicly read in the churches of the city. He admonished the ecclesiastics and monks not to frequent the houses of widows and virgins, and menaced their disobedience with the animadversion of the civil judge. The director was no longer permitted to receive any gift, or legacy, or inheritance from the liberality of his spiritual daughter; every testament contrary to this edict was declared null and void, and the illegal donation was confiscated for the use of the treasury. By a subsequent regulation it should seem that the same provisions were extended to nuns and bishops, and that all persons of the ecclesiastical order were rendered incapable of receiving any testamentary gifts and strictly confined to the natural and legal rights of inheritance.

As the guardian of domestic happiness and virtue, Valentinian applied this severe remedy to the growing evil. In the capital of the empire the females of noble and opulent houses possessed a very ample share of independent property; and many of those devout females had embraced the doctrines of Christianity not only with the cold assent of the understanding but with the warmth of affection and perhaps with the eagerness of fashion. They sacrificed the pleasures of dress and luxury and renounced, for the praise of chastity, the soft endearments of conjugal society. Some ecclesiastic of real or apparent sanctity was chosen to direct their timorous conscience and to amuse the vacant tenderness of their heart; and the unbounded confidence which they hastily bestowed was often abused by knaves and enthusiasts, who hastened from the extremities of the East to enjoy, on a splendid theatre, the privileges of the monastic profession. By their contempt of the world, they insensibly acquired its most desirable advantages: the lively attachment, perhaps, of a young and beautiful woman, the delicate plenty of an opulent household, and the respectful homage of the slaves, the freedmen, and the clients of a senatorial family. The immense fortunes of the Roman ladies were gradually consumed in lavish alms and expensive pilgrimages; and the artful monk, who had assigned himself the first or possibly the sole place in the testament of his spiritual daughter, still presumed to declare, with the smooth face of hypocrisy, that *he* was only the instrument of charity and the steward of the poor.

The lucrative but disgraceful trade, which was exercised by the clergy to defraud the expectations of the natural heirs, had provoked the indignation of a superstitious age; and two of the most respectable of the Latin fathers very honestly confess that the ignominious edict of Valentinian was just and necessary, and that the Christian priests had deserved to lose a privilege which was still enjoyed by comedians, charioteers, and the ministers of idols. But the wisdom and authority of the legislator are seldom victorious in a contest with the vigilant dexterity of private interest; and Jerom or Ambrose might patiently acquiesce in the justice of an ineffectual or salutary law. If the ecclesiastics were checked in the pursuit of personal emolument, they would exert a more laudable industry to increase the wealth of the church, and dignify their covetousness with the specious names of piety and patriotism.

Damasus, bishop of Rome, who was constrained to stigmatize the avarice of his clergy by the publication of the law of Valentinian, had the good sense, or the good fortune, to engage in his service the zeal and abilities of the learned Jerom; and the grateful saint has celebrated the merit and purity of a very ambiguous character.[5] But the splendid vices of the church of Rome under the reign of Valentinian and Damasus have been curiously observed by the historian Ammianus, who delivers his impartial sense in these expressive words: "The præfecture of Juventius was accompanied with peace and plenty, but the tranquillity of his government was soon disturbed by a bloody sedition of the distracted people. The ardour of Damasus and Ursinus to seize the episcopal seat surpassed the ordinary measure of human ambition. They contended with the rage of party; the quarrel was maintained by the wounds and death of their followers; and the præfect, unable to resist or to appease the tumult, was constrained by superior violence to retire into the suburbs. Damasus prevailed: the well-disputed victory remained on the side of his faction; one hundred and thirty-seven dead bodies were found in the Basilica of Sicininus, where the Christians hold their religious assemblies; and it was long before the angry minds of the people resumed their accustomed tranquillity. When I consider the splendour of the capital, I am not astonished that so valuable a prize should inflame the desires of ambitious men and produce the fiercest and most obstinate contests. The successful candidate is secure that he will be enriched by the offerings of matrons; that, as soon as his dress is composed with becoming care and elegance, he may proceed in his chariot through the streets of Rome; and that the sumptuousness of the Imperial table will not equal the profuse and delicate entertainments provided by the taste and at the expense of the Roman pontiffs.

"How much more rationally (continues the honest pagan) would those pontiffs consult their true happiness

5. The enemies of Damasus styled him *Auriscalpius Matronarum*, the ladies' ear-scratcher.

if, instead of alleging the greatness of the city as an
excuse for their manners, they would imitate the exemplary life of some provincial bishops, whose temperance
and sobriety, whose mean apparel and downcast looks,
recommend their pure and modest virtue to the Deity
and his true worshippers!" The schism of Damasus and
Ursinus was extinguished by the exile of the latter, and
the wisdom of the præfect Prætextatus restored the
tranquillity of the city. Prætextatus was a philosophic
pagan, a man of learning, of taste, and politeness, who
disguised a reproach in the form of a jest when he assured Damasus that if he could obtain the bishopric of
Rome, he himself would immediately embrace the Christian religion.[6] This lively picture of the wealth and luxury of the popes in the fourth century becomes the more
curious as it represents the intermediate degree between
the humble poverty of the apostolic fisherman and the
royal state of a temporal prince whose dominions extend
from the confines of Naples to the banks of the Po.

When the suffrage of the generals and of the army
committed the sceptre of the Roman empire to the
hands of Valentinian, his reputation in arms, his military
skill and experience, and his rigid attachment to the
forms as well as spirit of ancient discipline were the
principal motives of their judicious choice. The eagerness of the troops, who pressed him to nominate his
colleague, was justified by the dangerous situation of
public affairs; and Valentinian himself was conscious
that the abilities of the most active mind were unequal
to the defence of the distant frontiers of an invaded
monarchy. As soon as the death of Julian had relieved
the barbarians from the terror of his name, the most

6. It is more than probable that Damasus would not have
purchased his conversion at such a price.

sanguine hopes of rapine and conquest excited the nations of the East, of the North, and of the South. Their
inroads were often vexatious and sometimes formidable; but during the twelve years of the reign of Valentinian his firmness and vigilance protected his own
dominions, and his powerful genius seemed to inspire
and direct the feeble counsels of his brother. Perhaps
the method of annals would more forcibly express the
urgent and divided cares of the two emperors; but the
attention of the reader, likewise, would be distracted by
a tedious and desultory narrative. A separate view of
the five great theatres of war—I. Germany; II. Britain;
III. Africa; IV. The East; and V. The Danube—will impress a more distinct image of the military state of the
empire under the reigns of Valentinian and Valens.

I. GERMANY. The ambassadors of the Alemanni had
been offended by the harsh and haughty behaviour of
Ursacius, master of the offices, who by an act of unseasonable parsimony had diminished the value as well as
the quantity of the presents to which they were entitled,
either from custom or treaty, on the accession of a new
emperor. They expressed, and they communicated to
their countrymen, their strong sense of the national
affront. The irascible minds of the chiefs were exasperated by the suspicion of contempt, and the martial
youth crowded to their standard. Before Valentinian
could pass the Alps, the villages of Gaul were in flames;
before his general Dagalaiphus could encounter the
Alemanni, they had secured the captives and the spoil
in the forests of Germany. In the beginning of the ensuing year the military force of the whole nation, in deep
and solid columns, broke through the barrier of the
Rhine during the severity of a northern winter. Two
Roman counts were defeated and mortally wounded;

and the standard of the Heruli and Batavians fell into the hands of the conquerors, who displayed with insulting shouts and menaces the trophy of their victory.

The standard was recovered, but the Batavians had not redeemed the shame of their disgrace and flight in the eyes of their severe judge. It was the opinion of Valentinian that his soldiers must learn to fear their commander before they could cease to fear the enemy. The troops were solemnly assembled, and the trembling Batavians were enclosed within the circle of the Imperial army. Valentinian then ascended his tribunal, and, as if he disdained to punish cowardice with death, he inflicted a stain of indelible ignominy on the officers whose misconduct and pusillanimity were found to be the first occasion of the defeat. The Batavians were degraded from their rank, stripped of their arms, and condemned to be sold for slaves to the highest bidder. At this tremendous sentence the troops fell prostrate on the ground, deprecated the indignation of their sovereign, and protested that if he would indulge them in another trial they would approve themselves not unworthy of the name of Romans and of his soldiers. Valentinian, with affected reluctance, yielded to their entreaties: the Batavians resumed their arms, and with their arms the invincible resolution of wiping away their disgrace in the blood of the Alemanni.

The principal command was declined by Dagalaiphus; and that experienced general, who had represented, perhaps with too much prudence, the extreme difficulties of the undertaking, had the mortification, before the end of the campaign, of seeing his rival Jovinus convert those difficulties into a decisive advantage over the scattered forces of the barbarians. At the head of a well-disciplined army of cavalry, infantry, and light troops, Jovinus advanced with cautious and rapid steps to Scarponna, in the territory of Metz, where he surprised a large division of the Alemanni before they had time to run to their arms, and flushed his soldiers with the confidence of an easy and bloodless victory.

Another division, or rather army, of the enemy, after the cruel and wanton devastation of the adjacent country, reposed themselves on the shady banks of the Moselle. Jovinus, who had viewed the ground with the eye of a general, made his silent approach through a deep and woody vale, till he could distinctly perceive the indolent security of the Germans. Some were bathing their huge limbs in the river; others were combing their long and flaxen hair; others again were swallowing large draughts of rich and delicious wine. On a sudden they heard the sound of the Roman trumpet; they saw the enemy in their camp. Astonishment produced disorder; disorder was followed by flight and dismay; and the confused multitude of the bravest warriors was pierced by the swords and javelins of the legionaries and auxiliaries.

The fugitives escaped to the third and most considerable camp in the Catalaunian plains, near Châlons in Champagne; the straggling detachments were hastily recalled to their standard; and the barbarian chiefs, alarmed and admonished by the fate of their companions, prepared to encounter in a decisive battle the victorious forces of the lieutenant of Valentinian. The bloody and obstinate conflict lasted a whole summer's day, with equal valour and with alternate success. The Romans at length prevailed, with the loss of about twelve hundred men. Six thousand of the Alemanni were slain, four thousand were wounded; and the brave Jovinus, after chasing the flying remnant of their host as far as the banks of the Rhine, returned to Paris to receive the applause of his sovereign and the ensigns of the consulship for the ensuing year.

The triumph of the Romans was indeed sullied by their treatment of the captive king, whom they hung on a gibbet, without the knowledge of their indignant general. This disgraceful act of cruelty, which might be imputed to the fury of the troops, was followed by the deliberate murder of Withicab, the son of Vadomair, a German prince of a weak and sickly constitution but of a daring and formidable spirit. The domestic assassin was instigated and protected by the Romans; and the violation of the laws of humanity and justice betrayed their secret apprehension of the weakness of the declining empire. The use of the dagger is seldom adopted in public councils as long as they retain any confidence in the power of the sword.[7]

II. BRITAIN. Six years after the death of Constantine the destructive inroads of the Scots and Picts required the presence of his youngest son, who reigned in the Western empire. Constans visited his British dominions; but we may form some estimate of the importance of his achievements by the language of panegyric, which celebrates only his triumph over the elements, or, in other words, the good fortune of a safe and easy passage from the port of Boulogne to the harbour of Sandwich. The calamities which the afflicted provincials continued to experience from foreign war and domestic tyranny were aggravated by the feeble and corrupt administration of

7. *Editor's note:* Gibbon elaborates, at this point in the original, by describing one of Valentinian's campaigns against the Alemanni, the chain of fortifications which he constructed along the whole length of the Rhine, and his diligence in setting the barbarians against one another. This period also brought the first appearance of the Saxons, who as sea pirates ravaged the European coast and far up the navigable streams.

the eunuchs of Constantius; and the transient relief which they might obtain from the virtues of Julian was soon lost by the absence and death of their benefactor. The sums of gold and silver which had been painfully collected or liberally transmitted for the payment of the troops were intercepted by the avarice of the commanders; discharges, or at least exemptions, from the military service were publicly sold; the distress of the soldiers, who were injuriously deprived of their legal and scanty subsistence, provoked them to frequent desertion; the nerves of discipline were relaxed; and the highways were infested with robbers.

The oppression of the good and the impunity of the wicked equally contributed to diffuse through the island a spirit of discontent and revolt; and every ambitious subject, every desperate exile, might entertain a reasonable hope of subverting the weak and distracted government of Britain. The hostile tribes of the North, who detested the pride and power of the King of the World, suspended their domestic feuds; and the barbarians of the land and sea, the Scots, the Picts, and the Saxons, spread themselves with rapid and irresistible fury from the wall of Antoninus to the shores of Kent.

Every production of art and nature, every object of conveniences or luxury, which they were incapable of creating by labour or procuring by trade, was accumulated in the rich and fruitful province of Britain. A philosopher may deplore the eternal discord of the human race, but he will confess that the desire of spoil is a more rational provocation than the vanity of conquest. From the age of Constantine to that of the Plantagenets this rapacious spirit continued to instigate the poor and hardy Caledonians; but the same people whose generous humanity seems to inspire the songs of Ossian was disgraced by a savage ignorance of the virtues of peace and of the laws of war. Their southern neighbours have felt, and perhaps exaggerated, the cruel depredations of the Scots and Picts; and a valiant tribe of Caledonia, the Attacotti, the enemies and afterwards the soldiers of Valentinian, are accused by an eye-witness of delighting in the taste of human flesh. When they hunted the woods for prey, it is said that they attacked the shepherd rather than his flock, and that they curiously selected the most delicate and brawny parts both of males and females, which they prepared for their horrid repasts. If in the neighbourhood of the commercial and literary town of Glasgow a race of cannibals has really existed, we may contemplate in the period of the Scottish history the opposite extremes of savage and civilized life. Such reflections tend to enlarge the circle of our ideas, and to encourage the pleasing hope that New Zealand may produce in some future age the Hume of the Southern Hemisphere.

Every messenger who escaped across the British channel conveyed the most melancholy and alarming tidings to the ears of Valentinian, and the emperor was soon informed that the two military commanders of the province had been surprised and cut off by the barbarians. Severus, count of the domestics, was hastily despatched and as suddenly recalled by the court of Treves. The representations of Jovinus served only to indicate the greatness of the evil; and after a long and serious consultation the defence, or rather the recovery, of Britain was entrusted to the abilities of the brave Theodosius.

The exploits of that general, the father of a line of emperors, have been celebrated with peculiar complacency by the writers of the age; but his real merit deserved their applause, and his nomination was received by the army and province as a sure presage of approaching victory. He seized the favourable moment of navi-

gation and securely landed the numerous and veteran
bands of the Heruli and Batavians, the Jovians and the
Victors. In his march from Sandwich to London, Theodosius defeated several parties of the barbarians, released a multitude of captives, and, after distributing to
his soldiers a small portion of the spoil, established the
fame of disinterested justice by the restitution of the remainder to the rightful proprietors. The citizens of London, who had almost despaired of their safety, threw
open their gates; and, as soon as Theodosius had obtained from the court of Treves the important aid of a
military lieutenant and a civil governor, he executed
with wisdom and vigour the laborious task of the deliverance of Britain. The vagrant soldiers were recalled to
their standard, an edict of amnesty dispelled the public
apprehensions, and his cheerful example alleviated the
rigour of martial discipline.

The scattered and desultory warfare of the barbarians, who infested the land and sea, deprived him of the
glory of a signal victory; but the prudent spirit and consummate art of the Roman general were displayed in the
operations of two campaigns which successively rescued
every part of the province from the hands of a cruel and
rapacious enemy. The splendour of the cities and the
security of the fortifications were diligently restored by
the paternal care of Theodosius, who with a strong hand
confined the trembling Caledonians to the northern
angle of the island and perpetuated, by the name and
settlement of the new province of *Valentia,* the glories
of the reign of Valentinian. The voice of poetry and
panegyric may add, perhaps with some degree of truth,
that the unknown regions of Thule were stained with the
blood of the Picts, that the oars of Theodosius dashed
the waves of the Hyperborean ocean, and that the distant Orkneys were the scene of his naval victory over

the Saxon pirates. He left the province with a fair as well as splendid reputation, and was immediately promoted to the rank of master general of the cavalry by a prince who could applaud without envy the merit of his servants. In the important station of the Upper Danube the conqueror of Britain checked and defeated the armies of the Alemanni before he was chosen to suppress the revolt of Africa.

III. AFRICA. The prince who refuses to be the judge instructs his people to consider him as the accomplice of his ministers. The military command of Africa had been long exercised by Count Romanus, and his abilities were not inadequate to his station; but as sordid interest was the sole motive of his conduct, he acted on most occasions as if he had been the enemy of the province and the friend of the barbarians of the desert. The three flourishing cities of Oea, Leptis, and Sabrata, which under the name of Tripoli had long constituted a federal union, were obliged for the first time to shut their gates against a hostile invasion; several of their most honourable citizens were surprised and massacred, the villages and even the suburbs were pillaged, and the vines and fruit-trees of that rich territory were extirpated by the malicious savages of Gætulia.

The unhappy provincials implored the protection of Romanus; but they soon found that their military governor was not less cruel and rapacious than the barbarians. As they were incapable of furnishing the four thousand camels and the exorbitant present which he required before he would march to the assistance of Tripoli, his demand was equivalent to a refusal, and he might justly be accused as the author of the public calamity. In the annual assembly of the three cities they nominated two deputies to lay at the feet of Valentinian the customary offering of a gold victory and to accompany this tribute of duty, rather than of gratitude, with their humble complaint that they were ruined by the enemy and betrayed by their governor.

If the severity of Valentinian had been rightly directed, it would have fallen on the guilty head of Romanus. But the count, long exercised in the arts of corruption, had despatched a swift and trusty messenger to secure the venal friendship of Remigius, master of the offices. The wisdom of the Imperial council was deceived by artifice, and their honest indignation was cooled by delay. At length, when the repetition of complaint had been justified by the repetition of public misfortunes, the notary Palladius was sent from the court of Treves to examine the state of Africa and the conduct of Romanus. The rigid impartiality of Palladius was easily disarmed; he was tempted to reserve for himself a part of the public treasure which he brought with him for the payment of the troops; and from the moment that he was conscious of his own guilt he could no longer refuse to attest the innocence and merit of the count. The charge of the Tripolitans was declared to be false and frivolous, and Palladius himself was sent back from Treves to Africa with a special commission to discover and prosecute the authors of this impious conspiracy against the representatives of the sovereign. His inquiries were managed with so much dexterity and success that he compelled the citizens of Leptis, who had sustained a recent siege of eight days, to contradict the truth of their own decrees and to censure the behaviour of their own deputies. A bloody sentence was pronounced without hesitation by the rash and headstrong cruelty of Valentinian. The president of Tripoli, who had presumed to pity the distress of the province, was publicly executed at Utica, four distinguished citizens were put to death as the accomplices of the imaginary fraud, and the tongues of two others were cut out by the express order of the emperor. Romanus, elated by impunity and irritated by resistance, was still continued in the military command, till the Africans were provoked by his avarice to join the rebellious standard of Firmus, the Moor.

His father Nabal was one of. the richest and most powerful of the Moorish princes who acknowledged the supremacy of Rome. But as he left, either by his wives or concubines, a very numerous posterity, the wealthy inheritance was eagerly disputed; and Zamma, one of his sons, was slain in a domestic quarrel by his brother Firmus. The implacable zeal with which Romanus prosecuted the legal revenge of this murder could be ascribed only to a motive of avarice or personal hatred; but on this occasion his claims were just, his influence was weighty, and Firmus clearly understood that he must either present his neck to the executioner, or appeal from the sentence of the Imperial consistory to his sword and to the people. He was received as the deliverer of his country; and as soon as it appeared that Romanus was formidable only to a submissive province, the tyrant of Africa became the object of universal contempt. The ruin of Cæsarea, which was plundered and burned by the licentious barbarians, convinced the refractory cities of the danger of resistance; the power of Firmus was established, at least in the provinces of Mauritania and Numidia, and it seemed to be his only doubt whether he should assume the diadem of a Moorish king or the purple of a Roman emperor.

But the imprudent and unhappy Africans soon discovered that in this rash insurrection they had not sufficiently consulted their own strength or the abilities of their leader. Before he could procure any certain intelligence that the emperor of the West had fixed the choice of a general or that a fleet of transports was collected at the mouth of the Rhone, he was suddenly informed that the great Theodosius with a small band of veterans had landed near Igilgilis, or Gigeri, on the African coast, and the timid usurper sank under the ascendant of virtue and military genius. Though Firmus possessed arms and treasures, his despair of victory immediately reduced him to the use of those arts which, in the same country and in a similar situation, had formerly been practised by the crafty Jugurtha. He attempted to deceive by an apparent submission the vigilance of the Roman general, to seduce the fidelity of his troops, and to protract the duration of the war by successively engaging the independent tribes of Africa to espouse his quarrel or to protect his flight.

Theodosius imitated the example and obtained the success of his predecessor Metellus. When Firmus, in the character of a suppliant, accused his own rashness and humbly solicited the clemency of the emperor, the lieutenant of Valentinian received and dismissed him with a friendly embrace; but he diligently required the useful and substantial pledges of a sincere repentance, nor could he be persuaded by the assurances of peace to suspend for an instant the operations of an active war. A dark conspiracy was detected by the penetration of Theodosius, and he satisfied without much reluctance the public indignation which he had secretly excited. Several of the guilty accomplices of Firmus were abandoned, according to ancient custom, to the tumult of a military execution; many more, by the amputation of both their hands, continued to exhibit an instructive spectacle of horror; the hatred of the rebels was accompanied with fear, and the fear of the Roman soldiers was mingled with respectful admiration.

Amidst the boundless plains of Gætulia and the innumerable valleys of Mount Atlas, it was impossible to prevent the escape of Firmus; and if the usurper could have tired the patience of his antagonist, he would have secured his person in the depth of some remote solitude and expected the hopes of a future revolution. He was subdued by the perseverance of Theodosius, who had formed an inflexible determination that the war should end only by the death of the tyrant, and that every nation of Africa which presumed to support his cause should be involved in his ruin. At the head of a small body of troops, which seldom exceeded three thousand five hundred men, the Roman general advanced with a steady prudence, devoid of rashness or of fear, into the heart of a country where he was sometimes attacked by armies of twenty thousand Moors. The boldness of his charge dismayed the irregular barbarians; they were disconcerted by his seasonable and orderly retreats; they were continually baffled by the unknown resources of the military art; and they felt and confessed the just superiority which was assumed by the leader of a civilized nation.

When Theodosius entered the extensive dominions of Igmazen, king of the Isaflenses, the haughty savage required, in words of defiance, his name and the object of his expedition. "I am," replied the stern and disdainful count, "I am the general of Valentinian, the lord of the world, who has sent me hither to pursue and punish a desperate robber. Deliver him instantly into my hands; and be assured that if thou dost not obey the commands of my invincible sovereign, thou and the people over whom thou reignest shall be utterly extirpated." As soon as Igmazen was satisfied that his enemy had strength and resolution to execute the fatal menace, he consented to purchase a necessary peace by the sacrifice of a guilty fugitive. The guards that were placed to secure the person of Firmus deprived him of the hopes of escape, and the Moorish tyrant, after wine had extinguished the sense of danger, disappointed the insulting triumph of the Romans by strangling himself in the night. His dead body, the only present which Igmazen could offer to the conqueror, was carelessly thrown upon a camel; and Theodosius, leading back his victorious troops to Sitifi, was saluted by the warmest acclamations of joy and loyalty.

Africa had been lost by the vices of Romanus; it was restored by the virtues of Theodosius; and our curiosity may be usefully directed to the inquiry of the respective treatment which the two generals received from the Imperial court. The authority of Count Romanus had been suspended by the master general of the cavalry, and he was committed to safe and honourable custody till the end of the war. His crimes were proved by the most authentic evidence, and the public expected with some impatience the decree of severe justice. But the partial and powerful favour of Mellobaudes encouraged him to challenge his legal judges, to obtain repeated delays for the purpose of procuring a crowd of friendly witnesses, and finally to cover his guilty conduct by the additional guilt of fraud and forgery. About the same time the restorer of Britain and Africa, on a vague suspicion that his name and services were superior to the rank of a subject, was ignominiously beheaded at Carthage. Valentinian no longer reigned; and the death of Theodosius as well as the impunity of Romanus may justly be imputed to the arts of the ministers who abused the confidence and deceived the inexperienced youth of his sons.[8]

8. *Editor's note:* Gibbon continues here with a brief description of the African theatre in which the campaign of Theodosius occurred.

IV. THE EAST. The ignominious treaty which saved the army of Jovian had been faithfully executed on the side of the Romans; and as they had solemnly renounced the sovereignty and alliance of Armenia and Iberia, those tributary kingdoms were exposed without protection to the arms of the Persian monarch. Sapor entered the Armenian territories at the head of a formidable host of cuirassiers, of archers, and of mercenary foot; but it was the invariable practice of Sapor to mix war and negotiation, and to consider falsehood and perjury as the most powerful instruments of regal policy. He affected to praise the prudent and moderate conduct of the king of Armenia; and the unsuspicious Tiranus was persuaded, by the repeated assurances of insidious friendship, to deliver his person into the hands of a faithless and cruel enemy. In the midst of a splendid entertainment he was bound in chains of silver, as an honour due to the blood of the Arsacides; and after a short confinement in the Tower of Oblivion at Ecbatana he was released from the miseries of life either by his own dagger or by that of an assassin. The kingdom of Armenia was reduced to the state of a Persian province; the administration was shared between a distinguished satrap and a favourite eunuch; and Sapor marched without delay to subdue the martial spirit of the Iberians. Sauromaces, who reigned in that country by the permission of the emperors, was expelled by a superior force; and as an insult on the majesty of Rome the king of kings placed a diadem on the head of his abject vassal Aspacuras.

The city of Artogerassa was the only place of Armenia which presumed to resist the effort of his arms. The treasure deposited in that strong fortress tempted the avarice of Sapor; but the danger of Olympias, the wife or widow of the Armenian king, excited the public compassion and animated the desperate valour of her sub-

jects and soldiers. The Persians were surprised and repulsed under the walls of Artogerassa by a bold and
well-concerted sally of the besieged. But the forces of
Sapor were continually renewed and increased; the hopeless courage of the garrison was exhausted; the strength
of the walls yielded to the assault; and the proud conqueror, after wasting the rebellious city with fire and
sword, led away captive an unfortunate queen who, in
a more auspicious hour, had been the destined bride of
the son of Constantine.

Yet if Sapor already triumphed in the easy conquest
of two dependent kingdoms, he soon felt that a country is unsubdued as long as the minds of the people
are actuated by an hostile and contumacious spirit. The
satraps, whom he was obliged to trust, embraced the
first opportunity of regaining the affection of their countrymen and of signalizing their immortal hatred to the
Persian name. Since the conversion of the Armenians
and Iberians those nations considered the Christians as
the favourites, and the Magians as the adversaries, of
the Supreme Being; the influence of the clergy over a
superstitious people was uniformly exerted in the cause
of Rome; and as long as the successors of Constantine
disputed with those of Artaxerxes the sovereignty of the
intermediate provinces, the religious connection always
threw a decisive advantage into the scale of the empire.
A numerous and active party acknowledged Para, the
son of Tiranus, as the lawful sovereign of Armenia, and
his title to the throne was deeply rooted in the hereditary succession of five hundred years. By the unanimous
consent of the Iberians, the country was equally divided
between the rival princes; and Aspacuras, who owed his
diadem to the choice of Sapor, was obliged to declare
that his regard for his children, who were detained as
hostages by the tyrant, was the only consideration which

prevented him from openly renouncing the alliance of Persia.

The emperor Valens, who respected the obligations of the treaty and who was apprehensive of involving the East in a dangerous war, ventured with slow and cautious measures to support the Roman party in the kingdoms of Iberia and Armenia. Twelve legions established the authority of Sauromaces on the banks of the Cyrus. The Euphrates was protected by the valour of Arintheus. A powerful army, under the command of Count Trajan and of Vadomair, king of the Alemanni, fixed their camp on the confines of Armenia. But they were strictly enjoined not to commit the first hostilities, which might be understood as a breach of the treaty; and such was the implicit obedience of the Roman general that they retreated with exemplary patience under a shower of Persian arrows, till they had clearly acquired a just title to an honourable and legitimate victory.

Yet these appearances of war insensibly subsided in a vain and tedious negotiation. The contending parties supported their claims by mutual reproaches of perfidy and ambition; and it should seem that the original treaty was expressed in very obscure terms, since they were reduced to the necessity of making their inconclusive appeal to the partial testimony of the generals of the two nations who had assisted at the negotiations. The invasion of the Goths and Huns, which soon afterwards shook the foundations of the Roman empire, exposed the provinces of Asia to the arms of Sapor. But the declining age and perhaps the infirmities of the monarch suggested new maxims of tranquillity and moderation. His death, which happened in the full maturity of a reign of seventy years, changed in a moment the court and councils of Persia, and their attention was most probably engaged by domestic troubles and the distant efforts of a Carmanian war. The remembrance of ancient injuries was lost in the enjoyment of peace. The kingdoms of Armenia and Iberia were permitted, by the mutual though tacit consent of both empires, to resume their doubtful neutrality. In the first years of the reign of Theodosius a Persian embassy arrived at Constantinople to excuse the unjustifiable measures of the former reign and to offer, as the tribute of friendship or even of respect, a splendid present of gems, of silk, and of Indian elephants.[9]

V. THE DANUBE. During a peaceful interval of thirty years the Romans secured their frontiers and the Goths extended their dominions. The victories of the great Hermanric, king of the Ostrogoths and the most noble of the race of the Amali, have been compared by the enthusiasm of his countrymen to the exploits of Alexander, with this singular and almost incredible difference: that the martial spirit of the Gothic hero, instead of being supported by the vigour of youth, was displayed with glory and success in the extreme period of human life, between the age of fourscore and one hundred and ten years. The independent tribes were persuaded or compelled to acknowledge the king of the Ostrogoths as the sovereign of the Gothic nation; the chiefs of the Visigoths, or Thervingi, renounced the royal title and assumed the more humble appellation of *Judges;* and among those judges Athanaric, Fritigern, and Alavivus were the most illustrious, by their personal merit as well as by their vicinity to the Roman prov-

9. *Editor's note:* The lively adventures of Para, heir to the Armenian throne, are related at this point in the original. Para lived among the Romans; was befriended by them; eventually escaped from virtual imprisonment by them; and was ultimately assassinated by them at a Roman banquet at which he was a guest.

inces. These domestic conquests, which increased the military power of Hermanric, enlarged his ambitious designs. He invaded the adjacent countries of the North, and twelve considerable nations, whose names and limits cannot be accurately defined, successively yielded to the superiority of the Gothic arms.

The Heruli, who inhabited the marshy lands near the lake Mæotis, were renowned for their strength and agility; and the assistance of their light infantry was eagerly solicited and highly esteemed in all the wars of the barbarians. But the active spirit of the Heruli was subdued by the slow and steady perseverance of the Goths; and after a bloody action in which the king was slain, the remains of that warlike tribe became an useful accession to the camp of Hermanric. He then marched against the Venedi, unskilled in the use of arms and formidable only by their numbers, which filled the wide extent of the plains of modern Poland. The victorious Goths, who were not inferior in numbers, prevailed in the contest by the decisive advantages of exercise and discipline.

After the submission of the Venedi the conqueror advanced without resistance as far as the confines of the Æstii, an ancient people whose name is still preserved in the province of Esthonia. Those distant inhabitants of the Baltic coast were supported by the labors of agriculture, enriched by the trade of amber, and consecrated by the peculiar worship of the Mother of the Gods. But the scarcity of iron obliged the Æstian warriors to content themselves with wooden clubs; and the reduction of that wealthy country is ascribed to the prudence rather than to the arms of Hermanric. His dominions, which extended from the Danube to the Baltic, included the native seats and the recent acquisitions of the Goths; and he reigned over the greatest part of Germany and

Scythia with the authority of a conqueror and sometimes with the cruelty of a tyrant. But he reigned over a part of the globe incapable of perpetuating and adorning the glory of its heroes. The name of Hermanric is almost buried in oblivion; his exploits are imperfectly known; and the Romans themselves appeared unconscious of the progress of an aspiring power which threatened the liberty of the North and the peace of the empire.

The Goths had contracted an hereditary attachment for the Imperial house of Constantine, of whose power and liberality they had received so many signal proofs. They respected the public peace; and if an hostile band sometimes presumed to pass the Roman limit, their irregular conduct was candidly ascribed to the ungovernable spirit of the barbarian youth. Their contempt for two new and obscure princes, who had been raised to the throne by a popular election, inspired the Goths with bolder hopes; and while they agitated some design of marching their confederate force under the national standard, they were easily tempted to embrace the party of Procopius and to foment, by their dangerous aid, the civil discord of the Romans. The public treaty might stipulate no more than ten thousand auxiliaries; but the design was so zealously adopted by the chiefs of the Visigoths that the army which passed the Danube amounted to the number of thirty thousand men.

They marched with the proud confidence that their invincible valour would decide the fate of the Roman empire; and the provinces of Thrace groaned under the weight of the barbarians, who displayed the insolence of masters and the licentiousness of enemies. But the intemperance which gratified their appetites retarded their progress; and before the Goths could receive any certain intelligence of the defeat and death of Procopius, they perceived, by the hostile state of the country, that the civil and military powers were resumed by his successful rival. A chain of posts and fortifications, skilfully disposed by Valens or the generals of Valens, resisted their march, prevented their retreat, and intercepted their subsistence. The fierceness of the barbarians was tamed and suspended by hunger; they indignantly threw down their arms at the feet of the conqueror, who offered them food and chains; the numerous captives were distributed in all the cities of the East; and the provincials, who were soon familiarized with their savage appearance, ventured by degrees to measure their own strength with these formidable adversaries, whose name had so long been the object of their terror.

The king of Scythia (and Hermanric alone could deserve so lofty a title) was grieved and exasperated by this national calamity. His ambassadors loudly complained at the court of Valens of the infraction of the ancient and solemn alliance which had so long subsisted between the Romans and the Goths. They alleged that they had fulfilled the duty of allies by assisting the kinsman and successor of the emperor Julian; they required the immediate restitution of the noble captives; and they urged a very singular claim, that the Gothic generals marching in arms and in hostile array were entitled to the sacred character and privileges of ambassadors. The decent but peremptory refusal of these extravagant demands was signified to the barbarians by Victor, master general of the cavalry, who expressed with force and dignity the just complaints of the emperor of the East. The negotiation was interrupted, and the manly exhortations of Valentinian encouraged his timid brother to vindicate the insulted majesty of the empire.

The splendour and magnitude of this Gothic war are celebrated by a contemporary historian, but the events scarcely deserve the attention of posterity except as the preliminary steps of the approaching decline and fall of the empire. Instead of leading the nations of Germany and Scythia to the banks of the Danube, or even to the gates of Constantinople, the aged monarch of the Goths resigned to the brave Athanaric the danger and glory of a defensive war against an enemy who wielded with a feeble hand the powers of a mighty state. A bridge of boats was established upon the Danube, the presence of Valens animated his troops, and his ignorance of the art of war was compensated by personal bravery and a wise deference to the advice of Victor and Arintheus, his master generals of the cavalry and infantry. The operations of the campaign were conducted by their skill and experience; but they found it impossible to drive the Visigoths from their strong posts in the mountains, and the devastation of the plains obliged the Romans themselves to repass the Danube on the approach of winter. The incessant rains, which swelled the waters of the river, produced a tacit suspension of arms and confined the emperor Valens, during the whole course of the ensuing summer, to his camp of Marcianopolis.

The third year of the war was more favourable to the Romans and more pernicious to the Goths. The interruption of trade deprived the barbarians of the objects of luxury, which they already confounded with the necessaries of life; and the desolation of a very extensive tract of country threatened them with the horrors of famine. Athanaric was provoked or compelled to risk a battle, which he lost, in the plains; and the pursuit was rendered more bloody by the cruel precaution of the victorious generals, who had promised a large reward for the head of every Goth that was brought into the Imperial camp. The submission of the barbarians appeased the resentment of Valens and his council; the emperor listened with satisfaction to the flattering and eloquent remonstrance of the senate of Constantinople, which assumed for the first time a share in the public deliberations; and the same generals, Victor and Arintheus, who had successfully directed the conduct of the war were empowered to regulate the conditions of peace. The freedom of trade which the Goths had hitherto enjoyed was restricted to two cities on the Danube; the rashness of their leaders was severely punished by the suppression of their pensions and subsidies; and the exception, which was stipulated in favour of Athanaric alone, was more advantageous than honourable to the Judge of the Visigoths.

Athanaric, who on this occasion appears to have consulted his private interest without expecting the orders of his sovereign, supported his own dignity and that of his tribe in the personal interview which was proposed by the ministers of Valens. He persisted in his declaration that it was impossible for him, without incurring the guilt of perjury, ever to set his foot on the territory of the empire; and it is more than probable that his regard for the sanctity of an oath was confirmed by the recent and fatal examples of Roman treachery. The Danube, which separated the dominions of the two independent nations, was chosen for the scene of the conference. The emperor of the East and the Judge of the Visigoths, accompanied by an equal number of armed followers, advanced in their respective barges to the middle of the stream. After the ratification of the treaty and the delivery of hostages, Valens returned in triumph to Constantinople; and the Goths remained in a state of tranquillity about six years, till they were violently impelled against the Roman empire by an innumerable host of Scythians, who appeared to issue from the frozen regions of the North.

An early skirmish, before the full fury of the barbarian storm broke over the empire, cost Valentinian his life. A barbarian king had been lured to a Roman banquet and murdered; his tribe, the Quadi, retaliated by ravaging several Roman provinces; and Valentinian led most of the forces of the West in a campaign of vengeance. In a momentary lull in the war the ambassadors of the Quadi were led into Valentinian's presence to beg for clemency. In reply, the emperor "reviled . . . the baseness, their ingratitude, their insolence. His eyes, his voice, his colour, his gestures, expressed the violence of his ungovernable fury; and while his whole frame was agitated with convulsive passion a large blood-vessel suddenly burst in his body, and Valentinian fell speechless into the arms of his attendants." He died within a few minutes; and the government of the West passed into the hands of his son, Gratian.

Chapter XIII

(A.D. 365-398)

*Manners of the pastoral nations – Progress of the
Huns from China to Europe – Flight of the Goths
– They pass the Danube – Gothic war – Defeat
and death of Valens – Gratian invests Theodosius
with the eastern empire – His character and
success – Peace and settlement of the Goths –
Triumph of orthodoxy and final destruction of
paganism – Civil wars and death of Theodosius –
Final division of the empire between his sons*[1]

IN THE second year of the reign of Valentinian and
Valens, on the morning of the twenty-first day of
July, the greatest part of the Roman world was shaken
by a violent and destructive earthquake. The impression
was communicated to the waters; the shores of the Mediterranean were left dry by the sudden retreat of the sea;
great quantities of fish were caught with the hand; large
vessels were stranded on the mud; and a curious spectator amused his eye, or rather his fancy, by contemplating
the various appearance of valleys and mountains which
had never since the formation of the globe been exposed
to the sun. But the tide soon returned with the weight
of an immense and irresistible deluge, which was severely felt on the coasts of Sicily, of Dalmatia, of Greece,
and of Egypt; large boats were transported and lodged
on the roofs of houses, or at the distance of two miles

1. *Editor's note:* Chapters XXVI through XXIX of the
original.

510

from the shore; the people, with their habitations, were swept away by the waters; and the city of Alexandria annually commemorated the fatal day on which fifty thousand persons had lost their lives in the inundation.

This calamity, the report of which was magnified from one province to another, astonished and terrified the subjects of Rome, and their affrighted imagination enlarged the real extent of a momentary evil. They recollected the preceding earthquakes, which had subverted the cities of Palestine and Bithynia; they considered these alarming strokes as the prelude only of still more dreadful calamities; and their fearful vanity was disposed to confound the symptoms of a declining empire and a sinking world.

It was the fashion of the times to attribute every remarkable event to the particular will of the Deity; the alterations of nature were connected by an invisible chain with the moral and metaphysical opinions of the human mind; and the most sagacious divines could distinguish, according to the colour of their respective prejudices, that the establishment of heresy tended to produce an earthquake or that a deluge was the inevitable consequence of the progress of sin and error. Without presuming to discuss the truth or propriety of these lofty speculations, the historian may content himself with an observation which seems to be justified by experience: that man has much more to fear from the passions of his fellow-creatures than from the convulsions of the elements. The mischievous effects of an earthquake or deluge, a hurricane or the eruption of a volcano, bear a very inconsiderable proportion to the ordinary calamities of war, as they are now moderated by the prudence or humanity of the princes of Europe, who amuse their own leisure and exercise the courage of their subjects in the practice of the military art.

But the laws and manners of modern nations protect the safety and freedom of the vanquished soldier; and the peaceful citizen has seldom reason to complain that his life or even his fortune is exposed to the rage of war. In the disastrous period of the fall of the Roman empire, which may justly be dated from the reign of Valens, the happiness and security of each individual were personally attacked, and the arts and labours of ages were rudely defaced, by the barbarians of Scythia and Germany. The invasion of the Huns precipitated on the provinces of the West the Gothic nation, which advanced in less than forty years from the Danube to the Atlantic and opened a way by the success of their arms to the inroads of so many hostile tribes more savage than themselves.

A minute examination of the background of the barbarian peoples of eastern Asia, especially the Huns (whose talent for warfare Gibbon attributes to diet, mobility of habitation, and practice in the semi-military exercise of hunting), comprises the next section of the original. Long before the Christian era the Huns, who normally lived just north of the Great Wall of China, had carved out so extensive a dominion as to wield considerable power over the Chinese empire itself; but the Chinese emperor Vouti, of the Han dynasty, eventually humbled the Huns by a combination of military defeat and subverting their allies.

Thereafter the Huns appear to have split into three great groups: one remained in their native country, and were soon conquered and absorbed by another Tartar tribe known as the Sienpi; a second retired to land in the southwest of China assigned for their settlement by the Chinese emperor; while the third and most daring struck out for the West. This third group again split into

two, a southern branch that built an extensive civilization around the Caspian Sea, and a northern branch
which traversed the whole of Asia and eastern Europe
and, toward the end of the fourth century, suddenly appeared among the barbarian peoples along the north-
eastern borders of the Roman empire.

The Huns quickly conquered and absorbed the extensive Alani nation and then fell upon the horrified
Goths, who firmly believed that "the witches of Scythia
. . . had copulated in the desert with infernal spirits,
and that the Huns were the offspring of this execrable
conjunction." The Ostrogoths were next defeated, many
becoming subjects of the Huns; but the entire Visigoth
nation fled towards the banks of the Danube and "implored the protection of the Roman emperor of the
East."

After Valens had terminated the Gothic war with
some appearance of glory and success, he made a progress through his dominions of Asia and at length fixed
his residence in the capital of Syria. The five years which
he spent at Antioch were employed to watch, from a
secure distance, the hostile designs of the Persian monarch; to check the depredations of the Saracens and
Isaurians; to enforce, by arguments more prevalent than
those of reason and eloquence, the belief of the Arian
theology; and to satisfy his anxious suspicions by the
promiscuous execution of the innocent and the guilty.
But the attention of the emperor was most seriously engaged by the important intelligence which he received
from the civil and military officers who were entrusted
with the defence of the Danube. He was informed that
the North was agitated by a furious tempest; that the
irruption of the Huns, an unknown and monstrous race
of savages, had subverted the power of the Goths; and

that the suppliant multitudes of that warlike nation, whose pride was now humbled in the dust, covered a space many miles along the banks of the river. With out-stretched arms and pathetic lamentations they loudly deplored their past misfortunes and their present dan-ger; acknowledged that their only hope of safety was in the clemency of the Roman government; and most sol-emnly protested that, if the gracious liberality of the emperor would permit them to cultivate the waste lands of Thrace, they should ever hold themselves bound by the strongest obligations of duty and gratitude to obey the laws and to guard the limits of the republic. These assurances were confirmed by the ambassadors of the Goths, who impatiently expected from the mouth of Valens an answer that must finally determine the fate of their unhappy countrymen. The emperor of the East was no longer guided by the wisdom and authority of his elder brother, whose death happened towards the end of the preceding year; and as the distressful situ-ation of the Goths required an instant and peremptory decision, he was deprived of the favourite resource of feeble and timid minds, who consider the use of the dilatory and ambiguous measures as the most admirable efforts of consummate prudence.

As long as the same passions and interests subsist among mankind, the questions of war and peace, of jus-tice and policy, which were debated in the councils of antiquity, will frequently present themselves as the sub-ject of modern deliberation. But the most experienced statesman of Europe has never been summoned to con-sider the propriety or the danger of admitting or reject-ing an innumerable multitude of barbarians, who are driven by despair and hunger to solicit a settlement on the territories of a civilized nation. When that important proposition, so essentially connected with the public safety, was referred to the ministers of Valens, they were perplexed and divided; but they soon acquiesced in the flattering sentiment which seemed the most favourable to the pride, the indolence, and the avarice of their sovereign. The slaves who were decorated with the titles of præfects and generals dissembled or disregarded the terrors of this national emigration—so extremely different from the partial and accidental colonies which had been received on the extreme limits of the empire. But they applauded the liberality of fortune which had conducted, from the most distant countries of the globe, a numerous and invincible army of strangers to defend the throne of Valens, who might now add to the royal treasures the immense sums of gold supplied by the provincials to compensate their annual proportion of recruits.

The prayers of the Goths were granted, and their service was accepted by the Imperial court; and orders were immediately despatched by the civil and military governors of the Thracian diocese to make the necessary preparations for the passage and subsistence of a great people, till a proper and sufficient territory could be allotted for their future residence. The liberality of the emperor was accompanied, however, with two harsh and rigorous conditions, which prudence might justify on the side of the Romans, but which distress alone could extort from the indignant Goths. Before they passed the Danube they were required to deliver their arms; and it was insisted that their children should be taken from them and dispersed through the provinces of Asia, where they might be civilized by the arts of education, and serve as hostages to secure the fidelity of their parents.

During this suspense of a doubtful and distant negotiation the impatient Goths made some rash attempts to pass the Danube without the permission of the government whose protection they had implored. Their motions were strictly observed by the vigilance of the troops which were stationed along the river, and their foremost detachments were defeated with considerable slaughter; yet such were the timid councils of the reign of Valens that the brave officers who had served their country in the execution of their duty were punished by the loss of their employments, and narrowly escaped the loss of their heads.

The Imperial mandate was at length received for transportation over the Danube of the whole body of the Gothic nation; but the execution of this order was a task of labour and difficulty. The stream of the Danube, which in those parts is above a mile broad, had been swelled by incessant rains, and in this tumultuous passage many were swept away and drowned by the rapid violence of the current. A large fleet of vessels, of boats, and of canoes was provided; many days and nights they passed and repassed with indefatigable toil; and the most strenuous diligence was exerted by the officers of Valens that not a single barbarian, of those who were reserved to subvert the foundations of Rome, should be left on the opposite shore. It was thought expedient that an accurate account should be taken of their numbers; but the persons who were employed soon desisted, with amazement and dismay, from the prosecution of the endless and impracticable task; and the principal historian of the age most seriously affirms that the prodigious armies of Darius and Xerxes, which had so long been considered as the fables of vain and credulous antiquity, were now justified in the eyes of mankind by the evidence of fact and experience. A probable testimony has fixed the number of the Gothic warriors at two hundred thousand men; and if we can venture to add the just proportion of women, of children, and of slaves, the whole mass of people which composed this formidable emigration must have amounted to near a million of persons of both sexes and of all ages.

The children of the Goths, those at least of a distinguished rank, were separated from the multitude. They were conducted without delay to the distant seats assigned for their residence and education; and as the numerous train of hostages or captives passed through the cities, their gay and splendid apparel, their robust and martial figure, excited the surprise and envy of the provincials.

But the stipulation most offensive to the Goths and most important to the Romans was shamefully eluded. The barbarians, who considered their arms as the ensigns of honour and the pledges of safety, were disposed to offer a price which the lust or avarice of the Imperial officers was easily tempted to accept. To preserve their arms the haughty warriors consented with some reluctance to prostitute their wives or their daughters; the charms of a beauteous maid or a comely boy secured the connivance of the inspectors, who sometimes cast an eye of covetousness on the fringed carpets and linen garments of their new allies, or who sacrificed their duty to the mean consideration of filling their farms with cattle and their houses with slaves. The Goths, with arms in their hands, were permitted to enter the boats; and when their strength was collected on the other side of the river, the immense camp which was spread over the plains and the hills of the Lower Mæsia assumed a threatening and even hostile aspect. The leaders of the Ostrogoths, Alatheus and Saphrax, the guardians of their infant king, appeared soon afterwards on the northern banks of the Danube and immediately despatched their ambassadors to the court of Antioch to solicit, with the same professions of allegiance and gratitude, the same favour which had been granted to the suppliant Visigoths. The absolute refusal of Valens suspended their progress and discovered the repentance, the suspicions, and the fears of the Imperial council.

An undisciplined and unsettled nation of barbarians required the firmest temper and the most dexterous management. The daily subsistence of near a million of extraordinary subjects could be supplied only by constant and skilful diligence, and might continually be interrupted by mistake or accident. The insolence or the indignation of the Goths, if they conceived themselves to be the objects either of fear or of contempt, might urge them to the most desperate extremities; and the fortune of the state seemed to depend on the prudence as well as the integrity of the generals of Valens.

At this important crisis the military government of Thrace was exercised by Lupicinus and Maximus, in whose venal minds the slightest hope of private emolument outweighed every consideration of public advantage, and whose guilt was only alleviated by their incapacity of discerning the pernicious effects of their rash and criminal administration. Instead of obeying the orders of their sovereign and satisfying, with decent liberality, the demands of the Goths, they levied an ungenerous and oppressive tax on the wants of the hungry barbarians. The vilest food was sold at an extravagant price; and, in the room of wholesome and substantial provisions, the markets were filled with the flesh of dogs and of unclean animals who had died of disease. To obtain the valuable acquisition of a pound of bread the Goths resigned the possession of an expensive though serviceable slave; and a small quantity of meat was greedily purchased with ten pounds of a precious but useless metal. When their property was exhausted they continued this necessary traffic by the sale of their sons and daughters; and notwithstanding the love of freedom which animated every Gothic breast, they submitted to the humiliating maxim that it was better for their children to be maintained in a servile condition than to perish in a state of wretched and helpless independence.

The most lively resentment is excited by the tyranny of pretended benefactors, who sternly exact the debt of gratitude which they have cancelled by subsequent injuries; a spirit of discontent insensibly arose in the camp of the barbarians, who pleaded without success the merit of their patient and dutiful behaviour and loudly complained of the inhospitable treatment which they had received from their new allies. They beheld around them the wealth and plenty of a fertile province, in the midst of which they suffered the intolerable hardships of artificial famine. But the means of relief, and even of revenge, were in their hands, since the rapaciousness of their tyrants had left to an injured people the possession and the use of arms.

The clamours of a multitude, untaught to disguise their sentiments, announced the first symptoms of resistance and alarmed the timid and guilty minds of Lupicinus and Maximus. Those crafty ministers, who substituted the cunning of temporary expedients to the wise and salutary counsels of general policy, attempted to remove the Goths from their dangerous station on the frontiers of the empire and to disperse them in separate quarters of cantonment through the interior provinces. As they were conscious how ill they had deserved the respect or confidence of the barbarians, they diligently collected from every side a military force that might urge the tardy and reluctant march of a people who had not yet renounced the title or the duties of Roman subjects. But the generals of Valens, while their attention was solely directed to the discontented Visigoths, imprudently disarmed the ships and the fortifications which constituted the defence of the Danube. The fatal oversight was observed and improved by Alatheus and Saphrax, who anxiously watched the favourable moment of escaping from the pursuit of the Huns. By the help of such rafts and vessels as could be hastily procured, the leaders of the Ostrogoths transported without opposition their king and their army and boldly fixed an hostile and independent camp on the territories of the empire.

Under the name of *Judges,* Alavivus and Fritigern were the leaders of the Visigoths in peace and war; and the authority which they derived from their birth was ratified by the free consent of the nation. In a season of tranquillity their power might have been equal as well as their rank; but as soon as their countrymen were exasperated by hunger and oppression the superior abilities of Fritigern assumed the military command, which he was qualified to exercise for the public welfare. He restrained the impatient spirit of the Visigoths till the injuries and the insults of their tyrants should justify their resistance in the opinion of mankind; but he was not disposed to sacrifice any solid advantages for the empty praise of justice and moderation. Sensible of the benefits which would result from the union of the Gothic powers under the same standard, he secretly cultivated the friendship of the Ostrogoths; and while he professed an implicit obedience to the orders of the Roman generals, he proceeded by slow marches towards Marcianopolis, the capital of the Lower Mæsia, about seventy miles from the banks of the Danube.

On that fatal spot the flames of discord and mutual hatred burst forth into a dreadful conflagration. Lupicinus had invited the Gothic chiefs to a splendid enter-

tainment, and their martial train remained under arms
at the entrance of the palace. But the gates of the city
were strictly guarded; and the barbarians were sternly
excluded from the use of a plentiful market, to which
they asserted their equal claim of subjects and allies.
Their humble prayers were rejected with insolence and
derision; and as their patience was now exhausted, the
townsmen, the soldiers, and the Goths were soon involved in a conflict of passionate altercation and angry
reproaches. A blow was imprudently given; a sword was
hastily drawn; and the first blood that was spilled in this
accidental quarrel became the signal of a long and destructive war.

In the midst of noise and brutal intemperance Lupicinus was informed by a secret messenger that many of
his soldiers were slain and despoiled of their arms; and
as he was already inflamed by wine and oppressed by
sleep, he issued a rash command that their death should
be revenged by the massacre of the guards of Fritigern
and Alavivus. The clamorous shouts and dying groans
apprised Fritigern of his extreme danger; and, as he possessed the calm and intrepid spirit of a hero, he saw that
he was lost if he allowed a moment of deliberation to
the man who had so deeply injured him. "A trifling dispute," said the Gothic leader with a firm but gentle tone
of voice, "appears to have arisen between the two nations; but it may be productive of the most dangerous
consequences unless the tumult is immediately pacified
by the assurance of our safety and the authority of our
presence." At these words Fritigern and his companions
drew their swords, opened their passage through the un-
resisting crowd which filled the palace, the streets, and
the gates of Marcianopolis, and, mounting their horses,
hastily vanished from the eyes of the astonished Romans.
The generals of the Goths were saluted by the fierce

and joyful acclamations of the camp; war was instantly resolved, and the resolution was executed without delay. The banners of the nation were displayed according to the custom of their ancestors, and the air resounded with the harsh and mournful music of the barbarian trumpet. The weak and guilty Lupicinus, who had dared to provoke, who had neglected to destroy, and who still presumed to despise his formidable enemy, marched against the Goths at the head of such a military force as could be collected on this sudden emergency. The barbarians expected his approach about nine miles from Marcianopolis; and on this occasion the talents of the general were found to be of more prevailing efficacy than the weapons and discipline of the troops. The valour of the Goths was so ably directed by the genius of Fritigern that they broke, by a close and vigorous attack, the ranks of the Roman legions. Lupicinus left his arms and standards, his tribunes and his bravest soldiers, on the field of battle; and their useless courage served only to protect the ignominious flight of their leader.

"That successful day put an end to the distress of the barbarians and the security of the Romans; from that day the Goths, renouncing the precarious condition of strangers and exiles, assumed the character of citizens and masters, claimed an absolute dominion over the possessors of land, and held in their own right the northern provinces of the empire, which are bounded by the Danube." Such are the words of the Gothic historian, who celebrates with rude eloquence the glory of his countrymen. But the dominion of the barbarians was exercised only for the purposes of rapine and destruction. As they had been deprived by the ministers of the emperor of the common benefits of nature and the fair intercourse of social life, they retaliated the injustice on the subjects of the empire; and the crimes of Lupicinus were expiated by the ruin of the peaceful husbandmen of Thrace, the conflagration of their villages, and the massacre or captivity of their innocent families. The report of the Gothic victory was soon diffused over the adjacent country; and while it filled the minds of the Romans with terror and dismay, their own hasty imprudence contributed to increase the forces of Fritigern and the calamities of the province.

Some time before the great emigration a numerous body of Goths, under the command of Suerid and Colias, had been received into the protection and service of the empire. They were encamped under the walls of Hadrianople; but the ministers of Valens were anxious to remove them beyond the Hellespont, at a distance from the dangerous temptation which might so easily be communicated by the neighbourhood and the success of their countrymen. The respectful submission with which they yielded to the order of their march might be considered as a proof of their fidelity; and their moderate request of a sufficient allowance of provisions and of a delay of only two days was expressed in the most dutiful terms. But the first magistrate of Hadrianople, incensed by some disorders which had been committed at his country-house, refused this indulgence; and arming against them the inhabitants and manufacturers of a populous city, he urged with hostile threats their instant departure.

The barbarians stood silent and amazed, till they were exasperated by the insulting clamours and missile weapons of the populace; but when patience or contempt was fatigued, they crushed the undisciplined multitude, inflicted many a shameful wound on the backs of their flying enemies, and despoiled them of the splendid armour which they were unworthy to bear. The resemblance of their sufferings and their actions soon united

this victorious detachment to the nation of the Visigoths;
the troops of Colias and Suerid expected the approach
of the great Fritigern, ranged themselves under his
standard, and signalized their ardour in the siege of
Hadrianople. But the resistance of the garrison informed
the barbarians that in the attack of regular fortifications
the efforts of unskilful courage are seldom effectual.
Their general acknowledged his error, raised the siege,
declared that "he was at peace with stone walls," and
revenged his disappointment on the adjacent country.
He accepted with pleasure the useful reinforcement of
hardy workmen who laboured in the gold-mines of
Thrace for the emolument and under the lash of an unfeeling master; and these new associates conducted the
barbarians through the secret paths to the most sequestered places which had been chosen to secure the inhabitants, the cattle, and the magazines of corn.

With the assistance of such guides nothing could
remain impervious or inaccessible: resistance was fatal,
flight was impracticable, and the patient submission of
helpless innocence seldom found mercy from the barbarian conqueror. In the course of these depredations a
great number of the children of the Goths, who had
been sold into captivity, were restored to the embraces
of their afflicted parents; but these tender interviews,
which might have revived and cherished in their minds
some sentiments of humanity, tended only to stimulate
their native fierceness by the desire of revenge. They
listened with eager attention to the complaints of their
captive children, who had suffered the most cruel indignities from the lustful or angry passions of their masters, and the same cruelties, the same indignities, were
severely retaliated on the sons and daughters of the
Romans.

The imprudence of Valens and his ministers had in-

troduced into the heart of the empire a nation of enemies; but the Visigoths might even yet have been reconciled by the manly confession of past errors and the
sincere performance of former engagements. These healing and temperate measures seemed to concur with the
timorous disposition of the sovereign of the East; but on
this occasion alone Valens was brave, and his unseasonable bravery was fatal to himself and to his subjects. He
declared his intention of marching from Antioch to Constantinople to subdue this dangerous rebellion; and as
he was not ignorant of the difficulties of the enterprise,
he solicited the assistance of his nephew, the emperor
Gratian, who commanded all the forces of the West. The
veteran troops were hastily recalled from the defence of
Armenia; that important frontier was abandoned to the
discretion of Sapor; and the immediate conduct of the
Gothic war was entrusted, during the absence of Valens,
to his lieutenants, Trajan and Profuturus, two generals
who indulged themselves in a very false and favourable
opinion of their own abilities. On their arrival in Thrace
they were joined by Richomer, count of the domestics;
and the auxiliaries of the West that marched under his
banner were composed of the Gallic legions, reduced
indeed by a spirit of desertion to the vain appearances
of strength and numbers.

In a council of war which was influenced by pride
rather than by reason, it was resolved to seek and to
encounter the barbarians, who lay encamped in the
spacious and fertile meadows near the most southern of
the six mouths of the Danube. Their camp was surrounded by the usual fortification of waggons; and the
barbarians, secure within the vast circle of the enclosure,
enjoyed the fruits of their valour and the spoils of the
province. In the midst of riotous intemperance, the
watchful Fritigern observed the motions and penetrated

the designs of the Romans. He perceived that the numbers of the enemy were continually increasing; and as he understood their intention of attacking his rear as soon as the scarcity of forage should oblige him to remove his camp, he recalled to their standard his predatory detachments which covered the adjacent country.

As soon as they descried the flaming beacons they obeyed with incredible speed the signal of their leader; the camp was filled with the martial crowd of barbarians; their impatient clamours demanded the battle, and their tumultuous zeal was approved and animated by the spirit of their chiefs. The evening was already far advanced; and the two armies prepared themselves for the approaching combat, which was deferred only till the dawn of day. While the trumpets sounded to arms, the undaunted courage of the Goths was confirmed by the mutual obligation of a solemn oath; and as they advanced to meet the enemy, the rude songs which celebrated the glory of their forefathers were mingled with their fierce and dissonant outcries and opposed to the artificial harmony of the Roman shout. Some military skill was displayed by Fritigern to gain the advantage of a commanding eminence; but the bloody conflict, which began and ended with the light, was maintained on either side by the personal and obstinate efforts of strength, valour, and agility. The legions of Armenia supported their fame in arms, but they were oppressed by the irresistible weight of the hostile multitude; the left wing of the Romans was thrown into disorder, and the field was strewed with their mangled carcasses. This partial defeat was balanced, however, by partial success; and when the two armies at a late hour of the evening retreated to their respective camps, neither of them could claim the honours or the effects of a decisive victory.

The real loss was more severely felt by the Romans, in proportion to the smallness of their numbers; but the Goths were so deeply confounded and dismayed by this vigorous and perhaps unexpected resistance that they remained seven days within the circle of their fortifications. Such funeral rites as the circumstances of time and place would admit were piously discharged to some officers of distinguished rank; but the indiscriminate vulgar were left unburied on the plain. Their flesh was greedily devoured by the birds of prey, who in that age enjoyed very frequent and delicious feasts; and several years afterwards the white and naked bones which covered the wide extent of the fields presented to the eyes of Ammianus a dreadful monument of the battle of Salices.

The progress of the Goths had been checked by the doubtful event of that bloody day; and the Imperial generals, whose army would have been consumed by the repetition of such a contest, embraced the more rational plan of destroying the barbarians by the wants and pressure of their own multitudes. They prepared to confine the Visigoths in the narrow angle of land between the Danube, the desert of Scythia, and the mountains of Hæmus, till their strength and spirit should be insensibly wasted by the inevitable operation of famine. The design was prosecuted with some conduct and success; the barbarians had almost exhausted their own magazines and the harvests of the country; and the diligence of Saturninus, the master general of the cavalry, was employed to improve the strength and to contract the extent of the Roman fortifications. His labours were interrupted by the alarming intelligence that new swarms of barbarians had passed the unguarded Danube, either to support the cause or to imitate the example of Fritigern. The just apprehension that he himself might be surrounded and overwhelmed by the arms of hostile and unknown nations compelled Saturninus to relinquish the siege of the Gothic camp; and the indignant Visigoths, breaking from their confinement, satiated their hunger and revenge by the repeated devastation of the fruitful country which extends above three hundred miles from the banks of the Danube to the straits of the Hellespont.

The sagacious Fritigern had successfully appealed to the passions as well as to the interest of his barbarian allies; and the love of rapine and the hatred of Rome seconded, or even prevented, the eloquence of his ambassadors. He cemented a strict and useful alliance with the great body of his countrymen, who obeyed Alatheus and Saphrax as the guardians of their infant king; the long animosity of rival tribes was suspended by the sense of their common interest; the independent part of the nation was associated under one standard; and the chiefs of the Ostrogoths appear to have yielded to the superior genius of the general of the Visigoths. He obtained the formidable aid of the Taifalæ, whose military renown was disgraced and polluted by the public infamy of their domestic manners. Every youth, on his entrance into the world, was united by the ties of honourable friendship and brutal love to some warrior of the tribe; nor could he hope to be released from this unnatural connection till he had approved his manhood by slaying in single combat a huge bear or a wild boar of the forest.

But the most powerful auxiliaries of the Goths were drawn from the camp of those enemies who had expelled them from their native seats. The loose subordination and extensive possessions of the Huns and the Alani delayed the conquests and distracted the councils of that victorious people. Several of the hordes were allured by the liberal promises of Fritigern; and the rapid cavalry of Scythia added weight and energy to the steady and strenuous efforts of the Gothic infantry. The Sarmatians, who could never forgive the successor of Valentinian, enjoyed and increased the general confusion; and a seasonable irruption of the Alemanni into the provinces of Gaul engaged the attention and diverted the forces of the emperor of the West.[2]

The emperor Valens, who at length had removed his court and army from Antioch, was received by the people of Constantinople as the author of the public calamity. Before he had reposed himself ten days in the capital he was urged by the licentious clamours of the Hippodrome to march against the barbarians whom he had invited into his dominions; and the citizens, who are always brave at a distance from any real danger, declared with confidence that if they were supplied with arms, *they* alone would undertake to deliver the province from the ravages of an insulting foe.

The vain reproaches of an ignorant multitude hastened the downfall of the Roman empire; they provoked the desperate rashness of Valens, who did not find either in his reputation or in his mind any motives to support with firmness the public contempt. He was soon persuaded by the successful achievements of his lieutenants to despise the power of the Goths, who, by the diligence of Fritigern, were now collected in the neighbourhood of Hadrianople. The march of the Taifalæ had been intercepted by the valiant Frigerid; the king of those licentious barbarians was slain in battle and the suppliant captives were sent into distant exile to cultivate the lands of Italy, which were assigned for their settlement

2. *Editor's note:* In a brief passage here omitted, Gibbon describes Gratian's vigorous campaign against the Alemanni, who had hoped to use the Gothic threat to screen their own depredations in Gaul.

in the vacant territories of Modena and Parma. The exploits of Sebastian, who was recently engaged in the service of Valens and promoted to the rank of master general of the infantry, were still more honourable to himself and useful to the republic. He obtained the permission of selecting three hundred soldiers from each of the legions, and this separate detachment soon acquired the spirit of discipline and the exercise of arms which were almost forgotten under the reign of Valens. By the vigour and conduct of Sebastian, a large body of the Goths was surprised in their camp; and the immense spoil which was recovered from their hands filled the city of Hadrianople and the adjacent plain.

The splendid narratives which the general transmitted of his own exploits alarmed the Imperial court by the appearance of superior merit; and though he cautiously insisted on the difficulties of the Gothic war, his valour was praised, his advice was rejected; and Valens, who listened with pride and pleasure to the flattering suggestions of the eunuchs of the palace, was impatient to seize the glory of an easy and assured conquest. His army was strengthened by a numerous reinforcement of veterans; and his march from Constantinople to Hadrianople was conducted with so much military skill that he prevented the activity of the barbarians, who designed to occupy the intermediate defiles and to intercept either the troops themselves or their convoys of provisions. The camp of Valens, which he pitched under the walls of Hadrianople, was fortified, according to the practice of the Romans, with a ditch and rampart; and a most important council was summoned to decide the fate of the emperor and of the empire.

The party of reason and of delay was strenuously maintained by Victor, who had corrected, by the lessons of experience, the native fierceness of the Sarmatian character; while Sebastian, with the flexible and obsequious eloquence of a courtier, represented every precaution and every measure that implied a doubt of immediate victory as unworthy of the courage and majesty of their invincible monarch. The ruin of Valens was precipitated by the deceitful arts of Fritigern and the prudent admonitions of the emperor of the West. The advantages of negotiating in the midst of war were perfectly understood by the general of the barbarians; and a Christian ecclesiastic was despatched, as the holy minister of peace, to penetrate and to perplex the councils of the enemy. The misfortunes as well as the provocations of the Gothic nation were forcibly and truly described by their ambassador, who protested, in the name of Fritigern, that he was still disposed to lay down his arms or to employ them only in the defence of the empire, if he could secure for his wandering countrymen a tranquil settlement on the waste lands of Thrace and a sufficient allowance of corn and cattle. But he added, in a whisper of confidential friendship, that the exasperated barbarians were averse to these reasonable conditions, and that Fritigern was doubtful whether he could accomplish the conclusion of the treaty unless he found himself supported by the presence and terrors of an Imperial army.

About the same time Count Richomer returned from the West to announce the defeat and submission of the Alemanni; to inform Valens that his nephew advanced by rapid marches at the head of the veteran and victorious legions of Gaul; and to request, in the name of Gratian and of the republic, that every dangerous and decisive measure might be suspended till the junction of the two emperors should ensure the success of the Gothic war. But the feeble sovereign of the East was actuated only by the fatal illusions of pride and jealousy. He disdained the importunate advice; he rejected the humiliating aid; he secretly compared the ignominious, at least the inglorious, period of his own reign with the fame of a beardless youth; and Valens rushed into the field to erect his imaginary trophy before the diligence of his colleague could usurp any share of the triumphs of the day.

On the ninth of August, a day which has deserved to be marked among the most inauspicious of the Roman calendar, the emperor Valens, leaving under a strong guard his baggage and military treasure, marched from Hadrianople to attack the Goths, who were encamped about twelve miles from the city. By some mistake of the orders or some ignorance of the ground, the right wing or column of cavalry arrived in sight of the enemy whilst the left was still at a considerable distance; the soldiers were compelled, in the sultry heat of summer, to precipitate their pace; and the line of battle was formed with tedious confusion and irregular delay. The Gothic cavalry had been detached to forage in the adjacent country; and Fritigern still continued to practise his customary arts. He despatched messengers of peace, made proposals, required hostages, and wasted the hours, till the Romans, exposed without shelter to the burning rays of the sun, were exhausted by thirst, hunger, and intolerable fatigue. The emperor was persuaded to send an ambassador to the Gothic camp; the zeal of Richomer, who alone had courage to accept the dangerous commission, was applauded; and the count of the domestics, adorned with the splendid ensigns of his dignity, had proceeded some way in the space between the two armies when he was suddenly recalled by the alarm of battle.

The hasty and imprudent attack was made by Bacurius the Iberian, who commanded a body of archers and targeteers; and as they advanced with rashness, they retreated with loss and disgrace. In the same moment the flying squadrons of Alatheus and Saphrax, whose return was anxiously expected by the general of the Goths, descended like a whirlwind from the hills, swept across the plain, and added new terrors to the tumultuous but irresistible charge of the barbarian host. The event of the battle of Hadrianople, so fatal to Valens and to the empire, may be described in a few words: the Roman cavalry fled; the infantry was abandoned, surrounded, and cut in pieces. The most skilful evolutions, the firmest courage, are scarcely sufficient to extricate a body of foot encompassed on an open plain by superior numbers of horse; but the troops of Valens, oppressed by the weight of the enemy and their own fears, were crowded into a narrow space where it was impossible for them to extend their ranks or even to use with effect their swords and javelins. In the midst of tumult, of slaughter, and of dismay the emperor, deserted by his guards and wounded, as it was supposed, with an arrow, sought protection among the Lancearii and the Mattiarii, who still maintained their ground with some appearance of order and firmness. His faithful generals, Trajan and Victor, who perceived his danger, loudly exclaimed that all was lost unless the person of the emperor could be saved. Some troops, animated by their exhortation, advanced to his relief: they found only a bloody spot, covered with a heap of broken arms and mangled bodies, without being able to discover their unfortunate prince either among the living or the dead. Their search could not indeed be successful if there is any truth in the circumstances with which some historians have related the death of the emperor. By the care of his attendants, Valens was removed from the field of battle to a neighbouring cottage, where they attempted to dress his wound and to provide for his future safety. But this humble retreat was instantly surrounded by the enemy; they tried to force the door; they were provoked by a discharge of arrows from the roof; till at length, impatient of delay, they set fire to a pile of dry faggots and consumed the cottage with the Roman emperor and his train. Valens perished in the flames, and a youth, who dropped from the window, alone escaped to attest the melancholy tale and to inform the Goths of the inestimable prize which they had lost by their own rashness.

A great number of brave and distinguished officers perished in the battle of Hadrianople, which equalled in the actual loss, and far surpassed in the fatal consequences, the misfortune which Rome had formerly sustained in the fields of Cannæ. Two master generals of the cavalry and infantry, two great officers of the palace, and thirty-five tribunes were found among the slain; and the death of Sebastian might satisfy the world that he was the victim as well as the author of the public calamity. Above two-thirds of the Roman army were destroyed; and the darkness of the night was esteemed a very favourable circumstance, as it served to conceal the flight of the multitude and to protect the more orderly retreat of Victor and Richomer, who alone amidst the general consternation maintained the advantage of calm courage and regular discipline.[3]

3. *Editor's note:* But the Goths, as the original relates, were unable to take Hadrianople or any other major city and had to content themselves with ravaging the countryside from the very walls of Constantinople to the borders of Italy. For their part, the Romans added to the general bloodshed by calling together all the Gothic hostages scattered through the eastern provinces (see p. 517) and massacring the lot at one swoop. How far the "urgent consideration of the public safety . . . may operate to dissolve the natural obliga-

The emperor Gratian was far advanced on his march towards the plains of Hadrianople when he was informed, at first by the confused voice of fame and afterwards by the more accurate reports of Victor and Richomer, that his impatient colleague had been slain in battle and that two-thirds of the Roman army were exterminated by the sword of the victorious Goths. Whatever resentment the rash and jealous vanity of his uncle might deserve, the resentment of a generous mind is easily subdued by the softer emotions of grief and compassion; and even the sense of pity was soon lost in the serious and alarming consideration of the state of the republic. Gratian was too late to assist, he was too weak to revenge, his unfortunate colleague; and the valiant and modest youth felt himself unequal to the support of a sinking world. A formidable tempest of the barbarians of Germany seemed ready to burst over the provinces of Gaul, and the mind of Gratian was oppressed and distracted by the administration of the western empire. In this important crisis the government of the East and the conduct of the Gothic war required the undivided attention of a hero and a statesman. A subject invested with such ample command would not long have preserved his fidelity to a distant benefactor; and the Imperial council embraced the wise and manly resolution of conferring an obligation rather than of yielding to an insult. It was the wish of Gratian to bestow the purple as the reward of virtue; but at the age of nineteen it is not easy for a prince, educated in the supreme rank, to understand the true characters of his ministers and generals. He attempted to weigh with an impartial hand their various merits and defects; and whilst he checked the rash confidence of ambition, he distrusted

tions of humanity and justice is [remarks Gibbon] a doctrine of which I still desire to remain ignorant."

the cautious wisdom which despaired of the republic. As each moment of delay diminished something of the power and resources of the future sovereign of the East, the situation of the times would not allow a tedious debate.

The choice of Gratian was soon declared in favour of an exile, whose father, only three years before, had suffered, under the sanction of *his* authority, an unjust and ignominious death. The great Theodosius, a name celebrated in history and dear to the catholic church, was summoned to the Imperial court, which had gradually retreated from the confines of Thrace to the more secure station of Sirmium. Five months after the death of Valens the emperor Gratian produced before the assembled troops *his* colleague and *their* master, who, after a modest, perhaps a sincere, resistance, was compelled to accept amidst the general acclamations the diadem, the purple, and the equal title of Augustus. The provinces of Thrace, Asia, and Egypt, over which Valens had reigned, were resigned to the administration of the new emperor; but as he was specially entrusted with the conduct of the Gothic war, the Illyrian præfecture was dismembered and the two great dioceses of Dacia and Macedonia were added to the dominions of the Eastern empire.[4]

It is not without the most sincere regret that I must now take leave of an accurate and faithful guide, who has composed the history of his own times without indulging the prejudices and passions which usually affect the mind of a contemporary. Ammianus Marcellinus, who terminates his useful work with the defeat and

---

4. *Editor's note:* At this point in the original, Gibbon describes in some detail the education of the younger Theodosius and the overwhelming part that pure merit played in his accessi ⌐ to empire.

death of Valens, recommends the more glorious subject
of the ensuing reign to the youthful vigour and eloquence of the rising generation. The rising generation
was not disposed to accept his advice or to imitate his
example; and in the study of the reign of Theodosius we
are reduced to illustrate the partial narrative of Zosimus
by the obscure hints of fragments and chronicles, by the
figurative style of poetry or panegyric, and by the precarious assistance of the ecclesiastical writers, who in the
heat of religious faction are apt to despise the profane
virtues of sincerity and moderation. Conscious of these
disadvantages, which will continue to involve a considerable portion of the decline and fall of the Roman
empire, I shall proceed with doubtful and timorous
steps. Yet I may boldly pronounce that the battle of
Hadrianople was never revenged by any signal or decisive victory of Theodosius over the barbarians; and the
expressive silence of his venal orators may be confirmed
by the observation of the condition and circumstances
of the times.

The fabric of a mighty state which has been reared
by the labours of successive ages could not be overturned by the misfortune of a single day, if the fatal
power of the imagination did not exaggerate the real
measure of the calamity. The loss of forty thousand
Romans who fell in the plains of Hadrianople might
have been soon recruited in the populous provinces of
the East, which contained so many millions of inhabitants. The courage of a soldier is found to be the cheapest and most common quality of human nature; and
sufficient skill to encounter an undisciplined foe might
have been speedily taught by the care of the surviving
centurions. If the barbarians were mounted on the
horses and equipped with the armour of their vanquished enemies, the numerous studs of Cappadocia and

Spain would have supplied new squadrons of cavalry; the thirty-four arsenals of the empire were plentifully stored with magazines of offensive and defensive arms; and the wealth of Asia might still have yielded an ample fund for the expenses of the war. But the effects which were produced by the battle of Hadrianople on the minds of the barbarians and of the Romans extended the victory of the former and the defeat of the latter far beyond the limits of a single day. A Gothic chief was heard to declare, with insolent moderation, that for his own part he was fatigued with slaughter; but that he was astonished how a people who fled before him like a flock of sheep could still presume to dispute the possession of their treasures and provinces. The same terrors which the name of the Huns had spread among the Gothic tribes were inspired, by the formidable name of the Goths, among the subjects and soldiers of the Roman empire. If Theodosius, hastily collecting his scattered forces, had led them into the field to encounter a victorious enemy, his army would have been vanquished by their own fears; and his rashness could not have been excused by the chance of success. But the *great* Theodosius, an epithet which he honourably deserved on this momentous occasion, conducted himself as the firm and faithful guardian of the republic. He fixed his headquarters at Thessalonica, the capital of the Macedonian diocese, from whence he could watch the irregular motions of the barbarians and direct the operations of his lieutenants from the gates of Constantinople to the shores of the Hadriatic. The fortifications and garrisons of the cities were strengthened; and the troops, among whom a sense of order and discipline was revived, were insensibly emboldened by the confidence of their own safety. From these secure stations they were encouraged to make frequent sallies on the barbarians who infested the adjacent country; and as they were seldom allowed to engage without some decisive superiority either of ground or of numbers, their enterprises were for the most part successful; and they were soon convinced, by their own experience, of the possibility of vanquishing their *invincible* enemies.

The detachments of these separate garrisons were gradually united into small armies; the same cautious measures were pursued, according to an extensive and well-concerted plan of operations; the events of each day added strength and spirit to the Roman arms; and the artful diligence of the emperor, who circulated the most favourable reports of the success of the war, contributed to subdue the pride of the barbarians and to animate the hopes and courage of his subjects. If instead of this faint and imperfect outline we could accurately represent the counsels and actions of Theodosius in four successive campaigns, there is reason to believe that his consummate skill would deserve the applause of every military reader. The republic had formerly been saved by the delays of Fabius; and while the splendid trophies of Scipio in the field of Zama attract the eyes of posterity, the camps and marches of the dictator among the hills of Campania may claim a juster proportion of the solid and independent fame which the general is not compelled to share either with fortune or with his troops. Such was likewise the merit of Theodosius; and the infirmities of his body, which most unseasonably languished under a long and dangerous disease, could not oppress the vigour of his mind or divert his attention from the public service.

The deliverance and peace of the Roman provinces was the work of prudence rather than of valour; the prudence of Theodosius was seconded by fortune; and the emperor never failed to seize, and to improve, every favourable circumstance. As long as the superior genius of Fritigern preserved the union and directed the motions of the barbarians, their power was not inadequate to the conquest of a great empire. The death of that hero, the predecessor and master of the renowned Alaric, relieved an impatient multitude from the intolerable yoke of discipline and discretion. The barbarians, who had been restrained by his authority, abandoned themselves to the dictates of their passions; and their passions were seldom uniform or consistent. An army of conquerors was broken into many disorderly bands of savage robbers; and their blind and irregular fury was not less pernicious to themselves than to their enemies. Their mischievous disposition was shown in the destruction of every object which they wanted strength to remove or taste to enjoy; and they often consumed, with improvident rage, the harvests or the granaries which soon afterwards became necessary for their own subsistence. A spirit of discord arose among the independent tribes and nations, which had been united only by the bands of a loose and voluntary alliance. The troops of the Huns and the Alani would naturally upbraid the flight of the Goths, who were not disposed to use with moderation the advantages of their fortune; the ancient jealousy of the Ostrogoths and the Visigoths could not long be suspended; and the haughty chiefs still remembered the insults and injuries which they had reciprocally offered or sustained while the nation was seated in the countries beyond the Danube. The progress of domestic faction abated the more diffusive sentiment of national animosity; and the officers of Theodosius were instructed to purchase, with liberal gifts and promises, the retreat or service of the discontented party. The acquisition of Modar, a prince of the royal blood of the Amali, gave a bold and faithful champion to the cause of Rome. The illustrious deserter soon obtained the rank of master general, with an important command; surprised an army of his countrymen, who were immersed in wine and sleep; and after a cruel slaughter of the astonished Goths returned with an immense spoil and four thousand waggons to the Imperial camp.

In the hands of a skilful politician the most different means may be successfully applied to the same ends; and the peace of the empire, which had been forwarded by the divisions, was accomplished by the reunion of the Gothic nation. Athanaric, who had been a patient spectator of these extraordinary events, was at length driven by the chance of arms from the dark recesses of the woods of Caucaland. He no longer hesitated to pass the Danube; and a very considerable part of the subjects of Fritigern, who already felt the inconveniences of anarchy, were easily persuaded to acknowledge for their king a Gothic Judge whose birth they respected and whose abilities they had frequently experienced. But age had chilled the daring spirit of Athanaric; and instead of leading his people to the field of battle and victory, he wisely listened to the fair proposal of an honourable and advantageous treaty. Theodosius, who was acquainted with the merit and power of his new ally, condescended to meet him at the distance of several miles from Constantinople, and entertained him in the Imperial city with the confidence of a friend and the magnificence of a monarch. "The barbarian prince observed with curious attention the variety of objects which attracted his notice and at last broke out into a sincere and passionate exclamation of wonder. I now behold (said he) what I never could believe, the glories of this stupendous capital! And as he cast his eyes around, he viewed and he admired the commanding situation of the city, the strength and beauty of the walls and public edifices, the capacious harbour crowded with innumerable vessels, the perpetual concourse of distant nations, and the arms and discipline of the troops. Indeed (continued Athanaric), the emperor of the Romans is a god upon earth; and the presumptuous man who dares to lift his hand against him is guilty of his own blood."

The Gothic king did not long enjoy this splendid and honourable reception; and as temperance was not the virtue of his nation, it may justly be suspected that his mortal disease was contracted amidst the pleasures of the Imperial banquets. But the policy of Theodosius derived more solid benefit from the death than he could have expected from the most faithful services of his ally. The funeral of Athanaric was performed with solemn rites in the capital of the East; a stately monument was erected to his memory; and his whole army, won by the liberal courtesy and decent grief of Theodosius, enlisted under the standard of the Roman empire. The submission of so great a body of the Visigoths was productive of the most salutary consequences; and the mixed influence of force, of reason, and of corruption became every day more powerful and more extensive. Each independent chieftain hastened to obtain a separate treaty, from the apprehension that an obstinate delay might expose *him*, alone and unprotected, to the revenge or justice of the conqueror. The general, or rather the final, capitulation of the Goths may be dated four years, one month, and twenty-five days, after the defeat and death of the emperor Valens.[5]

5. *Editor's note:* In the original, Gibbon dilates at this point upon the adventures of the Ostrogoths, who disdained the treaty with Theodosius. They retreated into unknown fastnesses of the North; made and violated a treaty with the

The original treaty, which fixed the settlement of the Goths, ascertained their privileges, and stipulated their obligations, would illustrate the history of Theodosius and his successors. The series of their history has imperfectly preserved the spirit and substance of this singular agreement. The ravages of war and tyranny had provided many large tracts of fertile but uncultivated land for the use of those barbarians who might not disdain the practice of agriculture. A numerous colony of the Visigoths was seated in Thrace; the remains of the Ostrogoths were planted in Phrygia and Lydia; their immediate wants were supplied by a distribution of corn and cattle; and their future industry was encouraged by an exemption from tribute during a certain term of years.

The barbarians would have deserved to feel the cruel and perfidious policy of the Imperial court if they had suffered themselves to be dispersed through the provinces. They required and they obtained the sole possession of the villages and districts assigned for their residence; they still cherished and · propagated their native manners and language; asserted, in the bosom of despotism, the freedom of their domestic government; and acknowledged the sovereignty of the emperor without submitting to the inferior jurisdiction of the laws and magistrates of Rome. The hereditary chiefs of the tribes and families were still permitted to command their followers in peace and war; but the royal dignity was abolished, and the generals of the Goths were appointed and removed at the pleasure of the emperor. An army of forty thousand Goths was maintained for

emperor of the West; and eventually returned four years later to the Lower Danube, where one of the generals of Theodosius inflicted on them so severe a defeat as to cripple temporarily their fighting power as a nation.

the perpetual service of the empire of the East; and those haughty troops, who assumed the title of *Fœderati,* or allies, were distinguished by their gold collars, liberal pay, and licentious privileges. Their native courage was improved by the use of arms and the knowledge of discipline; and while the republic was guarded or threatened by the doubtful sword of the barbarians, the last sparks of the military flame were finally extinguished in the minds of the Romans.

Theodosius had the address to persuade his allies that the conditions of peace, which had been extorted from him by prudence and necessity, were the voluntary expressions of his sincere friendship for the Gothic nation.[6] A different mode of vindication or apology was opposed to the complaints of the people, who loudly censured these shameful and dangerous concessions. The calamities of the war were painted in the most lively colours; and the first symptoms of the return of order, of plenty, and security were diligently exaggerated. The advocates of Theodosius could affirm, with some appearance of truth and reason, that it was impossible to extirpate so many warlike tribes, who were rendered desperate by the loss of their native country; and that the exhausted provinces would be revived by a fresh supply of soldiers and husbandmen. The barbarians still wore an angry and hostile aspect; but the experience of past times might encourage the hope that they would acquire the habits of industry and obedience, that their manners would be polished by time, education, and the influence of Christianity, and that

6. The Gothic historian [Jornandes] represents his nation as innocent, peaceable men, slow to anger and patient of injuries. According to Livy, the Romans conquered the world in their own defence.

their posterity would insensibly blend with the great body of the Roman people.

Notwithstanding these specious arguments and these sanguine expectations, it was apparent to every discerning eye that the Goths would long remain the enemies, and might soon become the conquerors, of the Roman empire. Their rude and insolent behavior expressed their contempt of the citizens and provincials, whom they insulted with impunity. To the zeal and valour of the barbarians Theodosius was indebted for the success of his arms; but their assistance was precarious, and they were sometimes seduced by a treacherous and inconstant disposition to abandon his standard at the moment when their service was the most essential. During the civil war against Maximus a great number of Gothic deserters retired into the morasses of Macedonia, wasted the adjacent provinces, and obliged the intrepid monarch to expose his person and exert his power to suppress the rising flame of rebellion.

The public apprehensions were fortified by the strong suspicion that these tumults were not the effect of accidental passion but the result of deep and premeditated design. It was generally believed that the Goths had signed the treaty of peace with an hostile and insidious spirit, and that their chiefs had previously bound themselves by a solemn and secret oath never to keep faith with the Romans, [but] to maintain the fairest show of loyalty and friendship and to watch the favourable moment of rapine, of conquest, and of revenge. But as the minds of the barbarians were not insensible to the power of gratitude, several of the Gothic leaders sincerely devoted themselves to the service of the empire, or at least of the emperor; the whole nation was insensibly divided into two opposite factions, and much sophistry was employed in conversation and dispute to compare the obligations of their first and second engagements. The Goths who considered themselves as the friends of peace, of justice, and of Rome were directed by the authority of Fravitta, a valiant and honourable youth, distinguished above the rest of his countrymen by the politeness of his manners, the liberality of his sentiments, and the mild virtues of social life. But the more numerous faction adhered to the fierce and faithless Priulf, who inflamed the passions and asserted the independence of his warlike followers.

On one of the solemn festivals, when the chiefs of both parties were invited to the Imperial table, they were insensibly heated by wine till they forgot the usual restraints of discretion and respect and betrayed in the presence of Theodosius the fatal secret of their domestic disputes. The emperor, who had been the reluctant witness of this extraordinary controversy, dissembled his fears and resentment and soon dismissed the tumultuous assembly. Fravitta, alarmed and exasperated by the insolence of his rival, whose departure from the palace might have been the signal of a civil war, boldly followed him and, drawing his sword, laid Priulf dead at his feet. Their companions flew to arms, and the faithful champion of Rome would have been oppressed by superior numbers if he had not been protected by the seasonable interposition of the Imperial guards. Such were the scenes of barbaric rage which disgraced the palace and table of the Roman emperor; and as the impatient Goths could only be restrained by the firm and temperate character of Theodosius, the public safety seemed to depend on the life and abilities of a single man.

Of the momentous happenings of the age of Theodosius, which are recounted in detail in the original, none exceeded in importance the final triumph of the orthodox group among the Christians and the final effective destruction of paganism. "Let us," said Theodosius in the first of fifteen severe edicts aimed primarily at the Arians, "believe the sole deity of the Father, the Son, and the Holy Ghost, under an equal majesty and a pious trinity." Persons so believing might "assume the title of catholic Christians; and as we judge that all others are extravagant madmen, we brand them with the infamous name of heretics. . . ." The heretical sects were prohibited from meeting; their leaders were subject to heavy fines; and those who adhered to them were gradually disqualified from many employments, forbidden from making wills, etc. A major monument to the orthodox zeal of Theodosius was his destruction of Arianism in Constantinople, its principal seat and fortress.

Up to the reigns of Gratian and Theodosius, even the Christian emperors had permitted to exist relatively unimpaired "the ancient fabric of Roman superstition, which was supported by the opinions and habits of eleven hundred years." But Gratian withdrew such official rights, immunities, and revenues as still remained to the pagan priesthood, while Theodosius placed formally before the senate the question "whether the worship of Jupiter or that of Christ should be the religion of the Romans." Under heavy pressure from the emperor the vote in favour of Christianity was overwhelming; and it was followed in the provinces by the seizure or destruction of all pagan temples and consecrated grounds and the prohibition of all pagan assemblies, rites, and sacrifices.

But the pagans were to have their subtle revenge. As vast numbers of pagan proselytes thronged the churches, the churches accommodated them by slowly adopting, in the worship of saints and relics, an equivalent to the pagan mythology. "The most respectable bishops," says Gibbon, "had persuaded themselves that the ignorant rustics would more cheerfully renounce the superstitions of paganism if they found some resemblance, some compensation, in the bosom of Christianity. The religion of Constantine achieved in less than a century the final conquest of the Roman empire; but the victors themselves were insensibly subdued by the arts of their vanquished rivals."

In the political sphere Gratian did not long maintain the early promise he had shown as emperor of the West. Not long after he chose Theodosius as his eastern colleague, he perished at the hands of one Maximus, who raised the standard of rebellion in Britain; and the growing barbarian threat led Theodosius to accept Maximus temporarily as a colleague, though he specified that Gratian's younger brother Valentinian should reign over Italy, Africa, and western Illyricum. But Maximus ambitiously took possession of Italy also, driving Valentinian, his sister Galla, and his mother Justina to Theodosius for assistance. Their pleas were sharpened by Theodosius' eye for Galla's beauty; and, in Gibbon's words, "the celebration of the royal nuptials was the assurance and signal of the civil war." Maximus was rapidly defeated and executed; and in the brief period before Valentinian was again confirmed as emperor of the West the empire was once again guided by a single master.

Valentinian's youth and inexperience made him, however, an easy mark for an ambitious usurper. Once Theodosius had retired to Constantinople, the real reins of power were soon collected in the hands of one Arbogastes, a Frank who commanded the armies of Gaul. Valentinian was found strangled shortly after a quarrel *with Arbogastes, who raised an associate named Eugenius to the purple. Once again Theodosius put down a western usurper and controlled the whole empire. He died a few months later, leaving the empire to two weak young sons, and leaving the Romans "terrified by the impending dangers of a feeble and divided administration."*

Arcadius and Honorius, the sons who respectively inherited the eastern and western empires, managed to live up to all these fears, being themselves ruled for the most part by venal, avaricious, and incompetent courtiers. The one impressive figure of their reigns was the great general Stilicho, whom Theodosius had entrusted on his deathbed with the care of his sons and of the republic. Stilicho, who so excited the jealousy and fears of Arcadius as to be declared an enemy of the republic by the senate at Constantinople, had to put up with such obstacles as repeatedly defending his life against assassins hired by the eastern emperor; but he still managed to recover the African provinces from a Moorish rebel named Gildo, and he organized the only serious resistance to the barbarian flood. As for Honorius, he "passed the slumber of his life a captive in his palace, a stranger in his country, and the patient, almost the indifferent, spectator of the ruin of the western empire."

Chapter XIV

(A.D. 398-408)

Revolt of the Goths – They plunder Greece – Two great invasions of Italy by Alaric and Radagaisus – They are repulsed by Stilicho – The Germans overrun Gaul – Disgrace and death of Stilicho[1]

IF THE subjects of Rome could be ignorant of their obligations to the great Theodosius, they were too soon convinced how painfully the spirit and abilities of their deceased emperor had supported the frail and mouldering edifice of the republic. He died in the month of January; and before the end of the winter of the same year the Gothic nation was in arms. The barbarian auxiliaries erected their independent standard and boldly avowed the hostile designs which they had long cherished in their ferocious minds. Their countrymen, who had been condemned by the conditions of the last treaty to a life of tranquillity and labour, deserted their farms at the first sound of the trumpet and eagerly resumed the weapons which they had reluctantly laid down. The barriers of the Danube were thrown open; the savage warriors of Scythia issued from their forests; and the uncommon severity of the winter allowed the poet to remark "that they rolled their ponderous waggons over the broad and icy back of the indignant river." The unhappy natives of the provinces to the south of the Danube submitted to the calamities which, in the course of twenty years, were almost grown familiar to their

1. *Editor's note:* Chapter XXX of the original.

imagination; and the various troops of barbarians who
gloried in the Gothic name were irregularly spread from
the woody shores of Dalmatia to the walls of Constantinople.

The interruption, or at least the diminution, of the
subsidy which the Goths had received from the prudent
liberality of Theodosius was the specious pretence of
their revolt; the affront was embittered by their contempt for the unwarlike sons of Theodosius; and their
resentment was inflamed by the weakness or treachery
of the minister of Arcadius. The frequent visits of Rufinus[2] to the camp of the barbarians, whose arms and
apparel he affected to imitate, were considered as a
sufficient evidence of his guilty correspondence; and the
public enemy, from a motive either of gratitude or of
policy, was attentive amidst the general devastation to
spare the private estates of the unpopular præfect.

The Goths, instead of being impelled by the blind and
headstrong passions of their chiefs, were now directed
by the bold and artful genius of Alaric. That renowned
leader was descended from the noble race of the Balti,
which yielded only to the royal dignity of the Amali;
he had solicited the command of the Roman armies;
and the Imperial court provoked him to demonstrate
the folly of their refusal and the importance of their
loss. Whatever hopes might be entertained of the conquest of Constantinople, the judicious general soon
abandoned an impracticable enterprise. In the midst of
a divided court and a discontented people, the emperor
Arcadius was terrified by the aspect of the Gothic arms;
but the want of wisdom and valour was supplied by
the strength of the city; and the fortifications, both of
the sea and land, might securely brave the impotent and

2. *Editor's note:* A knavish minister appointed by Theodosius and retained by Arcadius.

random darts of the barbarians. Alaric disdained to trample any longer on the prostrate and ruined countries of Thrace and Dacia, and he resolved to seek a plentiful harvest of fame and riches in a province which had hitherto escaped the ravages of war.

The character of the civil and military officers on whom Rufinus had devolved the government of Greece confirmed the public suspicion that he had betrayed the ancient seat of freedom and learning to the Gothic invader. The proconsul Antiochus was the unworthy son of a respectable father; and Gerontius, who commanded the provincial troops, was much better qualified to execute the oppressive orders of a tyrant than to defend with courage and ability a country most remarkably fortified by the hand of nature. Alaric had traversed without resistance the plains of Macedonia and Thessaly as far as the foot of Mount Oeta, a steep and woody range of hills almost impervious to his cavalry. They stretched from east to west to the edge of the seashore, and left, between the precipice and the Malian Gulf, an interval of three hundred feet, which in some places was contracted to a road capable of admitting only a single carriage. In this narrow pass of Thermopylæ, where Leonidas and the three hundred Spartans had gloriously devoted their lives, the Goths might have been stopped or destroyed by a skilful general; and perhaps the view of that sacred spot might have kindled some sparks of military ardour in the breasts of the degenerate Greeks. The troops which had been posted to defend the straits of Thermopylæ retired, as they were directed, without attempting to disturb the secure and rapid passage of Alaric; and the fertile fields of Phocis and Bœotia were instantly covered by a deluge of barbarians, who massacred the males of an age to bear arms and drove away the beautiful females with the spoil and cattle of the flaming villages. The travellers who visited Greece several years afterwards could easily discover the deep and bloody traces of the march of the Goths; and Thebes was less indebted for her preservation to the strength of her seven gates than to the eager haste of Alaric, who advanced to occupy the city of Athens and the important harbour of the Piræus.

The same impatience urged him to prevent the delay and danger of a siege by the offer of a capitulation; and as soon as the Athenians heard the voice of the Gothic herald, they were easily persuaded to deliver the greatest part of their wealth as the ransom of the city of Minerva and its inhabitants. The treaty was ratified by solemn oaths and observed with mutual fidelity. The Gothic prince, with a small and select train, was admitted within the walls; he indulged himself in the refreshment of the bath, accepted a splendid banquet which was provided by the magistrate, and affected to show that he was not ignorant of the manners of civilized nations. But the whole territory of Attica, from the promontory of Sunium to the town of Megara, was blasted by his baleful presence; and if we may use the comparison of a contemporary philosopher, Athens itself resembled the bleeding and empty skin of a slaughtered victim. The distance between Megara and Corinth could not much exceed thirty miles; but the *bad road*, an expressive name which it still bears among the Greeks, was or might easily have been made impassable for the march of an enemy. The thick and gloomy woods of Mount Cithæron covered the inland country; the Scironian rocks approached the water's edge and hung over the narrow and winding path, which was confined above six miles along the seashore. The passage of those rocks, so infamous in every age, was terminated by the isthmus of Corinth; and a small body of firm and intrepid soldiers might have successfully defended a temporary entrenchment of five or six miles from the Ionian to the Ægean Sea.

The confidence of the cities of Peloponnesus in their natural rampart had tempted them to neglect the care of their antique walls; and the avarice of the Roman governors had exhausted and betrayed the unhappy province. Corinth, Argos, Sparta, yielded without resistance to the arms of the Goths, and the most fortunate of the inhabitants were saved by death from beholding the slavery of their families and the conflagration of their cities. The vases and statues were distributed among the barbarians with more regard to the value of the materials than to the elegance of the workmanship; the female captives submitted to the laws of war; the enjoyment of beauty was the reward of valour; and the Greeks could not reasonably complain of an abuse which was justified by the example of the heroic times. The descendants of that extraordinary people, who had considered valour and discipline as the walls of Sparta, no longer remembered the generous reply of their ancestors to an invader more formidable than Alaric. "If thou art a god, thou wilt not hurt those who have never injured thee; if thou art a man, advance—and thou wilt find men equal to thyself."

From Thermopylæ to Sparta the leader of the Goths pursued his victorious march without encountering any mortal antagonists; but one of the advocates of expiring paganism has confidently asserted that the walls of Athens were guarded by the goddess Minerva with her formidable Ægis and by the angry phantom of Achilles, and that the conqueror was dismayed by the presence of the hostile deities of Greece. In an age of miracles it would perhaps be unjust to dispute the claim of the historian Zosimus to the common benefit; yet it cannot be dissembled that the mind of Alaric was ill prepared to receive, either in sleeping or waking visions, the impressions of Greek superstition. The songs of Homer and the fame of Achilles had probably never reached the ear of the illiterate barbarian; and the Christian faith, which he had devoutly embraced, taught him to despise the imaginary deities of Rome and Athens. The invasion of the Goths, instead of vindicating the honours, contributed at least accidentally to extirpate the last remains of paganism; and the mysteries of Ceres, which had subsisted eighteen hundred years, did not survive the destruction of Eleusis and the calamities of Greece.

The last hope of a people who could no longer depend on their arms, their gods, or their sovereign was placed in the powerful assistance of the general of the West; and Stilicho, who had not been permitted to repulse, advanced to chastise the invaders of Greece. A numerous fleet was equipped in the ports of Italy, and the troops, after a short and prosperous navigation over the Ionian Sea, were safely disembarked on the isthmus near the ruins of Corinth. The woody and mountainous country of Arcadia, the fabulous residence of Pan and the dryads, became the scene of a long and doubtful conflict between two generals not unworthy of each other. The skill and perseverance of the Roman at length prevailed; and the Goths, after sustaining a considerable loss from disease and desertion, gradually retreated to the lofty mountain of Pholoe, near the sources of the Peneus and on the frontiers of Elis—a sacred country which had formerly been exempted from the calamities of war.

The camp of the barbarians was immediately besieged; the waters of the river were diverted into another channel; and while they laboured under the intolerable pressure of thirst and hunger, a strong line of circumvallation was formed to prevent their escape. After these precautions Stilicho, too confident of victory, retired to enjoy his triumph in the theatrical games and lascivious dances of the Greeks; his soldiers, deserting their standards, spread themselves over the country of their allies, which they stripped of all that had been saved from the rapacious hands of the enemy. Alaric appears to have seized the favourable moment to execute one of those hardy enterprises in which the abilities of a general are displayed with more genuine lustre than in the tumult of a day of battle. To extricate himself from the prison of Peloponnesus it was necessary that he should pierce the entrenchments which surrounded his camp; that he should perform a difficult and dangerous march of thirty miles, as far as the Gulf of Corinth; and that he should transport his troops, his captives, and his spoil over an arm of the sea which, in the narrow interval between Rhium and the opposite shore, is at least half a mile in breadth.

The operations of Alaric must have been secret, prudent and rapid, since the Roman general was confounded by the intelligence that the Goths, who had eluded his efforts, were in full possession of the important province of Epirus. This unfortunate delay allowed Alaric sufficient time to conclude the treaty which he secretly negotiated with the ministers of Constantinople. The apprehension of a civil war compelled Stilicho to retire, at the haughty mandate of his rivals, from the dominions of Arcadius; and he respected, in the enemy of Rome, the honourable character of the ally and servant of the emperor of the East.[3]

3. *Editor's note:* Gibbon digresses briefly, at this point in the original, to describe the popular orations of Synesius

While the downfall of the barbarians was the topic of popular conversation, an edict was published at Constantinople which declared the promotion of Alaric to the rank of master general of the Eastern Illyricum. The Roman provincials, and the allies who had respected the faith of treaties, were justly indignant that the ruin of Greece and Epirus should be so liberally rewarded. The Gothic conqueror was received as a lawful magistrate in the cities which he had so lately besieged. The fathers whose sons he had massacred, the husbands whose wives he had violated, were subject to his authority; and the success of his rebellion encouraged the ambition of every leader of the foreign mercenaries. The use to which Alaric applied his new command distinguished the firm and judicious character of his policy. He issued his orders to the four magazines and manufactures of offensive and defensive arms, Margus, Ratiaria, Naissus, and Thessalonica, to provide his troops with an extraordinary supply of shields, helmets, swords, and spears; the unhappy provincials were compelled to forge the instruments of their own destruction; and the barbarians removed the only defect which had sometimes disappointed the efforts of their courage.

The birth of Alaric, the glory of his past exploits, and the confidence in his future designs insensibly united the body of the nation under his victorious standards; and with the unanimous consent of the barbarian chieftains the master general of Illyricum was elevated, according to ancient custom, on a shield and solemnly proclaimed king of the Visigoths. Armed with this double power, seated on the verge of the two empires, he alternately sold his deceitful promises to the courts of Arcadius and

advising the court and the people how best to meet the barbarian menace.

Honorius till he declared and executed his resolution of invading the dominions of the West. The provinces of Europe which belonged to the eastern emperor were already exhausted, those of Asia were inaccessible, and the strength of Constantinople had resisted his attack. But he was tempted by the fame, the beauty, the wealth of Italy, which he had twice visited; and he secretly aspired to plant the Gothic standard on the walls of Rome and to enrich his army with the accumulated spoils of three hundred triumphs.

The scarcity of facts and the uncertainty of dates oppose our attempts to describe the circumstances of the first invasion of Italy by the arms of Alaric. His march, perhaps from Thessalonica through the warlike and hostile country of Pannonia as far as the foot of the Julian Alps; his passage of those mountains, which were strongly guarded by troops and entrenchments; the siege of Aquileia and the conquest of the provinces of Istria and Venetia, appear to have employed a considerable time. Unless his operations were extremely cautious and slow, the length of the interval would suggest a probable suspicion that the Gothic king retreated towards the banks of the Danube and reinforced his army with fresh swarms of barbarians before he again attempted to penetrate into the heart of Italy.[4]

The emperor Honorius was distinguished above his subjects by the pre-eminence of fear as well as of rank. The pride and luxury in which he was educated had not allowed him to suspect that there existed on the earth any power presumptuous enough to invade the repose of the successor of Augustus. The arts of flattery

4. *Editor's note:* Here is omitted a brief passage in which Gibbon describes the effect of the Gothic invasion upon the lives of two individuals, and the general sense of public consternation and despair.

concealed the impending danger till Alaric approached
the palace of Milan. But when the sound of war had
awakened the young emperor, instead of flying to arms
with the spirit or even the rashness of his age, he eagerly
listened to those timid counsellors who proposed to
convey his sacred person and his faithful attendants to
some secure and distant station in the provinces of
Gaul. Stilicho alone had courage and authority to resist
this disgraceful measure, which would have abandoned
Rome and Italy to the barbarians; but as the troops of
the palace had been lately detached to the Rhætian
frontier, and as the resource of new levies was slow and
precarious, the general of the West could only promise
that if the court of Milan would maintain their ground
during his absence he would soon return with an army
equal to the encounter of the Gothic king.

Without losing a moment (while each moment was
so important to the public safety), Stilicho hastily embarked on the Larian lake, ascended the mountains of
ice and snow amidst the severity of an Alpine winter,
and suddenly repressed, by his unexpected presence,
the enemy who had disturbed the tranquillity of Rhætia.
The barbarians, perhaps some tribes of the Alemanni,
respected the firmness of a chief who still assumed the
language of command; and the choice which he condescended to make of a select number of their bravest
youth was considered as a mark of his esteem and
favour. The cohorts who were delivered from the neighbouring foe diligently repaired to the Imperial standard;
and Stilicho issued his orders to the most remote troops
of the West to advance by rapid marches to the defence
of Honorius and of Italy. The fortresses of the Rhine
were abandoned, and the safety of Gaul was protected
only by the faith of the Germans and the ancient terror
of the Roman name. Even the legion which had been

stationed to guard the wall of Britain against the Caledonians of the North was hastily recalled, and a numerous body of the cavalry of the Alani was persuaded to engage in the service of the emperor, who anxiously expected the return of his general. The prudence and vigour of Stilicho were conspicuous on this occasion, which revealed at the same time the weakness of the falling empire. The legions of Rome, which had long since languished in the gradual decay of discipline and courage, were exterminated by the Gothic and civil wars; and it was found impossible without exhausting and exposing the provinces to assemble an army for the defence of Italy.

When Stilicho seemed to abandon his sovereign in the unguarded palace of Milan, he had probably calculated the term of his absence, the distance of the enemy, and the obstacles that might retard their march. He principally depended on the rivers of Italy, the Adige, the Mincius, the Oglio, and the Addua, which in the winter or spring, by the fall of rains or by the melting of the snows, are commonly swelled into broad and impetuous torrents. But the season happened to be remarkably dry, and the Goths could traverse without impediment the wide and stony beds, whose centre was faintly marked by the course of a shallow stream. The bridge and passage of the Addua was secured by a strong detachment of the Gothic army; and as Alaric approached the walls, or rather the suburbs, of Milan he enjoyed the proud satisfaction of seeing the emperor of the Romans fly before him.

Honorius, accompanied by a feeble train of statesmen and eunuchs, hastily retreated towards the Alps, with a design of securing his person in the city of Arles, which had often been the royal residence of his predecessors. But Honorius had scarcely passed the Po before he was overtaken by the speed of the Gothic cavalry; the urgency of the danger compelled him to seek a temporary shelter within the fortification of Asta, a town of Liguria or Piedmont situate on the banks of the Tanarus. The siege of an obscure place, which contained so rich a prize and seemed incapable of a long resistance, was instantly formed and indefatigably pressed by the king of the Goths; and the bold declaration which the emperor might afterwards make, that his breast had never been susceptible of fear, did not probably obtain much credit even in his own court.

In the last and almost hopeless extremity, after the barbarians had already proposed the indignity of a capitulation, the Imperial captive was suddenly relieved by the fame, the approach, and at length the presence of the hero whom he had so long expected. At the head of a chosen and intrepid vanguard Stilicho swam the stream of the Addua, to gain the time which he must have lost in the attack of the bridge; the passage of the Po was an enterprise of much less hazard and difficulty; and the successful action in which he cut his way through the Gothic camp under the walls of Asta revived the hopes and vindicated the honour of Rome. Instead of grasping the fruit of his victory, the barbarian was gradually invested on every side by the troops of the West, who successively issued through all the passes of the Alps; his quarters were straitened, his convoys were intercepted, and the vigilance of the Romans prepared to form a chain of fortifications and to besiege the lines of the besiegers. A military council was assembled of the long-haired chiefs of the Gothic nation; of aged warriors, whose bodies were wrapped in furs and whose stern countenances were marked with honourable wounds. They weighed the glory of persisting in their attempt against the advantage of securing their plunder, and they recommended the prudent measure of a seasonable retreat. In this important debate Alaric displayed the spirit of the conqueror of Rome; and after he had reminded his countrymen of their achievements and of their designs, he concluded his animating speech by the solemn and positive assurance that he was resolved to find in Italy either a kingdom or a grave.

The loose discipline of the barbarians always exposed them to the danger of a surprise; but instead of choosing the dissolute hours of riot and intemperance, Stilicho resolved to attack the Christian Goths whilst they were devoutly employed in celebrating the festival of Easter. The execution of the stratagem (or, as it was termed by the clergy, of the sacrilege) was entrusted to Saul, a barbarian and a pagan who had served, however, with distinguished reputation among the veteran generals of Theodosius. The camp of the Goths, which Alaric had pitched in the neighbourhood of Pollentia, was thrown into confusion by the sudden and impetuous charge of the Imperial cavalry; but in a few moments the undaunted genius of their leader gave them an order and a field of battle, and, soon as they had recovered from their astonishment, the pious confidence that the God of the Christians would assert their cause added new strength to their native valour. In this engagement, which was long maintained with equal courage and success, the chief of the Alani, whose diminutive and savage form concealed a magnanimous soul, approved his suspected loyalty by the zeal with which he fought and fell in the service of the republic; and the fame of this gallant barbarian has been imperfectly preserved in the verses of Claudian, since the poet who celebrates his virtue has omitted the mention of his name. His death was followed by the flight and dismay of the squadrons which he commanded; and the defeat of the wing of cavalry might have decided the victory of Alaric if Stilicho had not immediately led the Roman and barbarian infantry to the attack.

The skill of the general and the bravery of the soldiers surmounted every obstacle. In the evening of the bloody day the Goths retreated from the field of battle, the entrenchments of their camp were forced, and the scene of rapine and slaughter made some atonement for the calamities which they had inflicted on the subjects of the empire. The magnificent spoils of Corinth and Argos enriched the veterans of the West; the captive wife of Alaric, who had impatiently claimed his promise of Roman jewels and patrician handmaids, was reduced to implore the mercy of the insulting foe; and many thousand prisoners, released from the Gothic chains, dispersed through the provinces of Italy the praises of their heroic deliverer. The triumph of Stilicho was compared by the poet, and perhaps by the public, to that of Marius, who in the same part of Italy had encountered and destroyed another army of Northern barbarians. The huge bones and the empty helmets of the Cimbri and of the Goths would easily be confounded by succeeding generations; and posterity might erect a common trophy to the memory of the two most illustrious generals who had vanquished, on the same memorable ground, the two most formidable enemies of Rome.

The eloquence of Claudian has celebrated with lavish applause the victory of Pollentia, one of the most glorious days in the life of his patron; but his reluctant and partial muse bestows more genuine praise on the character of the Gothic king. His name is indeed branded with the reproachful epithets of pirate and robber, to which the conquerors of every age are so justly entitled; but the poet of Stilicho is compelled to acknowledge that Alaric possessed the invincible temper of mind which rises superior to every misfortune and derives new resources from adversity. After the total defeat of his infantry he escaped, or rather withdrew, from the field of battle with the greatest part of his cavalry entire and unbroken. Without wasting a moment to lament the irreparable loss of so many brave companions, he left his victorious enemy to bind in chains the captive images of a Gothic king and boldly resolved to break through the unguarded passes of the Apennine, to spread desolation over the fruitful face of Tuscany, and to conquer or die before the gates of Rome.

The capital was saved by the active and incessant diligence of Stilicho; but he respected the despair of his enemy and, instead of committing the fate of the republic to the chance of another battle, he proposed to purchase the absence of the barbarians. The spirit of Alaric would have rejected such terms, the permission of a retreat and the offer of a pension, with contempt and indignation; but he exercised a limited and precarious authority over the independent chieftains, who had raised him for *their* service above the rank of his equals; they were still less disposed to follow an unsuccessful general, and many of them were tempted to consult their interest by a private negotiation with the minister of Honorius. The king submitted to the voice of his people, ratified the treaty with the empire of the West, and repassed the Po with the remains of the flourishing army which he had led into Italy. A considerable part of the Roman forces still continued to attend his motions; and Stilicho, who maintained a secret correspondence with some of the barbarian chiefs, was punctually appraised of the designs that were formed in the camp and council of Alaric. The king of the Goths, ambitious to signalize his retreat by some splendid achievement, had resolved to occupy the important city of Verona, which commands the principal passage of the Rhætian Alps; and, directing his march through the territories of those German tribes whose alliance would restore his exhausted strength, to invade on the side of the Rhine the wealthy and unsuspecting provinces of Gaul.

Ignorant of the treason which had already betrayed his bold and judicious enterprise, he advanced towards the passes of the mountains, already possessed by the Imperial troops, where he was exposed almost at the same instant to a general attack in the front, on his flanks, and in the rear. In this bloody action, at a small distance from the walls of Verona, the loss of the Goths was not less heavy than that which they had sustained in the defeat of Pollentia; and their valiant king, who escaped by the swiftness of his horse, must either have been slain or made prisoner if the hasty rashness of the Alani had not disappointed the measures of the Roman general. Alaric secured the remains of his army on the adjacent rocks and prepared himself with undaunted resolution to maintain a siege against the superior numbers of the enemy, who invested him on all sides. But he could not oppose the destructive progress of hunger and disease; nor was it possible for him to check the continual desertion of his impatient and capricious barbarians. In this extremity he still found resources in his own courage, or in the moderation of his adversary; and the retreat of the Gothic king was considered as the deliverance of Italy. Yet the people, and even the clergy, incapable of forming any rational judgment of the business of peace and war, presumed to arraign the policy of Stilicho, who so often vanquished, so often surrounded, and so often dismissed the implacable en-

emy of the republic. The first moment of the public
safety is devoted to gratitude and joy, but the second
is diligently occupied by envy and calumny.

The citizens of Rome had been astonished by the
approach of Alaric; and the diligence with which they
laboured to restore the walls of the capital confessed
their own fears and the decline of the empire. After
the retreat of the barbarians Honorius was directed to
accept the dutiful invitation of the senate and to celebrate in the Imperial city the auspicious era of the
Gothic victory and of his sixth consulship. The suburbs
and the streets, from the Milvian bridge to the Palatine
mount, were filled by the Roman people, who in the
space of an hundred years had only thrice been honoured with the presence of their sovereigns. While their
eyes were fixed on the chariot where Stilicho was
deservedly seated by the side of his royal pupil, they
applauded the pomp of a triumph which was not
stained, like that of Constantine or of Theodosius, with
civil blood. The procession passed under a lofty arch,
which had been purposely erected: but in less than
seven years the Gothic conquerors of Rome might read,
if they were able to read, the superb inscription of that
monument, which attested the total defeat and destruction of their nation.[5]

While Italy rejoiced in her deliverance from the
Goths, a furious tempest was excited among the nations
of Germany, who yielded to the irresistible impulse that
appears to have been gradually communicated from the

5. *Editor's note:* The most noteworthy result of Honorius's
visit to Rome, discussed at greater length in the original,
was his final prohibition of the contests of gladiators in the
amphitheatre. Upon quitting Rome he transferred the Imperial residence to Ravenna, chosen as "an inaccessible
fortress . . . where he might securely remain, while the
open country was covered by a deluge of barbarians."

eastern extremity of the continent of Asia.[6] The chain of events is interrupted, or rather is concealed, as it passes from the Volga to the Vistula, through the dark interval which separates the extreme limits of the Chinese and of the Roman geography. Yet the temper of the barbarians and the experience of successive emigrations sufficiently declare that the Huns, who were oppressed by the arms of the Geougen, soon withdrew from the presence of an insulting victor. The countries towards the Euxine were already occupied by their kindred tribes; and their hasty flight, which they soon converted into a bold attack, would more naturally be directed towards the rich and level plains through which the Vistula gently flows into the Baltic sea. The North must again have been alarmed and agitated by the invasion of the Huns; and the nations who retreated before them must have pressed with incumbent weight on the confines of Germany. The inhabitants of those regions which the ancients have assigned to the Suevi, the Vandals, and the Burgundians might embrace the resolution of abandoning to the fugitives of Sarmatia their woods and morasses, or at least of discharging their superfluous numbers on the provinces of the Roman empire.

About four years after the victorious Toulun had assumed the title of Khan of the Geougen, another barbarian, the haughty Rhodogast, or Radagaisus, marched from the northern extremities of Germany almost to the gates of Rome and left the remains of his army to achieve the destruction of the West. The Vandals, the

6. *Editor's note:* At this point in the original, Gibbon describes the growth of a warlike Tartar group called the Geougen, which pressed upon the westward-moving Huns and conquered those in the territory north of the Caspian Sea.

Suevi, and the Burgundians formed the strength of this mighty host; but the Alani, who had found an hospitable reception in their new seats, added their active cavalry to the heavy infantry of the Germans; and the Gothic adventurers crowded so eagerly to the standard of Radagaisus that, by some historians, he has been styled the King of the Goths. Twelve thousand warriors, distinguished above the vulgar by their noble birth or their valiant deeds, glittered in the van; and the whole multitude, which was not less than two hundred thousand fighting men, might be increased by the accession of women, of children, and of slaves to the amount of four hundred thousand persons. This formidable emigration issued from the same coast of the Baltic which had poured forth the myriads of the Cimbri and Teutones to assault Rome and Italy in the vigour of the republic. After the departure of those barbarians their native country, which was marked by the vestiges of their greatness, long ramparts and gigantic moles, remained during some ages a vast and dreary solitude, till the human species was renewed by the powers of generation and the vacancy was filled by the influx of new inhabitants. The nations who now usurp an extent of land which they are unable to cultivate would soon be assisted by the industrious poverty of their neighbours, if the government of Europe did not protect the claims of dominion and property.

The correspondence of nations was in that age so imperfect and precarious that the revolutions of the North might escape the knowledge of the court of Ravenna till the dark cloud which was collected along the coast of the Baltic burst in thunder upon the banks of the Upper Danube. The emperor of the West, if his ministers disturbed his amusements by the news of the impending danger, was satisfied with being the occasion and the spectator of the war. The safety of Rome was entrusted to the counsels and the sword of Stilicho; but such was the feeble and exhausted state of the empire that it was impossible to restore the fortifications of the Danube or to prevent by a vigorous effort the invasion of the Germans. The hopes of the vigilant minister of Honorius were confined to the defence of Italy. He once more abandoned the provinces, recalled the troops, pressed the new levies, which were rigorously exacted and pusillanimously eluded; employed the most efficacious means to arrest or allure the deserters; and offered the gift of freedom and of two pieces of gold to all the slaves who would enlist. By these efforts he painfully collected from the subjects of a great empire an army of thirty or forty thousand men, which in the days of Scipio or Camillus would have been instantly furnished by the free citizens of the territory of Rome. The thirty legions of Stilicho were reinforced by a large body of barbarian auxiliaries; the faithful Alani were personally attached to his service; and the troops of Huns and of Goths, who marched under the banners of their native princes Huldin and Sarus, were animated by interest and resentment to oppose the ambition of Radagaisus.

The king of the confederate Germans passed without resistance the Alps, the Po, and the Apennine, leaving on one hand the inaccessible palace of Honorius securely buried among the marshes of Ravenna, and on the other the camp of Stilicho, who had fixed his headquarters at Ticinum, or Pavia, but who seems to have avoided a decisive battle till he had assembled his distant forces. Many cities of Italy were pillaged or destroyed; and the siege of Florence by Radagaisus is one of the earliest events in the history of that celebrated republic, whose firmness checked and delayed the unskilful fury of the barbarians.

The senate and people trembled at their approach within an hundred and eighty miles of Rome, and anxiously compared the danger which they had escaped with the new perils to which they were exposed. Alaric was a Christian and a soldier, the leader of a disciplined army, who understood the laws of war, who respected the sanctity of treaties, and who had familiarly conversed with the subjects of the empire in the same camps and the same churches. The savage Radagaisus was a stranger to the manners, the religion, and even the language of the civilized nations of the South. The fierceness of his temper was exasperated by cruel superstition; and it was universally believed that he had bound himself by a solemn vow to reduce the city into a heap of stones and ashes, and to sacrifice the most illustrious of the Roman senators on the altars of those gods who were appeased by human blood. The public danger, which should have reconciled all domestic animosities, displayed the incurable madness of religious faction. The oppressed votaries of Jupiter and Mercury respected, in the implacable enemy of Rome, the character of a devout pagan; loudly declared that they were more apprehensive of the sacrifices than of the arms of Radagaisus; and secretly rejoiced in the calamities of their country, which condemned the faith of their Christian adversaries.

Florence was reduced to the last extremity, and the fainting courage of the citizens was supported only by the authority of St. Ambrose, who had communicated in a dream the promise of a speedy deliverance. On a sudden they beheld from their walls the banners of Stilicho, who advanced with his united force to the relief of the faithful city, and who soon marked that fatal spot for the grave of the barbarian host.

The apparent contradictions of those writers who

variously relate the defeat of Radagaisus may be reconciled without offering much violence to their respective
testimonies. Orosius and Augustin, who were intimately
connected by friendship and religion, ascribe this miraculous victory to the providence of God rather than to
the valour of man. They strictly exclude every idea of
chance or even of bloodshed and positively affirm that
the Romans, whose camp was the scene of plenty and
idleness, enjoyed the distress of the barbarians slowly
expiring on the sharp and barren ridge of the hills of
Fæsulæ, which rise above the city of Florence. Their
extravagant assertion that not a single soldier of the
Christian army was killed or even wounded may be dismissed with silent contempt; but the rest of the narrative of Augustin and Orosius is consistent with the
state of the war and the character of Stilicho. Conscious
that he commanded the *last* army of the republic, his
prudence would not expose it in the open field to the
headstrong fury of the Germans. The method of surrounding the enemy with strong lines of circumvallation,
which he had twice employed against the Gothic king,
was repeated on a larger scale and with more considerable effect. The examples of Cæsar must have been
familiar to the most illiterate of the Roman warriors;
and the fortifications of Dyrrachium, which connected
twenty-four castles by a perpetual ditch and rampart
of fifteen miles, afforded the model of an entrenchment
which might confine and starve the most numerous host
of barbarians. The Roman troops had less degenerated
from the industry than from the valour of their ancestors; and if the servile and laborious work offended the
pride of the soldiers, Tuscany could supply many thousand peasants who would labour, though perhaps they
would not fight, for the salvation of their native country.

The imprisoned multitude of horses and men was

gradually destroyed by famine rather than by the sword; but the Romans were exposed during the progress of such an extensive work to the frequent attacks of an impatient enemy. The despair of the hungry barbarians would precipitate them against the fortifications of Stilicho; the general might sometimes indulge the ardour of his brave auxiliaries, who eagerly pressed to assault the camp of the Germans; and these various incidents might produce the sharp and bloodly conflicts which dignify the narrative of Zosimus and the Chronicles of Prosper and Marcellinus. A seasonable supply of men and provisions had been introduced into the walls of Florence, and the famished host of Radagaisus was in its turn besieged.

The proud monarch of so many warlike nations, after the loss of his bravest warriors, was reduced to confide either in the faith of a capitulation or in the clemency of Stilicho. But the death of the royal captive, who was ignominiously beheaded, disgraced the triumph of Rome and of Christianity; and the short delay of his execution was sufficient to brand the conqueror with the guilt of cool and deliberate cruelty. The famished Germans who escaped the fury of the auxiliaries were sold as slaves, at the contemptible price of as many single pieces of gold; but the difference of food and climate swept away great numbers of those unhappy strangers; and it was observed that the inhuman purchasers, instead of reaping the fruits of their labour, were soon obliged to provide the expense of their interment. Stilicho informed the emperor and the senate of his success and deserved a second time the glorious title of Deliverer of Italy.

The fame of the victory, and more especially of the miracle, has encouraged a vain persuasion that the whole army, or rather nation, of Germans who migrated from the shores of the Baltic miserably perished under the walls of Florence. Such indeed was the fate of Radagaisus himself, of his brave and faithful companions, and of more than one third of the various multitude of Sueves and Vandals, of Alani and Burgundians, who adhered to the standard of their general. The union of such an army might excite our surprise, but the causes of separation are obvious and forcible: the pride of birth, the insolence of valour, the jealousy of command, the impatience of subordination, and the obstinate conflict of opinions, of interests, and of passions among so many kings and warriors who were untaught to yield or to obey. After the defeat of Radagaisus two parts of the German host, which must have exceeded the number of one hundred thousand men, still remained in arms between the Apennine and the Alps or between the Alps and the Danube. It is uncertain whether they attempted to revenge the death of their general; but their irregular fury was soon diverted by the prudence and firmness of Stilicho, who opposed their march and facilitated their retreat, who considered the safety of Rome and Italy as the great object of his care, and who sacrificed with too much indifference the wealth and tranquillity of the distant provinces. The barbarians acquired, from the junction of some Pannonian deserters, the knowledge of the country and of the roads, and the invasion of Gaul, which Alaric had designed, was executed by the remains of the great army of Radagaisus.

Yet if they expected to derive any assistance from the tribes of Germany who inhabited the banks of the Rhine their hopes were disappointed. The Alemanni preserved a state of inactive neutrality, and the Franks distinguished their zeal and courage in the defence of the empire. In the rapid progress down the Rhine, which was the first act of the administration of Stilicho, he had applied himself with peculiar attention to secure the alliance of the warlike Franks and to remove the irreconcilable enemies of peace and of the republic. Marcomir, one of their kings, was publicly convicted before the tribunal of the Roman magistrate of violating the faith of treaties. He was sentenced to a mild but distant exile in the province of Tuscany; and this degradation of the legal dignity was so far from exciting the resentment of his subjects that they punished with death the turbulent Sunno, who attempted to revenge his brother, and maintained a dutiful allegiance to the princes who were established on the throne by the choice of Stilicho.

When the limits of Gaul and Germany were shaken by the northern emigration, the Franks bravely encountered the single force of the Vandals, who, regardless of the lessons of adversity, had again separated their troops from the standard of their barbarian allies. They paid the penalty of their rashness; and twenty thousand Vandals, with their king Godigisclus, were slain in the field of battle. The whole people must have been extirpated if the squadrons of the Alani, advancing to their relief, had not trampled down the infantry of the Franks, who after an honourable resistance were compelled to relinquish the unequal contest. The victorious confederates pursued their march, and on the last day of the year, in a season when the waters of the Rhine were most probably frozen, they entered without opposition the defenceless provinces of Gaul. This memorable passage of the Suevi, the Vandals, the Alani, and the Burgundians, who never afterwards retreated, may be considered as the fall of the Roman empire in the countries beyond the Alps; and the barriers which had so long separated the savage and the civilized nations of the earth were from that fatal moment levelled with the ground.

While the peace of Germany was secured by the attachment of the Franks and the neutrality of the Alemanni, the subjects of Rome, unconscious of their approaching calamities, enjoyed the state of quiet and prosperity which had seldom blessed the frontiers of Gaul. Their flocks and herds were permitted to graze in the pastures of the barbarians; their huntsmen penetrated without fear or danger into the darkest recesses of the Hercynian wood. The banks of the Rhine were crowned, like those of the Tiber, with elegant houses and well-cultivated farms; and if a poet descended the river he might express his doubt on which side was situated the territory of the Romans. This scene of peace and plenty was suddenly changed into a desert; and the prospect of the smoking ruins could alone distinguish the solitude of nature from the desolation of man. The flourishing city of Metz was surprised and destroyed, and many thousand Christians were inhumanly massacred in the church. Worms perished after a long and obstinate siege; Strasbourg, Spires, Rheims, Tournay, Arras, Amiens, experienced the cruel oppression of the German yoke; and the consuming flames of war spread from the banks of the Rhine over the greatest part of the seventeen provinces of Gaul. That rich and extensive country, as far as the ocean, the Alps, and the Pyrenees, was delivered to the barbarians, who drove before them in a promiscuous crowd the bishop, the senator, and the virgin, laden with the spoils of their houses and altars.[7]

7. *Editor's note:* The original further recounts here the seditions of Britain—in which two pretenders were elevated and then assassinated—before a common soldier, possessing

The poet, whose flattery has ascribed to the Roman eagle the victories of Pollentia and Verona, pursues the hasty retreat of Alaric from the confines of Italy with a horrid train of imaginary spectres, such as might hover over an army of barbarians which was almost exterminated by war, famine, and disease. In the course of this unfortunate expedition the king of the Goths must indeed have sustained a considerable loss, and his harassed forces required an interval of repose to recruit their numbers and revive their confidence. Adversity had exercised and displayed the genius of Alaric; and the fame of his valour invited to the Gothic standard the bravest of the barbarian warriors, who from the Euxine to the Rhine were agitated by the desire of rapine and conquest. He had deserved the esteem, and he soon accepted the friendship, of Stilicho himself. Renouncing the service of the emperor of the East, Alaric concluded with the court of Ravenna a treaty of peace and alliance by which he was declared master general of the Roman armies throughout the præfecture of Illyricum, as it was claimed, according to the true and ancient limits, by the minister of Honorius.

The execution of the ambitious design, which was either stipulated or implied in the articles of the treaty, appears to have been suspended by the formidable irruption of Radagaisus; and the neutrality of the Gothic king may perhaps be compared to the indifference of Cæsar, who in the conspiracy of Catiline refused either to assist or to oppose the enemy of the republic. After the defeat of the Vandals, Stilicho resumed his pretensions to the provinces of the East, appointed civil magistrates for the administration of justice and of the

the fortunate name of Constantine, achieved enough success to rule over Britain as well as Spain and those cities of Gaul which had not succumbed to the barbarians.

finances, and declared his impatience to lead to the gates of Constantinople the united armies of the Romans and of the Goths. The prudence, however, of Stilicho, his aversion to civil war, and his perfect knowledge of the weakness of the state may countenance the suspicion that domestic peace rather than foreign conquest was the object of his policy, and that his principal care was to employ the forces of Alaric at a distance from Italy.

This design could not long escape the penetration of the Gothic king, who continued to hold a doubtful and perhaps a treacherous correspondence with the rival courts, who protracted, like a dissatisfied mercenary, his languid operations of Thessaly and Epirus and who soon returned to claim the extravagant reward of his ineffectual services. From his camp near Æmona, on the confines of Italy, he transmitted to the emperor of the West a long account of promises, of expenses, and of demands, called for immediate satisfaction, and clearly intimated the consequences of a refusal. Yet if his conduct was hostile his language was decent and dutiful. He humbly professed himself the friend of Stilicho and the soldier of Honorius, offered his person and his troops to march without delay against the usurper of Gaul, and solicited, as a permanent retreat for the Gothic nation, the possession of some vacant province of the western empire.

The political and secret transactions of two statesmen who laboured to deceive each other and the world must forever have been concealed in the impenetrable darkness of the cabinet if the debates of a popular assembly had not thrown some rays of light on the correspondence of Alaric and Stilicho. The necessity of finding some artificial support for a government which, from a principle not of moderation but of weakness, was reduced to negotiate with its own subjects had insensibly revived

the authority of the Roman senate; and the minister of
Honorius respectfully consulted the legislative council
of the republic. Stilicho assembled the senate in the
palace of the Cæsars, represented in a studied oration
the actual state of affairs, proposed the demands of the
Gothic king, and submitted to their consideration the
choice of peace or war. The senators, as if they had been
suddenly awakened from a dream of four hundred years,
appeared on this important occasion to be inspired by
the courage rather than by the wisdom of their predecessors. They loudly declared, in regular speeches or
in tumultuary acclamations, that it was unworthy of
the majesty of Rome to purchase a precarious and disgraceful truce from a barbarian king; and that, in the
judgment of a magnanimous people, the chance of ruin
was always preferable to the certainty of dishonor. The
minister, whose pacific intentions were seconded only
by the voices of a few servile and venal followers, attempted to allay the general ferment by an apology for
his own conduct, and even for the demands of the
Gothic prince. "The payment of a subsidy, which had
excited the indignation of the Romans, ought not (such
was the language of Stilicho) to be considered in the
odious light either of a tribute or of a ransom extorted
by the menaces of a barbarian enemy. Alaric had faithfully asserted the just pretensions of the republic to the
provinces which were usurped by the Greeks of Constantinople; he modestly required the fair and stipulated
recompense of his services; and if he had desisted from
the prosecution of his enterprise, he had obeyed in his
retreat the peremptory though private letters of the emperor himself. These contradictory orders (he would not
dissemble the errors of his own family) had been procured by the intercession of Serena. The tender piety of
his wife had been too deeply affected by the discord

of the royal brothers, the sons of her adopted father; and the sentiments of nature had too easily prevailed over the stern dictates of the public welfare."

These ostensible reasons, which faintly disguise the obscure intrigues of the palace of Ravenna, were supported by the authority of Stilicho and obtained, after a warm debate, the reluctant approbation of the senate. The tumult of virtue and freedom subsided; and the sum of four thousand pounds of gold was granted, under the name of a subsidy, to secure the peace of Italy and to conciliate the friendship of the king of the Goths. Lampadius alone, one of the most illustrious members of the assembly, still persisted in his dissent; [he] exclaimed with a loud voice, "This is not a treaty of peace but of servitude," and escaped the danger of such bold opposition by immediately retiring to the sanctuary of a Christian church.

But the reign of Stilicho drew towards its end, and the proud minister might perceive the symptoms of his approaching disgrace. The generous boldness of Lampadius had been applauded; and the senate, so patiently resigned to a long servitude, rejected with disdain the offer of invidious and imaginary freedom. The troops, who still assumed the name and prerogatives of the Roman legions, were exasperated by the partial affection of Stilicho for the barbarians; and the people imputed to the mischievous policy of the minister the public misfortunes which were the natural consequence of their own degeneracy.

Yet Stilicho might have continued to brave the clamours of the people, and even of the soldiers, if he could have maintained his dominion over the feeble mind of his pupil. But the respectful attachment of Honorius was converted into fear, suspicion, and hatred. The crafty Olympius, who concealed his vices under the mask

of Christian piety, had secretly undermined the benefactor by whose favour he was promoted to the honourable offices of the Imperial palace. Olympius revealed to the unsuspecting emperor, who had attained
the twenty-fifth year of his age, that he was without
weight or authority in his own government and artfully
alarmed his timid and indolent disposition by a lively
picture of the designs of Stilicho, who already meditated
the death of his sovereign with the ambitious hope of
placing the diadem on the head of his son Eucherius.
The emperor was instigated by his new favourite to
assume the tone of independent dignity; and the minister was astonished to find that secret resolutions were
formed in the court and council which were repugnant
to his interest or to his intentions. Instead of residing in
the palace of Rome, Honorius declared that it was his
pleasure to return to the secure fortress of Ravenna. On
the first intelligence of the death of his brother Arcadius,
he prepared to visit Constantinople and to regulate with
the authority of a guardian the provinces of the infant
Theodosius. The representation of the difficulty and
expense of such a distant expedition checked this strange
and sudden sally of active diligence; but the dangerous
project of showing the emperor to the camp of Pavia,
which was composed of the Roman troops, the enemies
of Stilicho and his barbarian auxiliaries, remained fixed
and unalterable. The minister was pressed by the advice
of his confidant Justinian, a Roman advocate of a lively
and penetrating genius, to oppose a journey so prejudi-
cial to his reputation and safety. His strenuous but
ineffectual efforts confirmed the triumph of Olympius;
and the prudent lawyer withdrew himself from the impending ruin of his patron.

In the passage of the emperor through Bologna a
mutiny of the guards was excited and appeased by the

secret policy of Stilicho, who announced his instructions
to decimate the guilty and ascribed to his own intercession the merit of their pardon. After this tumult
Honorius embraced for the last time the minister whom
he now considered as a tyrant and proceeded on his way
to the camp of Pavia, where he was received by the
loyal acclamations of the troops who were assembled
for the service of the Gallic war. On the morning of the
fourth day he pronounced, as he had been taught, a
military oration in the presence of the soldiers, whom
the charitable visits and artful discourses of Olympius
had prepared to execute a dark and bloody conspiracy.
At the first signal they massacred the friends of Stilicho,
the most illustrious officers of the empire: two Prætorian
præfects, of Gaul and of Italy; two masters general of
the cavalry and infantry; the master of the offices, the
quæstor, the treasurer, and the count of the domestics.
Many lives were lost, many houses were plundered; the
furious sedition continued to rage till the close of the
evening; and the trembling emperor, who was seen in
the streets of Pavia without his robes or diadem, yielded
to the persuasions of his favourite, condemned the
memory of the slain, and solemnly approved the innocence and fidelity of their assassins.

The intelligence of the massacre of Pavia filled the
mind of Stilicho with just and gloomy apprehensions,
and he instantly summoned in the camp of Bologna a
council of the confederate leaders who were attached to
his service and would be involved in his ruin. The impetuous voice of the assembly called aloud for arms and
for revenge; to march, without a moment's delay, under
the banners of a hero whom they had so often followed
to victory; to surprise, to oppress, to extirpate the guilty
Olympius and his degenerate Romans; and perhaps to
fix the diadem on the head of their injured general.

Instead of executing a resolution which might have been justified by success, Stilicho hesitated till he was irrecoverably lost. He was still ignorant of the fate of the emperor; he distrusted the fidelity of his own party; and he viewed with horror the fatal consequences of arming a crowd of licentious barbarians against the soldiers and people of Italy.

The confederates, impatient of his timorous and doubtful delay, hastily retired with fear and indignation. At the hour of midnight Sarus, a Gothic warrior renowned among the barbarians themselves for his strength and valour, suddenly invaded the camp of his benefactor, plundered the baggage, cut in pieces the faithful Huns who guarded his person, and penetrated to the tent where the minister, pensive and sleepless, meditated on the dangers of his situation. Stilicho escaped with difficulty from the sword of the Goths, and after issuing a last and generous admonition to the cities of Italy to shut their gates against the barbarians, his confidence or his despair urged him to throw himself into Ravenna, which was already in the absolute possession of his enemies. Olympius, who had assumed the dominion of Honorius, was speedily informed that his rival had embraced, as a suppliant, the altar of the Christian church. The base and cruel disposition of the hypocrite was incapable of pity or remorse; but he piously affected to elude rather than to violate the privilege of the sanctuary. Count Heraclian, with a troop of soldiers, appeared at the dawn of day before the gates of the church of Ravenna. The bishop was satisfied by a solemn oath that the Imperial mandate only directed them to secure the person of Stilicho; but as soon as the unfortunate minister had been tempted beyond the holy threshold he produced the warrant for his instant execution. Stilicho supported with calm resignation the injurious names of traitor and parricide, repressed the unseasonable zeal of his followers, who were ready to attempt an ineffectual rescue, and with a firmness not unworthy of the last of the Roman generals submitted his neck to the sword of Heraclian.

The servile crowd of the palace, who had so long adored the fortune of Stilicho, affected to insult his fall; and the most distant connection with the master general of the West, which had so lately been a title to wealth and honours, was studiously denied and rigorously punished. His family, united by a triple alliance with the family of Theodosius, might envy the condition of the meanest peasant. The flight of his son Eucherius was intercepted; and the death of that innocent youth soon followed the divorce of Thermantia, who filled the place of her sister Maria, and who, like Maria, had remained a virgin in the Imperial bed. The friends of Stilicho who had escaped the massacre of Pavia were persecuted by the implacable revenge of Olympius, and the most exquisite cruelty was employed to extort the confession of a treasonable and sacrilegious conspiracy. They died in silence; their firmness justified the choice, and perhaps absolved the innocence, of their patron; and the despotic power which could take his life without a trial and stigmatize his memory without a proof has no jurisdiction over the impartial suffrage of posterity.

The services of Stilicho are great and manifest; his crimes, as they are vaguely stated in the language of flattery and hatred, are obscure, at least, and improbable. About four months after his death an edict was published, in the name of Honorius to restore the free communication of the two empires, which had been so long interrupted by the *public enemy*. The minister whose fame and fortune depended on the prosperity of the state was accused of betraying Italy to the barbarians, whom he repeatedly vanquished at Pollentia, at Verona, and before the walls of Florence. His pretended design of placing the diadem on the head of his son Eucherius could not have been conducted without preparations or accomplices; and the ambitious father would not surely have left the future emperor, till the twentieth year of his age, in the humble station of tribune of the notaries. Even the religion of Stilicho was arraigned by the malice of his rival. The seasonable and almost miraculous deliverance was devoutly celebrated by the applause of the clergy, who asserted that the restoration of idols and the persecution of the church would have been the first measure of the reign of Eucherius. The son of Stilicho, however, was educated in the bosom of Christianity, which his father had uniformly professed and zealously supported. Serena had borrowed her magnificent necklace from the statue of Vesta; and the pagans execrated the memory of the sacrilegious minister by whose order the Sibylline books, the oracles of Rome, had been committed to the flames. The pride and power of Stilicho constituted his real guilt. An honourable reluctance to shed the blood of his countrymen appears to have contributed to the success of his unworthy rival; and it is the last humiliation of the character of Honorius that posterity has not condescended to reproach him with his base ingratitude to the guardian of his youth and the support of his empire.[8]

8. *Editor's note:* Gibbon continues here with a brief critical dissertation upon the poet Claudian, who had sung Stilicho's praises and who soon followed him in disgrace and death.

Chapter XV

(A.D. 408-410)

Invasion of Italy by Alaric – Manners of the Roman senate and people – Rome is thrice besieged, and at length pillaged, by the Goths – General observations on the fall of the Roman empire in the West[1]

THE incapacity of a weak and distracted government may often assume the appearance and produce the effects of a treasonable correspondence with the public enemy. If Alaric himself had been introduced into the council of Ravenna, he would probably have advised the same measures which were actually pursued by the ministers of Honorius. The king of the Goths would have conspired, perhaps with some reluctance, to destroy the formidable adversary by whose arms, in Italy as well as in Greece, he had been twice overthrown. *Their* active and interested hatred laboriously accomplished the disgrace and ruin of the great Stilicho. The valour of Sarus, his fame in arms, and his personal or hereditary influence over the confederate barbarians could recommend him only to the friends of their country who despised or detested the worthless characters of Turpilio, Varanes, and Vigilantius. By the pressing instances of the new favourites, these generals, unworthy as they had shown themselves of the name of soldiers, were promoted to the command of the cavalry, of the infantry, and of the domestic troops. The Gothic

1. *Editor's note:* From chapters XXXI and XXXVIII of the original.

prince would have subscribed with pleasure the edict which the fanaticism of Olympius dictated to the simple and devout emperor. Honorius excluded all persons who were adverse to the catholic church from holding any office in the state, obstinately rejected the service of all those who dissented from his religion, and rashly disqualified many of his bravest and most skilful officers who adhered to the pagan worship or who had imbibed the opinions of Arianism.

These measures, so advantageous to an enemy, Alaric would have approved and might perhaps have suggested; but it may seem doubtful whether the barbarian would have promoted his interest at the expense of the inhuman and absurd cruelty which was perpetrated by the direction, or at least with the connivance, of the Imperial ministers. The foreign auxiliaries who had been attached to the person of Stilicho lamented his death; but the desire of revenge was checked by a natural apprehension for the safety of their wives and children, who were detained as hostages in the strong cities of Italy, where they had likewise deposited their most valuable effects. At the same hour, and as if by a common signal, the cities of Italy were polluted by the same horrid scenes of universal massacre and pillage, which involved in promiscuous destruction the families and fortunes of the barbarians. Exasperated by such an injury, which might have awakened the tamest and most servile spirit, they cast a look of indignation and hope towards the camp of Alaric and unanimously swore to pursue with just and implacable war the perfidious nation that had so basely violated the laws of hospitality. By the imprudent conduct of the ministers of Honorius the republic lost the assistance and deserved the enmity of thirty thousand of her bravest soldiers; and the weight of that formidable army, which alone might have determined the event of the war, was transferred from the scale of the Romans into that of the Goths.

In the arts of negotiation, as well as in those of war, the Gothic king maintained his superior ascendant over an enemy whose seeming changes proceeded from the total want of counsel and design. From his camp on the confines of Italy, Alaric attentively observed the revolutions of the palace, watched the progress of faction and discontent, disguised the hostile aspect of a barbarian invader, and assumed the more popular appearance of the friend and ally of the great Stilicho—to whose virtues, when they were no longer formidable, he could pay a just tribute of sincere praise and regret. The pressing invitation of the malcontents, who urged the king of the Goths to invade Italy, was enforced by a lively sense of his personal injuries; and he might speciously complain that the Imperial ministers still delayed and eluded the payment of the four thousand pounds of gold which had been granted by the Roman senate either to reward his services or to appease his fury. His decent firmness was supported by an artful moderation, which contributed to the success of his designs. He required a fair and reasonable satisfaction; but he gave the strongest assurances that, as soon as he had obtained it, he would immediately retire. He refused to trust the faith of the Romans unless Aëtius and Jason, the sons of two great officers of state, were sent as hostages to his camp; but he offered to deliver in exchange several of the noblest youths of the Gothic nation.

The modesty of Alaric was interpreted by the ministers of Ravenna as a sure evidence of his weakness and fear. They disdained either to negotiate a treaty or to assemble an army, and with a rash confidence, derived only from their ignorance of the extreme danger, irretrievably wasted the decisive moments of peace and

war. While they expected in sullen silence that the barbarians should evacuate the confines of Italy, Alaric with
bold and rapid marches passed the Alps and the Po,
hastily pillaged the cities of Aquileia, Altinum, Con-
cordia, and Cremona, which yielded to his arms, increased his forces by the accession of thirty thousand
auxiliaries, and, without meeting a single enemy in the
field, advanced as far as the edge of the morass which
protected the impregnable residence of the emperor of
the West. Instead of attempting the hopeless siege of
Ravenna, the prudent leader of the Goths proceeded to
Rimini, stretched his ravages along the seacoast of the
Hadriatic, and meditated the conquest of the ancient
mistress of the world.

An Italian hermit, whose zeal and sanctity were respected by the barbarians themselves, encountered the
victorious monarch and boldly denounced the indignation of Heaven against the oppressors of the earth; but
the saint himself was confounded by the solemn assever-
ation of Alaric that he felt a secret and preternatural
impulse which directed, and even compelled, his march
to the gates of Rome. He felt that his genius and his
fortune were equal to the most arduous enterprises; and
the enthusiasm which he communicated to the Goths insensibly removed the popular and almost superstitious
reverence of the nations for the majesty of the Roman
name. His troops, animated by the hopes of spoil, followed the course of the Flaminian way, occupied the
unguarded passes of the Apennine, descended into the
rich plains of Umbria, and as they lay encamped on
the banks of the Clitumnus might wantonly slaughter
and devour the milk-white oxen which had been so long
reserved for the use of Roman triumphs. A lofty situation and a seasonable tempest of thunder and lightning
preserved the little city of Narni; but the king of the

Goths, despising the ignoble prey, still advanced with unabated vigour, and after he had passed through the stately arches adorned with the spoils of barbaric victories he pitched his camp under the walls of Rome.

During a period of six hundred and nineteen years the seat of empire had never been violated by the presence of a foreign enemy. The unsuccessful expedition of Hannibal served only to display the character of the senate and people: of a senate degraded rather than ennobled by the comparison of an assembly of kings; and of a people to whom the ambassador of Pyrrhus ascribed the inexhaustible resources of the Hydra. Each of the senators in the time of the Punic war had accomplished his term of military service either in a subordinate or a superior station; and the decree which invested with temporary command all those who had been consuls or censors or dictators gave the republic the immediate assistance of many brave and experienced generals. In the beginning of the war the Roman people consisted of two hundred and fifty thousand citizens of an age to bear arms. Fifty thousand had already died in the defence of their country, and the twenty-three legions which were employed in the different camps of Italy, Greece, Sardinia, Sicily, and Spain required about one hundred thousand men. But there still remained an equal number in Rome and the adjacent territory who were animated by the same intrepid courage, and every citizen was trained from his earliest youth in the discipline and exercises of a soldier. Hannibal was astonished by the constancy of the senate, who, without raising the siege of Capua or recalling their scattered forces, expected his approach. He encamped on the banks of the Anio, at the distance of three miles from the city; and he was soon informed that the ground on which he had pitched his tent was sold for an adequate price at a public auction and that a body of troops was dismissed by an opposite road to reinforce the legions of Spain. He led his Africans to the gates of Rome, where he found three armies in order of battle prepared to receive him; but Hannibal dreaded the event of a combat from which he could not hope to escape unless he destroyed the last of his enemies, and his speedy retreat confessed the invincible courage of the Romans.[2]

The accurate description of the city, which was composed in the Theodosian age, enumerates one thousand seven hundred and eighty houses, the residence of wealthy and honourable citizens. Many of these stately mansions might almost excuse the exaggeration of the poet—that Rome contained a multitude of palaces, and that each palace was equal to a city, since it included within its own precincts everything which could be subservient either to use or luxury: markets, hippodromes, temples, fountains, baths, porticoes, shady groves, and artificial aviaries. The historian Olympiodorus, who represents the state of Rome when it was besieged by the Goths, continues to observe that several of the richest senators received from their estates an annual income of four thousand pounds of gold, above one hundred and sixty thousand pounds sterling, without computing the stated provision of corn and wine, which, had they been sold, might have equalled in value one-third of the money. Compared to this immoderate wealth, an ordinary revenue of a thousand or fifteen hundred pounds of gold might be considered as no more than adequate to the dignity of the senatorian rank, which required many expenses of a public and ostentatious kind. Several ex-

2. *Editor's note:* Before launching into the description of the city that follows immediately, in the original Gibbon begins with a brief history of Rome's most eminent family, the Anician line.

amples are recorded in the age of Honorius of vain and popular nobles who celebrated the year of their prætorship by a festival which lasted seven days and cost above one hundred thousand pounds sterling.

The estates of the Roman senators, which so far exceed the proportion of modern wealth, were not confined to the limits of Italy. Their possessions extended far beyond the Ionian and Ægean seas to the most distant provinces: the city of Nicopolis, which Augustus had founded as an eternal monument of the Actian victory, was the property of the devout Paula; and it is observed by Seneca that the rivers which had divided hostile nations now flowed through the lands of private citizens. According to their temper and circumstances the estates of the Romans were either cultivated by the labour of their slaves or granted, for a certain and stipulated rent, to the industrious farmer. The economical writers of antiquity strenuously recommend the former method wherever it may be practicable; but if the object should be removed by its distance or magnitude from the immediate eye of the master, they prefer the active care of an old hereditary tenant, attached to the soil and interested in the produce, to the mercenary administration of a negligent, perhaps an unfaithful, steward.

The opulent nobles of an immense capital, who were never excited by the pursuit of military glory and seldom engaged in the occupations of civil government, naturally resigned their leisure to the business and amusements of private life. At Rome commerce was always held in contempt; but the senators, from the first age of the republic, increased their patrimony and multiplied their clients by the lucrative practice of usury, and the obsolete laws were eluded or violated by the mutual inclinations and interest of both parties. A considerable mass of treasure must always have existed at Rome, either in the current coin of the empire or in the form of gold and silver plate; and there were many sideboards in the time of Pliny which contained more solid silver than had been transported by Scipio from vanquished Carthage. The greater part of the nobles, who dissipated their fortunes in profuse luxury, found themselves poor in the midst of wealth and idle in a constant round of dissipation. Their desires were continually gratified by the labour of a thousand hands, of the numerous train of their domestic slaves, who were actuated by the fear of punishment, and of the various professions of artificers and merchants, who were more powerfully impelled by the hopes of gain.

The ancients were destitute of many of the conveniences of life which have been invented or improved by the progress of industry; and the plenty of glass and linen has diffused more real comforts among the modern nations of Europe than the senators of Rome could derive from all the refinements of pompous or sensual luxury. Their luxury and their manners have been the subject of minute and laborious disquisition; but as such inquiries would divert me too long from the design of the present work, I shall produce an authentic state of Rome and its inhabitants which is more peculiarly applicable to the period of the Gothic invasion. Ammianus Marcellinus, who prudently chose the capital of the empire as the residence the best adapted to the historian of his own times, has mixed with the narrative of public events a lively representation of the scenes with which he was familiarly conversant. The judicious reader will not always approve the asperity of censure, the choice of circumstances, or the style of expression; he will perhaps detect the latent prejudices and personal resentments which soured the temper of Ammianus himself; but he will surely observe, with philosophic curiosity, the interesting and original picture of the manners of Rome.

"The greatness of Rome (such is the language of the historian) was founded on the rare and almost incredible alliance of virtue and of fortune. The long period of her infancy was employed in a laborious struggle against the tribes of Italy, the neighbours and enemies of the rising city. In the strength and ardour of youth she sustained the storms of war, carried her victorious arms beyond the seas and the mountains, and brought home triumphal laurels from every country of the globe. At length, verging towards old age, and sometimes conquering by the terror only of her name, she sought the blessings of ease and tranquillity. The Venerable City, which had trampled on the necks of the fiercest nations and established a system of laws, the perpetual guardians of justice and freedom, was content, like a wise and wealthy parent, to devolve on the Cæsars, her favourite sons, the care of governing her ample patrimony. A secure and profound peace, such as had been once enjoyed in the reign of Numa, succeeded to the tumults of a republic; while Rome was still adored as the queen of the earth, and the subject nations still reverenced the name of the people and the majesty of the senate.

"But this native splendour (continues Ammianus) is degraded and sullied by the conduct of some nobles who, unmindful of their own dignity and of that of their country, assume an unbounded licence of vice and folly. They contend with each other in the empty vanity of titles and surnames, and curiously select or invent the most lofty and sonorous appellations—Reburrus or Fabunius, Pagonius or Tarrasius—which may impress the ears of the vulgar with astonishment and respect. From a vain ambition of perpetuating their memory, they affect to multiply their likeness in statues of bronze and marble; nor are they satisfied unless those statues are covered with plates of gold, an honourable distinction first granted to Acilius the consul after he had subdued by his arms and counsels the power of king Antiochus. The ostentation of displaying, of magnifying perhaps, the rent-roll of the estates which they possess in all the provinces, from the rising to the setting sun, provokes the just resentment of every man who recollects that their poor and invincible ancestors were not distinguished from the meanest of the soldiers by the delicacy of their food or the splendour of their apparel. But the modern nobles measure their rank and consequence according to the loftiness of their chariots and the weighty magnificence of their dress. Their long robes of silk and purple float in the wind; and as they are agitated, by art or accident, they occasionally discover the under garments, the rich tunics embroidered with the figures of various animals. Followed by a train of fifty servants and tearing up the pavement, they move along the streets with the same impetuous speed as if they travelled with post-horses; and the example of the senators is boldly imitated by the matrons and ladies, whose covered carriages are continually driving round the immense space of the city and suburbs. Whenever these persons of high distinction condescend to visit the public baths, they assume on their entrance a tone of loud and insolent command, and appropriate to their own use the conveniences which were designed for the Roman people. If in these places of mixed and general resort they meet any of the infamous ministers of their pleasures, they express their affection by a tender embrace, while they proudly decline the salutations of their fellow-citizens, who are not permitted to aspire above the honour of kissing their hands or their knees. As soon as they have indulged themselves in the refreshment of

the bath, they resume their rings and the other ensigns
of their dignity, select from their private wardrobe of
the finest linen, such as might suffice for a dozen persons, the garments the most agreeable to their fancy,
and maintain till their departure the same haughty demeanour which perhaps might have been excused in the
great Marcellus after the conquest of Syracuse.

"Sometimes, indeed, these heroes undertake more arduous achievements: they visit their estates in Italy
and procure themselves, by the toil of servile hands, the
amusements of the chase. If at any time, but more especially on a hot day, they have courage to sail in their
painted galleys from the Lucrine lake to their elegant
villas on the seacoast of Puteoli and Caieta, they compare their own expeditions to the marches of Cæsar and
Alexander. Yet should a fly presume to settle on the
silken folds of their gilded umbrellas, should a sunbeam
penetrate through some unguarded and imperceptible
chink, they deplore their intolerable hardships and lament in affected language that they were not born in
the land of the Cimmerians, the regions of eternal darkness. In these journeys into the country the whole body
of the household marches with their master. In the same
manner as the cavalry and infantry, the heavy and the
light armed troops, the advanced guard and the rear,
are marshalled by the skill of their military leaders, so
the domestic officers, who bear a rod as an ensign of
authority, distribute and arrange the numerous train of
slaves and attendants. The baggage and wardrobe move
in the front and are immediately followed by a multitude of cooks and inferior ministers employed in the
service of the kitchens and of the table. The main body
is composed of a promiscuous crowd of slaves, increased
by the accidental concourse of idle or dependent plebeians. The rear is closed by the favourite band of

eunuchs, distributed from age to youth according to the order of seniority. Their numbers and their deformity excite the horror of the indignant spectators, who are ready to execrate the memory of Semiramis for the cruel art which she invented of frustrating the purposes of nature and of blasting in the bud the hopes of future generations.

"In the exercise of domestic jurisdiction the nobles of Rome express an exquisite sensibility for any personal injury and a contemptuous indifference for the rest of the human species. When they have called for warm water, if a slave has been tardy in his obedience, he is instantly chastised with three hundred lashes; but should the same slave commit a wilful murder, the master will mildly observe that he is a worthless fellow, but that if he repeats the offence he shall not escape punishment. Hospitality was formerly the virtue of the Romans, and every stranger who could plead either merit or misfortune was relieved or rewarded by their generosity. At present, if a foreigner, perhaps of no contemptible rank, is introduced to one of the proud and wealthy senators, he is welcomed indeed in the first audience with such warm professions and such kind inquiries that he retires enchanted with the affability of his illustrious friend and full of regret that he had so long delayed his journey to Rome, the native seat of manners as well as of empire. Secure of a favourable reception, he repeats his visit the ensuing day and is mortified by the discovery that his person, his name, and his country are already forgotten. If he still has resolution to persevere, he is gradually numbered in the train of dependents and obtains the permission to pay his assiduous and unprofitable court to a haughty patron incapable of gratitude or friendship, who scarcely deigns to remark his presence, his departure, or his return.

"Whenever the rich prepare a solemn and popular entertainment, whenever they celebrate with profuse and pernicious luxury their private banquets, the choice of the guests is the subject of anxious deliberation. The modest, the sober, and the learned are seldom preferred; and the nomenclators, who are commonly swayed by interested motives, have the address to insert in the list of invitations the obscure names of the most worthless of mankind. But the frequent and familiar companions of the great are those parasites who practise the most useful of all arts, the art of flattery; who eagerly applaud each word and every action of their immortal patron, gaze with rapture on his marble columns and variegated pavements, and strenuously praise the pomp and elegance which he is taught to consider as a part of his personal merit. At the Roman tables the birds, the squirrels, or the fish, which appear of an uncommon size, are contemplated with curious attention; a pair of scales is accurately applied to ascertain their real weight; and while the more rational guests are disgusted by the vain and tedious repetition, notaries are summoned to attest by an authentic record the truth of such a marvellous event. Another method of introduction into the houses and society of the great is derived from the profession of gaming, or, as it is more politely styled, of play. The confederates are united by a strict and indissoluble bond of friendship, or rather of conspiracy; a superior degree of skill in the *Tesserarian* art (which may be interpreted the game of dice and tables) is a sure road to wealth and reputation. A master of that sublime science, who in a supper or assembly is placed below a magistrate, displays in his countenance the surprise and indignation which Cato might be supposed to feel when he was refused the prætorship by the votes of a capricious people.

"The acquisition of knowledge seldom engages the curiosity of the nobles, who abhor the fatigue and disdain the advantages of study; and the only books which they peruse are the Satires of Juvenal and the verbose and fabulous histories of Marius Maximus. The libraries which they have inherited from their fathers are secluded, like dreary sepulchres, from the light of day. But the costly instruments of the theatre, flutes, and enormous lyres, and hydraulic organs, are constructed for their use; and the harmony of vocal and instrumental music is incessantly repeated in the palaces of Rome. In those palaces sound is preferred to sense, and the care of the body to that of the mind. It is allowed as a salutary maxim that the light and frivolous suspicion of a contagious malady is of sufficient weight to excuse the visits of the most intimate friends; and even the servants who are despatched to make the decent inquiries are not suffered to return home till they have undergone the ceremony of a previous ablution. Yet this selfish and unmanly delicacy occasionally yields to the more imperious passion of avarice. The prospect of gain will urge a rich and gouty senator as far as Spoleto; every sentiment of arrogance and dignity is subdued by the hopes of an inheritance, or even of a legacy, and a wealthy childless citizen is the most powerful of the Romans. The art of obtaining the signature of a favourable testament, and sometimes of hastening the moment of its execution, is perfectly understood; and it has happened that in the same house, though in different apartments, a husband and a wife, with the laudable design of overreaching each other, have summoned their respective lawyers to declare at the same time their mutual but contradictory intentions.

"The distress which follows and chastises extravagant luxury often reduces the great to the use of the most humiliating expedients. When they desire to borrow, they employ the base and supplicating style of the slave in the comedy; but when they are called upon to pay, they assume the royal and tragic declamation of the grandsons of Hercules. If the demand is repeated they readily procure some trusty sycophant, instructed to maintain a charge of poison or magic against the insolent creditor, who is seldom released from prison till he has signed a discharge of the whole debt. These vices, which degrade the moral character of the Romans, are mixed with a puerile superstition that disgraces their understanding. They listen with confidence to the predictions of haruspices, who pretend to read in the entrails of victims the signs of future greatness and prosperity; and there are many who do not presume either to bathe or to die, or to appear in public, till they have diligently consulted, according to the rules of astrology, the situation of Mercury and the aspect of the moon. It is singular enough that this vain credulity may often be discovered among the profane sceptics who impiously doubt or deny the existence of a celestial power."

In populous cities which are the seat of commerce and manufactures, the middle ranks of inhabitants, who derive their subsistence from the dexterity or labour of their hands, are commonly the most prolific, the most useful, and in that sense the most respectable part of the community. But the plebeians of Rome, who disdained such sedentary and servile arts, had been oppressed from the earliest times by the weight of debt and usury; and the husbandman, during the term of his military service, was obliged to abandon the cultivation of his farm. The lands of Italy, which had been originally divided among the families of free and indigent proprietors, were insensibly purchased or usurped by the avarice of the nobles; and in the age which preceded the fall of the republic, it was computed that only two thousand citizens were possessed of any independent substance. Yet as long as the people bestowed by their suffrages the honours of the state, the command of the legions, and the administration of wealthy provinces, their conscious pride alleviated in some measure the hardships of poverty; and their wants were seasonably supplied by the ambitious liberality of the candidates, who aspired to secure a venal majority in the thirty-five tribes, or the hundred and ninety-three centuries, of Rome.

But when the prodigal commons had imprudently alienated not only the use, but the inheritance, of power, they sank under the reign of the Cæsars into a vile and wretched populace, which must in a few generations have been totally extinguished if it had not been continually recruited by the manumission of slaves and the influx of strangers. As early as the time of Hadrian it was the just complaint of the ingenuous natives that the capital had attracted the vices of the universe and the manners of the most opposite nations. The intemperance of the Gauls, the cunning and levity of the Greeks, the savage obstinacy of the Egyptians and Jews, the servile temper of the Asiatics, and the dissolute, effeminate prostitution of the Syrians were mingled in the various multitude, which, under the proud and false denomination of Romans, presumed to despise their fellow-subjects and even their sovereigns who dwelt beyond the precincts of the Eternal City.

Yet the name of that city was still pronounced with respect; the frequent and capricious tumults of its inhabitants were indulged with impunity; and the successors of Constantine, instead of crushing the last remains of the democracy by the strong arm of military power, embraced the mild policy of Augustus and studied to relieve the poverty and to amuse the idleness of an innumerable people. For the convenience of the lazy plebeians, the monthly distributions of corn were converted into a daily allowance of bread; a great number of ovens were constructed and maintained at the public expense; and at the appointed hour each citizen, who was furnished with a ticket, ascended the flight of steps which had been assigned to his peculiar quarter or division and received, either as a gift or at a very low price, a loaf of bread of the weight of three pounds for the use of his family. The forests of Lucania, whose acorns fattened large droves of wild hogs, afforded as a species of tribute a plentiful supply of cheap and wholesome meat. During five months of the year a regular allowance of bacon was distributed to the poorer citizens; and the annual consumption of the capital, at a time when it was much declined from its former lustre, was ascertained, by an edict of Valentinian the Third, at three millions six hundred and twenty-eight thousand pounds.

In the manners of antiquity the use of oil was indispensable for the lamp as well as for the bath, and the annual tax which was imposed on Africa for the benefit of Rome amounted to the weight of three millions of pounds, to the measure, perhaps, of three hundred thousand English gallons. The anxiety of Augustus to provide the metropolis with sufficient plenty of corn was not extended beyond that necessary article of human subsistence; and when the popular clamour accused the dearness and scarcity of wine, a proclamation was issued by the grave reformer to remind his subjects that no man could reasonably complain of thirst, since the aqueducts of Agrippa had introduced into the city so many copious streams of pure and salubrious water. This rigid sobriety was insensibly relaxed; and although the generous design of Aurelian does not appear to have been executed, in its full extent, the use of wine was allowed on very easy and liberal terms. The administration of the public cellars was delegated to a magistrate of honourable rank, and a considerable part of the vintage of Campania was reserved for the fortunate inhabitants of Rome.

The stupendous aqueducts, so justly celebrated by the praises of Augustus himself, replenished the *Thermæ*, or baths, which had been constructed in every part of the city with Imperial magnificence. The baths of Antoninus Caracalla, which were open at stated hours for the indiscriminate service of the senators and the people, contained above sixteen hundred seats of marble; and more than three thousand were reckoned in the baths of Diocletian. The walls of the lofty apartments were covered with curious mosaics that imitated the art of the pencil in the elegance of design and the variety of colours. The Egyptian granite was beautifully encrusted with the precious green marble of Numidia; the perpetual stream of hot water was poured into the capacious basins through so many wide mouths of bright and massy silver; and the meanest Roman could purchase, with a small copper coin, the daily enjoyment of a scene of pomp and luxury which might excite the envy of the kings of Asia. From these stately palaces issued a swarm of dirty and ragged plebeians, without shoes and without a mantle, who loitered away whole days in the street or Forum to hear news and to hold disputes, who dissipated in extravagant gaming the miserable pittance of their wives and children, and spent the hours of the night in obscure taverns and brothels in the indulgence of gross and vulgar sensuality.

But the most lively and splendid amusement of the idle multitude depended on the frequent exhibition of public games and spectacles. The piety of Christian princes had suppressed the inhuman combats of gladiators, but the Roman people still considered the Circus as their home, their temple, and the seat of the republic. The impatient crowd rushed at the dawn of day to secure their places, and there were many who passed a sleepless and anxious night in the adjacent porticoes. From the morning to the evening, careless of the sun or of the rain, the spectators, who sometimes amounted to the number of four hundred thousand, remained in eager attention, their eyes fixed on the horses and charioteers, their minds agitated with hope and fear for the success of the colours which they espoused; and the happiness of Rome appeared to hang on the event of a race.

The same immoderate ardour inspired their clamours and their applause as often as they were entertained with the hunting of wild beasts and the various modes of theatrical representation. These representations in modern capitals may deserve to be considered as a pure and elegant school of taste, and perhaps of virtue. But the Tragic and Comic Muse of the Romans, who seldom aspired beyond the imitation of Attic genius, had been almost totally silent since the fall of the republic; and their place was unworthily occupied by licentious farce, effeminate music, and splendid pageantry. The pantomimes, who maintained their reputation from the age of Augustus to the sixth century, expressed without the use of words the various fables of the gods and heroes of antiquity; and the perfection of their art, which sometimes disarmed the gravity of the philosopher, always excited the applause and wonder of the people. The vast and magnificent theatres of Rome were filled by three thousand female dancers and by three thousand singers, with the masters of the respective choruses. Such was the popular favour which they enjoyed that, in a time of scarcity when all strangers were banished from the city, the merit of contributing to the public pleasures exempted them from a law which was strictly executed against the professors of the liberal arts.

It is said that the foolish curiosity of Elagabalus attempted to discover, from the quantity of spiders' webs, the number of the inhabitants of Rome. A more rational method of inquiry might not have been undeserving of the attention of the wisest princes, who could easily have resolved a question so important for the Roman government and so interesting to succeeding ages. The births and deaths of the citizens were duly registered; and if any writer of antiquity had condescended to mention the annual amount, or the common average, we might now produce some satisfactory calculation which would destroy the extravagant assertions of critics and perhaps confirm the modest and probable conjectures of philosophers. The most diligent researches have collected only the following circumstances, which, slight and imperfect as they are, may tend in some degree to illustrate the question of the populousness of ancient Rome.

1. When the capital of the empire was besieged by the Goths, the circuit of the walls was accurately measured by Ammonius, the mathematician, who found it equal to twenty-one miles. It should not be forgotten that the form of the city was almost that of a circle, the geometrical figure which is known to contain the largest space within any given circumference.

2. The architect Vitruvius, who flourished in the Augustan age, and whose evidence on this occasion has peculiar weight and authority, observes that the innumerable habitations of the Roman people would have spread themselves far beyond the narrow limits of the city; and that the want of ground, which was probably contracted on every side by gardens and villas, sug-

gested the common though inconvenient practice of raising the houses to a considerable height in the air. But
the loftiness of these buildings, which often consisted
of hasty work and insufficient materials, was the cause
of frequent and fatal accidents; and it was repeatedly
enacted by Augustus, as well as by Nero, that the height
of private edifices within the walls of Rome should not
exceed the measure of seventy feet from the ground.

3. Juvenal laments, as it should seem from his own
experience, the hardships of the poorer citizens, to
whom he addresses the salutary advice of emigrating
without delay from the smoke of Rome, since they might
purchase in the little towns of Italy a cheerful, com-
modious dwelling at the same price which they annually
paid for a dark and miserable lodging. House-rent was
therefore immoderately dear: the rich acquired at an
enormous expense the ground which they covered with
palaces and gardens; but the body of the Roman people
was crowded into a narrow space; and the different
floors and apartments of the same house were divided,
as it is still the custom of Paris and other cities, among
several families of plebeians.

4. The total number of houses in the fourteen regions
of the city is accurately stated in the description of
Rome composed under the reign of Theodosius, and
they amount to forty-eight thousand three hundred and
eighty-two. The two classes of *domus* and of *insulæ* into
which they are divided include all the habitations of the
capital of every rank and condition, from the marble
palace of the Anicii, with a numerous establishment of
freedmen and slaves, to the lofty and narrow lodging-
house where the poet Codrus and his wife were permitted to hire a wretched garret immediately under the
tiles. If we adopt the same average which, under similar
circumstances, has been found applicable to Paris, and

indifferently allow about twenty-five persons for each house of every degree, we may fairly estimate the inhabitants of Rome at twelve hundred thousand—a number which cannot be thought excessive for the capital of a mighty empire, though it exceeds the populousness of the greatest cities of modern Europe.

Such was the state of Rome under the reign of Honorius, at the time when the Gothic army formed the siege, or rather the blockade, of the city. By a skilful disposition of his numerous forces, who impatiently watched the moment of an assault, Alaric encompassed the walls, commanded the twelve principal gates, intercepted all communication with the adjacent country, and vigilantly guarded the navigation of the Tiber, from which the Romans derived the surest and most plentiful supply of provisions. The first emotions of the nobles and of the people were those of surprise and indignation that a vile barbarian should dare to insult the capital of the world; but their arrogance was soon humbled by misfortune; and their unmanly rage, instead of being directed against an enemy in arms, was meanly exercised on a defenceless and innocent victim. Perhaps in the person of Serena the Romans might have respected the niece of Theodosius, the aunt, nay even the adoptive mother, of the reigning emperor; they abhorred the widow of Stilicho, and they listened with credulous passion to the tale of calumny which accused her of maintaining a secret and criminal correspondence with the Gothic invader. Actuated or overawed by the same popular frenzy, the senate, without requiring any evidence of her guilt, pronounced the sentence of her death. Serena was ignominiously strangled; and the infatuated multitude were astonished to find that this cruel act of injustice did not immediately produce the retreat of the barbarians and the deliverance of the city.

That unfortunate city gradually experienced the distress of scarcity and at length the horrid calamities of famine. The daily allowance of three pounds of bread was reduced to one-half, to one-third, to nothing; and the price of corn still continued to rise in a rapid and extravagant proportion. The poorer citizens, who were unable to purchase the necessaries of life, solicited the precarious charity of the rich; and for a while the public misery was alleviated by the humanity of Læta, the widow of the emperor Gratian, who had fixed her residence at Rome and consecrated to the use of the indigent the princely revenue which she annually received from the grateful successors of her husband. But these private and temporary donatives were insufficient to appease the hunger of a numerous people, and the progress of famine invaded the marble palaces of the senators themselves. The persons of both sexes who had been educated in the enjoyment of ease and luxury discovered how little is requisite to supply the demands of nature and lavished their unavailing treasures of gold and silver to obtain the coarse and scanty sustenance which they would formerly have rejected with disdain. The food the most repugnant to sense or imagination, the aliments the most unwholesome and pernicious to the constitution, were eagerly devoured and fiercely disputed by the rage of hunger. A dark suspicion was entertained that some desperate wretches fed on the bodies of their fellow-creatures whom they had secretly murdered; and even mothers (such was the horrid conflict of the two most powerful instincts implanted by nature in the human breast), even mothers are said to have tasted the flesh of their slaughtered infants! Many thousands of the inhabitants of Rome expired in their houses or in the streets for want of sustenance; and as the public sepulchres without the walls were in the power of the enemy,

the stench which arose from so many putrid and unburied carcasses infected the air, and the miseries of
famine were succeeded and aggravated by the contagion
of a pestilential disease.

The assurances of speedy and effectual relief, which
were repeatedly transmitted from the court of Ravenna,
supported for some time the fainting resolution of the
Romans, till at length the despair of any human aid
tempted them to accept the offers of a preternatural deliverance. Pompeianus, præfect of the city, had been
persuaded, by the art or fanaticism of some Tuscan di-
viners, that by the mysterious force of spells and sacrifices they could extract the lightning from the clouds
and point those celestial fires against the camp of the
barbarians. The important secret was communicated to
Innocent, the bishop of Rome; and the successor of St.
Peter is accused, perhaps without foundation, of preferring the safety of the republic to the rigid severity of
the Christian worship. But when the question was agitated in the senate, when it was proposed as an essential condition that those sacrifices should be performed
in the Capitol by the authority and in the presence of
the magistrates, the majority of that respectable assembly, apprehensive either of the Divine or of the Imperial
displeasure, refused to join in an act which appeared
almost equivalent to the public restoration of paganism.

The last resource of the Romans was in the clemency,
or at least in the moderation, of the king of the Goths.
The senate, who in this emergency assumed the supreme
powers of government, appointed two ambassadors to
negotiate with the enemy. This important trust was delegated to Basilius, a senator of Spanish extraction already
conspicuous in the administration of provinces, and to
John, the first tribune of the notaries, who was peculiarly
qualified by his dexterity in business as well as by his

former intimacy with the Gothic prince. When they were introduced into his presence they declared, perhaps in a more lofty style than became their abject condition, that the Romans were resolved to maintain their dignity either in peace or war, and that if Alaric refused them a fair and honourable capitulation he might sound his trumpets and prepare to give battle to an innumerable people exercised in arms and animated by despair. "The thicker the hay, the easier it is mowed," was the concise reply of the barbarian; and this rustic metaphor was accompanied by a loud and insulting laugh, expressive of his contempt for the menaces of an unwarlike populace enervated by luxury before they were emaciated by famine.

He then condescended to fix the ransom which he would accept as the price of his retreat from the walls of Rome: *all* the gold and silver in the city, whether it were the property of the state or of individuals; *all* the rich and precious movables; and *all* the slaves who could prove their title to the name of *barbarians*. The ministers of the senate presumed to ask, in a modest and suppliant tone, "If such, O king! are your demands, what do you intend to leave us?" "YOUR LIVES," replied the haughty conqueror; they trembled and retired. Yet before they retired a short suspension of arms was granted, which allowed some time for a more temperate negotiation. The stern features of Alaric were insensibly relaxed; he abated much of the rigour of his terms, and at length consented to raise the siege on the immediate payment of five thousand pounds of gold, of thirty thousand pounds of silver, of four thousand robes of silk, of three thousand pieces of fine scarlet cloth, and of three thousand pounds weight of pepper. But the public treasury was exhausted; the annual rents of the great estates in Italy and the provinces were intercepted by the calamities of war; the gold and gems had been exchanged, during the famine, for the vilest sustenance; the hoards of secret wealth were still concealed by the obstinacy of avarice; and some remains of consecrated spoils afforded the only resource that could avert the impending ruin of the city. As soon as the Romans had satisfied the rapacious demands of Alaric they were restored in some measure to the enjoyment of peace and plenty. Several of the gates were cautiously opened; the importation of provisions from the river and the adjacent country was no longer obstructed by the Goths; the citizens resorted in crowds to the free market which was held during three days in the suburbs; and while the merchants who undertook this gainful trade made a considerable profit, the future subsistence of the city was secured by the ample magazines which were deposited in the public and private granaries.

A more regular discipline than could have been expected was maintained in the camp of Alaric; and the wise barbarian justified his regard for the faith of treaties by the just severity with which he chastised a party of licentious Goths who had insulted some Roman citizens on the road to Ostia. His army, enriched by the contributions of the capital, slowly advanced into the fair and fruitful province of Tuscany, where he proposed to establish his winter-quarters; and the Gothic standard became the refuge of forty thousand barbarian slaves who had broken their chains and aspired, under the command of their great deliverer, to revenge the injuries and the disgrace of their cruel servitude. About the same time he received a more honourable reinforcement of Goths and Huns, whom Adolphus, the brother of his wife, had conducted at his pressing invitation from the banks of the Danube to those of the Tiber, and who had cut their way, with some difficulty and loss, through the superior numbers of the Imperial troops. A victorious leader, who united the daring spirit of a barbarian with the art and discipline of a Roman general, was at the head of an hundred thousand fighting men; and Italy pronounced with terror and respect the formidable name of Alaric.

At the distance of fourteen centuries we may be satisfied with relating the military exploits of the conquerors of Rome without presuming to investigate the motives of their political conduct. In the midst of his apparent prosperity Alaric was conscious, perhaps, of some secret weakness, some internal defect; or perhaps the moderation which he displayed was intended only to deceive and disarm the easy credulity of the ministers of Honorius. The king of the Goths repeatedly declared that it was his desire to be considered as the friend of peace and of the Romans. Three senators, at his earnest request, were sent [as] ambassadors to the court of Ravenna to solicit the exchange of hostages and the conclusion of the treaty; and the proposals which he more clearly expressed during the course of the negotiations could only inspire a doubt of his sincerity, as they might seem inadequate to the state of his fortune. The barbarian still aspired to the rank of master general of the armies of the West; he stipulated an annual subsidy of corn and money; and he chose the provinces of Dalmatia, Noricum, and Venetia for the seat of his new kingdom, which would have commanded the important communication between Italy and the Danube.

If these modest terms should be rejected, Alaric showed a disposition to relinquish his pecuniary demands and even to content himself with the possession of Noricum, an exhausted and impoverished country perpetually exposed to the inroads of the barbarians of Germany. But the hopes of peace were disappointed by the weak obstinacy or interested views of the minister Olympius. Without listening to the salutary remonstrances of the senate, he dismissed their ambassadors under the conduct of a military escort too numerous for a retinue of honour and too feeble for an army of defence. Six thousand Dalmatians, the flower of the Imperial legions, were ordered to march from Ravenna to Rome, through an open country which was occupied by the formidable myriads of the barbarians. These brave legionaries, encompassed and betrayed, fell a sacrifice to ministerial folly; their general, Valens, with an hundred soldiers, escaped from the field of battle; and one of the ambassadors, who could no longer claim the protection of the law of nations, was obliged to purchase his freedom with a ransom of thirty thousand pieces of gold. Yet Alaric, instead of resenting this act of impotent hostility, immediately renewed his proposals of peace, and the second embassy of the Roman senate, which derived weight and dignity from the presence of Innocent, bishop of the city, was guarded from the dangers of the road by a detachment of Gothic soldiers.[3]

While the emperor and his court enjoyed with sullen pride the security of the marshes and fortifications of Ravenna, they abandoned Rome, almost without defence, to the resentment of Alaric. Yet such was the moderation which he still preserved or affected that as he moved with his army along the Flaminian way he successively despatched the bishops of the towns of Italy to reiterate his offers of peace and to conjure the emperor that he would save the city and its inhabitants from hostile fire and the sword of the barbarians. These

3. *Editor's note:* At this point in the original, Gibbon expands with a discussion of some of the foolish and criminal intrigues that continued in the court of Honorius despite the proximity of the barbarian armies.

impending calamities were, however, averted, not indeed by the wisdom of Honorius but by the prudence or humanity of the Gothic king, who employed a milder though not less effectual method of conquest. Instead of assaulting the capital he successfully directed his efforts against the port of Ostia, one of the boldest and most stupendous works of Roman magnificence. The accidents to which the precarious subsistence of the city was continually exposed in a winter navigation and an open road had suggested to the genius of the first Cæsar the useful design which was executed under the reign of Claudius. The artificial moles which formed the narrow entrance advanced far into the sea and firmly repelled the fury of the waves, while the largest vessels securely rode at anchor within three deep and capacious basins which received the northern branch of the Tiber about two miles from the ancient colony of Ostia. The Roman port insensibly swelled to the size of an episcopal city, where the corn of Africa was deposited in spacious granaries for the use of the capital. As soon as Alaric was in possession of that important place he summoned the city to surrender at discretion; and his demands were enforced by the positive declaration that a refusal, or even a delay, should be instantly followed by the destruction of the magazines on which the life of the Roman people depended. The clamours of that people and the terror of famine subdued the pride of the senate; they listened without reluctance to the proposal of placing a new emperor on the throne of the unworthy Honorius; and the suffrage of the Gothic conqueror bestowed the purple on Attalus, præfect of the city. The grateful monarch immediately acknowledged his protector as master general of the armies of the West; Adolphus, with the rank of count of the domestics, obtained the custody of the person of Attalus; and the two hostile nations seemed to be united in the closest bands of friendship and alliance.

The gates of the city were thrown open, and the new emperor of the Romans, encompassed on every side by the Gothic arms, was conducted in tumultuous procession to the palace of Augustus and Trajan. After he had distributed the civil and military dignities among his favourites and followers, Attalus convened an assembly of the senate, before whom, in a formal and florid speech, he asserted his resolution of restoring the majesty of the republic and of uniting to the empire the provinces of Egypt and the East which had once acknowledged the sovereignty of Rome. Such extravagant promises inspired every reasonable citizen with a just contempt for the character of an unwarlike usurper, whose elevation was the deepest and most ignominious wound which the republic had yet sustained from the insolence of the barbarians. But the populace, with their usual levity, applauded the change of masters. The public discontent was favourable to the rival of Honorius; and the sectaries, oppressed by his persecuting edicts, expected some degree of countenance, or at least of toleration, from a prince who in his native country of Ionia had been educated in the pagan superstition and who had since received the sacrament of baptism from the hands of an Arian bishop.

The first days of the reign of Attalus were fair and prosperous. An officer of confidence was sent with an inconsiderable body of troops to secure the obedience of Africa; the greatest part of Italy submitted to the terror of the Gothic powers; and though the city of Bologna made a vigorous and effectual resistance, the people of Milan, dissatisfied perhaps with the absence of Honorius, accepted with loud acclamations the choice of the Roman senate. At the head of a formidable army Alaric

conducted his royal captive almost to the gates of Ravenna; and a solemn embassy of the principal ministers
—of Jovius, the Prætorian præfect, of Valens, master
of the cavalry and infantry, of the quæstor Potamius,
and of Julian, the first of the notaries—was introduced
with martial pomp into the Gothic camp. In the name
of their sovereign they consented to acknowledge the
lawful election of his competitor and to divide the provinces of Italy and the West between the two emperors.
Their proposals were rejected with disdain; and the
refusal was aggravated by the insulting clemency of
Attalus, who condescended to promise that if Honorius
would instantly resign the purple he should be permitted to pass the remainder of his life in the peaceful
exile of some remote island.

So desperate indeed did the situation of the son of
Theodosius appear to those who were the best acquainted with his strength and resources that Jovius and
Valens, his minister and his general, betrayed their trust,
infamously deserted the sinking cause of their benefactor, and devoted their treacherous allegiance to the service of his more fortunate rival. Astonished by such examples of domestic treason, Honorius trembled at the
approach of every servant, at the arrival of every messenger. He dreaded the secret enemies who might lurk
in his capital, his palace, his bedchamber; and some
ships lay ready in the harbour of Ravenna to transport
the abdicated monarch to the dominions of his infant
nephew, the emperor of the East.

But there *is* a Providence (such at least was the opinion of the historian Procopius) that watches over innocence and folly, and the pretensions of Honorius to its
peculiar care cannot reasonably be disputed. At the moment when his despair, incapable of any wise or manly
resolution, meditated a shameful flight, a seasonable

reinforcement of four thousand veterans unexpectedly landed in the port of Ravenna. To these valiant strangers, whose fidelity had not been corrupted by the factions of the court, he committed the walls and gates of the city, and the slumbers of the emperor were no longer disturbed by the apprehension of imminent and internal danger. The favourable intelligence which was received from Africa suddenly changed the opinions of men and the state of public affairs. The troops and officers whom Attalus had sent into that province were defeated and slain, and the active zeal of Heraclian maintained his own allegiance and that of his people. The faithful count of Africa transmitted a large sum of money, which fixed the attachment of the Imperial guards; and his vigilance in preventing the exportation of corn and oil introduced famine, tumult and discontent into the walls of Rome.

The failure of the African expedition was the source of mutual complaint and recrimination in the party of Attalus, and the mind of his protector was insensibly alienated from the interest of a prince who wanted spirit to command or docility to obey. The most imprudent measures were adopted without the knowledge or against the advice of Alaric, and the obstinate refusal of the senate to allow in the embarkation the mixture even of five hundred Goths betrayed a suspicious and distrustful temper which in their situation was neither generous nor prudent. The resentment of the Gothic king was exasperated by the malicious arts of Jovius, who had been raised to the rank of patrician, and who afterwards excused his double perfidy by declaring without a blush that he had only *seemed* to abandon the service of Honorius more effectually to ruin the cause of the usurper. In a large plain near Rimini, and in the presence of an innumerable multitude of Romans and barbarians, the wretched Attalus was publicly despoiled of the diadem and purple; and those ensigns of royalty were sent by Alaric as the pledge of peace and friendship to the son of Theodosius. The officers who returned to their duty were reinstated in their employments, and even the merit of a tardy repentance was graciously allowed; but the degraded emperor of the Romans, desirous of life and insensible of disgrace, implored the permission of following the Gothic camp in the train of a haughty and capricious barbarian.

The degradation of Attalus removed the only real obstacle to the conclusion of the peace, and Alaric advanced within three miles of Ravenna to press the irresolution of the Imperial ministers, whose insolence soon returned with the return of fortune. His indignation was kindled by the report that a rival chieftain, Sarus, the personal enemy of Adolphus and the hereditary foe of the house of Balti, had been received into the palace. At the head of three hundred followers that fearless barbarian immediately sallied from the gates of Ravenna, surprised and cut in pieces a considerable body of Goths, re-entered the city in triumph, and was permitted to insult his adversary by the voice of a herald, who publicly declared that the guilt of Alaric had forever excluded him from the friendship and alliance of the emperor.

The crime and folly of the court of Ravenna was expiated a third time by the calamities of Rome. The king of the Goths, who no longer dissembled his appetite for plunder and revenge, appeared in arms under the walls of the capital; and the trembling senate, without any hopes of relief, prepared by a desperate resistance to delay the ruin of their country. But they were unable to guard against the secret conspiracy of their slaves and domestics, who either from birth or interest were attached to the cause of the enemy. At the hour of midnight the Salarian gate was silently opened, and the inhabitants were awakened by the tremendous sound of the Gothic trumpet. Eleven hundred and sixty-three years after the foundation of Rome, the Imperial city, which had subdued and civilized so considerable a part of mankind, was delivered to the licentious fury of the tribes of Germany and Scythia.

The conquest of the Eternal City by the Goths did not of course mean the "fall of Rome" in any precise sense. Gibbon himself observes that "the vestiges of the Gothic invasion were almost obliterated" in less than seven years and that "the venerable matron replaced her crown of laurel, which had been ruffled by the storms of war, and was still amused in the last moment of her decay with the prophecies of revenge, of victory, and of eternal dominion."

But observe the mortal wounds that had been inflicted. Across the face of Gaul, Italy, and Spain swirled a cloud of barbarian conquerors—Goths, Burgundians, Vandals, Huns, etc.—whose character was but thinly disguised by the term of "guests" of the Romans. Of all the western empire, only Africa for a brief time stood unsullied by barbarian hands; but a successful expedition of the Vandals under Genseric, aided by Moors, Donatist fanatics, slaves, and deserters, soon took possession of that granary of Europe. The obvious helplessness of the western empire, as it was penetrated at will by divers barbarian swarms, led the island of Britain and the French maritime provinces between the Seine and the Loire to split off from the empire and set up independent governments.

And to whom could the western empire turn in its distress? Even more fatal than the pressure of the barbarians had been the splitting of the once-united empire into eastern and western fragments. The eastern empire could hardly be called "Roman" by any wild stretch of the word: it was an absolute monarchy whose princes "measured their greatness by the servile obedience of their people"—a people "equally incapable of guarding their lives and fortunes against the assault of the barbarians or of defending their reason against the terrors of superstition." Under 'these circumstances it mattered not too much that Italy was overrun by Attila the Hun, the "Scourge of God," or that Rome was pillaged by seafaring Vandal pirates from their newly conquered African bases. Other barbarian peoples could easily have performed those dreadful offices undeterred by a Roman government that "appeared every day less formidable to its enemies, more odious and oppressive to its subjects." For the torch of Rome was flickering low; before A.D. *500 Italy was in the hands of Odoacer, her first barbarian king; and soon thereafter Gibbon interrupts the flow of his narrative to give the following epitaph on the demise of the western empire.*

General Observations on the Fall of the Roman Empire in the West

The Greeks, after their country had been reduced into a province, imputed the triumphs of Rome not to the merit but to the *Fortune* of the republic. The inconstant goddess, who so blindly distributes and resumes her favours, had *now* consented (such was the language of envious flattery) to resign her wings, to descend from her globe, and to fix her firm and immutable throne on the banks of the Tiber. A wiser Greek [Polybius], who has composed with a philosophic spirit the memorable history of his own times, deprived his countrymen of this vain and delusive comfort by opening to their view the deep foundations of the greatness of Rome. The fidelity of the citizens to each other and to the state was confirmed by the habits of education and the prejudices of religion. Honour, as well as virtue, was the principle of the republic; the ambitious citizens laboured to deserve the solemn glories of a triumph; and the ardour of the Roman youth was kindled into active emulation as often as they beheld the domestic images of their ancestors. The temperate struggles of the patricians and plebeians had finally established the firm and equal balance of the constitution, which united the freedom of popular assemblies with the authority and wisdom of a senate and the executive powers of a regal magistrate. When the consul displayed the standard of the republic, each citizen bound himself, by the obligation of an oath, to draw his sword in the cause of his country till he had discharged the sacred duty by a military service of ten years. This wise institution continually poured into the field the rising generations of freemen and soldiers; and their numbers were reinforced by the warlike and populous states of Italy, who after a brave resistance had yielded to the valour and embraced the alliance of the Romans.

The sage historian, who excited the virtue of the younger Scipio and beheld the ruin of Carthage, has accurately described their military system, their levies, arms, exercises, subordination, marches, encampments, and the invincible legion, superior in active strength to the Macedonian phalanx of Philip and Alexander. From these institutions of peace and war Polybius has deduced the spirit and success of a people incapable of fear and impatient of repose. The ambitious design of conquest, which might have been defeated by the seasonable conspiracy of mankind, was attempted and achieved; and the perpetual violation of justice was maintained by the political virtues of prudence and courage. The arms of the republic, sometimes vanquished in battle, always victorious in war, advanced with rapid steps to the Euphrates, the Danube, the Rhine, and the ocean; and the images of gold, or silver, or brass that might serve to represent the nations and their kings were successively broken by the *iron* monarchy of Rome.

The rise of a city which swelled into an empire may deserve, as a singular prodigy, the reflection of a philosophic mind. But the decline of Rome was the natural and inevitable effect of immoderate greatness. Prosperity ripened the principle of decay; the causes of destruction multiplied with the extent of conquest; and as soon as time or accident had removed the artificial supports, the stupendous fabric yielded to the pressure of its own weight. The story of its ruin is simple and obvious; and instead of inquiring *why* the Roman empire was destroyed, we should rather be surprised that it had subsisted so long. The victorious legions, who in distant wars acquired the vices of strangers and mercenaries, first oppressed the freedom of the republic and afterwards violated the majesty of the purple. The emperors, anxious for their personal safety and the public peace, were reduced to the base expedient of corrupting the discipline which rendered them alike formidable to their sovereign and to the enemy; the vigour of the military government was relaxed and finally dissolved by the partial institutions of Constantine; and the Roman world was overwhelmed by a deluge of barbarians.

The decay of Rome has been frequently ascribed to the translation of the seat of empire; but this history has already shown that the powers of government were *divided* rather than *removed.* The throne of Constantinople was erected in the East; while the West was still possessed by a series of emperors who held their residence in Italy and claimed their equal inheritance of the legions and provinces. This dangerous novelty impaired the strength and fomented the vices of a double reign; the instruments of an oppressive and arbitrary system were multiplied; and a vain emulation of luxury, not of merit, was introduced and supported between the degenerate successors of Theodosius. Extreme distress, which unites the virtue of a free people, embitters the factions of a declining monarchy. The hostile favourites of Arcadius and Honorius betrayed the republic to its common enemies; and the Byzantine court beheld with indifference, perhaps with pleasure, the disgrace of Rome, the misfortunes of Italy, and the loss of the West. Under the succeeding reigns the alliance of the two empires was restored; but the aid of the Oriental Romans was tardy, doubtful, and ineffectual; and the national schism of the Greeks and Latins was enlarged by the perpetual difference of language and manners, of interests, and even of religion. Yet the salutary event approved in some measure the judgment of Constantine. During a long period of decay his impregnable city repelled the victorious armies of barbarians, protected the wealth of Asia, and commanded, both in peace and war, the important straits which connect the Euxine and Mediterranean Seas. The foundation of Constantinople more essentially contributed to the preservation of the East than to the ruin of the West.

As the happiness of a *future* life is the great object or religion, we may hear without surprise or scandal that the introduction, or at least the abuse, of Christianity had some influence on the decline and fall of the Roman empire. The clergy successfully preached the doctrines of patience and pusillanimity; the active virtues of society were discouraged; and the last remains of military spirit were buried in the cloister. A large portion of public and private wealth was consecrated to the specious demands of charity and devotion, and the soldiers' pay was lavished on the useless multitudes of both sexes who could only plead the merits of abstinence and chastity. Faith, zeal, curiosity, and more earthly passions of malice and ambition kindled the flame of theological discord; the church and even the state were distracted by religious factions, whose conflicts were sometimes bloody and always implacable; the attention of the emperors was diverted from camps to synods; the Roman world was oppressed by a new species of tyranny, and the persecuted sects became the secret enemies of their country.

Yet party spirit, however pernicious or absurd, is a principle of union as well as of dissension. The bishops, from eighteen hundred pulpits, inculcated the duty of passive obedience to a lawful and orthodox sovereign; their frequent assemblies and perpetual correspondence maintained the communion of distant churches; and the benevolent temper of the Gospel was strengthened, though confined, by the spiritual alliance of the catholics. The sacred indolence of the monks was devoutly embraced by a servile and effeminate age; but if superstition had not afforded a decent retreat, the same vices would have tempted the unworthy Romans to desert, from baser motives, the standard of the republic. Religious precepts are easily obeyed which indulge and sanctify the natural inclinations of their votaries; but the pure and genuine influence of Christianity may be traced in its beneficial though imperfect effects on the barbarian p oselytes of the North. If the decline of the Roman empire was hastened by the conversion of Constantine, his victorious religion broke the violence of the fall and mollified the ferocious temper of the conquerors.

This awful revolution may be usefully applied to the instruction of the present age. It is the duty of a patriot to prefer and promote the exclusive interest and glory of his native country; but a philosopher may be permitted to enlarge his views and to consider Europe as one great republic whose various inhabitants have attained almost the same level of politeness and cultivation. The balance of power will continue to fluctuate, and the prosperity of our own or the neighbouring kingdoms may be alternately exalted or depressed; but these partial events cannot essentially injure our general state of happiness, the system of arts and laws and manners which so advantageously distinguish, above the rest of mankind, the Europeans and their colonies. The savage nations of the globe are the common enemies of civilized society; and we may inquire, with anxious curiosity, whether Europe is still threatened with a repetition of those calamities which formerly oppressed the arms and institutions of Rome. Perhaps the same reflections will illustrate the fall of that mighty empire, and explain the probable causes of our actual security.

The Romans were ignorant of the extent of their dangers and the number of their enemies. Beyond the Rhine and Danube the northern countries of Europe and Asia were filled with innumerable tribes of hunters and shepherds, poor, voracious, and turbulent, bold in arms and impatient to ravish the fruits of industry. The barbarian world was agitated by the rapid impulse of war, and the peace of Gaul or Italy was shaken by the distant revolutions of China. The Huns, who fled before a victorious enemy, directed their march towards the West; and the torrent was swelled by the gradual accession of captives and allies. The flying tribes who yielded to the

Huns assumed in *their* turn the spirit of conquest; the endless column of barbarians pressed on the Roman empire with accumulated weight; and if the foremost were destroyed the vacant space was instantly replenished by new assailants. Such formidable emigrations no longer issue from the North; and the long repose, which has been imputed to the decrease of population, is the happy consequence of the progress of arts and agriculture. Instead of some rude villages thinly scattered among its woods and morasses, Germany now produces a list of two thousand three hundred walled towns; the Christian kingdoms of Denmark, Sweden, and Poland have been successively established; and the Hanse merchants, with the Teutonic knights, have extended their colonies along the coast of the Baltic as far as the Gulf of Finland. From the Gulf of Finland to the Eastern Ocean, Russia now assumes the form of a powerful and civilized empire. The plough, the loom, and the forge are introduced on the banks of the Volga, the Oby, and the Lena; and the fiercest of the Tartar hordes have been taught to tremble and obey. The reign of independent barbarism is now contracted to a narrow span; and the remnant of Calmucks or Uzbecks, whose forces may be almost numbered, cannot seriously excite the apprehensions of the great republic of Europe. Yet this apparent security should not tempt us to forget that new enemies and unknown dangers may *possibly* arise from some obscure people, scarcely visible in the map of the world. The Arabs or Saracens, who spread their conquests from India to Spain, had languished in poverty and contempt till Mahomet breathed into those same bodies the soul of enthusiasm.

The empire of Rome was firmly established by the singular and perfect coalition of its members. The subject nations, resigning the hope and even the wish of independence, embraced the character of Roman citizens; and the provinces of the West were reluctantly torn by the barbarians from the bosom of their mother country. But this union was purchased by the loss of national freedom and military spirit; and the servile provinces, destitute of life and motion, expected their safety from the mercenary troops and governors who were directed by the orders of a distant court. The happiness of an hundred millions depended on the personal merit of one or two men, perhaps children, whose minds were corrupted by education, luxury, and despotic power. The deepest wounds were inflicted on the empire during the minorities of the sons and grandsons of Theodosius; and after those incapable princes seemed to attain the age of manhood they abandoned the church to the bishops, the state to the eunuchs, and the provinces to the barbarians. Europe is now divided into twelve powerful though unequal kingdoms, three respectable commonwealths, and a variety of smaller though independent states; the chances of royal and ministerial talent are multiplied, at least, with the number of its rulers; and a Julian or Semiramis may reign in the North, while Arcadius and Honorius again slumber on the thrones of the South. The abuses of tyranny are restrained by the mutual influence of fear and shame; republics have acquired order and stability; monarchies have imbibed the principles of freedom, or at least of moderation; and some sense of honour and justice is introduced into the most defective constitutions by the general manners of the times. In peace, the progress of knowledge and industry is accelerated by the emulation of so many active rivals; in war, the European forces are exercised by temperate and undecisive contests. If a savage conqueror should issue from the deserts of Tartary, he must repeatedly vanquish the robust peasants of Russia, the numerous armies of Germany, the gallant nobles of France, and the intrepid freemen of Britain, who, perhaps, might confederate for their common defence. Should the victorious barbarians carry slavery and desolation as far as the Atlantic Ocean, ten thousand vessels would transport beyond their pursuit the remains of civilized society; and Europe would revive and flourish in the American world, which is already filled with her colonies and institutions.

Cold, poverty, and a life of danger and fatigue fortify the strength and courage of barbarians. In every age they have oppressed the polite and peaceful nations of China, India, and Persia, who neglected, and still neglect, to counterbalance these natural powers by the resources of military art. The warlike states of antiquity, Greece, Macedonia, and Rome, educated a race of soldiers: exercised their bodies, disciplined their courage, multiplied their forces by regular evolutions, and converted the iron which they possessed into strong and serviceable weapons. But this superiority insensibly declined with their laws and manners; and the feeble policy of Constantine and his successors armed and instructed, for the ruin of the empire, the rude valour of the barbarian mercenaries. The military art has been changed by the invention of gunpowder, which enables man to command the two most powerful agents of nature, air and fire. Mathematics, chemistry, mechanics, architecture, have been applied to the service of war, and the adverse parties oppose to each other the most elaborate modes of attack and of defence. Historians may indignantly observe that the preparations of a siege would found and maintain a flourishing colony; yet we cannot be displeased that the subversion of a city should be a work of cost and difficulty, or that an industrious people should be protected by those arts which survive and supply the decay of military virtue. Cannon and fortifications now form an impregnable barrier against the Tartar horse; and Europe is secure from any future irruption of barbarians, since, before they can conquer, they must cease to be barbarous. Their gradual advances in the science of war would always be accompanied, as we may learn from the example of Russia, with a proportionable improvement in the arts of peace and civil policy; and they themselves must deserve a place among the polished nations whom they subdue.

Should these speculations be found doubtful or fallacious, there still remains a more humble source of comfort and hope. The discoveries of ancient and modern navigators, and the domestic history or tradition of the most enlightened nations, represent the *human savage* naked both in mind and body, and destitute of laws, of arts, of ideas, and almost of language. From this abject condition, perhaps the primitive and universal state of man, he has gradually arisen to command the animals, to fertilize the earth, to traverse the ocean, and to measure the heavens. His progress in the improvement and exercise of his mental and corporeal faculties has been irregular and various, infinitely slow in the beginning and increasing by degrees with redoubled velocity; ages of laborious ascent have been followed by a moment of rapid downfall; and the several climates of the globe have felt the vicissitudes of light and darkness. Yet the experience of four thousand years should enlarge our hopes and diminish our apprehensions. We cannot determine to what height the human species may aspire in their advance towards perfection; but it may safely be presumed that no people, unless the face of nature is changed, will relapse into their original barbarism.

The improvements of society may be viewed under a threefold aspect: 1. The poet or philosopher illustrates his age and country by the efforts of a *single* mind; but these superior powers of reason or fancy are rare and spontaneous productions, and the genius of Homer or Cicero or Newton would excite less admiration if they could be created by the will of a prince or the lessons of a preceptor. 2. The benefits of law and policy, of trade and manufactures, of arts and sciences, are more solid and permanent; and *many* individuals may be qualified, by education and discipline, to promote in their respective stations the interest of the community. But this general order is the effect of skill and labour; and the complex machinery may be decayed by time or injured by violence. 3. Fortunately for mankind, the more useful or at least more necessary arts can be performed without superior talents or national subordination, without powers of *one* or the union of *many*. Each village, each family, each individual, must always possess both ability and inclination to perpetuate the use of fire and of metals; the propagation and service of domestic animals; the methods of hunting and fishing; the rudiments of navigation; the imperfect cultivation of corn or other nutritive grain; and the simple practice of the mechanic trades. Private genius and public industry may be extirpated, but these hardy plants survive the tempest and strike an everlasting root into the most unfavourable soil. The splendid days of Augustus and Trajan were eclipsed by a cloud of ignorance, and the barbarians subverted the laws and palaces of Rome. But the scythe, the invention or emblem of Saturn, still continued annually to mow the harvests of Italy; and the human feasts of the Læstrigons have never been renewed on the coast of Campania.

Since the first discovery of the arts, war, commerce,

and religious zeal have diffused among the savages of
the Old and New World these inestimable gifts. They
have been successively propagated; they can never be
lost. We may therefore acquiesce in the pleasing conclusion that every age of the world has increased and
still increases the real wealth, the happiness, the knowledge, and perhaps the virtue of the human race.

Chapter XVI

Excerpts from the Latter Half of the Original Work

But the monumental job of the historian was far from done. This volume so far represents a condensation of approximately the first half of the History of the Decline and Fall of the Roman Empire. In the original, Gibbon continues by describing the long course of the empire in the East, the rise of Mohammedanism, the story of the once-barbarian tribes who settled and built nations amid the ruins of the West, the Crusades, the transient conquests of Genghis Khan and Tamerlane— in short, every major historical current that began in the original Roman empire, supplanted it, developed from it, occurred in the same geographical area, or affected that area in any significant way. Space considerations alone would require eliminating the great bulk of the second half of the original. However, the reader's loss at the omission is not so great as it might appear, for three reasons: (1) The subsequent discovery of new sources regarding this long period, as already noted in the introduction, has made this section of the original less valuable than the first half; (2) the average reader's requirements will be satisfied by a connected narrative which concludes with the extinction of the empire in the West; and (3) Gibbon himself most seriously considered concluding his history at this point. Therefore the final few pages of this volume will consist of brief selections from the second half of the original, chosen partly for their general interest and literary merit and partly to illustrate the breadth and versatility of the historian.

1. The Eastern Empire in the Sixth Century: I. Portrait of an Empress; II. The Factions of the Hippodrome[1]

I. In the exercise of supreme power, the first act of Justinian was to divide it with the woman whom he loved, the famous Theodora, whose strange elevation cannot be applauded as the triumph of female virtue. Under the reign of Anastasius the care of the wild beasts maintained by the green faction at Constantinople was entrusted to Acacius, a native of the isle of Cyprus, who from his employment was surnamed the master of the bears. This honourable office was given after his death to another candidate, notwithstanding the diligence of his widow, who had already provided a husband and a successor. Acacius had left three daughters, Comito, Theodora, and Anastasia, the eldest of whom did not then exceed the age of seven years. On a solemn festival these helpless orphans were sent by their distressed and indignant mother, in the garb of suppliants, into the midst of the theatre; the green faction received them with contempt, the blues with compassion; and this difference, which sunk deep into the mind of Theodora, was felt long afterwards in the administration of the empire.

As they improved in age and beauty, the three sisters were successively devoted to the public and private pleasures of the Byzantine people; and Theodora, after following Comito on the stage in the dress of a slave, with a stool on her head, was at length permitted to

1. *Editor's note:* From Chapter XL of the original.

exercise her independent talents. She neither danced, nor sang, nor played on the flute; her skill was confined to the pantomime art; she excelled in buffoon characters; and as often as the comedian swelled her cheeks and complained with a ridiculous tone and gesture of the blows that were inflicted, the whole theatre of Constantinople resounded with laughter and applause. The beauty of Theodora was the subject of more flattering praise and the source of more exquisite delight. Her features were delicate and regular; her complexion, though somewhat pale, was tinged with a natural colour; every sensation was instantly expressed by the vivacity of her eyes; her easy motions displayed the graces of a small but elegant figure; and either love or adulation might proclaim that painting and poetry were incapable of delineating the matchless excellence of her form. But this form was degraded by the facility with which it was exposed to the public eye and prostituted to licentious desire. Her venal charms were abandoned to a promiscuous crowd of citizens and strangers of every rank and of every profession; the fortunate lover who had been promised a night of enjoyment was often driven from her bed by a stronger or more wealthy favourite; and when she passed through the streets, her presence was avoided by all who wished to escape either the scandal or the temptation. The satirical historian has not blushed to describe the naked scenes which Theodora was not ashamed to exhibit in the theatre. After exhausting the arts of sensual pleasure[2] she most ungratefully murmured against the parsimony of Nature;[3] but her mur-

2. At a memorable supper thirty slaves waited round the table; ten young men feasted with Theodora. Her charity was *universal*.

3. She wished for a *fourth* altar on which she might pour libations to the god of love.

murs, her pleasures, and her arts must be veiled in the obscurity of a learned language.

After reigning for some time the delight and contempt of the capital, she condescended to accompany Ecebolus, a native of Tyre, who had obtained the government of the African Pentapolis. But this union was frail and transient; Ecebolus soon rejected an expensive or faithless concubine; she was reduced at Alexandria to extreme distress; and in her laborious return to Constantinople every city of the East admired and enjoyed the fair Cyprian, whose merit appeared to justify her descent from the peculiar island of Venus. The vague commerce of Theodora, and the most detestable precautions, preserved her from the danger which she feared; yet once, and once only, she became a mother. The infant was saved and educated in Arabia by his father, who imparted to him on his death-bed that he was the son of an empress. Filled with ambitious hopes, the unsuspecting youth immediately hastened to the palace of Constantinople and was admitted to the presence of his mother. As he was never more seen, even after the decease of Theodora, she deserves the foul imputation of extinguishing with his life a secret so offensive to her imperial virtue.

In the most abject state of her fortune and reputation, some vision, either of sleep or of fancy, had whispered to Theodora the pleasing assurance that she was destined to become the spouse of a potent monarch. Conscious of her approaching greatness, she returned from Paphlagonia to Constantinople; assumed, like a skilful actress, a more decent character; relieved her poverty by the laudable industry of spinning wool; and affected a life of chastity and solitude in a small house, which she afterwards changed into a magnificent temple. Her beauty, assisted by art or accident, soon attracted, cap-

tivated, and fixed the patrician Justinian, who already
reigned with absolute sway under the name of his uncle.
Perhaps she contrived to enhance the value of a gift
which she had so often lavished on the meanest of mankind; perhaps she inflamed, at first by modest delays
and at last by sensual allurements, the desires of a lover
who, from nature or devotion, was addicted to long
vigils and abstemious diet. When his first transports had
subsided she still maintained the same ascendant over
his mind by the more solid merit of temper and understanding.

Justinian delighted to ennoble and enrich the object
of his affection; the treasures of the East were poured
at her feet, and the nephew of Justin was determined,
perhaps by religious scruples, to bestow on his concubine the sacred and legal character of a wife. But
the laws of Rome expressly prohibited the marriage of
a senator with any female who had been dishonoured
by a servile origin or theatrical profession; the empress
Lupicina, or Euphemia, a barbarian of rustic manners
but of irreproachable virtue, refused to accept a prostitute for her niece; and even Vigilantia, the superstitious
mother of Justinian, though she acknowledged the wit
and beauty of Theodora, was seriously apprehensive lest
the levity and arrogance of that artful paramour might
corrupt the piety and happiness of her son. These obstacles were removed by the inflexible constancy of Justinian. He patiently expected the death of the empress;
he despised the tears of his mother, who soon sunk
under the weight of her affliction; and a law was promulgated, in the name of the emperor Justin, which
abolished the rigid jurisprudence of antiquity. A glorious repentance (the words of the edict) was left open
for the unhappy females who had prostituted their persons on the theatre, and they were permitted to contract

a legal union with the most illustrious of the Romans. This indulgence was speedily followed by the solemn nuptials of Justinian and Theodora; her dignity was gradually exalted with that of her lover; and as soon as Justin had invested his nephew with the purple, the patriarch of Constantinople placed the diadem on the heads of the emperor and empress of the East. But the usual honours which the severity of Roman manners had allowed to the wives of princes could not satisfy either the ambition of Theodora or the fondness of Justinian. He seated her on the throne as an equal and independent colleague in the sovereignty of the empire, and an oath of allegiance was imposed on the governors' of the provinces in the joint names of Justinian and Theodora. The eastern world fell prostrate before the genius and fortune of the daughter of Acacius. The prostitute who, in the presence of innumerable spectators, had polluted the theatre of Constantinople, was adored as a queen in the same city by grave magistrates, orthodox bishops, victorious generals, and captive monarchs.

Those who believe that the female mind is totally depraved by the loss of chastity will eagerly listen to all the invectives of private envy or popular resentment which have dissembled the virtues of Theodora, exaggerated her vices, and condemned with rigour the venal or voluntary sins of the youthful harlot. From a motive of shame or contempt, she often declined the servile homage of the multitude, escaped from the odious light of the capital, and passed the greatest part of the year in the palaces and gardens which were pleasantly seated on the seacoast of the Propontis and the Bosphorus. Her private hours were devoted to the prudent as well as grateful care of her beauty, the luxury of the bath and table, and the long slumber of the evening and the morning. Her secret apartments were occupied by the favourite women and eunuchs, whose interests and passions she indulged at the expense of justice; the most illustrious personages of the state were crowded into a dark and sultry antechamber; and when at last, after tedious attendance, they were admitted to kiss the feet of Theodora, they experienced, as her humour might suggest, the silent arrogance of an empress or the capricious levity of a comedian. Her rapacious avarice to accumulate an immense treasure may be excused by the apprehension of her husband's death, which could leave no alternative between ruin and the throne; and fear as well as ambition might exasperate Theodora against two generals who, during a malady of the emperor, had rashly declared that they were not disposed to acquiesce in the choice of the capital.

But the reproach of cruelty, so repugnant even to her softer vices, has left an indelible stain on the memory of Theodora. Her numerous spies observed and zealously reported every action, or word, or look injurious to their royal mistress. Whomsoever they accused were cast into her peculiar prisons, inaccessible to the inquiries of justice; and it was rumoured that the torture of the rack or scourge had been inflicted in the presence of a female tyrant insensible to the voice of prayer or of pity. Some of these unhappy victims perished in deep unwholesome dungeons; while others were permitted, after the loss of their limbs, their reason, or their fortune, to appear in the world the living monuments of her vengeance, which was commonly extended to the children of those whom she had suspected or injured. The senator or bishop whose death or exile Theodora had pronounced was delivered to a trusty messenger, and his diligence was quickened by a menace from her own mouth. "If you fail in the execution of my commands, I swear by him who liveth forever that your skin shall be flayed from your body."

If the creed of Theodora had not been tainted with heresy, her exemplary devotion might have atoned, in the opinion of her contemporaries, for pride, avarice, and cruelty; but if she employed her influence to assuage the intolerant fury of the emperor, the present age will allow some merit to her religion and much indulgence to her speculative errors. The name of Theodora was introduced with equal honour in all the pious and charitable foundations of Justinian; and the most benevolent institution of his reign may be ascribed to the sympathy of the empress for her less fortunate sisters, who had been seduced or compelled to embrace the trade of prostitution. A palace on the Asiatic side of the Bosphorus was converted into a stately and spacious monastery, and a liberal maintenance was assigned to five hundred women who had been collected from the streets and brothels of Constantinople. In this safe and holy retreat they were devoted to perpetual confinement; and the despair of some, who threw themselves headlong into the sea, was lost in the gratitude of the penitents who had been delivered from sin and misery by their generous benefactress.

The prudence of Theodora is celebrated by Justinian himself; and his laws are attributed to the sage counsels of his most reverend wife, whom he had received as the gift of the Deity. Her courage was displayed amidst the tumult of the people and the terrors of the court. Her chastity, from the moment of her union with Justinian, is founded on the silence of her implacable enemies; and although the daughter of Acacius might be satiated with love, yet some applause is due to the firmness of a mind which could sacrifice pleasure and habit to the stronger sense either of duty or interest. The wishes and prayers of Theodora could never obtain the blessing of a lawful son, and she buried an infant daughter, the sole off-spring of her marriage. Notwithstanding this disappointment, her dominion was permanent and absolute; she preserved, by art or merit, the affections of Justinian; and their seeming dissensions were always fatal to the courtiers who believed them to be sincere.

Perhaps her health had been impaired by the licentiousness of her youth; but it was always delicate, and she was directed by her physicians to use the Pythian warm-baths. In this journey the empress was followed by the Prætorian præfect, the great treasurer, several counts and patricians, and a splendid train of four thousand attendants. The highways were repaired at her approach; a palace was erected for her reception; and as she passed through Bithynia she distributed liberal alms to the churches, the monasteries, and the hospitals, that they might implore Heaven for the restoration of her health. At length, in the twenty-fourth year of her marriage and the twenty-second of her reign, she was consumed by a cancer; and the irreparable loss was deplored by her husband, who, in the room of a theatrical prostitute, might have selected the purest and most noble virgin of the East.

II. A material difference may be observed in the games of antiquity: the most eminent of the Greeks were actors, the Romans were merely spectators. The Olympic stadium was open to wealth, merit, and ambition; and if the candidates could depend on their personal skill and activity, they might pursue the footsteps of Diomede and Menelaus and conduct their own horses in the rapid career. Ten, twenty, forty chariots were allowed to start at the same instant; a crown of leaves was the reward of the victor, and his fame, with that of his family and country, was chanted in lyric strains more durable than monuments of brass and marble. But a senator, or even a citizen, conscious of his dignity, would have blushed to expose his person or his horses in the Circus of Rome. The games were exhibited at the expense of the republic, the magistrates, or the emperors; but the reins were abandoned to servile hands; and if the profits of a favourite charioteer sometimes exceeded those of an advocate, they must be considered as the effects of popular extravagance, and the high wages of a disgraceful profession.

The race, in its first institution, was a simple contest of two chariots, whose drivers were distinguished by *white* and *red* liveries: two additional colours, a light *green* and a cerulean *blue,* were afterwards introduced; and as the races were repeated twenty-five times, one hundred chariots contributed in the same day to the pomp of the Circus. The four *factions* soon acquired a legal establishment and a mysterious origin, and their fanciful colours were derived from the various appearances of nature in the four seasons of the year: the red dog-star of summer, the snows of winter, the deep shades of autumn, and the cheerful verdure of the spring. Another interpretation preferred the elements to the seasons, and the struggle of the green and blue was supposed to represent the conflict of the earth and sea. Their respective victories announced either a plentiful harvest or a prosperous navigation, and the hostility of the husbandmen and mariners was somewhat less absurd than the blind ardour of the Roman people, who devoted their lives and fortunes to the colour which they had espoused.

Such folly was disdained and indulged by the wisest princes; but the names of Caligula, Nero, Vitellius,

Verus, Commodus, Caracalla, and Elagabalus were enrolled in the blue or green factions of the Circus; they
frequented their stables, applauded their favourites,
chastised their antagonists, and deserved the esteem of
the populace by the natural or affected imitation of their
manners. The bloody and tumultuous contest continued
to disturb the public festivity till the last age of the
spectacles of Rome; and Theodoric, from a motive of
justice or affection, interposed his authority to protect
the greens against the violence of a consul and a patrician who were passionately addicted to the blue faction
of the Circus.

Constantinople adopted the follies, though not the
virtues, of ancient Rome, and the same factions which
had agitated the Circus raged with redoubled fury in
the Hippodrome. Under the reign of Anastasius this
popular frenzy was inflamed by religious zeal; and the
greens, who had treacherously concealed stones and
daggers under baskets of fruit, massacred at a solemn
festival three thousand of their blue adversaries. From
the capital this pestilence was diffused into the provinces and cities of the East, and the sportive distinction
of two colours produced two strong and irreconcilable
factions, which shook the foundations of a feeble government. The popular dissensions, founded on the most
serious interest or holy pretence, have scarcely equalled
the obstinacy of this wanton discord, which invaded the
peace of families, divided friends and brothers, and
tempted the female sex, though seldom seen in the
Circus, to espouse the inclinations of their lovers or to
contradict the wishes of their husbands. Every law,
either human or divine, was trampled under foot; and
as long as the party was successful, its deluded followers appeared careless of private distress or public calamity. The licence, without the freedom, of d   ɔcracy was

revived at Antioch and Constantinople, and the support of a faction became necessary to every candidate for civil or ecclesiastical honours.

A secret attachment to the family or sect of Anastasius was imputed to the greens; the blues were zealously devoted to the cause of orthodoxy and Justinian, and their grateful patron protected above five years the disorders of a faction whose seasonable tumults overawed the palace, the senate, and the capitals of the East. Insolent with royal favour, the blues affected to strike terror by a peculiar and barbaric dress—the long hair of the Huns, their close sleeves and ample garments, a lofty step, and a sonorous voice. In the day they concealed their two-edged poniards, but in the night they boldly assembled in arms and in numerous bands, prepared for every act of violence and rapine. Their adversaries of the green faction, or even inoffensive citizens, were stripped and often murdered by these nocturnal robbers, and it became dangerous to wear any gold buttons or girdles, or to appear at a late hour in the streets of a peaceful capital. A daring spirit, rising with impunity, proceeded to violate the safeguard of private houses; and fire was employed to facilitate the attack or to conceal the crimes of these factious rioters. No place was safe or sacred from their depredations; to gratify either avarice or revenge they profusely spilled the blood of the innocent; churches and altars were polluted by atrocious murders; and it was the boast of the assassins that their dexterity could always inflict a mortal wound with a single stroke of their dagger. The dissolute youth of Constantinople adopted the blue livery of disorder; the laws were silent, and the bonds of society were relaxed; creditors were compelled to resign their obligations; judges to reverse their sentence; masters to enfranchise their slaves; fathers to supply the extravagance of their children; noble matrons were prostituted to the lust of their servants; beautiful boys were torn from the arms of their parents; and wives, unless they preferred a voluntary death, were ravished in the presence of their husbands.

The despair of the greens, who were persecuted by their enemies and deserted by the magistrate, assumed the privilege of defence, perhaps of retaliation; but those who survived the combat were dragged to execution, and the unhappy fugitives, escaping to woods and caverns, preyed without mercy on the society from whence they were expelled. Those ministers of justice who had courage to punish the crimes and to brave the resentment of the blues became the victims of their indiscreet zeal: a præfect of Constantinople fled for refuge to the holy sepulchre; a count of the East was ignominiously whipped; and a governor of Cilicia was hanged, by the order of Theodora, on the tomb of two assassins whom he had condemned for the murder of his groom and a daring attack upon his own life.

An aspiring candidate may be tempted to build his greatness on the public confusion, but it is the interest as well as duty of a sovereign to maintain the authority of the laws. The first edict of Justinian, which was often repeated and sometimes executed, announced his firm resolution to support the innocent and to chastise the guilty of every denomination and colour. Yet the balance of justice was still inclined in favour of the blue faction by the secret affection, the habits, and the fears of the emperor; his equity, after an apparent struggle, submitted without reluctance to the implacable passions of Theodora; and the empress never forgot or forgave the injuries of the comedian. At the accession of the younger Justin the proclamation of equal and rigorous justice indirectly condemned the partiality of the former reign. "Ye blues, Justinian is no more! Ye greens, he is still alive!"

A sedition, which almost laid Constantinople in ashes, was excited by the mutual hatred and momentary reconciliation of the two factions. In the fifth year of his reign Justinian celebrated the festival of the Ides of January. The games were incessantly disturbed by the clamorous discontent of the greens; till the twenty-second race the emperor maintained his silent gravity; at length, yielding to his impatience, he condescended to hold, in abrupt sentences and by the voice of a crier, the most singular dialogue that ever passed between a prince and his subjects. Their first complaints were respectful and modest; they accused the subordinate ministers of oppression and proclaimed their wishes for the long life and victory of the emperor. "Be patient and attentive, ye insolent railers!" exclaimed Justinian; "be mute, ye Jews, Samaritans, and Manichæans!" The greens still attempted to awaken his compassion. "We are poor, we are innocent, we are injured, we dare not pass through the streets: a general persecution is exercised against our name and colour. Let us die, O emperor! but let us die by your command and for your service!" But the repetition of partial and passionate invectives degraded, in their eyes, the majesty of the purple; they renounced allegiance to the prince who refused justice to his people, lamented that the father of Justinian had been born, and branded his son with the opprobrious names of a homicide, an ass, and a perjured tyrant. "Do you despise your lives?" cried the indignant monarch. The blues rose with fury from their seats, their hostile clamours thundered in the Hippodrome, and their adversaries, deserting the unequal contest, spread terror and despair through the streets of Constantinople.

At this dangerous moment seven notorious assassins of both factions, who had been condemned by the præfect, were carried round the city and afterwards transported to the place of execution in the suburb of Pera. Four were immediately beheaded; a fifth was hanged; but when the same punishment was inflicted on the remaining two the rope broke, they fell alive to the ground, the populace applauded their escape, and the monks of St. Conon, issuing from the neighbouring convent, conveyed them in a boat to the sanctuary of the church. As one of these criminals was of the blue, and the other of the green, livery, the two factions were equally provoked by the cruelty of their oppressor or the ingratitude of their patron, and a short truce was concluded till they had delivered their prisoners and satisfied their revenge. The palace of the præfect, who withstood the seditious torrent, was instantly burned, his officers and guards were massacred, the prisons were forced open, and freedom was restored to those who could only use it for the public destruction.

A military force which had been despatched to the aid of the civil magistrate was fiercely encountered by an armed multitude, whose numbers and boldness continually increased; and the Heruli, the wildest barbarians in the service of the empire, overturned the priests and their relics, which from a pious motive had been rashly interposed to separate the bloody conflict. The tumult was exasperated by this sacrilege; the people fought with enthusiasm in the cause of God; the women, from the roofs and windows, showered stones on the heads of the soldiers, who darted firebrands against the houses; and the various flames, which had been kindled by the hands of citizens and strangers, spread without control over the face of the city. The conflagration involved the cathedral of St. Sophia, the baths of Zeuxippus, a part of the palace from the first entrance to the altar of Mars, and the long portico from the palace to the forum of Constantine; a large hospital, with the sick patients, was consumed; many churches and stately edifices were destroyed; and an immense treasure of gold and silver was either melted or lost. From such scenes of horror and distress the wise and wealthy citizens escaped over the Bosphorus to the Asiatic side, and during five days Constantinople was abandoned to the factions, whose watchword, *Nika, vanquish!* has given a name to this memorable sedition.

As long as the factions were divided, the triumphant blues and desponding greens appeared to behold with the same indifference the disorders of the state. They agreed to censure the corrupt management of justice and the finance; and the two responsible ministers, the artful Tribonian and the rapacious John of Cappadocia, were loudly arraigned as the authors of the public misery. The peaceful murmurs of the people would have been disregarded; they were heard with respect when the city was in flames; the quæstor and the præfect were instantly removed, and their offices were filled by two senators of blameless integrity. After this popular concession Justinian proceeded to the Hippodrome to confess his own errors and to accept the repentance of his grateful subjects; but they distrusted his assurances, though solemnly pronounced in the presence of the holy Gospels; and the emperor, alarmed by their distrust, retreated with precipitation to the strong fortress of the palace.

The obstinacy of the tumult was now imputed to a secret and ambitious conspiracy, and a suspicion was entertained that the insurgents, more especially the green faction, had been supplied with arms and money by Hypatius and Pompey, two patricians who could neither forget with honour nor remember with safety that they were the nephews of the emperor Anastasius. Capriciously trusted, disgraced, and pardoned by the jealous levity of the monarch, they had appeared as loyal servants before the throne, and during five days of the tumult they were detained as important hostages; till at length, the fears of Justinian prevailing over his prudence, he viewed the two brothers in the light of spies, perhaps of assassins, and sternly commanded them to depart from the palace. After a fruitless representation that obedience might lead to involuntary treason, they retired to their houses; and in the morning of the sixth day Hypatius was surrounded and seized by the people, who, regardless of his virtuous resistance and the tears of his wife, transported their favourite to the forum of Constantine and, instead of a diadem, placed a rich collar on his head. If the usurper, who afterwards pleaded the merit of his delay, had complied with the advice of his senate and urged the fury of the multitude, their first irresistible effort might have oppressed or expelled his trembling competitor. The Byzantine palace enjoyed a free communication with the sea, vessels lay ready at the garden stairs, and a secret resolution was already formed to convey the emperor with his family and treasures to a safe retreat at some distance from the capital.

Justinian was lost, if the prostitute whom he raised from the theatre had not renounced the timidity as well as the virtues of her sex. In the midst of a council where Belisarius was present, Theodora alone displayed the spirit of a hero; and she alone, without apprehending his future hatred, could save the emperor from the imminent danger and his unworthy fears. "If flight," said the consort of Justinian, "were the only means of safety, yet I should disdain to fly. Death is the condition of our birth, but they who have reigned should never survive the loss of dignity and dominion. I implore Heaven that I may never be seen, not a day, without my diadem and purple; that I may no longer behold the light when I cease to be saluted with the name of queen. If you resolve, O Cæsar! to fly, you have treasures; behold the sea, you have ships; but tremble lest the desire of life should expose you to wretched exile and ignominious death. For my own part, I adhere to the maxim of antiquity that the throne is a glorious sepulchre."

The firmness of a woman restored the courage to deliberate and act, and courage soon discovers the resources of the most desperate situation. It was an easy and a decisive measure to revive the animosity of the factions; the blues were astonished at their own guilt and folly that a trifling injury should provoke them to conspire with their implacable enemies against a gracious and liberal benefactor; they again proclaimed the majesty of Justinian; and the greens, with their upstart emperor, were left alone in the Hippodrome. The fidelity of the guards was doubtful, but the military force of Justinian consisted in three thousand veterans, who had been trained to valour and discipline in the Persian and Illyrian wars. Under the command of Belisarius and Mundus, they silently marched in two divisions from the palace, forced their obscure way through narrow passages, expiring flames, and falling edifices, and burst open at the same moment the two opposite gates of the Hippodrome. In this narrow space the disorderly and affrighted crowd was incapable of resisting on either side a firm and regular attack; the blues signalized the fury of their repentance, and it is computed that above thirty thousand persons were slain in the merciless and promiscuous carnage of the day. Hypatius was dragged from his throne and conducted with his brother Pompey to the feet of the emperor; they implored his clemency, but their crime was manifest, their innocence uncertain, and Justinian had been too much terrified to forgive. The next morning the two nephews of Anastasius, with eighteen illustrious accomplices of patrician or consular rank, were privately executed by the soldiers, their bodies were thrown into the sea, their palaces razed, and their fortunes confiscated. The Hippodrome itself was condemned during several years to a mournful silence; with the restoration of the games the same disorders revived, and the blue and green factions continued to afflict the reign of Justinian and to disturb the tranquillity of the eastern empire.

2. Mohammed and the Rise of Islam[4]

The base and plebeian origin of Mohammed is an unskilful calumny of the Christians, who exalt instead of degrading the merit of their adversary. His descent from Ismael was a national privilege or fable; but if the first steps of the pedigree are dark and doubtful, he could produce many generations of pure and genuine nobility. He sprung from the tribe of Koreish and the family of Hashem, the most illustrious of the Arabs, the princes of Mecca, and the hereditary guardians of the Caaba. The grandfather of Mohammed was Abdol Motalleb, the son of Hashem, a wealthy and generous citizen who relieved the distress of famine with the supplies of commerce. Mecca, which had been fed by the liberality of the father, was saved by the courage of a son. The kingdom of Yemen was subject to the Christian princes of Abyssinia; their vassal Abrahah was provoked

4. *Editor's note:* From Chapter L of the original.

by an insult to avenge the honour of the cross; and the holy city was invested by a train of elephants and an army of Africans. A treaty was proposed; and in the first audience the grandfather of Mohammed demanded the restitution of his cattle. "And why," said Abrahah, "do you not rather implore my clemency in favour of your temple, which I have threatened to destroy?" "Because," replied the intrepid chief, "the cattle is my own; the Caaba belongs to the gods, and *they* will defend their house from injury and sacrilege." The want of provisions, or the valour of the Koreish, compelled the Abyssinians to a disgraceful retreat; their discomfiture has been adorned with a miraculous flight of birds, who showered down stones on the heads of the infidels; and the deliverance was long commemorated by the era of the elephant.

The glory of Abdol Motalleb was crowned with domestic happiness; his life was prolonged to the age of one hundred and ten years; and he became the father of six daughters and thirteen sons. His best beloved Abdallah was the most beautiful and modest of the Arabian youth; and in the first night, when he consummated his marriage with Amina, of the noble race of the Zahrites, two hundred virgins are said to have expired of jealousy and despair. Mohammed, the only son of Abdallah and Amina, was born at Mecca four years after the death of Justinian and two months after the defeat of the Abyssinians, whose victory would have introduced into the Caaba the religion of the Christians. In his early infancy he was deprived of his father, his mother, and his grandfather; his uncles were strong and numerous; and in the division of the inheritance the orphan's share was reduced to five camels and an Æthiopian maid-servant. At home and abroad, in peace and war, Abu Taleb, the most respectable of his uncles, was

the guide and guardian of his youth; in his twenty-fifth
year he entered into the service of Cadijah, a rich and
noble widow of Mecca, who soon rewarded his fidelity
with the gift of her hand and fortune. The marriage contract, in the simple style of antiquity, recites the mutual
love of Mohammed and Cadijah, describes him as the
most accomplished of the tribe of Koreish, and stipulates
a dowry of twelve ounces of gold and twenty camels,
which was supplied by the liberality of his uncle. By this
alliance the son of Abdallah was restored to the station
of his ancestors; and the judicious matron was content
with his domestic virtues, till, in the fortieth year of his
age, he assumed the title of a prophet and proclaimed
the religion of the Koran.

According to the tradition of his companions, Mohammed was distinguished by the beauty of his person,
an outward gift which is seldom despised except by
those to whom it has been refused. Before he spoke, the
orator engaged on his side the affections of a public or
private audience. They applauded his commanding presence, his majestic aspect, his piercing eye, his gracious
smile, his flowing beard, his countenance that painted
every sensation of the soul, and his gestures that enforced each expression of the tongue. In the familiar
offices of life he scrupulously adhered to the grave and
ceremonious politeness of his country; his respectful attention to the rich and powerful was dignified by his
condescension and affability to the poorest citizens of
Mecca; the frankness of his manner concealed the artifice
of his views; and the habits of courtesy were imputed
to personal friendship or universal benevolence. His
memory was capacious and retentive; his wit easy and
social; his imagination sublime; his judgment clear,
rapid, and decisive. He possessed the courage both of
thought and action; and although his designs might

gradually expand with his success, the first idea which he entertained of his divine mission bears the stamp of an original and superior genius.

The son of Abdallah was educated in the bosom of the noblest race, in the use of the purest dialect of Arabia; and the fluency of his speech was corrected and enhanced by the practice of discreet and seasonable silence. With these powers of eloquence, Mohammed was an illiterate barbarian. His youth had never been instructed in the arts of reading and writing; the common ignorance exempted him from shame or reproach, but he was reduced to a narrow circle of existence and deprived of those faithful mirrors which reflect to our mind the minds of sages and heroes. Yet the book of nature and of man was open to his view, and some fancy has been indulged in the political and philosophical observations which are ascribed to the Arabian *traveller*. He compares the nations and the religions of the earth; discovers the weakness of the Persian and Roman monarchies; beholds with pity and indignation the degeneracy of the times; and resolves to unite under one God and one king the invincible spirit and primitive virtues of the Arabs. Our more accurate inquiry will suggest that, instead of visiting the courts, the camps, the temples of the East, the two journeys of Mohammed into Syria were confined to the fairs of Bostra and Damascus; that he was only thirteen years of age when he accompanied the caravan of his uncle; and that his duty compelled him to return as soon as he had disposed of the merchandise of Cadijah. In these hasty and superficial excursions the eye of genius might discern some objects invisible to his grosser companions; some seeds of knowledge might be cast upon a fruitful soil; but his ignorance of the Syriac language must have checked his curiosity; and I cannot perceive in the life or writings of Mohammed that his prospect was far extended beyond the limits of the Arabian world.

From every region of that solitary world the pilgrims of Mecca were annually assembled by the calls of devotion and commerce; in the free concourse of multitudes, a simple citizen in his native tongue might study the political state and character of the tribes, the theory and practice of the Jews and Christians. Some useful strangers might be tempted or forced to implore the rights of hospitality; and the enemies of Mohammed have named the Jew, the Persian, and the Syrian monk, whom they accuse of lending their secret aid to the composition of the Koran. Conversation enriches the understanding, but solitude is the school of genius; and the uniformity of a work denotes the hand of a single artist. From his earliest youth Mohammed was addicted to religious contemplation; each year, during the month of Ramadan, he withdrew from the world and from the arms of Cadijah; in the cave of Hera, three miles from Mecca, he consulted the spirit of fraud or enthusiasm whose abode is not in the heavens but in the mind of the prophet. The faith which, under the name of *Islam*, he preached to his family and nation is compounded of an eternal truth and a necessary fiction: THAT THERE IS ONLY ONE GOD, AND MOHAMMED IS THE APOSTLE OF GOD.

The creed of Mohammed is free from suspicion or ambiguity, and the Koran is a glorious testimony to the unity of God. The prophet of Mecca rejected the worship of idols and men, of stars and planets, on the rational principle that whatever rises must set, that whatever is born must die, that whatever is corruptible must decay and perish. In the Author of the universe his rational enthusiasm confessed and adored an infinite and eternal being, without form or place, without issue or similitude, pres-

ent to our most secret thoughts, existing by the necessity
of his own nature, and deriving from himself all moral
and intellectual perfection. These sublime truths, thus
announced in the language of the prophet, are firmly
held by his disciples and defined with metaphysical precision by the interpreters of the Koran.

A philosophic atheist might subscribe the popular
creed of the Mohammedans, a creed too sublime perhaps for our present faculties. What object remains for
the fancy, or even the understanding, when we have
abstracted from the unknown substance all ideas of time
and space, of motion and matter, of sensation and reflection? The first principle of reason and revelation was
confirmed by the voice of Mohammed; his proselytes,
from India to Morocco, are distinguished by the name of
Unitarians; and the danger of idolatry has been prevented by the interdiction of images. The doctrine of
eternal decrees and absolute predestination is strictly
embraced by the Mohammedans; and they struggle with
the common difficulties, *how* to reconcile the prescience
of God with the freedom and responsibility of man, *how*
to explain the permission of evil under the reign of
infinite power and infinite goodness.

The God of nature has written his existence on all his
works, and his law in the heart of man. To restore the
knowledge of the one, and the practice of the other, has
been the real or pretended aim of the prophets of every
age; the liberality of Mohammed allowed to his predecessors the same credit which he claimed for himself;
and the chain of inspiration was prolonged from the fall
of Adam to the promulgation of the Koran. During that
period some rays of prophetic light had been imparted
to one hundred and twenty-four thousand of the elect,
discriminated by their respective measure of virtue and
grace; three hundred and thirteen apostles were sent

with a special commission to recall their country from
idolatry and vice; one hundred and four volumes have
been dictated by the Holy Spirit; and six legislators of
transcendent brightness have announced to mankind the
six successive revelations of various rites but of one immutable religion. The authority and station of Adam,
Noah, Abraham, Moses, Christ, and Mohammed rise in
just gradation above each other; but whosoever hates or
rejects any one of the prophets is numbered with the
infidels.

The writings of the patriarchs were extant only in the
apocryphal copies of the Greeks and Syrians; the conduct of Adam had not entitled him to the gratitude or
respect of his children; the seven precepts of Noah were
observed by an inferior and imperfect class of the proselytes of the synagogue; and the memory of Abraham
was obscurely revered by the Sabians in his native land
of Chaldæa. Of the myriads of prophets, Moses and
Christ alone lived and reigned, and the remnant of the
inspired writings was comprised in the books of the
Old and New Testament. The miraculous story of Moses
is consecrated and embellished in the Koran, and the
captive Jews enjoy the secret revenge of imposing their
own belief on the nations whose recent creeds they
deride. For the author of Christianity the Mohammedans
are taught by the prophet to entertain a high and mysterious reverence. "Verily, Christ Jesus, the son of Mary,
is the apostle of God, and his word, which he conveyed
unto Mary, and a Spirit proceeding from him: honourable in this world, and in the world to come; and one of
those who approach near to the presence of God." The
wonders of the genuine and apocryphal Gospels are
profusely heaped on his head, and the Latin church has
not disdained to borrow from the Koran the immaculate
conception of his virgin mother.

Yet Jesus was a mere mortal; and at the day of judgment his testimony will serve to condemn both the Jews, who reject him as a prophet, and the Christians, who adore him as the Son of God. The malice of his enemies aspersed his reputation and conspired against his life; but their intention only was guilty; a phantom or a criminal was substituted on the cross; and the innocent saint was translated to the seventh heaven. During six hundred years the Gospel was the way of truth and salvation; but the Christians insensibly forgot both the laws and the example of their founder, and Mohammed was instructed by the Gnostics to accuse the church as well as the synagogue of corrupting the integrity of the sacred text. The piety of Moses and of Christ rejoiced in the assurance of a future Prophet, more illustrious than themselves: the evangelic promise of the *Paraclete,* or Holy Ghost, was prefigured in the name and accomplished in the person of Mohammed, the greatest and the last of the apostles of God.

The communication of ideas requires a similitude of thought and language. The discourse of a philosopher would vibrate without effect on the ear of a peasant; yet how minute is the distance of *their* understandings if it be compared with the contact of an infinite and a finite mind, with the word of God expressed by the tongue or the pen of a mortal? The inspiration of the Hebrew prophets, of the apostles and evangelists of Christ, might not be incompatible with the exercise of their reason and memory; and the diversity of their genius is strongly marked in the style and composition of the books of the Old and New Testament. But Mohammed was content with a character more humble, yet more sublime, of a simple editor; the substance of the Koran, according to himself or his disciples, is uncreated and eternal, subsisting in the essence of the Deity and inscribed with a pen of light on the table of his everlasting decrees. A paper copy, in a volume of silk and gems, was brought down to the lowest heaven by the angel Gabriel, who under the Jewish economy had indeed been despatched on the most important errands; and this trusty messenger successively revealed the chapters and verses to the Arabian prophet.

Instead of a perpetual and perfect measure of the divine will, the fragments of the Koran were produced at the discretion of Mohammed; each revelation is suited to the emergencies of his policy or passion; and all contradiction is removed by the saving maxim that any text of Scripture is abrogated or modified by any subsequent passage. The word of God and of the apostle was diligently recorded by his disciples on palm-leaves and the shoulder-bones of mutton; and the pages, without order or connection, were cast into a domestic chest in the custody of one of his wives. Two years after the death of Mohammed the sacred volume was collected and published by his friend and successor Abubeker; the work was revised by the caliph Othman, in the thirtieth year of the Hegira; and the various editions of the Koran assert the same miraculous privilege of a uniform and incorruptible text. In the spirit of enthusiasm or vanity the prophet rests the truth of his mission on the merit of his book, audaciously challenges both men and angels to imitate the beauties of a single page, and presumes to assert that God alone could dictate this incomparable performance.

This argument is most powerfully addressed to a devout Arabian whose mind is attuned to faith and rapture, whose ear is delighted by the music of sounds, and whose ignorance is incapable of comparing the productions of human genius. The harmony and copiousness of style will not reach, in a version, the European infidel; he will peruse with impatience the endless incoherent rhapsody of fable and precept and declamation, which seldom excites a sentiment or an idea, which sometimes crawls in the dust, and is sometimes lost in the clouds. The divine attributes exalt the fancy of the Arabian missionary; but his loftiest strains must yield to the sublime simplicity of the book of Job, composed in a remote age, in the same country, and in the same language. If the composition of the Koran exceeds the faculties of a man, to what superior intelligence should we ascribe the Iliad of Homer or the Philippics of Demosthenes?

In all religions the life of the founder supplies the silence of his written revelation: the sayings of Mohammed were so many lessons of truth, his actions so many examples of virtue, and the public and private memorials were preserved by his wives and companions. At the end of two hundred years the *Sonna,* or oral law, was fixed and consecrated by the labours of Al Bochari, who discriminated seven thousand two hundred and seventy-five genuine traditions from a mass of three hundred thousand reports of a more doubtful or spurious character. Each day the pious author prayed in the temple of Mecca and performed his ablutions with the water of Zemzem; the pages were successively deposited on the pulpit and the sepulchre of the apostle; and the work has been approved by the four orthodox sects of the Sonnites.

The talents of Mohammed are entitled to our applause, but his success has perhaps too strongly attracted our admiration. Are we surprised that a multitude of proselytes should embrace the doctrine and the passions of an eloquent fanatic? In the heresies of the church the same seduction has been tried and repeated from the time of the apostles to that of the reformers. Does it seem incredible that a private citizen should grasp the sword and the sceptre, subdue his native country, and erect a monarchy by his victorious arms? In the moving picture of the dynasties of the East, a hundred fortunate usurpers have arisen from a baser origin, surmounted more formidable obstacles, and filled a larger scope of empire and conquest. Mohammed was alike instructed to preach and to fight; and the union of these opposite qualities, while it enhanced his merit, contributed to his success. The operation of force and persuasion, of enthusiasm and fear, continually acted on each other till every barrier yielded to their irresistible power. His voice invited the Arabs to freedom and victory, to arms and rapine, to the indulgence of their darling passions in this world and the other; the restraints which he imposed were requisite to establish the credit of the prophet and to exercise the obedience of the people; and the only objection to his success was his rational creed of the unity and perfections of God.

It is not the propagation but the permanency of his religion that deserves our wonder: the same pure and perfect impression which he engraved at Mecca and Medina is preserved, after the revolutions of twelve centuries, by the Indian, the African, and the Turkish proselytes of the Koran. If the Christian apostles, St. Peter or St. Paul, could return to the Vatican, they might possibly inquire the name of the Deity who is worshipped with such mysterious rites in that magnificent temple. At Oxford or Geneva they would experience less surprise, but it might still be incumbent on them to peruse the catechism of the church and to study the orthodox commentators on their own writings and the words of their Master. But the Turkish dome of St. Sophia, with an increase of splendour and size, represents the humble tabernacle erected at Medina by the hands of Mohammed. The Mohammedans have uniformly withstood the temptation of reducing the object of their faith and devotion to a level with the senses and imagination of man. "I believe in one God, and Mohammed the apostle of God," is the simple and invariable profession of Islam. The intellectual image of the Deity has never been degraded by any visible idol; the honours of the prophet have never transgressed the measure of human virtue; and his living precepts have restrained the gratitude of his disciples within the bounds of reason and religion. The votaries of Ali have, indeed, consecrated the memory of their hero, his wife, and his children, and some of the Persian doctors pretend that the divine essence was incarnate in the person of the Imams; but their superstition is universally condemned by the Sonnites, and their impiety has afforded a seasonable warning against the worship of saints and martyrs.

The metaphysical questions on the attributes of God and the liberty of man have been agitated in the schools of the Mohammedans as well as in those of the Christians; but among the former they have never engaged the passions of the people or disturbed the tranquillity of the state. The cause of this important difference may be found in the separation or union of the regal and sacerdotal characters. It was the interest of the caliphs, the successors of the prophet and commanders of the faithful, to repress and discourage all religious innovations; the order, the discipline, the temporal and spiritual ambition of the clergy are unknown to the Moslems; and the sages of the law are the guides of their conscience and the oracles of their faith. From the Atlantic to the Ganges the Koran is acknowledged as the fundamental code not only of theology but of civil and criminal jurisprudence; and the laws which regulate the actions and the property of mankind are guarded by the infallible and immutable sanction of the will of God. This religious servitude is attended with some practical disadvantage; the illiterate legislator has been often misled by his own prejudices and those of his country; and the institutions of the Arabian desert may be ill adapted to the wealth and numbers of Ispahan and Constantinople. On these occasions the Cadi respectfully places on his head the holy volume and substitutes a dexterous interpretation more apposite to the principles of equity and the manners and policy of the times.

His beneficial or pernicious influence on the public happiness is the last consideration in the character of Mohammed. The most bitter or most bigoted of his Christian or Jewish foes will surely allow that he assumed a false commission to inculcate a salutary doctrine, less perfect only than their own. He piously supposed, as the basis of his religion, the truth and sanctity of their prior revelations, the virtues and miracles of their founders. The idols of Arabia were broken before the throne of God; the blood of human victims was expiated by prayer and fasting and alms, the laudable or innocent arts of devotion; and his rewards and punishments of a future life were painted by the images most congenial to an ignorant and carnal generation. Mohammed was, perhaps, incapable of dictating a moral and political system for the use of his countrymen; but he breathed among the faithful a spirit of charity and friendship, recommended the practice of the social virtues, and checked by his laws and precepts the thirst of revenge and the oppression of widows and orphans. The hostile tribes were united in faith and obedience, and the valour which had been idly spent in domestic quarrels was vigorously directed against a foreign enemy.

Had the impulse been less powerful, Arabia, free at home and formidable abroad, might have flourished under a succession of her native monarchs. Her sovereignty was lost by the extent and rapidity of conquest. The colonies of the nation were scattered over the East and West, and their blood was mingled with the blood of their converts and captives. After the reign of three caliphs the throne was transported from Medina to the valley of Damascus and the banks of the Tigris; the holy cities were violated by impious war; Arabia was ruled by the rod of a subject, perhaps of a stranger; and the Bedoweens of the desert, awakening from their dream of dominion, resumed their old and solitary independence.

3. Fall of Constantinople (A.D. 1453) and Final Downfall of the Eastern Empire[5]

Another Mohammed, by name Mohammed the Second, a vigorous ruler of the Ottoman Turks in the fifteenth century, was destined to complete the extinction of the Roman empire in the East. Little remained of that empire save a thin sliver of territory on the European side of the Bosphorus, mainly the suburbs of Constantinople; and that city itself was so shrunken, both in size and in public spirit, that Phranza, chamberlain and secretary to the last emperor, Constantine Palæologus, could by a diligent census discover only four thousand nine hundred and seventy citizens willing and able to bear arms in the city's defence. Counting foreign auxiliaries, a garrison of perhaps seven or eight thousand soldiers defended the walls of Constantinople in its last siege by some two hundred and fifty thousand

5. *Editor's note:* From Chapter LXVIII of the original.

*Moslems; the description of that siege is one of Gibbon's
more memorable passages.*

Of the triangle which composes the figure of Constantinople the two sides along the sea were made inaccessible to an enemy—the Propontis by nature and the
harbour by art. Between the two waters, the basis of
the triangle, the land side, was protected by a double
wall and a deep ditch of the depth of one hundred feet.
Against this line of fortification, which Phranza, an eye-
witness, prolongs to the measure of six miles, the Ottomans directed their principal attack; and the emperor,
after distributing the service and command of the most
perilous stations, undertook the defence of the external
wall. In the first days of the siege the Greek soldiers
descended into the ditch or sallied into the field; but
they soon discovered that, in the proportion of their
numbers, one Christian was of more value than twenty
Turks; and after these bold preludes they were prudently content to maintain the rampart with their missile weapons. Nor should this prudence be accused of
pusillanimity. The nation was indeed pusillanimous and
base, but the last Constantine deserves the name of
a hero; his noble band of volunteers was inspired with
Roman virtue, and the foreign auxiliaries supported the
honour of the western chivalry. The incessant volleys of
lances and arrows were accompanied with the smoke,
the sound, and the fire of their musketry and cannon.
Their small arms discharged at the same time either five,
or even ten, balls of lead of the size of a walnut; and
according to the closeness of the ranks and the force of
the powder, several breastplates and bodies were trans-
pierced by the same shot.

But the Turkish approaches were soon sunk in
trenches or covered with ruins. Each day added to the

science of the Christians, but their inadequate stock of gunpowder was wasted in the operations of each day. Their ordnance was not powerful either in size or number; and if they possessed some heavy cannon, they feared to plant them on the walls lest the aged structure should be shaken and overthrown by the explosion. The same destructive secret had been revealed to the Moslems, by whom it was employed with the superior energy of zeal, riches, and despotism. The great cannon of Mohammed has been separately noticed, an important and visible object in the history of the times; but that enormous engine was flanked by two fellows almost of equal magnitude. The long order of the Turkish artillery was pointed against the walls; fourteen batteries thundered at once on the most accessible places; and of one of these it is ambiguously expressed that it was mounted with one hundred and thirty guns, or that it discharged one hundred and thirty bullets. Yet in the power and activity of the sultan we may discern the infancy of the new science. Under a master who counted the moments, the great cannon could be loaded and fired no more than seven times in one day. The heated metal unfortunately burst; several workmen were destroyed, and the skill of an artist was admired who bethought himself of preventing the danger and the accident by pouring oil, after each explosion, into the mouth of the cannon.

The first random shots were productive of more sound than effect; and it was by the advice of a Christian that the engineers were taught to level their aim against the two opposite sides of the salient angles of a bastion. However imperfect, the weight and repetition of the fire made some impression on the walls; and the Turks, pushing their approaches to the edge of the ditch, attempted to fill the enormous chasm and to build a road to the assault. Innumerable fascines and hogsheads and trunks of trees were heaped on each other; and such was the impetuosity of the throng that the foremost and the weakest were pushed headlong down the precipice and instantly buried under the accumulated mass. To fill the ditch was the toil of the besiegers; to clear away the rubbish was the safety of the besieged; and after a long and bloody conflict the web that had been woven in the day was still unravelled in the night. The next resource of Mohammed was the practice of mines, but the soil was rocky; in every attempt he was stopped and undermined by the Christian engineers; nor had the art been yet invented of replenishing those subterraneous passages with gunpowder and blowing whole towers and cities into the air.

A circumstance that distinguishes the siege of Constantinople is the reunion of the ancient and modern artillery. The cannon were intermingled with the mechanical engines for casting stones and darts; the bullet and the battering-ram were directed against the same walls; nor had the discovery of gunpowder superseded the use of the liquid and unextinguishable fire. A wooden turret of the largest size was advanced on rollers; this portable magazine of ammunition and fascines was protected by a threefold covering of bulls' hides; incessant volleys were securely discharged from the loopholes; in the front three doors were contrived for the alternate sally and retreat of the soldiers and workmen. They ascended by a staircase to the upper platform, and, as high as the level of that platform, a scaling-ladder could be raised by pulleys to form a bridge and grapple with the adverse rampart.

By these various arts of annoyance, some as new as they were pernicious to the Greeks, the tower of St. Romanus was at length overturned; after a severe struggle the Turks were repulsed from the breach and interrupted by darkness, but they trusted that with the return of light they should renew the attack with fresh vigour and decisive success. Of this pause of action, this interval of hope, each moment was improved by the activity of the emperor and Justiniani, who passed the night on the spot and urged the labours which involved the safety of the church and city. At the dawn of day the impatient sultan perceived, with astonishment and grief, that his wooden turret had been reduced to ashes, the ditch was cleared and restored, and the tower of St. Romanus was again strong and entire. He deplored the failure of his design and uttered a profane exclamation that the word of the thirty-seven thousand prophets should not have compelled him to believe that such a work, in so short a time, could have been accomplished by the infidels.

The generosity of the Christian princes was cold and tardy; but in the first apprehension of a siege Constantine had negotiated, in the isles of the Archipelago, the Morea, and Sicily, the most indispensable supplies. As early as the beginning of April five great ships equipped for merchandise and war would have sailed from the harbour of Chios had not the wind blown obstinately from the north. One of these ships bore the Imperial flag; the remaining four belonged to the Genoese; and they were laden with wheat and barley, with wine, oil, and vegetables, and above all with soldiers and mariners for the service of the capital. After a tedious delay a gentle breeze, and on the second day a strong gale, from the south carried them through the Hellespont and the Propontis; but the city was already invested by sea and land, and the Turkish fleet, at the entrance of the Bosphorus, was stretched from shore to

shore in the form of a crescent, to intercept, or at least
to repel, these bold auxiliaries.

The reader who has present to his mind the geographical picture of Constantinople will conceive and
admire the greatness of the spectacle. The five Christian
ships continued to advance with joyful shouts and a full
press both of sails and oars against the hostile fleet of
three hundred vessels; and the rampart, the camp, the
coasts of Europe and Asia, were lined with innumerable
spectators, who anxiously awaited the event of this momentous succour. At the first view that event could not
appear doubtful; the superiority of the Moslems was
beyond all measure or account, and in a calm their numbers and valour must inevitably have prevailed. But
their hasty and imperfect navy had been created not by
the genius of the people but by the will of the sultan;
in the height of their prosperity the Turks have acknowledged that, if God had given them the earth, he had
left the sea to the infidels; and a series of defeats, a
rapid progress of decay, had established the truth of
their modest confession. Except eighteen galleys of some
force, the rest of their fleet consisted of open boats,
rudely constructed and awkwardly managed, crowded
with troops and destitute of cannon; and since courage
arises in a great measure from the consciousness of
strength, the bravest of the Janizaries might tremble on
a new element.

In the Christian squadron five stout and lofty ships
were guided by skilful pilots and manned with the
veterans of Italy and Greece, long practised in the arts
and perils of the sea. Their weight was directed to sink
or scatter the weak obstacles that impeded their passage; their artillery swept the waters; their liquid fire
was poured on the heads of the adversaries who, with

the design of boarding, presumed to approach them; and the winds and waves are always on the side of the ablest navigators. In this conflict the Imperial vessel, which had been almost overpowered, was rescued by the Genoese; but the Turks, in a distant and a closer attack, were twice repulsed with considerable loss. Mohammed himself sat on horseback on the beach, to encourage their valour by his voice and presence, by the promise of reward, and by fear more potent than the fear of the enemy. The passions of his soul and even the gestures of his body seemed to imitate the actions of the combatants; and, as if he had been the lord of nature, he spurred his horse with a fearless and impotent effort into the sea. His loud reproaches and the clamours of the camp urged the Ottomans to a third attack, more fatal and bloody than the two former; and I must repeat, though I cannot credit, the evidence of Phranza, who affirms from their own mouth that they lost above twelve thousand men in the slaughter of the day. They fled in disorder to the shores of Europe and Asia, while the Christian squadron, triumphant and unhurt, steered along the Bosphorus and securely anchored within the chain of the harbour.

In the confidence of victory, they boasted that the whole Turkish power must have yielded to their arms; but the admiral, or captain bashaw, found some consolation for a painful wound in his eye by representing that accident as the cause of his defeat. Baltha Ogli was a renegade of the race of the Bulgarian princes; his military character was tainted with the unpopular vice of avarice; and under the despotism of the prince or people, misfortune is a sufficient evidence of guilt. His rank and services were annihilated by the displeasure of Mohammed. In the royal presence, the captain bashaw was extended on the ground by four slaves and received one hundred strokes with a golden rod; his death had been pronounced, and he adored the clemency of the sultan, who was satisfied with the milder punishment of confiscation and exile.

The introduction of this supply revived the hopes of the Greeks and accused the supineness of their western allies. Amidst the deserts of Anatolia and the rocks of Palestine, the millions of the Crusades had buried themselves in a voluntary and inevitable grave; but the situation of the Imperial city was strong against her enemies and accessible to her friends; and a rational and moderate armament of the maritime states might have saved the relics of the Roman name and maintained a Christian fortress in the heart of the Ottoman empire. Yet this was the sole and feeble attempt for the deliverance of Constantinople; the more distant powers were insensible of its danger; and the ambassador of Hungary, or at least of Huniades, resided in the Turkish camp, to remove the fears and to direct the operations of the sultan.

It was difficult for the Greeks to penetrate the secret of the divan; yet the Greeks are persuaded that a resistance so obstinate and surprising had fatigued the perseverance of Mohammed. He began to meditate a retreat; and the siege would have been speedily raised if the ambition and jealously of the second vizier had not opposed the perfidious advice of Calil Bashaw, who still maintained a secret correspondence with the Byzantine court. The reduction of the city appeared to be hopeless unless a double attack could be made, from the harbour as well as from the land, but the harbour was inaccessible; an impenetrable chain was now defended by eight large ships, more than twenty of a smaller size, with several galleys and sloops; and, instead of forcing this barrier, the Turks might appre-

hend a naval sally and a second encounter in the open
sea.

In this perplexity the genius of Mohammed conceived
and executed a plan of a bold and marvellous cast, of
transporting by land his lighter vessels and military
stores from the Bosphorus into the higher part of the
harbour. The distance is about ten miles; the ground is
uneven, and was overspread with thickets; and, as the
road must be opened behind the suburb of Galata, their
free passage or total destruction must depend on the
option of the Genoese. But these selfish merchants were
ambitious of the favour of being the last devoured, and
the deficiency of art was supplied by the strength of
obedient myriads. A level way was covered with a broad
platform of strong and solid planks; and to render them
more slippery and smooth, they were anointed with the
fat of sheep and oxen. Fourscore light galleys and
brigantines of fifty and thirty oars were disembarked
on the Bosphorus shore, arranged successively on rollers,
and drawn forwards by the power of men and pulleys.
Two guides or pilots were stationed at the helm and
the prow of each vessel, the sails were unfurled to the
winds, and the labour was cheered by song and accla-
mation. In the course of a single night this Turkish fleet
painfully climbed the hill, steered over the plain, and
was launched from the declivity into the shallow waters
of the harbour, far above the molestation of the deeper
vessels of the Greeks.

The real importance of this operation was magnified
by the consternation and confidence which it inspired;
but the notorious, unquestionable fact was displayed
before the eyes, and is recorded by the pens, of the two
nations. A similar stratagem had been repeatedly practised by the ancients; the Ottoman galleys (I must again
repeat) should be considered as large boats; and if we

compare the magnitude and the distance, the obstacles and the means, the boasted miracle has perhaps been equalled by the industry of our own times. As soon as Mohammed had occupied the upper harbour with a fleet and army, he constructed in the narrowest part a bridge, or rather mole, of fifty cubits in breadth and one hundred in length; it was formed of casks and hogsheads, joined with rafters, linked with iron, and covered with a solid floor. On this floating battery he planted one of his largest cannon, while the fourscore galleys, with troops and scaling-ladders, approached the most accessible side, which had formerly been stormed by the Latin conquerors.

The indolence of the Christians has been accused for not destroying these unfinished works; but their fire, by a superior fire, was controlled and silenced; nor were they wanting in a nocturnal attempt to burn the vessels as well as the bridge of the sultan. His viligance prevented their approach: their foremost galliots were sunk or taken; forty youths, the bravest of Italy and Greece, were inhumanly massacred at his command; nor could the emperor's grief be assuaged by the just though cruel retaliation of exposing from the walls the heads of two hundred and sixty Musulman captives.

After a siege of forty days the fate of Constantinople could no longer be averted. The diminutive garrison was exhausted by a double attack; the fortifications, which had stood for ages against hostile violence, were dismantled on all sides by the Ottoman cannon; many breaches were opened, and near the gate of St. Romanus four towers had been levelled with the ground. For the payment of his feeble and mutinous troops, Constantine was compelled to despoil the churches with the promise of a fourfold restitution; and his sacrilege offered a new reproach to the enemies of the union. A spirit of discord

impaired the remnant of the Christian strength; the
Genoese and Venetian auxiliaries asserted the pre-eminence of their respective service; and Justiniani and the
great duke, whose ambition was not extinguished by
the common danger, accused each other of treachery
and cowardice.

During the siege of Constantinople the words of peace
and capitulation had been sometimes pronounced, and
several embassies had passed between the camp and
the city. The Greek emperor was humbled by adversity
and would have yielded to any terms compatible with
religion and royalty. The Turkish sultan was desirous
of sparing the blood of his soldiers, still more desirous
of securing for his own use the Byzantine treasures; and
he accomplished a sacred duty in presenting to the
Gabours the choice of circumcision, of tribute, or of
death. The avarice of Mohammed might have been
satisfied with an annual sum of one hundred thousand
ducats, but his ambition grasped the capital of the East;
to the prince he offered a rich equivalent, to the people
a free toleration or a safe departure; but after some
fruitless treaty he declared his resolution of finding
either a throne or a grave under the walls of Constantinople. A sense of honour and the fear of universal reproach forbade Palæologus to resign the city into the
hands of the Ottomans; and he determined to abide
the last extremities of war.

Several days were employed by the sultan in the
preparations of the assault; and a respite was granted
by his favourite science of astrology, which had fixed
on the twenty-ninth of May as the fortunate and fatal
hour. On the evening of the twenty-seventh he issued
his final orders, assembled in his presence the military
chiefs, and dispersed his heralds through the camp to
proclaim the duty and the motives of the perilous enter-

prise. Fear is the first principle of a despotic government; and his menaces were expressed in the Oriental style, that the fugitives and deserters, had they the wings of a bird, should not escape from his inexorable justice. The greatest part of his bashaws and Janizaries were the offspring of Christian parents; but the glories of the Turkish name were perpetuated by successive adoption; and in the gradual change of individuals, the spirit of a legion, a regiment, or an *oda*, is kept alive by imitation and discipline. In this holy warfare the Moslems were exhorted to purify their minds with prayer, their bodies with seven ablutions, and to abstain from food till the close of the ensuing day. A crowd of dervishes visited the tents to instil the desire of martyrdom and the assurance of spending an immortal youth amidst the rivers and gardens of paradise and in the embraces of the black-eyed virgins. Yet Mohammed principally trusted to the efficacy of temporal and visible rewards. A double pay was promised to the victorious troops. "The city and the buildings," said Mohammed, "are mine; but I resign to your valour the captives and the spoil, the treasures of gold and beauty; be rich and be happy. Many are the provinces of my empire; the intrepid soldier who first ascends the walls of Constantinople shall be rewarded with the government of the fairest and most wealthy; and my gratitude shall accumulate his honours and fortunes above the measure of his own hopes." Such various and potent motives diffused among the Turks a general ardour, regardless of life and impatient for action; the camp re-echoed with the Moslem shouts of "God is God: there is but one God, and Mohammed is the apostle of God"; and the sea and land, from Galata to the seven towers, were illuminated by the blaze of their nocturnal fires.

Far different was the state of the Christians, who

with loud and impotent complaints deplored the guilt
or the punishment of their sins. The celestial image of
the Virgin had been exposed in solemn procession, but
their divine patroness was deaf to their entreaties. They
accused the obstinacy of the emperor for refusing a
timely surrender, anticipated the horrors of their fate,
and sighed for the repose and security of Turkish servitude. The noblest of the Greeks and the bravest of the
allies were summoned to the palace to prepare them,
on the evening of the twenty-eighth, for the duties and
dangers of the general assault. The last speech of Palæologus was the funeral oration of the Roman empire; he
promised, he conjured, and he vainly attempted to infuse the hope which was extinguished in his own mind.
In this world all was comfortless and gloomy, and
neither the Gospel nor the church have proposed any
conspicuous recompense to the heroes who fall in the
service of their country. But the example of their prince
and the confinement of a siege had armed these warriors
with the courage of despair; and the pathetic scene is
described by the feelings of the historian Phranza, who
was himself present at this mournful assembly. They
wept, they embraced; regardless of their families and
fortunes, they devoted their lives; and each commander,
departing to his station, maintained all night a vigilant
and anxious watch on the rampart. The emperor and
some faithful companions entered the dome of St.
Sophia, which in a few hours was to be converted into
a mosque, and devoutly received with tears and prayers the sacrament of the holy communion. He reposed
some moments in the palace, which resounded with
cries and lamentations; solicited the pardon of all whom
he might have injured; and mounted on horseback to
visit the guards and explore the motions of the enemy.
The distress and fall of the last Constantine are more

glorious than the long prosperity of the Byzantine Cæsars.

In the confusion of darkness an assailant may sometimes succeed; but in this great and general attack the military judgment and astrological knowledge of Mohammed advised him to expect the morning, the memorable twenty-ninth of May in the fourteen hundred and fifty-third year of the Christian era. The preceding night had been strenuously employed; the troops, the cannon, and the fascines were advanced to the edge of the ditch, which in many parts presented a smooth and level passage to the breach; and his fourscore galleys almost touched, with the prows and their scaling-ladders, the less defensible walls of the harbour. Under pain of death, silence was enjoined; but the physical laws of motion and sound are not obedient to discipline or fear; each individual might suppress his voice and measure his footsteps; but the march and labour of thousands must inevitably produce a strange confusion of dissonant clamours, which reached the ears of the watchmen of the towers.

At daybreak, without the customary signal of the morning gun, the Turks assaulted the city by sea and land; and the similitude of a twined or twisted thread has been applied to the closeness and continuity of their line of attack. The foremost ranks consisted of the refuse of the host, a voluntary crowd who fought without order or command; of the feebleness of age or childhood, of peasants and vagrants, and of all who had joined the camp in the blind hope of plunder and martyrdom. The common impulse drove them onwards to the wall; the most audacious to climb were instantly precipitated; and not a dart, not a bullet, of the Christians was idly wasted on the accumulated throng. But their strength and ammunition were exhausted in this laborious defence; the ditch was filled with the bodies of the slain; they supported the footsteps of their companions; and of this devoted vanguard the death was more serviceable than the life. Under their respective bashaws and sanjaks, the troops of Anatolia and Romania were successively led to the charge; their progress was various and doubtful, but after a conflict of two hours the Greeks still maintained and improved their advantage; and the voice of the emperor was heard, encouraging his soldiers to achieve by a last effort the deliverance of their country.

In that fatal moment the Janizaries arose, fresh, vigorous, and invincible. The sultan himself, on horseback, with an iron mace in his hand, was the spectator and judge of their valour; he was surrounded by ten thousand of his domestic troops, whom he reserved for the decisive occasion; and the tide of battle was directed and impelled by his voice and eye. His numerous ministers of justice were posted behind the line, to urge, to restrain, and to punish; and if danger was in the front, shame and inevitable death were in the rear of the fugitives. The cries of fear and of pain were drowned in the martial music of drums, trumpets, and attaballs; and experience has proved that the mechanical operation of sounds, by quickening the circulation of the blood and spirits, will act on the human machine more forcibly than the eloquence of reason and honour. From the lines, the galleys, and the bridge the Ottoman artillery thundered on all sides; and the camp and city, the Greeks and the Turks, were involved in a cloud of smoke which could only be dispelled by the final deliverance or destruction of the Roman empire. The single combats of the heroes of history or fable amuse our fancy and engage our affections; the skilful evolutions of war may inform the mind and improve a necessary though pernicious science. But in the uniform and odious pictures of a general assault, all is blood and horror and confusion; nor shall I strive, at the distance of three centuries and a thousand miles, to delineate a scene of which there could be no spectators, and of which the actors themselves were incapable of forming any just or adequate idea.

The immediate loss of Constantinople may be ascribed to the bullet or arrow which pierced the gauntlet of John Justiniani. The sight of his blood, and the exquisite pain, appalled the courage of the chief, whose arms and counsels were the firmest rampart of the city. As he withdrew from his station in quest of a surgeon, his flight was perceived and stopped by the indefatigable emperor. "Your wound," exclaimed Palæologus, "is slight, the danger is pressing, your presence is necessary; and whither will you retire?" "I will retire," said the trembling Genoese, "by the same road which God has opened to the Turks"; and at these words he hastily passed through one of the breaches of the inner wall. By this pusillanimous act he stained the honours of a military life; and the few days which he survived in Galata, or the isle of Chios, were embittered by his own and the public reproach. His example was imitated by the greatest part of the Latin auxiliaries, and the defence began to slacken when the attack was pressed with redoubled vigour. The number of the Ottomans was fifty, perhaps a hundred, times superior to that of the Christians; the double walls were reduced by the cannon to a heap of ruins; in a circuit of several miles some places must be found more easy of access or more feebly guarded; and if the besiegers could penetrate in a single point, the wh le city was irrecoverably lost.

The first who deserved the sultan's reward was Hassan the Janizary, of gigantic stature and strength. With his scimitar in one hand and his buckler in the other,

he ascended the outward fortification; of the thirty Janizaries who were emulous of his valour, eighteen perished in the bold adventure. Hassan and his twelve
companions had reached the summit; the giant was precipitated from the rampart; he rose on one knee and was
again oppressed by a shower of darts and stones. But
his success had proved that the achievement was possible; the walls and towers were instantly covered with
a swarm of Turks; and the Greeks, now driven from the
vantage ground, were overwhelmed by increasing multitudes. Amidst these multitudes the emperor, who accomplished all the duties of a general and a soldier, was
long seen and finally lost. The nobles who fought round
his person sustained till their last breath the honourable
names of Palæologus and Cantacuzene; his mournful
exclamation was heard, "Cannot there be found a Christian to cut off my head?" and his last fear was that of
falling alive into the hands of the infidels. The prudent
despair of Constantine cast away the purple; amidst the
tumult he fell by an unknown hand, and his body was
buried under a mountain of the slain.

After his death resistance and order were no more;
the Greeks fled towards the city, and many were pressed
and stifled in the narrow pass of the gate of St.
Romanus. The victorious Turks rushed through the
breaches of the inner wall, and as they advanced into
the streets they were soon joined by their brethren, who
had forced the gate Phenar on the side of the harbour.
In the first heat of the pursuit about two thousand Christians were put to the sword; but avarice soon prevailed
over cruelty, and the victors acknowledged that they
should immediately have given quarter if the valour of
the emperor and his chosen bands had not prepared
them for a similar opposition in every part of the capital.
It was thus, after a siege of fifty-three days, that Con-

stantinople, which had defied the power of Chosroes, the Chagan, and the caliphs, was irretrievably subdued by the arms of Mohammed the Second. Her empire only had been subverted by the Latins; her religion was trampled in the dust by the Moslem conquerors.

The tidings of misfortune fly with a rapid wing; yet such was the extent of Constantinople that the more distant quarters might prolong some moments the happy ignorance of their ruin. But in the general consternation, in the feelings of selfish or social anxiety, in the tumult and thunder of the assault, a sleepless night and morning must have elapsed; nor can I believe that many Grecian ladies were awakened by the Janizaries from a sound and tranquil slumber. On the assurance of the public calamity, the houses and convents were instantly deserted; and the trembling inhabitants flocked together in the streets, like a herd of timid animals, as if accumulated weakness could be productive of strength, or in the vain hope that amid the crowd each individual might be safe and invisible.

From every part of the capital they flowed into the church of St. Sophia; in the space of an hour the sanctuary, the choir, the nave, the upper and lower galleries were filled with the multitudes of fathers and husbands, of women and children, of priests, monks, and religious virgins; the doors were barred on the inside, and they sought protection from the sacred dome which they had so lately abhorred as a profane and polluted edifice. Their confidence was founded on the prophecy of an enthusiast or impostor that one day the Turks would enter Constantinople and pursue the Romans as far as the column of Constantine in the square before St. Sophia; but that this would be the term of their calamities; that an angel would descend from heaven with a sword in his hand and would deliver the empire, with that celestial weapon, to a poor man seated at the foot of the column. "Take this sword," would he say, "and avenge the people of the Lord." At these animating words the Turks would instantly fly, and the victorious Romans would drive them from the West, and from all Anatolia, as far as the frontiers of Persia. It is on this occasion that Ducas, with some fancy and much truth, upbraids the discord and obstinacy of the Greeks. "Had that angel appeared," exclaims the historian, "had he offered to exterminate your foes if you would consent to the union of the church, even then, in that fatal moment, you would have rejected your safety or have deceived your God."

While they expected the descent of the tardy angel the doors were broken with axes; and as the Turks encountered no resistance their bloodless hands were employed in selecting and securing the multitude of their prisoners. Youth, beauty, and the appearance of wealth attracted their choice; and the right of property was decided among themselves by a prior seizure, by personal strength, and by the authority of command. In the space of an hour the male captives were bound with cords, the females with their veils and girdles. The senators were linked with their slaves, the prelates with the porters of the church, and young men of a plebeian class with noble maids whose faces had been invisible to the sun and their nearest kindred. In this common captivity the ranks of society were confounded, the ties of nature were cut asunder, and the inexorable soldier was careless of the father's groans, the tears of the mother, and the lamentations of the children. The loudest in their wailings were the nuns, who were torn from the altar with naked bosoms, outstretched hands, and dishevelled hair; and we should piously believe that few could be tempted to prefer the vigils of the harem to those of the monastery. Of these unfortunate Greeks, of these domestic animals, whole strings were rudely driven through the streets; and as the conquerors were eager to return for more prey, their trembling pace was quickened with menaces and blows.

At the same hour a similar rapine was exercised in all the churches and monasteries, in all the palaces and habitations, of the capital; nor could any place, however sacred or sequestered, protect the persons or the property of the Greeks. Above sixty thousand of this devoted people were transported from the city to the camp and fleet, exchanged or sold according to the caprice or interest of their masters, and dispersed in remote servitude through the provinces of the Ottoman empire. Among these we may notice some remarkable characters. The historian Phranza, first chamberlain and principal secretary, was involved with his family in the common lot. After suffering four months the hardships of slavery he recovered his freedom; in the ensuing winter he ventured to Adrianople and ransomed his wife from the *mir bashi*, or master of the horse; but his two children, in the flower of youth and beauty, had been seized for the use of Mohammed himself. The daughter of Phranza died in the seraglio, perhaps a virgin; his son, in the fifteenth year of his age, preferred death to infamy and was stabbed by the hand of the royal lover. A deed thus inhuman cannot surely be expiated by the taste and liberality with which he released a Grecian matron and her two daughters, on receiving a Latin ode from Philelphus, who had chosen a wife in that noble family. The pride or cruelty of Mohammed would have been most sensibly gratified by the capture of a Roman legate; but the dexterity of Cardinal Isidore eluded the search, and he escaped from Galata in a plebeian habit.

The chain and entrance of the outward harbour was

still occupied by the Italian ships of merchandise and war. They had signalized their valour in the siege; they embraced the moment of retreat, while the Turkish mariners were dissipated in the pillage of the city. When they hoisted sail, the beach was covered with a suppliant and lamentable crowd; but the means of transportation were scanty; the Venetians and Genoese selected their countrymen; and notwithstanding the fairest promises of the sultan, the inhabitants of Galata evacuated their houses and embarked with their most precious effects.

In the fall and the sack of great cities an historian is condemned to repeat the tale of uniform calamity; the same effects must be produced by the same passions; and when those passions may be indulged without control, small, alas! is the difference between civilized and savage man. Amidst the vague exclamations of bigotry and hatred, the Turks are not accused of a wanton or immoderate effusion of Christian blood; but according to their maxims (the maxims of antiquity), the lives of the vanquished were forfeited; and the legitimate reward of the conqueror was derived from the service, the sale, or the ransom of his captives of both sexes. The wealth of Constantinople had been granted by the sultan to his victorious troops, and the rapine of an hour is more productive than the industry of years. But as no regular division was attempted of the spoil, the respective shares were not determined by merit; and the rewards of valour were stolen away by the followers of the camp, who had declined the toil and danger of the battle. The narrative of their depredations could not afford either amusement or instruction; the total amount, in the last poverty of the empire, has been valued at four millions of ducats; and of this sum a small part was the property of the Venetians, the Genoese, the Florentines, and the merchants of Ancona. Of these foreigners the stock was improved in quick and perpetual circulation; but the riches of the Greeks were displayed in the idle ostentation of palaces and wardrobes, or deeply buried in treasures of ingots and old coin, lest it should be demanded at their hands for the defence of their country.

The profanation and plunder of the monasteries and churches excited the most tragic complaints. The dome of St. Sophia itself, the earthly heaven, the second firmament, the vehicle of the cherubim, the throne of the glory of God, was despoiled of the oblations of ages; and the gold and silver, the pearls and jewels, the vases and sacerdotal ornaments, were most wickedly converted to the service of mankind. After the divine images had been stripped of all that could be valuable to a profane eye, the canvas or the wood was torn, or broken, or burned, or trod under foot, or applied in the stables or the kitchen to the vilest uses. The example of sacrilege was imitated, however, from the Latin conquerors of Constantinople; and the treatment which Christ, the Virgin, and the saints had sustained from the guilty catholic might be inflicted by the zealous Musulman on the monuments of idolatry.

Perhaps, instead of joining the public clamour, a philosopher will observe that in the decline of the arts the workmanship could not be more valuable than the work, and that a fresh supply of visions and miracles would speedily be renewed by the craft of the priest and the credulity of the people. He will more seriously deplore the loss of the Byzantine libraries, which were destroyed or scattered in the general confusion: one hundred and twenty thousand manuscripts are said to have disappeared; ten volumes might be purchased for a single ducat; and the same ignominious price, too high perhaps for a shelf of theology, included the whole works

of Aristotle and Homer, the noblest productions of the
science and literature of ancient Greece. We may reflect
with pleasure that an inestimable portion of our classic
treasures was safely deposited in Italy, and that the
mechanics of a German town had invented an art which
derides the havoc of time and barbarism.

From the first hour of the memorable twenty-ninth of
May, disorder and rapine prevailed in Constantinople
till the eighth hour of the same day, when the sultan
himself passed in triumph through the gate of St. Romanus. He was attended by his viziers, bashaws, and
guards, each of whom (says a Byzantine historian) was
robust as Hercules, dexterous as Apollo, and equal in
battle to any ten of the race of ordinary mortals. The
conqueror gazed with satisfaction and wonder on the
strange though splendid appearance of the domes and
palaces, so dissimilar from the style of Oriental architecture. In the Hippodrome, or *atmeidan,* his eye was attracted by the twisted column of the three serpents; and
as a trial of his strength he shattered with his iron mace
or battle-axe the under jaw of one of these monsters,
which in the eyes of the Turks were the idols or talis-
mans of the city. At the principal door of St. Sophia,
he alighted from his horse and entered the dome; and
such was his jealous regard for that monument of his
glory that, on observing a zealous Musulman in the act
of breaking the marble pavement, he admonished him
with his scimitar that if the spoil and captives were
granted to the soldiers, the public and private buildings
had been reserved for the prince.

By his command the metropolis of the Eastern church
was transformed into a mosque; the rich and portable
instruments of superstition had been removed; the
crosses were thrown down; and the walls, which were
covered with images and mosaics, were washed and

purified and restored to a state of naked simplicity. On the same day, or on the ensuing Friday, the *muezin*, or crier, ascended the most lofty turret and proclaimed the *ezan*, or public invitation, in the name of God and his prophet; the imam preached; and Mohammed the Second performed the *namaz* of prayer and thanksgiving on the great altar where the Christian mysteries had so lately been celebrated before the last of the Cæsars. From St. Sophia he proceeded to the august but desolate mansion of a hundred successors of the great Constantine, but which in a few hours had been stripped of the pomp of royalty. A melancholy reflection on the vicissitudes of human greatness forced itself on his mind, and he repeated an elegant distich of Persian poetry: "The spider has wove his web in the Imperial palace, and the owl hath sung her watch-song on the towers of Afrasiab."

4. The Ruins of Rome in the Fifteenth Century, and Conclusion of the Whole Work[6]

In the last days of Pope Eugenius the Fourth, two of his servants, the learned Poggius and a friend, ascended the Capitoline hill, reposed themselves among the ruins of columns and temples, and viewed from that commanding spot the wide and various prospect of desolation. The place and the object gave ample scope for moralizing on the vicissitudes of fortune, which spares neither man nor the proudest of his works, which buries empires and cities in a common grave; and it was agreed that, in proportion to her former greatness, the fall of

6. *Editor's note:* From Chapter LXXI of the original.

Rome was the more awful and deplorable. "Her primeval state, such as she might appear in a remote age, when Evander entertained the stranger of Troy, has been delineated by the fancy of Virgil. This Tarpeian rock was then a savage and solitary thicket; in the time of the poet it was crowned with the golden roofs of a temple; the temple is overthrown, the gold has been pillaged, the wheel of fortune has accomplished her revolution, and the sacred ground is again disfigured with thorns and brambles. The hill of the Capitol, on which we sit, was formerly the head of the Roman empire, the citadel of the earth, the terror of kings, illustrated by the footsteps of so many triumphs, enriched with the spoils and tributes of so many nations. This spectacle of the world, how is it fallen! how changed! how defaced! The path of victory is obliterated by vines, and the benches of the senators are concealed by a dunghill. Cast your eyes on the Palatine hill and seek among the shapeless and enormous fragments the marble theatre, the obelisks, the colossal statues, the porticoes of Nero's palace; survey the other hills of the city, the vacant space is interrupted only by ruins and gardens. The forum of the Roman people, where they assembled to enact their laws and elect their magistrates, is now enclosed for the cultivation of pot-herbs or thrown open for the reception of swine and buffaloes. The public and private edifices that were founded for eternity lie prostrate, naked, and broken, like the limbs of a mighty giant; and the ruin is the more visible, from the stupendous relics that have survived the injuries of time and fortune. . . ."

When Petrarch first gratified his eyes with a view of those monuments whose scattered fragments so far surpass the most eloquent descriptions, he was astonished at the supine indifference of the Romans themselves; he was humbled rather than elated by the discovery that, except his friend Rienzi and one of the Colonna, a stranger of the Rhone was more conversant with these antiquities than the nobles and natives of the metropolis. The ignorance and credulity of the Romans are elaborately displayed in the old survey of the city which was composed about the beginning of the thirteenth century; and without dwelling on the manifold errors of name and place, the legend of the Capitol may provoke a smile of contempt and indignation.

"The Capitol," says the anonymous writer, "is so named as being the head of the world, where the consuls and senators formerly resided for the government of the city and the globe. The strong and lofty walls were covered with glass and gold and crowned with a roof of the richest and most curious carving. Below the citadel stood a palace, of gold for the greatest part, decorated with precious stones, and whose value might be esteemed at one-third of the world itself. The statues of all the provinces were arranged in order, each with a small bell suspended from its neck; and such was the contrivance of art-magic that if the province rebelled against Rome the statue turned round to that quarter of the heavens, the bell rang, the prophet of the Capitol reported the prodigy, and the senate was admonished of the impending danger."

A second example, of less importance though of equal absurdity, may be drawn from the two marble horses led by two naked youths, which have since been transported from the baths of Constantine to the Quirinal hill. The groundless application of the names of Phidias and Praxiteles may perhaps be excused; but these Grecian sculptors should not have been removed above four hundred years from the age of Pericles to that of Tiberius; they should not have been transformed into two philosophers or magicians, whose nakedness was the symbol of truth and knowledge, who revealed to the emperor his most secret actions, and, after refusing all pecuniary recompense, solicited the honour of leaving this eternal monument of themselves.

Thus awake to the power of magic, the Romans were insensible to the beauties of art. No more than five statues were visible to the eyes of Poggius; and of the multitudes which chance or design had buried under the ruins, the resurrection was fortunately delayed till a safer and more enlightened age. The Nile, which now adorns the Vatican, had been explored by some labourers in digging a vineyard near the temple, or convent, of the Minerva; but the impatient proprietor, who was tormented by some visits of curiosity, restored the unprofitable marble to its former grave. The discovery of a statue of Pompey, ten feet in length, was the occasion of a lawsuit. It had been found under a partition wall; the equitable judge had pronounced that the head should be separated from the body to satisfy the claims of the contiguous owners; and the sentence would have been executed if the intercession of a cardinal and the liberality of a pope had not rescued the Roman hero from the hands of his barbarous countrymen.

But the clouds of barbarism were gradually dispelled, and the peaceful authority of Martin the Fifth and his successors restored the ornaments of the city as well as the order of the ecclesiastical state. The improvements of Rome since the fifteenth century have not been the spontaneous produce of freedom and industry. The first and most natural root of a great city is the labour and populousness of the adjacent country, which supplies the materials of subsistence, of manufactures, and of foreign trade. But the greater part of the Campagna of Rome is reduced to a dreary and desolate wilderness; the over-

grown estates of the princes and the clergy are cultivated by the lazy hands of indigent and hopeless vassals;
and the scanty harvests are confined or exported for the
benefit of a monopoly. A second and more artificial
cause of the growth of a metropolis is the residence of
a monarch, the expense of a luxurious court, and the
tributes of dependent provinces. These provinces and
tributes had been lost in the fall of the empire; and if
some streams of the silver of Peru and the gold of Brazil
have been attracted by the Vatican, the revenues of the
cardinals, the fees of office, the oblations of pilgrims and
clients, and the remnant of ecclesiastical taxes afford a
poor and precarious supply, which maintains, however,
the idleness of the court and city. The population of
Rome, far below the measure of the great capitals of
Europe, does not exceed one hundred and seventy thousand inhabitants; and within the spacious enclosure of
the walls, the largest portion of the seven hills is overspread with vineyards and ruins.

The beauty and splendour of the modern city may
be ascribed to the abuses of the government, to the
influence of superstition. Each reign (the exceptions are
rare) has been marked by the rapid elevation of a new
family, enriched by the childless pontiff at the expense
of the church and country. The palaces of these fortunate nephews are the most costly monuments of elegance and servitude; the perfect arts of architecture,
painting, and sculpture have been prostituted in their
service; and their galleries and gardens are decorated
with the most precious works of antiquity, which taste
or vanity has prompted them to collect. The ecclesiastical revenues were more decently employed by the popes
themselves in the pomp of the catholic worship; but it
is superfluous to enumerate their pious foundations of
altars, chapels, and churches, since these lesser stars are

eclipsed by the sun of the Vatican, by the dome of St. Peter, the most glorious structure that ever has been applied to the use of religion. The fame of Julius the Second, Leo the Tenth, and Sixtus the Fifth is accompanied by the superior merit of Bramante and Fontana, of Raphael and Michelangelo; and the same munificence which had been displayed in palaces and temples was directed with equal zeal to revive and emulate the labours of antiquity. Prostrate obelisks were raised from the ground and erected in the most conspicuous places; of the eleven aqueducts of the Cæsars and consuls, three were restored; the artificial rivers were conducted over a long series of old or of new arches, to discharge into marble basins a flood of salubrious and refreshing waters; and the spectator, impatient to ascend the steps of St. Peter's, is detained by a column of Egyptian granite which rises between two lofty and perpetual fountains to the height of one hundred and twenty feet. The map, the description, the monuments of ancient Rome have been elucidated by the diligence of the antiquarian and the student; and the footsteps of heroes, the relics not of superstition but of empire, are devoutly visited by a new race of pilgrims from the remote and once savage countries of the North.

Of these pilgrims, and of every reader, the attention will be excited by a History of the Decline and Fall of the Roman Empire, the greatest, perhaps, and most awful scene in the history of mankind. The various causes and progressive effects are connected with many of the events most interesting in human annals: the artful policy of the Cæsars, who long maintained the name and image of a free republic; the disorders of military despotism; the rise, establishment, and sects of Christianity; the foundation of Constantinople; the division of the monarchy; the invasion and settlements of the barbarians of Germany and Scythia; the institutions of the civil law; the character and religion of Mohammed; the temporal sovereignty of the popes; the restoration and decay of the western empire of Charlemagne; the crusades of the Latins in the East; the conquests of the Saracens and Turks; the ruin of the Greek empire; the state and revolutions of Rome in the middle ages. The historian may applaud the importance and variety of his subject; but while he is conscious of his own imperfections, he must often accuse the deficiency of his materials. It was among the ruins of the Capitol that I first conceived the idea of a work which has amused and exercised near twenty years of my life, and which, however inadequate to my own wishes, I finally deliver to the curiosity and candour of the public.

Lausanne
June 27, 1787

THE
ROMAN EMPIRE
IN THE
AGE OF THE ANTONINES
(SECOND CENTURY A.D.)